DRUGS

SECOND EDITION

HARRY AVIS
Sierra College

Life

WCB Brown & Benchmark
P U B L I S H E R S

Madison, Wisconsin • Dubuque, Iowa • Indianapolis, Indiana
Melbourne, Australia • Oxford, England

Book Team

Editor *Chris Rogers*
Developmental Editor *Susan J. McCormick*
Production Editor *Suzanne M. Guinn*
Designer *Eric Engelby*
Art Editor *Rachel Imsland*
Photo Editor *Robin Storm*
Art Processor *Rachel Imsland*

Brown & Benchmark
PUBLISHERS

A Division of Wm. C. Brown Communications, Inc.

Vice President and General Manager *Thomas E. Doran*
Executive Managing Editor *Ed Bartell*
Executive Editor *Edgar J. Laube*
Director of Marketing *Kathy Law Laube*
National Sales Manager *Eric Ziegler*
Marketing Manager *Pamela Cooper*
Advertising Manager *Jodi Rymer*
Director of Production *Vickie Putman Caughron*
Manager of Visuals and Design *Faye M. Schilling*
Design Manager *Jac Tilton*
Art Manager *Janice Roerig*

Publishing Services Manager *Karen J. Slaght*
Permissions/Records Manager *Connie Allendorf*

Wm. C. Brown Communications, Inc.

Chairman Emeritus *Wm. C. Brown*
Chairman and Chief Executive Officer *Mark C. Falb*
President and Chief Operating Officer *G. Franklin Lewis*
Corporate Vice President, Operations *Beverly Kolz*
Corporate Vice President, President of WCB Manufacturing *Roger Meyer*

Copyedited by Jean Pascual

Cover Image: Arents Collections
The New York Public Library
Astor, Lenox and Tilden Foundations

Library of Congress Catalog Card Number: 92–72170

ISBN 0–697–12598–X

Printed in the United States of America by Wm. C. Brown Communications, Inc.,
2460 Kerper Boulevard, Dubuque, IA 52001

10 9 8 7 6 5 4 3 2 1

CONTENTS

• • •

11

THE LEGAL DRUGS II: PRESCRIPTION MEDICATION 356

12

DRUGS AND THE LAW 384

13

SUBSTANCE ABUSE AND SUBSTANCE ABUSE TREATMENT 428

14

DRUG EDUCATION AND DRUG ABUSE PREVENTION 464

TO MY FELLOW STUDENTS

As you read this book, I hope you will keep an open mind, an inquiring spirit, and a healthy skepticism about everything I have written. Critical thinking is a phrase you will undoubtedly hear many times during your college career, and it may seem to you, at times, that you have heard the phrase so often that it has lost all meaning. However, I can think of few areas in which critical thinking skills are so essential as they are in the questions that arise from the use of drugs in our society.

I address you as "fellow students" because I feel we all have something to contribute to each other in our understanding of drugs. I have been teaching for more than twenty years and I still evaluate each semester on the basis of not only what I feel I have succeeded in teaching my students, but also on what my students have taught me. There is scarcely a paragraph in this book that does not reflect some insight which I have gained from my students or have learned from pursuing questions that students have asked me.

I do not expect you will agree with everything you read in this book. Indeed, I would disappointed if you did. Some of you will feel that I am too sympathetic to those who use drugs; others may feel that I overemphasize the dangers of drug use. If you disagree with what I have written or with what your instructor says, it is my honest hope that you will pursue your concerns and find arguments to support your opinions. If you wish to share them with me, I would appreciate reading them.

One of the most profound changes in our educational system is that the "typical" college student is no longer necessarily between eighteen and twenty-one. This book is written with that change in mind. To the younger students: You will find references in this book to events that occurred in what might seem like the far distant past and written in a way that assumes you should have some familiarity with them. Ask your older friends, parents, or relatives to explain what these occurences meant to *them*. To the more mature students: Some of the material you will read will seem obvious or redundant. Ask your children or the younger students in your class to describe what it is like for them to face the issues of adulthood and responsibility for the first time.

Every generation thinks that *theirs* is the most complicated and pressured in all history. I certainly would not want to be twenty-one and faced with the choices younger people must make. But I am sure my parents felt the same way, just as I am sure that the current group of twenty-one-year-olds will feel the same way in 2015.

In Voltaire's novel, *Candide,* written in 1759, the philosopher Pangloss assures us that everything happens for the best in the best of all possible worlds. *Candide* is a satire on what Voltaire thought was a naive point of view. Voltaire's theme has relevance for the issue of drug use and abuse. In the best of all possible worlds of the twentieth century, there would be no drug abuse (or perhaps even drug use), and everyone would act responsibly.

Unfortunately, we live in an imperfect world. No culture has ever been totally drug free and there are no signs that our society will be different, high-minded slogans and wishful thinking to the contrary. While recognizing that we can never make reality conform to our ideals, we must, nevertheless, do all we can to reduce the frightful impact of drug abuse on our society. As Pangloss says at the end of the novel, after many adventures, "We must tend our garden, meaning, probably, that hard work is more profitable than speculation. It is going to take more hard work than Pangloss or Voltaire could have imagined to deal with our drug issues. If this book helps you understand some of these issues, it will have served its purpose.

PREFACE

• • •

My reasons for writing the first edition of this textbook stemmed from my frustration over twenty years of teaching at thirteen different colleges and universities throughout the United States. Along with many of the readers of this preface, I had seen enormous changes take place in teaching, textbooks, and students. Nowhere were these changes as apparent as in the teaching of a course on drugs. I felt at the time, as I do now, that this course is both extremely important and extremely challenging. I can think of no other course taught at the undergraduate level in which knowledge is accumulating so rapidly.

Instructors in this course cannot afford the luxury of notes that are even one year out of date. Our knowledge base is changing, our attitudes toward drug use are undergoing rapid alteration, and political events also influence how a course needs to be taught. Since the first edition was written, cocaine use (as well as use of most other drugs) has declined in many segments of the population, and important events are emerging that relate to treatment and prevention.

One of the areas that was of comparatively little importance a few years ago has emerged as a primary concern for those studying drug use—the conflict between the legal and the treatment approach to drug abuse prevention. As a result of this change and as a result of suggestions by reviewers, colleagues, and students, I added a chapter on drugs and the law.

This second edition has been substantially updated, of course, and benefits from the suggestions of many of my students as well as professionals who have been so kind as to write me. I have tried to incorporate their suggestions, retain the best material, and eliminate my most glaring mistakes without changing the basic point of view that I tried to get across in the first edition. Without being an advocate for any perspective and without worrying about "political correctness," I maintain the reasons for not abusing drugs are so self-evident that there is no need for half truths.

My mother-in-law used to say "if wishes were horses beggars would ride," meaning that wishful thinking and reality rarely coincide. Simply repeating an incorrect statement does not make it true. Two statements which permeate much of the current drug abuse literature are good examples. First, there *is* a difference between drug use and drug abuse. Good reasons exist for not using some drugs under any circumstances, but occasional use is not synonymous with abuse if either term is to have any meaning. To fail to recognize this distinction can lead to grave consequences.

The second concern deals with the legal classification of drugs. To me, the evidence is irrefutable that the rationale for making some drug use illegal while permitting or encouraging other drug use stems as much from the attitude of society as it does from scientific fact. Society has the right to say it disapproves of the use of a particular drug and to pass laws prohibiting its use. At the same time, the reason for that prohibition needs to be presented honestly. No statement in this book should be construed as promoting any drug use, legal or illegal. But at the same time, I have reported the facts as I have been able to gather them.

Other, less controversial considerations also have had an influence on both my choice of subject matter and the tone of this book. In particular, I have tried to write a book which reflects the diversity of students currently attending college. In my college, the average age of students is twenty-eight, many are married with children, and most work at least part-time. I have written this text with a wide range of students in mind: the forty-year-old insurance salesman who is returning to school because he wants to change careers, the newly divorced woman who is struggling with the issues of child care and the necessity of finding a job to support her family, the first semester freshman just out of high school who is used to daily classes, highly structured courses, and frequent reviews, and the quiet student in the back of the class whose father was an alcoholic and who is taking my class to find out why. Throw in the usual assortment of curiosity seekers, students trying to fill a requirement, and those who need a class at the hour I am teaching it, and you have quite a melange.

I wrote this textbook, in part, because I was dissatisfied for various reasons with those already available. While there are many good texts that an instructor can adopt, none, I felt, had the following features that I feel are needed for a superior textbook. Some come close, but I sincerely believe that mine is the only one with all of these. I hope that you, the instructor, and you, the student, agree. I would be interested in hearing from you with your assessment of how well I have succeeded.

1. A good text must acknowledge the diversity of students now attending college. The photos I have chosen, the examples I have used, and the general tone of this book is meant to appeal to many different types of students. I have not been too concerned about "readability," or the reading level of this book. There is a glossary of important terms in the back of the book and since the "typical" student no longer exists, I have concentrated on making communication clear rather than relying on some formula to measure reading level.
2. A good text must be interesting to read. The style of this book is meant to be rather informal. I want the student to enjoy reading the material as well as to learn the

facts presented. I feel the best way to accomplish this goal is to write to the reader as I would address my class. While the subject of drug abuse is no laughing matter, the approach to understanding drug use in our society does not have to be unrelentingly grim. The more approachable a text is, the more likely a student is to read it. My choice of topics for the ''You Read It Here First'' and ''In Depth'' inserts reflect my determination to make this book enjoyable to read.

3. A good text must be current. In the field of drug use and abuse, six months is often the same as six years in other fields. I have chosen references that are current or reflect current thinking. The references I have chosen tend to come from sources that are likely to be available to the student. The citations also reflect my attitude toward the scholarly aspects of textbook writing. I could reference nearly every sentence I have written, but I feel that doing so slows down the average reader who is more interested in the facts being presented. Some chapters contain many references, others only a few. Any potentially controversial statement has been thoroughly researched and referenced, however, and I have tried to present both sides of numerous issues. In addition, the inclusion of ''You Read It Here First'' is an attempt to project what I see as the major issues on drugs that are emerging.

4. A good text must be objective and realistic. While studies have shown that the fact-oriented approach to drug use and abuse so common in the seventies did not have a significant impact on the drug problem, there is no evidence that either wishful thinking or an approach that relies on legal sanctions will be any more successful. I have tried to present the facts about drug use and abuse without moralizing, and some of the findings may be surprising. This approach may lead to controversy in your class and, if so, I hope it encourages students to critically read the available literature.

5. A good textbook should have a broad perspective. In addition to the obvious relationship of drug use to medicine and psychology, the issue of drug use in our culture has had significant impact on our history, our literature, our legal system, and even our popular music. I have retained the historical background to drug use and have broadened the cultural base since the first edition. Not all instructors will feel these points are important, but I cannot imagine how some topics, such as the hallucinogens, for example, could be taught without them.

6. A good text should help the instructor teach the course as well as the student to learn. While I do not choose a book because of its ancillary features, I will not stick with a book that does not have good supplementary materials. In particular, I think the test bank is second in importance only to the book itself. In the Instructors Manual, you will find at least fifty multiple choice questions per chapter, twenty true-false, and ten essay questions. In addition, there is a supplemental reading list of articles and books I have found useful, a list of audiovisual materials and their sources, and a listing of important journals, newsletters, and other sources of up-to-date information.

ORGANIZATION AND CONTENT

Keeping in mind the goal and intended audience for this book, the lower division undergraduate or community college student without significant background in psychology, biology, or public health, the organization and content of this book have been structured to stimulate interest and thought. If I were writing an encyclopedic text on drugs, I would have included longer sections on antipsychotics and other prescription drugs which have little abuse potential. I would also have expanded the section on the sedative hypnotics. Had the course for which I am writing this book been a course on *drugs* I would have included material on contraceptives and other drugs that have little or no psychoactive effect. Had I intended this book primarily as an introductory text in the public health or criminal justice areas I would have gone into greater detail on public policy as it relates to each topic.

My decision-making process concerning which drugs and topics to include or leave out were based on three criteria: (1) Did the drugs have a significant psychoactive component? If not, were they so much a part of culture that they warranted discussion anyway—hence the inclusion of aspirin and some of the OTC drugs? (2) Did the drugs have a significant abuse potential? (3) Did the issues raised by use of a particular drug reflect the attitudes of our society toward drug use in general—hence the inclusion of steroids and so called aphrodisiacs? Doubtless many instructors will disagree with some of my choices, but I feel this book is broad enough to meet most instructors' needs.

APPROACH

To repeat what I wrote at the beginning of this preface, no statement in this text should be interpreted as a justification for drug use of any kind, either licit or illicit. In fact, I have explicitly pointed out that every drug has the potential for harm, if misused. However, it is equally true that virtually no drug is, by itself, invariably harmful.

The solution to the drug problem requires an approach at many levels. Legal sanctions against drug use have never worked when there was a demand for the drug in question. Societal disapproval reduces the demand for some people, but for others who identify with a deviant life style,

disapproval may be an impetus for drug use. Education is important but is not sufficient in itself, if it is based on the unrealistic assumption that reasonable people do not commit unreasonable acts. Finally, treatment is essential for those who are already abusers, but the ultimate goal must be prevention.

In chapter 14, I discuss the three levels of drug abuse programs. It is my belief that an integration of these three levels is our best hope. My goal in writing this book has been to help the student gain an understanding of the complexities involved in dealing with drugs in our society and to gain an appreciation of the fact that the task is neither easy nor going to be solved by any single, simplistic approach, whether it be drastically increased legal sanctions or legalization.

ACKNOWLEDGEMENT

No one has ever written a textbook without recognizing explicitly or implicity the influence of numerous individuals and sources. The intellectual influences that shape this book go back to 1962 and my first psychology class with Larry Gulick who, perhaps more than anyone else, showed me that teaching could be an intellectually rewarding and highly stimulating career.

The personal influences that are reflected in this book begin with my parents, Harry and Margaret Avis, who made it possible for me to become what I am. My wife, Julie, has been a source of support, inspiration, and a model of patience. In addition to maintaining her own several careers, she has provided me the time and privacy to write this book, put up with my peculiar personal and work habits, and, in short, made it possible for this book to have been written.

My students have shaped the writing of both editions of this book over many years. Their questions have astounded me and their interest has sustained me. Teaching is the most intellectually stimulating occupation I could imagine, and it is so because of the students who face us each day. To all of them, I owe a debt of gratitude.

I also owe a debt of gratitude to the people at Brown & Benchmark. In particular, Chris Rogers, who had the confidence in me to get this project off the ground in the first place and Susie McCormick, who wields a velvet whip with just the right sting. Having honed procrastination to a fine art, I am astounded at how much others accomplish in so short a time.

The mistakes in this book are my responsibility. There would have been far more, however, without the able assistance of the reviewers of this book in its various stages. I hope all of them recognize their contributions, without which this book would have been impossible. I would like to especially thank

Dan Duquette
University of Wisconsin—LaCrosse

Paul Kulkosky
University of Southern Colorado

Chrystyna Kosarchyn
Longwood College

Melvin Wallace
McHenry County College

Terry Blumenthal
White Forest University

Roger Seehafer
Purdue University

Roseanne Benson
George Mason University

The National Institute of Drug Abuse, National Institute of Alcoholism and Alcohol Abuse, Office of Substance Abuse Prevention, and the Office of Smoking and Health provided me with innumerable materials.

Harry Avis

1

• • •

INTRODUCTION
TO
DRUGS

• • •

OBJECTIVES

When you have finished studying this chapter you should:

1. Be able to describe the patterns of drug use.
2. Know why primary reinforcement is important in understanding drug use.
3. Be able to discuss the role that secondary reinforcement plays in determining drug use.
4. Be able to list the reinforcements that maintain drug use.
5. Be able to discuss the controversy concerning the relationship between drug use and personality.
6. Know how drug use is related to age and life-style changes.
7. Know how the legality or illegality of a given drug affects its use.
8. Know how the availability of a drug affects its use.
9. Know the difference between the agent/host and the deviance approach to understanding drug use.
10. Be able to discuss the three patterns of drug use.
11. Know why it is sometimes difficult to interpret the results of drug surveys.

KEY TERMS

advocacy figures
Amanita muscaria
circumstantial–situational use
compulsive use
consensus estimates
desire for self-improvement
desire to enhance physical performance
desire to enhance sensory awareness
desire to facilitate social interaction
Drug-Free Workplace Act
Ecstasy
experimental use
influence of media
influence of medicine
influence of religion
intensified use
law of supply and demand
National Commission on Marijuana and Drug Abuse
negative reinforcement
PCP
peer approval
premorbid personality
primary reinforcement
pruno
secondary reinforcement
positive reinforcement
social-recreational

Dad got up in the morning and put the ———— on. He reached into the medicine cabinet for some ———— but stopped when he remembered that he was scheduled to take a urine test for his job—he had heard that ———— can make him test positive for marijuana. He took two ———— instead, along with ———— and ———— for his high blood pressure. Mom got up shortly after and reached for the ———— pot, but she remembered that ———— has been linked to fibrous breast tumors so she put on some water for herbal ————. After her ———— she put a piece of ———— chewing gum in her mouth because she was trying to stop ————. Bethany, their daughter, had been up since 5:00 A.M. finishing her paper on *Drug Abuse in Intact Families* and since her eyes were irritated from her VDT, she put some ———— in them. She took two ———— for the headache she got from drinking ———— with her boyfriend the night before. After George took his shower he put some ———— on his injured knee, and took ———— because he had seen on television that it was good for preventing colds.

During lunch hour, Dad played racquetball at the health club and took a "Power Pak" ———— with his protein smoothee. Mom had a glass of ———— at lunch because her client was an account executive for a wine distributing company. When they got home from work, Mom and Dad had a glass of ———— each since it was Friday. Dad didn't mention that he had stopped off with Jim and had a ————. Just before bed Dad took a ———— for constipation and Mom took some ———— she asked her doctor to write a prescription for after hearing about it in a television commercial. Bethany brushed her teeth carefully so the folks wouldn't notice that she had smoked a ———— with her boyfriend, and George hurried upstairs to his room, so his parents wouldn't smell the ———— that he drank at the party his girlfriend had since her parents were away for the weekend.

As Mom drifted off to sleep, she whispered to Dad, "I can sleep so much better these days, now that we've gotten health-oriented. Remember how much we used to worry about our kids using drugs? Our good example must have paid off."

While this scenario may not be typical of most households, it is not too farfetched. Federal and state governments spend billions of dollars combatting drug abuse, while television, radio, and print ads warn us of the dangers of drugs; public figures, from wives of former presidential candidates to athletes and movie stars, discuss their own addictions at great length. If we can believe the various polls which seem to appear weekly, occasional use of illegal drugs is down, alcohol use is on the decline, and cigarette smoking is at an all-time low.

On the other hand, we are at the same time assaulted by commercials that tell us we can solve all our problems, from dandruff to depression to unpopularity, by taking drugs. Even drugs that can be obtained only by prescription are now being advertised. Furthermore, the same newspapers and magazines that report a decline in legal and casual drug use report that among abusers, drug use is actually increasing! Have we won or lost the war on drugs? Are we really significantly reducing our drug use, or are we switching our preferences and underestimating (or lying about) our use? What really is the distinction between ''good'' and ''bad'' drugs, drug use and abuse, alcohol, nicotine, and ''other drugs''?

One of the difficulties in understanding the drug problem is that we tend to ignore a simple fact: drug taking among human beings is virtually universal. The use of drugs is recorded in our earliest written histories and continues today. Now, as in the past, some of these drugs are taken to relieve physical symptoms or to combat disease, some for religious reasons or for enlightenment, and some are taken for pure enjoyment. Of course, there are those impossible-to-define examples of drug taking. According to at least one report, Kung Fu experts in Indonesia are supposed to drink kerosene to demonstrate their dedication (Diamond, 1990). Can we obtain the same goals without drugs? Is drug taking an innate characteristic of humans? The question *why* we take drugs may be the most important underlying issue in the controversy over drugs.

WHY DO WE TAKE DRUGS?

Psychiatrists, sociologists, and psychologists write reams of articles, appear on talk shows, and give speeches offering reasons why people use drugs. The reasons they give are complex and seem profound. Alienation from the mainstream of culture, adolescent rebellion, unresolved Oedipal complexes, dread of the future, and unconscious suicidal impulses are mentioned. One simple reason, based on sound psychological theory, is rarely mentioned.

Imagine Kimberly Jones rolling some marijuana into a joint. At that moment is she worried about dying in a nuclear holocaust or freezing in a nuclear winter? Is she disturbed by our inability to bring peace to the Mideast, or is she, like most teenagers, unable to find Kuwait on a map? Is she trying to make a statement about her independence from her parents when they, who are in their early forties, spent the Summer of Love, 1967, in San Francisco shocking *their* parents by living together and smoking marijuana?

If you were to ask *her* you might get a different answer. She smokes marijuana because she enjoys it; it makes her feel good. Psychologists use the term **reinforcement** to describe such reasons. Of course, other factors entered into her decision to smoke marijuana, but consider this: If she were motivated primarily by alienation or a desire for risk taking, why does she smoke marijuana instead of taking phencyclidine (PCP)? PCP is far more dangerous, and the laws against its use are far more severe so she would be much more daring if she used it. However, PCP doesn't make you feel as good. For similar reasons, no one snorts Drano, and probably no amount of

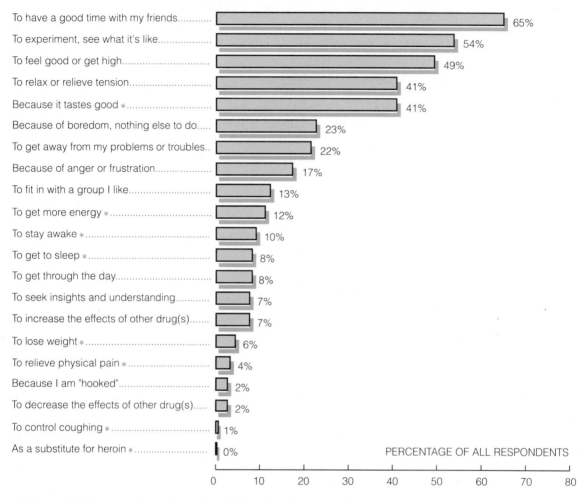

Reason for Use of Any Drug, Classes of 1983 and 1984, Combined

Reason	Percentage
To have a good time with my friends............	65%
To experiment, see what it's like.................	54%
To feel good or get high............................	49%
To relax or relieve tension..........................	41%
Because it tastes good *............................	41%
Because of boredom, nothing else to do.....	23%
To get away from my problems or troubles..	22%
Because of anger or frustration...................	17%
To fit in with a group I like...........................	13%
To get more energy *...................................	12%
To stay awake *..	10%
To get to sleep *..	8%
To get through the day................................	8%
To seek insights and understanding...........	7%
To increase the effects of other drug(s).......	7%
To lose weight *...	6%
To relieve physical pain *............................	4%
Because I am "hooked"................................	2%
To decrease the effects of other drug(s).....	2%
To control coughing *..................................	1%
As a substitute for heroin *.........................	0%

PERCENTAGE OF ALL RESPONDENTS

*Indicates that this reason is not relevant for all of the drugs.

FIGURE 1.1

Notice how many responses have something to do with "feeling good" or "having a good time."

peer pressure could get anyone to shoot up talcum powder, at least not more than once.

Although speculation about why people use drugs is rampant, data are scarce. Surprisingly, very few studies have actually *asked* people why they use drugs. One notable exception is an ongoing study of high school students. This study has been sampling almost 20,000 subjects a year for ten years. Along with questions of which drugs are used and how frequently, Johnston and O'Malley (1986) asked these students *why* they used the drugs they did. Their answers are revealing.

The overwhelming percentage of responses reflected some aspect of feeling good. When all drugs were combined, four of the five most common answers were: "To have a good time with my friends," "To feel good or get high,'' ''To relax or relieve tension,'' and ''Because it tastes good.'' Just as revealing is the other response: ''To experiment ... to see what it is like.''

Another study of high school students showed similar results, linking alcohol and marijuana use to four factors: (1) enhance positive affect and creativity, (2) reduce negative affect, (3) social cohesion, and (4) addiction (Newcomb, Chou, Bentler, & Huba, 1988). The first three factors were the most important, indicating that, for most high school students at least, alcohol and marijuana use is not motivated by the need to find something to get them through the day. We need to explore the term reinforcement to further our understanding of the reasons why people use drugs.

Primary Reinforcement

Although the precise definition is far more complicated, a reinforcer can be thought of as any stimulus or event that will increase the likelihood of a behavior. Since we all repeat behaviors that have been associated in the past with feeling good (or at least better), feeling good can be thought of as a reinforcer. Some stimuli and events seem to have intrinsic reinforcing properties. Food when you are hungry, water when you are thirsty, and, sex just about anytime are reinforcers that we do not have to learn to appreciate. Food, water, air, and sex are considered primary reinforcers. It is not too farfetched to add ''feeling good'' to this list. Primary reinforcers are very powerful in controlling behavior.

Virtually everyone has experienced the pleasurable effects of a glass of wine, a cold beer, or a mixed drink. If we believe the reports of those who have free-based or snorted cocaine, smoked crack, or even inhaled nitrous oxide (laughing gas), the effect is pleasurable indeed. These experiences are called **positive reinforcers,** experiences that we seek because they make us feel good. But there are also **negative reinforcers**, and these also are very powerful in controlling behavior.

Negative reinforcers are things that relieve pain or discomfort. We take the drug aspirin not because it makes us feel good but because it makes us feel less bad. For heroin addicts, addicted cigarette smokers, and many problem drinkers, the motivation for their behavior is not to feel good, but to feel normal. In fact, with these drugs the user long ago may have ceased to feel the positive reinforcing effects that got him or her started in the first place. Now the user is motivated solely by the relief of discomfort.

Secondary Reinforcement

Primary reinforcement is a powerful force in determining drug use, but it is by no means the only factor. We must also consider the role of **secondary reinforcement.** Secondary reinforcers gain their power to modify behavior through their association with primary reinforcers. Money is a secondary reinforcer. It has no value in itself, but becomes valuable when it is associated with primary reinforcers. With it I can obtain primary reinforcement, so I work hard to obtain money. Other common secondary reinforcers are praise, recognition, and, of course, grades. Drug use is motivated by secondary as well as primary reinforcement. Perhaps the most powerful secondary reinforcer for drug use is peer approval.

Peer Approval

In the late sixties, marijuana use was associated (among some groups) with a particular political, aesthetic, and philosophical point of view. Those who smoked marijuana (called "dope" in those days), felt they were part of a particular (and obviously superior) subculture that was "cool." Smoking dope meant you were against war and for equality. Smoking a joint with others was like the secret handshake you learned to admit you to a grade school club.

In the early 1980s many young, urban professionals (yuppies) snorted cocaine through straws after chopping the "coke" with a single-edged razor. At the time, cocaine was thought to be relatively harmless, although it was very expensive. It was a sign of affluence and sophistication to be able to afford coke and know how to use it.

Of course, peer approval for *non-use* also influences behavior. Health consciousness is at an all time high (some might call it a fad) for many individuals, and for these people, at least, considerable peer pressure exists for abstinence from all drugs: not just the illegal drugs, but alcohol and nicotine and even caffeine. Have you ever noticed the disapproving expressions on the faces of some shoppers when they look in the shopping cart of the person in front of them in the line at the supermarket and see a carton of cigarettes, a pound of coffee, and a quart of vodka?

Peer pressure, peer approval, and peer disapproval are frequently cited as important factors in preventing drug abuse, but caution must be used in defining these terms. Many well-meaning people, including all too many professionals, assume that the term "peer" refers to everyone of the same age. This mistake is particularly common when the targeted peer group consists of adolescents. Yet adolescents, more so than perhaps any age group, vary widely among themselves. Does the adolescent who uses drugs (a "stoner" in many high schools) consider the campus president of a service club a "peer"? Will the disapproval of the head cheerleader stop Sammy Stoner from inhaling nitrous oxide at a Grateful Dead concert?

Other influences that shape drug use in our culture that are harder to classify as primary or secondary reinforcers include the media, religion, and medicine. Still other important factors exist as well, including the desire to enhance sensory awareness, the desire for self-exploration, the desire to facilitate social interaction, and the desire to increase performance. The influence of many of these will be discussed in detail in later chapters, but needs to be introduced here.

Influence of the Media

Television, popular music, and print journalism tell us what drugs are popular, who uses them, how to use them, and what effects to expect. In some cases the media may stand accused of creating a demand for a drug. A case in point is Ecstasy, a drug the media "discovered" in 1985, although it had been around for many years (see chapter 5). Few people knew of it until newspapers and magazines ran features on it. After these appeared, legislators and law enforcement agencies banded together to stop the "new" menace, the drug was made illegal, and a black market quickly developed. How

All of these young people are the same age, but are they really peers? Would they accept or reject advice from each other?

important was the media in creating interest in this drug? A more recent arrival that may also go the same route is "ice," also discussed in chapter 5.

Influence of Religion

Most religions use drugs in their rituals. In some, such as the Native American church that uses the hallucinogen peyote, the role is central; in others, such as the Catholic church and some Protestant denominations, drug use is restricted to communion wine. Organized religion also recognizes the role of drugs for social or recreational purposes; most churches serve coffee at get-togethers and some even serve alcoholic beverages.

The attitude of organized religion plays a crucial role in understanding drug use within a culture. Rituals are important in every religion and also in drug use. To a great extent these rituals help define drug use within a culture. Hallucinogenic drugs are an important part of many Native American cultures, but recreational use of these drugs is rare. In general, drugs that are confined to religious ritual use are unlikely to be abused (Davis, 1986).

Religion may also have a paradoxical effect. Fundamental Christian denominations frown on any alcohol use, and one would expect less alcohol use in areas dominated by such groups. Although this seems to be the case, problems associated with alcohol abuse are actually higher in these areas than in parts of the country where more moderate views prevail (Linsky, Colby, & Strauss, 1986).

Influence of Medicine

Almost every patient going to a physician with a complaint expects to be given a prescription for a drug. Even in cultures where going to a medical doctor is the exception rather than the rule, witch doctors, *curanderos,* or herbalists fill the same role. Taking drugs is seen as the normal way of curing

Religion plays an important role in most people's lives. The attitudes of religion toward drug use help shape our attitudes.

disease, so taking drugs to relieve conditions that bring discomfort seems equally normal. If aspirin relieves my headache, why can't some other drug relieve my boredom? Furthermore, in the last several years, many disorders previously thought to be "psychological" or the result of "neuroses" such as phobias and obsessive-compulsive disorders (see chapter 13) have been treated with psychiatric medication (Kessler & Pines, 1990). Advertisements for drugs available only by prescription but directed at the average person have also increased, raising concern among many professionals (Peck, 1990).

Desire to Enhance Sensory Awareness

During the sixties and early seventies, many people who went to a rock concert smoked marijuana. Before and during the performance, some in the audience would get "high" in the belief that it would increase their enjoyment of the music. Such practices are not confined to any particular group. Artists have long sought ways of changing their perception of reality. In the 1840s in France, a club was formed consisting of Baudelaire, Dumas, and other writers and artists. They smoked hashish, a potent form of marijuana, and wrote about their impressions. In the early 1960s another group of writers, among them Ken Kesey, about whom we will read later, began experimenting with LSD and other drugs for the same purposes. Alcoholic beverages are commonly used to enhance sensory awareness. Have you ever heard the expression, "A meal without wine is like a day without sunshine"?

This photograph was taken at a rock concert in the 1960s. Use of marijuana and hallucinogens, such as LSD, was common at such events.

Alcoholic beverages in small amounts may increase the enjoyment of food, music, and even sex.

Desire to Enhance Physical Performance

Athletes are under great pressure to take drugs to enhance their innate capabilities, and they may use techniques ranging from blood-doping to drugs such as amphetamines and steroids (see chapters 3 and 12). According to some authorities at least half the athletes who competed at the Olympics in Seoul in 1988 may have used drugs to enhance their performance. Many of these drugs are the product of sophisticated underground research, and a constant battle exists between the drug users and those trying to detect use.

The everyday use of drugs to enhance physical performance is not limited to track stars, football players, and other athletes, however. Truck drivers know about bennies (amphetamines), students regularly use over-the-counter drugs such as NoDoz and Vivarin (which contain caffeine), and your Uncle John may have "just one more cup of coffee" before he drives home after Christmas dinner.

The United States military has long recognized the value of stimulant and sedative drugs. Astronaut Gordon Cooper took an amphetamine during the return flight of the Apollo rocket that landed on the moon, and recent

Could these people enjoy themselves as much if their glasses were filled with soft drinks?

reports indicate that such drugs, along with sedatives to promote sleep, are still prescribed to pilots of the United States Air Force (Brawley, 1988).

Desire for Self-Exploration

One of the major tasks of adolescence is to establish a sense of identity, which entails a long period of self-exploration; for many of us, the process of self-exploration continues throughout life. For centuries this task has been aided by drugs. In the sixties, psychedelic drugs were assumed to provide such insight, and Timothy Leary urged adolescents of that age to "turn on, tune in, and drop out." LSD was supposed to reveal profound truths about oneself.

One common report of the LSD experience is a supposedly deeper understanding of the universe and a feeling of "oneness." Before we credit Timothy Leary and his associate Richard Alpert (later known as Baba Ram Dass) with being gurus of inner truth, consider the story of Oliver Wendell Holmes (1809–1894), poet, novelist, essayist, and professor of medicine at Harvard University. In an address he gave to the Phi Beta Kappa honor society in 1870, he reported:

> I once inhaled a pretty full dose of ether with the determination to put on record at the earliest moment of regaining consciousness, the thought I should find uppermost in my mind. The mighty music of the triumphal march into consciousness reverberated through my brain, and filled me with a sense of infinite possibilities which made me an archangel for a moment. The veil of eternity was lifted. The one great truth which underlies all human experience and is the key to all the mysteries that philosophy has sought in vain to solve flashed upon me in a sudden revelation. Henceforth all was clear: a few words had lifted my intelligence to the level of the knowledge of the cherubim. As my natural condition returned, I remembered my resolution; and staggering to my desk, I wrote, in ill-shaped straggling characters, the all-embracing truth still glimmering in my consciousness. The words were these (children may smile; the wise will ponder); 'a strong smell of turpentine prevails throughout' (quoted in Brecher, p. 316).

in depth

Drug Use in Animals

Although we tend to associate drug taking with *human* behavior, anyone who has ever observed animals should be aware that drug taking is not confined to our species. Moreover, animals seem to take drugs for many of the same reasons that humans do. For example, many animals get drunk on alcohol. As you will read in chapter 5, fermentation is a natural process and animals eating fermented fruits exhibit behavior indistinguishable from that of altogether too many people on New Year's Eve. Whether they seek out the fermented fruit for its carbohydrates and sugar content, or for the effect of the alcohol itself, is difficult to determine. They may accept the intoxication as a necessary result of eating the fruit. However, Siegel (1989) has gathered enough evidence to suggest that at least some animals, like elephants and raccoons, seem to enjoy the intoxicating effect of the alcohol.

Animals seem to ingest other drugs willingly as well. Plants have evolved various defenses against animals, and some produce chemicals called secondary compounds. As many as 10,000 such chemicals may exist. They can cause illness and death, but it seems that eating some of these secondary compounds produces behavior that in humans would clearly be labeled addictive. For example, horses and cattle develop a sometimes fatal attraction to a variety of plants including those known as locoweed and star thistle. They seek out these plants and continue to eat them even after experiencing severe toxic symptoms. Other secondary compounds seem to be hallucinogenic and some animals seek these out. There is even evidence that animals recognize that some secondary compounds have medicinal properties. Observations of animals that are ill indicate that some seem to be attracted to specific plants. These plants have medicinal properties in humans which are effective in treating the symptoms that the animals display (Cowen, 1990). Is it possible that humans first learned about the mind-altering properties of plants by observing animals?

*Desire to Facilitate
Social Interaction*

Television commercials rarely show anyone drinking alone. A group of impossibly handsome young men gather at an elegant bar after a game of soccer and watch a football game. A magazine ad shows a beautiful woman handing her dashing-looking boss a cognac, while the night lights of the city can be seen through the huge window behind them. For social drinkers, the question, "Would you like a drink?" is probably the second or third sentence hosts utter to guests, right after "Hi, how are you?" and "Glad you made it."

Many people feel the disinhibiting effects of alcohol are essential for conversation, hence the cocktail party. Taking a drug like alcohol can aid in social interaction by reducing anxiety, and sharing an illegal drug can help form a bond among users. Heroin addicts frequently share their drug and their needles. Despite widespread knowledge that needle sharing is a primary means of transmitting AIDS, this behavior has proven difficult to stop, in part because sharing is seen as a sign of friendship. In the 1960s, smoking marijuana served a similar bonding process. Many of those who attacked the

Yellowjackets Get Drunk and Sting Humans

United Press International

Monmouth, Ore.
If you are stung by a yellowjacket this season, there is a good chance it is drunk.

Researchers said yellowjackets get a buzz in the fall from eating fruit that has begun to ferment.

Jim Thompson, a botanist for Miles-Hollister-Stier Laboratories in Monmouth, said yellowjackets usually are responsible for insect stings this time of year. They like to eat fruit that falls to the ground as the weather gets cold, he said.

The fruit is fermenting and "the little buggers get bombed out of their minds," Thompson said.

David Turner, the Oregon Agriculture Department's chief of beehive inspections, agreed, saying fermenting juice "tends to make them a little whoopie."

Doctors report more bee stings in the fall than any other time of year.

establishment and were opposed to the Vietnam War, who felt the pace of integration was too slow, and who rebelled against middle class conventions, smoked marijuana as a further indication of their alienation.

Desire to Alter Consciousness

Another reason for taking drugs is so simple it is easy to overlook; the desire to alter consciousness. This desire may be the basis for drug use by animals (Siegal, 1989) and it certainly is a powerful motivator among humans. The desire to alter consciousness may stem from an attempt to gain profound mystical or religious insights, such as is seen in the peyote and psilocybin ceremonies of some Native American tribes. Artists have used drugs to alter their consciousness in order to gain creative insight.

The desire to alter one's consciousness may have less lofty motivation as well, and drug use is but one means. As a child in grammar school, I can remember "dryering." One of us would climb in a dryer while a friend would (I'd hoped) put the heat control on "low" and insert a dime. While this practice has little else to recommend it, it did make you dizzy. Perhaps you remember hyperventilating or some other equally silly behavior. While some of the techniques used may seem dangerous or bizarre, the fact that virtually everyone has experimented with altering consciousness speaks to the importance of this motive.

Even as "normal" adults, we pay good money to jump out of perfectly good airplanes, jump from bridges with bungee cords attached to our ankles, or ski slopes that are rated one step higher than we really are qualified for. One common element in all these behaviors is that they alter consciousness, and drug taking may be seen as a shortcut to the same result. The fact that drug taking (or skydiving) serves other purposes as well does not reduce the importance of the desire to alter consciousness as a motivating force.

HOW EXTENSIVE IS DRUG USE?

Having established some of the reasons *why* people use drugs, we need to ask *who* uses them. The answer is obvious and simple: virtually everyone. The many purposes for which drugs are taken virtually guarantee that someone, somewhere, is taking a drug as you read this page.

Every culture seems to have its preferred, as well as its outlawed, drugs. Many anthropologists believe that as soon as a culture moved from the hunter-gatherer stage and developed agriculture, the process of fermentation was discovered. Alcoholic beverages can be made from anything that contains sugar (or that can be converted to sugar, like starch), and require only the presence of yeast cells which float in the air. The Anglo-Saxons made mead out of honey, pygmies in Africa make beer out of bananas, Indians make pulque out of cactus, and prisoners in the United States make "pruno" out of vegetable scraps.

Pruno Recipe

Never use pears or bananas

2 tumbler water
16 oranges cut in quarters then cut again, squeeze and use peel, pulp and all
1 lb sugar
pinch of yeast
In warm setting takes 3 days Cooler may take up to five days
Never use metal
Use plastic bag with straw or ? to let fumes excape. Don't let straw touch pruno. Fruit will float on top, pruno on bottom.
Fruit can be used over 4 or 5 times to make a new batch.

This recipe was obtained from a prisoner at Folsom Correctional Facility in California and is printed exactly as written by him, misspellings and all. The author had the opportunity to sample a batch confiscated at the prison, but as it smelled like the residue at the bottom of a garbage can that had been sitting in the hot sun for several days, I passed. Officers at the facility report that prisoners often get so drunk on pruno that they become violently ill. Apparently the odor of a prisoner after a pruno binge is not to be believed. Since the highest possible percentage of alcohol that could be produced by such a method is 14 percent, and since most prisoners are experienced drinkers, either they must consume large quantities of pruno, or the effects of set and setting operate. Anyone for a glass of Chateau de Folsom Pruno, vintage Thursday?

The Native American is often upheld as a paragon of virtue, living at one with nature. Many writers with more compassion than knowledge have claimed that alcohol was largely responsible for the decline in Native American culture. In fact, many tribes made alcoholic beverages, although distilled alcohol was unknown. The poverty, unemployment, and high rate of alcoholism seen in some tribes can better be explained by systematic exploitation, displacement, and massacre by the white man than as a result of the introduction of high proof alcoholic beverages.

Native Americans discovered and used more than 100 hallucinogenic drugs found in native plants (Davis, 1986). Siberian natives discovered that the fungus **Amanita muscaria** causes an alteration of consciousness when mixed with reindeer milk and wild blueberries. The strength of the desire to alter one's consciousness can be appreciated by the fact that one of the tribes, the Koryak, discovered that the active substance in this fungus is excreted unchanged in the urine. Those who partake of the psychedelic blueberry-mushroom milkshake save their urine for others to drink. It is estimated that the active hallucinogenic substance remains potent even when the urine is drunk five times (Dobkin de Rios, 1984).

The extent of drug use in the United States is difficult to determine. Most surveys target a particular group, such as high risk individuals, college students, or young adolescents. Very few have attempted to ask about legal as well as illegal drug use and, at the same time, sample a wide age range. One exception is the Household Survey of Drug Use conducted by the U.S. Department of Health and Human Services. The patterns of drug use over the last few years may be seen in Table 1.1.

An examination of the data in Table 1.1 would seem to indicate that drug use in the United States is declining. Note that according to these figures 13 percent of 18–25-year-olds are current users of marijuana, compared to 35.4 percent in 1979. "Only" 2 percent report recent cocaine use, compared to 9.3 percent in 1979. Concerning legal drugs, 63.6 percent are current users of alcohol and 32.2 percent users of cigarettes. This compares to 75.9 percent and 42.6 percent in 1979. Similar but smaller decreases can be seen in those that the National Institute of Drug Abuse refers to as "older

Table 1.1 Current (Past Month) Drug Use: 1972–1991

Youth Age 12–17

	1972	1974	1976	1977	1979	1982	1985	1988	1990	1991
Any Illicit Use	—	—	—	—	17.6	12.7	14.9	9.2	8.1	6.8
Marijuana	7.0	12.0	12.3	16.6	16.7	11.5	12.0	6.4	5.2	4.3
Hallucinogens	1.4	1.3	0.9	1.6	2.2	1.4	1.2	0.8	0.9	0.8
Cocaine	0.6	1.0	1.0	0.8	1.4	1.6	1.5	1.1	0.6	0.4
Heroin	*	*	*	*	*	*	*	0.1	*	0.1
Nonmedical use of										
Stimulants	—	1.0	1.2	1.3	1.2	2.6	1.6	1.2	1.0	0.5
Sedatives	—	1.0	*	0.8	1.1	1.3	1.0	0.6	0.9	0.5
Tranquilizers	—	1.0	1.1	0.7	0.6	0.9	0.6	0.2	0.5	0.3
Analgesics	—	—	—	—	0.6	0.7	1.6	0.9	1.4	1.1
Alcohol	—	34.0	32.4	31.2	37.2	30.2	31.0	25.2	24.5	20.3
Cigarettes	—	25.0	23.4	22.3	12.1+	14.7	15.3	11.8	11.6	10.8

Young Adults Age 18–25

	1972	1974	1976	1977	1979	1982	1985	1988	1990	1991
Any Illicit Use	—	—	—	—	37.1	30.4	25.7	17.8	14.9	15.4
Marijuana	27.8	25.2	25.0	27.4	35.4	27.4	21.8	15.5	12.7	13.0
Hallucinogens	—	2.5	1.1	2.0	4.4	1.7	1.9	1.9	0.8	1.2
Cocaine	—	3.1	2.0	3.7	9.3	6.8	7.6	4.5	2.2	2.0
Heroin	—	*	*	*	*	*	*	0.1	0.1	0.1
Nonmedical use of										
Stimulants	—	3.7	4.7	2.5	3.5	4.7	3.7	2.4	1.2	0.8
Sedatives	—	1.6	2.3	2.8	2.8	2.6	1.6	0.9	0.7	0.6
Tranquilizers	—	1.2	2.6	2.4	2.1	1.6	1.6	1.0	0.5	0.6
Analgesics	—	—	—	—	1.0	1.0	1.8	1.5	1.2	1.5
Alcohol	—	69.3	69.0	70.0	75.9	70.9	71.4	65.3	63.3	63.6
Cigarettes	—	48.8	49.4	47.3	42.6+	39.5	36.8	35.2	31.5	32.2

Adults Age 26 and Older

	1972	1974	1976	1977	1979	1982	1985	1988	1990	1991
Any Illicit Use	—	—	—	—	6.5	7.5	8.5	4.9	4.6	4.5
Marijuana	2.5	2.0	3.5	3.3	6.0	6.6	6.1	3.9	3.6	3.3
Hallucinogens	—	*	*	*	*	*	*	*	0.1	0.1
Cocaine	—	*	*	*	0.9	1.2	2.0	0.9	0.6	0.8
Heroin	—	*	*	*	*	*	*	*	*	*
Nonmedical use of										
Stimulants	—	*	*	0.6	0.5	0.6	0.7	0.5	0.3	0.2
Sedatives	—	*	0.5	*	*	*	0.6	0.3	0.1	0.3
Tranquilizers	—	*	*	*	*	*	1.0	0.6	0.2	0.4
Analgesics	—	—	—	—	*	*	0.9	0.4	0.6	0.5
Alcohol	—	54.5	56.0	54.9	61.3	59.8	60.6	54.8	52.3	52.5
Cigarettes	—	39.1	38.4	38.7	36.9+	34.6	32.8	29.8	27.7	28.2

— Estimate not available

* Low precision—no estimate shown

+ Includes only persons who ever smoked at least 5 packs.

Source: Department of Health & Human Services, National Household Survey on Drugs, *Drugs And Drug Abuse Education*, November/December, 1991, p. 104.

Table 1.2 Estimates of Emergency Room Drug Abuse Episodes of Top-Ranking Drugs 1988, 1989, 1990, and 1991 (First and Second Quarters)

Metropolitan Area	Total 1988	Total 1989	Total 1990	1990 4th Quarter	Jan.–Mar. 91*	Apr.–June 91*
Total ER Drug Abuse Episodes	416,962	425,904	371,208	89,325	96,406	100,381
Alcohol-in-Combination	120,117	125,861	115,162	26,878	28,921	30,397
Cocaine	104,732	110,013	80,355	19,381	22,282	25,370
Heroin/Morphine	39,026	41,656	33,884	7,510	8,465	9,432
Acetaminophen	24,288	29,667	25,422	6,496	7,208	7,528
Aspirin	23,570	23,435	19,188	5,156	6,083	5,192
Marijuana/Hashish	20,708	20,703	15,706	3,546	4,372	4,820
Diazepam	18,268	17,032	14,836	3,087	3,696	3,396
Ibuprofen	15,425	16,537	16,299	4,017	4,209	4,253
Alprazolam	16,571	14,946	15,846	3,726	3,628	4,654
Amitriptyline	9,049	10,497	8,642	2,247	2,381	1,778
Acetaminophen/Codeine	8,980	9,981	8,222	2,512	1,746	1,782
Methamphetamine Speed	9,345	8,722	5,236	963	1,220	1,350
O.T.C. sleep aids	8,362	8,517	7,984	1,759	1,543	1,510
PCP/PCP combinations	12,966	8,042	4,408	954	921	1,020
d-Propoxyphene	7,899	7,552	7,417	1,808	1,666	2,158
Lorazepam	4,953	7,056	7,625	1,797	1,664	1,680
Diphenhydramine	6,155	6,787	6,483	1,792	1,681	1,662
Phenobarbital	3,095	4,395	3,668	567	998	554
Triazolam	6,028	4,381	3,801	919	974	1,085
Hydantoin	3,705	4,913	4,026	732	720	596

*Estimates for this time period are provisional.

Source: NIDA, Drug Abuse Warning Network, *Drugs & Drug Abuse Education*, November/December, 1991, p. 106.

adults''—those over twenty-six. These decreases reflect what seems to be an ongoing trend, but note that the downward trend has leveled off in the last two or three years.

While the overall reported use of drugs has declined, an ominous trend seems to be developing. The most recent data suggest that emergency room admissions for drug episodes have dramatically increased for most drugs, as can be seen in Table 1.2. These data suggest that while *use* may be declining *abuse* seems to be increasing. Are we or aren't we winning the war on drugs?

The concept of *social desirability* applies to a number of situations, including responding to drug surveys. People tend to give what they consider the socially desirable answer on questionnaires and surveys. When drug use was considered more socially acceptable, a tendency existed for people to *overestimate* their drug use; now that many people consider drug use socially unacceptable, they may have a tendency to *underestimate* their use. If these figures are low estimates, what should be made of the House-holds Survey's finding that nearly 40 percent of Americans over the age of

Table 1.3 Trends in Lifetime and Current Use of Drugs by High School Seniors

Drug	Lifetime			Current		
	1988	1989	1990	1988	1989	1990
Any illicit use	54	51	48	21	20	17
Marijuana	47	44	41	18	17	14
Inhalants	17	18	18	03	02	03
Hallucinogens	09	09	09	02	02	02
Cocaine	12	10	09	03	03	02
Opiates	10	10	10	02	02	02
Stimulants	20	19	18	05	04	04
Sedatives	08	07	05	01	02	01
Tranquilizers	09	08	07	02	01	01
Alcohol	92	91	90	63	60	57
Cigarettes	66	66	64	29	29	29
Steroids	NA	03	03	NA	01	01

Note: Lifetime use means "ever used" while current use refers to use in the last thirty days. The term "opiates" includes heroin. NA stands for Not Available, meaning the data were not collected in 1988. All data were rounded off to the nearest whole percentage.

twelve have tried illicit drugs at least once, and 13 percent report using an illicit drug in the last year?!

The results of a survey of high school seniors show similar trends in drug use, at least for those remaining in school. When compared to previous years, reported use of legal and illegal drugs has either remained the same or declined. Whether this trend will continue or level off remains to be seen.

Table 1.3 shows the results of the questionnaire that has been answered by more than 15,000 students a year since the first year it was given. Such a large sample is most impressive, but remember that not everyone completes high school. Do high school dropouts have higher or lower rates of drug use? Furthermore, the same concept of social desirability applies to high school seniors as to adults; if it is socially unacceptable to admit drug use, do students tell the truth?

The National Household Survey includes the age group twelve to seventeen, but generally, nationwide studies of younger students are lacking. Many local communities and most states do compile such data, however, and a little searching will probably reveal a survey in your area. One study, done in Placer County, California, in 1991 is probably fairly representative (Table 1.4).

Other measures of drug use, or to be more correct, drug abuse, indicate that rather than declining, the drug problem may be getting worse. Nearly half of the 1.4 million prisoners in jails and prisons are incarcerated for alcohol or other drug related offenses, and the jail population is increasing so rapidly that at the current rate one half of the population of the United States will be incarcerated by the year 2053! Drug convictions account for most of the increase in the population. A study released by the United States

Table 1.4   Use of Various Drugs by 7th, 8th, and 9th Grade Students, Placer County, California

Drug	7th Grade	8th Grade	9th Grade
Marijuana	06	20	20
Inhalants	11	11	05
Hallucinogens	02	06	08
Cocaine	02	04	05
Stimulants	03	06	10
Tranquilizers	05	03	03
Alcohol	48	58	59
Cigarettes	23	33	34

Use is defined as at least once in the past six months.
Source: Placer County, CA, Office of Education.

Senate Judiciary Committee at about the same time as the Household Survey in 1991 claims that the incidence of cocaine addiction is nearly four times as great as the NIDA survey would indicate, and the rate of heroin use is nearly double.

The difference between these estimates is probably due to several factors. It may be that experimental use of drugs is declining, but drug *abuse* is increasing. It may be that each of these measures samples different populations. It may even be due to the fact that surveys and other estimates are influenced by subtle or not-so-subtle political pressure to make it appear that drug use is declining and thus we are winning the war on drugs, or that drug abuse is at an all-time high and we have failed in our war.

WHY DO PEOPLE CHOOSE A PARTICULAR DRUG?

Now that we have seen some reasons why people use drugs and who uses them, we need to consider *why* individuals choose to use which drugs. The principles of primary reinforcement and secondary reinforcement explain in part *why* drugs are used. Other factors, however, enter into the decision of *which* drug to use. Three factors seem particularly important: the user's personality, the legality or illegality of a drug, and the availability of a drug.

Personality Characteristics

Personality characteristics interact closely with motivation for drug use. Some people seem to prefer stimulants, some euphoriants, and some depressants. While this statement may seem obvious, it is difficult to prove. Moreover, extensive use of one drug can lead to use of another class of drugs to counteract the first. Cocaine users, for example, use heroin, barbituates, or alcohol to prolong the euphoria and decrease the unpleasant effects of the drug. In the past, drug users tended to have a preferred drug, but within the last ten to twenty years the polydrug abuser has come on the scene, one who indiscriminately uses and abuses various types and classes of drugs.

Moreover, drug use and especially drug abuse cause personality changes, and the vast majority of studies have looked at personality characteristics of drug users *after* they started using drugs. While numerous studies

• YOU READ IT HERE FIRST •

Because of federal regulations, college campuses and virtually all other public institutions have adopted a drug-free workplace policy, and there is increasing pressure to make access to legal drugs such as tobacco and alcohol more difficult on campuses. While this public health approach seems laudable, a danger does exist. Assume that college students will continue to drink alcoholic beverages despite education and official policy—a not unreasonable assumption supported by research (Meacci, 1990; Williams, Kirkman-Liff, & Szivek, 1990). Does restricting access to alcohol reduce the amount drunk or does it merely alter the location at which it is drunk? When the author was a college student during the Punic Wars, possession of alcoholic beverages on campus resulted in immediate dismissal. Consequently, on weekends especially, students gathered off-campus in more or less hidden locations to drink and then drove back to campus. Many students made sure their blood alcohol level was high enough to get them through the evening. Not only were we driving after drinking but we were drinking relatively large quantities in a short time period—a pattern that is clearly abusive. Do you feel that your college's policy towards alcohol and other drugs could actually unintentionally increase abusive patterns of consumption? If so, what can be done?

show that drug abusers are depressed, passive, and antisocial, studies that examine people before they start abusing drugs usually show no difference in *premorbid* personality between those who were moderate users and those who became abusers (Valliant, 1983; O'Connor & Berry, 1990). **Premorbid personality** refers to the user's personality characteristics before drug use became a problem.

Perhaps the most prevalent view of drug use is the **deviance model** which views drug use (especially illegal drug use) as a sign of abnormality or social maladjustment. The deviance model presumes that drug use is a symptom of an underlying psychological problem. This viewpoint, despite its current popularity, was first challenged more than forty years ago (Lindesmith, 1947; Winich, 1986) and is difficult to maintain in light of the fact that, as discussed above, nearly 40 percent of Americans more than twelve years old have used an illegal drug. Is it reasonable to assume that 40 percent of the population of the United States is deviant?

Furthermore, those who have used an illegal drug occasionally do not seem to be much different from those who have not. In fact, one study, which as you might expect, raised a storm of controversy, found that those who engaged in occasional use of drugs, typically marijuana, were actually the best adjusted of the students surveyed. Those who were heavy users were the worst off, not surprisingly, showing emotional problems and alienation, but those who had never used a drug by the age of eighteen seemed to be more anxious than the occasional user and more lacking in social skills (Shedler & Block, 1990).

Other studies, though not as dramatic, have also shown that the choice to use a drug, experimentally at least, is not necessarily an indication of psychological maladjustment, and that the reasons why some people use drugs and others do not are extremely complex. The choice to use or not use a drug is deeply embedded in cultural, religious, parental, and peer values, but neither these factors nor personality traits can in themselves predict drug use.

One reason that the deviance model has been maintained for so long is that studies show that those presenting themselves to drug and alcohol abuse treatment centers show a very high rate of psychiatric disorders (Ross, Glaser, & Germanson, 1988; Regier, Farmer, Rae, et al, 1990). Similarly, drug abuse among adolescents is a significant risk factor in suicidal behavior (Crumley, 1990). Treatment professionals see so many drug and alcohol abusers with psychiatric histories that they conclude that psychiatric disorders *cause* the drug abuse. However, it is not clear whether the relationship is causal; it may also be that those with psychological problems are more likely to abuse drugs.

Legality or Illegality

For some people, making a drug illegal decreases the likelihood that they will use it. For others, however, the illegality of a drug poses no deterrent, and for still others it might increase the attractiveness of the drug. A person convicted of a drug related felony, for example, is barred from many occupations and may lose voting and driving privileges. If, however, a person is unemployed, feels alienated from society, or already is an offender, the fear of arrest will not be as effective.

Making a drug illegal does not substantially decrease the demand for a drug once the drug has become established in a culture. Alcohol, marijuana, and cocaine demonstrate this fact quite clearly. The imposition of Prohibition in 1920 did not substantially alter use of alcohol among established drinkers. Similarly, marijuana and cocaine are both illegal drugs, yet the demand for them fuels an illegal drug industry that yields more than $30 billion a year for those involved in it. It should also be noted that the illegality of a drug has little to do with its **toxicity.** Nicotine, used by more than 60 million people in the United States, is a deadly poison, and addiction to cigarettes is directly responsible for 350,000 deaths a year. On the other hand, there have never been any deaths directly attributable to the use of marijuana or LSD. The legality or illegality of a drug often is more a statement by society about which drugs it will permit than it is a rational policy based on scientific evidence.

Availability of a Drug

When it is difficult to get heroin, addicts seek out codeine. The curves of amphetamine and cocaine use are almost exactly opposite; when amphetamine use is high, cocaine use is low (Brecher, 1972). When alcohol availability was limited in Ireland in the late nineteenth century, many turned to drinking ether, as others did during Prohibition in the United States (Brecher, 1972).

FARLEY by Phil Frank

For an individual willing to spend the money, any drug is available. However, a good argument could be made that too ready availability of a drug fosters its use. Alcohol is a good case in point. In many states, alcoholic beverages can be purchased at a bewildering variety of stores, from supermarkets to gas stations. In other states, availability is much more restricted. Would it help the incidence of alcohol abuse if sales were restricted for everyone?

Since the late 1980s two opposing forces have been meeting head on. First, there are those who feel that decreasing the availability of alcohol will decrease its use. This is the public health approach and involves three elements; the environment, the agent, and the host. The agent, of course, is the drug, in this case alcohol. The environment refers to the physical and social setting where alcohol and other drug purchase and use take place (Mosher, 1990). This approach emphasizes the importance of all three elements.

Those who feel that reducing availability of a drug—alcohol, for example—will reduce the number of those who have problems point out that it is hypocritical to wage campaigns against drinking and driving and then sell beer and wine in convenience stores that are often attached to gas stations (Ryan & Segars, 1987). Another tactic favored by the public health approach involves increasing the price of the drug through taxes or, in the case of illicit drugs, reducing supply.

This approach is opposed by those who think that the appropriate target is the host, especially the abuser. This argument maintains that since it is the abuser who is responsible for the majority of alcohol problems, it is unfair to restrict availability for the person who drinks responsibly. Needless to say, the alcohol industry supports this approach, accounting for the large number of "safe and sane" drinking advertisements sponsored by the alcohol industry. The conflict between those who wish to restrict access to legal drugs, such as cigarettes and alcohol, and those who oppose such efforts in

If this customer can buy beer at a gas station, what is to prevent him from drinking it on the way home?

the name of personal freedom or corporate profit, is sure to heat up in the years to come.

PATTERNS OF DRUG USE

The pattern of drug use varies from culture to culture, among individuals within each culture, and during the life span of the individual drug user. In order to understand drug use we must consider each of these elements.

Drug Use in a Cultural Context

Some cultures condone or encourage use and even abuse of alcohol, and others have strict prohibitions against its use. In some cultures, ritual use of hallucinogens is expected as part of puberty rites; in others, hallucinogen use is punished by imprisonment. In some cultures, regular smoking of opium is considered normal, while in others, possession of narcotics is punishable by death. Living in a given culture shapes our attitudes toward drugs. The use of alcohol, because it is so widespread, provides a good example of how patterns of drug use are affected by cultural attitudes.

Unlike American society, most cultures view alcohol use as a means to an end, not the end itself, and drinking without eating is rare. In Italy, wine is considered food, and the author can testify that in Spain, even though what we would call bars seem to be everywhere, drinking without eating is considered unusual, and intoxication is rarely seen. Even in today's Americanized world, cocktail lounges as we know them are relatively rare in Europe. Ours is perhaps the only Western culture in which the caption to the following photograph would make sense.

Another way in which drug use is controlled by a culture is through ceremonial use. Even without religious connotations many people control their drug use by setting aside a time and place and see their use as being highly structured. From the use of kava in the South Pacific island of Tonga, to drinking tea in England, ceremonial use of drugs serves many purposes

FIGURE 1.2
My hobby is drinking. On the weekends I enjoy getting together with my friends and boozing.

(Bott, 1987; Hazan, 1987). Zinberg (1984) summarized many years of research (both his and others') and concluded that through ceremonial rituals, some people are even capable of occasional use of such drugs as heroin or opium, drugs usually seen as highly addictive.

Patterns of Drug Use among Individuals

Many people take drugs from the moment they wake up until they go to sleep. Consider a cigarette smoker who also drinks coffee and alcohol. That person's system is never without one drug or another. A heroin addict is looked at with pity or scorn, depending on one's perspective, because he/she shoots up three or four times a day. Yet a heavy smoker does the equivalent in every couple of minutes!

Just as one swallow does not make a summer, neither does one swallow make an alcoholic or a drug addict. Instead of a broad gulf between "us" and "them," studies of patterns of drug use indicate that the issue is far more complicated. Polich, Ellickson, Reuter, and Kahan (1984) have identified four generally accepted patterns of drug use: non-use, experimental use, regular use, and heavy use. Non-use is self-explanatory but the other distinctions are important and need to be discussed.

Experimental Use

Experimental use is defined as ten or fewer experiences with a given drug and is usually motivated by curiosity or peer pressure. Experimental use, by definition, does not become repeated use for a number of reasons, including lack of access to the drug, failure to appreciate its psychotropic effect (it doesn't make the user feel good), or a lack of contact with the using culture.

Regular Use

This type of use is typical of drug use by most people. The primary motivation is the desire to share pleasurable experiences with friends. It might also be defined as **social-recreational.** Further purposes include (a) the desire to attain a degree of euphoria, (b) increased enjoyment of other activities, and (c) as a social lubricant. Also included in regular use is a type of drug use that might be defined as **circumstantial-situational.** Circumstantial-situational use occurs in the context of coping with a problem or some serious pressure. Graduate students preparing for exams, truck drivers making a long haul, and bodybuilders getting ready for a contest are likely to ingest drugs in this manner. Generally, though unfortunately not always, this type of drug use is limited to the circumstance or the situation. It can, however, lead to a pattern of coping with any situation by using a drug.

Heavy Use

Circumstantial-situational and social-recreational use are limited; heavy use (also called intensive or compulsive) is not. The person involved here uses drugs in an attempt to obtain relief from a persistent problem or in order to maintain a certain level of performance. This type of drug use should be considered dysfunctional. These users may be functioning in society, but dependence is present and daily use is a normal habit. They seem to have expanded circumstantial-situational use to nearly every circumstance and situation.

For heavy users the emphasis is on avoiding discomfort rather than experiencing pleasure. Social functioning has decreased, and the individual has to take the drug to have any semblance of normal functioning. The social setting no longer influences drug use; drug use determines the social setting. The individual finds settings to justify behavior that might, in other contexts, be seen as abnormal.

Several points need to be emphasized here. First, there is no reason to assume that these patterns are necessarily sequential. Many individuals remain social-recreational or circumstantial-situational users for a lifetime (Zinberg, 1982). Some individuals do start out using a drug occasionally and then go on to compulsive use, but most do not.

The second point is that use of any particular drug is not necessarily linked to any particular pattern. There are experimental users of heroin and compulsive users of caffeine. There are circumstantial-situational users of marijuana and intensified users of tranquilizers. Drug use cannot be considered out of the context of the pattern of use.

A third point needs to be made. For some groups, such as adolescents, virtually any drug use is illegal, even those drugs that are legal for adults. The drinking age is twenty-one in all states and most states have passed laws restricting cigarette sales to minors. For the rest of us, use of illicit drugs is, by definition, illegal.

The Office of Substance Abuse Prevention (OSAP) of the Alcohol, Drug Abuse and Mental Health Administration opposes the use of such terms as social-recreational use since they argue that there can be no recreational use of illegal substances. For them, all use is abuse. OSAP feels that taking such a stand will help reverse the public acceptance of some types of drug use.

While no one, especially the author of this textbook, wants to appear to advocate the use of any drug, the fact remains that research has clearly demonstrated that occasional, circumstantial, situational or whatever-you-choose-to-call-it drug use occurs, and occurs without significant harm for some people. Not all use is abuse (Newcomb & Bentler, 1989). Considerable evidence exists that experimental use, especially in adolescence, is not associated with serious consequences (Newcomb & Bentler, 1988) and, as you have read, some researchers have even concluded that experimental users are psychologically as healthy if not healthier than abstainers.

Drug Use across the Life Span

Not only do individuals differ in their drug use but a given person may alter his or her pattern and choice of drugs in the course of a lifetime (Fillmore, 1988). If we examine the alcohol or other drug use of a person at a given point in time, even if in the course of that survey we attempt to determine the length of drug use, we may be getting a false picture. Studies in which the pattern of drug use is measured over a period of time (called a longitudinal study) indicate that alcohol and drug use patterns vary considerably depending on, among other things, the age and personal circumstances of the user.

In addition, periods of transition in a person's life such as divorce, marriage, death of a spouse, or onset of middle age are often when patterns of alcohol and drug use may fluctuate. It is essential therefore to consider the passage of time as a significant factor in estimating and understanding drug use. An otherwise stable and normal individual may be labeled a drug abuser based on the pattern of drug use for a short period of time. Conversely, of course, those who have a long pattern of drug abuse can and do moderate or even stop drug use for surprisingly long periods.

Many people, especially adolescents, experiment with drug use as a result of social influence. Basically stable, healthy, young adults whose values are largely conventional and who live in a context where drug use is not acceptable, usually give up the experimentation of their adolescence (Kandel & Raveis, 1989). Several nominees for justice of the Supreme Court, a vice president of the United States, and many other prominent public figures have admitted to experimental use of marijuana in their youth. Presumably, these youthful indiscretions have not hindered their later performance.

METHODS OF DETERMINING DRUG USE

Any number of sources exist for estimating the amount of drug use, the cost of drug abuse to industry, and other kinds of data that flood the popular press. Often these data conflict. Do we really know where we stand on drug use in the United States? Where do these data come from?

The way in which data are collected undoubtedly influences the findings. In the questionnaire method, for example, respondents are simply asked to report the type and frequency of drug use. Most questionnaires distinguish between categories such as "ever used," "currently use," "used within the last thirty days," or "use daily," but what about the drug user whose use fluctuates with circumstances? What about the person who used to use a drug but stopped? What about the person who lies, as most people do on questionnaires?

Another common method of obtaining data is the interview method. Instead of relying on subjects to fill out forms, researchers ask questions about drug use face-to-face. Properly conducted interviews are quite effective, since the person conducting the interview can follow up on topics that might come up during the interview and can clarify any difficulty the subject may have in understanding the questions. Like the questionnaire method, however, verifying the accuracy of the information given is difficult, if not impossible.

Ingenious methods have been developed to increase the validity of interviews and questionnaires, but they remain flawed. In fact, these two techniques for data collection can produce different results. Even the setting makes a difference. In a study done with adolescents, a questionnaire administered in a home setting revealed less drug use than the same questionnaire administered in school (Rootman & Smart, 1985).

Indirect methods of estimating drug use have also been used, but they have their problems as well. We can easily estimate how much alcohol is sold legally in the United States by examining alcohol sales tax revenues. Disregarding the amount of illegal, untaxed alcohol consumed, such a figure tells us nothing about the patterns of use.

If you convert the amount of alcohol sold in the United States into per capita consumption, the figure amounts to several drinks per day per person who admits to drinking. This amount does not correlate with self-reports and fails to consider that alcohol use varies among individuals. Other estimates indicate that 50 percent of the alcohol is consumed by 10 percent of the population, making the average drinker's consumption far less than several drinks daily.

With illegal drugs, estimating patterns of use with indirect methods is virtually impossible. The amount of cocaine smuggled into the United States, the amount of marijuana grown here, or the extent of heroin use can only be estimated, and the agencies doing the estimating rarely have hard figures to substantiate them. Furthermore, they are under considerable pressure to adjust those figures to reflect either the extent of the problem (if they need more money) or their success in combatting it (if they are called on to justify their budgets).

The same problem is seen whenever accurate data are difficult to obtain, such as estimates of date rape or child neglect. Data presented to demonstrate a point of view are called **advocacy figures** and are usually weighted in the direction that the advocate is promoting.

For example, the cost to society of drug use is often stated to be in excess of $100 billion. One way to come up with such a figure is to look at the absentee rates, accident records, hospitalization costs, and other data of acknowledged drug abusers and then use this figure to estimate a cost for society at large. However, these numbers are nothing more than guesses and suffer from a basic flaw; they assume that if the drug abuser were not using drugs, that he/she would be a productive member of society. Maybe users would be absent just as much straight as when using.

No matter how flawed they are, however, nearly all published statistics are better than consensus estimates. Have you ever noticed that users of a particular drug, or believers in a particular religion, for that matter, tend to overestimate the numbers of users/followers? If you know no one who uses heroin, your estimates of heroin use are likely to be low. If you come from an area where heroin use is more common, your estimate will be higher. We tend to associate with those like us and make judgments based on the behavior of those around us.

After considering all of the factors involved in drug use, we can see that there are no simplistic answers to the problem of drug use and abuse. Given the pervasiveness of drug use, we would have to be incredibly naive to believe that society can ever reasonably expect to be completely drug free. The goal of this book is to help the reader develop a perspective that will allow him or her to understand some of the issues involved. All of us need to be able to make informed, intelligent decisions as a person, parent, and member of society. In fact, we have no choice. As the existential philosophers have pointed out, not choosing is also a choice. The alternative to being informed is the decision to remain ignorant.

SUMMARY

Most people use drugs of some kind, either legal or illegal. The reasons for this drug use are complex and cannot be reduced to a simplistic formula. Concepts such as primary and secondary reinforcement can help explain some drug use, but other factors need to be considered as well.

The roles of the media, religion, and medicine need to be considered, as do peer influences. Surrounded as we are by constant examples of drug taking, the fact that some of us abuse these drugs should come as no surprise. In fact, the distinction between drug use and abuse is often difficult to determine. Virtually any drug can be abused, and some people appear to be able to use even supposedly highly addicting drugs on an occasional basis.

Patterns of drug use need to be considered when attempting to understand the issue of drug abuse. Different cultures have different attitudes toward drugs, and drug use varies across the life span. Drug use is not synonymous with abuse. All too often well meaning people confuse experimental use with compulsive use. Even the political and legal systems of our society sometimes fail to recognize these distinctions.

Much of what we think we know about drugs is inaccurate and this misinformation extends to the question of the extent of drug use. Various methods of determining who uses which drug yield different results. People lie, forget, and misinterpret questions about their drug use, making accurate estimation very difficult.

REFERENCES

Brecher, E. (1972). *Licit and illicit drugs.* Boston: Little, Brown.

Crumley, F. E. (1990). Substance abuse and adolescent suicidal behavior. *Journal of the American Medical Association, 263,* 3051–956.

Davis, W. (1985). Hallucinogenic plants and their use in traditional society: An overview. *Cultural Survival Quarterly, 9,* 2–4.

Diamond, J. (1990). Kung Fu kerosene drinking. *Natural History,* August, 20–24.

Dobkin de Rios, M. (1984). *Hallucinogens: Cross cultural perspectives.* Albuquerque: University of New Mexico Press.

Fillmore, K. (1988). *Alcohol use across the life course: A critical review of 70 years of international longitudinal research.* Toronto: Addiction Research Foundation.

Janofsky, W. J., & Alfano, P. Half of Seoul athletes may have used banned drugs. *Sacramento Bee,* November 17, 1988. Reprinted from *The New York Times.*

Johnston, L., & O'Malley, P. (1986). Why do the nation's students use drugs and alcohol? Self-reported reasons from nine national surveys. *Journal of Drug Issues, 16,* 29–66.

Kandel, D., & Raveis, V. (1989). Cessation of illicit drug use in young adulthood. *Archives of General Psychiatry, 46,* 109–16.

Kessler, D., & Pines, W. (1990). The federal regulation of prescription drug advertising and promotion. *Journal of the American Medical Association, 18,* 2409–15.

Lindesmith, A. (1947). *Opiate Addiction.* Bloomington: Principia Press.

Linsky, A., Colby, J., & Strauss, M. (1986). Drinking norms and alcohol-related problems in the United States. *Journal of Alcohol Studies, 47,* 384–93.

Newcomb, M., & Bentler, P. (1988). Impact of adolescent drug use and social support on problems of young adults: A longitudinal study. *Journal of Abnormal Psychology, 97,* 64–75.

Newcomb, M., & Bentler, P. (1989). Substance use and abuse among children and teenagers. *American Psychologist, 44,* 242–48.

Newcomb, M., Chou, C., Bentler, P., & Huba, G. (1988). Cognitive motivators for use among adolescents: Longitudinal tests of gender differences and predictors of change in drug use. *Journal of Counseling Psychology, 35,* 426–38.

O'Conner, L., & Berry, S. (1990). The drug of choice phenomenon: Why addicts start using their preferred drugs. *Journal of Psychoactive Drugs, 22,* 305–10.

O'Gorman, P. A. The conflict between personal ideology and prevention programs. *Alcohol Health and Research World, 12(4),* 298–301.

Peck, C. (1991). FDA regulation of prescription drug advertising. *Journal of the American Medical Association, 264,* 2424–25.

Polich, J. M., Ellickson, P. L., Reuter, P., & Kahan, J. P. (1984). *Strategies for Controlling Adolescent Drug Use.* Santa Monica, CA: Rand Corporation.

Regier, D., Farmer, M., Rae, D., Locke, B., Keith, S., Judd, L., & Goodwin, F. (1990). Comorbidity of mental disorders with alcohol and other drug abuse. *Journal of the American Medical Association, 264,* 2511–18.

Rootman, I., & Smart, R. (1985). A comparison of alcohol, tobacco and drug use as determined from household/school surveys. *Drug and Alcohol Dependence, 16,* 89–94.

Ross, H. E., Glaser, F. B., & Germanson, T. (1988). The prevalence of psychiatric disorders in patients with alcohol and other drug problems. *Archives of General Psychiatry, 45,* 1023–31.

Ryan, B., & Segars, L. (1987). Minimarts and maxiproblems: The relationship between purchase and consumption location. *Alcohol Health and Research World, 12,* 27–29.

Shedler, J., & Block, J., (1990). Adolescent drug use and psychological health: A longitudinal inquiry. *American Psychologist 45,* 613–30.

Siegel, R. (1989). *Intoxication.* New York: E. P. Dutton.

Valliant, G. (1983). *The Natural History of Alcoholism.* Boston: Harvard University Press.

Winick, C. (1986). The deviance model of drug-taking behavior: A critique. In B. Segal (Ed.), *Perspectives on drug use in the United States,* pp. 29–50. New York: Haworth Press.

Zinberg, N., & Harding, W. (1982). Introduction-control and intoxicant use: A theoretical and practical overview. In N. Zinberg & W. Harding (Eds.), *Control over intoxicant use: Pharmacological, Psychological and Social Considerations,* pp. 13–35. New York: Human Sciences Press.

Zinberg, N. (1984). *Drug, set and setting.* New Haven: Yale University Press.

2

• • •

THE PHARMACOLOGY OF DRUG ACTION

• • •

OBJECTIVES

When you have finished studying this chapter you should:

1. Be able to define what a drug is.
2. Be able to name the routes of administration of a drug and the advantages and disadvantages of each.
3. Know why titration is an important concept in understanding drug use.
4. Be able to discuss the importance of lipid solubility.
5. Understand how the half life of a drug affects the patterns of drug use.
6. Be able to tell how the concept of threshold is related to a drug's effect.
7. Know the concept of the "lock and key principle".
8. Be able to discuss time relationships of drugs.
9. Know how individual differences affect the action of a drug.
10. Be able to discuss the concept of addiction.
11. Know the difference between psychological and physiological dependence.
12. Be able to discuss four types of tolerance.
13. Know why placebo effects are so important in understanding the effects of drugs.
14. Know how set and setting affect a person's response to a drug.
15. Know how set and setting contribute to a drug's effects.
16. Be able to classify drugs into their respective categories.

KEY TERMS

acute tolerance
addiction
behavioral tolerance
binding
blood/brain barrier
buccal
chippers
cross-tolerance
dependence
diffusion
DMSO
double blind
ED50
ethnic differences
half life
inhalation
intravenous
intramuscular
LD
lipid solubility
lock-and-key principle
mainlining
osmosis
parenteral
physiological tolerance
placebo
psychoactive
psychological dependence
reductionism
reverse tolerance
route of administration
set
setting
specificity
subcutaneous route
substance abuse
teratogenic
threshold
titration
tolerance
transdermal
withdrawal

I n order to understand how drugs affect behavior, it is essential to understand how they affect the body. The study of how drugs affect the body is called pharmacology and is one of the oldest sciences. Sumerian clay tablets date back to 3000 B.C. and include prescriptions for treatment of many diseases (Ansel, 1985). The most famous set of prescriptions is an Egyptian papyrus which includes such ingredients as jackal fat, boiled thigh bones, and crocodile dung. Also included in these remedies, however, were valuable drugs such as opium and castor oil, among others.

Some medicines and treatments prescribed in ancient times are still in use today. The ancient physicians of India advised reserpine for treatment of hypertension, aseptic surgery (in which precautions are taken to prevent infection), and vaccination for smallpox—all of this more than 2,500 years ago and some 2,000 years before being discovered by "enlightened" Western medicine (Levine, 1983).

The logical way to start a chapter on pharmacology is to define the term **drug**—not an easy task, as the word has many meanings and connotations. A pharmacologist would insist that I am taking a drug right now, since I am drinking coffee as I write this paragraph. The pharmacologist would also classify heroin, aspirin, and nicotine as drugs, while the average person often thinks of "drugs" and "illegal drugs" as synonymous. No standard definition can encompass all the meanings of the word. Although the definition is imperfect, the term *drug* will be used to describe any chemical substance taken to cure or prevent disease, to enhance mental or physical performance, or to escape from or cope with reality.

In this book we are most interested in chemical substances that alter behavior or change consciousness. We will call these substances **psychoactive** drugs. Many drugs that are taken for other purposes have psychoactive effects. Propranolol, for example, is a drug taken to reduce blood pressure. As discussed in chapter 3, it is also an effective antianxiety drug and is used in the treatment of some phobias (Noyes, 1982). Similarly, many steroids, antihistamines, and over-the-counter medications normally taken to relieve the symptoms of disease have strong psychoactive effects.

In addition, many substances that we do not normally consider drugs nevertheless meet the above definition. A cup of tea or coffee, a glass of wine, or a cigarette all contain drugs. We need to remember that these frequently used and socially approved substances which we ingest daily are, in fact, drugs. Even many foods contain chemical substances that in another context are considered drugs.

Both the Indian in this pottery figure from Ecuador and the young man are using the buccal route of administration. The more things change, the more they remain the same.

HOW DRUGS WORK

With few exceptions, psychoactive drugs first need to be transported to the brain in order to be effective. In nearly every case the mode of transport is the bloodstream. The varied **routes of administration** are methods of getting drugs into the bloodstream. The drug is then absorbed into the brain and into cell tissue where it exerts its effect. Finally, the action of the drug is terminated and the drug is excreted. Understanding the details of these processes is essential to understanding the effects of psychoactive drugs.

Routes of Administration

There are a number of pathways by which psychoactive drugs can reach the brain and exert their effects. Each has its advantages and disadvantages. The form in which the drug is administered is determined in part by the intended route of administration. Conversely, some drugs come in a form which dictates the route of administration. Crack and ''ice'' differ from cocaine and methamphetamine, for example, primarily because they are in a form which permits them to be absorbed through inhalation. On the other hand, since alcohol is a liquid, it is most readily absorbed by the oral route of administration.

Oral Route

Oral administration is a convenient, and the most frequent, route of administration. The effect of drugs administered this way however, can be variable since several factors influence the rate of absorption. The three most important factors are the concentration of the drug being absorbed, the stomach contents of the person taking the drug, and the presence or absence of enzymes which can metabolize certain drugs.

The rate of absorption is affected by the *concentration* of the drug. High concentrations of a drug are often absorbed more slowly than more moderate concentrations. A shot of 100 proof bourbon taken straight, for example, will be absorbed more slowly than the same amount of bourbon in a mixed drink. The same is true for aspirin. Many people take aspirin with only a sip of water. Because the concentration of aspirin is high (assuming, of course that it even goes into solution) the drug is absorbed more slowly than if taken with a full glass of water.

Stomach content also influences the effects of a drug. The stomach functions as a storage place and processes food for absorption by the small intestine. Therefore, stomach contents determine how long a given drug will remain there. Furthermore, the digestive acids in the stomach can influence absorption by interacting with the drug taken. Finally, the presence of enzymes in the stomach can affect absorption by metabolizing the drug taken.

Until quite recently, for example, it was accepted that the primary route of metabolism of alcohol was in the liver and the contribution of the tissues of the gastrointestinal tract was minimal. However, now it is believed that substantial metabolism of alcohol takes place in the stomach due to the presence of the enzyme, alcohol dehydrogenase (Frezza, Padova, Pozzato, et al, 1990; Lieber, 1991). The significance of this finding is discussed in chapter 5.

Titration. Another problem with the oral route of administration is that compared with inhalation or injection, the oral route is slow. Peak blood alcohol levels are not reached until about forty-five minutes after ingestion, while with inhalation the drug reaches the brain in seconds. The slow speed of absorption and the variability with which absorption takes place with the oral route makes **titration** very difficult. The ability to titrate, or adjust the concentration of a drug, is one of the factors that differentiates the experienced from the inexperienced user.

For example, most people report that the most pleasurable effects of alcohol occur at blood alcohol levels of 0.02–0.05 (the equivalent of one or two standard drinks for a 150–pound male drinking on an empty stomach). Because of the variables involved, however, it is difficult to reach and remain at this level. Most drinkers have had the experience of feeling nothing shortly after the first drink, drink one or two more too quickly, and then feeling intoxicated.

The experienced drug user is usually better at titrating than the novice user. This knowledge, or ability, is quite valuable and, in reality, is the essence of responsible drug use. How do you know when enough of a drug is enough? If we could answer, one could go a long way toward solving the drug problem we have today. If we accept the idea that, at least for some drugs, drug use is not synonymous with drug abuse, the concept of titration is an important one.

FIGURE 2.1

The villi increase surface area of the intestine so that drugs and nutrients may be more readily absorbed.

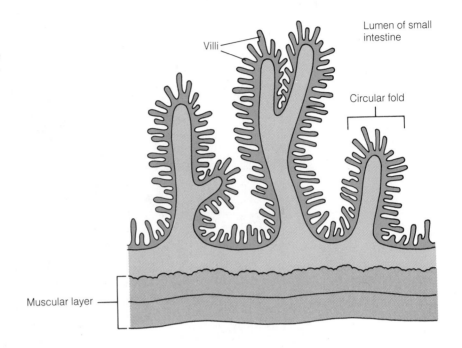

Buccal Route. Despite the disadvantages, the oral route of administration is very popular, and many drugs are taken orally. Although we associate the word "oral" with "mouth," drug absorption takes place along the entire gastrointestinal tract. In the mouth, the thin layer of cells called the epithelium and the intricate network of blood vessels are conducive to rapid absorption. Most substances do not remain in the mouth for long, however, so normally only a small percentage of total absorption occurs this way. If the drug is kept in the mouth, of course, then these membranes can function. Bolivian Indians absorb cocaine this way, and those who chew tobacco or use tobacco pouches absorb nicotine through this route. This route is sometimes called the **buccal** route of administration.

Sublingual Route. If the **sublingual** route of administration is used, the drug to be absorbed is placed under the tongue. Several prescription drugs are marketed in this form, and over-the-counter sublingual preparations are becoming popular as well. One advantage of this route is that drugs absorbed this way do not pass through the liver before going to the heart. Thus not only does the drug reach the brain faster, but it is not metabolized by the liver until *after* it reaches the brain. Another advantage is that drugs can be taken this way which would be irritating elsewhere in the gastrointestinal tract. Drugs to treat migraine and some heart conditions are commonly administered sublingually.

The next major site of absorption is the stomach. Some absorption of drugs does take place in there although the percentage is small compared to

FIGURE 2.2
Heroin, as seen above, can be found in many forms. At the top of the picture are rubber balloons sometimes used to smuggle heroin. These are swallowed and passed through the gastrointestinal tract.

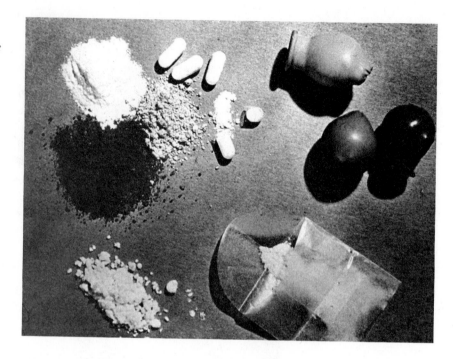

that of the intestine (Levine, 1983). For most drugs the primary site of absorption is the small intestine, which is also the site of absorption of digested food. The inner layer of the intestine is composed of villae, or folds, that greatly increase the surface area of the intestine and thus increase the rate of absorption (see figure 2.1). Once absorbed into the veins of the gastrointestinal tract, the drug taken by the oral route passes through the liver before getting to the heart and being distributed throughout the body. The passage of the drug down the gastrointestinal tract and then through the veins to the liver and finally to the heart accounts for the relatively slow absorption compared to some other routes of administration.

Drugs taken in tablet or capsule form have to be in solution before they can be absorbed. A drug that is difficult to dissolve will be absorbed slowly, if at all. This phenomenon has lead to the development of time release capsules. Various coatings are used to ensure a gradual release of the drug over a period of hours. In most cases, a drug in solution is absorbed within thirty minutes. With coatings, the time of absorption can be prolonged so that a single capsule could release its drug over an eight-hour period.

If the coating surrounding the drug is completely insoluble, the drug will pass through the entire digestive tract and be excreted unchanged. Drug smugglers take advantage of this fact and fill prophylactics or rubber balloons with heroin or cocaine and induce others to swallow them before gaining entry to a country. These ''mules,'' as they are called, then clear

Users of drugs such as heroin and cocaine often use the intravenous route.

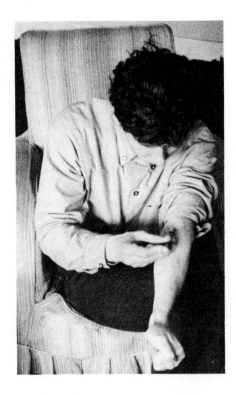

customs and excrete the balloons with the drug inside, unaffected by its journey across the border or through the digestive tract. Unhappily for the mules, however, the balloons or prophylactics sometimes break, and several would-be smugglers have died when a large quantity of heroin or cocaine was suddenly released in the intestinal tract (Joynt & Mikhael, 1985).

Parenteral Use

Parenteral use refers to injection of drugs directly into the body, not to the use of drugs by parents. The word **parenteral** literally means ''outside the intestine.'' Drugs can be injected into or beneath the skin, into muscles, or directly into the veins or arteries. Drugs can be injected into the heart, the spine, bone, abdominal cavity, joints, or any organ. Under rare circumstances, drugs can even be injected direct›y into the brain. As might be imagined, each of these uses has its advantages and disadvantages.

Intravenous Route. Since the bloodstream is the route by which drugs are distributed throughout the body, the most practical method of drug administration would be to introduce the drug directly into the bloodstream. The term used to describe this method is the **intravenous** route of administration. In this method a hypodermic syringe is filled with a solution and the needle introduced into a vein, usually in the forearm.

Once in the bloodstream of the venous system, the drug goes to the heart, from the heart the blood carrying the drug goes to the lungs, then back to the heart and then through the arteries to the organs and structures of the body. Capillaries form the link between the arteries and veins, and the veins carry the blood back to the heart. The circulating bloodstream distributes the drug to all parts of the body within one minute after injection, so the effect of the drug is virtually instantaneous.

The intravenous route has several advantages. Precise measurement of the amount of drug introduced is possible, since all intervening steps to absorption into the bloodstream have been bypassed. Titration, therefore, is easy. The concentration of the drug is not affected by stomach contents or digestive acids, and drugs that may be irritating to tissues can be administered.

In emergencies where speed is important, the intravenous route can be lifesaving. Furthermore, evidence suggests that part of the pleasant effect of any drug is the speed with which a drug is absorbed into tissue, especially brain tissue. The more rapid the change, apparently, the more pleasant the effect. Since the drug is injected directly into a vein, the concentration of the drug can be quite high and that change in concentration can be achieved quite rapidly. Consequently, absorption in the target organ is quite rapid. No wonder then, that the intravenous route is the preferred method of administration among many "serious" drug users.

Disadvantages to the parenteral route exist as well. For example, once a drug has been administered intravenously, it cannot be retrieved. With oral administration drugs can be removed by pumping the stomach, inducing vomiting, or by enemas and laxatives. Even with other parenteral routes, the rate of absorption can be slowed. However, since no method yet exists for removing the drug from the bloodstream once it is there, the intravenous route is dangerous, with drug overdose always a possibility.

Other disadvantages include the fact that not all drugs are soluble in fluids which can be injected in the body. Concentration of some drugs may be irritating to the blood vessels. Of course, the risk of acquiring an infection such as hepatitis or AIDS is considerable as well.

Subcutaneous Route. A rich layer of blood vessels exists just below the epidermis, or skin. Drugs can be injected between this cutaneous layer and the layer of blood vessels. These injections are **subcutaneous.** Absorption by this route is slower than the intravenous route. The chief advantage of subcutaneous absorption is that the rate of absorption can be controlled. For example, when you go to a dentist and receive an injection of an anesthetic into the gum around a tooth, the drug would normally be rapidly absorbed. However, included in the injection is a drug that constricts blood vessels, thus decreasing the rate of absorption and increasing the duration of the anesthesia.

The subcutaneous route is popular with recreational drug users who refer to the technique as "skin popping." It is often the intermediate step in heroin use. Heroin addicts often start out by smoking the drug and then

One assumes (and hopes) that this photograph of an intramuscular injection reflects a legal use of drugs.

"progress" to skin popping before beginning intravenous use, or "mainlining."

The subcutaneous route is not without problems. Some drugs irritate subcutaneous membranes, making injection painful. Use of nonsterile or even sterile needles can lead to abscesses. Nevertheless, subcutaneous injection is safer than intravenous use.

Intramuscular Route. The **intramuscular** route of administration is familiar to most of us from childhood and countless hospital jokes, because the buttock muscle is often used. In fact, any large muscle group is suitable, and favorite sites include the upper arm and thigh as well as the buttock. In the forties and fifties, when the percentage of heroin in the average "bag" was much higher, intramuscular injection was a common route of administration of the narcotics.

The intramuscular injection route is commonly used when immediate response is not desired and when a large volume of a drug or an irritating substance is to be injected. As long as a blood vessel is not accidentally penetrated, the relative location of the site of injection is unimportant, making intramuscular use safe and easy.

The characteristics of intramuscular use—slowness of absorption, a high safety factor, and ease of administration—have lead to two fairly recent developments in drug use. In the first method, a drug to be absorbed is dissolved in oil, and the oil is then injected into a muscle. Absorption is slow because the drug has to diffuse from the oil suspension. The oil serves as a

FIGURE 2.3
Drugs absorbed by the oral route must be transported from the gastrointestinal (G.I.) tract to the liver to the heart to the lungs, and back to the heart before they get to the brain. Inhalation gets drugs to the brain much faster because they go from the lungs to the heart to the brain.

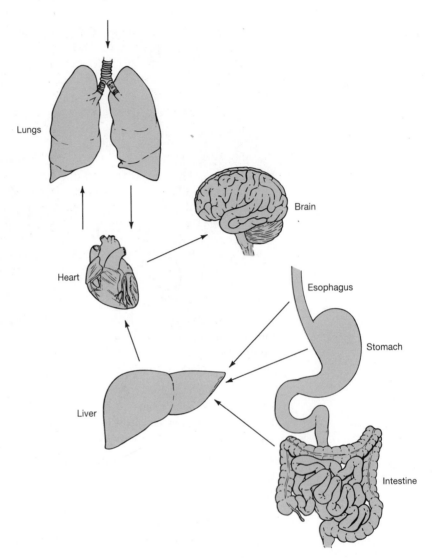

reservoir of the drug. Testing is currently being conducted to determine whether this technique would be effective as a method of birth control.

The second development is the styrette. Self injection is a difficult task. Most people have an aversion to sticking a needle into their bodies, yet there are times when injection is essential. The styrette is a spring-loaded mechanism that contains a needle and a standard dose of a drug. The spring is triggered by placing the styrette in contact with the skin or clothing. The needle is then driven forward, driving the needle into the muscle and injecting the drug.

Inhalation

The three most common routes of drug absorption for humans are oral, parenteral, and inhalation. Administration by **inhalation** is quite rapid because of the extensive network of blood vessels in the lungs. The normal function of this collection of capillaries is to absorb oxygen; however, many other molecules such as those of drugs also can be transported. Drugs readily absorbed by the capillaries in the lungs include anesthetic gases, such as nitrous oxide, nicotine, THC (the primary active ingredient in marijuana), and cocaine when it is used as "freebase" or "crack."

Moreover, as can be seen in figure 2.3 the venous blood supply from the lungs goes directly to the heart and then is pumped to the tissues of the body through the arteries. Compare a molecule of drug absorbed this way with one absorbed into the bloodstream through the intestine which must pass through the liver, travel to the heart, then to the lungs, back to the heart, and finally to the tissues. No wonder the inhalation route is so rapid.

Small molecules such as anesthetic gases are absorbed into the blood quite rapidly. Nicotine, THC, and cocaine are fairly large molecules, however, and it should be difficult for them to pass into the bloodstream. Exactly how they are absorbed is not entirely clear, but they obviously are. The rapid increase in drug level produced by inhalation seems to be highly reinforcing, and the deeper the drug is inhaled, the more the contact with the capillaries in the lungs. Watch a fellow student who is a cigarette smoker after a long class. He or she will walk outside, light up, and inhale deeply. Then watch for a change in facial expression to see how rapidly nicotine reaches the brain.

Mucous Membranes

Absorption also can occur across any **mucous membrane.** There are two routes, vaginal and anal, that are relatively uncommon but possible modes of administration. Rectal suppositories are sometimes administered to unconscious patients in hospitals, and some "chippers" or recreational users of opiate drugs use this route because they think they will be less likely to develop nausea.

Indians of the Mayan culture before the Spanish Conquest and some tribes today administer alcohol and hallucinogenic drugs by means of an enema (Diamond, 1990). The advantage of this method over the oral route (it isn't too difficult to think of several disadvantages) is that, like the buccal route, drugs absorbed rectally (or vaginally) bypass the liver; the veins go directly to the heart.

Intravaginal absorption of drugs has been suggested as basis for the folk belief in flying witches (Davis, 1985). The formula below is purported to be a "recipe" that enables "witches" to fly. Some researchers believe that these substances were introduced into the vagina during the notorious witches' sabbaths. Legend has it that this was accomplished by means of a broomstick. After intravaginal absorption of these substances, the witches might readily report that they could "fly."

Traditional English Flying Ointment

3 grams annamthol
30 grams betel
50 grams extract of opium
15 grams of cinquefoil
15 grams henbane
15 grams belladonna
15 grams hemlock
250 grams cannabis indica
5 grams cantharidin
Blend with oil of your choice; baby fat, vaseline, safflower oil or
butter (Jong, 1983).

Opium and hemlock induce a drowsy stupor. Henbane and belladonna contain hyoscine derivatives, notably scopolamine, which causes hallucinations and amnesia. Cannabis indica is marijuana, and cantharidin is the infamous Spanish Fly. Such a combination of drugs, combined with the expectations of those who take them, could easily lead to the illusion of flying. Of course, in high doses most of these drugs are also fatal.

Similarly, some couples engage in oral-genital sex involving introduction of cocaine into the vaginal cavity. Rapid absorption of the drug would be expected because blood vessels dilate during sexual excitement. At least one death has been attributed to this practice when a lethal dose of cocaine was absorbed.

Transdermal

Another relatively uncommon means of drug absorption occurs across the skin barrier or **transdermally.** The external layer of skin is a very effective barrier against absorption, but it is not perfect. Cuts and abrasions expose blood vessels so that drugs which are placed on the surface of the skin can be absorbed directly. In fact, the "flying ointment" described above was also supposedly rubbed on the skin. In the past, skin lesions were far more common than they are today, so any substance applied to the skin would probably be readily absorbed.

Dimethyl sulfoxide, or **DMSO,** is a curious chemical compound that is readily transported across the skin barrier. In addition it is widely used in industry because it is a very powerful solvent. Any drug dissolved in DMSO would be absorbed into the bloodstream if DMSO were rubbed on the skin. Although DMSO is often used by athletes because it has been touted as a cure for muscle strains and arthritis, it does not seem to have caught on with the drug using population.

One interesting, but probably fictitious, story about transdermal absorption concerns Jimi Hendrix, a well known popular music figure of the sixties who died of a reputed drug overdose in September, 1970. He is supposed to have placed LSD in the headband that he wore during performances. His

New Ways to Administer Drugs

All of the common ways of administering drugs are nonspecific, meaning that a drug is absorbed and then transported throughout the body. In addition, every means of administration has drawbacks. New developments in molecular biology and other scientific fields have enabled researchers to devise new ways of delivering drugs that eliminate at least some of the drawbacks.

The problem of specificity, the need to get a drug to a precise part of the body, has been aided by the development of discs. These discs degrade naturally and, in doing so, release a drug. Used experimentally to release small amounts of neurotransmitters to specific areas of the brain, this technique would seem to have considerable promise in Alzheimer's disease, believed to be related to a deficiency of acetylcholine (see chapter 3). Similar implants are available that, as they dissolve, release contraceptive hormones. One, a matchstick-sized implant, can prevent conception for up to four years and was approved in 1990.

Transdermal patches have recently become popular and are used to deliver scopolamine (to fight seasickness), nitroglycerine (for patients with chest pain due to heart conditions), and, most recently, nicotine for helping smokers overcome their habit (Segal, 1991; Transdermal Nicotine Study Group, 1991).

The most technologically complex methods involve mechanical pumps that can be implanted in the body and deliver drugs at very precise doses and rates. It may even be possible to develop feedback mechanisms that will regulate the output of these pumps. One such pump has been available since 1982 for treating liver cancer and a new pump has recently been approved for administering morphine to those in severe pain.

On a less technical level, nasal sprays are also being developed that will deliver drugs more rapidly to the bloodstream. As we have seen, the nasal cavity is richly supplied with blood vessels. Large drug molecules cannot penetrate this barrier, but recent advances in biochemistry have combined these molecules with a form of detergent which makes them pass into the bloodstream more rapidly. This method is presently being tested for administering insulin and contraceptives.

While these techniques have not been adapted to illegal, recreational, or psychoactive drug use, it is probably only a question of time. To the extent that the greatest reinforcement is gained from absorbing drugs as rapidly as possible, some of these techniques are likely to be adapted by drug users in the future.

sweat is supposed to have dissolved the LSD which then was absorbed through the skin.

TRANSPORT AND DISTRIBUTION

For a drug to have a psychoactive effect, it is essential that it be absorbed into the bloodstream and distributed to the brain; these are the processes of **transport** and **distribution.** For all routes of administration except the intravenous, the first step is transport across the barrier created by the membrane composing the blood vessel. The blood vessels contain a fatty, or *lipid,* layer, and in order to get into the bloodstream the drug must pass through this layer. Drugs that dissolve readily in fat are more easily absorbed, and

FIGURE 2.4
Various methods of drug administration. The oral route of administration is slow because the drug must pass several barriers before it reaches the bloodstream. Inhalation and intravenous injection bypass these barriers.

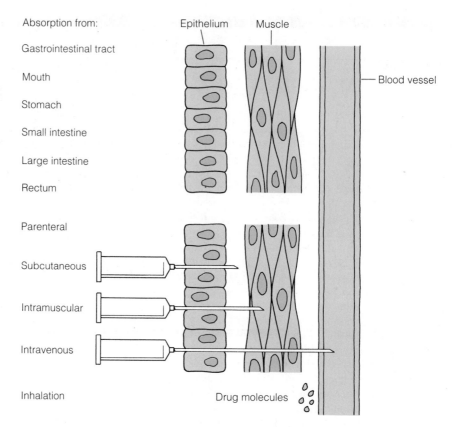

Absorption from:

Gastrointestinal tract

Mouth

Stomach

Small intestine

Large intestine

Rectum

Parenteral

Subcutaneous

Intramuscular

Intravenous

Inhalation

Epithelium   Muscle

Blood vessel

Drug molecules

lipid solubility is one of the most important criteria for determining a drug's potency.

Once in the bloodstream, distribution is rapid, but there is an additional barrier. Protein molecules circulate through the bloodstream also, and many chemical substances are attracted to these molecules. The extent to which drugs "bind" to these molecules helps determine their potency; alcohol, for example, does not bind readily and so is effective at relatively low concentrations. Other drugs bind more readily and so are less potent. Only unbound drugs can leave the bloodstream.

In addition to being bound to protein molecules, drugs can be filtered out by the kidney or metabolized by the liver. The drug that is absorbed into the bloodstream, and escapes being bound, filtered, or metabolized, faces another problem. The capillaries of the brain are different than those in most parts of the body. They seem to be denser and prevent the diffusion of many substances into the neurons of the brain. The **blood/brain barrier** is an important factor in understanding which drugs are behaviorally active. Drugs that cannot pass into the brain obviously do not have a major psychoactive effect.

The pregnant woman in this photo is smoking crack; crack use is thought to be harmful to the fetus.

Penicillin, for example, is a useful drug for fighting infection. It does not pass the blood/brain barrier, which is a good thing; were it not for the blood/brain barrier, this drug would be unusable since it causes convulsions when injected directly into the brain.

Most drugs pass the placental barrier in pregnant women. The blood vessels of the pregnant woman and the blood vessels of the developing embryo and fetus are very close to each other. Normally, waste products from the fetus pass into the maternal bloodstream while oxygen, protein, and other necessary substances pass into the fetal bloodstream. Since a pregnant woman using drugs has a higher concentration of the drug in her bloodstream it will pass into the embryo or fetus. Such substances which can cause developmental abnormalities are called **teratogens.** Alcohol, nicotine, cocaine, and amphetamine all pass readily and the consequences can be tragic.

The circulating drug also passes into the milk of the nursing mother and hence to the baby. Babies nursed by mothers who drink alcohol absorb alcohol, while cocaine and amphetamine pass even more rapidly to the infant. The extent of the problem of drug absorption by infants has not received extensive investigation but the danger is real.

TERMINATION OF DRUG ACTION

Once taken up by the tissues from the bloodstream, the process of diffusion guarantees that the concentration of a drug will eventually reach equilibrium. That is, it will be the same in both tissue and blood until something happens to eliminate the drug.

Termination of drug action normally takes place when the drug is eliminated by the kidney or metabolized by the liver. Lesser routes of termination involve respiration through the lung and excretion from the skin. The amount of time required for half the drug to be eliminated is called the drug's **half life.**

Some drugs, like cocaine, have a half life measured in minutes, while others, such as marijuana, are absorbed by tissue and bound to fatty deposits, making diffusion back into the bloodstream a slow process. Depending on the detection method and the amount initially ingested, marijuana, for example, can be detected up to twenty-eight days after use (Hawkes & Chiang, 1986).

In the kidney, drug elimination primarily occurs by means of diffusion. The higher concentrations of drug or its metabolite in the bloodstream pass by means of osmosis into the renal tubules, and the drug then is excreted in the urine. This means of termination of drug action forms the basis for urinalysis tests. As we shall see in chapter 12, a urine test may indicate the presence of the drug itself or of a metabolite of the drug. Other substances that produce the same or similar metabolites can produce a positive reaction in the urine test and thus result in what is called a *false positive*.

The liver, on the other hand, removes drugs from the bloodstream by more active processes, breaking them down into substances that can then be excreted. The way in which the liver breaks down various drugs is discussed in individual chapters. The breakdown products of various drugs can be excreted in feces, urine, or any of several other means.

Elimination of a drug through the lungs is the basis for Breathalyzer tests for alcohol consumption. A person suspected of driving under the influence of alcohol is asked to blow into a machine which analyzes the alcohol content of the expired air. This test is an accurate measure of blood alcohol because of the principles of diffusion. The alcohol in the bloodstream diffuses across the blood vessel wall into the air sacs. When breath is expelled, it carries with it the molecules of alcohol. It is a simple procedure, then, to convert the amount of alcohol measured into an estimate of blood alcohol level. Since it is only an *estimate* of blood alcohol level, it is less accurate than a direct measurement. In fact, recent evidence suggests that the most commonly used Breathalyzer equipment yields an estimate 10 percent below the actual blood alcohol level (Simpson, 1989, 1990).

Incidentally, the elimination of alcohol through the lungs also explains why alcohol can be detected on a drinker's breath long after the last drink was consumed. Even though many people believe that some alcoholic beverages cannot be detected on the breath, once any alcoholic beverage, beer, wine, vodka, or bourbon, is absorbed, ethyl alcohol circulates in the bloodstream. As long as any alcohol remains, it can be detected, regardless of its source.

GENERAL PRINCIPLES OF DRUG ACTION

In order to understand how a drug works, we must consider a number of physiological and psychological factors that influence drug action.

Dose-Response Relationship

For a drug to have an effect, there must be an adequate concentration of the drug in the system. For many drugs, however, the effect the drug produces is not always directly proportional to its concentration. In other words, one aspirin given to an adult will not relieve a headache half as well as two aspirin. There exists for most drugs a minimum concentration necessary to produce a given effect. This concentration is called the **threshold** dose.

Once past this dose, the effect of increasing the concentration depends on the drug. For some drugs the effect is close to linear; that is, increasing the dosage by a certain percent will increase the effect of the drug by the same percent. For many drugs, however, the dose-response relationship is nonlinear. With aspirin, once the threshold dose is reached, increasing the concentration has little effect. In the same way that one-quarter of an aspirin will not help a minor headache at all, four aspirin will not relieve a severe headache faster or better than two.

Considerable individual variability exists with drugs, and a given dose will affect individuals differently. One way of expressing this variability is by means of the ED_{50}. This term stands for the amount of a drug necessary to produce an effect in 50 percent of the population tested. The amount required to have a lethal effect is called the **LD,** or **lethal dose.**

One method of estimating the safety of a drug is by means of the *Standard Safety Margin* (SSM) which is expressed as SSM = (LD_1 − ED_{99})/ED_{99} × 100, where LD_1 is the lethal dose for 1 percent of the population, and ED_{99} is the effective dose for 99 percent of the population. The higher this number, the safer the drug (see figure 2.5). For example, Librium (chlordiazepoxide) has a lower SSM than Valium (diazepam), which in turn has a lower SSM than Miltown (meprobamate).

One problem with estimating the safety of a drug is the problem of **tolerance,** which is discussed in detail on page 54. As a person uses a drug he or she becomes accustomed to its effects, and more and more is required to have the desired behavioral effect. The lethal dose may not, however, increase as rapidly, so the safety margin for the tolerant individual may be much less than for the experimental user.

Receptor Binding

Chapter 3 discusses in detail the effects of drugs on the brain. In order to understand some principles of drug action, however, it is necessary to introduce the **lock-and-key principle** here. Many nerve cells have receptors that are sensitive to various drugs because the drugs in some way resemble a naturally occurring substance that the cell is sensitive to. These drugs operate on the lock-and-key principle in which the drug can be thought of as the "key" that either fits into the "lock," causing the nerve cell to be more sensitive and more likely to discharge, or "jams" the lock, preventing the "door" from opening and the nerve cell from discharging. Drugs that are readily accepted by the receptor are said to have high affinity and are potent at low doses.

If the receptor for a drug exists on a neuron or cell of an organ, the drug can affect the functioning of that cell. Often, cells in different parts of

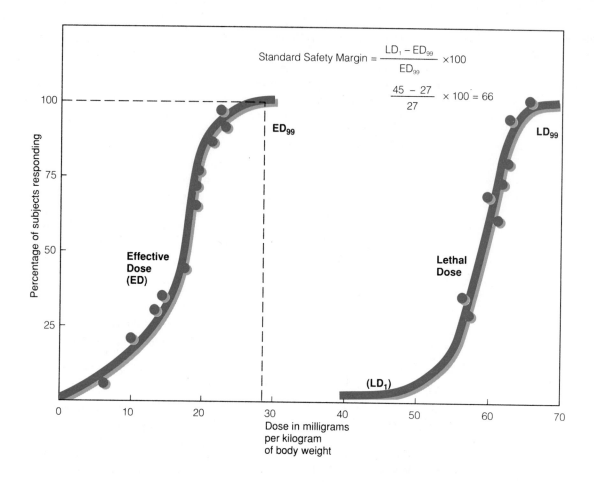

$$\text{Standard Safety Margin} = \frac{LD_1 - ED_{99}}{ED_{99}} \times 100$$

$$\frac{45 - 27}{27} \times 100 = 66$$

FIGURE 2.5

A diagram of a hypothetical drug. Follow the dotted lines to see that the effective dose for 99% of all subjects was 27 mg/kg. The lethal dose for 1% was 45 mg/kg. A SSM of 66 indicates that this is not a safe drug.

the body have similar receptors so drugs can affect many organ systems. The degree to which a drug affects specific portions of the body is called the drug's **specificity.** Most psychoactive drugs have a relative lack of specificity.

Because of this lack of specificity, a given drug can have many effects. Undesirable drug effects are called side effects. Remember, though, that whether an effect is a "side" effect or the main effect is largely a matter of definition. Antihistamines, for example, sold to relieve allergies, have a "side effect" of causing drowsiness. Antihistamines sold as sleeping tablets have the "side effect" of drying up the nasal passages and causing stuffiness.

Time-Response Relationship

The time-response relationship of a drug has three components: the latency of onset, the time to peak effect, and the duration of action. When cocaine is snorted, the effect is almost immediate, occurring within seconds, but the duration is only twenty to thirty minutes. When marijuana is eaten in the form of brownies, the latency to onset can be more than an hour, and the duration of

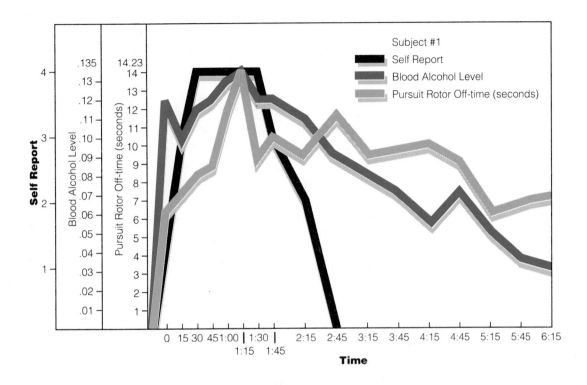

FIGURE 2.6

In an experiment, a subject was asked to report the level of intoxication experienced while a physical measure of intoxication, a breathalyzer, recorded BAL. At the same time the subject attempted to track a moving light with a pen as a measure of physical impairment. You can see that the subject's estimate of intoxication declined far more rapidly than did the actual impairment or BAL.

action can last for several hours. Some barbiturates have both a very rapid onset of action and a very long duration of action, so no general rules exist.

For most psychoactive drugs, the latency of onset is determined by the speed with which a drug is absorbed, distributed through the body, and taken up by the target organ, usually the brain. Injection directly into the bloodstream and inhalation both produce rapid rates of absorption and distribution, while the oral route is relatively slow. Time release capsules, of course, produce even slower rates.

The time to peak effect is the length of time required for the drug to have its maximum effect and is related to the speed with which receptors on the target organ are filled (see figure 2.6). With alcohol, the time to peak effect is approximately forty-five minutes after oral ingestion on an empty stomach, while with drugs like cocaine and heroin, the time to peak effect may be measured in seconds, especially if they are inhaled.

The duration of action of a drug depends in part on how long the drug remains in contact with the receptor. The strength of the bond between the drug and its receptor site, the rate at which the drug is eliminated, and the extent to which absorption continues to take place all affect the duration of action.

The duration of action is not the same as the **half life** of a drug, as defined on page 48. A drug may remain bound to the receptor site after it has been virtually eliminated from the blood, resulting in a duration of longer than the half life. On the other hand, the drug may have a shorter duration of action than half life if the drug is released from the receptor sites before it is eliminated from the blood. Cocaine is an example of the latter. Its psychological effects last only twenty minutes or so, although its half life in the blood is considerably longer. To further complicate matters, there is the concept of **acute tolerance,** discussed on page 54. Briefly, acute tolerance means that the effect of a drug is more noticeable while it is being absorbed than when it is being metabolized.

Individual Differences

Dose-response relationships and time-response relationships are biochemical phenomena that are tempered by individual differences. Women absorb drugs differently from men, young people differently from the elderly, and thin people differently from the obese. These individual differences in response to drugs are important.

Age

Drug effects differ as a function of age. Not only are the young and the elderly lighter than adults, but both groups are affected differently for other reasons. Infants and young children lack certain enzymes, making them more responsive to some drugs (Eveloff, 1970; McKim & Mishara, 1987).

In the elderly the response to a given drug is likely to be greater for a number of reasons. The elderly have a decreased cardiac output. This means that drugs will be retained longer in the bloodstream. Both liver and kidney functioning are usually diminished, so that these, the primary routes of excretion and metabolism, are less efficient. The elderly also have a higher percentage of body fat to lean muscle than younger people, meaning that the fat stores act as a drug reservoir (Lifshitz & Kline, 1970).

Weight

Response to a given drug is a function of the concentration of the drug within the system, which itself is a function of the total mass of the system. This means that a 200–pound male would respond differently to a single shot of tequila than a 100–pound female. Figure 2.7 illustrates the relationship of weight to blood concentration for alcohol.

Weight is not the only factor to be considered. Most drugs are more readily absorbed into muscle fiber than fatty tissue, so an athlete whose body mass is largely muscle would be less responsive to a drug than a person of the same weight whose body mass is largely fat. The fatty tissue would not absorb the drug as readily, leaving more in the blood. Once absorbed into fatty tissue, however, drugs are released more slowly from these stores, so a drug would have a longer duration of action for an obese person than for a muscular person of the same weight.

Sex

The weight of the average woman is less than that of the average man, and a higher percentage of that weight is represented by fat rather than muscle. It follows then that many drugs have a greater impact on women than men.

In addition, the hormonal differences between men and women can affect the response to a given drug and, as you have already read, there are sex differences in the amount and location of enzymes which metabolize drugs.

FIGURE 2.7

This chart is conservative and does not take into consideration stomach contents, need, and other factors.

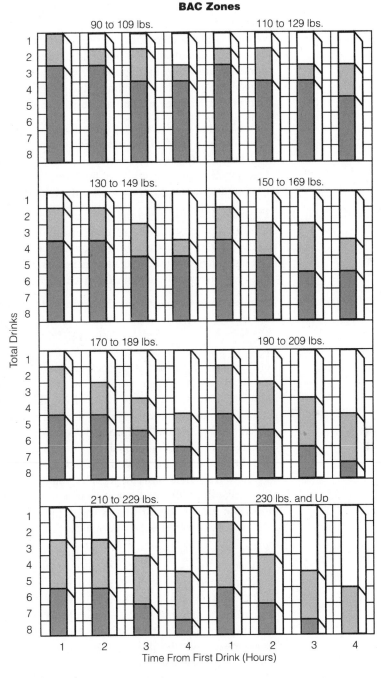

BAC Zones

Legend:

☐ [.01%–.04%] Seldom illegal

▨ [.05%–.09%] May be illegal in some states

[.05%–.09%] Illegal if under 18 years old in most states

■ [.10% Up] Definitely illegal in all states

Ethnicity

As a result of recent guidelines suggested by various federal agencies, there is an increasing amount of investigation on the differences in drug effects in various ethnic groups. The Native American population has a very high incidence of alcoholism, and some feel there may be a genetic basis for this. Some Asians seem to respond differently to alcohol as compared to Caucasians. These and other findings may have important implications for understanding differences in drug abuse in different cultural and ethnic groups.

Tolerance

The concept of **tolerance** is quite complicated since the term is used to describe a number of phenomena. For example, we can speak of physiological and behavioral tolerance, acute and chronic tolerance, cross-tolerance, even reverse tolerance. In every case, however, the term refers to the fact that a given dose of drug has a different effect, depending on the experience of the user.

Physiological Tolerance

Physiological tolerance involves an adaptive mechanism at the biochemical level that affects the rate of drug metabolism and elimination and the sensitivity of the receptors and secondary messenger systems (Abood, 1984 NIDA). Physiological tolerance develops to a wide range of drugs, but it does not completely explain the phenomenon of tolerance.

Behavioral Tolerance

Another form of tolerance is **behavioral tolerance,** also an adaptive process, but at a different level. Behavioral tolerance is familiar to those who drink alcohol. A given blood alcohol level will likely produce much different effects in a twenty-year-old college student on spring break and a forty-year-old college professor at a cocktail party. Part of this difference can be attributed to the longer drinking history of the professor and hence physiological tolerance. Much of it, however, is behavioral tolerance.

Over the course of years, the forty-year-old has discovered what a given level of alcohol will do and how to minimize the behavioral effects of alcohol use. Slurred pronunciation is compensated for by speaking less and avoiding troublesome phrases. Effects on balance and walking are controlled by more deliberate movements. The young student, however, has not learned these adaptive skills and hence appears more intoxicated. Conversely and for the same reason, the 20-year-old may be better at disguising how high he or she may be after smoking marijuana.

Acute Tolerance

Acute tolerance occurs when the effect of a drug diminishes during a single episode of drug use. With cocaine it is clear that the psychological effect of a given blood level is much greater before than after the peak of absorption of the drug (Van Dycke & Byck, 1982). The same is true for alcohol. For some drugs subsequent administration of the same drug results in less and less psychological effect, as long as the drug remains in the system. This phenomenon will be discussed in the chapter on stimulants and may be related to the fact that nearly all receptors become occupied with the drug, so that increasing the amount taken has little additional effect.

Cross-Tolerance

Cross-tolerance occurs when one has developed physiological tolerance to one drug and shows a similar tolerance to other drugs. Cross-tolerance exists, for example, between alcohol and the barbiturates, most hallucinogenics with each other, and with the various types of amphetamine-like stimulant drugs. Cross-tolerance implies that similar physiological mechanisms are operating in the adaptation to various drugs. Behavioral cross-tolerance also probably occurs, but it is seldom studied and is difficult to distinguish from physiological cross-tolerance.

Reverse Tolerance

Finally, **reverse tolerance** is a term used to describe the fact that users can become more rather than less sensitive to the effects of a given drug. Sometimes this is the result of a breakdown in the system that metabolizes the drug, such as in the case of prolonged heavy drinking that results in liver damage. The damaged liver is no longer able to detoxify the alcohol, so it builds up in the blood, and a small amount that the problem drinker would not even have noticed years earlier now causes severe symptoms.

On other occasions, as with cocaine, reverse tolerance is believed to be caused by "kindling," where frequent administration of the drug sensitizes the brain to its effects (Post, Weiss, Pert & Uhde, 1987). Learning is also thought to play a role in the development of reverse tolerance. Many first-time users of marijuana report little or no effect of the drug, while regular users may get high from marijuana that contains virtually no THC. Apparently users learn to pay attention to the cues associated with being "high" and come to value that experience.

Dependence

Dependence is another term that is widely used in many different contexts. Strictly speaking, the term refers to a physiological process by which the body requires the presence of the drug for normal functioning. Without the drug, the user experiences **withdrawal,** the classic symptom of dependence. Withdrawal refers to physical symptoms that result from discontinuation of a drug. A hangover is thought by some to be a withdrawal symptom. Heroin withdrawal is familiar to most of us from television programs and movies, even though these scenes have little to do with reality.

Physical dependence does not account for all forms of dependence, however, and an additional term is often used. **Psychological dependence** refers to a craving for a drug that does not have a basis in physiology. Long after all evidence of physiological dependence is gone, most heavy smokers report a continuing craving for a cigarette. The psychological dependence may be related to the remembered pleasurable effects of the drug, the ritual of drug use, habit, or any of a number of reasons. Regardless of its cause, psychological dependence is real and often quite strong. Caffeine is another example of a drug that causes strong psychological dependence (as well as, some think, physical dependence).

The Problem of "Addiction"

Definitions of **addictions** widely accepted just a few years ago recently have been revised. The classic definition involved the presence of both tolerance

• YOU READ IT HERE FIRST •

Addiction as a Defense

The United States Supreme Court has ruled several times that while alcoholism is a disease, a person who is intoxicated is still responsible for his or her actions, the rationale basically being that he or she made the choice to drink initially. Recently, this concept has been challenged from several directions relating not only to alcohol but also to other drugs.

One of the most well publicized cases of addiction as a defense came about in 1990, when three airline pilots were charged with flying an airplane while intoxicated. The captain, who had consumed at least fifteen drinks containing rum the night before, had a BAL of .12 after he had successfully landed the plane. The other two officers had BALs of .06 and .04 when measured in the morning (they had stopped drinking at 2:00 A.M.). The flight captain attempted to defend himself by claiming that he was an alcoholic and since he had been drinking heavily for many years, he was able to function at a BAL which would incapacitate a less experienced drinker (Forensic Drug Abuse Advisor, 1990). You probably remember that he was found guilty, but the defense may come up again.

Another possibility for the addiction as defense line of reasoning lies in the concept of a "blackout." Blackouts occur when a person has been drinking heavily and cannot remember events that occurred during the drinking episode. Is a person under such circumstances considered responsible for his/her ac-

tions? At present, yes, but some have suggested that the concept at least be considered (Sweeney, 1990).

Virtually everyone is indignant over stories of "crack babies," babies born with cocaine in their bodies. On the one hand many courts have held that the mother was guilty of child abuse, the child was removed from the family and the mother placed in jail. If the woman was genuinely addicted to cocaine, however, and if she did not have adequate treatment facilities available to her, should she be punished? Should women who test positive for drug use be forced to undergo treatment as some have suggested (Chavkin, 1991)?

Before you answer too quickly, what about a woman who does not stop smoking cigarettes, thus running the risk of a small baby (smoking mothers have smaller babies than nonsmoking mothers)? Should she be required to stop smoking or be prosecuted as well? What about the mother who doesn't eat properly or who drinks occasionally?

What about the bodybuilder who is taking steroids, since steroids are thought to increase aggressiveness? Is "roid rage" a defense? It has been tried several times with mixed results, was permitted as a defense, and may have influenced the jury (Forensic Drug Abuse Advisor, 1991). Is there such a thing as "not guilty by reason of addiction?"

and physical dependence that was demonstrated by signs of withdrawal when the drug was not present. Unless both tolerance and physical dependence were seen, the drug was not considered addictive.

Recently the concept of addiction has been widened to include psychological and social aspects. In fact, some have argued that addiction is not a biological process at all but a means of adapting to the environment. Furthermore, the concept of addiction as a biological process or disease is not only wrong, but does far more harm than good (Peele & Brodsky, 1991).

Some of the arguments against a disease model of addiction may be found in chapter 4.

To the extent that the term has any meaning at all, addiction must be considered as resulting from several routes including biological, social, and psychological elements (Sunderwith, 1985). We all have an unfortunate tendency to **reductionism;** explaining complex events with a few simple concepts. We look for the causes of aggression or mental disorders in the biochemistry of the brain. We try to explain why John divorced Mary by saying he was experiencing a mid-life crisis, and we seek the answer to addiction at the level of the neuron in the brain.

No one explanation can possibly suffice for such complex behaviors, however. Addiction may in part be maintained by changes in the neuron, but also is undoubtedly influenced by society's view of addiction and the results that addiction produces for the individual. None of these and the many other possible factors that maintain addiction can be explained at the level of the neuron. Because the term is so difficult to define, it will be used sparingly in this book. The terms *abuse* and *dependence* are easier to define and will be used instead.

PSYCHOLOGICAL ASPECTS OF DRUG USE

In addition to the pharmacological factors affecting drug use, we must consider other, less biologically based, aspects of drugs. For want of a better term, these are usually called "psychological" factors, although some have a physiological component as well.

Placebo Effect

Imagine a substance with no known side effects that is 60 percent as effective as morphine in relieving some types of pain, is easily administered, is virtually free, and is not addicting. Wouldn't its "discovery" make headlines? Such a drug already exists. It is plain water. Research has shown that an injection of sterile water is nearly as effective as an injection of morphine for relief of post-surgical abdominal pain (Ornstein & Sobell, 1987).

You are probably familiar with the term **placebo,** which means in Latin "I will please" and think that it refers to the sugar pill the physician sometimes gives to patients that he thinks are faking their illness. Placebo effects are quite real, however, and a person who responds to a placebo is not a malingerer or weak willed. Any drug is more likely to be effective if the person believes in it. To that extent all drugs have a placebo effect.

Researchers are aware of placebo effects and their strength. When testing drugs, they use a design called the **double blind** procedure. Both the drug to be tested and an inert substance are given either to the same subject at different times or to different subjects. Neither the researchers nor the subjects know when the active drug is being given. To be considered effective, the drug being tested must be superior to the placebo control. As we shall see in later chapters, many widely used drugs are only slightly superior to placebos, and some cannot be distinguished from them.

Placebo effects also enter into our response to psychoactive drugs, both legal and illegal. In one study, users of cocaine were unable to distinguish between it and a simple local anesthetic with no central nervous system effect (Van Dyke and Byck, 1982). Similarly, regular heavy users of marijuana got high smoking marijuana from which all of the primary active ingredient (THC) had been removed (Jones, 1971).

Placebo effects on pain seem to have a physiological basis. The pain-relieving effects of an inert drug are greatly reduced when the patient first receives naloxone, a drug that blocks the action of morphine and endorphin, the natural pain reliever (Ornstein & Sobel, 1987). If the placebo effect were not real, how could another drug reverse the effect?

Set and Setting

The concepts of **set** and **setting** are crucial to understanding how drugs work. These concepts help explain many otherwise surprising drug effects. Set refers to the expectation of what a drug will do. If I believe that tequila makes me mean and brandy makes me mellow, I have induced a set. When I drink either of these, I am, therefore, predisposed to become either mean or mellow.

The set of the user helps to determine whether a given effect of a drug will be perceived as pleasant or unpleasant and is impossible to eliminate. Albert Hofmann was probably the first, and one of the few people ever, to experience LSD without a set of what it should do. He was experimenting with a series of compounds, one of which turned out to be LSD (see chapter 8 for the full story). After unknowingly ingesting the drug, he left work and went home. His subsequent experiences were, therefore, unaltered by the knowledge that he had taken a hallucinogenic drug.

The United States Army and the Central Intelligence Agency conducted a series of experiments along the same line when their researchers gave hallucinogenic drugs to unknowing subjects and observed their reaction. One of these experiments is reported to have lead to the suicide of one of the participants, who thought he was becoming insane. Since nearly everyone else takes a drug with some expectations of what it will do, the set a person has goes a long way toward explaining a drug's effect.

The term setting refers to the effect of the circumstances surrounding the drug use. Two glasses of wine in a dark, quiet room with soft music playing would make me sleepy, but the same amount of alcohol consumed as beer at a football game might make me a shouting, gesturing fan. Zinberg (1984) believes that set and setting are the most powerful factors that distinguish between drug use and drug abuse.

Setting is an extremely important concept in understanding the various effects of the so-called hallucinogenic or psychedelic drugs. In the earliest research with these drugs careful attention was paid to the setting in which the drugs were taken, along with careful instructions designed to produce a positive set. Perhaps as a result, serious adverse effects were relatively rare. As the popularity of these drugs increased, more uninformed people began using them, and less attention was paid to set and setting. During their height of popularity, the late 1960s, "bad trips" became more common. Similarly, it is not uncommon to read newspaper reports of a person being arrested or detained for being under the influence of a drug and then becoming so unstable that they have to be hospitalized. Anyone who has ever been arrested knows that jail is a frightening place under the best of circumstances. For someone who is under the influence of a psychedelic drug, the experience could easily be overwhelming.

CATEGORIES OF DRUGS

We have seen that the effects of drugs vary depending on dose, set, setting, and a host of other factors. It is difficult therefore to devise a categorization of drugs that is completely accurate. Table 2.1 shows the principal psychoactive drugs. Various terms need to be explained in order to understand the table. Note also that many of these drugs have uses other than their psychoactive properties.

Opiates

Opiates, as we shall see in chapter 9, are synthetic and natural derivatives of opium and have been used for centuries, both as medicine and for psychoactive use. In general they produce a drowsy, relaxed state, although sudden ingestion of a large quantity can produce euphoria.

Marijuana

Marijuana is sometimes classified as a hallucinogenic, but little evidence exists to support this classification. The subjective effects of marijuana are hard to describe, but true hallucinations are rare. One term sometimes used to describe this drug is *euphoriant,* although euphoria is not the exclusive property of this drug, nor is it the inevitable result of its use. Because of its historic and economic significance, as well as its complex effects, it will be placed in its own category.

Hallucinogenics

Hallucinogenics, as we shall see in chapter 8, are also somewhat misnamed. True hallucinations do not occur at low doses for most of these drugs. The major effect of all of these substances is alteration of sensory input. A wide class of drugs which affects serotonin, acetylcholine, and the catecholamines have hallucinogenic properties. The effect of these drugs can be quite dramatic, especially if the set and setting are appropriate.

Stimulants

Stimulants include such common drugs as caffeine as well as such illicit drugs as cocaine. All affect alertness and some can produce a sense of well-being or even euphoria. They are among the most commonly used drugs in society. Many have a strong dependence potential and at high doses can be lethal. Note that according to federal regulations, cocaine is officially a narcotic drug.

Depressants

Depressants do the opposite of the stimulants; they decrease alertness. Alcohol can be classified as a depressant, as can the so called "minor" tranquilizers such as Valium and Librium. Another class of depressants are those prescribed as sleeping pills. You may sometimes see the term sedative-hypnotic for

Table 2.1 The Principal Psychoactive Drugs				
Classification	Physical Dependence	Psychological Dependence	Tolerance	Effects
Opiates: heroin, morphine, codeine, methadone, meperidine, others	yes	yes	yes	euphoria, drowsiness, nausea
Cannabis: marijuana, hashish, tetrahydrocannabinol	unknown	yes	yes	euphoria, increased appetite, relaxed inhibitions
Hallucinogens: LSD, mescaline, psilocybin, phencyclidine, others	none	unknown	yes	illusion, hallucinations, distorted perceptions
Stimulants: amphetamine, cocaine, xanthines, others	possible	yes	yes	increase of alertness, blood pressure, heart rate, euphoria
Depressants: barbiturates, benzodiazepines, others	yes	yes	yes	slurred speech, disorientation
Alcohol: gin, vodka, beer, wine, others	yes	yes	yes	slurred speech, disorientation
Nicotine: cigarettes, pipes, snuff	yes	yes	yes	varies: may produce relaxation or stimulation

these drugs. The term hypnotic used in this context can be confusing, because it refers to inducing sleep rather than producing a state of hypnosis.

Alcohol and Cigarettes

Alcohol and cigarettes are such common drugs that they deserve categories of their own, even though nicotine is a stimulant and alcohol a depressant. Their effects are far more complex than their simple pharmacological properties would indicate. Each is discussed in a separate chapter in this book.

In this chapter we have seen that the answer to the question, "What will this drug do to me if I take it?" is very complicated. Physiological, pharmacological, and psychological factors all combine to influence your response to any drug. In the next chapter we will discuss in detail how drugs act on the body and the brain.

SUMMARY

Drugs that alter behavior or change consciousness are known as psychoactive drugs. In order to be effective they must be transported to the brain, and the routes of administration are the means for accomplishing this task. The most common route is the oral route, while other means of administration include injection and absorption by inhaling the vapors of drugs (perhaps the most rapid route). Every route of administration has its advantages and disadvantages.

The next major concern is that of transport and distribution. The lipid solubility of a drug plays an important role in the transport and distribution of most drugs. Final distribution into the brain for most psychoactive drugs is accomplished primarily by osmosis. The blood/brain barrier is a major hurdle for the absorption of most drugs.

Once taken up by tissue, drug action must be terminated. Termination of drug action primarily takes place in the liver and kidney, although drug action may be terminated by other means.

Some factors that contribute to the effect a drug will have include the dose-response relationship, time-response relationship, individual differences, tolerance, and the extent of receptor binding. Other considerations include the age, sex, and weight of the user. Tolerance can take many forms and the result may be to make a drug either more or less effective.

Dependence is an important concept that is often misunderstood. It is an integral part of the definition of addiction. Recent understanding of the role that some drugs play on psychological factors has lead to a broadening of the concept of addiction. At the same time, the entire concept of addiction as a disease has come under attack.

No understanding of the pharmacology of drug use would be complete without consideration of the placebo effect. Long thought to be ''in the mind,'' placebo effects are often real physiological phenomena. Placebo effects can often be nearly as strong as the actual drug effects. Set and setting also play an important role in determining what effect a drug will have. The same drug may be interpreted as producing elation or terror, depending on the expectations of the user and the nature of his/her surroundings.

Drugs are difficult to classify because they have different effects depending on the time since administration, dose, psychological, and other factors influence what a given drug will do in any set or setting.

REFERENCES

Chavkin, W. (1991). Mandatory treatment for drug use during pregnancy. *Journal of the American Medical Association, 266,* 1556–61.

Diamond, J. (1990). Kung Fu kerosene drinking. *Natural History, July,* 20–24.

Eveloff, H. H. (1970). Pediatric psychopharmacology. In W. G. Clark & J. del Giudice (Eds.), *Principles of Psychopharmacology,* (pp. 683–94). New York: Academic Press.

Frezza, M., Padova, C., Pozzato, G., Terpin, M., Baraona, E., & Lieber, C. (1990). High blood alcohol levels in women: The role of decreased gastric alcohol dehydrogenase activity and first pass metabolism. *New England Journal of Medicine, 322,* 95–99.

Hawkes, R. L., & Chiang, C. N. (1986). Urine testing for drugs of abuse. *National Institute of Drug Abuse Research Monograph 73.*

Jones, R. T. (1971). Marijuana-induced ''high'': Influence of expectation, setting and previous drug experience. *Pharmacological Reviews, 23,* 359–69.

Jong, E. (1983). *Witches.* New York: Harry N. Abrams.

Joynt, B. P., & Mikhael, N. Z. (1985). Sudden death of a heroin body packer. *Journal of Analytical Toxicology, 9,* 238–49.

Karch, S. (Ed.) (1990). Pilots found guilty of drunken flying; Novel defense proposed. *The Forensic Drug Abuse Advisor, 2,* 78–80.

Karch, S. (Ed.) (1991). Roid rage: Do anabolic steroids make people psychotic? *The Forensic Drug Abuse Advisor 3,* 1–3.

Levine, R. R. (1983). *Pharmacology: Drug actions and reactions,* 3d ed. Boston: Little, Brown.

Lieber, C. (1991). Hepatic, metabolic and toxic effects of ethanol: 1991 update. *Alcoholism: Clinical and Experimental Research, 15,* 573–92.

Lifshitz, K., & Kline, N. S. (1970). Psychopharmacology in geriatrics. In W. G. Clark & J. del Guidice (Eds.), *Principles of psychopharmacology,* (pp. 695–706). New York: Academic Press.

McKim, W. A., & Mishara, B. L. (1987). *Drugs and aging.* Toronto and Vancouver: Butterworth.

Noyes, R. (1982). Beta blocking drugs and anxiety. *Psychosomatics, 23,* 155–63.

Ornstein, R., & Sobell, D. (1987). *The Healing Brain.* New York: Simon & Schuster.

Peele, S., & Brodsky, A. (1991). *The truth about addiction and recovery.* New York: Simon & Schuster.

Post, R. M., Weiss, S. R. B., Pert, A., & Uhde, T. (1987). Chronic cocaine administration; sensitization and kindling effects. In S. Fisher, A. Raskin, & E. H. Uhlenhuth (Eds.), *Cocaine,* (pp. 109–73). New York: Oxford University Press.

Segal, M. (1991) Patches, pumps and timed release: new ways to deliver drugs. *FDA Consumer, 25,* 13–15.

Simpson, G. (1990). Absorption time, alcoholic beverage type and breath analysis, *Journal of Analytical Toxicology, 14,* 393–95.

Simson, G. (1989). Do breathalyzer tests really underestimate blood alcohol concentration? *Journal of Analytical Toxicology, 13,* 120–23.

Sunderwirth, S. G. Biological mechanisms: Neurotransmission and addiction. In H. B. Milkman & H. J. Shaffer (Eds.), *The addictions: Multidisciplinary perspective and treatment,* (pp. 11–20). Lexington, MA: Lexington Books.

Sweeney, D. (1990). Alcoholic blackouts: Legal implications. *Journal of Substance Abuse Treatment, 7,* 155–59.

Transdermal Nicotine Study Group (1991) Transdermal nicotine for smoking cessation. *Journal of the American Medical Association, 266,* 3133–39.

Van Dyke, C., & Byck, R. (1982). Cocaine. *Scientific American, 246,* 128–41.

Weiss, R. (1988). Delivering the goods. *Science News, 133,* 360–62.

Zinberg, N. E. (1984). *Drug set and setting: The basis for controlled intoxicant use.* New Haven and London: Yale University Press.

3

• • •

DRUGS AND PHYSIOLOGY

• • •

OBJECTIVES

When you have finished studying this chapter you should:

1. Be able to identify the major portions of the central and peripheral nervous systems.
2. Know how a nerve impulse is transmitted from a dendrite to an end button.
3. Understand how chemical transmission at the synapse is related to drug effects.
4. Understand the principle of binding.
5. Be able to differentiate between neurotransmitter, neuromodulators, and neurohormones.
6. Be able to discuss the function of acetylcholine in both the peripheral and central nervous systems.
7. Know how serotonin affects behavior.
8. Be able to discuss the role of catecholamines in drug use.
9. Know how peptides affect neural transmission.
10. Understand the role of the hypothalamus and limbic system in mediating drug effects.
11. Be able to discuss the role of the brain stem in arousal.
12. Know what aphrodisiacs are and how drug use affects sexual functioning.
13. Understand the relationship between the sympathetic and parasympathetic portions of the nervous system.
14. Know how anabolic steroids work and why they are dangerous.

KEY TERMS

acetylcholine
amyl nitrite
anabolic steroids
androgen
aphrodisiacs
ARAS
autonomic nervous system
axon
basal ganglia
beta blockers
brain stem
cantharidin
catecholamine
cell body
central nervous system
cortex
Creutzfeld-Jakob disease
curare
dendrite
diuretics
dopamine
end button
endogenous
endorphin
enkephalin
epinephrine
ergogenic aids
feminization syndrome
gamma-aminobutyric acid
glutamic acid
gynecomastia
high density lipoproteins
hirsutism
homeostatis
human growth hormone

hypothalamus
isobutyl nitrite
Kaposi's sarcoma
limbic system
malathion
mandrake
medial forebrain bundle
morphine
neurohormones
neuromodulators
neurotransmitters
nicotine
norepinephrine
opioid peptides
opium
peliosis
peptides
pituitary
polarized
postsynaptic
prescursor
presynaptic
reticular formation
re-uptake
second messenger system
serotonin
Spanish fly
substance P
synapse
testicular atrophy
testosterone
tryptophan
tyrosine
vasopressin
vesicles

I n the previous chapter, you learned some of the principles of pharmacology and how they relate to the topics in this text. In this chapter you will
gain an understanding of how drugs operate at various levels of physiological functioning, from the level of individual cells to that of integrated systems. Our uniqueness as a species and as individuals of that species cannot
be understood without considering the physiology of the central and peripheral nervous system. Similarly, the effects of drugs cannot be understood
without considering how these drugs interact with the physiology of the
nervous system. If I were to remove your brain and replace it with mine,
who would *you* be? Drugs have very specific effects on the nervous system.
Understanding how the nervous system works, therefore, goes a long way to
understanding how drugs work.

An enormous amount of research has been done on the structure and
function of the nervous system, the anatomy of the neuron, and the role of
neurotransmitters in mediating behavior. Rather than cite individual research
articles to establish each point in this chapter, citations have been limited to
specific important studies. For more general information, Carlson (1991),
Shepherd (1988), Levitan & Kaczmarek (1991), and Cooper, Bloom, & Roth
(1986) were the main sources for the discussion which follows.

THE STRUCTURE OF THE NERVOUS SYSTEM

Figure 3.1 illustrates how the human nervous system is organized. Drugs can
and do affect the functioning of all parts of the nervous system as well as
individual organs. However, we will be most concerned with the effects of
drugs on the **central nervous system**—composed of the brain and spinal
cord, which are in turn composed of nerve cells called neurons.

In figure 3.2 you can see the structure of a typical neuron. The purpose
of the neuron is to transmit information, and this task is accomplished by
both electrical and chemical processes. Within the neuron, information is
transmitted electrically through the exchange of ions, while transmission between neurons occurs chemically. Drugs affect both of these processes.

The Level of the Neuron

The **dendrite** receives information from other neurons, and the **cell body**
transmits that information to the **axon.** The axon carries the information to
the **end button,** which releases **neurotransmitters** that cross the **synapse** to
another dendrite or cell body (see figure 3.3). Drugs can affect any one of
these steps, but most of the psychoactive drugs exert their effect at the level
of the synapse.

The nerve impulse travels down the axon and reaches the end button.
The **vesicles** containing neurotransmitters move toward the wall of the neuron and release the neurotransmitters into the synapse (the word *synapse* is

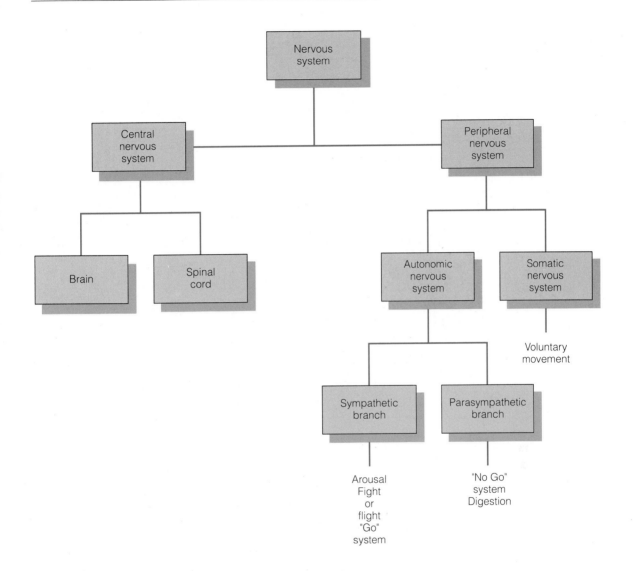

FIGURE 3.1

The structure of the nervous system.

Greek and means space). This portion of the neuron (the end button, vesicles, and cell wall) is referred to as the **presynaptic area.** Once the neurotransmitter is released, it crosses the synapse to the **postsynaptic area.** The postsynaptic membrane contains the postsynaptic receptors for the various neurotransmitters.

The *lock-and-key principle* described briefly in the previous chapter explains how neural messages are transmitted, as well as how many drugs work. Because of its chemical structure, a neurotransmitter has an affinity for a specialized portion of the postsynaptic membrane. Normally, that membrane is **polarized,** which means that an electrical charge has built up. The

FIGURE 3.2
A ''typical'' neuron.

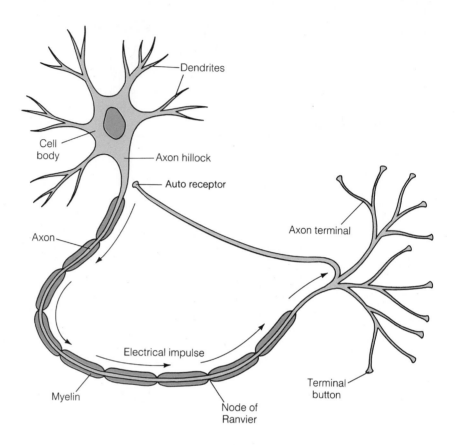

neurotransmitter, the key, attaches to the receptor area, the lock, and produces a charge in the membrane so that ions can flow through and alter the
electrical charge that has built up. If that charge is great enough, the entire
neuron discharges—the door opens.

Neurotransmitters that increase the likelihood of a neuron firing are
called excitatory, but neurotransmitters can be inhibitory as well. If the neurotransmitter fits into the postsynaptic receptor and causes an increased flow
of a different chemically-charged molecule, the neuron becomes less likely
to fire. A number of drugs, such as alcohol and the benzodiazepines, (see
chapter 11) alter the functioning of inhibitory neurotransmitters.

Some neurotransmitters are excitatory. They make the neuron more
likely to discharge, while others are inhibitory, increasing the electrical potential of the cell wall and decreasing the likelihood that the cell will
discharge. Further complicating the issue, excitatory and inhibitory potentials
occur on the same membrane so that whether a nerve impulse is propagated
depends on the *summation* of excitatory and inhibitory neurotransmitters.

Yet another way in which neurotransmitters work is to indirectly open
ion channels through what is called the **second messenger system.** As figure

FIGURE 3.3

The structure of the synapse.

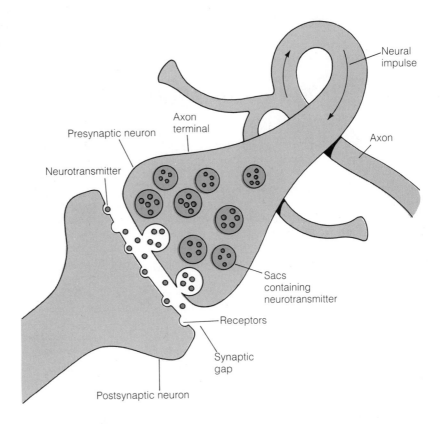

Neural impulse

Axon terminal

Presynaptic neuron

Axon

Neurotransmitter

Sacs containing neurotransmitter

Receptors

Synaptic gap

Postsynaptic neuron

3.5 shows, some postsynaptic receptors have enzymes attached to them. When the receptor is occupied by a neurotransmitter or drug, this enzyme is released and through a complicated process indirectly alters the resting potential of the cell membrane in its vicinity. The second messenger system functions more indirectly by sensitizing the nerve cell than it does directly by producing an action potential. Caffeine is believed to exert part of its action by altering the second messenger system.

In addition to the postsynaptic receptor, many neurons also contain *autoreceptors,* located on any part of the cell. Autoreceptors respond to the neurotransmitter that the neuron releases. Neurons releasing acetylcholine, for example, have autoreceptors for acetylcholine on various portions of the cell wall. Autoreceptors function to regulate the synthesis of the neurotransmitter, and most decrease its production. What seems to be involved, therefore, is a feedback mechanism: the presence of a neurotransmitter in the extracellular space inhibits the production of that neurotransmitter, whereas a relative lack would serve to increase production.

As complicated as the description above may seem, it is simple compared to what happens when looking at higher levels of organization: "At the molecular level, an explanation of the action of a drug is often possible,

Propagation of the Nerve Impulse

The process by which a nerve impulse is propagated is quite complicated, but even a simplified explanation goes a long way toward aiding our understanding of how drugs work. Think of the axon as being filled with intracellular fluid and bathed in extracellular fluid. Found in these fluids are charged molecules called *ions*. When table salt (NaCl), for example, is dissolved in water, it forms two groups of charged particles—the sodium ions (positively-charged cations) and the chlorine ions (negatively-charged anions). In neurons, there are four important ions: protein and chloride anions (with a negative charge) as well as sodium cations and potassium cations (with a positive charge).

These ions are not evenly distributed in intra- and extracellular fluids. The concentration of protein anions and potassium cations is greater inside the axon, and the concentration of sodium and chlorine ions is greater in the extracellular space. The result of this imbalance is that the inside of the axon is negatively charged relative to the outside and is called the *resting potential*.

You probably remember that such an imbalance should lead to *diffusion*—with the positive ions moving inward across the membrane that makes up the axon wall, and the negative ions moving outward until there is no difference in the concentration of the ions and, hence, no electrical charge. Diffusion, however, does not occur because the wall of the axon is *semipermeable,* meaning that it stops the large protein molecules from diffusing outward and prevents most of the sodium ions from diffusing inward.

Another reason the inside of the neuron has a charge of /ms/70 mv relative to the outside is the *sodium potassium pump*. The sodium potassium pump is an active process made up of thousands of protein molecules that pick up sodium ions inside the axon and exchange them for potassium ions outside the axon. Since the ratio of exchange is three sodium for two potassium ions, the net result is an increase in the negative charge inside the axon.

An *action potential* occurs when this semipermeable membrane becomes suddenly permeable. In the wall of the axon are *ion channels* that do exactly what their name implies. When the sodium ion channel opens up, for example, sodium ions rush into the intracellular space. Now the inside is actually positive relative to the outside. The next thing that happens is that the sodium ion channel closes, and the potassium ion channel opens up, with the result that the positive potassium ions flow outward. With the aid of the sodium potassium pump, the original charge is then restored and the axon is ready to "fire" again. The sudden influx and efflux of ions causes other ion channels to open and the action potential is propagated down the axon.

What causes the ion channels to open up in the first place? Neurotransmitters attach to the postsynaptic receptor and open special ion channels. Depending on which ion channels are opened, the neurotransmitters can either increase or decrease the resting potential of the cell membrane. When these local charges in the resting potential become sufficiently large, then ion channels on the axon open up and an action potential results. Cocaine, along with other local anesthetics, exerts its effect by making the axonal membrane more permeable to sodium and potassium when the neuron is in a resting stage and by somehow changing the sodium ion channel so that the sodium ions do not flow freely into the intracellular space during the action potential. Therefore the action potential cannot occur and the nerve cell does not fire. If the nerve cell in question is a pain fiber, anesthesia results.

FIGURE 3.4

The appropriate neurotransmitter, because of its molecular structure, fits like a "key" into the "lock" of the postsynaptic receptor.

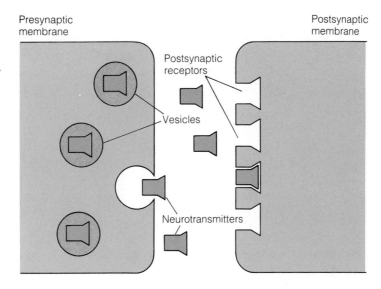

Presynaptic membrane

Postsynaptic membrane

Postsynaptic receptors

Vesicles

Neurotransmitters

at the cellular level, an explanation is sometimes possible, but at a behavioral level our ignorance is abysmal'' (Cooper, Bloom, & Roth, 1986, p. 4).

Just *how* abysmal our ignorance is will become apparent as we explore the various classes of drugs. The reader should keep the above quote in mind when reading the oversimplified discussion of drugs in the popular media. The complex actions of cocaine on humans, for example, cannot be explained by a description of this drug on the release and re-uptake of a few neurotransmitters. For example, some antidepressants have the same biochemical effect as cocaine and yet are not stimulants, while cocaine is not an antidepressant in any real sense of the term.

In addition to neurotransmitters, two other types of chemical substances need to be discussed. The role of neurotransmitters in the propagation of the nerve impulse is relatively well understood. The roles of neuromodulators and neurohormones are only beginning to be explored but promise new frontiers in the understanding of drugs and their action.

Neuromodulators operate in a complicated way that is not well understood. They exert their effect at a distance from the neuron that secretes them and seem to act on the second messenger system. You are undoubtedly familiar with one neuromodulator which is also a neurotransmitter: endorphin.

Neurohormones also operate at a distance from the neurons that secrete them. Some neurohormones are secreted into the bloodstream while others are circulated by other means. Dopamine is a neurotransmitter in some parts of the brain and a neurohormone in others. Neurohormones are essential in the regulation of growth and maturation, sexual and maternal behavior, and aggression. The role of neurohormones in determining the effects of such drugs as alcohol is just now beginning to be explored.

FIGURE 3.5

When the neurotransmitter attaches to the postsynaptic receptor, a second messenger system is activated, which alters the permeability of the postsynaptic membrane as well as affecting the cell nucleus.

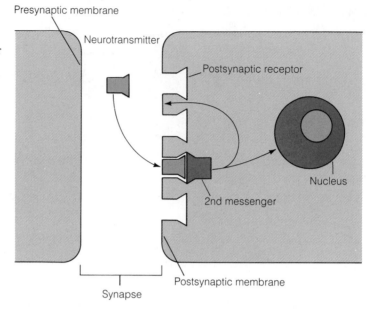

Presynaptic membrane

Neurotransmitter

Postsynaptic receptor

Nucleus

2nd messenger

Postsynaptic membrane

Synapse

Neurotransmitter Systems

Having just demonstrated that it is impossible to talk in simplistic terms of neurotransmitters, neuromodulators, and neurohormones, we will now do exactly that and discuss several important neurotransmitters. The list of neurotransmitters seems to grow weekly, and the more that is found out about them, the less seems to be known. For our purposes, however, a few relatively simple principles are sufficient. Our primary interest, after all, is how drugs alter neurotransmitters, not the exact way that they work.

Drugs act several ways to alter transmitters. A drug may alter the production of a neurotransmitter, its release or re-uptake, or alter the storage. In addition, drugs can act at the postsynaptic site by mimicking a neurotransmitter, or by occupying the receptor sites and preventing the cell from firing. Drugs also can affect the sensitivity of the cell membrane. Obviously, even at the level of the synapse drug effects are complex.

At least two dozen neurotransmitters are presumed to exist but luckily only a few are well understood, and these will be discussed.

Acetylcholine

Imagine you are walking through a jungle in South America. An Indian aims a blow pipe at you, and you feel the prick of a dart. In a short period of time all your muscles go limp, and you fall. Since you need the muscles in your chest and diaphragm to breath, you stop breathing. Eventually you cannot even move your eyelids. However, you can see, hear, and feel everything that is happening around you. You are completely conscious—immobilized, but conscious. At last you slip into a coma and die.

The drug you just absorbed through the subcutaneous or intramuscular route was **curare,** a drug extracted from the bark of the tree. Curare blocks in depth

Neurotransmitters and Food

Health food enthusiasts have been claiming for many years that the food we eat affects our behavior. Many people believe, for example, that sugar and carbohydrates can make children hyperactive, despite the fact that most carefully controlled studies show no such link. Some researchers have explored the relationship between nutrients in food, their relationship to neurotransmitters, and their effect on behavior.

At the outset it should be noted that the effects found are small and subtle, which should not be surprising. Basically, the typical research paradigm is to have the subject ingest the precursors of known neurotransmitters and then measure their effect. Since the precursors are involved in many reactions in the body, relatively little gets to the brain. These precursors must then somehow affect neurotransmitter systems, which themselves are quite subtle. Nevertheless there is some evidence that precursors of three neurotransmitters may affect behavior.

Tyramine, a precursor of norepinephrine has been shown to have some effect on mood and may help relieve some of the symptoms of depression. Lecithin, the precursor of acetylcholine, which is one of the primary neurotransmitters in the hippocampus and which has been implicated in memory, may also have some effect on memory in some people. You cannot take a bottle of lecithin just before an exam and expect it to help you get an A, nor can you eat a hamburger (which contains tyramine) and expect it to relieve your depression. However, the research evidence does demonstrate that food can be viewed as a drug.

One amino acid, tryptophan, has had much wider application and has been the center of a recent controversy. As you will recall from page 75 tryptophan is the precursor of serotonin, a major inhibitory neurotransmitter in the brain. You also read that milk and bananas are rich in tryptophan. Until 27 November 1989, tryptophan was available in tablet form from health food stores and many supermarkets. It was sold as a food supplement, getting around the FDA restrictions on over-the-counter drugs. Millions of people took tryptophan for years as a self-treatment for depression, insomnia, and premenstrual syndrome, even though the FDA had not approved it for these purposes.

In October of 1989, however, the New Mexico Health and Environment Department and the Centers for Disease Control in Atlanta were notified of three patients who were suffering from myalgia (muscle pain) and eosinophilia (an excess of white blood cells). Within a few weeks, two-hundred-and-eighty-seven cases had been reported, and the FDA recalled all products in which tryptophan was an ingredient. Since the recall in 1989, new cases have fallen virtually to zero (Swygert, Maes, Sewell, et al, 1990).

As of 1991, over 1,500 cases of eosinophilia-myalgia syndrome, as it came to be called, had been reported, along with twenty-seven deaths. Since people had been taking tryptophan for many years, the suddenness of the outbreak suggested something other than tryptophan itself. As it turns out, it appears some kind of contaminant was responsible. All of the tryptophan sold in the United States is produced in Japan by six companies. One of these companies uses a genetically altered strain of bacteria to produce tryptophan, and it appears that batches from this company are responsible for most if not all of the cases (Slutsker, Hoesley, Miller, et al, 1990; Centers for Disease Control, 1990; Belongia, Hedberg, Gleich et al, 1990).

Although only a small percentage of those taking the contaminated product became ill, the risk was serious for those who did, and the ban on the sale of tryptophan continues, at least until the exact nature of the cause of this condition is clear. Throughout this book you will read example after example of the importance of being an informed consumer of any drug, legal or illegal.

the action of **acetylcholine** released from a neuron that synapses on a muscle. The vesicle in these neurons secretes acetylcholine, causing the muscle to contract.

Curare is a competitive blocker in that it "fools" the postsynaptic receptor on the wall of the muscle into accepting it, but it does not open the ion channel and hence the muscle does not contract. Eventually, curare will be released from the postsynaptic receptor, and acetylcholine, which does open the ion channel, will takes its place. When that happens the muscle will again contract. Long before this happens, however, the victim is usually dead. Curare does not pass the blood/brain barrier, and does not affect the brain. Consequently, the victim remains conscious during the entire experience.

Acetylcholine is the primary neurotransmitter at the neuromuscular junction, but is also active in the brain. Systems of neurons that contain acetylcholine are called cholinergic, and cholinergic systems are involved in a number of behaviors. As we shall see, drugs that block the action of acetylcholine can cause memory loss, and Alzheimer's disease, a progressive disease that results in memory loss, has been associated with a reduction of acetylcholine receptors in the brain. The molecule of acetylcholine acts both as a first and as a second messenger. At the neuromuscular junction it operates primarily as a first messenger while its actions in the brain are those of a second messenger.

Blocking the action of acetylcholine in the brain not only causes memory loss but can cause hallucinations. A number of plants contain substances that block the action of acetylcholine and hence cause hallucinations. Among these plants are datura and the hallucinogenic mushroom Amanita muscaria. See chapter 8 for a more detailed description of the anticholinergic hallucinogens.

Acetylcholine, Nerve Gas, and Insecticide. Acetylcholine is metabolized by an enzyme *cholinesterase* which exists in the synapse. Drugs which destroy this enzyme are called cholinesterase inhibitors. When a cholinesterase inhibitor is somehow absorbed, the postsynaptic membrane is stimulated by the constant release of acetylcholine. Since this action is primarily at the neuromuscular junction, the result is involuntary muscle contractions. Eventually, respiratory depression and death occur after a long period of seizures.

During the war with Iraq in 1991, you saw pictures of soldiers wearing gas masks and camouflage suits. The Iraqi army was believed to have stockpiles of various chemical weapons, including *nerve gas*. Nerve gas is a cholinesterase inhibitor, which actually destroys the existing cholinesterase in the body. Initial treatment for nerve gas poisoning consists of injections of atropine, which blocks the action of acetylcholine.

Insecticides are also cholinesterase inhibitors and are functionally similar to nerve gas. Think of that the next time you spray your roses. Malathion, for example, is one of the most widely used insecticides, even

U.S. Soldiers in Iraq wore gas masks to protect themselves from nerve gas poisoning and other chemical warfare.

though it is an inactive compound, meaning that malathion itself has no biological action. In both humans and animals, however, it is converted to malaoxon, which is a cholinesterase inhibitor. Malaoxon is more stable in insects than in humans, who rapidly convert it to an inactive compound (Levine, 1983). Thus the active drug builds up in insects. Given a sufficiently high dose of malathion or other factors, a similar buildup is possible in humans.

Suppose you decide not to expose yourself to nerve gas, and reach for the "organic" insecticides. Most of these contain nicotine, which mimics the action of acetylcholine at the neuromuscular junction, so the effect is the same. Nicotine is an extremely potent poison, as anyone who has smoked one cigarette knows. There is more than enough nicotine in a pack of unfiltered cigarettes to kill a human. Cigarette smokers have become tolerant to the effects of nicotine, but the inexperienced user can become quite ill as a result of exposure to nicotine.

Serotonin

Serotonin is widely distributed throughout the body. It functions as a neurotransmitter in many parts of the brain and is involved in the release of neurohormones in the hypothalamus. Serotonin-containing neurons are believed to be involved in the regulation of mood, eating, and pain. Recently a great deal of interest has focused on the role of serotonin in depression, and at least two drugs have been marketed as antidepressants because they primarily affect the serotonin system (see chapter 11). The role of serotonin in understanding drug action is discussed in later chapters.

When you were four or five and couldn't fall asleep, your mother might have told you to take a hot bath and drink a glass of warm milk. Now that you are an adult, you probably smile fondly in remembrance of such old-fashioned beliefs. Although it is unlikely that the milk had any real effect, Mother nevertheless had something going for her. Serotonin is generally considered an inhibitory transmitter. In the reticular formation it is thought to slow the functioning of neurons that alert the cortex to incoming stimuli. Therefore, any drug that increases the amount of serotonin in the brain should reduce alertness.

Milk is rich in **tryptophan,** an amino acid that the brain converts to 5 hydroxytryptophan, also known as serotonin. In other words, when you drink a glass of milk, you are ingesting a substance (called a **precursor**) from which the brain naturally produces a sedative. Until 1989, tryptophan was sold in health food stores and recommended as a ''natural'' sleeping pill. Some studies support its effectiveness. How did Mom figure all that out anyway?

In addition to operating at the level of the upper brain stem, serotonin has other effects that are not well understood. At least three different serotonin receptors exist, and drugs such as LSD which affect this system have hallucinogenic properties (Jacobs, 1987). No simple relationship exists between hallucinogenic drugs and the serotonin system, as might be expected from a system that is widely distributed in the brain.

Catecholamines

The term **catecholamine** refers to several neurotransmitters and neurohormones that are similar in structure, since they all contain a *catechol* nucleus, hence the name. You don't have to have studied three semesters of organic chemistry to realize that the molecules shown in figure 3.6 are remarkably similar. They are all catecholamines, and all function as neurotransmitters or neurohormones. **Dopamine** and **norepinephrine** are found extensively in the brain while **epinephrine** is found in higher percentages in the bloodstream.

An enormous amount of research has been done on the relationship between the catecholamines and drugs and a great deal has been learned about the way these neurotransmitters work. Figure 3.7 may seem formidable but it helps to explain how different drugs work.

Catecholamines are released from the vesicles and cross the synapse where they bind to the postsynaptic receptor. The action of the catecholamines is terminated in two ways. If the catecholamine leaks from the synapse, it is metabolized by an enzyme. Most often, however, the catecholamine is taken back up into the presynaptic membrane (a process called re-uptake). Once inside the cell, it is absorbed back into the vesicles, the original recycling plant. There is also an enzyme that metabolizes catecholamines inside the presynaptic cell.

The catecholamines are regulated in a number of ways. Consequently, drugs can affect catecholamine metabolism at any of these steps. As we shall see in the chapter on stimulants, some of the different effects of drugs can be attributed to the manner in which they affect metabolism.

Since the catecholamines are linked to our emotional states, the alternating elation and depression that occurs with amphetamine and cocaine can in part be understood at the biochemical level. Apparently both drugs cause an initial increase in catecholamines in the synapse, followed by a reduction. The depletion of catecholamines is known to be related to depression, while an increase is thought to relate to excitation. This topic will be discussed in detail in chapters 5 and 11.

FIGURE 3.6

You do not have to be a biochemist to see that these three molecules are very similar.

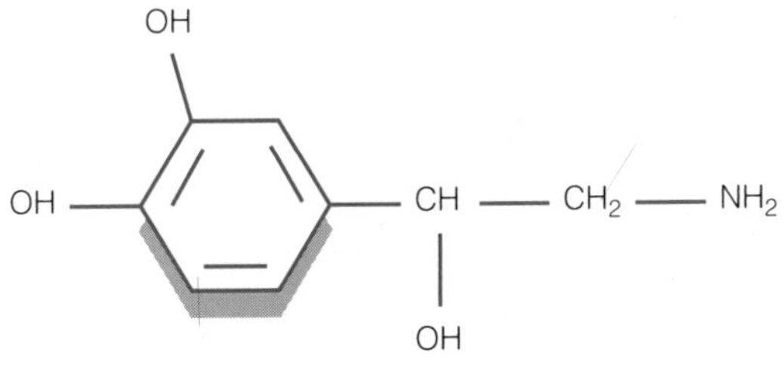

Norepinephrine

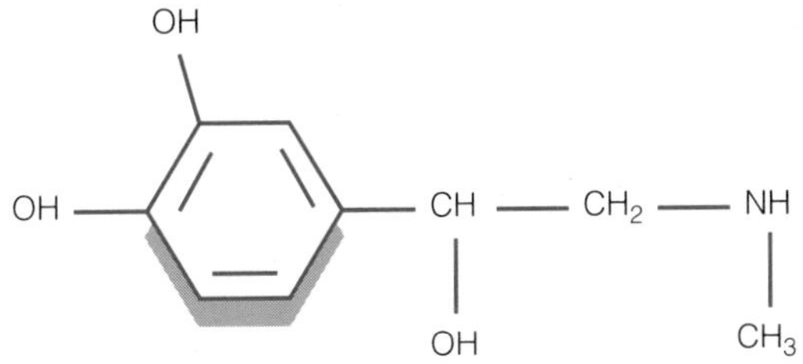

Epinephrine

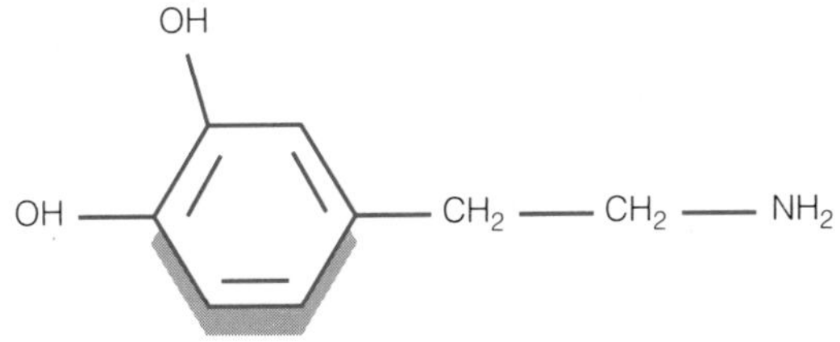

Dopamine

Peptides

The term **peptide** is used to describe a large number of substances that may function as neurotransmitters, neurohormones, neuromodulators, or all three. Peptides are a sequence of amino acids. A peptide containing a long sequence of amino acids (over 100) is called a protein, while shorter ones are called polypeptides. The best known series of polypeptides is popularly known collectively as **endorphins.** Even scientists working in the field use this word casually but when serious refer to them as opiate peptides.

The Endorphins (Oops, opiate peptides). Morphine is derived from opium, one of the oldest drugs known, and morphine and its derivatives have a wide range of uses. Although morphine was synthesized more than 100 years ago, little was known about how it works until recently.

Some drugs work because they resemble a naturally occurring neurotransmitter. Morphine looked like no neurotransmitter known at that time. Other drugs work because they alter the metabolism of a neurotransmitter. Morphine does that but not in any consistent way that would explain its effects.

FIGURE 3.7

Using norepinephrine (NE) as an example, the diagram shows some of the ways drugs can affect catecholamine metabolism. Keep in mind that this diagram is simplified.
1. Drugs can affect the synthesis of NE.
2. Drugs can cause a slow release of NE from the vesicle depleting these stores.
3. Drugs can cause vesicles to increase the release of NE into the synapse.
4. Drugs can prevent the vesicles from absorbing NE.
5. Inhibiting MAO (monoamine oxidase) which normally metabolizes NE will result in an increase in turnover.
6. Drugs can block the re-uptake of NE into the presynaptic neuron.
7. Drugs can mimic the effect of NE.
8. Drugs can occupy the receptor sites for NE and prevent the "lock" from fitting into the "key."

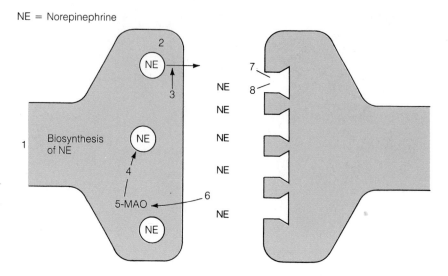

NE = Norepinephrine

When researchers discovered that morphine was bound to a postsynaptic receptor, the race was on. The discovery of the postsynaptic receptor for morphine was important because it meant that there existed in the brain a naturally occurring morphine-like substance. Either that or over the course of millions of years of evolution, we evolved a receptor that had no function until opium was discovered about 3,000 years ago.

Shortly after the discovery of the postsynaptic receptor, the substance that the brain itself produced was discovered and found to be a peptide. Shortly after *that* various similar substances were found. The word **endorphin** comes from endogenous (naturally occurring) morphine-like substances (endogenous + morphine = endorphin). The study of the opiate peptides is extremely complex and beyond the scope of this textbook. In brief, however, there are at least three different groups of opiate peptides, and five different receptors for them in the brain alone. The peptides and receptors are found in many areas of the brain, including the hypothalamus, the pituitary, the limbic system, and the pain pathways.

As you might expect, the opiate peptides have been linked to many different behaviors, with most of the evidence being rather flimsy. Strong evidence exists, however, that they relieve the emotional component of pain. As we shall see in chapter 11, pain is very complex. Some pain, while severe, is easier to tolerate than other pain. Morphine and the opiate peptides apparently help us tolerate pain while still feeling it. One of the receptors, the delta receptor, is found in the limbic system which mediates mood. Another receptor, the mu receptor, is found in the part of the brain that actually mediates pain, the periaqueductal gray matter (page 85).

Other peptides include **substance P,** also involved in the perception of pain, vasopressin, which has been shown to be involved in memory, insulin,

• YOU READ IT HERE FIRST •

Smart Drugs

In 1988, the Food and Drug Administration issued a ruling allowing individuals to purchase drugs that are not approved for use in the United States. The purchaser can purchase only a three month's supply, must specify that the drugs are for personal use, and are being used with the approval of a physician. In part, this ruling came about as a result of pressure from AIDS activists but the ruling has had an unexpected result.

You may now purchase several books extolling the virtues of "smart drugs." In addition there are companies that are only too willing to sell you these drugs, bypassing the usual prescription regulations by appealing to the FDA ruling. How do these drugs work? Are they for real? As is the case with virtually every drug, there is a wide difference of opinion about their safety and effectiveness; advocates, who, of course, tend to be users (or sellers) maintain that the drugs work for them, at least, while most researchers are more than a little skeptical.

Some of the drugs are approved for legitimate uses by the Food and Drug Administration while others can be obtained only through mail-order houses in Europe and Mexico. They include *piracetam*, which is supposed to increase blood flow between the right and left hemisphere and hence improve creativity, *ergoloid mesylate* (Hydergine), given to elderly people with memory deficits, *vasopressin,* an antidiuretic taken by diabetics, and *dehydroepiandrosterone* (DHEA), a hormone that causes some nerve cells to grow. The rationale for using these drugs differs from drug to drug. Piracetam is supposed to work by increasing blood supply, Hydergine might have some slight ef-

fect on memory loss and alertness in those with Alzheimer's or related diseases, vasopressin is a neurotransmitter linked to memory, and DHEA levels do decrease with age.

The reason most scientists and physicians are skeptical is that there is no reason to believe that because a drug improves functioning in a person with an organic brain deficit, the same drug will improve memory in a healthy young person. Merely increasing the blood supply to the brain or absorbing a neurotransmitter is no guarantee that these changes can be incorporated into normal brain functioning. No carefully controlled scientific studies support the position that "smart drugs" work, and most have significant side effects ranging from increased bowel movements to insomnia to increased facial hair growth in women. The normal human brain is functioning at an amazing level of complexity and efficiency; taking a "smart pill" is probably no more likely to improve your mental performance than changing your brand of gasoline is your car's performance.

For those who don't want to risk prescription drugs, "smart drinks" are also available. At least in California, there are even clubs you can go to read about smart drugs while listening to music and dancing. No alcohol is served, but you can purchase amino-acid-loaded smart drinks instead. While smart drinks are unlikely to have any benefit except to those who sell them, you would undoubtedly rather see someone getting behind the wheel of a car who had just drunk a Psuperpsonic Cybertonic (no kidding, the actual name!) than six shots of tequila followed by a few beers.

and an endogenous substance that resembles the antianxiety drug Librium. The next time you eat ''hot'' food containing chile peppers or curry, keep in mind that what you are really doing is increasing the firing in substance P receptors. Capsaicin is the chemical found in ''hot'' food and increases available substance P. The food you are eating is not really hot; what you are feeling is really pain. If you doubt this, *gently* rub a small slice of jalapeño chile pepper on your skin.

The discovery of how peptides function as neurotransmitters caused a major shift in the way scientists looked at neurotransmission. Until recently, one of the established principles of neuronal function was that a neuron secreted one and only one neurotransmitter and that the postsynaptic receptor responded to only one neurotransmitter. It is now recognized that peptides are secreted by neurons that also produce other neurotransmitters and that these peptides cross the synapse and interact in a complex way with the postsynaptic receptor. Just how they interact is not clear, but they may be released only when the cell is firing rapidly, thus increasing firing of the postsynaptic neuron.

The Amino Acid Transmitters

Amino acids are used by all cells in the brain in the process of protein synthesis. Some neurons also secrete them as neurotransmitters. Amino acids are found in the most primitive of organisms and are widely distributed in the brain. One, **glutamic acid,** is excitatory and the other, **gamma-aminobutyric acid** (GABA), is inhibitory. A third amino acid, **glycine,** also functions as an inhibitory neurotransmitter, primarily in the spinal cord and lower part of the brain. The bacteria that causes tetanus secretes a substance that blocks glycine synthesis. Since glycine is an inhibitory neurotransmitter affecting motor function, the result is continuous contraction of muscles, hence the term ''lockjaw.''

Many readers have experienced the effects of an excess of glutamic acid since monosodium glutamate (MSG) is used in Chinese food and can lead to flushing and jaw pain—known as the *Chinese food syndrome*. Monosodium glutamate is glutamic acid in salt form. Glutamic acid is also believed to be involved in memory.

Gamma-aminobutyric acid is an inhibitory neurotransmitter. Alcohol and the benzodiazepines such as Valium and Librium operate by attaching to part of the GABA receptor and facilitating the ion exchange that reduces the likelihood of the cell firing. As you will read in chapter 11, there appears to be a naturally occurring substance secreted by neurons in time of stress that does just what the benzodiazepines and alcohol do. The best way to remember how these drugs work is that they increase the inhibitory effect of GABA.

MAJOR DIVISIONS OF THE NERVOUS SYSTEM

Referring to figure 3.1 we can see that there are basically three parts to the nervous system: the central, the peripheral, and the autonomic. Drugs exert their primary effect on the central and autonomic nervous systems, so this brief discussion will focus on these two. Students of physiology know that these three parts are not really separate, but for our purposes they can be so treated.

The Central Nervous System

The **central nervous system** consists of the spinal cord and brain. The spinal cord carries messages from the brain to the muscles and organs of the body and transmits impulses from them back to the brain.

Brain Stem

As the spinal cord joins the brain there is a swelling called the *brain stem* that is composed of two structures, the *medulla* and the *pons*. In addition, part of the reticular formation (see figure 3.9) is found within the medulla and pons. The brain stem has many functions, including regulation of the cardiovascular system (in conjunction with the hypothalamus) and control of muscle tone (together with the cerebellum). Two functions, one essential and the other seemingly trivial, are important in our understanding of drugs: the brain stem controls breathing and initiates vomiting.

When you were young you probably had the experience of paying attention to your breathing and then wondering if you were going to die if you stopped. Needless to say, since you are reading this, you didn't, and you have the brain stem to thank for that. Cells in the brain stem maintain breathing without your awareness. A number of drugs, including the opiates and alcohol, are respiratory depressants, which means that they can inhibit breathing rate, and respiratory depression is a common cause of death from drug overdose. Even cocaine, normally considered a stimulant, can ultimately cause death by respiratory depression brought on by exhaustion.

Vomiting may not seem like a particularly useful function, but it can be lifesaving. The vomiting center in the brain stem triggers vomiting to rid the stomach of potential poisons. This center can be triggered by various drugs, including alcohol. Excessive drinking can lead to nausea and vomiting. Inexperienced drinkers who suddenly ingest more than they are used to drinking are especially prone to this most unpleasant experience sometimes called "worshipping the porcelain god."

In addition, some drugs reduce the vomit reflex. Dramamine is an over-the-counter drug used for this purpose, and marijuana also is effective as an *antiemetic* (the technical term). In fact, as we shall see in chapter 6, Marinol, a drug that contains the active substance in marijuana, has recently been marketed for this express purpose. Scopolamine, an anticholinergic drug that in low doses is antiemetic and in high doses is hallucinogenic, is marketed as a transdermal patch.

Reticular Formation

The **reticular formation** is a large structure that begins in the medulla and ends at the midbrain and plays an important role in sleep, arousal, attention, and muscle movement. Along with two other parts of the brain closely associated with the reticular formation, the locus coeruleus and the raphe nuclei, the reticular formation is an important site of action for many drugs. Drugs which affect serotonin and norepinephrine act in part on these structures.

Amino Acids, Peptides, and Addiction

Drugs of all kinds alter the biochemical metabolism of the brain. Those who abuse drugs must alter this biochemistry even more. In chapter 13 you will read about biochemical theories of addiction, but for present purposes, consider the possibility that drugs produce a long-lasting change in the brain chemistry so that normal function may not return for a long time (six months to a year or more). If drugs alter the metabolism of the brain, might the recovering addict be helped by nutrients and supplements that help restore that balance?

Although this is a new area of research, it does show some promise. In double blind studies, nutritional supplements which increase levels of enkephalin, serotonin, GABA, and dopamine were shown to relieve some of the stress associated with long-term withdrawal from alcohol, and a similar combination was shown to be effective for cocaine withdrawal (Trachtenberg & Blum, 1988; Blum, Trachtenberg, Elliot, Dingler, Sexton, Samuels, & Cataldie, 1989).

Similar findings have been reported for other combinations of amino acids and vitamins (Lieber, 1991). There is no single cure for addiction, and no one should expect that popping a handful of pills is going to overcome an addiction; nevertheless, nutritional supplements may play a future role in relapse prevention and the treatment of addiction.

Amphetamine, for example, increases alertness and decreases sleepiness. Sometimes users of high doses of amphetamines concentrate on something so hard they repeat an action over and over for minutes at a time. Amphetamine works on the reticular formation and the locus coeruleus because many of the neurons contain norepinephrine, and amphetamine causes the release of norepinephrine. There is some evidence to suggest that the locus coeruleus is specifically involved in controlling attention to external stimuli.

Serotonin-containing neurons are found in the raphe nucleus and the reticular formation. When these are damaged experimentally, animals experience insomnia. Drugs such as tryptophan increase levels of serotonin and hence promote sleep. Parts of the reticular formation are also involved in various stages of dream, or REM, sleep.

Hypothalamus

Stick the tip of your tongue as far back in your mouth as it will go; then touch the roof of your mouth. A short distance above that point lies a very important part of the brain called the **hypothalamus.** The thalamus distributes various sensory input to various parts of the cortex. The hypothalamus is the part of the brain below the thalamus (hypo = below).

This area of the brain is rich in cell bodies called nuclei, which control and regulate a number of functions. Homeostasis is the process by which the body maintains a steady state. In many animals, if the blood sugar level is too low, the hypothalamus senses this and helps initiate behavior that leads

FIGURE 3.8

The nervous system can be divided into the central nervous system (brain and spinal cord) and the peripheral nervous system (the nerves that branch out to all parts of the body from the central nervous system).

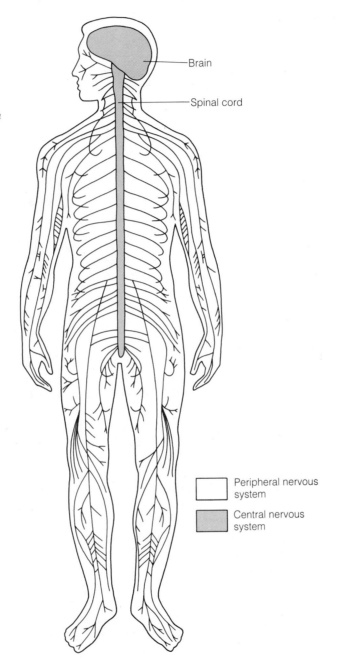

Brain

Spinal cord

☐ Peripheral nervous system

▨ Central nervous system

FIGURE 3.9

A cross section of the brain.

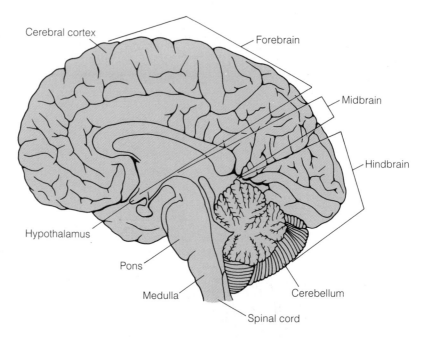

to eating. If blood sugar level is high, then another portion of the hypothalamus responds, and food-seeking behavior decreases. Regulation of hunger also involves peptides produced in the intestine and is quite complicated. The hypothalamus also is important in regulating temperature and cardiovascular functioning, as well as aggressive and sexual behavior.

In addition, the hypothalamus is the link between the brain and the **autonomic nervous system** which is composed of the sympathetic and parasympathetic branches. The sympathetic branch of the autonomic nervous system increases blood supply to the brain and to the muscles, decreases the blood supply to the digestive system, and initiates other changes that prepare the animal to fight or to flee. The parasympathetic branch of the autonomic nervous system is operating when we are digesting food, at rest, or in general, in a nonaroused state. Remember how you felt after last Thanksgiving's dinner?

Yet another function of the hypothalamus is to influence the **pituitary,** or master gland, of the body. The pituitary secretes a number of hormones that influence many organ systems in the body. Control of the pituitary is accomplished by neurons from the hypothalamus, as well as by neurohormones secreted by cells there.

The hypothalamus is richly supplied with blood vessels, so drugs often affect the hypothalamus before reaching other portions of the brain. Drugs that alter the functioning of the hypothalamus can affect homeostatic mechanisms such as temperature, eating, and sex, the autonomic nervous system, and the entire hormonal system of the body.

Limbic System and Medial Forebrain Bundle

These two structures are often linked together. Along with the hypothalamus, they regulate emotions and other complex behaviors that occur at a low level of conscious awareness. As anyone who was ever stopped by a policeman and who tried to appear calm knows, you do not have much conscious control over emotions such as fear, and they seem to occur without our awareness.

The **medial forebrain bundle** system is particularly important in understanding drug effects, because numerous experiments have shown that rats will press a bar to obtain stimulation of this area of the brain. They will press a bar in preference to food, water, or sex, and will tolerate high levels of electric shock to their feet in order to obtain this reward. These findings have led to much speculation that some drugs are rewarding because they increase firing in this system.

Basal Ganglia

Complex movement of the body requires the coordination of opposing muscles. Without this coordination, spasms and trembling would occur. The basal ganglia are cells that accomplish this task of coordination. They form a pathway on either side of the thalamus.

The basal ganglia contain neurons that use dopamine or acetylcholine as a neurotransmitter, and an imbalance of either can raise havoc with smooth movement of the body. Parkinson's disease is believed to be caused by a loss of dopamine-containing neurons in the basal ganglia. Individuals with Parkinson's disease develop a gradually increased tremor of the hands and head. Eventually, the muscles become rigid. People with Parkinson's disease have extreme difficulty in performing slow, steady movements like walking, but may still be capable of rapid movements such as catching a ball thrown at them.

Drugs that affect either acetylcholine or dopamine can produce tremors and spasms by affecting the basal ganglia. Drugs used to treat schizophrenia can induce Parkinson-like behavior and one "designer drug" (a synthetic compound used in place of heroin and called China White) has been linked to brain damage similar to that seen with Parkinson's disease. Apparently a substance similar to China White can be produced inadvertently during its synthesis and this toxic substance destroys the brain cells of the basal ganglia. Chapter 9 treats these topics in depth.

Periaqueductal Gray Matter

Many neuroanatomical terms appear unnecessarily complex and impossible to pronounce or remember until they are examined carefully. The **periaqueductal gray matter** is one such phrase. Ventricles are hollow chambers within the brain that are filled with cerebrospinal fluid. There are four ventricles connected to each other and to the central canal of the spinal cord. The cerebral aqueduct connects the third and fourth ventricles, which in turn connect to the central canal of the spinal cord. Surrounding the central aqueduct are cell bodies that, unlike axons, are gray in color. Therefore the formidable term—periaqueductal gray matter—merely refers to the cell bodies (gray matter) around the central aqueduct (peri- means around, aqueduct means aqueduct).

Electrical stimulation of the periaqueductal gray matter in humans or animals results in analgesia or loss of pain sensation. Part of the analgesic action of the opiates described above involves this important area of the brain. The periaqueductal gray matter is also involved in behavior such as fighting and mating.

Cortex

The outer surface of the brain is called the cortex. More than any other part of the brain it provides us with the experiences that make us different from other animals. No other animal has as complex a cortex; the percentage of the total brain taken up by the cortex is greatest in humans.

The cortex is involved in vision, motor movement, sensory perception, hearing, speech, and higher cognitive functions. The cortex is divided into several lobes that have varied and individual functions, as can be seen in figure 3.9. Because of the complexity of the cortex, it is not surprising that virtually all psychoactive drugs exert their effect at least in part through the cortex.

The various parts of the brain do not function independently of each other. The reticular formation sends input to the cortex. The cortex controls muscle movement by way of the basal ganglia and cerebellum. The limbic system affects our emotional response to events, and the hypothalamus and medulla monitor functions of which we are normally not aware. It has been said that, ultimately, every neuron in the brain is connected to every other neuron. Therefore a drug cannot affect just one part of the brain in exclusion to all others. In addition, the various parts of the brain are involved in experiencing and altering the perception of the effect of the drug.

We can see how complicated the interaction of drugs, the brain, and behavior are by looking at sex, one of the simplest and at the same time most complicated of all behaviors. Both the modern and ancient folklore of drugs is full of stories about drugs that will affect sexuality. Although the rhetoric associated with the war on drugs rarely mentions sex and drugs, it is safe to say that more expense and effort has been spent trying to modify sexual function with drugs than any other behavior. How successful has all this effort been?

Drugs, Sex, and Aphrodisiacs

Aphrodisiacs are named after Aphrodite, the Greek goddess of love. But *love* is rarely included in the definition of an aphrodisiac. An *anaphrodisiac* is any agent that decreases sexual desire. In addition to sexual *desire*, aphrodisiacs are often thought of as increasing sexual *performance*.

As Shakespeare and others have warned us for thousands of years, desire and performance are not the same thing. When we try to determine whether there is such a thing as an aphrodisiac, therefore, we must keep in mind these multiple meanings. Finally, we must add to the above definitions

FIGURE 3.10

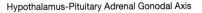

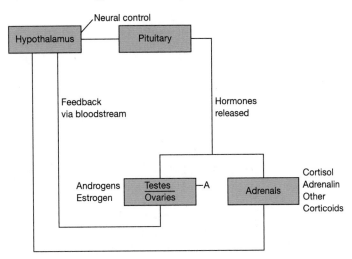

the possibility that drugs can enhance the pleasurable sensory experiences associated with sex, without necessarily affecting either desire or performance.

History of Aphrodisiacs

Aphrodisiacs are mentioned in the Bible. After all, Adam and Eve ate the forbidden fruit (the Bible does not mention the type of fruit; Milton, the English poet, is responsible for the belief that it was an apple) and became aware of their nakedness. Mandrake, which you will read about in chapter 8, has long been considered an aphrodisiac, and is mentioned in Genesis. The context leaves no doubt as to its use.

The *Kama Sutra* is a Hindu manuscript written sometime between the first and fourth centuries A.D. It has achieved a reputation for eroticism that has little to do with its actual contents. The aphrodisiacs that are mentioned in this book are largely based on magical belief.

One supposed aphrodisiac mentioned in the *Kama Sutra* is a combination of milk and honey, among other ingredients. While it might only taste good, it might also have an invigorating effect in someone who was malnourished and thus have some value. On the other hand, at least one anaphrodisiac was probably quite effective—the *Kama Sutra* recommends mixing a special potion with donkey excrement and dumping it on a maiden to prevent her from marrying (Taberner, 1985)!

The Classic Aphrodisiacs Today

While there is little market for the skin of the forehead of a hippopotamus today (Pliny of Rome recommended its use), the sale of other supposed aphrodisiacs is still a million dollar industry, as can be seen in the newspaper excerpt in figure 3.11.

FIGURE 3.11
San Francisco Chronicle,
February 11, 1988. Copyright
1988 Chronicle Publishing
Co., San Francisco, CA.

> A state Department of Fish and Game investigation is continuing into a Chinatown apothecary where wardens seized 886 animal items. They included 351 seal and tiger penises, dried and fresh abalone, a rhinoceros horn and a stuffed bear. Many of the items seized in Tuesday's raid are used in Chinese medicine as aphrodisiacs.

Powdered rhinoceros horn and seal or tiger penises clearly rely on what is called the doctrine of signatures for their supposed effect. The doctrine of signatures is the folk belief that "like cures like." For example, if you eat the heart of an animal you will become brave. The rhinoceros is thought to be the source of the myth of the unicorn, long considered a symbol of sexuality. The horn also is supposed to serve as protection against poisoning. The choice of seal or tiger penis is fairly obvious, but a stuffed bear?

The most famous of all aphrodisiacs, at least to generations of young adolescents, is Spanish fly. Since nearly everyone has heard at least one lurid story about the supposed effects of this drug and dismissed it as juvenile fantasy, you may be surprised to know that Spanish fly is real. Its active ingredient is known, and a preparation of Spanish fly still has some medical use. It would take a very bizarre stretch of imagination to consider its effects as sexually stimulating, however.

Spanish fly is, in fact, a beetle, and, while it is found in Spain, it also is common in other Mediterranean countries. The beetles commonly known as Spanish fly are blister beetles; when dried and crushed and mixed with alcohol, Spanish fly will cause irritation, inflammation, and eventual blistering when applied to the skin. The active substance in Spanish fly is cantharidin and is used to remove warts (Swinyard & Pathak, 1980).

A low dose of Spanish fly taken orally has an effect similar to eating several hot chile peppers. At higher doses, there is a burning sensation in the mouth, stomach cramps, and diarrhea. Death can result from ingestion of as little as 32 mg and is the result of kidney failure (Taberner, 1985).

It is hard to imagine how an extract used to raise blisters or remove warts or that causes massive diarrhea and kidney failure, along with blood in the urine, could have gained such a reputation as an aphrodisiac. Nevertheless, the reputation of Spanish fly continues until the present time. The author recently saw an advertisement for "genuine spurious Spanish fly."

Common Drugs and Sex

Many drugs have gained a reputation for increasing or decreasing sexual desire or performance. None seem to be successful as aphrodisiacs, and those that have the most famous reputations for doing so, seem, in fact, to be the exact opposite. The only positive effect of any drug in regards to sex seems to lie in its ability to enhance sensory awareness. If we restrict the meaning of the term aphrodisiac to this almost trivial definition, several drugs may qualify.

Alcohol. **Alcohol** may be the most famous aphrodisiac of all, even though it is actually exactly the opposite. Both the short-term and the long-term effects of alcohol intake are harmful to sexual performance for both men and women, but nevertheless the myth persists. How could a drug that demonstrably impairs every physical measure of sexual functioning have gained such a reputation?

The answer, of course, lies in the effect of alcohol on higher psychological processes, such as inhibition and memory. While alcohol might have an adverse effect on what we *can* do, it may permit us to act out our fantasies of what we *want* to do.

Alcohol and Men. Numerous well designed studies have demonstrated that the short- and long-term effects of alcohol on virtually every aspect of male sexual performance are negative. While there is some evidence that alcohol affects the likelihood that males will *express* sexual feelings, especially in a social setting, measures of physiological arousal, as well as anecdotal evidence, reveals that most males perform less well sexually when intoxicated (Clark, 1952; Farkas & Rosen, 1976). The crucial factor seems to be that males think they are more sexually aroused when they think they have been drinking, even though they definitely are not.

Prolonged use of alcohol leads to both impotence and what is called "feminization syndrome." Estrogen levels in males increase, while testosterone levels decrease, leading to a female pattern of body fat, reduction of the size of the testes, **gynecomastia** (breast development), and other symptoms. This particular pattern may be the result of liver disease, such as cirrhosis, although there is evidence for direct involvement (Van Thiel & Gavaler, 1985).

Heavy alcohol consumption results in decreased sperm production, decreased sperm motility, and a higher incidence of malformed sperm. Thus, even if the heavy drinker is capable of sex, he is far more likely than the moderate or nondrinker to be sterile (Van Thiel & Lester, 1976; Abel, 1985).

Alcohol and Women. The effects of alcohol on the developing fetus are discussed in chapter 4. Alcohol has harmful effects on other aspects of female sexual functioning as well. Menstrual irregularities are common among heavy-drinking women, and there is evidence that women who drink heavily experience earlier menopause.

Spontaneous abortions are more common among heavy-drinking women. Even among "social drinkers," the rate of abortion is greater than among those who drink infrequently or not at all. Among heavier drinkers, as few as three drinks a day can increase the risk of spontaneous abortion by a factor of more than three (Harlap & Shiono, 1980).

Inhalants. Amyl and **isobutyl nitrite** are known as "poppers" and are frequently considered aphrodisiacs, especially among homosexual males. Sold as "room deodorizers," the trade names are more revealing: Rush, Heart-on, and Locker Room. Medically, amyl nitrite is used as a vasodilator in the treatment of congestive heart failure. In the normal individual, the nitrites cause an increase in heart rate, dizziness, and a decrease in blood pressure.

When used as an aphrodisiac, they are inhaled shortly before orgasm. They are called poppers because the substance is contained in a glass vial which the user breaks and then inhales the fumes. Users report that poppers make their orgasms longer and intensify the experience. Some users also report an intense headache after the effect of the popper has worn off (Schwartz, 1988).

It is difficult to imagine why a sudden dilation of blood vessels would be seen as pleasant or why poppers are considered aphrodisiacs. Perhaps the sudden drop in blood pressure, the dizziness, and the flushing are interpreted, given the set and setting, as pleasant. No evidence exists to suggest that poppers have any direct effect on sexual performance. In fact, there is one report of use of amyl nitrite to cause an unwanted erection to subside (Welti & Brodsky, 1980).

Furthermore, there seems to be a relationship between poppers and AIDS. Poppers may make practices such as anal sex, which is considered to increase the risk for transmission of AIDS, more pleasant (Mudd, 1977; Able, 1985). There also seems to be a direct relationship between poppers and **Kaposi's sarcoma,** a form of cancer prevalent in AIDS patients (Ostrow, 1987). The nature of the relationship is unclear, but poppers may depress the immune system or may be directly carcinogenic (Haverkos, 1988).

Stimulants. Cocaine and amphetamine have a virtually universal reputation as aphrodisiacs, even though medical evidence suggests that they may cause impotence. The effects of these drugs on sexual performance seem to depend on the definition of performance, as well as on the method of ingestion and the duration of use.

In males, with occasional use, these drugs can cause delayed ejaculation, which may or may not be seen as positive. Prolonged use results in loss of sexual interest and impotence. Females generally report that sexual interest and performance are not especially enhanced for them (Abel, 1984). Cocaine also acts as a local anesthetic and is sometimes applied to the penis or vagina. The resulting decrease in sensation may further delay ejaculation in males, but may deaden sensation in women.

The combination of anesthesia and the increased physical activity that accompanies cocaine ingestion may cause physical damage to the vagina and adjacent structures during sex when both women and their partners use the drug. There are other dangers as well. One bizarre case has been reported in which a man administered cocaine intraurethrally to enhance sexual performance. The reaction was so severe that both legs and nine fingers had to be amputated. In addition, he suffered "autoamputation" of his penis (Maher, Perry & Sutton, 1988).

Marijuana and the Hallucinogens. Marijuana and the hallucinogenic drugs such as LSD do not have a direct effect upon sexual behavior. There is no evidence that any of these drugs can increase sexual performance or desire. The controversial studies showing that chronic use of marijuana can decrease testosterone levels even suggest the opposite point of view (see chapter 6). Nevertheless, these drugs are commonly assumed to be aphrodisiacs.

The answer to this apparent dilemma probably lies in the general effects of these drugs on perception and mood. While they may not have a direct effect on sexual behavior, the fact that they are intensifiers of experience may account for their reputation. Sexual pleasure may very well be indirectly enhanced by drugs that cause depersonalization, euphoria, and a release of inhibitions. In this regard, the drugs would best be seen as having an indirect, rather than direct, effect.

Narcotics. Even though the initial "rush" of an injected narcotic has been described as being similar to an orgasm, few drugs fit the definition of anaphrodisiacs as well as the narcotics. The true narcotic addict has little or no interest in sex, and this phenomenon has sometimes been suggested as a reason for continuing opiate use (Platt & Labate, 1986). Furthermore, the combination of chronic malnutrition, abscesses, hepatitis, and the other results of illicit drug injection are not conducive to a lifestyle of hedonism and sexuality.

Prescription Drugs and Sex. A number of prescription drugs affect sexuality, but unfortunately, they all have an adverse effect. All too often, those taking them may not realize that a drug taken for a heart condition, for example, could cause sexual dysfunction. Furthermore, those who do make the connection may discontinue the use of the drug without mentioning the reason to their physician, behavior that could result in the deterioration of their health or even death.

A variety of antihypertensives can cause sexual problems in males; the evidence is less clear in women. As a general rule the drugs used to treat more severe forms of high blood pressure are more likely to cause sexual dysfunction than those used to treat less severe cases, but impotence, in particular, has been reported for virtually every kind of antihypertensive drug (Buffam, 1986). Although the effects of antihypertensives on sexuality are well known to physicians, many men are reluctant to report such a side effect to their doctors.

Drugs used to treat depression also can affect sexual performance. Rather than impotence, these drugs tend to cause delayed ejaculation, although impotence has been reported. In women, these drugs have been associated with orgasmic difficulties (Buffam, 1986).

Drugs used to treat the psychoses also have a tendency to cause sexual difficulties. Even drugs used to treat glaucoma and ulcers have been reported to affect sexuality (Buffam, 1986). For some of these drugs, the reasons for their effects are easy to understand. Many block norepinephrine, which is essential for sexual arousal, while others are anticholinergic, affecting the system responsible for orgasms. The reasons for the effects of the others on sexuality is less clear, but may be indirect.

In addition to the direct effect of these drugs on sexual performance, the conditions for which these drugs are being taken can also cause problems. A depressed person may not be as interested in sex because of his or her depression, so even mild side effects of antidepressants may intensify the problem. People with hypertension may be going through personal crises, and the stress may interfere with sexual function. Furthermore, any illness or medical condition that results in chronic pain may decrease sexual interest. Nevertheless, many prescription drugs can affect sexual functioning, and this fact deserves wider recognition.

Is There a Real Aphrodisiac?

While the number of actual cases reported is quite small, there have been reports in the medical literature that some drugs have side effects that could be interpreted as aphrodisiac. Fluoxetine (Prozac) and clonidine (Catapres) have both been associated with a rather peculiar effect. Women taking these drugs have reported spontaneous orgasms just after yawning (McClean, Forsyth, & Apkin, 1983; Klein, 1989). One woman reported twenty-four in a two hour period! Before you rush out to find these drugs, remember that they are prescription drugs prescribed for depression and obsessive compulsive behavior respectively. Also keep in mind that a greater percentage of people taking these drugs reported sexual difficulties.

Bupropion (Wellbutrin) is another antidepressant. Some patients taking this drug have reported an increase in sexual desire. Of course, depression is often accompanied by a decrease in sexual desire so the aphrodisiac effect might simply be a lifting of the depression. From time to time you will see reports in the popular literature about the effects of various drugs on sexual behavior. Usually these are case histories involving at most a few subjects and the publicity given them probably is as much a function of the media as it is an actual breakthrough.

Yohimbine, an extract of the bark of a tree, has been widely reported to increase both sexual desire and sexual performance in males. In one study, it improved sexual performance in 46 percent of those with psychogenic (psychologically based) impotence (Reid, Surridge, Morales, Condra, Harris, & Owen, 1987).

One drug, Papaverine, is quite effective in increasing arousal by producing a prolonged erection in men. The only problem is that it has to be injected directly into the penis! Despite this apparent drawback, it is prescribed with some regularity.

It should be noted that with the exception of yohimbine, these drugs are prescription medications and have significant side effects. Self-medication is not only foolish but potentially dangerous. These drugs seem to be useful to a greater or lesser extent in *restoring* sexual functioning to those who have problems. For the majority of the population, the most powerful aphrodisiac remains the imagination.

The Peripheral Nervous System

As can be seen in figure 3.1, the peripheral nervous system consists of the autonomic and somatic nervous systems. We are most concerned with the autonomic nervous system which itself is composed of two subsystems, the sympathetic and parasympathetic branches.

Og, the cave man, has just finished his dinner of mammoth stew and walks outside his cave to look around. He sits on a rock and thinks "It can't get much better than this." Just then he hears a sound in the forest and looks up. He sees the eyes of a saber-toothed tiger gleaming in the moonlight. Without thinking, Og grabs his club (which he has conveniently been carrying with him), swings it over his head, screams at the animal, and charges toward it. It retreats, snarling, into the gloom of the woods. Og stares after it, panting, puts his club against the rock he had been sitting on, breathes a sigh of relief, and relaxes.

The events described above illustrate the interaction of the central and peripheral nervous systems. The central nervous system (CNS) was responsible for perceiving the danger and instructing the body what to do, the peripheral nervous system for carrying out the instructions of the CNS. The autonomic nervous system (ANS) contributed by preparing the body both for the flight or fight response, and for the relaxation that preceded and followed Og's escapade.

The sympathetic portion of the ANS prepares the body for flight or fight. It increases blood supply to the brain and to the muscles, releases adrenalin, increases heart rate and blood pressure, dilates the pupils, and releases glucose into the bloodstream. The parasympathetic nervous portion does the opposite. It decreases blood supply to the brain and muscles (increasing the supply to the stomach and intestine), lowers heart rate and blood pressure and, in general, prepares the body to relax and digest food.

Drugs have differential effects on these two systems. The stimulant drugs, in particular, increase the action of the sympathetic branch. Many of the effects of cocaine, amphetamine, and caffeine, for example, can be attributed to the stimulant effects on the sympathetic branch of the autonomic nervous system.

THE ENDOCRINE SYSTEM

The CNS responds rapidly, the ANS more slowly, and the endocrine system most slowly of all. The endocrine system is composed of a number of structures that release hormones into the bloodstream. These are called the ductless glands because they secrete their hormones directly into the bloodstream instead of the hormones passing through "ducts," as is the case in most glands. The endocrine system regulates a number of functions, but only a few will be discussed here.

The *adrenal glands* secrete a number of hormones related to the fight or flight syndrome. Adrenalin, or **epinephrine,** is one of them. When the sympathetic portion of the autonomic nervous system is active, adrenalin is released into the bloodstream. Many drugs, such as the stimulants, also cause release of adrenalin, and a few, such as some drugs used to control blood pressure, reduce the body's response to adrenalin. In addition to adrenalin, the adrenal glands secrete inflammatory and anti-inflammatory hormones that are also involved in the fight or flight syndrome.

The **pituitary,** a structure in the center of the brain, is often called the "master gland" because it not only releases hormones, but also regulates the actions of many other glands. Among its most important functions are to regulate the production of sex hormones by the ovaries and testes, to stimulate growth, and to maintain fluid balance. Many drugs have effects on these functions. Alcohol, for example, increases urination because it blocks the formation of a hormone that slows the formation of urine.

The pancreas secretes insulin which aids the cells in the uptake of sugar. Insulin, therefore, is important in the regulation of blood sugar levels. A common problem in heavy drinkers is hypoglycemia, or low blood sugar. Alcohol impairs the ability of the body to regulate blood sugar levels, as we shall see. Figure 3.12 shows some of the glands of the endocrine system and common drugs that affect them.

As you just read, the pituitary is the master gland of the body, secreting a number of hormones and neurohormones. At the beginning of this chapter you read about neurotransmitters, neuromodulators, and neurohormones. Most of these chemical substances alter the membrane potential of a neuron. Some, however, penetrate into a cell and have a direct effect on its function. Such chemicals are called steroids. Steroids attach directly to the nucleus of the cell and alter synthesis of protein and other substances necessary for the functioning of the cell. Those steroids that increase muscle size are called anabolic steroids.

Ergogenic Aids and Steroids

Along with the desire to enhance sexual performance, the desire to enhance physical performance is one of man- (and woman-) kind's greatest desires. Similarly, drugs have been used to accomplish this goal. Ergogenic drugs are drugs which enhance physical performance. Far too many athletes have had their careers or even their lives shortened by the use of illegal drugs, and most sports organizations have very strict rules about the use of such drugs, but use continues. A large number of drugs exist which will increase athletic performance, including amphetamines, beta blockers, and others, but the primary drugs of concern for most athletes are the anabolic steroids.

FIGURE 3.12

Locations of major endocrine glands.

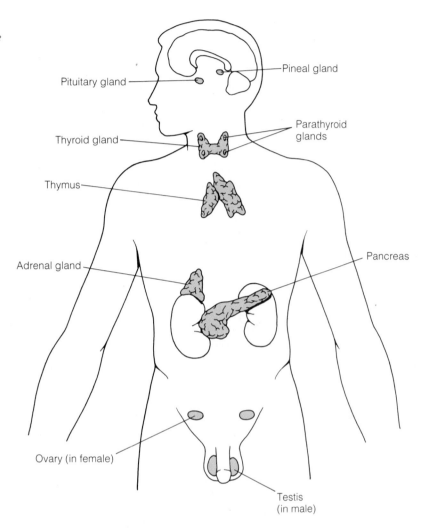

Pituitary gland

Pineal gland

Thyroid gland

Parathyroid glands

Thymus

Adrenal gland

Pancreas

Ovary (in female)

Testis (in male)

Anabolic Steroids

In addition to the obvious physical differences in primary sex characteristics, men differ from women in other ways as well. The average male has greater muscle strength, lung capacity, and endurance than the average female. While part of these differences are cultural, genetic and hormonal differences also play a role. Specifically, the male sex hormones, primarily testosterone, are responsible for some of the differences in strength between men and women.

The male sex hormones are responsible not only for the maintenance of secondary male sex characteristics, such as deeper voice, body hair, and male pattern of body fat, but also for muscle strength and size. The so-called **anabolic steroids** supposedly affect only the development of muscles. Hence, athletes taking steroids presumably are stimulating only the factors responsible for muscle growth. In fact, however, the story is much more complicated.

The common anabolic steroids are synthetic derivatives of testosterone manufactured by adding a molecule to the male hormone. Presumably, these drugs will have only muscle-building (anabolic) properties, splitting off this property from the aspect of testosterone that affects male secondary sex characteristics. However, high doses of the steroids simulate the effects of testosterone itself (Council on Scientific Affairs, 1988).

Use of steroids seems to be increasing. Any number of articles in the popular press have reported the use of steroids by professional athletes. Some estimates place use of steroids among competitive athletes as high as 50 percent, with some sports such as weight lifting even higher. Even more alarming are reports of steroid use by adolescents. Various studies report different frequencies of use, but a figure of 10 percent of male high school students is near the average (Council on Scientific Affairs, 1990).

Steroid abuse is considered to be such a problem that Congress passed the Anabolic Steroids Control Act of 1990, mandating that as of 27 February 1991, these drugs were placed in Schedule III of the Controlled Substances Abuse Act. Schedule III drugs have recognized medical uses, but also have moderate abuse potential. The maximum offense for trafficking or illegal dispensing of anabolic steroids is five years in jail and a $250,000 fine.

Negative Effects of Steroids. The hypothalamus monitors the levels of hormones in the blood. Apparently the steroids, especially at the levels taken by athletes, fool the hypothalamus and cause it to signal to the body to stop producing testosterone. Some of the circulating steroids are converted to estrogen, and produce gynecomastia, or breast development, in males, which, incidentally, is often permanent and may have to be surgically remedied after the athlete has stopped competing. Testicular atrophy (a decrease in the size of the testes) also occurs, and sperm production decreases (Voy, 1986).

In addition to these effects, called feminization, steroids can cause bone growth to cease in adolescents, stunting the teenager's growth. Steroids can also cause the development of **peliosis,** or cysts of blood, in the liver, which can rupture and cause hemorrhaging. Peliosis is considered a serious problem to those engaged in contact sports. Jaundice and even liver cancer have been linked to steroid use as well.

Steroids also drastically reduce the amount of high density lipoproteins (HDL) in the blood. HDL is the "good" cholesterol and helps protect against heart attack. Normal HDL levels can be reduced by 90 percent in athletes taking steroids (Council on Scientific Affairs, 1988).

The problem for women taking steroids is equally grim. Steroids can cause an increase in growth of body hair (hirsutism), an increase in growth of the clitoris, and other unpleasant side effects. Most of these effects do not go away when the athlete stops taking the drug. Some relatively minor side effects, such as decreased sperm production in men and disruption of

Can this woman, who does not take steroids, compete against those women who do?

menstruation for women, may be reversed after the athlete stops taking steroids, but the most serious ones tend to be permanent (Council on Scientific Affairs, 1990). Although it may be difficult to believe, many women athletes seem to find these changes acceptable when weighed against the benefits (Strauss, Mariah, & Ligget, 1985).

Positive Effects. These drugs must have some positive effects or athletes would not continue to take them. Early studies of the effects of steroids failed to show that they aided muscle development or strength. Psychological factors play such an important role in athletic performance that the effect of steroids was attributed to the placebo effect discussed in the previous chapter. At least, researchers and medical doctors claimed that steroids had no real effect.

Athletes themselves knew better, however. One reason why early studies failed to show that steroids were effective was that it is unethical to give the kinds of doses that some athletes regularly take. Using a principle called "stacking," athletes will take several different kinds of steroids and then taper off just prior to a performance (or a drug test). The principles behind stacking are based on experience, not scientific knowledge, and consequently can be dangerous. The fact remains, however, that steroids can increase muscle mass, strength, and endurance.

Are Steroids Addicting? Given that virtually all athletes know that steroids can be harmful, why do they continue to take them? Some psychological reasons are discussed later, but the possibility exists that they may be physically

Ben Johnson was stripped of his Olympic gold medal when it was discovered he had used steroids.

addicting. Long-term use can lead to a preoccupation with the drugs, drug craving, and an inability to stop even after negative effects have begun to appear. Depression is common among those who stop abruptly, and there is evidence for physiological tolerance and dependence as well (Kaskin & Kleber, 1989). Dissatisfaction with body appearance seems to be the motivating factor for those who later go on to abuse these drugs and those who are most dissatisfied seem to be most likely to abuse them. In one study, nearly 60 percent of users met the medical criteria for dependence (Brower, Blow, Young & Hill, 1991).

Psychological factors also play a role in steroid use. Steroid users sometimes develop a denial system. They deny that the drugs actually cause harm since they themselves may know many people who use them and know only a few who have experienced harmful side effects. Of course, the side effects may not occur for years after the drugs are first used.

The drug users may claim that they have a right to their drug use, since even if the drugs are harmful, they are harming only themselves. Besides, others are using them as well and they have to use steroids in order to keep up. Additionally, many steroid users resort to blaming those who criticize them for their drug use. Doctors don't participate in the kind of sports that steroid users do; thus, doctors and others who warn of the dangers of drug use are seen as misinformed. As is often the case with a subculture of whatever makeup, the users often view themselves, paradoxically, as superior to the supposed "experts."

Psychological Effects of Steroids. In addition to putting on weight and adding muscle mass, steroids apparently have psychological effects as well. Steroid users report feelings of well-being and even euphoria. They reported having increased sexual desire. On the negative side, many reports exist of increased aggressiveness, irritability, and even psychotic symptoms. Sleep disturbances and frightening dreams have also been reported.

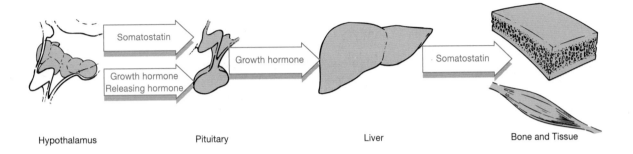

Hypothalamus   Pituitary   Liver   Bone and Tissue

Regulation of production of growth hormone. Somatostatin inhibits release of growth hormone; GHRH causes its release from the pituitary; growth hormone effects organs other than liver.

Since steroids were classified as Schedule III drugs, they have become harder to come by. No ethical physician would prescribe them, so they are sold by unscrupulous people who have a close relationship to athletes. Where they get their supply is another question and numerous reports suggest that a black market exists for the manufacture and sale of these drugs. Some are made in Mexico and smuggled in. Increasingly, bogus steroids designed to resemble the real thing are showing up in gyms. Ironically, it may be that the increasing popularity of steroids among some people has produced a positive effect; the majority of "steroids" are inert fakes, thus reducing the risk to the user (The Forensic Drug Abuse Advisor, 1991).

Other Ergogenic Aids

Athletes also use a wide variety of other drugs to enhance their performance. A relatively new phenomenon is the use of growth hormone. Growth hormone is normally secreted by the pituitary and is partly responsible for the growth spurt seen in adolescents. Dwarfs, for example, can sometimes be aided by growth hormone to reach a near normal height.

Until 1985, human growth factor was available in small doses and at great cost from the National Hormone and Pituitary Program in Baltimore, Maryland. Some also was available commercially. Human growth factor (HGH) was extremely expensive and difficult to obtain because it had to be extracted from human cadavers. In 1985, that source of HGH dried up when it was discovered that the hormone had been contaminated with a rare virus that causes a degenerative brain condition called **Creutzfeld-Jakob disease** (Fradkin, Schonberger, & Mills, et al, 1991).

Genetic engineering came to the rescue, however, in the form of recombinant DNA, and it is now possible to mass produce this hormone. Such production would, of course, reduce the cost considerably. It is estimated that the cost of treatment is about $20,000 per year for up to five years. There is currently debate in the medical literature about the use of synthetic growth hormone to treat short children whose shortness is not the result of growth hormone deficiency (Lantos, Siegler, & Cuttler, 1989). While the debate, which centers on the expense and the unknown long-term effects goes on, another problem has emerged.

The manufacturers of HGH claim that they are extraordinarily cautious in their distribution of this product and ensure that it is given only to those who are truly short of stature. Nevertheless there are widespread reports of its use by athletes (Council on Scientific Affairs—American Medical Association, 1988).

The actual extent of growth hormone use by athletes is difficult to estimate, and much of the purported use is undoubtedly of fake products such as animal growth hormone sold by unscrupulous "gym rats." Furthermore, its effectiveness has never been clearly established. One inducement to its use is that none of the tests currently used to detect drug use is sensitive to HGH. To the extent that it is being used it should be a matter of serious concern, both for the obvious ethical issues involved as well as for health concerns.

Growth hormone causes an enlargement of all parts of the body, including the skin, tongue, and internal organs. In adolescents HGH can add several inches to a person's height, which may be a temptation to prospective basketball players. In adults, its use can lead to enlargement of the tendons and connective tissue, a condition known as acromegaly. Additional side effects from its use include high blood pressure and diabetes (Voy, 1986; Wadler & Hainline, 1989).

Other banned drugs that are used by athletes include (1) antihypertensives, known as beta blockers, which slow the heartbeat, thus enabling target shooters to take steadier aim; (2) amphetamines, taken to delay fatigue and to promote "get up;" (3) caffeine, taken for the same purpose; and (4) diuretics, for weight loss (Wadler & Hainline, 1989). Perhaps the most bizarre example (although air is not a "drug") is the report that swimmers inject air into their lower bowel to gain buoyancy, and hence a competitive edge (Dyment, 1987).

It may be surprising that caffeine was one of the drugs banned at the 1988 Olympics, although some caffeine was permitted. An athlete could be eliminated from competition after taking the equivalent of six cups of coffee very quickly (or three No-Doz). The reason for the ban is that studies have shown that caffeine can increase performance in some sports.

Table 3.1 shows a list of the drugs banned at the 1988 Olympics. Testing for these drugs can run to several hundred dollars per test, and athletes and coaches can be quite ingenious in discovering ways to cheat the tests. So long as split seconds separate the winners from the losers and so long as society rewards only the winners, attempts to gain an edge will continue. Just how far these attempts will go remains to be seen.

SUMMARY

The neuron is the main building block of the central nervous system. Most psychoactive drugs exert their effects at the level of the neuron. The primary means of communication between neurons is through the release of neurotransmitters from vesicles in the presynaptic portion of the neuron. Although several dozen neurotransmitters have been proposed, seven are of primary importance in studying drugs' effects: acetylcholine, serotonin, dopamine, norepinephrine, peptides, and the amino acids. Another important, although

Table 3.1 Drugs Banned at the 1988 Olympics

Psychomotor Stimulant Drugs
  Amphetamine
  Benzphetamine
  Chlorphentermine
  Cocaine
  Diethylpropion
  Dimethylamphetamine
  Ethylamphetamine
  Fencamfamin
  Meclofenoxate
  Methylamphetamine
  Methylphenidate
  Norpseudoephedrine
  Pemoline
  Phendimetrazine
  Phenmetrazine
  Phentermine
  Pipradol
  Prolintane
  And related compounds
Sympathomimetic Amines
  Chlorprenaline
  Ephedrine
  Etafedreine
  Isoetharine
  Isoprenaline
  Methoxyphenamine
  Methylephedrine
  And related compounds

**Miscellaneous Central Nervous
System Stimulants**
  Amiphenazole
  Bemigride
  Caffeine
  Cropropamide
  Crolethamide
  Doxapram
  Ethamivan
  Leptazol
  Nikethamide
  Picrotoxine
  Strychnine
  And related compounds
Narcotic Analgesics
  Anileridine
  Codeine
  Dextroaoriamide
  Dihydrocodeine
  Dipipanoe
  Ethylmorphine
  Heroin
  Hydrocodone
  Hydromorphone
  Levorphanol
  Methadone
  Morphine
  Oxocodone
  Oxomorphone

  Pentazocine
  Pethidine
  Phenazocine
  Piminodine
  Thebacon
  Trimeperidine
  And related compounds
Anabolic Steroids
  Clostebol
  Dehydrochlormethyl-testosterone
  Fluoxymesterone
  Mesterolone
  Methenolone
  Methandienone
  Methyltestosterone
  Nandrolone
  Norethandrolone
  Oxymesterone
  Oxymetholone
  Stanozolol
  Testosterone
  And related compounds

Note that caffeine is on this list.
Source: Adapted from Dyment, 1987.

poorly understood, means of regulating neuronal action is through neuro-modulators. Some peptides are both neurotransmitters and neuromodulators. Neurohormones act most slowly, and their relationship to drug effects is just beginning to be explored.

Various drugs affect the central and peripheral nervous systems. The brain stem controls vegetative functions such as breathing and is often implicated in deaths due to drug overdose. Vomiting is another important function of the brain stem. The reticular formation is involved in arousing the cortex. Stimulant drugs often affect this structure. The hypothalamus and pituitary form a system which helps regulate hormones in the body. The limbic system is involved in emotional behavior and may be a reward center for drugs in the brain. The periaqueductal gray matter and the basal ganglia are involved in pain and in motor movement respectively. The cortex enables us to have conscious awareness, to think, and to plan ahead, among other functions. Nearly all psychoactive drugs affect the cortex.

Sexual behavior, one of humanity's most popular pastimes, is the result of psychological and physiological factors. The search for a magic elixir to stimulate sexual behavior has been going on since ancient times. Unfortunately, no simple pill exists that will coordinate such an enormously complex interaction of mind and body.

The peripheral nervous system is also involved in arousal. Some drugs affect the sympathetic and some the parasympathetic portion of the autonomic nervous system. Drugs increasing sympathetic nervous system arousal cause excitation, those increasing parasympathetic arousal decrease excitation.

The endocrine system is a relatively slow acting system which regulates hormonal production. Drugs affect this by altering this regulatory process. Steroid and human growth factor, alcohol, and other drugs affect the endocrine system in subtle and complicated ways that are only beginning to be understood.

Nevertheless, just as with sex, athletes and others have long sought a pill that will make them stronger. Unlike sex, such pills do exist, but the physical cost is horrible.

REFERENCES

Abel, E. (1985). *Psychoactive drugs and sex.* New York: Plenum Press.

Baum, R. (1985, September 9). New variety of street drugs poses growing problem. *Chemical and Engineering News.*

Belongia, E., Hedberg, C., & Gleich, G. (1990). An investigation of the cause of the eosinophilia myalgia syndrome associated with tryptophan use. *New England Journal of Medicine, 323,* 357–64.

Blum, K., Trachtenberg, M., Elliott, C., Dingler, M., Sexton, R., Samuels, A., & Cataldie, L. (1989). Enkephalinase inhibition and recursor amino acid loading improves inpatient treatment of alcohol and polydrug abusers; Double-blind placebo controlled study of nutritional adjunct SAAVE. *Alcohol, 5,* 481–93.

Brower, K., Blow, F., Young, J., & Hill, E. (1991). Symptoms and correlates of anabolic steroid dependencies. *British Journal of Addictions, 86,* 759–68.

Brown, R., Blum, K., & Trachtenberg, M. (1990). Neurodynamics of relapse prevention: A neuronutrient approach to outpatient DUI offenders. *Journal of Psychoactive Drugs, 22,* 173–84.

Buffum, S. (1986). Pharmacosexology update: Prescription drugs and sexual function. *Journal of Psychoactive Drugs, 18,* 97–105.

Carlson, N. (1991). *Physiology and behavior (4th ed.)* Boston: Allyn and Bacon, Inc.

Centers for Disease Control (1990). Analysis of L-tryptophan for the etiology of eosinophilia-myalgia syndrome. *Journal of the American Medical Association, 264,* 1656.

Clark, R. A. (1952). The projective measurement of experimentally induced levels of sexual motivation. *Journal of Experimental Psychology, 44,* 391–99.

Cooper, J., Bloom, F., & Roth, R. (1986). *The biochemical basis of neuropharmacology.* New York and Oxford: Oxford University Press.

Council on Scientific Affairs, The American Medical Association (1988). Drug abuse in athletes: Anabolic steroids and human growth hormone. *Journal of the American Medical Association, 259,* 1703–05.

Council on Scientific Affairs, The American Medical Association (1990). Medical and nonmedical uses of anabolic-androgenic steroids. *Journal of the American Medical Association, 264,* 2923–27.

Dyment, P. (1987). The adolescent athlete and ergogenic aids. *Journal of Adolescent Health Care, 8,* 68–73.

Farkas, G. M., & Rosen, R. C. (1976). Effect of alcohol in elicited male sexual response. *Journal of Studies on Alcohol, 37,* 265–72.

Fradkin, J., Schonberger, L., Mills, J., Gunn, W., Piper, V., Wysoski, P., Thomson, R., Durako, S., & Brown, P. (1991). Creutzfeldt-Jakob disease in pituitary growth hormone recipients in the United States. *Journal of the American Medical Association, 265,* 880–86.

Fuller, J. R., & La Fountain, M. (1987). Performance-enhancing drugs in sports: A different form of drug abuse. *Adolescence, 22,* 969–76.

Harlap, S., & Shiono, P. (1980). Alcohol, smoking and incidence of spontaneous abortions in the first and third trimester. *Lancet, 2,* 173–76.

Hartman, E., Cravens, J., & List, S. (1974). Hypnotic effects of l-tryptophan. *Archives of General Psychiatry, 31,* 395–98.

Haverkos, H. (1988). Epidemiological studies—Kaposi's Sarcoma *vs* opportunistic infection among homosexual men with AIDS. *National Institute of Drug Abuse Research Monographs, 83,* 96–106.

Jacobs, B. (1987). How hallucinogenic drugs work. *American Scientist, 75,* 386–92.

Kashkin, K., & Kleber, H. (1989). Hooked on hormones? An anabolic steroid addiction hypothesis. *Journal of the American Medical Association, 262,* 3166–70.

Klein, D. (1989). Repeated observations of yawning, clitoral engorgement and orgasm associated with fluoxetin administration. *Journal of Clinical Psychopharmacology, 9,* 384.

Lantos, J., Siegler, M., & Cuttler, L. (1989). Ethical issues in growth hormone therapy. *Journal of the American Medical Association, 261,* 1020–24.

Levine, R. (1983). *Pharmacology: Drug action and reaction (3d ed.).* Boston and Toronto: Little, Brown.

Levitan, R., & Kaczmarek, L. (1991). *The neuron, cell and molecular biology.* New York: Oxford University Press.

Lieber, C. (1991). Hepatic metabolic and toxic effects of ethanol: 1991 update. *Alcoholism: Clinical and Experimental Research, 15,* 573–92.

McLean, J. D., Forsyth, R. G., & Apkin, I. A. (1983). Unusual side effects of clomipramine. *Canadian Journal of Psychiatry, 28,* 569–70.

Mahler, J., Perry, S., & Sutton, B. (1988). Intraurethral cocaine administration. *Journal of the American Medical Association, 259,* 3126.

Moertel, C., Reitemeier, R., & Gage, R. (1963). A controlled clinical evaluation of antiemetic drugs. *Journal of the American Medical Association, 186,* 116–18.

Mudd, J. W. (1977). *American Journal of Psychiatry, 134,* 922.

Murray, T. H. (1987). The ethics of drugs in sports. In R. M. Strauss (Ed.), *Drugs and performance in sports,* (pp. 11–22). Philadelphia: W. B. Saunders.

Ostrow, D. (1987). Barriers to the recognition of links between drugs and alcohol abuse and AIDS. In *Acquired immune deficiency syndrome and chemical dependency,* (pp. 87–153). Washington, D.C.: National Institute of Alcohol Abuse and Alcoholism, Department of Health and Human Services.

Pasternak, G. (1988). Multiple morphine and enkephalin receptors and the relief of pain. *Journal of the American Medical Association, 259,* 1362–66.

Platt, J. (1986). *Heroin addiction: Theory research and treatment.* Malabar, FL: Robert E. Krieger Publishing Company.

Reid, K., Surridge, D., Morales, A., Condra, M., Harris, C., Owen, J., & Fennemore, J. (1987, August 22). Double blind trial of yohimbine in the treatment of psychogenic impotence. *The Lancet,* 422–23.

Schwartz, R. (1988). Deliberate inhalation of isobutyl nitrite during adolescence. *National Institute of Drug Abuse Research Monograph 83,* 81–85.

Shepherd, G. (1988). *Neurobiology (2d ed.).* New York: Oxford University Press.

Slutsker, L., Hoesey, F., Miller, L., et al (1990). Eosinophilia—myalgia syndrome associated with exposure to tryptophan from a single manufacturer. *Journal of the American Medical Association, 264,* 213–17.

Strauss, R. H., Mariah, T., Liggett, M. S. (1985). Anabolic steroid use and perceived effects in ten weight-trained women athletes. *Journal of the American Medical Association, 253,* 2871–73.

Swinyard, E. A., & Pathak, M. A. (1980). Surface-acting drugs. In A. G. Gilman, L. S. Goodman, and A. Gilman (Eds.), *The pharmacological basis of therapeutics (6th ed.),* (pp. 951–53). New York: Macmillan.

Swygert, L., Maes, E., Sewell, L., Miller, L., Fack, H., & Kilbourne, E. (1990). Eosinophilia-myalgia syndrome: Results of national surveillance. *Journal of the American Medical Association, 264,* 1698–1703.

Taberner, P. J. (1985). *Aphrodisiacs: The science and the myth.* Philadelphia: University of Pennsylvania Press.

Taylor, P. (1980). Neuromuscular blocking agents. In A. Gilman, L. Goodman, & A. Goodman (Eds.), *The pharmacological basis of therapeutics.* New York: Macmillan.

The Forensic Drug Abuse Advisor (1991). 'Roid rip off: Analysis of black market steroids. *3,* 24–25.

Trachtenberg, M., & Blum, K. (1988). Improvement of cocaine-induced neuromodulator deficits by the neuronutrient Tropamine. *Journal of Psychoactive Drugs, 20,* 315–31.

Van Thiel, D. H., & Gavaler, J. S. (1985). Endocrine effects of chronic alcohol use: Hypothalamic, pituitary, gonadal axis. In R. E. Tarter and D. H. Van Thiel (Eds.), (pp. 69–81). *Alcohol and the brain: Chronic effects.* New York and London: Plenum Press.

Van Thiel, D. H., & Lester, R. (1976). Alcoholism: Its effects on hypothalamic-pituitary-gonadal functions. *Gastroenterology, 71,* 318–27.

Voy, R. (1986). Illicit drugs and the athlete. *American Pharmacy, 26,* 39– 45.

Wadler, G., & Hainline, B. (1989). *Drugs and the athlete.* Philadelphia: F. A. Davis Company.

Welti, R. S. and Brodsky, J. B. (1980). Treatment of intraoperative penile tumescence. *Journal of Urology, 124,* 925–26.

4

• • •

ALCOHOL—THE GREAT AMERICAN DRUG

• • •

OBJECTIVES

When you have finished studying this chapter you should:

1. Know how alcohol was produced in the past.
2. Know the difference between fermentation and distillation.
3. Be able to trace attitudes toward alcohol use from the past to the present.
4. Know what did and didn't happen during Prohibition.
5. Know the ethanol content of various alcoholic beverages.
6. Be able to discuss the factors that affect alcohol absorption.
7. Know the routes of metabolism of ethanol and how it affects the liver.
8. Understand how sex, weight, and percentage of body fat affect alcohol absorption.
9. List the immediate effects of alcohol.
10. Know the symptoms of Fetal Alcohol Syndrome.
11. Be able to discuss how alcohol consumption affects thinking.
12. Know what factors might predispose someone to becoming a problem drinker.
13. Understand the differences between alcoholism, alcohol abuse, and alcohol dependence.
14. Be able to recognize three measures of alcohol problem drinking.

KEY TERMS

acetaldehyde
ACOA
acute alcohol amnesia
alcohol abuse
alcohol dependence
alcoholic fatty liver
alcoholic hepatitis
amethystic agent
anterograde amnesia
blackout
blood alcohol level
CAGE
cirrhosis
congener
distillation
equivalency
fetal alcohol syndrome
fetal alcohol effects
holiday heart syndrome
male-limited
Michigan Alcoholism Screening Test
milieu-limited
monoamine oxidase
NA beer
Prohibition
proof
teratogenic drug
Wernicke-Korsakoff's syndrome

Dear Congressman: How do you stand on whiskey?

My Dear Friend:

I had not intended to discuss this controversial subject at this time. However, I want you to know that I do not shun a controversy. On the contrary, I will take a stand on any issue at any time regardless of how fraught with controversy it may be. You have asked me how I feel about whiskey: here is how I stand on the question.

If when you say whiskey, you mean the devil's brew, the poison curse, the bloody monster that defiles innocence, dethrones reason, destroys the home, creates misery and poverty, yea, literally takes the bread from the mouths of little children, if you mean the evil drink that topples the Christian man and woman from the pinnacles of righteous, gracious living into the bottomless pit of degradation and despair, shame, helplessness, and hopelessness, then certainly I am against it with all of my power.

BUT, if when you say whiskey you mean the oil of conversation, the philosophic wine, the ale that is consumed when good fellows get together, that puts a song in their hearts and laughter on their lips and the warm glow of contentment in their eyes, if you mean Christmas cheer, if you mean the stimulating drink that puts the spring in the old man's step on a frosty morning, if you mean that drink that enables a man to magnify his job and happiness and forget, if only for a little while, life's great tragedies and heartbreaks, if you mean that drink that the sale of which pours into our treasuries untold millions of dollars which are used to provide tender care for our little children, our blind and deaf, our pitiful aged and infirm, to build highways, hospitals and schools, then I am certainly in favor of it.

This is my stand and I will not compromise.

Your Congressman

(reprinted from Dundes and Pagter, 1975)

The above "letter" is from a collection of folk humor and is thought to date from the 1920s. Its writer intended it as humor, but it nevertheless demonstrates a basic split in the thinking of many toward alcohol. On the one hand, alcohol is the commonest psychoactive drug known. Alcoholic drinks are mentioned in the earliest writings that have been preserved; clear evidence of beer and wine dates back 5,000 years.

On the other hand, alcoholic beverages also are seen as dangerous substances, and the warnings against excessive use go back just as far. In this chapter, we will explore the role of alcohol in society, the effects of alcohol on the body, and the issue of problem drinking and alcoholism. It is not farfetched to say that the solution to the "drug problem" in American society lies in the resolution of the "alcohol" problem. If our society can develop a rational attitude toward alcohol, such as exists in other societies, we probably can do the same for other drugs.

HISTORY OF ALCOHOL USE

The first mention of alcoholic beverages coincides with the first written documents. All that is needed to produce alcoholic beverages is yeast, the spores of which are always present in the air; sugar, water, and warm temperatures. The combination of these conditions leads to fermentation, which is a natural phenomenon. Therefore, alcohol is spontaneously produced in nature with great frequency. Bees and bears get drunk on fermented honey, elephants get smashed on fermented fruit, and birds get so drunk they can't fly from eating fermented berries (Siegal, 1988). Primitive man was a careful observer of animals. Maybe we learned to drink from watching animals get drunk?

Egyptians had taverns and warnings against staying too long in them thousands of years ago (National Institute of Alcohol and Alcohol Abuse, 1980). The Greeks, Hebrews, and Romans of ancient times were quite familiar with wine. The Bible has several words for wine and passages recommending its use, as well as warnings against excessive consumption. In the New Testament, Paul advises Timothy, "Drink no longer water, but use a little wine for thy stomach's sake" (1 Timothy 5:23). In the Old Testament, Proverbs says, "Procure strong drink for a man about to perish, wine for the heart that is full of bitterness. Let him drink and forget his misfortune and remember his misery no more" (Proverbs 31:6–7), and in Ecclesiastes 31:27 it says, "Wine is as good as life to a man."

Of course, like the Romans and Egyptians the writers of the Bible also knew of the dangers of wine. The same book of Proverbs tells us, "It is not for kings to drink wine; nor for princes strong drink. Lest they drink and forget the law; and pervert the judgement of any of the afflicted" (Proverbs 31: 4–5), and another verse, Proverbs 20:1, warns us, "Wine is a mocker, strong drink is raging." Incidentally, the Hebrew word that is usually translated as "strong drink" does not mean what we call hard liquor, since wine was the strongest beverage available until the Middle Ages. It may refer to wine mixed with opium.

In the process of fermentation, yeast turns sugar into alcohol and carbon dioxide. The process continues until all the sugar is gone or until the concentration of alcohol kills the yeast cells. Since an alcohol concentration of 12–15 percent is sufficient to kill yeast cells, the natural process of fermentation cannot yield a drink with an alcohol content higher than about 14 percent. In order to produce a higher concentration, someone had to develop the artificial process of distillation.

The discovery of distillation is usually attributed to the Arabs at the beginning of the Middle Ages. In fact, the Egyptians first discovered the process, but since distilled beverages were reserved for the nobility, their

Old woodcut.

process remained a secret until the Arabs rediscovered it (Abel, 1987). The Arabian scientists were not looking for a quicker way to get drunk, but for the ''essence'' of wine, which was considered a valuable medicine, as well as an essential beverage. In fact, the term *alcohol* comes from the Arabic *Al Kohl,* which simply means ''the essence.''

Through successive distillations and coolings, it is possible to produce nearly pure alcohol. Since concentrated alcohol absorbs water, the limit is 95 percent pure alcohol which is known as laboratory grade ethanol and sold under brand names such as Everclear in some states. Most distilled beverages, as we shall see, are mixed with water, coloring agents, and various other substances that alter their taste and have an alcohol content of about 40–50 percent.

Traditionally, alcoholic beverages were drunk as much for health as for recreational reasons. Tea became popular because it was one of the few non-alcoholic beverages that could be drunk safely. Until recently, water supplies were nearly always contaminated, so the fact that the alcohol in beer or wine killed most bacteria was of great importance. Furthermore, the yeast and other products that remain after fermentation provide numerous vitamins and minerals that are essential to health. Brewer's yeast, the spent yeast that results from the fermentation of beer, is still used in numerous food products.

Alcohol in American Society

Our image of a New England Puritan is a dark-suited dour man with a perpetual frown who would never think of drinking. In fact, however, the

This old engraving shows how common drinking was among people of every age. The beverage "punch" contained alcohol but was not thought to be "drinking," which usually meant distilled liquor.

Puritans disdained neither beer nor hard liquor, although they frowned on drunkenness. The Puritans considered alcohol a gift from God; drunkenness was condemned but the drunkard was viewed leniently. Attempts were made to reform drunkards in order to save their souls (Austin, 1978). They were also shrewd businessmen and developed the "Triangle Trade" that involved brewing rum from molasses in New England, shipping it to Africa where it was traded for slaves, who were in turn transported to the West Indies where they were traded for molasses that was shipped to New England and so forth.

The production and consumption of alcohol played an important role in American society from its inception. After the War for Independence, the boundaries of the United States began to expand and transportation rapidly became an important issue. Grain grown in Maryland, Kentucky, Virginia, and western Pennsylvania might cost more to transport to eastern markets than the farmers could get for selling it. They learned that if they converted their grain into whiskey, they could make a substantial profit.

Distilleries soon sprouted in many of these areas, perhaps the most famous being in Bourbon County, Kentucky, where the Reverend Elijah Craig discovered that putting his distilled product in charred oak barrels for a while improved the taste of the whiskey. His product came to be called bourbon, although it could as easily have been called craig.

Consumption of alcohol reached a peak in America in the early 1800s when it is estimated that the average drinker consumed more than six ounces of hard liquor or its equivalent per day. Never before or since have we been such tipplers. This high level of consumption spawned the most successful antidrug movement in history. The temperance movement of the 1800s reduced alcohol consumption by three quarters in just ten years. It should be

noted that the movement was a *temperance* movement; the goal was to reduce, not eliminate alcohol use (Rorbaugh, 1979).

A variety of political, economic, and religious factors combined to
alter the path of this movement into a *prohibition* movement, and temperance became synonymous with prohibition (Tyrell, 1979). The movement
was so successful that the Eighteenth Amendment to the Constitution was
ratified in 1919, prohibiting the manufacture, sale, or importation of "intoxicating liquors" for "beverage purposes." Possession, note carefully, was
still legal.

Prohibition is widely seen as a dismal failure, and it certainly did not
live up to the hopes of its proponents. First of all, most Americans did not
support the law. Therefore, manufacture, sale, and importation continued virtually without hesitation, and respect for the legal system was severely damaged. A flourishing illegal trade sprang up, with speakeasies (bars where
illegal alcohol was sold) and moonshiners (manufacturers of illegal alcohol)
everywhere. In Canada, where alcoholic beverages were legal, huge profits
were made by supplying "rumrunners."

Since there were no laws against home brewing many people made
their own. According to the Prohibition Bureau's estimate, 700 million gallons of beer were brewed at home in 1929 (Maddox, 1979). Stores sold
malt, hops, and bricks of grape concentrate that could be made into beer or
wine. Even distillation was not difficult, and a thriving business in the sale
of small stills grew up shortly after Prohibition.

In fairness, however, it should be noted that in the beginning of Prohibition, alcohol-related deaths did decrease as did the more overt signs of
alcohol problem drinking. It wasn't until about 1930 that alcohol related
problems approached pre-Prohibition levels. Prohibition was not a total failure, but it was doomed for the simple reason that most drinkers did not want
to stop. Although Prohibition was repealed in 1933, it left a legacy. Organized crime had developed an elaborate network to meet the needs of the
drinking public, and profits made were funneled into other concerns, both
legitimate and illegitimate. The lesson of Prohibition is that no law can succeed unless it is supported by the people it affects. Some experts in the field
of drug abuse feel we have not yet learned this lesson.

WHO DRINKS WHAT AND HOW MUCH

We are nowhere near the tippling society we were in the 1830s nor do we
drink as much as do those in some other countries. Nevertheless, most people drink at least occasionally, and far too many drink enough to cause problems for themselves and others. What is normal drinking and how much
does the "average" person actually drink? The answer to this question is
not at all easy to determine.

The most accurate reports of the amount of alcohol consumed are
based on the amount of alcohol produced and on tax receipts, since alcohol is
taxed in every state. However, these figures only show the total consumption of
alcohol—minus spillage, breakage, moonshining, and home production, of

Table 4.1 Per Capita Consumption of Alcohol In Gallons

	1966	1968	1970	1972	1974	1976	1978	1980	1982	1984
Beer	16.5	17.3	18.5	19.7	21.3	21.6	23.1	24.3	24.4	23.9
Wine	1.0	1.1	1.5	1.6	1.7	1.7	1.9	2.1	2.2	2.3
Liquor	1.6	1.7	1.9	1.9	2.0	2.0	2.0	2.0	1.9	1.9

	1986	1988	1990
Beer	24.1	23.7	23.4
Wine	2.4	2.2	2.0
Liquor	1.8	1.6	1.4

Liquor refers to distilled spirits. Translating these figures into consumption per day, the ''average'' person (man, woman, child, and alcohol abuser) consumes 1.3 standard drinks per day!

Source: Beverage Industry, 1991

course. This population includes newborn babies, your 85-year-old grandmother who has a glass of sherry on Thanksgiving and Christmas, the 21-year-old college student who drinks a six-pack a day during spring break, and the estimated 10 percent of the population that the National Institute of Alcoholism and Alcohol Abuse claims accounts for 50 percent of all alcohol consumed.

Nevertheless such data is useful in that it can reveal overall trends of alcohol consumption. In the table 4.1 you will see the per capita consumption of beer, wine, and hard liquor for the last twenty-five years. As you can see, consumption of all three is down from earlier peaks in the last ten years. The decline is most noticeable in hard liquor. Before we start patting ourselves on the back, however, we should note that per capita consumption of beer and wine is still considerably higher than it was in 1966, while retreating back to virtually the same level for distilled spirits.

The decline is due to many factors. The average age of the population is increasing, particularly in the age group over fifty, and older people drink less than those in their twenties. We seem to be going through a period of relative health consciousness as well, and many people are moderating their consumption for this reason. Taxes on alcoholic beverages are a favorite source of revenue for governments trying to avoid increasing income taxes. Per capita estimates, however, do not answer the question of who drinks what.

The decision to drink alcohol is affected by age, religious belief, marital status, sex, and numerous other variables. The obvious way to determine how much a person drinks is to ask. However, self-report is rarely accurate. Heavy drinkers may be expected to underestimate their alcohol consumption, some young drinkers overestimate in order to appear more sophisticated, and even the definition of ''a drink'' makes self-report questionable. If you come home and pour eight ounces of bourbon into a glass do you count that as one drink or eight?

Billboards, television, and the print media have been promoting the concept of *equivalency*. One martini purchased at a bar, one glass of wine from the same place, and one glass of beer have the same amount of alcohol, about .6 ounce of absolute alcohol. This rule should not be followed too strictly, however, since there are variations. The next time you have the opportunity, check the alcohol content of various beverages sold in liquor or package stores. One popular brand of "canned cocktails" sells a vodka or gin martini with nearly six ounces of 40 proof liquor for the same price as a mixed cocktail such as a screwdriver that contains one ounce of 80 proof vodka. Also, there are wine coolers that contain 5 percent alcohol and very similar drinks that contain 20 percent.

An individual's pattern of drinking also needs to be considered. College students, for example, tend toward what might be considered binge drinking, drinking very little during the week and then heavily on weekends. If you drink fourteen drinks on Saturday, are you in the same category as someone who drinks two drinks every day?

According to recent estimates, more than 113 million people in the United States drink alcohol, yet few know anything at all about its effects. Table 4.2 lists a number of commonly held assumptions about alcohol and alcohol abuse that are wrong. So much misunderstanding is remarkable given the amount of money spent on alcohol education.

TYPES OF ALCOHOLIC BEVERAGES

Chemically speaking, what we call alcohol is ethyl alcohol with a chemical formula usually written as C_2H_5OH. There are a number of other forms of alcohol that also affect the body, as we shall see later, but ethanol, as it is also called, is the most important.

Alcoholic beverages come in many types and differ widely in their ethanol content. Beer is the word used to refer to alcoholic beverages made from grain. Sprouted barley (malt) is added to grain to convert the carbohydrates in the grain to sugar, and yeast converts the sugar to alcohol. Wine is made from fruit juices with a high sugar content such as grape juice. Note that sake, or rice "wine," really should be called beer since it is made from a grain.

In the United States, beer has an alcohol content of no more than 5 percent. Any product with a greater alcohol content must be called something else, such as malt liquor. Wine has an alcohol content of from 8–14 percent, although port and sherry have more. Hard liquor is typically 40–50 percent alcohol, although some alcoholic beverages have even more.

Alcohol content is sometimes expressed as **proof.** The word is short for *gunpowder proof,* meaning gunpowder test. Potential buyers would test the distiller's product by pouring it on gunpowder and attempting to light it. If the alcohol content was at least 50 percent the gunpowder would burn, otherwise the water would put out the flame. Thus, distilled spirits that burned passed the gunpowder proof were called 100 proof. You may rest assured that they contained no *more* than 50 percent alcohol. In time, then,

Table 4.2

All of these statements are *false*. How many do you believe?

1. Alcohol is a stimulant.
2. If you are cold, a stiff drink will warm you up.
3. If you mix various kinds of drinks you will become intoxicated more quickly than if you stick to one kind.
4. You can sober up by taking a cold shower and drinking lots of coffee.
5. The best cure for a hangover is more of the same (the hair of the dog).
6. Drinking martinis or manhattans in a bar will get you drunk faster than drinking beer or wine.
7. You can't be an alcoholic if you drink only beer.
8. Most alcoholics are found on skid row.
9. People who drink, even when they know it is causing them problems, simply are weak-willed.
10. Alcoholism cannot be treated: Once a drunk, always a drunk.

the term proof came to mean twice the percentage of alcohol; 80 proof is 40 percent alcohol, and so on.

Sherry is a "fortified wine." It can be made by adding any alcohol to slightly-sweetened wine, although expensive sherry is fortified with fine brandy. The finest sherry is made in the Jerez region of southern Spain, and the term sherry is believed to come from the Arab pronunciation of this name of Jerez. Port, which originally came from Portugal, is a fortified red wine. Port and sherry have an alcohol content of about 20 percent. Since they can be made cheaply and are stronger than wine, they are popular among some heavy drinkers, especially those with little money.

What we call liquor is produced through the process of distillation. Vodka is nothing more than pure ethanol distilled from a variety of sources and diluted with water. By U.S. federal law it must be filtered or treated so that it has no taste or smell. Gin is similar except that it is flavored with juniper berries or other herbs. Bourbon is made from corn and aged in charred oak barrels to give it its distinctive taste, while Scotch is made from malt and grain and aged in barrels formerly used for sherry. Part of its distinctive flavor comes from the malt that is dried over burning peat. Rum is made from sugarcane and/or molasses (Keller, McCormick, & Efron, 1982).

ABSORPTION, DISTRIBUTION, AND METABOLISM OF ALCOHOL

In order to describe the effects of alcohol some measure of the concentration of alcohol in the body is needed. Usually the standard measure is the concentration of alcohol in the blood. For reasons that will become clear later in this chapter, blood alcohol level is usually measured as the concentration in veins as opposed to arteries. Urine tests and Breathalyzers convert their values to estimates of blood alcohol.

Alcohol is almost invariably ingested by the oral route of administration and most absorption takes place in the small intestine. In order to obtain clear-cut results, laboratory studies of absorption typically involve subjects

• YOU READ IT HERE FIRST •

The beverage industry markets a bewildering variety of beverages containing alcohol. In some states, you can purchase alcohol that is 90 percent pure grain alcohol. In all states, you can buy distilled beverages that are at least 50 percent alcohol as well as regular and fortified wine, beer, and malt liquor, wine coolers, fruit drinks with alcohol added, and so on. One recent trend is toward "alcoholic" beverages that contain no alcohol!

As you saw in Table 4.1, the greatest overall decline in consumption of alcohol beverages has been in those with the highest alcohol content, distilled spirits. Beer consumption is down, but very slightly. Furthermore, sales of "light" beer have increased dramatically in the last few years. Following the trend to its logical extreme, sales of **nonalcoholic beer** have gone from virtually nonexistent to sales of over 1.2 million barrels in 1991 (compared to 180 million barrels of regular beer). Every major domestic beer producer and many foreign brewers have introduced NA beer, as it is called in the trade.

If beer is made by fermenting grain in the presence of sugar and yeast, how do you get nonalcoholic beer? Keep in mind that alcohol is lighter than water. The most common method is to brew beer in the ordinary way, then centrifuge it and use evaporation equipment to remove the alcohol. The result is a mild beverage that has most of the taste that beer drinkers seem to like. Since it has less than 0.5 percent alcohol (basically it has *no* alcohol), brewers do not have to pay the normal tax levied on alcoholic beverages.

Who drinks NA beer? It is advertised in a way to suggest that you can enjoy the taste of a brew and still stay "sharp," presumably meaning sober. The industry has targeted it toward those who for medical reasons cannot drink alcohol, such as diabetics, pregnant women, and even designated drivers who choose not to drink. A market undoubtedly exists as well among former heavy drinkers who don't like the sweet taste of ordinary sodas or other substitutes. The beverage industry is unlikely to go after former alcohol abusers, however, for obvious reasons.

Is NA beer a fad? Only time will tell, but many retailers report that people are buying NA beer *and* regular beer. It might be a good idea if you are planning a long afternoon/evening party where beer will be served to urge drinkers to switch to the NA variety on occasion. By the way, NA beer is not new, although it is being widely advertised for the first time using the same avenues as for regular beer. In the past, drinkers were known to buy such beer and add their own distilled spirits, usually grain alcohol or vodka—a practice called "needling."

drinking diluted pure alcohol on an empty stomach after a period of fasting. While this drinking pattern is not unknown outside the laboratory, most people who drink have variable amounts of food in their stomachs, and usually drink beverage alcohol such as beer, wine, or mixed drinks. Therefore laboratory studies may not compare directly with the experiences of social or even abusive drinkers.

Alcohol is lipid soluble, and the presence of food in the stomach, especially if the food contains fat, will slow the rate of absorption. Therefore, the same amount of alcohol consumed by two drinkers of equal weight will be absorbed more rapidly by someone who is drinking on an empty stomach than by someone who has just eaten a salad made with olive oil followed by a greasy bacon cheeseburger. Whether these two drinkers ultimately will reach the same level of alcohol in the blood is still an unresolved question (Simpson, 1990).

The type of alcoholic beverage consumed also affects absorption. As a rule, wine and beer are absorbed more slowly than distilled beverages, although two other factors must be considered. Carbonation increases the rate of absorption, while alcoholic beverages that are very strong (over 100 proof) are actually absorbed more slowly. Therefore, the alcohol in a glass of champagne would be absorbed more rapidly than that in a shot of 120–proof rum.

Mood can also influence the rate of absorption, since emotions influence the amount of time it takes the contents of the stomach to empty into the intestine. Strong moods are likely to cause the stomach to "dump" its contents into the small intestine, thus speeding up the rate of absorption since the intestine absorbs alcohol more efficiently than the stomach.

Once absorbed into the bloodstream in the intestine or stomach, alcohol is transported to the heart, to the lungs, back to the heart, and then to the body as described in chapter 2. Remember, however, that blood from the intestine first passes through the liver, where some of the alcohol is metabolized.

Imagine a dose of alcohol drunk on an empty stomach. The alcohol is absorbed into the arterial system, but has not yet reached the heart and hence the venous system. In this phase called the *absorptive phase,* concentrations of alcohol are higher in the arterial system than in the venous system. After several drinks, our imaginary drinker stops, and as time passes, absorption of alcohol stops. Now the concentration of alcohol is the same for both arteries as veins. As the liver metabolizes alcohol brought to it by the arteries, the ratio changes and the concentration of alcohol in the venous system is higher than in the arterial system. During this phase, called the *post-absorptive phase,* the blood alcohol concentration is falling.

While the above paragraph may seem confusing, the discussion has important implications to someone who drinks alcohol. If you consume a large amount of alcohol rapidly and are tested soon after consumption, your **blood alcohol level** may be low. If, however, there is a delay before you are tested, your blood alcohol concentration has a chance to rise, and if the delay is sufficiently long it may begin to fall again. Therefore it is important to know how recently someone has consumed alcohol in order to obtain an accurate picture of their degree of intoxication.

Distribution of alcohol is accomplished quite rapidly by the bloodstream, and alcohol reaches all the tissues of the body. It is absorbed differently into different tissue, however, so different people will respond differently to a given amount of alcohol. Muscle absorbs more alcohol than fat. Therefore, Mary Sue, a slightly overweight twenty-one-year-old, who weighs 140 pounds and is five feet, four inches, will be more strongly affected by a drink than Bill, twenty-two, a skinny six-footer who also tips the scales at 140. Women typically have a higher percentage of body fat than men, and obese people obviously have even more. Therefore Bill has

Table 4.3 Estimated Blood-Alcohol Concentrations

Estimated potential blood-alcohol concentration in one hour*

Alcoholic beverages	Alcohol content %	Normal measures dispensed	One drink Body weight				Two drinks Body weight				Three drinks Body weight			
			100	140	180	220	100	140	180	220	100	140	180	220
Ale	5	12 oz.	0.05	0.04	0.03	0.02	0.08	0.06	0.05	0.05	0.11	0.09	0.08	0.07
Malt Beverage	7	12 oz.	0.06	0.05	0.04	0.03	0.09	0.07	0.06	0.05	0.15	0.12	0.09	0.08
Regular Beer	4	12 oz.	0.04	0.03	0.02	0.02	0.07	0.05	0.04	0.03	0.10	0.08	0.06	0.05
Wines														
Fortified: (port, muscatel, etc.)	18	3 oz.	0.04	0.03	0.02	0.02	0.07	0.05	0.04	0.03	0.10	0.08	0.06	0.05
Natural: red, white, champagne	12	3 oz.	0.03	0.03	0.02	0.02	0.06	0.05	0.04	0.03	0.08	0.06	0.04	0.04
Cider (hard)	10	3 oz.	0.05	0.04	0.03	0.02	0.08	0.06	0.05	0.05	0.11	0.09	0.08	0.07
Liqueurs														
Strong: sweet, syrupy	40	1 oz.	0.03	0.03	0.02	0.02	0.07	0.05	0.04	0.03	0.08	0.06	0.05	0.05
Medium: fruit brandies	25	2 oz.	0.04	0.03	0.02	0.02	0.08	0.06	0.04	0.04	0.10	0.08	0.06	0.06
Distilled spirits brandy; cognac; rum; scotch; vodka; whiskey	45	1 oz.	0.04	0.03	0.02	0.02	0.07	0.05	0.04	0.03	0.09	0.07	0.06	0.05
Mixed drinks & cocktails Strong: Martini; Manhattan	30	3½ oz.	0.08	0.06	0.04	0.04	0.15	0.12	0.09	0.08	0.22	0.16	0.12	0.10
Medium: Old Fashioned; Alexander	15	4 oz.	0.05	0.04	0.03	0.02	0.08	0.06	0.05	0.05	0.11	0.09	0.08	0.07
Light: High Ball sweet & sour mixes; tonics	7	8 oz.	0.05	0.04	0.03	0.02	0.08	0.06	0.05	0.04	0.12	0.09	0.07	0.06

Source: U.S. Department of Transportation, "First Aid for the Drunken Driver Begins in Your Office," GPO 717–793, pp. 3–4.
*For each hour additional subtract 0.15% from the number shown.

proportionately more muscle than Mary to absorb the alcohol, leaving less in the bloodstream.

Once absorbed by the body, alcohol does virtually nothing except provide calories, a source of energy for the cell. Alcohol provides no nutrients, vitamins, or protein. The caloric content of alcohol is, however, often sufficient to reduce a drinker's appetite. For a short period of time heavy drinkers can get their entire caloric need from alcohol without ingesting any real food.

This, then, adds nutritional deficiencies to the toxic effects of the alcohol. It is not uncommon for heavy drinkers to obtain more than half of their caloric intake from alcohol.

Until recently, it was thought that alcohol was metabolized almost exclusively in the liver, with some excreted unchanged in the urine, sweat, or by exhalation. Recently, however, it was discovered that a substantial proportion of alcohol is metabolized in the stomach by alcohol dehydrogenase, the same enzyme found in the liver. Furthermore, this metabolism is substantially greater in males than in females, and in light or moderate drinkers than in heavy drinkers or alcoholics. What this means is that after all other factors such as weight and percent body fat are taken into consideration, blood alcohol concentrations after consumption of a given amount of alcohol are higher for women and heavy drinkers than for light drinkers and men. Furthermore, virtually no metabolism of alcohol occurred in the stomach of women alcoholics (Frezza, Padova, Pozzato, et al, 1990).

The discovery of the presence of gastric alcohol dehydrogenase also explains the results of a study that anyone who drinks should bear in mind. Subjects who were given two aspirin on a full stomach and then drank alcohol had blood alcohol levels 26 percent higher than those who drank without taking the aspirin (Roine, Gentry, Hernandez-Munoz, Baraona, & Lieber, 1990). Apparently, the aspirin prevented the breakdown of alcohol by alcohol dehydrogenase in the stomach. How many times have you eaten, taken two aspirin, and then had a few drinks? It is possible that you could be legally intoxicated or impaired much more easily than if you had not taken the aspirin.

When alcohol reaches the liver, it is metabolized by the same enzyme found in the stomach, alcohol dehydrogenase, to acetaldehyde and then to acetate, carbon dioxide, and water. **Acetaldehyde** is a toxic chemical which can cause immediate symptoms such as nausea and vomiting as well as long-term effects such as liver damage.

In heavy drinkers there is a second metabolic pathway for alcohol involving an enzyme that the liver specifically produces after long-term consumption. This system, called the microsomal ethanol oxidizing system, helps explain why heavy drinkers may metabolize high doses of alcohol more rapidly. The same system also contributes to the production of acetaldehyde and may contribute to the liver damage seen in heavy drinkers.

Unlike absorption, metabolism of alcohol occurs independently of body weight and is independent of the amount of alcohol consumed. In the following diagram you will see the changes in blood alcohol level of a hypothetical individual who consumed a large amount of alcohol rapidly. Note that even though many hours have passed, the individual is still legally intoxicated the morning after consumption.

The liver can metabolize the equivalent of approximately three-quarters of an ounce of hard liquor, or the equivalent in beer or wine per hour. If you consume more than that amount, your blood alcohol level will increase—which is, of course, the whole point of recreational drinking. It is

Table 4.4 Nutritional Content of Alcoholic Beverages

Food nutrient**	Type of beverage and quantity†					
	Beer 12oz.	Rum 1.5 oz.	Whiskey 1.5 oz.	Martin 2oz.	Manhattan 2 oz.	Wines§ 4 oz.
Calories	175.0	150.0	110.0	160.0	160.0	160.0
Calories from alcohol	125.0	150.0	110.0	110.0	110.0	145.0
Protein (g)	2.0	0.0	0.0	0.0	0.0	0.0
Fat (g)	0.0	0.0	0.0	0.0	0.0	0.0
Carbohydrate (g)	12.0	0.0	0.0	0.0	0.0	4.2
Thiamine (mg)	0.1	0.0	0.0	0.0	0.0	0.0
Nicotinic acid (mg)	0.75	0.0	0.0	0.0	0.0	0.0
Riboflavin (mg)	10.0	0.0	0.0	0.0	0.0	0.0
Ascorbic acid (mg)	0.0	0.0	0.0	0.0	0.0	0.0
Folic acid (mg)	0.0	0.0	0.0	0.0	0.0	0.0

Source: Adapted from Kenneth L. Jones, Louis Shainberg, and Curtis O. Byer, *Drugs and Alcohol,* 2nd ed. (San Francisco: Harper and Row, 1973), p. 125.

**Approximate amounts only.

†Quantities—as most often consumed.

§Dry wine—20% alcoholic content

also important to remember the concept of **equivalency.** Many people believe that beer and wine are less intoxicating because they have a lower alcohol content than hard liquor. The volume consumed, however, makes up for this lower concentration.

If you consume a large amount of alcohol rapidly and then slow down your consumption to one drink an hour, your blood alcohol level will not go down at all. In figure 4.2, see what happens when a 115-pound woman has three beers in an hour and then has only two ounces of wine an hour for the next five hours. At the end of six hours she is still legally intoxicated. This is because the one drink an hour that she is absorbing is maintaining her blood alcohol level.

If you were to ask Mary Sue how she felt at the end of that six hours, she would probably reply that she felt sober and perfectly in control. This phenomenon is known as *acute tolerance.* Another aspect of acute tolerance is that drinkers generally feel less intoxicated on the descending curve of blood alcohol than on the ascending curve. What this means is that our hypothetical drinker in figure 4.1 would not have felt particularly intoxicated at eight in the morning after his night of binging, even though he was still legally drunk.

Research on the phenomenon of acute tolerance demonstrates that motor tasks, cognitive performance, and reaction time are all less affected by alcohol when the BAL is falling than when rising (Jones & Vega, 1972; Leblanc, Kalant, & Gibbins, 1975). Remember, however, that from a legal point of view, the criterion is *blood alcohol level* and it makes no difference whether BAL is measured on the ascending or descending curve.

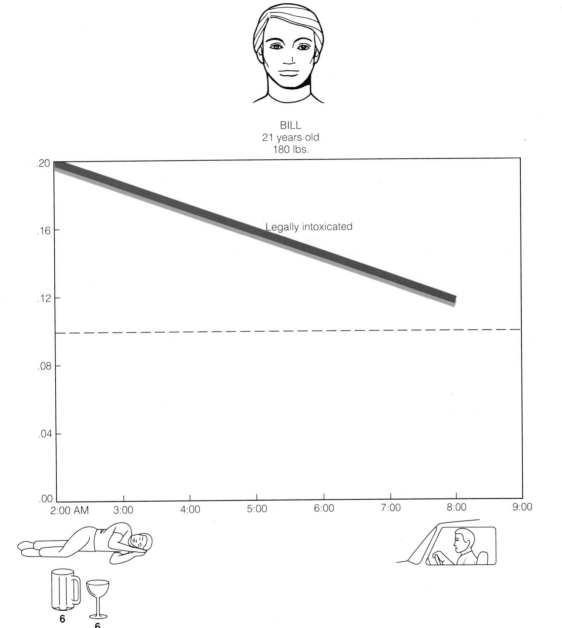

BILL
21 years old
180 lbs.

Legally intoxicated

Figure 4.1

On Saturday night Bill celebrated his twenty-first birthday with six shots of tequila and six beer chasers. He went to ''sleep'' at 2:00 A.M. with a BAL of .20. He woke Sunday morning feeling fine but he has not sobered up yet. On the way to church at 8:00 A.M., Bill is stopped and arrested; his BAL is .11.

MARY SUE
21 years old
115 lbs.

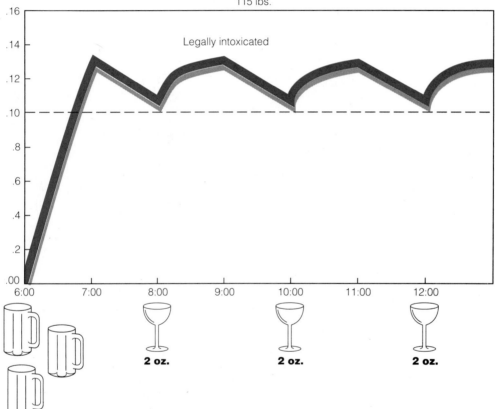

Figure 4.2

Mary Sue drank three beers around 6 P.M. She felt intoxicated so she didn't drink anything else until 8 P.M., when she had just two ounces of wine. She had two ounces of wine at 10 P.M. and at midnight. Although she probably feels fine, she has, in fact, been legally intoxicated since 6:30. The two ounces of wine every two hours was enough to maintain her blood alcohol level above .10.

Table 4.5 Blood-Alcohol Concentrations and Depressant Effects on the Central Nervous System

Blood-alcohol concentration	Number of drinks consumed	Effects that often occur
.04%	1–2	Lowered efficiency of the cortex, or brain covering, in the uppermost part of the brain Some impairment of judgment Release of restraints and inhibitions Feelings of warmth, relaxation, and buoyancy Slight change in existing mood Increased heart rate
.06	3–4	Continued depression of the cortex Disruption of judgment Some loss of coordination Less concern about environment Feelings of warmth Mental relaxation Relaxation of inhibitions
.10	5–6	Reduced operation of those parts of the brain controlling movement Impairment of fine coordination skills Delayed reaction time Exaggerated emotions Noticeable clumsiness Talkativeness Impairment of peripheral vision Presumptive evidence of "impaired ability" to operate motor vehicle in all states
.16	6–8	Progressive deterioration of higher cortical functions and some motor activities Staggering Slurred speech Blurred vision Serious loss of judgment and coordination Unmistakable abnormality of gross bodily and mental functions
.20	8–10	Lowered midbrain functioning Feeling of need to lie down Inability to walk or dress without help Tears or rage with little provocation Double vision
.30	10–15	Reduced functioning of lower portion of brain—intoxication marked by increasing difficulty in maintaining motor function High degree of uninhibited behavior

Source: Hafen & Brog, 1983.

Amethystic Agents

No way exists of speeding up the metabolism of alcohol, but considerable research has been done on drugs which will at least counteract some of its effects. Such "sobering up" drugs are called **amethystic agents.** One such drug gained a great deal of publicity when it was first announced. The manufacturer's name for the drug is Ro 15–4513, and it was reported to

The Hangover

In Spanish, it is *la cruda* (the "rawness"), in German, it is *katzenjammer* (wailing of cats). In whatever language, it is most unpleasant and since most languages have colloquial terms for it, quite common. Interestingly, despite all of the research done on the effects of alcohol, its cause remains somewhat of a mystery.

The symptoms of a hangover are familiar to most drinkers: headache, upset stomach, anxiety, depression, thirst, and in severe cases, an almost overwhelming desire to crawl into a hole and die. The theories about what causes a hangover are about as numerous as the supposed cures for it.

People who get hangovers often smoke too much, stay up too late, and engage in other behaviors not likely to be conducive to feeling well the next day. In addition to fatigue and perhaps guilt, however, certain physiological phenomena have been linked to feeling "raw" the next morning. One is the role of congeners. **Congeners** are forms of alcohol other than ethanol. Methanol is a congener, as are other alcohols referred to as *fusel oils*. These congeners are metabolized more slowly than ethanol and are more toxic. When you drink alcoholic beverages, your body metabolizes ethanol first; when all the ethanol is gone, it begins on the congeners, and the toxic byproducts contribute to the feeling we call a hangover.

Support for the congener theory of hangover comes from the finding that alcohol beverages rich in them produce worse hangovers than beverages such as vodka, which is pure alcohol and water (Chapman, 1970; Pawan, 1972). Congeners are the product of distillation, and some are added for taste. Ironically, the cheaper the liquor the fewer the congeners. Vodka has almost no congeners, while bourbon and scotch contain higher levels. Expensive bourbon and scotch contain even more.

Alcohol also upsets water balance in the body since it inhibits the antidiuretic hormone resulting in excess urination and a disturbed electrolyte balance the next day. Drinking several glasses of water will relieve the thirst that results but cannot shorten the hangover. Many people report that drinking too much gives them a headache. In all probability, this is the result of dilation of blood vessels in the brain (perhaps because of a reaction to congeners); coffee will help contract the blood vessels and reduce the pain (Hafen & Brog, 1983). Antacids (see chapter 10) will relieve the upset stomach that results from the effects of alcohol on the gastrointestinal tract.

Many fancy "cures" for hangovers have been devised but none work. Time is the only cure for a hangover: time for the liver to metabolize the congeners, time for the electrolyte balance to be restored, time for the irritation of the gastrointestinal tract to lessen. "Hair of the dog that bit you"—more alcohol the morning after—might temporarily relieve some of the symptoms, since ethyl alcohol is metabolized preferentially over other forms of alcohol, but simply prolongs the eventual onset. Moreover, morning drinking is a major indicator of problem drinking.

counter some of the intoxicating effects of alcohol in animals (Suzdak, Glowa, Crawley, Schwartz, Skolnick, & Paul, 1986). This drug is not likely to be placed on the market, since it does not counteract the other effects of alcohol on the body not mediated by the GABA system. In addition, it causes seizures.

Other drugs may eventually prove to be of some use. Naloxone, (an opiate antagonist) can reverse alcohol-induced respiratory depression and coma, while ibuprofen (see Chapter 10), lithium (Chapter 12), and thyrotropin-releasing hormone (which acts on the thyroid) have been shown to reduce some of the effects of intoxication. Since alcohol affects every part of the body and brain, it is unlikely that a single sobering-up pill will ever be discovered (Litten & Allen, 1991). Besides, imagine the impact on the individual and society of a drug that would enable drinkers to drink as much as they want and then take another drug and appear normal.

PHYSIOLOGICAL EFFECTS OF ALCOHOL CONSUMPTION

The effects of alcohol are dose related, meaning that different blood alcohol levels have quantitatively, as well as qualitatively, different effects. Keeping in mind that tolerance plays an important role in the effects of alcohol, table 4.5 lists the primary behavioral effects of various blood alcohol levels.

If you drink alcoholic beverages, think back to your most recent episode of drinking, and estimate your blood alcohol level from table 4.5. Do the reported effects seem similar to your own recollection of how you felt or behaved? If not, remember that alcohol impairs perception, which is, in a way, lucky since most of us feel that we are suave, debonair, and chic when our BALs are around .05. In fact, we are nothing more than slightly tipsy. However, our companions are probably similarly intoxicated, so *their* perception is equally distorted. If you have ever been the designated driver with a group of people who have been drinking, you know that being sober around a bunch of drunks is, in itself, a sobering experience.

Cardiovascular Effects

Alcohol has a number of effects on the cardiovascular system. It can affect the heart directly, causing degeneration of the heart muscle; it can induce irregular heart rhythm (cardiac arrhythmia); it can cause an increase in blood pressure and increase the possibility of heart attack or stroke. All of these effects are dose related, of course, and most can be reversed upon abstinence.

Alcohol has a direct effect on the heart muscle, because it metabolizes alcohol forming a group of compounds called fatty acid ethyl esters that reduce the energy capacity of the muscle. Alcohol also induces other changes that reduce the energy capacity of the heart as well as affecting its ability to contract.

Drinking and withdrawal from alcohol also increase the irritability of the heart, leading to cardiac arrhythmia. Even short-term alcohol abuse can lead to cardiac arrhythmia. There is a condition called **holiday heart syndrome,** which is characterized by premature heartbeats and disturbances of the heart rhythm (Ettinger, Wu, & De La Cruz, 1978). It is called "holiday heart syndrome" because it can be produced in sensitive individuals after only a few days of heavy drinking. Since the symptoms seem similar to a heart attack, emergency rooms are quite familiar with the condition after

Violence at baseball games, as a result of drunkenness, has led several teams to set up special "family" sections, cut off beer sales after the 6th inning, and forbid sales to fans who are intoxicated.

such holidays as Thanksgiving, Christmas, and New Year's, when drinkers are likely to overindulge for a period of days.

Alcohol also contributes to high blood pressure. Even moderate amounts of alcohol can cause increases in blood pressure, and those who report drinking three to five drinks a day have higher blood pressure than those who drink less (Klatsky, Friedman & Siegelaub, 1977). For those who drink heavily (six or more drinks a day) the incidence of high blood pressure is twice that of light drinkers or abstainers. High levels of alcohol intake also increase the risk of stroke and other cerebrovascular problems.

A major effect that every drinker has experienced is dilation of peripheral blood vessels. This dilation produces a sensation of warmth that can be quite misleading. On television you sometimes see football fans in the coldest of weather, barechested, screaming, and cheering for their team. You assume that they are "feeling no pain" because of tailgate parties and alcohol consumption during the game. But it is important to note that these same fans are risking a severe case of hypothermia. The blood that fills the peripheral blood vessels has to come from somewhere, and it comes from the inner body.

Core temperatures actually decrease in individuals exposed to cold after consuming alcohol, although the subjects report feeling warm. Hypothermia, as a result of alcohol intoxication, can lead to death. This risk can be quite real for those who drink and then travel long distances, especially on foot. One study, for example, found that Native Americans in New Mexico who could not purchase alcohol on the reservation were thirty times more likely to die of hypothermia than other New Mexico residents, and 90 percent of those who died were highly intoxicated (Gallaher, Fleming,

Berger, & Sewell, 1992). Of course all drinkers are also running the risk of a drunken driving conviction, harming an innocent victim, getting in an accident, or being injured in a fall.

Yes, you may be saying to yourself, but there is *some* good that comes of moderate drinking as it relates to the cardiovascular system. After all, what about those studies that show that occasional drinking *lowers* low density cholesterol (the bad stuff) and raises high density lipoproteins (the good stuff)? What about those studies that show that moderate drinkers live longer than either nondrinkers or heavy drinkers? Unfortunately, those data are not as clear-cut as the popular press and advertisements make out. When researchers look at many studies and consider all the factors that could account for these differences, they are not convinced that alcohol is the responsible factor. This is not to say that moderate alcohol consumption *doesn't* do the good things it is supposed to, just that the available research does not permit a conclusion one way or the other (Pohorecky, 1990; Regan, 1990; Shafer, 1990; Veenstra, Van de Pol, & Schafsama, 1990).

Effects on the Liver

The liver is the primary site for the metabolism of alcohol, so it should be obvious that heavy alcohol use can seriously affect it. The three major liver problems associated with drinking are **fatty liver, alcoholic hepatitis,** and **cirrhosis,** or scarring. These three conditions are not progressive stages of liver injury due to heavy drinking, but can all occur concurrently in the same person. Furthermore, the most serious form, cirrhosis, can develop without any evidence of hepatitis. Finally, both fatty liver and hepatitis are reversible, but cirrhosis is not. Therefore in order to understand the effects of alcohol on the liver, we must consider all three conditions.

One immediate result of stress is the release of fat from fatty tissue. Fat, of course, provides calories. Alcohol, because it is a stressor, causes a release of fat from fatty or adipose tissue. In the drinker, however, the liver, which normally regulates the amount of fat in the bloodstream, is busy metabolizing the ingested alcohol, so it stores the excess fat in the liver. Anytime you drink faster than your body can metabolize the alcohol, fatty stores are building up in your liver (Goldstein, 1983). This condition is known as alcoholic fatty liver and occurs in virtually every heavy drinker.

How much do you have to drink before you begin to experience this condition? Evidence suggests that alcoholic fatty liver can develop after even a weekend of what some would consider relatively light drinking (Rubin & Lieber, 1968). Five or six drinks a day for several days can produce fatty liver in males, while as few as two drinks may produce the same effect in females (Grant, Dufour & Harford, 1988). If the drinker abstains, the liver can metabolize the fat and return to normal in two or three days (see figure 4.3).

Alcoholic hepatitis is a much more serious condition that is often overlooked. Alcoholic hepatitis can be accompanied by high fever and loss of appetite, nausea, vomiting, and confusion. These symptoms may occur after

FIGURE 4.3

The liver can metabolize many poisons. For those susceptible to the effects of alcohol, however, excessive alcohol use can lead to cirrhosis.
(Adapted from "Alcoholic Hepatitis, Facts You Should Know" from the U.S. Dept. of Health and Human Services, Public Health Services.)

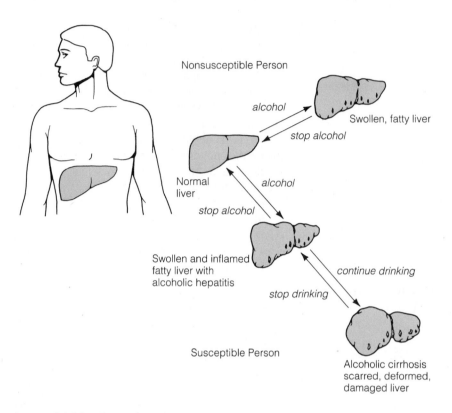

Nonsusceptible Person

alcohol

stop alcohol

Swollen, fatty liver

Normal liver

alcohol

stop alcohol

Swollen and inflamed fatty liver with alcoholic hepatitis

continue drinking

stop drinking

Susceptible Person

Alcoholic cirrhosis scarred, deformed, damaged liver

heavy drinking has stopped and may get worse for days or weeks after the drinker has "gone on the wagon." Often, however, episodes of alcohol hepatitis go unrecognized, ignored, or hidden. Standard liver tests may or may not indicate hepatitis. Repeated episodes of hepatitis are now believed to be responsible for the development of cirrhosis in susceptible individuals.

Cirrhosis of the liver and related alcohol-induced liver diseases are the commonest cause of illness and death from alcohol abuse (West, Maxwell, & Noble, 1984; Frank & Raicht, 1985). Cirrhosis means scarring, and this condition is found in 50 percent or more of drinkers who consume about the equivalent of a quart of liquor a day for twenty or more years. For those who drink less the incidence is much lower, probably not more than 15 percent.

Treatment for hepatitis is largely supportive, meaning that with rest and abstinence from alcohol, the liver will recover. Conversely, there is no real treatment for cirrhosis, and the mortality rate approaches 50 percent or more. The biggest problem is to get the alcohol-dependent person to stop drinking. While it would seem that rational people told they must stop drinking or die would stop, the fact is that abstinence, even in those with liver trouble, is difficult to achieve.

The way in which alcohol damages the liver is gradually becoming clear. Other drug use, nutrition, differences in hormonal systems, as well as possible genetic susceptibility, are all factors. We now know that chronic ingestion of alcohol itself can produce cirrhosis even in drinkers whose diet is adequate; it was previously thought that malnutrition was the primary cause of this disease. Nevertheless, depletion of vitamin A by alcohol does play a role, although an adequate amount of this vitamin will not prevent cirrhosis (Lieber, 1991).

In chronic heavy drinkers, the microsomal pathway for metabolism of alcohol contributes to liver damage by increasing the buildup of acetaldehyde, which is toxic to the liver. In addition, this pathway also converts other drugs and chemicals, such as solvents, some painkillers, and prescription drugs, to toxic metabolites. Such a conversion seems to take place only through the microsomal pathway (Lieber, 1991). The fact that not all drinkers develop liver damage suggests that genetics also plays a role.

If there is any "good news" about recent research on alcohol and the liver, it is that laboratory studies indicate that some nutrients taken in high doses may protect the liver from alcohol damage. No controlled studies exist to determine whether these nutrients could protect heavy drinkers, but the possibility does exist (Lieber, 1991).

The mortality rate due to cirrhosis has been declining in the United States and elsewhere in the world, but it still is the ninth leading cause of death in this country. The death rate from cirrhosis for males is twice that for females, but women traditionally drink less than men. For women who do drink, susceptibility to alcohol-related liver damage seems to be greater. Women develop alcohol-related liver problems with lower levels of consumption, and alcohol-dependent women actually show a higher rate of liver problems than do alcohol-dependent men.

The reasons for these sex differences are not clear, but the recent finding that women have lower levels of alcohol dehydrogenase in the stomach may partially explain them. If women do not metabolize alcohol in the stomach as well as men, more enters the venous system to be carried to the liver. Thus the liver has to work harder to metabolize alcohol. Other factors undoubtedly play a role as well, of course; body weight, immune systems differences, and hormonal differences have been implicated.

Gastrointestinal and Nutritional Effects

Chronic alcohol intake has a harmful effect on the entire gastrointestinal tract. It damages the mucous membranes and can cause inflammation of the esophagus, chronic stomach irritation, and problems with absorption in the intestine. Because of its irritant effect, it can cause hemorrhage of the esophagus, a condition that is usually fatal. Alcohol combined with aspirin is particularly harmful to the stomach. Alcohol also affects intestinal motility and can cause diarrhea.

Alcohol abuse is a major cause in chronic pancreatitis, or inflammation of the pancreas—the organ that produces digestive enzymes and insulin (U.S. Department of Health and Human Services, 1990). Alcohol inhibits all

• YOU READ IT HERE FIRST •

One of the major advances in medical science in recent years has been in the field of transplant surgery. Obscured by the publicity over a few spectacular successes (and failures) of multiple organ transplantation is the fact that organ transplantation is now an accepted practice. The availability of donors, however, is always less than the number of those needing a transplant and when an organ becomes available someone must decide who gets the organ. As remaining technical problems are solved, look for demand to increase and along with the demand, controversy over who deserves the transplant (Cohen & Benjamin, 1991; Moss & Siegler, 1991).

As you have read, alcohol is toxic to the liver, and cirrhosis is the ninth leading cause of death in the United States. Liver transplantation is feasible, and more than 1,000 were performed in 1990. But with over 30,000 needing a transplant, difficult decisions must be made (Evans, Orians, & Ascher, 1992). Does an "alcoholic" who has "willfully" destroyed his/her liver "deserve" a new one when the relapse rate is so high, or should the available liver instead be given to someone—preferably a beautiful young child—whose liver has been damaged by disease or a genetic defect?

If you read the sentence with the intended emphasis as indicated by the quotation marks, the issue seems clear, but as always, there is another side. If alcoholism is a disease, the alcoholic is just as deserving as little Tiffany. Are you sure that your answer is not tinged by a moral disapproval of heavy drinking? Since smoking causes lung cancer, should we give smokers a second chance?

Furthermore, how far should we go in determining the suitability for a transplant? What if there were two people in need of a liver, Julia a thirty-five-year-old brain surgeon, and Richard, a seventy-year-old retired janitor. Your answer might depend on whether or not Richard was your father. Would your answer be different if you knew that, of the problem drinkers who have received a new liver, most have stopped drinking? Despite the millions of dollars spent every year to change people's attitudes toward alcohol and other drug abuse, issues such as these can demonstrate that most of us still have ambivalent attitudes toward drug use.

---

of the enzymes normally produced, thus further contributing to the malabsorption so common in chronic alcohol users.

Combine the gastrointestinal effects of chronic alcohol abuse with the fact that alcohol is a source of calories, and it is easy to see why the abuser will suffer nutritional deficiencies. Alcohol may account for more than ten percent of the total caloric intake of adult drinkers, and the percentage is even higher for heavy drinkers and alcohol abusers. Alcohol interferes with the metabolism of proteins, carbohydrates, lipids, most vitamins, and many minerals, and impairs absorption of many nutrients. Table 4.6 shows the minimal amount of time it takes for depletion of nutrients to occur in the heavy drinker.

Central Nervous System

Alcohol, because it is lipid soluble, moves from the bloodstream into the brain. The effects of alcohol on the cells of the brain has been an exciting area of research that is beginning to yield important findings. Alcohol is taken up by the cell membrane of individual neurons and alters the delicate balance of the membrane, causing the membrane to become less stable. These

Table 4.6 Minimal Time of Heavy Alcohol Use for Depletion of Nutrients To Occur

2–4 Weeks	4–12 Weeks	12–16 Weeks	6 Months or Longer
folate	niacin	ascorbic acid	calcium
magnesium	nicotinamide	long-life proteins	copper
potassium	pantothenate		retinol
zinc	phosphorous		selenium
short-life proteins	pyridoxine		25-hydroxy D
	riboflavin		vitamin B_{12}
	thiamine		vitamin E
	medium-life proteins		vitamin K

Source: Adapted from Iber & Panda, 1986.

changes in fluidity account for some of the effects of alcohol, especially at high doses, but do not explain the effects of alcohol at lower doses, those that most of us are likely to have experienced (Tabakoff, Hoffman, & Petersen, 1990; U. S. Department of Health and Human Services, 1990). The effects of low doses of alcohol are just now beginning to be understood and seem to involve various neurotransmitters.

You will recall from chapter 3 that gamma-aminobutyric acid (GABA) is an inhibitory neurotransmitter. GABA interacts with the postsynaptic receptor, causing the neuron to be less sensitive to other neurotransmitters. Alcohol increases the ability of GABA to inhibit cell functioning. Furthermore, evidence exists to suggest that the GABA receptor adapts to the presence of alcohol, and that various forms of alcohol that have different intoxicating effects affect the GABA receptor in different ways (Tabakoff, Hoffman, and Petersen, 1990; U. S. Department of Health and Human Services, 1990).

Frequently, especially in popular literature, you will read that alcohol abuse and dependence has been "explained" by the effect of alcohol on endorphin receptors. Alcohol is supposed to act like morphine or heroin, thus accounting for the craving that supposedly occurs after alcohol withdrawal.

This theory is strengthened by the fact that some of the effects of morphine are similar to alcohol, and many opiate addicts turn to alcohol abuse when they stop using narcotics. Furthermore, some individuals at risk to develop alcohol problems have lower levels of endorphins, and small doses of morphine make the effects of alcohol more pleasant (Reid, 1990). Nevertheless, other studies in animals and humans are equally convincing that the relationship between endorphins and alcohol is far from simple.

The alcohol-endorphin hypothesis is a good example of an idea that remains popular despite evidence to contradict it because it would simplify things if it were true. It also fits into the current popular interest in endorphins. A complex relationship may also exist between alcohol abuse and endorphins, but theories in the popular press are far too simplistic.

Alcohol also has an effect on other neurotransmitters, especially serotonin, which plays a role in depression and aggressive behavior, and norepinephrine, but the precise relationship is not at all clear and much of the evidence is confusing. Another neurotransmitter affected by alcohol is glutamate, which was also discussed in chapter 3. Glutamate is an excitatory neurotransmitter, and it should not be surprising to learn that alcohol inhibits the activity of glutamate.

Perhaps you are getting an overall picture: Alcohol increases the effect of inhibitory transmitters and inhibits excitatory transmitters. The inhibitory effect of alcohol on glutamate is important because glutamate is believed to play a role in learning and memory, and we shall see shortly that alcohol affects memory. The glutamate receptor is found in the hippocampus, a structure known to be involved in memory. The excitatory effects of glutamate are believed to be partially responsible for seizures in the brain, a not uncommon result of alcohol withdrawal. Research on the effects of alcohol on glutamate is one of the most promising avenues for understanding its effects (Litten & Allen, 1991).

Another area of research that is quite new, but shows potential for understanding how alcohol works, is the study of the effect of alcohol on the second messenger system described in chapter 3. For now, too little is known about how alcohol affects this system to make any definite statements, but the effect of alcohol may also be explained in part by its ability to alter the binding of neurotransmitters such as serotonin, norepinephrine, and adenosine which in turn stimulate the second messenger system.

Effects on the Endocrine System

As we saw above, alcohol is a stressor, and the importance of this fact is just beginning to be understood. In general, the endocrine effects of alcohol are consistent with this finding, and form the basis for important studies on the genetic aspects of problem drinking that will be discussed later.

Stress is mediated by the connection between the pituitary and the adrenal glands. Researchers have known for a long time that alcohol acts at the level of the pituitary, rather than the adrenal glands (Forbes & Duncan, 1951). Animals and humans show individual differences in their endocrine responses to alcohol, and these differences seem to have a genetic basis (Kakihana, Noble, & Butte, 1968). Basically, alcohol administration causes a rise in plasma corticosteroid, hormones that are released when humans or animals are under stress.

With chronic use of alcohol, nearly all endocrine glands are affected, producing changes in hormone levels and perhaps even the metabolism of the braithe brain. Excess amounts of cortisol, a stress hormone, are secreted during heavy alcohol use. The endocrine system, of course, mediates many of the sexual problems that plague heavy drinkers (Litten & Allen, 1991). With alcohol withdrawal, the endocrine system is severely disturbed, which may account for some of the symptoms. In particular, the hypothalamus-pituitary-adrenal system you read about in chapter 3 is affected, as is norepinephrine metabolism.

Effects on Sexual Performance

A virtually universal belief exists in our society that alcohol is an aphrodisiac, in spite of overwhelming evidence to the contrary. Shakespeare knew this when he had the porter in Macbeth say to Macduff of "drink"—"Lechery, sir, it provokes, and unprovokes; it provokes the desire, but it takes away the performance: . . . it makes him and it mars him; it persuades him and disheartens him; makes him stand to and not stand to . . . ." As is so often the case with Shakespeare, here he is repeating in iambic pentameter what he borrowed (some would say plagiarized) from older sources.

The effects of alcohol on sex in both men and women have been noted by numerous authorities since the time of Aristotle, who wrote, "Those who are drunk are incapable of sexual intercourse." Alexander the Great is reported to have drunk so much "that he had no appetite for sexual indulgence" (quoted in Abel, 1985).

For women, alcohol was almost universally seen as a dangerous aphrodisiac. In ancient Rome, drinking by women was punishable by death and equated with adultery! In the Talmud (the commentary on the first five books of the Old Testament that forms the basis of Jewish law) it says, "One glass of wine is becoming to a woman, two are somewhat degrading, and if she has three glasses she solicits coitus" (quoted in Abel, 1985).

As a general rule, increasing blood alcohol levels leads to an increase in perceived sexual arousal (up to a point), but to a decrease in strength of erection and time to orgasm for males, and to corresponding vaginal changes and time to orgasm for females (Farkas & Rosen, 1976; Wilson & Lawson, 1976, 1978; Malatesta, Pollack, Wilbanks, & Adams, 1979; Malatesta, Crotty, Pollack, & Peacock, 1982). Alcohol also releases inhibitions and this effect is both physiological and psychological (Crowe & George, 1989).

If the acute effects of alcohol on sexual functioning were not enough to give you pause, the effects of chronic alcohol abuse certainly will. In the male, alcohol reduces testosterone synthesis (Ellingboe & Varanelli, 1979; Johnston, Chiao, & Gavaler, 1981). Even short-term alcohol abuse can result in lowered testosterone levels. In one study a decrease was found after the consumption of the equivalent of a pint of whiskey a day for three days (Van Thiel, 1983).

The chronic alcohol abuser often develops atrophy of the testes, impotence, and infertility (Van Thiel, Gavaler, Cobb, & Chiao, 1982; Schiavi, 1990). Furthermore, estrogen synthesis is increased, resulting in feminization (decreased body hair, breast development, and the female pattern of body fat). The impotence is often permanent, even if the abuser stops drinking and testosterone levels return to normal. As many as 60 percent of male alcoholics report impotence (Crowe & George, 1989).

In women, chronic alcohol intake is associated with menstrual difficulties, higher rates of gynecological surgery, infertility, and loss of secondary sex characteristics (Wilsnack, Klassen, & Wilsnack, 1984). These differences were seen in women who reported drinking approximately four or more drinks daily.

Fetal Alcohol Syndrome

Fetal alcohol syndrome, as we know it, was first clearly described in the early 1970s (Jones, Smith, Ulleland, & Streissguth, 1973; Jones & Smith, 1973); since then over 5,000 studies have been published (Abel & Sokol, 1990). We now know that alcohol is a **teratogenic drug,** causing a wide range of physical and behavioral defects. The vast majority of the available research has been done on animals; with humans, the studies are indirect.

The most severe type of defect is known as fetal alcohol syndrome, which produces a group of defects including facial malformations, growth deficiencies, and intellectual deficits (Streissguth & LaDue, 1985). The most common facial malformations can be seen in figure 4.4 and include abnormally small head (microcephaly), narrow eyes (short palpebral fissures), missing ridges on the upper lip just between the nose and lip (indistinct philtrum), and a thin upper lip (Streissguth & LaDue, 1985).

Growth deficiencies also are common in these children, and they are often severely retarded. More subtle changes include problems paying attention and lower-than-average, while still normal, I.Q. scores. In addition, maternal drinking has been associated with lower birth weight, higher rates of spontaneous abortion, greater susceptibility to infection, impaired ability to feed, and other problems (Streissguth, Barr, & Sampson, 1989).

Severe fetal alcohol syndrome (FAS) continues into adolescence and adulthood. In one study, patients diagnosed as having FAS as children, had an average I.Q. of 68, with academic functioning at the second to fourth grade level. They showed poor judgement, were distractable, and in general severely maladjusted (Streissguth, Aase, Clarren, Randels, LaDue, & Smith, 1991). It seems likely that for many cases of FAS, the damage is irreversible and severe.

Children with only some symptoms of FAS are said to have suspected **fetal alcohol effects** (FAE). No definite statements can be made about when during pregnancy alcohol exerts its effects, but defects related to physical features seem related to alcohol abuse early in fetal growth, while mental and behavioral problems are more likely the result of either continued abuse or abuse later in pregnancy.

The mechanism by which alcohol produces FAS and FAE is not known, but evidence points to three possibilities; impaired placental blood flow, a direct effect of alcohol on cell functioning in the fetus, and disruption of prostaglandin balance (Schenker, Becker, Randall, et al, 1990). Prostaglandins are important fatty acids that are intimately involved in fetal growth (as well as pain perception and seemingly everything else). These possibilities are not mutually exclusive.

Despite the dramatic effects just described, the issue of FAS and FAE is not as clear-cut as might be expected. First of all, the actual incidence of fetal alcohol syndrome is less than would be expected if there were a simple relationship between alcohol and birth defects. The most recent estimates available indicate the rate worldwide at about 0.33 cases per 1,000 live births (Abel & Sokol, 1991). Even among those diagnosed as heavy drinkers, the rate is "only" 25 per 1,000 live births. In actual numbers this translates into

FIGURE 4.4
Common facial characteristics of children with FAS. Features labeled on the left are seen frequently; those on the right are less specific to this syndrome.

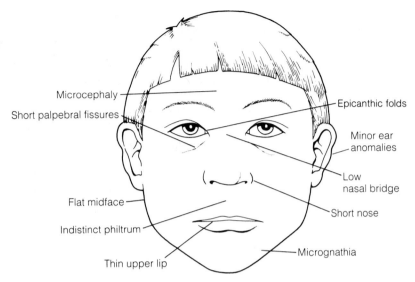

Microcephaly

Short palpebral fissures

Epicanthic folds

Minor ear anomalies

Low nasal bridge

Flat midface

Short nose

Indistinct philtrum

Thin upper lip

Micrognathia

1,200 cases of FAS in the United States each year with an estimated cost of treating this condition as $74.6 million.

When the diagnosis of FAE is included, of course, the rate is much higher, but the fact is that most babies born even to heavy drinkers do not show obvious effects of FAS or FAE (U. S. Department of Health and Human Services, 1990). Furthermore, most heavy-drinking pregnant women also use other drugs, and diagnosis of FAE is very difficult (Abel & Sokol, 1991).

In the past and even now, many pregnant women drink and have children with no apparent problems, although they *seem* to be drinking less (Serdulla, Williamson, Kendreck, Anda, & Byers, 1991). The absence of obvious problems does not mean that no fetal alcohol effects exist in apparently normal children, however. Fetal alcohol syndrome and fetal alcohol effects probably represent two points on a continuum of problems that result from alcohol abuse during pregnancy. Other, more subtle behavioral problems may be difficult to measure, but still present. For example, one study of mothers who consumed two or more drinks a day during pregnancy had children who, at age seven, scored an average of seven points lower on I.Q. tests. (Streissguth, Barr, & Sampson, 1990).

Moreover, all the studies reported rely on self-report which is notoriously unreliable, with underreporting being the rule (Ernhart, Morrow-Tlucak, Sokol, & Martin, 1988). This problem makes it difficult to give advice about possible safe limits on drinking. An overwhelming number of studies of various drinking populations report, furthermore, that the pattern of drinking is more important in predicting problems than total consumption. For example, seven drinks on one day is likely to have a more serious effect on the fetus than one drink a day for seven days.

Given all the confusion, is there *any* amount of alcohol that a pregnant woman can drink without worrying about birth defects? Because of the seriousness of fetal alcohol syndrome and how little we know of the factors involved that cause it, virtually every researcher would agree with the U. S. Surgeon General's recommendation that women who are pregnant should not drink and should be aware of the alcohol content of foods and drugs. Nevertheless, you should keep in mind that if your mother drinks alcoholic beverages, chances are she drank during your development as an embryo and fetus. No clear evidence links small amounts of alcohol to birth defects, but no clear evidence exists to suggest that alcohol has no effect. Why take the risk?

The Immune System and Cancer

Alcohol abusers are at higher risk for many infectious diseases, especially tuberculosis (Smith & Palmer, 1976). The evidence suggests that alcohol impairs the ability of the body to recognize and fight foreign bodies such as bacteria and viruses. In addition, the alcohol abuser often has nutritional deficiencies that further decrease the ability to fight infection. The relationship between alcohol and AIDS is unclear, especially because the major at-risk populations for AIDS are also high-risk populations for alcohol abuse, but any stressor with a known effect on the immune system like alcohol would probably contribute to the development of the disease.

Alcohol abusers are also at higher risk for various kinds of cancer, particularly cancers that are related to the gastrointestinal tract (Lieber, Seitz, Garro, & Worner, 1979). Alcohol has been implicated in the following tumors: oral cavity, tongue, pharynx, larynx, esophagus, stomach, liver, lung, pancreas, colon, and rectum. Most smokers drink, and many drinkers smoke, and the smoking drinker is at particular risk, especially if he/she is poor (Elwood, Pearson, Skippen, & Jackson, 1984). One mechanism by which alcohol is thought to increase the incidence of cancer is by inhibiting the absorption of carcinogenic substances, thus permitting them to be distributed to sensitive organs (Swann, Coe, & Mace, 1984).

ALCOHOL AND THINKING

Alcohol has a disruptive effect on thinking, as nearly everyone knows and most have experienced. The disruption of memory is particularly noticeable and has been demonstrated both in laboratory and clinical settings. Some of the observed effects of alcohol on memory are controversial, but if the research is accurate, the findings should be of considerable concern.

Consumption of alcohol causes memory disruption during the time that alcohol is in the bloodstream. The amount of alcohol necessary to produce **acute alcohol amnesia** is not exceptionally high. Impairment is reliably reported at BALs as low as .08 (Carpenter & Ross, 1965; Hashtroudi, Parker, DeLisis, Wyatt, & Mutter, 1983). In fact, anyone who has consumed four or five drinks in a given drinking session has probably experienced memory impairment for some of the events that happened during that time (Hashtroudi & Parker, 1986). The primary effect seems to be on learning new material, such as what a drinking partner said during that time, while more familiar information, such as your partner's name, is unaffected (Birnbaum, Parker, Hartley, & Noble, 1978; Miller, Adesso, Fleming, Gino, & Lauerman, 1978).

Acute alcohol amnesia should not be confused with the **blackout** that occurs when a problem drinker has several drinks, appears normal to those around him, but has no subsequent memory of anything that has happened during the time he was drinking. Blackouts can occur for hours and even days. While the ability to recall the past and to remember well-practiced skills is not impaired, there is complete and total loss of recall for any events occurring during the blackout.

In the last few years psychologists have demonstrated that there are various types of memory that involve different parts of the brain and different neurotransmitters. No one is quite sure how alcohol affects each of these to form either the short- or long-lasting memory deficits just described but they are real.

Chronic alcohol abuse over a long period of time can result in a condition called **Wernicke-Korsakoff's syndrome,** which is the result both of alcohol abuse and thiamine deficiency (Institute of Medicine, 1987). Excessive alcohol use results in a thiamine (vitamin B_1) deficiency. Thiamine is essential for the normal functioning of the nervous system, and thiamine deficiency results in widespread central nervous system damage. This condition is referred to as Wernicke's encephalopathy. Treatment with thiamine, rest, and other medical treatment can often reverse Wernicke encephalopathy, and the symptoms are much more dramatic than with Korsakoff's psychosis.

Korsakoff's psychosis, or alcohol amnestic disorder (Diagnostic and Statistical Manual III, 1980), can occur together with or separate from Wernicke's disease. Korsakoff's psychosis is primarily a disorder of memory, with the major symptom being **anterograde amnesia,** or the inability to retain new information that has been learned since the onset of the disease. In other words, the person with Korsakoff's syndrome can remember facts that occurred or things learned earlier in life, but cannot remember for more than a few seconds or minutes anything that has occurred recently. The person often confabulates, or makes up facts, to cover the memory deficit and becomes angry when these facts are questioned.

In order to develop Korsakoff's syndrome, one has to drink heroic quantities of alcohol for years and ignore one's diet. A more important question is whether there is a continuum of alcohol-induced deficit. In other words, does a little drinking daily cause a little deficit and so on, culminating in Korsakoff's syndrome, or does one have to be an alcohol abuser to show cognitive deficits?

The available evidence is not clear, but what does exist suggests that there is real concern over the cognitive effects of social drinking (Parsons, 1986; Williams & Skinner, 1990). Moreover, there is evidence to suggest that the impairment seen does not require a lifetime of drinking in order to show up. Several researchers have found evidence that social drinkers scored worse on tests of cognitive functioning (Parker & Noble, 1977; MacVane, Butters, Montgomery & Farber, 1982; Hannon, Day, Butler, Larson, & Casey, 1983), and some have found evidence in social drinkers of brain damage that was partially reversed when the drinkers abstained (Cala, Jones, Burns, Davis, Stenhouse, & Mastaglia, 1983).

In a recent large-scale study of young social drinkers, there was little sign of impairment. However, even in these subjects, who were between ages eighteen and twenty-four, there was some indication that high quantity consumption might cause problems in the future (Bates & Tracy, 1990). This finding is consistent with most studies showing that occasional, but heavy, drinking is more consistently associated with impairment (for whatever reason) than is steadier, but lighter, drinking. The threshold seems to be close to five or more drinks on a given occasion. It should therefore be a matter of concern to everyone that young people are likely to drink infrequently (once a week or less), but fairly heavily when they do. The weekend party atmosphere typical of young adults is not conducive to either health or normal cognitive functioning.

A number of factors could explain these results without resorting to a direct effect of alcohol intake. For example, those with poorer cognitive functioning may drink more, or perhaps those who are under stress may not only drink more but perform more poorly on cognitive tasks. There may be a genetic link to both heavier drinking and poorer cognitive functioning. Finally, the result may be due to the fact that those who are regular social drinkers are likely to have consumed alcohol fairly recently, and the cognitive deficits may be the result of a temporary impairment (Parsons, 1986).

Although both the short term and the long term effects of alcohol abuse can be quite tragic, and although the supposed beneficial effects of moderate drinking may be overstated, it is important to note that all is not hopeless. The human body has a remarkable ability to repair itself and, given half a chance, it will do just that. Alcohol abusers who achieve abstinence and maintain it have no higher mortality rates than nonabusers. On the other hand, those that relapse have nearly five times the mortality rate of nonabusers (Bullock, Reed, & Grant, 1992).

ALCOHOL ABUSE AND ALCOHOLISM

The vast majority of drinkers have no problem with alcohol. It does not impair their functioning, nor are their lives shortened by it. Approximately 10 percent of all drinkers, however, develop serious problems related to alcohol use. They drink far more than their friends; it is estimated that 10 percent of drinkers drink 50 percent of the alcohol (NIAAA,1987), and that they suffer physically, socially, and personally from its use. This combination of events creates an enormous economic problem.

Before beginning this discussion of alcohol abuse, it is necessary to define the terminology that will be used. The words *alcoholic* and *alcoholism* are widely used, even by professionals, to describe those whose alcohol use results in serious psychological, physical, or social impairment. The terms, however, are imprecise and difficult to define. In addition, when the term alcoholism is used there is a tendency to think of the phrase "disease of alcoholism." So widespread has the phrase become that it may be surprising to find that the disease concept of alcoholism is one of the most hotly debated topics in the field of drug abuse.

Is Alcoholism a Disease?

All of the following prestigious organizations refer to alcoholism as a disease in their publications intended for the public: the American Medical Association, American Psychiatric Association, American Public Health Association, American Hospital Association, American Psychological Association, National Association of Social Workers, World Health Organization, American College of Physicians, the National Institute of Alcoholism and Alcohol Abuse, and the National Institute of Mental Health. In addition, in a 1982 poll, 79 percent of Americans said alcoholism was a disease that required medical treatment (Peele, 1984).

On the other hand, the cause of this "disease" remains a mystery and it does not fit the classic medical definition of a disease. None of the theories that you may have heard of (and perhaps assumed "proven") has stood up to investigation. No evidence exists that alcoholism is caused by allergies, hypoglycemia, vitamin deficiency, or metabolic disorders (Vaillant, 1985).

More recent explanations concern a possible genetic component: disorders of alcohol metabolism and differences in brain chemistry between alcohol abusers and the nonabusing population. None of these, however, really explains why some people abuse alcohol and deteriorate, some abuse alcohol for awhile and stop, some shift their abuse to other drugs, some exhibit the classic symptoms of alcoholism, and some drink heavily with no signs of social or health problems.

Some of the objections to the disease concept of alcoholism may be summarized as follows. First, alcohol abuse is under voluntary control: We do not choose to have a fever. Second, the idea that the disease of alcoholism leads to an uncontrollable desire to drink or an inability to stop once drinking starts, has never been adequately demonstrated. Third, drinking behavior represents a continuum from light through moderate to excessive. A disease, on the other hand, either exists or it doesn't. You don't get a little plague. Fourth, the disease concept of alcoholism plays down the important role played by such societal factors as socioeconomic status, role modeling, and availability of alcohol. Finally, diseases have physical treatments and cures. Alcoholism itself is not treated medically, although the physical consequences of heavy drinking are. As one of the most noted authorities in the field has said, in effect, that even if alcoholism is a medical disease, both its cause and treatment are social (Vaillant, 1988).

The concept of alcoholism as a disease has support from many powerful forces in our society. If alcoholism is a disease it can be treated by medical doctors in medical facilities, and health insurance will pay for much of it. If alcoholism is a disease that a small percentage of drinkers have but the majority don't, then the alcohol industry is justified in spending millions in advertisement to attract the sensible, "normal" drinker. If alcoholism is a disease then the millions of people suffering from it need not feel guilty over their inability to control their drinking.

If alcoholism is not a disease, then we are wasting billions of dollars a year on medical treatment of a nondisease. If alcoholism is not a disease, then anyone could become an alcohol abuser, and the alcohol industry would find it hard to justify encouraging anyone to drink. If alcoholism is not a disease then everything most problem drinkers have been taught is wrong, and even most alcohol abuse counselors would have to change their approach.

With so much invested in maintaining the disease concept of alcoholism, it is not difficult to see that anyone taking a different approach will be met with considerable opposition. Yet such approaches do exist and should be examined with an open mind. Alternatives to a strict disease approach have emphasized behavioral and cultural factors (Nathan, Marlatt, & Loberg, 1978; Peele, 1984). Recently, a model of alcohol dependence has been developed which emphasizes the role of cognition (Marlatt, 1987). In this model, emphasis is placed on what the drinker *thinks* alcohol is going to do and on the concept that alcohol has a two-phase effect; at low doses it is a stimulant (in the behavioral sense), and at high doses a depressant.

In an attempt to make diagnosis of alcohol problem drinking more quantifiable, the third edition of the Diagnostic and Statistical Manual (DSM) of the American Psychiatric Association (a publication that attempts to define mental disorders) avoids the use of the term "alcoholic" and, instead, makes a distinction between **alcohol abuse** and **alcohol dependence.** The DSM III describes objective criteria for these two labels which are relatively easy to apply. The criteria can be found in table 4.7.

The controversy over whether alcoholism is a disease will continue for many years in professional literature. What is important to remember on a practical, personal level is that if alcoholism is a disease and you have it, you will not be able to control your drinking and you have to stop drinking. If alcoholism is not a disease and you can't control your drinking for whatever reason, you have to stop drinking. The result, therefore, is the same regardless of the cause. Of course, by the same token, if you can control your drinking, you don't have a problem whether or not alcoholism is a disease.

Who Are the Problem Drinkers?

If 10 percent of the population drinks 50 percent of the alcohol, preventing alcohol abuse would seem to be a simple problem; find those 10 percent and help them. However, that 10 percent is not easy to spot. Alcohol abusers are black, white, and Oriental; young, old, and middle-aged; rich, poor, and in-between; male and female; highly educated and abysmally ignorant. In short, alcohol abusers are just like you and me. In fact, they may *be* you and me.

Table 4.7   DSM-III Criteria

Alcohol Abuse

A. Pattern of pathological alcohol use: need for daily use of alcohol for adequate functioning; inability to cut down or stop drinking; repeated efforts to control or reduce excess drinking; binges (remaining intoxicated throughout the day for at least 2 days); occasional consumption of a fifth of spirits; amnesic periods for events occurring while intoxicated (blackouts); continuation of drinking despite a serious alcohol-related physical disorder; drinking of nonbeverage alcohol
B. Impairment in social or occupation functioning due to alcohol use; e.g., violence while intoxicated, absence from work, loss of job, legal difficulties, arguments with family or friends because of excessive alcohol use
C. Duration of symptoms of at least one month

Alcohol Dependence

A. Either a pattern of pathological alcohol use (as above) or impairment in social or occupational functioning due to alcohol use (as above)
B. Either tolerance or withdrawal
Tolerance: need for markedly increased amounts of alcohol to achieve the desired effect or markedly diminished effect with regular use of the same amount
Withdrawal: development of alcohol withdrawal (e.g., morning "shakes" and malaise relieved by drinking) after cessation of or reduction in drinking

---

We do know that some people are more likely than others to become problem drinkers, but in every population there are those who do not drink, those who drink sensibly, and those who abuse alcohol.

Sociocultural Factors   Can you tell from your background whether you are likely to be at risk to be a problem drinker? The answer to this question is complex, with your physiology, your genetics, the culture in which you live, and your own experiences in life contributing to the answer. Generally speaking, however, a few factors emerge.

Sex Differences   Typically, women drink less than men and traditionally have had far fewer problems with drinking. Recently, however, there has been an increase in drinking problems in women between thirty-five and sixty-four (NIAAA, 1987). As we saw above, when women do drink to excess, they are more likely to suffer physical problems (Gallant, 1990; Schenker, 1990). There are also ethnic differences in problem drinking among women. Black women are less likely to drink than white women, although those who do are more likely to be alcohol abusers. Asian women, on the other hand, are the most likely to be complete abstainers and the least likely to have problems if they do drink.

Ethnic Differences   American Indians have high rates of alcohol abuse and alcohol-related problems. A common belief is that the metabolism of American Indians is somehow different than that of Caucasians, and this predisposes them to alcoholism. However, the preponderance of evidence suggests that there are *no* differences between Native Americans and other people regarding the physiology of alcohol (Lujan, 1992). Presumably, there are no genetic differences between various Indian tribes and yet the rate of alcoholism among them differs widely. A more likely explanation for the high rate of alcoholism among Indians is cultural.

A widespread belief exists that a physiological basis for low rates of alcohol abuse is seen in Asians and Asian-Americans. About 50 percent of Asians lack a type of enzyme that metabolizes acetaldehyde, the toxic byproduct of alcohol metabolism. When people lacking this, drink, acetaldehyde builds up rapidly, producing unpleasant symptoms such as rapid pulse, nausea, and skin flushing. These effects may serve as a powerful stimulus to remind the drinker that further alcohol intake will result in even more unpleasant symptoms.

Although many Asians do lack this enzyme and the rate of alcohol abuse is low, it is too simplistic to conclude a cause-and-effect relationship. First, many American Indians also flush and their rate of alcoholism is high. Second, use of alcohol and incidence of problem drinking varies widely within Asian populations, and this variation is not related to the presence or absence of the acetaldehyde molecule. Most important, however, is that large differences in alcohol abuse exist between men and women alcoholics in Asian populations, but there are no sex differences in enzyme availability. Other factors such as social or cultural influences are probably more important in explaining the low rate of alcohol abuse (Johnson & Nagoshi, 1990).

Hispanics or Latinos make up a substantial portion of our population; if the illegal alien population is included the figure may exceed twenty million. Hispanics show a higher than average rate of alcohol abuse and alcohol-related physical problems, even though a high percentage of Hispanic women do not drink. The percentage of women who do not drink is more than offset by a high rate of drinking by Hispanic men, with a corresponding high rate of mortality from cirrhosis of the liver. Furthermore, evidence suggests that the traditional social and cultural values among Hispanics, which serve to help reduce alcohol use in women, gradually break down with exposure to Anglo society, with the result that alcohol problems are more common among Hispanic women who have the greatest exposure to American society (Eden & Aguilar, 1989).

Complicating the issue of alcohol problems for Hispanics are cultural and historical factors. Since before the conquest by the Spanish, drinking alcoholic beverages in Mexico, and Central and South America was seen as being an important way of identifying with other members of the social group. In addition, the concept of *machismo,* better known in our society as the adjective *macho,* also contributes to the prevalence of drinking problems (Eden & Aguilar, 1989). It might be acceptable and even "macho" to drink a great deal. Other factors that might contribute to alcohol use among Hispanics is the high rate of unemployment, changing social values, and the conflict between the traditional Hispanic values of close family ties and the American emphasis on individual achievement.

Alcoholism is one of the most important health problems in the African-American community. Many believe that the problems with alcohol account for the lower life expectancy compared to whites (69.5 years as compared to 75.3 for whites) and for the higher rates of death due to homicide, liver problems, heart disease, and various cancers associated with heavy drinking (Brown & Tooley, 1989).

Given these problems it may be surprising that the rate of alcohol use is actually lower among African-Americans than among whites. African-American youth and women, in particular, use alcohol less than their white counterparts and even though the rate in adult males is similar, more African-Americans are abstainers. This discrepancy is probably due to several factors. Those who do use alcohol often become heavy drinkers or use other drugs, and those who develop health or drinking problems may not have the same access to health care as do whites (OSAP, 1990). Socioeconomic factors also play a role in that the lowest rates of alcohol use and abuse are seen in the highest socioeconomic groups.

Genetic Factors The fact that alcohol abuse runs in families has been observed for centuries. Caution is needed, however, in interpreting the cause of this relationship. Approximately 30 percent of alcohol abusers have parents who are also alcoholics; only 5 percent of nonalcoholics reported alcohol-abusing parents (Cotton, 1979). This question arises, however: Is the influence one of modeling or of genetics? A strong, logical, argument would be that growing up in a family where alcohol abuse is common would lead the children to engage in the same behaviors simply as a result of observation. At the same time, demonstration that genetics plays a role would go a long way in explaining why only some members of a given family develop alcohol problems.

Although the popular press and altogether too many professionals who should know better state that the genetic link to alcohol abuse has been proven, the actual evidence indicates that the relationship is far from simple. No one who reads the literature objectively could deny that for some at least there is a genetic component, but the genetic component, even in high-risk individuals, is only one factor among many.

The strongest evidence for the genetic link comes from adoption and twin studies and from research on animals bred for susceptibility to excessive alcohol intake. In general, adoption studies look at whether adopted children's drinking is more like that of their biological or adoptive parent. Twin studies look for *concordance,* or evidence, of greater similarities between identical and fraternal twins. Both sets of studies reveal a genetic component, but also indicate that the environment plays a role.

Adoption studies have suggested that there are two types of alcohol abuse that have a genetic component. The first type is called Type I, **milieu-limited.**

This rather imposing term applies to drinkers who had at least one parent of either sex who was a problem drinker and who grew up in an environment that was conducive to heavy drinking. The Type I alcoholic has fairly mild symptoms, is rarely involved in criminal activity, and has a condition that, while marked by a genetic predisposition, has to have an environmental releaser for it to occur. In adoption studies, the Type I individual growing up in a family where problem drinking did not occur was no more likely to be a problem drinker than the control population. However, exposure to a heavy drinking environment seems to bring out the latent tendencies. Type I alcohol abusers also seem to share certain personality characteristics as well. They are thought to avoid novelty and harmful situations, and to be concerned about the thoughts and feelings of others. Females as well as males seem to show Type I problem drinking (U. S. Department of Health and Human Services, 1990).

Type II, **male-limited,** is seen only in males and seems to be independent of environmental influence. Type II seems to be more severe and is associated with criminal activity. It has an early onset (in the teens or early twenties) as opposed to the later onset of Type I. Males born in families where there is Type I alcoholism are nine times as likely than the control population to become alcohol abusers, even when they are adopted into normal families. In contrast to Type Is, Type II alcoholics seem to be impulsive, uninhibited, and not to have close social contacts. Although daughters born to Type I alcoholic males do not show a higher than normal incidence of problem drinking, they do often have a history of vague physical conditions involving pain and discomfort (U. S. Department of Health and Human Services, 1990).

Animal studies have shown that it is possible to breed lines of rats and mice that show different susceptibilities to alcohol. Some strains of rats prefer alcohol and some don't, some strains of mice are more responsive to alcohol than others, and these tendencies can be transmitted genetically. By studying the differences between strains of mice and rats, researchers have identified neurochemical differences which may be related to alcohol-seeking behavior. Remember, however, that human behavior is far more complex than that of rats and mice, and it is too simple to expect that the complex factors that go into alcohol abuse in humans can be explained by these types of experiments.

Occasionally, a study comes along demonstrating a clear genetic link to some complex human behavior. Subsequent studies fail to confirm these findings, but the negative reports rarely get the same publicity as do the positive ones. In 1990, a report was published showing that 69 percent of alcoholics, as opposed to 20 percent of nonalcoholics, had a particular gene for a receptor for the neurotransmitter dopamine (Blum, Noble, Sheridan, et al, 1990). This study was exciting because it fit into several prevailing theories about the genetic transmission of alcoholism. Unfortunately, subsequent research has failed to support the initial report (Bolos, Dean, Lucas, et al, 1990).

Adult Children of Alcoholics

Until fairly recently, the effects of alcohol abuse on the family has focused on the *children* living at home. Research on links between alcohol abuse and fetal alcohol syndrome, attention deficit disorder, child abuse, truancy, delinquency, and the like has been widespread and there are numerous self-help groups such as Alateen to help children deal with an alcoholic parent. The children of alcoholics use the medical care system at far higher rates than children of nonalcoholics. They are more likely to be admitted to hospitals, stay longer, and cost the system more. Most of the excess cost is related to substance abuse and mental health problems (Children of Alcoholics Foundation, 1990).

The problems that the alcoholic parent causes can have an impact long after his/her children have become adults, however. First of all, children of alcoholics are at greater risk for alcoholism themselves. Perhaps just as important, however, they almost always have grown up in a severely disordered family. They may have experienced enormous inconsistencies in parental affection, sometimes been the victim of sexual and physical abuse, and often have suffered neglect. They have had to deal with the deception of the alcoholic parent and often feel excessive responsibility for maintaining the family. They have had to take care of the alcoholic parent and have experienced shame because of his or her behavior.

Some adult children of alcoholics have banded together and call themselves **ACOAs** (Adult Children Of Alcoholics). ACOAs try to help each other deal with the characteristics that many ACOAs seem to have in common; low self-esteem, excessive feelings of responsibility, difficulty in giving and receiving love, and depression. Many ACOAs also report feeling guilty when they assert themselves, say they find it difficult to deal with authority, and are terrified of abandonment.

One issue that seems central to the lives of many ACOAS is that of control. They seem to react to the stress of interpersonal and psychological conflicts by increasing their efforts to control events. Loss of control results in feelings of failure and self-deprecation. This desperate need to control is seen as a result of the alcoholic parent's own conflicts about control (Cermak & Rosenfeld, 1987).

ACOAs have joined in these self-help groups because they feel they have similar problems. However, it is also true that "if it's not broken, you don't fix it." Do these self-identified ACOAs represent all adults who grew up in an alcoholic family? In order to establish that ACOAs have specific problems associated with their upbringing it is necessary to show that their problems are different from those of people growing up in other dysfunctional or even normal families.

It should be reassuring that although data examining large groups of people who either did or did not come from alcoholic families are hard to come by, but what evidence does exist indicates that ACOAs may not inevitably be different from children in more stable families. Tweed and Ryff (1991) have shown that on most characteristics ACOAs are similar to other adults, although they do show more depression and anxiety. Even the depression and anxiety are within normal limits, however.

An alternative point of view suggests that some ACOAs, instead of developing problems actually are more resilient (Werner, 1985). Resilient children have, or develop, certain characteristics that seem to protect them from the disadvantages of growing up in an alcoholic family. Among these characteristics are intelligence, achievement orientation, a belief that they are responsible for their own behavior (called an internal locus of control), and a belief in their own capacity to help themselves. One very important common element in these resilient children was the absence of conflict in the first two years of the child's life (Werner, 1985).

No one would deny that living in a home with an alcoholic parent is difficult, but again you must remember that in human behavior in general and in alcohol and drug-related issues in particular, nothing is certain. Those who have problems in later life may have experienced more severe abuse or neglect, they may interpret it differently, or they may have been the particular target of the alcoholic parent. No one is predetermined to grow up troubled, normal, or resilient, and everyone responds in different ways to problems.

Further research has revealed that the link between the dopamine receptor and ''alcoholism'' may not be specific to alcohol abuse in that the same abnormality is frequently seen with conditions such as attention deficit disorder (see chapter 5) and autism, a serious neurological condition evidenced by bizarre behavior and a lack of ability to respond to others (Comings, Comings, & Muhleman, 1991). The best guess about the relationship of this specific gene to alcoholism is that it does not cause the condition, but makes it worse if it is present (Cloninger, 1991).

Numerous studies have attempted to show differences between the children of alcoholics and the children of nonalcoholics on a number of different measures, both physiological and psychological. This research is promising, but so confusing that no definite conclusions should be drawn. It seems that as soon as a difference is found, another study is reported which contradicts it. One area of research that looked promising in the past were studies of differences in brain wave activity between sons of alcoholics and sons of nonalcoholics. Much was made of these in the popular press. Unfortunately, more recent studies have tempered earlier enthusiasm (Newlin & Thomson, 1990).

What seems to emerge from this bewildering array of studies is that sons (but probably not daughters) of alcoholics show a different response to alcohol. They find it more rewarding because they are more sensitive to the positive effects of alcohol that predominate when BAL is rising and are less sensitive to the anxiety and other negative feelings that predominate when BAL is falling (Newlin & Thomson, 1990).

Even if research were to show a clear link between genetic factors and alcohol abuse, it does not completely explain why some become alcohol abusers and others don't. Remember that even if 30 percent of alcoholics had an alcoholic parent, 70 percent did not. Even if children of alcoholics have three to four times the risk of becoming alcoholic, most children of alcoholics do *not* go on to problem drinking. A genetic factor may predispose someone to become an alcohol abuser but it is not a sentence of death.

Furthermore, a real danger exists if you believe that the genetic component is more important than it is. If you believe you have the gene you may develop a sense of fatalism and feel you are doomed to alcoholism, and it may become a self-fulfilling prophecy. On the other hand, if you have no history of alcohol abuse in your family you may feel you are immune and conclude you do not have to be concerned. What *is* exciting about this research is the possibility of finding a marker, or a way of determining who might be at greater risk to become an alcoholic.

Patterns and Progress of Alcohol Problem Drinking

There are probably as many different patterns of problem drinking as there are problem drinkers, and the development of the problem can follow many paths. Some problem drinkers never drink alone; some do most of their drinking alone. Some drink only wine, some only beer, some only hard liquor, and some mix wine, beer, and hard liquor together and drink it. When desperate, alcoholics will resort to mouthwash, rubbing alcohol, hair tonic, after-shave lotion, and canned cooking fuel (Sterno). Some even become dependent on this "nonbeverage alcohol" (Egbert, Reed, Powell, Liskow, & Liese, 1985).

Various classification systems have been developed to describe the "typical" alcohol abuser and the "typical" pattern of alcohol abuse. While these have some value they are not as widely used as in the past, in part because they may give a false sense of confidence to those who do not fit the criteria, and in part because no classification system could ever describe every alcohol abuser.

Identifying Problem Drinkers

If alcohol abuse can take an almost infinite variety of forms, can you identify problem drinking in yourself or in others? Numerous tests exist to detect the presence of problem drinking, and most of them rely on self-report; the drinker is asked to answer questions about his own drinking honestly. Since most problem drinkers are experts at denial you might expect that these tests would be useless. Surprisingly, however, many of these tests are reasonably accurate in detecting problem drinking. One reason for this is that, despite their own highly developed denial mechanisms, problem drinkers simply do not realize how little other people drink in comparison.

One of the simplest, and quite accurate, measures of problem drinking is the **CAGE** questionnaire. CAGE is a **mnemonic,** or memory device, for remembering four questions: Have you ever tried to Cut back on your drinking? Are you Annoyed at criticisms about your drinking? Do you ever feel Guilty about drinking? Have you ever had an Eye-opener? Anyone who answers yes to any of these questions is likely to be an alcohol abuser, and this simple test is more accurate in detecting alcohol abusers than biochemical measures (American Journal of Medicine, 1987).

A more comprehensive test is the **Michigan Alcoholism Screening Test** (MAST) which is shown in table 4.8. Anyone scoring more than five on this test is presumed to have a drinking problem. Should you take the test? Maybe you should ask someone close to you to answer the questions for you as they think you *should* answer them.

These and other tests (a large number exist) are useful as screening devices for identifying alcohol abusers in a large population and may be helpful in breaking down the denial system of problem drinkers. However, they really aren't necessary. The simplest rule of thumb is "if you think you have a drinking problem, you do." Treatment of alcohol problem drinking is dealt with in detail in chapter 13.

SUMMARY

Alcohol is a potent drug that has been around since humans first evolved. Warnings about its abuse and praise to its effects can both be found in the earliest written records. The production of the many various types of alcoholic drinks is limited only by the ingenuity of its manufacturers, and alcohol even occurs naturally.

Table 4.8   The Michigan Alcoholism Screening Test (MAST) Questionnaire

Question:	Points
1. Do you feel you are a normal drinker?	2*
2. Have you ever awakened the morning after some drinking the night before and found that you could not remember a part of the evening before?	2
3. Does your wife, husband (or parents) ever worry or complain about your drinking?	1
4. Can you stop drinking without a struggle after one or two drinks?	2*
5. Do you ever feel bad about your drinking?	1
6. Do friends or relatives think you are a normal drinker?	2
7. Do you ever try to limit your drinking to certain times of the day or to certain places?	0
8. Are you always able to stop drinking when you want to?	2*
9. Have you ever attended a meeting of Alcoholics Anonymous (AA)?	5
10. Have you gotten into fights when drinking?	1
11. Has drinking ever created problems with you and your wife or husband?	2
12. Has your wife or husband (or other family member) ever gone to anyone for help about your drinking?	2
13. Have you ever lost friends or girlfriends or boyfriends because of drinking?	2
14. Have you ever gotten into trouble at work because of drinking?	2
15. Have you ever lost a job because of drinking?	2
16. Have you ever neglected your obligations, your family, or your work for two or more days in a row because you were drinking?	2
17. Do you ever drink before noon?	1
18. Have you ever been told you have liver trouble? Cirrhosis?	2
19. Have you ever had delirium tremens (DTs), severe shaking, heard voices or seen things that weren't there after heavy drinking?	5
20. Have you every gone to anyone for help about your drinking?	5
21. Have you ever been in a hospital because of drinking?	5
22. Have you ever been a patient in a psychiatric hospital or on a psychiatric ward of a general hospital where drinking was part of the problem?	2
23. Have you ever been seen at a psychiatric or mental health clinic, or gone to a doctor, social worker or clergyman for help with an emotional problem in which drinking played a part?	5
24. Have you ever been arrested even for a few hours because of drunk behavior?	2 (each arrest)
25. Have you ever been arrested for drunk driving?	2

Scoring: For each "yes" for all questions except 1, 4, and 8, give yourself the points indicated. For question 1, 4, and 8, (marked with an asterisk) give yourself the points indicated for a "no" answer.

How do you compare? In a study by Selzer (1971), 95% of the control group, 45% of those arrested for drunk driving, and only 2% of those hospitalized for alcoholism scored between 0–4 points. Based on this and other findings, a score of "5" or better is generally considered to indicate a person with a drinking problem.

Source: Selzer, 1971.

The physiology of the absorption, metabolism, and excretion of alcohol is well understood by science but subject to numerous misconceptions by the average person. Absorption can be affected by a number of factors including body weight, stomach contents, and sex, but metabolism is a constant. It may take twice as much alcohol to get a 200-pound male legally intoxicated as it does a 100-pound female, but both will require the same amount of time before they are sober.

Alcohol affects virtually every organ in the body, and alcohol abuse has particularly devastating effects on the liver and the brain. Sexual functioning is also negatively affected despite common belief. Alcohol abuse is a major medical and social concern but is surprisingly difficult to define. Genetic and cultural factors, learning, and physiology all play a role in alcohol abuse.

There is no "typical" alcohol abuser and no "typical" form of alcohol abuse. Even the widely accepted idea that alcoholism is a disease is disputed by many. Evidence exists to suggest that traditional beliefs concerning alcohol use and abuse have hindered understanding of the phenomenon and, more importantly, made it more difficult to help the alcohol abuser. Recent findings in the field of alcohol abuse have begun to change our understanding of alcohol abuse in ways that will ultimately help one of our most important health and social problems.

REFERENCES

Abel, E. (1984). *Fetal alcohol syndrome and fetal alcohol effects.* New York: Plenum Press.

Abel, E. (1985). *Psychoactive drugs and sex.* New York: Plenum Press.

Abel, E. (1987). *Alcohol wordlore and folklore.* Buffalo, NY: Prometheus Press.

Abel, E. & Sobel, R. (1991). A revised conservative estimate of the incidence of fetal alcohol syndrome and its economic impact. *Alcoholism: Clinical and Experimental Research 15,* 514–24.

Armor, D. J., Polich, J. M. & Stanbul, H. B. (1978). *Alcoholism and treatment.* New York: Wiley.

Ashley, M. J. (1985). Alcohol consumption, ischemic heart disease and cerebrovascular disease. *Journal of Studies on Alcohol, 46,* 869–87.

Bates, M., & Tracy, J. (1990). Cognitive functioning in young "social drinkers": Is there impairment to detect? *Journal of Abnormal Psychology, 99,* 242–49.

Birbaum, I. M., Parker, E. S., Hartley, J. T., & Noble, E. P. (1975). Alcohol and memory: Retrieval processes. *Journal of Learning and Verbal Behavior, 17,* 325–35.

Blum, K., Noble, E. P., Sheridan, P. J., et al (1990). Alleged association of human dopamine D_2 receptor gene in alcoholism. *Journal of the American Medical Association, 263,* 2055–59.

Bohman, M. (1978). Some genetic aspects of alcoholism and criminality. *Archives of General Psychiatry, 35,* 269–76.

Bolos, A., Dean, M., Lucas, T., Derge, S., Ramsberg, M., Brown, G., & Goldman, D. (1990). Population and pedigree studies reveal a lack of association between the dopamine D_2 receptor gene and alcoholism. *Journal of the American Medical Association, 264,* 3156–60.

Brown, R., & Tooley, J. (1989). Alcoholism in the black community. In G. W. Lawson and A. W. Lawson (Eds.), pp. 115–31. *Alcoholism and substance abuse in special populations.* Rockville, MD: Aspen Publishers.

Buchsbaum, M. S., Coursey, R. D., & Murphy, D. L. (1976). The biochemical high-risk paradigm: Behavioral and familial correlates of blood platelet monoamine oxidase activity. *Science, 194,* 339–41.

Bullock, K. D., Reed, R. J., & Grant, I. (1992). Reduced mortality in alcoholics who achieve long term abstinence. *Journal of the American Medical Association, 267,* 668–72.

Cala, L. A., Jones, B., Burns, P., Davis, R. E., Stenhouse, N., & Mastaglia, F. L. (1983). Results of computerized tomography, psychometric testing and dietary studies on social drinkers with an emphasis on recovery after abstinence. *Medical Journal of Australia, 26,* 64–69.

Carlen, P. L., Wilkinson, D. A., Wortsman, G., & Holgate, R. (1984). Partially reversible cerebral atrophy and functional improvement in recently abstinent alcoholics. *Canadian Journal of Neurological Science, 11,* 441–46.

Carpenter, J. A., & Ross, B. M. (1965). Effect of alcohol on short term memory. *Quarterly Journal of the Studies of Alcohol, 26,* 561–79.

Cermak, T. L., & Rosenfeld, A. A. (1987). Therapeutic considerations with adult children of alcoholics. In M. Bean-Bayog & B. Stimmel (Eds.), pp. 17–32. *Children of Alcoholics.* New York and London: Haworth Press.

Cloninger, C. R., Bohman, M., & Sigvardsson, S. (1981). Inheritance of alcohol abuse. *Archives of General Psychiatry, 38,* 861–68.

Cloninger, C. R. (1991). D_2 dopamine receptor gene is associated but not linked with alcoholism. *Journal of the American Medical Association, 266,* 1833–34.

Cohen, C., & Benjamin, M. (1991). Alcoholism and liver transplantation. *Journal of the American Medical Association, 265,* 1299—1301.

Cole-Harding, S., & Wilson, J. R. (1987). Ethanol metabolism in men and women. *Journal of Studies on Alcohol, 48,* 380–87.

Comings, D. E., Comings, B. G., Muhleman, D., et al, (1991). The dopamine D_2 receptor locus as a modifying gene in neuropsychiatric disorders. *Journal of the American Medical Association, 266,* 1793–1800.

Crowe, L., & George, W. (1989). Alcohol and human sexuality: Review and integration. *Psychological Bulletin, 105,* 374–86.

Diagnostic and statistical manual of mental disorders (1980), 3d ed. Washington, D.C.: American Psychiatric Association.

Dundes, A., & Payter, C. R. (1975). *Urban folklore from the paperwork empire.* Austin, TX: American Folklore Society.

Durand, D., & Carlen, P. L. (1984). Impairment of long term potentiation in rat hippocampus following ethanol treatment. *Brain Research, 308,* 325–32.

Eden, S. L., & Aguilar, R. J. (1989). The Hispanic chemically dependent client: Consideratons for diagnosis and treatment. In G. W. Lawson & A. W. Lawson (Eds.). *Alcoholism and substance abuse in special populations.* Rockville, MD: Aspen Publications.

Egbert, A. A., Reed, J. S., Powell, B. J., Liskow, B. I., & Liese, B. S. (1985). Alcoholics who drink mouthwash: The spectrum of nonbeverage alcohol use. *Journal of Studies on Alcohol, 46,* 473–80.

Ellinboe, J., & Varanelli, C. E. (1979). Ethanol inhibits testosterone biosynthesis by direct action on Leydig cells. *Research Communication in Chemistry, Pathology and Pharmacology, 24,* 87–102.

Elwood, J. M., Pearson, J. C. G., Skipper, D. H., & Jackson, S. M. (1984). Alcohol, smoking, social and occupational factors in the aetiology of cancer of the oral cavity, pharynx, and larynx. *International Journal of Cancer, 34,* 603–12.

Ernhardt, C., Morrow-Tlucak, Sokol, R., & Martin, S. (1991). Underreporting of alcohol use in pregnancy. *Alcoholism: Clinical and Experimental Research, 12,* 506–11.

Ettinger, P. O., Wu, C. F., & De La Cruz, C. (1978). Arrhythmias and the "holiday heart": Alcohol associated cardiac rhythm disorders. *American Heart Journal, 95,* 555–62.

Evans, R. W., Orians, C. E., Ascher, N. L. (1992). The potential supply of organ donors. *Journal of the American Medical Association, 267,* 239–46.

Farkas, G. M., & Rosen, R. C. (1976). Effect of alcohol on elicited male sexual response. *Journal of Studies on Alcohol, 37,* 265–72.

Forbes, J. C., & Duncan, G. M. (1951). The effect of acute alcohol intoxication in the adrenal glands of rats and guinea pigs. *Quarterly Journal of Studies of Alcohol, 12,* 355–59.

Frank, D., & Raicht, R. F. (1985). Alcohol in induced liver disease. *Alcohol, Clinical Experimental Research, 9,* 661-82.

Freund, G. (1985). Neuropathology of alcohol abuse. In R. E. Tarter and D. H. Van Thiel (Eds.), pp. 3–18. *Alcohol and the brain: Chronic effects.* New York: Plenum Press.

Gallaher, M. M., Fleming, D. W., Berger, L. R., & Sewell, C. M. (1992). Pedestrian and hypothermia deaths among Native Americans in New Mexico: between bar and home. *Journal of the American Medical Association, 267,* 1345–1348.

Gallant, D. (1990). The female alcohol abuser: Vulnerability to multiple organ damage. *Alcoholism, Clinical and Experimental Research, 14,* 260.

Goldstein, D. B. (1983). *Pharmacology of Alcohol.* New York and London: Oxford University Press.

Hafen, B., & Brog, M. (1983). *Alcohol.* St. Paul and New York: West Publishing.

Hannon, R., Butler, C. P., Day, C. L., Khar, S. A., Quitaarno, L. A., Butler, A. M., & Meredith, L. A. (1985). Alcohol use and cognitive function in men and women college students. In M. Galanter (Ed.), pp. 241–52. *Recent developments in alcoholism volume 3: High risk studies. Prostaglandins and leukotrienes, cardiovascular effects and cerebral functions in social drinkers.* New York: Plenum Press.

Hannon, R., Day C. L., Butler, A. M., Larson, A. J. & Casey, M. (1983). Alcohol consumption and cognitive functioning in college students. *Journal of Studies on Alcohol, 44,* 283–98.

Hashtroudi, S., & Parker, E. S. (1986). Acute alcohol amnesia: What is remembered and what is forgotten. *Research Advances in Alcohol and Drug Problems: Volume 9,* 179–207. New York: Plenum Press.

Hashtroudi, S., Parker, E. S., Dolisi, L. E., & Wyatt, R. T. (1983). On elaboration and alcohol. *Journal of Verbal Learning and Verbal Behavior, 22,* 164–73.

Hilton, M. E., & Clark, W. B. (1987). Changes in American drinking patterns and problems, 1967–1984. *Journal of Studies on Alcohol, 48,* 515–22.

Hunt, W. A. (1985). *Alcohol and biological membranes.* New York: Guilford Press.

Institute of Medicine (1987). *Report of a study: Causes and consequences of alcohol problems*. An agenda for research. Washington: National Academy Press.

Jellinek, E. M. (1952). Phases of alcohol addiction. *Quarterly Journal of the Studies of Alcohol, 13,* 673–84.

Jellinek, E. M. *The Disease Concept of Alcoholism*. New Haven: Hillhouse Press.

Johnson, R., & Nagoshi, C. (1990). Asians, Asian-Americans and alcohol. *Journal of Psychoactive Drugs, 22,* 52–65.

Johnston, D. E., Chiao, Y. B., & Gavaler, J. S. (1981). Inhibition of testosterone synthesis by ethanol and acetaldehyde. *Biochemical Pharmacology, 30,* 1827–31.

Jones, K. L., & Smith, D. W. (1973). Recognition of the fetal alcohol syndrome in early infancy. *Lancet, 2,* 999–1001.

Jones, K. L., Smith, D. W., Ulleland, C. N., & Streissguth, A. P. (1973). Patterns of malformation in offspring of chronic alcoholic mothers. *Lancet, 1,* 1267–71.

Jones, B., and Vega, A. (1972). Cognitive performance measured on the ascending and descending limb of the blood alcohol curve. *Psychopharmacologia,* 99–114.

Kakihawa, R., Noble, E. P., & Butte, J. C. (1968). Corticosterone response to ethanol in inbred strains of mice. *Nature, 218,* 360–61.

Keller, M., McCormick, M., & Efron, V. (1982). *A dictionary of words about alcohol*. New Brunswick, NJ: Rutgers Center of Alcohol Studies.

Klatsky, A. L., Friedman, G. D., & Siegelaub, B. (1973). Alcohol consumption and blood pressure: Kaiser permanente multiphase health examination data. *New England Journal of Medicine, 296,* 1194–1200.

Kress, Y. (1989). Special issue of adult children of alcoholics. In G. W. Lawson and A. W. Lawson (Eds.), pp. 139–64. *Alcoholism and substance abuse in special populations*. Rockville, MD: Aspen Publications.

Lee, H. (1963). *How dry we were: Prohibition revisited*. Englewood Cliffs, NJ: Prentice-Hall.

Leigh, B. (1990). The relationship of sex-related alcohol expectations to alcohol consumption and sexual behavior. *British Journal of Addiction, 85,* 919–28.

Leland, J. (1976). *Firewater myths: North American Indians drinking and alcohol addiction*. New Brunswick, NJ: Rutgers Center of Alcohol Studies.

Lieber, C., Seitz, H., Garro, A., & Worner, T. (1979). Alcohol-related diseases and carcinogenesis. *Cancer Research, 39,* 2863–86.

Lieber, C. (1991). Hepatic, metabolic, and toxic effects of ethanol: 1991 update. *Alcoholism: Clinical and Experimental Research, 15,* 573–92.

Lujan, C. (1992). Alcohol-related deaths of American Indians. *Journal of the American Medical Association, 267,* 1384.

McMullen, P. A., Saint Cyr, J. A., & Carlen, P. L. (1984). Morphological alterations in rat hippocamal pyramidal cell dendrites resulting from chronic ethanol consumption and withdrawal. *Journal of Comparative Neurology, 225,* 111–18.

Macvane, J., Butters, N., Montgomery, K., & Farber, J. (1982). Cognitive functioning in men social drinkers. *Journal of Studies on Alcohol, 43,* 81–95.

Maddox, R. (1979). The war against demon rum. *American History Illustrated*, June, pp. 113–17. Historical Times Incorporated.

Malatesta, V., Pollack, R., Wilbanks, W., & Adams, H. (1979). Alcohol effects on the orgasmic-ejaculatory response in human males. *Journal of Sex Research, 15,* 101–107.

Malatesta, V., Pollack, R., Crotty, T., & Peacock, L. (1982). Acute alcohol intoxication and the female orgasmic response. *Journal of Sex Research, 18,* 1–17.

Marlatt, G. A. (1987). Alcohol, expectancy and emotional states. *Alcohol Health and Research World, 11,* 10–13; 80–81.

Mayfield, D., McCleod, G., & Hall, P. (1974). The CAGE questionnaire: Validation of a new alcoholism instrument. *American Journal of Psychiatry, 131,* 1121–23.

Miller, M. E., Adesso, V. J., Fleming, J. P., Gino, F., & Lauerman, R. (1978). Effects of alcohol on storage and retrieval processes on heavy social drinkers. *Journal of Experimental Psychology: Human Learning and Memory, 4,* 245–55.

Moore, D. T. (1985). Animal models. *Alcohol Health and Research World, 9,* 10–12.

Moore, D. T. (1987). A class lesson in alcoholic malnutrition. *Alcohol Health and Research World, 2,* 58–59;73.

Moss, A., & Siegler, M. (1991). Should alcoholics compete equally for liver transplantation? *Journal of the American Medical Association, 265,* 1295–98.

Nanson, J., & Hiscock, M. (1990). Attention deficit in children exposed to alcohol prenatally. *Alcoholism: Clinical and Experimental Research, 14,* 656–61.

National Institute on Alcohol Abuse and Alcoholism (1980). *Facts about Alcohol and Alcoholism.* Washington, D.C.: U.S. Government Printing Office.

National Institute of Alcohol Abuse and Alcoholism (1983). *Fifth Special Report to the United States Congress.* Washington, D.C.: U. S. Government Printing Office.

National Institute of Alcohol Abuse and Alcoholism (1989). *Alcohol and Cognition.* Washington, D.C.: U.S. Government Printing Office.

Newlin, D., & Thomson, J. (1990). Alcohol challenges with the sons of alcoholics; A critical review and analysis. *Psychological Bulletin, 108,* 383–402.

Office of Substance Abuse Prevention (1990). *The fact is—Alcohol and other drug use is a special concern for African American families and communities.* Washington, D.C.: U.S. Government Printing Office.

Parker, E. S. & Noble, E. P. (1977). Alcohol consumption and cognitive function in social drinkers. *Journal of Studies on Alcohol, 38,* 1224–32.

Parson, O. A. (1986). Cognitive function in sober social drinkers: A review and critique. *Journal of Studies on Alcohol, 49,* 101–114.

Peele, S. (1991). The cultural context of psychological approaches to alcoholism: Can we control the effects of alcohol? *American Psychologist, 39,* 1337–49.

Pohorecky, L. (1990). Interaction of alcohol and stress at the cardiovascular level. *Alcohol, 7,* 537–46.

Pollock, V. E., Volavka, J., Goodwin, D. W., Sarnoff, A. M., Babrielli, W. F., Knop, J., & Schulsinger, F. (1983). The electroencephalogram after alcohol adminsitration in men at risk for alcoholism. *Archives of General Psychiatry, 40,* 857–61.

Porjesz, N., & Beylester, H. (1985). Human brain electrophysiology and alcoholism. In R. T. Tarter and D. H. Van Thiel (Eds.), pp. 139–82. *Alcohol and the brain: Chronic effects.* New York, Plenum Press.

Raymond, C. A. (1987). Birth defect linked with specific level of maternal alcohol use but abstinence is still the best policy. *Journal of the American Medical Association, 258,* 177–78.

Reed, T. D. (1985). Ethnic differences in alcohol use. *Social Biology, 32,* 195–209.

Regan, T. (1990). Alcohol and the cardiovascular system. *Journal of the American Medical Association, 264,* 377–81.

Roine, R., Gentry, T., Hernandez-Munoz, R., Baraona, E., Lieber, C. (1990). Aspirin increases blood-alcohol concentrations in humans after ingestion of ethanol. *Journal of the American Medical Association, 264,* 2406–08.

Ron, M. M. (1983). The alcoholic brain: CT scan and psychological findings. *Psychological Medicine Monograph Supplement 3,* Cambridge, England: Cambridge University Press.

Rorabaugh, W. (1979). *The alcoholic republic: An American tradition.* New York and Oxford: Oxford University Press.

Rubin, E., & Libon, C. S. (1968). Alcohol induced hepatitis injury in nonalcoholic volunteers. *New England Journal of Medicine, 278,* 869–76.

Schenker, S. (1990). The risk of alcohol intake in men and women. *New England Journal of Medicine, 322,* 127–29.

Schenker, S., Becker, H., & Randall, C. (1991). Fetal alcohol syndrome: Current status of pathogenesis. *Alcoholism: Clinical and Experimental Research, 14,* 635–47.

Schiavi (1990). Chronic alcoholism and human sexual dysfunction. *Journal of Sex and Marital Therapy, 16,* 23–31.

Searles, J. S. (1988). The role of genetics in the pathogenesis of alcoholism. *Journal of Abnormal Psychology, 97,* London: 153–67.

Seltman, C. (1980). *Wine in the ancient world.* London: Routledge and Kegan Paul.

Senior, J., & O'Rourke, S. (1988). *Alcoholic hepatitis: Facts you should know.* U. S. Department of Health and Human Services.

Serdulla, M., Williamson, D., Kendrick, J., Anda, A., & Byers, T. (1991). Trends in alcohol consumption by pregnant women. *Journal of American Medical Association, 265,* 876–79.

Seventh special report to the United States Congress on alcohol and health (1990). U. S. Department of Health and Human Services.

Shafer, A. (1990). Alcohol mortality: A review of prospective studies. *British Journal of Addiction, 85,* 837–47.

Siegel, R. K. (1988). *Intoxication,* New York: E. P. Dutton.

Simpson, G. (1990). Absorption time, alcoholic beverage type and breath analysis. *Journal of Analytic Toxicology, 14,* 393–95.

Sixth special report to the United States Congress on alcohol and health (1987). U. S. Department of Health and Human Services.

Smith, F. F., & Palmer, D. L. (1979). Alcoholism, infection and altered host defenses: A review of clinical and experimental observations. *Journal of Chronic Disease, 29,* 35–49.

Sokol, B. J., Miller, S. I., & Reed, C. (1980). Alcohol abuse during pregnancy: An epidemiologic study. *Alcoholism: Clinical and Experimental Research, 4,* 135–45.

Streissguth, A. P., Aase, J., Clarren, S., Randels, S., LaDue, R., & Smith, D. (1991). Fetal alcohol syndrome in adolescents and adults. *Journal of the American Medical Association, 265,* 1961–67.

Streissguth, A. P., Barr, H. M., & Martin, D. C. (1984). Alcohol exposure in utero and defects in children during the first four years of life. In R. Porter, M. O'Conner, and J. Whelan (Eds.), pp. 176–96. *Mechanisms of alcohol damage in utero.* CIBA Foundation Symposium, *105.* London: Pitman Publishers, LTD.

Streissguth, A. P., Barr, H., & Sampson, P. D. 1990. Moderate alcohol exposure: Effect on child IQ and learning problems at age 7 1/2 years. *Alcohol: Clinical and Experimental Research, 14,* 662–69.

Streissguth, A. P., Clarren, S. K., & Jones, K. L. (1984). A 10 year follow-up of the first children described as having fetal alcohol syndrome. *Alcoholism: Clinical and Experimental Research, 8,* 21.

Streissguth, A. P., Clarren, S. K., & Jones, K. L. (1985). Natural history of the fetal alcohol syndrome: A 10 year follow-up of eleven patients. *Lancet, 15,* 85–91.

Streissguth, A. P., & LaDue, R. A. (1985). Psychological and behavioral effects in children prenatally exposed to alcohol. *Alcohol Health and Research World, 10,* 6–12.

Suzdak, P., Glowa, J., Crawley, N., Schwartz, R., Skolnick, P., & Paul, W. (1963). A selective imidazobenzodiazepine antagonist of ethanol in the rat. *Science, 234,* 1243–47.

Swann, P. F., Coe, A. M., & Mace, R. (1984). Ethanol and diemethylnitrosamine and diethylnitrosamine metabolism and disposition in the rat. Possible relevance to the influence of ethanol on human cancer incidence. *Carcinogenesis, 5,* 1337–43.

Teichman, M., Richman, S., & Fine, E. (1987). Dose/duration effect: Relationship between alcohol consumption and cerebral atrophy: A psychological and neurological evaluation. *American Journal of Drug and Alcohol Abuse, 13,* 357–63.

Tweed, S. H., & Ryff, C. D. (1991). Adult children of alcoholics: Profiles of wellness amidst distress. *Journal of Studies on Alcohol, 52,* 133–41.

Vaillant, G. E. (1983). *The natural history of alcoholism.* Cambridge and London: Harvard University Press.

Van Thiel, D. H., Lipsitz, H. D., & Porter, L. E. (1981). Gastrointestinal and hepatic manifestations of chronic alcoholism. *Gastroenterology, 81,* 594–615.

Van Thiel, D. H. (1983). Ethanol: Its adverse effects upon the hypothalamic-pituitary gonadal axis. *Journal of Laboratory and Clinical Medicine, 101,* 21–33.

Van Thiel, D. H., Gavaler, S. S., Cobb, C. F., & Chiao, V. B. (1982). Effects of ethanol on the hypothalamic-pituitary gonadal axis. In A. L. Von Knorring, M. Bohman, L. Von Knorring, & L. Oreland (Eds.), pp. 57–58. (1985). Platelet MAO activity as a biological marker in subgroups of alcoholism. *Acta Psychiatrica Scandinavica, 72.*

Veenstra, J., Van de Pol, H., Schaafsma, G. (1990). Moderate alcohol consumption and platelet aggregation in healthy middle-aged men. *Alcohol, 7,* 547–49.

Werner, E. E. (1986). Resilient children of alcoholics: A longitudinal study from birth to age 18. *Journal of Studies on Alcohol, 47,* 34–40.

West, L. J., Maxwell, D. S., & Noble, E. P. (1985). Alcoholism. *Annals of Internal Medicine, 100,* 405–16.

Williams, C., & Skinner, A. (1990). The cognitive effect of alcohol abuse: A controlled study. *British Journal of Addiction, 85,* 911–17.

Williams, M. (1986). Alcohol and ethnic minorities. Native Americans—An update. *Alcohol Health and Research World, 11,* 5–6.

Wilsnack, S. C., Klasseen, A. D., & Wilsnack, R. W. (1984). Drinking and reproductive dysfunction among women in a 1981 national survey. *Alcoholism: Clinical and Experimental Research, 8,* 451–58.

Wilson, G., & Lawson, D. (1976a). Effects of alcohol on sexual arousal in women. *Journal of Abnormal Psychology, 85,* 476–89.

Wilson, G., & Lawson, D. (1976b). Expectancies, alcohol and sexual arousal in male social drinkers. *Journal of Abnormal Psychology, 85,* 587–94.

Woodside, M. (1988). Research on children of alcoholics: Past and future. *British Journal of Addiction, 83,* 785–92.

5

• • •

THE
STIMULANTS

• • •

OBJECTIVES

When you have finished studying this chapter you should:

1. Know why stimulants are so commonly used in our society.
2. Know the primary effects of the stimulants.
3. Be able to name the major stimulants.
4. Be able to name three xanthines.
5. Understand the effects of caffeine.
6. Be able to discuss the relative effects of the three xanthines.
7. Know how cocaine became popular.
8. Understand how the dependence potential of cocaine-containing substances relates to concentration of the drug in the substance.
9. Be able to discuss the dependence potential of cocaine.
10. Know how cocaine works as an anesthetic.
11. Understand the primary physiological effects of cocaine.
12. Understand how cocaine affects neurotransmitter systems.
13. Be able to discuss the similarities and differences between cocaine and amphetamine.
14. Know the medical uses for amphetamine in the past and the present.
15. Be able to discuss the effects of amphetamine on the body.
16. Know how Ecstasy and amphetamines are related.
17. Be able to discuss the physiological effects of MDMA.

KEY TERMS

adenosine
d and l amphetamine
aphrodisiac
attention deficit disorder
basuca
benzedrine
body packers
bronchodilators
caffeine
coca
crack
crank
dysphoria
Ecstasy
Elavil
euphoria
freebase
"ice"
kindling
lethal dose
look-alike drugs
MDA
MDMA
methamphetamine
mules
narcolepsy
Quetzalcoatl
septum
speed
stereotypy
tachycardia
theobromine
theophylline
Triavil
uppers
xanthine

S timulants are the most widely used drugs in our society. Use begins in early childhood and continues through old age. Multiple doses are taken daily by the vast majority of the population, with little thought of the consequences. The stimulants are not only widely used, but they are also promoted through all forms of advertising and are an integral part of our culture.

What is being described here, of course, are legal drugs such as caffeine and nicotine that usually are not even considered drugs. Other stimulants such as amphetamine and cocaine, are illegal, and the penalty for possession of them is a felony; yet caffeine and cocaine are both stimulants. Why is one considered harmless and the other a major menace? What, in fact, is a stimulant? How do they act? Are they addictive? Why do we take them? In this chapter we will explore these and other questions, the answers to which will be surprisingly complex.

WHAT DO STIMULANTS DO?

The primary effect of all the stimulants is on the arousal system (see chapter 3). Stimulants operate at all levels of the central nervous system to increase alertness, decrease appetite, relieve fatigue, and, in general, make the user feel better. No wonder they are called "uppers."

The sheer number of individual stimulant drugs is astounding—reflecting, perhaps, on the need of our society for something to help "keep you going." Most of the stimulants can be divided into three major groups: the xanthines, including the active ingredients in coffee, tea and chocolate; cocaine and its derivatives; and amphetamine and its structural analogues. A fourth, nicotine, is so important that it is dealt with separately in chapter 7.

THE MAJOR STIMULANTS

Does it seem odd to lump coffee and tea together with cocaine and amphetamine? It shouldn't, for as we shall see they share many properties. In fact, these drugs have been used interchangeably in various cultures for centuries.

The Xanthines

While the term **xanthine** may not be familiar, xanthine-containing beverages enjoy worldwide popularity. From guaraná in Brazil and máte in other parts of South America to tea in England, from chocolate among the Aztecs to coffee throughout the world, the xanthines are widely enjoyed. Furthermore, an examination of the history of these stimulants reveals that they have long been recognized as potent drugs, not just as the mild social beverages they are considered to be in the twentieth century.

The most important xanthines are caffeine, theophylline, and theobromine. These are the active compounds in coffee, tea, and chocolate, respectively. They are similar in their chemical structures and have similar

These beverages from around the world are usually drunk hot.

physiological effects. Each, however, is different in some respects. To further complicate the issue, caffeine is found in preparations of both tea and chocolate as well as in coffee. To avoid confusion in our discussion of the xanthines, we will refer to them by their more common names.

Coffee

According to legend, the first use of what we now call coffee was the result of an order by none other than Mohammed, the founder of the Moslem religion. Somehow he is supposed to have found out that a goatherder named Kaldi had told his imam, or priest, that his goats had stayed awake jumping about all night after eating the berries of a particular plant. The imam and Kaldi are supposed to have made a drink out of the berries and danced around with Kaldi's goats. Mohammed then is supposed to have told the imam to give the drink to the other priests to help them stay awake during their long religious vigils.

Coffee use spread throughout the world and became extremely popular in England, France, and Germany. Bach wrote a cantata to its joys, Voltaire is said to have drunk forty cups a day of a combination of coffee and chocolate, and even in the twentieth century popular songs are still being written that extol its virtues.

We drink far less coffee in the United States than formerly. In the table below you can see the trend of coffee use over the last twenty-five years. Does this change mean that we are consuming less caffeine? Not necessarily, because the consumption of soft drinks has skyrocketed in that same time.

Note that soft drink use has more than doubled while **coffee** consumption is down to 68 percent in the last twenty-five years. Assuming that 80 percent of soft drinks contain caffeine and the average caffeine content is 50 mg and that the average five-ounce cup of coffee contains 100 mg, per capita yearly

Table 5.1 Consumption per person (in gallons)

	1966	1968	1970	1972	1974	1976	1978	1980	1982	1984	1986
Soft Drinks	19.1	21.4	22.7	25.3	26.4	28.6	32.1	34.2	35.6	38.8	42.1
Coffee	37.4	37.0	35.7	35.2	33.8	29.4	27.0	27.4	26.6	26.4	25.8
Tea	4.0	4.7	5.2	6.0	6.1	7.4	7.7	7.3	7.5	7.2	7.3

	1988	1990
Soft Drinks	46.0	47.5
Coffee	25.4	25.2
Tea	7.4	7.2

Source: *Beverage Industry*, 1991

consumption of caffeine has decreased from 478 grams to about 341 grams (about 10 ounces) of pure caffeine!

Soft Drinks

The soft drink industry has been a growth industry in the United States for many years. Almost everyone drinks some kind of soft drink, and the choices are numerous. One thing that most have in common is caffeine. While most of us would hesitate before offering children a cup of coffee, we think nothing of giving them a Pepsi or a Coke.

Advertisers recently seem to have discovered what pharmacologists have known all along: caffeine is a drug, and they have directed their campaigns accordingly. Combined with an emphasis on fitness and weight consciousness that has led to the artificial sweetener, soft drink companies now offer us a bewildering array of possibilities. You can drink old Coke, new Coke, cherry Coke, Coke with and without sugar, Coke with and without caffeine, and every combination of these; you can drink Seven-Up, Pepsi in all its forms, as well as several other cola drinks. There is even Jolt, with its advertising slogan, "All of the sugar and twice the caffeine."

About 5 percent of the caffeine in the "cola" drinks comes from the leaf of the cola plant; the rest of the caffeine in these drinks and all of the caffeine in the others must be added. Where does it come from? What do you think they do with all the caffeine left over when they decaffeinate coffee?

In table 5.4 you can find the caffeine content of various popular beverages. Examine these amounts in light of the fact that toxic effects of caffeine have been seen with as little as one gram of the drug (Rall, 1980), and fatalities have been reported when three grams have been ingested, although five grams is the generally accepted lethal dose. The toxic effects of caffeine include insomnia, headaches, diarrhea, frequent urination, mood swings, and depression. Since some heavy coffee drinkers consume six or more cups of coffee a day, one wonders how often caffeine toxicity goes unrecognized.

A selection of stimulant beverages that are most often drunk cold. The Russian version of Pepsi is third from the right.

Tea

The legend surrounding the origin of tea, like that of coffee, recognizes its stimulant properties and has a religious basis. Daruma, the founder of Buddhism, is supposed to have fallen asleep meditating one day. Out of shame he cut off his eyelids and where they fell, the tea plant grew. Whatever its origin, the blended leaves, buds, and flowers of Camelia sinensis (the botanical name for tea) helped to alter the path of history.

In the twentieth century, it is difficult to imagine the political and economic impact that tea had on Europe in the seventeenth and eighteenth centuries. Over thirty million pounds were consumed in England alone by 1800 (Hobhouse, 1986). Tea also played a pivotal role in our American Revolution. The fact that we are a nation of coffee drinkers can be traced in large part to the economic importance of tea in colonial America.

Why was tea such an important commodity? We take indoor plumbing, safe drinking water, and modern medicine for granted, yet these were unknown in most parts of the world for most of recorded history. Until the introduction of tea, coffee, and chocolate into Europe in the 1650s, virtually the only safe beverages were those containing enough alcohol to kill most harmful bacteria. Most people, therefore, drank alcoholic beverages morning, noon, and night. Imagine the impact of beverages that used boiled water (making them safe to drink), with a distinctive taste and stimulant effects. No wonder they changed the course of history (Hobhouse, 1986).

In some ways, tea is a more potent drug than coffee, and some brands of tea contain more caffeine than some types of coffee, as shown in table 5.4.

● in depth ● ●

Coffee, Tea, and the American Revolution

The American colonists were an independent lot who paid little attention to the edicts of the British crown. In order to establish some control over the colonies, King George III declared that the East Indian Company would have a monopoly over the legal tea trade and that only merchants loyal to the crown would be permitted to purchase the drug. Furthermore, a tax of three pence per pound was to be levied. The tax was ordered merely to demonstrate the right of the British government to tax the colonies.

The New England colonies, especially, were deeply divided over the new rules. Some switched to drinking coffee to show their defiance of the king.

Others were Loyalists who didn't mind paying what was a very small tax. Everything reached a head on 16 December 1773, when a group of colonists disguised as Mohawk Indians threw the entire cargo of three East India ships into the Boston Harbor. Similar ''tea parties'' were held in New York, Philadelphia, Annapolis, Savannah, and Charleston. The British retaliated by closing the port of Boston. The Declaration of Independence was written and signed shortly thereafter. Anyone who drank tea, then, was probably a Loyalist. Real Americans drank coffee.

Theophylline, the other xanthine found in tea, is medically used as a treatment for asthma. As a **bronchodilator,** it is the primary ingredient in more than sixty prescription drugs. It dilates blood vessels and speeds up the heart rate. In the summer of 1988, however, the Food and Drug Administration removed theophylline from the list of approved over-the-counter (OTC) drugs, because they could find no evidence that it was effective at the dosage levels found in OTC products. It is still available in higher doses as a prescription drug.

Theophylline is even more toxic than caffeine. According to the Drug Abuse Warning Network report for 1986, reports of theophylline overdose were twice as frequent as caffeine overdose. There were more deaths attributed to caffeine overdose than to theophylline overdose, but you should remember caffeine use, from coffee to over-the-counter stimulants, is far more common than use of theophylline. The amount of theophylline required to cause death is not likely to be approached by any normal tea drinker, but deaths, accidental and otherwise, have occurred.

Chocolate

Perhaps no beverage seems as innocuous as a cup of hot chocolate. Chocolate bars, chocolate-covered raisins, and a box of chocolates bring back memories of our childhood. Nevertheless, chocolate was considered a sacred drink by the Aztecs, and only the greatest noblemen were permitted to drink it.

The legend associated with chocolate is that Quetzacoatl, the man-god of the Aztecs, lived with the children of the sun god in paradise. He returned with **cacao** seeds, which he cultivated in his garden. He ate the seeds and fermented the pulp of the fruit, which supposedly inspired him to gather disciples and teach them astronomy, agriculture, and medicine (Ott, 1985).

Montezuma, the Aztec ruler at the time of the Spanish conquest, reportedly drank fifty goblets of what we call chocolate a day out of golden cups, which he then gave to the poor after one use. The Spanish conquistadors were astonished to learn that the chocolate bean was the money of the Aztecs. The gold they had in abundance was not used for currency. Instead, duty and tribute were paid in cacahuatl beans.

The Spanish did not readily take to chocolate drinking, as the beverage the Aztecs drank was bitter and flavored with hot chile peppers. It also was reported to have had a froth, or scum, on top as a result of being stirred rapidly with a whisk. It was probably also quite thick, and consequently not at all like the hot chocolate we know (Ott, 1985).

The conquistadors apparently believed that chocolate was an aphrodisiac and, according to one source, there was concern that consumption of chocolate by priests would inflame their passion and so should be considered a violation of their triple vows of poverty, chastity, and obedience (Ott, 1985). As you read in chapter 3, even though they are useless, aphrodisiacs have a history that goes back to antiquity. You may laugh at the idea of chocolate as an aphrodisiac, but what about the tradition of giving chocolates on Valentine's Day?

The active ingredient in chocolate is **theobromine,** although chocolate contains small amounts of caffeine as well. Theobromine is a xanthine like theophylline and caffeine, although it is far less potent. Compared to caffeine, theobromine is a weak central nervous system stimulant. For example, it does not affect sleep latency. Also unlike theophylline and caffeine, theobromine has no current medical use, although it is a diuretic and, like the other xanthines, it does increase heart rate (Dorfman & Jarvik, 1970).

Pharmacology and Physiology of the Xanthines

The xanthines are a class of drugs having several physiological effects. They are central nervous stimulants, although theobromine is far less active in this regard than caffeine or theophylline. They stimulate the respiratory centers in the medulla (see chapter 3) and induce nausea and vomiting at high doses. In the cardiovascular system they increase heart rate, dilate peripheral blood vessels, and constrict blood vessels in the brain. In addition, they relax smooth muscles, especially in the bronchial tubes and produce increased urination. Minor effects include an increase in stomach acid secretion and an increase in the basal metabolic rate (Goodman & Gilman, 1980).

The three members of the class—caffeine, theophylline, and theobromine—vary in the extent to which they produce the above effects. However,

Table 5.2 The Relative Strengths of the Various Xanthines	
Physiological Effect	**Order of Potency**
Increase in metabolic rate	Caffeine (others ineffective)
Bronchodilation	Theophylline (others ineffective)
Diuretic action	Theophylline most effective, followed by theobromine and caffeine
Cardiac muscle stimulant	Theophylline most effective, followed by theobromine and caffeine
Muscle capacity for work	Caffeine is most effective followed by theophylline and theobromine
Respiratory stimulant	Caffeine is most effective, followed by theophylline and theobromine
CNS stimulant	Caffeine is equal to theophylline, both are more potent than theobromine

all show cross-tolerance, meaning that a person habituated to one of these drugs will be habituated to the others. The relative effectiveness of the three xanthines is shown in table 5.2.

Absorption of the xanthines by the oral route is rapid, with peak action occurring about two hours after ingestion for theophylline and forty-five minutes for caffeine. The half life, or time required for excretion of one half of a dose of xanthine, varies from three-and-a-half hours for caffeine to eight or nine hours for theophylline. The primary route of metabolism is the liver, and damage to the liver can substantially increase the half life of the xanthines. Since it is the most commonly used xanthine and the one which has been most carefully studied, the discussion which follows is limited to caffeine.

Caffeine Toxicity

Caffeine is not a harmless drug. As you read on page 160, the lethal dose of caffeine is about 5 grams if taken orally. Since a cup of coffee contains 75–125 milligrams of caffeine, you would have to drink at least forty cups of coffee very quickly to reach that amount. Fatal doses have been consumed, however, when a large quantity of ''look-alike'' capsules were ingested (Garriott, Simmons, Poklis, & Mackell, 1985). These pills are designed to resemble amphetamine tablets and capsules but contain only caffeine. They are sold to unsuspecting users as ''black beauties'' or other street names for amphetamine. In at least one case, a fatality occurred when the seller swallowed the pills to avoid arrest.

Far more common and usually unrecognized is **caffeinism**—a toxic reaction to caffeine. The most easily recognized symptom of caffeinism is anxiety. Approximately 10–20 percent of caffeine users develop symptoms of anxiety and this condition is most common in those who consume more than 500 mg a day. Depression is another symptom linked to caffeine use.

Although the evidence is far from clear, those suffering from depression seem to be heavier users of caffeine than those who are not depressed.

Sleep disturbance is so commonly known to be an effect of caffeine that many people take it for just that purpose. Most people believe that caffeine before bedtime will keep them awake. This belief has been demonstrated in laboratory studies. Furthermore, caffeine seems to disturb the deeper stages of sleep, which may contribute to both depression and increased use of caffeine the next day. Other, rarer, conditions that may be linked to caffeinism include diarrhea, rapid heart beat, and even delusions and delirium (Greden, 1989).

Tolerance and Dependence

Common sense tells us that tolerance occurs with caffeine; isn't that why we restrict coffee drinking in children while we as adults consume large quantities of caffeine? Tolerance to many of the effects of caffeine has been demonstrated and caffeinism is most likely to be seen in occasional users.

Dependence also occurs with caffeine and withdrawal symptoms are seen when caffeine use is abruptly stopped. Headache and fatigue are the commonest symptoms, but anxiety, diarrhea, irritability, vomiting, and muscle pain have also been reported (Griffiths & Woodson, 1988). Further evidence for dependence comes from the fact that its severity depends on the amount of caffeine normally consumed, the observation that withdrawal is relieved by administration of caffeine, and caffeine is more effective than other drugs in reducing the symptoms (Griffiths & Woodson, 1989). We saw in chapter 2 that tolerance and dependence were the classic signs of addiction, so it is not unreasonable to state that caffeine can be addicting.

The amount of caffeine required to produce tolerance and dependence is a matter of debate, with estimates ranging from as little as 100 to as much as 1,000 milligrams a day. The consensus is probably in the vicinity of 350–500 milligrams a day over a period of months or longer. Since caffeine is found in so many different substances, 500 milligrams a day is not a difficult amount to reach. Table 5.3 is a questionnaire to help you determine your own caffeine consumption. Could you be on the path to being a caffeine addict or are you already there? To give you a frame of reference, Johnson-Greene, Fatis, Sonnek, and Shawchuck (1988) found that about 10 percent of the college students in their survey used more than 500 mg of caffeine a day.

Since headache is one of the symptoms of caffeine withdrawal, does it seem curious that many over-the-counter medications sold for headache relief contain substantial amounts of caffeine? If you have a caffeine withdrawal headache are you actually making your dependence worse by taking these pills? In chapter 11 you will see that many patent medicines of the nineteenth century contained morphine. When people took enough of these medicines they became dependent and when they stopped they experienced withdrawal. It was common to interpret these withdrawal symptoms as an illness that could be relieved by more of the same patent medicine. Have things really changed all that much?

Table 5.3   Caffeine Consumption Questionnaire

Estimate your intake of caffeine by filling in the appropriate blanks. Multiply the total number of servings/tablets by the caffeine content for each row and then add the column on the right. Divide by seven to get your daily average intake of caffeine.

	Morning 6–12 noon	Afternoon 12 noon–6 PM	Evening 6 PM–2 AM	Night 2 AM–6 AM	Total
Coffee 5 oz servings (week)	_____	_____	_____	_____	_____
Regular Brewed					
Percolated (110 mg)	_____	_____	_____	_____	_____
Drip brewed (150 mg)	_____	_____	_____	_____	_____
Regular instant (65 mg)	_____	_____	_____	_____	_____
Decaffeinated					
Brewed (4.5 mg)	_____	_____	_____	_____	_____
Instant (2.0 mg)	_____	_____	_____	_____	_____
Tea (45 mg) 5 oz servings (week)	_____	_____	_____	_____	_____
Cocoa (13 mg) 5 oz servings (week)	_____	_____	_____	_____	_____
Chocolate (6 mg) 5 oz servings (week)	_____	_____	_____	_____	_____
Soft drinks 12 oz servings (week)					
Coca-Cola (42 mg)	_____	_____	_____	_____	_____
Dr. Pepper (61 mg)	_____	_____	_____	_____	_____
Mountain Dew (49 mg)	_____	_____	_____	_____	_____
Mr. Pibb (57 mg)	_____	_____	_____	_____	_____
Tab (45 mg)	_____	_____	_____	_____	_____
Pepsi Cola (35 mg)	_____	_____	_____	_____	_____
Diet Pepsi (34 mg)	_____	_____	_____	_____	_____
RC Cola (36 mg)	_____	_____	_____	_____	_____
Mello Yello (32 mg)	_____	_____	_____	_____	_____
Jolt (75 mg)	_____	_____	_____	_____	_____
Over-the-Counter Drugs Tablets per week					
Vivarin (200 mg)	_____	_____	_____	_____	_____
NoDoz (100 mg)	_____	_____	_____	_____	_____
Excedrin (65 mg)	_____	_____	_____	_____	_____
Vanquish (33 mg)	_____	_____	_____	_____	_____
Anacin (32 mg)	_____	_____	_____	_____	_____
Dristan (16.2 mg)	_____	_____	_____	_____	_____
Dexatrim (200 mg)	_____	_____	_____	_____	_____

Grand total of caffeine in mgs/7 = Caffeine intake/day
Not all beverages or pills have been listed. Estimate your intake and their caffeine content from this table.

Set, the term discussed in chapter 2, also plays a role in caffeine use. Several studies have shown that the expectation of taking caffeine can be sufficient to produce many of the symptoms of caffeine use. One study found that those who thought they were getting caffeine (in fact they received a cellulose filled capsule) thought they were more alert, had less of a headache,

Table 5.4 Caffeine Content

Prescription Drugs	Milligrams Caffeine
Cafergot (for migraine headache)	100
Fiorinal (for tension headache)	40
Soma Compound (pain relief, muscle relaxant)	32
Darvon Compound (pain relief)	32.4

Nonprescription Drugs

Weight-Control Aids	
Codexin	
Dex-A-Diet II	200
Dexatrim, Dexatrim Extra Strength	200
Dietac capsules	200
Maximum Strength Appedrine	100
Prolamine	140
Alertness Tablets	
Nodoz	100
Vivarin	200
Analgesic/Pain Relief	
Anacin, Maximum Strength Anacin	32
Excedrin	65
Midol	32.4
Vanquish	33
Diuretics	
Aqua-Ban	100
Maximum Strength Aqua-Ban Plus	200
Permathene H2 Off	200
Cold/Allergy Remedies	
Coryban-D capsules	30
Triaminicin tablets	30
Dristan Decongestant tablets and Dristan A-F decongestant tablets	16.2
Duradyne-Forte	30

Soft Drinks

Brand	Milligrams Caffeine (12 oz. serving)
Sugar-Free Mr. PIBB	58.8
Mountain Dew	54.0
Mello Yello	52.8
TAB	46.8
Coca-Cola	45.6
Diet Coke	45.6
Shasta Cola	44.4
Shasta Cherry Cola	44.4
Shasta Diet Cola	44.4
Mr. PIBB	40.8
Dr. Pepper	39.6
Sugar-Free Dr. Pepper	39.6
Big Red	38.4

Continued on next page

Table 5.4—*Continued*	
Sugar-Free Big Red	38.4
Pepsi-Cola	38.4
Aspen	36.0
Diet Pepsi	36.0
Pepsi Light	36.0
RC Cola	36.0
Diet Rite	36.0
Kick	31.2
Canada Dry Jamaica Cola	30.0
Canada Dry Diet Cola	1.2

Beverages and Foods

Item	Milligrams Caffeine	
	Average	**Range**
Coffee (5-oz. cup)		
Brewed, drip method	115	60–180
Brewed, percolator	80	40–170
Instant	65	30–120
Decaffeinated, brewed	3	2–5
Decaffeinated, instant	2	1–5
Tea (5-oz. cup)		
Brewed, major U.S. brands	40	20–90
Brewed, imported brands	60	25–110
Instant	30	25–50
Iced (12-oz. glass)	70	67–76
Cocoa beverage (5-oz. cup)	4	2–20
Chocolate milk beverage (8 oz.)	5	2–7
Milk chocolate (1 oz.)	6	1–15
Dark chocolate, semi-sweet (1 oz.)	20	5–35
Baker's chocolate (1 oz.)	26	26
Chocolate-flavored syrup (1 oz.)	4	4

Source: FDA's National Center from Drugs and Biologics; FDA, Food Additive Chemistry Evaluation Branch, based on evaluations of existing literature on caffeine levels.

and could think better (Christensen, White, Krietsch, & Steele, 1990). On the other hand, some subjects who thought they were drinking regular coffee and got a cup of decaf, showed withdrawal symptoms, an outcome which showed evidence of physiological addiction withdrawal symptoms unaffected by set.

Assuming that caffeine does produce tolerance and dependence, does it matter? Can prolonged consumption of caffeine cause health problems? What do we caffeine addicts (the author estimates his use at about 700 mg a day) have to worry about? In other words, how safe is caffeine?

How Safe Is Caffeine?   You have probably read the studies in the popular press which appear to link caffeine to various medical conditions. These studies are difficult to evaluate, however, for many reasons. Caffeine use is so widespread that it is difficult to find a control group of subjects who do not use caffeine and yet are similar in other ways to the rest of society. Furthermore, caffeine use has been linked to alcohol use and cigarette smoking (Soeken & Bausell, 1989). Caffeine use seems to be part of a pattern of drug use and other life-style behaviors that may interact in a complicated way.

Taking into consideration many different factors, the overall news is good. There is little evidence that moderate amounts of coffee are harmful to a healthy adult. That statement is not the same thing as saying caffeine is harmless, because high doses can present problems for anyone, and caffeine should be avoided by some people.

Caffeine and Heart Disease. Given that caffeine is a central nervous stimulant that can increase heart rate and blood pressure and given its wide use in many forms, it should not be surprising that many researchers have suggested a link between caffeine and cardiovascular problems. Most of these studies are flawed for various reasons. Carefully controlled studies indicate that at moderate levels, at least, caffeine seems not to increase the risk of heart disease.

In a longitudinal study of more than 50,000 men, for example, even consumption of large amounts of caffeine (four or more cups a day) had no significant relationship to cardiovascular problems. Interestingly, consumption of high doses of decaffeinated coffee *was* associated with slightly higher risk of disease. The increased risk was small but significant (Grobbee, Rimm, Gionvanucci, et al, 1990).

Many doctors routinely advise patients with irregular heart beat (cardiac arrhythmia) to abstain from coffee. In a recent laboratory study, however, no relationship was seen between caffeine consumption and arrhythmia even in patients with a history of this condition (Chelsky, Cutler, Griffith, et al, 1990). Of course, these two studies do not mean that caffeine is completely harmless. The first study looked at health care professionals, all of whom were male and between the ages of forty and seventy-five. In the second study, the effect of caffeine was measured by causing arrhythmia in a laboratory setting. Whether these data can be applied to *everyone* in every setting is an open question.

Virtually everyone is aware of cholesterol and many people are concerned about their cholesterol level. Although the relationship between cholesterol level and heart disease is complex, high cholesterol levels do increase the risk of heart disease. Therefore, you should be aware that at least one study has found that subjects who drank approximately five cups of coffee showed significant increases in cholesterol levels (both low and high density) compared to those who drank decaffinated coffee, no coffee, or two cups a day (Fried, Levine, Kwiterovich, Diamond, Wilder, et al., 1992). This was a short-term controlled study, and whether this increase can be considered a health risk is not clear, but studies like these do point out the fact once again, that no drug can be considered completely harmless.

Caffeine and Cancer. MacMahon, Yen, Trichopolous, Warren, and Nardi (1981) found that coffee drinkers are at a higher risk for cancer of the pancreas than nondrinkers. However, additional studies have found no such link. The incidence of cancer of the pancreas is not high to begin with, so the increased risk, if there is one, is probably small.

Caffeine and Breast Tumors. Some women develop fibrous tumors of the breast. These can be painful. Many doctors advise women who are susceptible to them to avoid caffeine, and some studies have supported the relationship (Minton, 1985). However, a recent study of a large group of women has failed to find a link (Lubin, Ron, Wax, Black, Funaro, & Shitrit, 1985).

Caffeine and Pregnancy. Caffeine does cross the placental barrier and animal studies have indicated that it is teratogenic (capable of causing birth defects) in animals, but these data are difficult to interpret. In one study, for example, pregnant female rats were given the equivalent of 100 cups of coffee a day. Human studies have shown conflicting evidence, but there seems to be a possible link between caffeine use and both spontaneous abortions and low birth weight (Heller, 1987). Of course, women should probably limit or restrict all drug use during pregnancy.

Another controversy surrounds decaffeinated coffee. Many people who wish to avoid caffeine have switched to decaf. In the United States, most coffee is decaffeinated by using a solvent, methylene chloride, formerly an ingredient in hair spray. Inhalation of methylene chloride has been shown to produce cancer in laboratory animals. However, it did not cause cancer when the animals drank the solution, and besides, very little remains in decaf. Methylene chloride is approved by the FDA for this use. Another method of caffeine extract, the water method, is used more extensively in Europe. However, decaf made this way is usually more expensive. Switching to decaf will not prevent an increased flow of stomach acid, however, and those with ulcers or heartburn should avoid even decaf.

Behavioral Effects of Caffeine

Research into the behavioral effects of caffeine has found that performance on some tasks is enhanced and on others it is impaired (when high doses are given). Most studies have given subjects large doses of caffeine, typically 100–500 mg. Looking back at table 5.4, 500 mg is the equivalent of four or more cups of coffee. As a result these findings may not reflect the experience of the typical caffeine user. Recently, however, researchers have begun using more moderate doses with the finding that caffeine does just about what you would expect. It increases reaction time and increases performance on a vigilance task.

The practical significance of this is that even the caffeine content of one can of soda is sufficient to make a person more alert and react more quickly (Lieberman, Wurtman, Emde, Roberts, & Coviella, 1987). Of course, most people seem to know this from experience, since coffee or soda is

The bowl in the hand of this pottery figure holds coca leaves. The figure's other hand holds a limestick, which helps extract the cocaine from the leaf.

often taken by automobile drivers. It is nice to know, however, that science has confirmed what we already thought we knew.

Another belief that some people hold, unfortunately for them (and others), is that caffeine can sober you up after drinking too much alcohol. There is an old saying that what you have when a drunk takes a shower and drinks black coffee is a clean, wide-awake, drunk. Folk mythology aside, however, moderate amounts of caffeine do seem to improve alertness and peripheral responses in someone who has a moderate (.05) BAL (Burns & Moskowitz, 1990). Of course, other, more important, elements of driving are unaffected by caffeine so no one should ever drink and drive. Moreover, the relationship is quite complicated and completely eliminated at higher BALs.

If we all recognize coffee nerves, and if caffeine can in fact be fatal, why do most of us consider it an innocuous drug? First of all, it is legal and socially acceptable. Second, it is usually taken orally in a weak solution that minimizes its potentially harmful effects. People who take the drug, furthermore, do not perceive themselves as getting high, but have come to appreciate the taste and the fact that it does increase their performance. Coca leaves

Crack is often smoked in pipes. The rapid absorption leads to strong dependency potential.

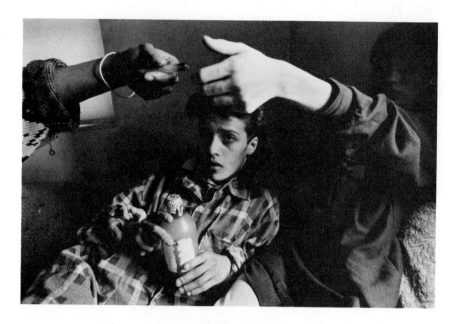

fulfill the same purpose for the many Indians of Peru and Bolivia, as we shall see.

Cocaine

It is 6:00 A.M. A cold wind blows across the Altiplano in Bolivia. In a small house in the mountains above Cochabamba, Jesus Maria Juarez reaches into a small bag, a *chuspa,* hanging on a string around his neck. He takes some leaves, mixes them with a little wood ash from his fire, adds some lime, puts the wad into his mouth and starts his day. Several times that day, whenever he feels hungry or tired, he will reach into his chuspa for a few more leaves.

About 10:00 A.M., during a break, Benacio Sanchez lights up his *basuca,* takes a few drags, and then goes back to pounding the leaves lying on the floor of the building hidden in one of the barrios (neighborhoods) of Bogotá, Colombia. He is making coca paste that will be refined into cocaine in another laboratory. After smoking some of his own product, he works faster and doesn't feel nearly as tired.

After a hard day at the office trying to make sales contacts, George unwinds at his neighborhood bar drinking a beer with a friend. His friend suggests that they go into the men's room to snort a line and then go to a party. George follows him eagerly.

It's midnight on 42nd Street near Times Square in New York. The three men huddle in a doorway as the rain pours down. One of them reaches into his coat pocket, takes out a pipe, puts a small amount of a substance into the bowl, lights it with his butane lighter, and greedily breathes in the fumes. Suddenly, he feels much better and he begins to laugh.

The chuspa, *a bag worn around the neck contains coca leaves.*

The four individuals were separated by thousands of miles and a chasm of cultural and racial differences, but they had one thing in common: they were all taking the same drug, cocaine.

The History of Cocaine The history of cocaine and cocaine use provides insight into a number of the factors that contribute to drug use and abuse. Set and setting are important, as is technology, which developed stronger and stronger forms of cocaine. Moreover, the media, socioeconomic factors, and even geopolitics played significant roles.

Coca leaves, from which cocaine is derived, have been used by the Indians of what we now call Bolivia, Ecuador, Peru, Colombia, and parts of Argentina for perhaps five thousand years (Shultes, 1987). The coca leaves are dried and then chewed. Wood ash or lime, when available, is added to the leaves, since saliva is acidic and would neutralize much of the effect of the cocaine, which is an alkaloid. The leaves are chewed to reduce hunger and increase energy. Although originally restricted to the nobility, coca leaves have been in use by the lower classes at least since the time of the Spanish Conquest (Schultes, 1987).

The Indians clearly understood the practical significance of the coca leaf. The Incas of South America had an empire that extended for two thousand miles, with an extensive mail service. Their "mailmen" were runners who had to cover long distances at high altitudes. They were provided with coca leaves to give them energy. There were even supplies of coca leaves stored at various stops along the way. The "postal authorities" recognized the functional and ritual use of coca leaves and warned their postmen that they were only to use the leaves just before they left and while they were on their "postal route" (Opler, 1970).

Coca-leaf chewing never caught on with the Spanish conquistadors. They permitted its use by the Indians to enable them to work harder, but did not seem to take up the habit themselves. Perhaps the esthetics of a wad of leaves in the mouth and the constant spitting and chewing offended them. An early observer of the Indians, Matienzo, wrote in 1567: "If we are surprised to see them carrying in their mouths such a crude and unsavory substance . . . they, too, are surprised to see the eating of garlic, olives, and radishes . . . trying them, they spit them out . . . ." (Gelles, 1986).

The Modern History of Cocaine

In the nineteenth century there were enormous advances in chemistry. One of these was the isolation of cocaine from the coca leaf by a chemist in Germany, Niemann, about 1859. This chemical eventually came to the attention of a well-known figure in psychology, Sigmund Freud.

In 1884, Freud was a young doctor specializing in neurology at a hospital in Vienna. One of his professors had done research on the local anesthetic properties of cocaine, but Freud, who was prone to depression, was more interested in the central stimulating effects. He tried the drug himself and wrote a paper which in English is titled "On Coca," hailing it a wonder drug for the treatment of impotence, depression, and fatigue. He also felt it was useful in the treatment of morphine addiction.

The use of cocaine spread throughout Europe, but within a short time, reports of cocaine dependence began to surface until, one year later, in 1885, Freud was accused of having unleashed the "third scourge of humanity" on mankind, the first two being alcohol and opiate addiction. Humiliated, Freud stopped recommending the drug (Allen, 1987).

Cocaine was a common ingredient in many patent medicines and remedies until the beginning of the twentieth century. One such "tonic" in particular, made a wealthy man out of Angelo Mariani, a French chemist who mixed an extract of coca leaf with wine to make Vin Mariani. His product was enormously successful and was recommended by celebrities like John Philip Sousa, the bandleader, and the actress Sarah Bernhardt. He was even awarded a medal by Pope Leo XIII for his contribution to mankind.

After the debacle brought on by Sigmund Freud, use of cocaine was for a time mostly restricted to medicine and "nerve tonics." Eventually, though, recreational cocaine use began to increase again, and the next epidemic lead the president of the United States to declare: "The misuse of cocaine is undoubtedly an American habit, the most threatening of the drug habits that has ever appeared in this country, and there is no uncertain feeling in every State and municipality of the country that the habit will continue to spread . . . ." (Erickson, Adlaf, Murray, & Smart, 1987). These modern-sounding phrases were actually those of President Taft in 1910.

Despite being classified (incorrectly) as a narcotic drug along with opium, heroin, and morphine by the Harrison Act of 1914 (see chapter 12), cocaine use continued into the twenties and thirties. In fact, its use was relatively common until amphetamines came along. Amphetamine replaced cocaine for a time because it was cheaper, longer acting, and easier to obtain.

We have seen that the most recent outbreak of cocaine use was hardly unique in history; there have been others before and there will probably be more in the future. What was unique was that new methods of administering cocaine were developed—helping to make cocaine a more readily abused drug.

With a concentration of about 2 percent, it is hard to imagine how one could absorb enough cocaine from coca leaf to get much of a rush. Indians who chew it constantly do so for relief from hunger and for energy. Their "set" is that the leaf is to be used for utilitarian purposes. The pure extract of the coca leaf is, however, another story. When it is either injected or snorted, absorption is quite rapid and the danger of dependence increases. The most recent cocaine epidemic introduced a new method of using the drug, **freebasing,** which involves inhaling the virtually pure cocaine. Since inhalation is a very efficient method of absorbing a drug, dependency develops rapidly.

The surface area of the lungs is the size of a tennis court. When cocaine is mixed with ether and heated, the residue contains a higher proportion of the cocaine molecule than does the powder. This mixture is then smoked to produce a very short acting but intense experience. This form of "freebasing" was very popular among cocaine users for a short period of time in the early 1980s. It was called freebasing because it involved separating the cocaine molecule (an alkaloid or base) from the form in which it is normally found, combined with a salt. Ether freebasing was quickly supplanted by "crack."

Crack is very similar to ether freebasing except that the cocaine is mixed with ordinary baking soda, creating a lump that is then smoked. Heating ether can be quite dangerous, as many people both famous and obscure have found out. Crack is much safer to use than ether-extracted freebase—at least one doesn't risk going up in flames. Crack use became popular in many urban areas in 1985 and 1986. As we shall see below, the reasons for its popularity were as much economic as pharmacological.

Another method of smoking cocaine has yet to gain a significant foothold in the United States. In South America and in the Bahamas, however, **basuca** smoking is quite common. An early step in the extraction of cocaine from coca leaf is to make coca paste that contains cocaine sulfate, kerosene, sulfuric acid, manganese, and other substances (Ensing, 1985; Noya, 1987). The paste is called basuca and is mixed either with tobacco or with marijuana (Gomez, 1987). Basuca smoking is associated with a wide variety of psychological and physiological disorders and is considered a serious health problem by many (Jeri, 1987).

You don't need to be an expert in drug use to understand that a major reason for the high abuse potential resulting from injecting, snorting, or smoking cocaine, is that a massive amount of the drug is absorbed with great rapidity. With freebasing or smoking crack on the scene, we seem to have reached the final "logical" step. Coca leaf chewing results in a slow, steady, absorption of the drug with little abuse potential. Short of injecting the cocaine molecule directly into the active sites in the brain by means of cannula, it is hard to imagine a more rapid method of administration than crack. No wonder the abuse potential is so high.

Pharmacology and Physiology of Cocaine

What is this thing called cocaine, anyway? The molecule is shown in figure 5.1, but its structure doesn't help much in understanding its effects on the brain. In fact, for a drug as widely used and studied there is still considerable mystery about how it works.

Cocaine has two primary effects: as a local anesthetic and as a central nervous system stimulant. Both of these effects are important in understanding cocaine use.

Imagine what going to the dentist was like before the discovery of local anesthetics. Would you sit through a filling, let alone an extraction, without some form of anesthetic? The discovery of the anesthetic properties of cocaine was at least as important to the profession of dentistry as it was to other medical specialties. Local anesthetics used in dentistry are all variations of the cocaine molecule. Cocaine itself is still used occasionally in surgery and dentistry although it has largely been supplanted by drugs with fewer central nervous system (CNS) effects.

As we saw in chapter 3, the exact mechanism by which cocaine exerts its anesthetic effects is not entirely known. Cocaine and the other local anesthetics apparently are absorbed by the axon membrane and increase the threshold for depolarization by blocking the channel through which the ions pass.

Cocaine action is terminated when the drug is absorbed by the bloodstream from the axon wall. Therefore, especially in dentistry, vasoconstrictors also are injected to prolong the anesthetic action by slowing the rate of absorption. As cocaine is absorbed into the bloodstream it acts as a CNS stimulant, increasing heart rate and causing a release of adrenalin. In sensitive people this stimulation has been known to cause cardiac arrest, and deaths have been reported from injections of what would otherwise be considered a harmless dose of a "local" anesthetic.

If the action of cocaine were limited to altering the threshold of the action potential in sensory and motor nerves, its production would hardly be responsible for the potential destabilization of several South American countries, and it would not have generated a multi-billion dollar illegal industry.

The *central* effects of cocaine involve increases in blood pressure, body temperature, and heart rate but, even so, are not particularly striking. What is striking is the reported psychological effect. Users report feeling a sense of power, an increase in energy and euphoria. This effect was noted as early as 1859 when an Italian physician reported that "borne on the wings of two coca leaves, I flew about in the spaces of 77,438 worlds, each one more splendid than the others . . . . I prefer a life of ten years with coca to

FIGURE 5.1

Cocaine (and antidepressants) prevent the reuptake of norepinephrine and dopamine into the presynaptic membrane.

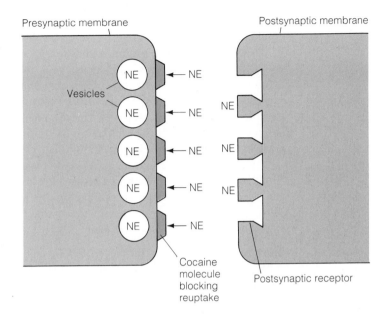

one of a hundred thousand without it'' (Erickson, Adlaf, Murray, & Smart, 1987). And all he did was chew coca leaves!

One of the most striking effects of cocaine is its short duration of action. Most users report that the stimulant effects of cocaine last about twenty minutes. The half life (the time at which half of the drug has been inactivated or removed from the bloodstream) is closer to forty-five to ninety minutes. The euphoric effect of cocaine correlates with blood levels only when the drug level is rising. After it has begun to fall, the user often reports **dysphoria** or depression (Van Dyck & Byck 1982).

You should recall from chapter 2 that the technical term for this occurrence is acute tolerance. Like so many other effects of cocaine, no one really knows why it occurs. The crucial factor may be the rate of change since cocaine is absorbed more rapidly than it is metabolized. Perhaps the receptors in the neuron become saturated or filled with the cocaine molecule and no more can get in, or perhaps high levels of cocaine are being maintained in the bloodstream when the drug is metabolized because the neurons are releasing it back into the bloodstream (Van Dyck & Byck, 1982). Obviously, no one really understands how the pharmacology of cocaine relates to the behavioral effects (Woods, Winger, & France, 1987).

Another curious fact about cocaine is that in laboratory studies, users often confuse local anesthetics with no central nervous systems effects, and even a placebo with real cocaine (Van Dyck & Byck, 1982). Perhaps regular users become classically conditioned to the stimuli associated with cocaine use. In other words they associate the euphoria produced by the drug with preparing it, snorting, or smoking it, and all the associated paraphernalia that go along with its use.

Cocaine is clearly a drug with strong reinforcing properties. Animals willingly bar press and learn other behaviors to obtain cocaine. In fact, they do so even when the doses they obtain are clearly toxic (Woods, Winger, & France, 1987). Unfortunately, the more sensational aspects of this research have been blown out of proportion by the popular press. While animals can be induced to respond in ways that are harmful to them, the so-called "compulsive" behavior cannot be equated to that of the cocaine abuser.

As we shall see below, cocaine affects several neurotransmitter systems, especially those which are involved in the reward pathways and centers in the brain. Animal research strongly suggests that the reinforcing properties of cocaine are at least partially due to stimulations of these pathways and centers (Kornetsky & Bain, 1987).

Mechanism of Action. The mechanism of action for the central effects of cocaine are still a matter of debate. Cocaine prevents the re-uptake of norepinephrine and dopamine into the presynaptic membrane, thereby increasing the amount of either catecholamine in the synapse. Until quite recently this inhibition of re-uptake, seen in figure 5.1, was considered to be the mode of action of cocaine. However, antidepressants (**Elavil** and **Triavil** are two examples) also inhibit the uptake of norepinephrine, and there is no black market for these drugs, since they are not considered stimulants, and those who take them do not report the euphoric effects characteristic of cocaine.

Cocaine administration has been linked to changes in GABA (Gale, 1984), and there is some evidence for a link between cocaine and peptides (Gale, 1984; Hammer & Hazeltine, 1984). Cocaine also affects the metabolism of serotonin (Hammer & Hazelton, 1984). Given the complex interaction of set and setting, individual differences, and the interaction of various neurotransmitter systems, it is simplistic to assume that the action of cocaine in the human could ever be reduced to a biochemical level.

Metabolism and Elimination of Cocaine. The primary site of metabolism of cocaine is the liver, where it is converted to benzoylecgonine and ecgonine methyl ester. (In case you wonder where scientists get names like this, consider that the chemical name for cocaine is *benzoylmethylecgonine*.) Nearly 80 percent of cocaine seems to be metabolized and excreted in this manner. Some cocaine is excreted unchanged in the urine, but this route is of minor importance. The metabolism is quite rapid and the half life of cocaine in circulation ranges from 15 to 120 minutes, depending on how it has been administered. Continued use of high doses of cocaine can lead to accumulation in body tissues because cocaine is fat soluble. At least one study found that cocaine and its metabolites could be detected for up to ten to fifteen days after last use (Cone & Weddington, 1989).

In laboratory animals, high or repeated dosages of cocaine can lead to death by liver failure. Apparently, at least one step in the metabolism of cocaine produces a toxic substance which can destroy the liver and kill the animal several days after the last injection (Roberts, James, Simmons, & Harbison, 1987). The common use of cocaine with other drugs has lead to concern since they may potentiate the danger of liver damage from cocaine.

Alcohol presents particular problems because it combines with cocaine to form a metabolite called cocaethylene. This metabolite is nearly as toxic as cocaine and works at the same centers in the brain. Alcohol is so common in our society and most drug users are polydrug users. More than half of the victims of cocaine-associated deaths in one study had significant amounts of cocaethylene. This metabolite also appears to be quite toxic to the liver (The Forensic Drug Abuse Advisor, 1991; Randall, 1992).

How Dangerous Is Cocaine?

Only a few years ago cocaine was considered to be a relatively harmless drug when used recreationally. There was thought to be little social cost (National Commission on Marijuana and Drug Abuse, 1973). Most references concluded that addiction was not possible, although psychological dependence might occur. Now, however, cocaine is considered an exceedingly dangerous drug; one authority has written, "Society must understand the horror of cocaine and accept the fact that the price for one small white line or one small rock can also have another price, the cost of a life" (Turner, 1987).

The truth of the matter is that the danger of cocaine depends on a number of factors. We shall look at some of these factors within the context of the acute and chronic effects of cocaine use.

Acute Effects. The lethal dose of cocaine has never been adequately determined, for the obvious reason that we cannot use humans for this type of research. The only human evidence we have comes from reports of death after ingestion by users or by smugglers.

Individuals are sometimes induced to smuggle cocaine into the country inside their body cavities. These individuals are called **body packers** or **mules.** Several have died suddenly, with massive quantities of cocaine found in their stomachs and intestines (Wetli & Mittleman, 1981). Users also have died after accidental overdoses when the drug was intentionally taken (Winek, Wahba, Rozin, & Janssen, 1987). Under such circumstances, a postmortem (after death) study is done and concentrations of cocaine are determined. These studies are of little use in determining the lethal dose in the recreational users, however, since the amount ingested cannot readily be estimated from such data.

In animals, the lethal dose varies widely, both between and within species. Dogs are more sensitive to cocaine than are rats or mice. The human equivalent of a lethal dose for a rat is up to seven grams, while for the dog it seems to be slightly more than one gram (Smart & Anglin, 1987). Humans seem closer to dogs than rats since one gram seems to be the generally accepted lethal dose for cocaine when taken orally, with as little as 20 mg when given intravenously (Nanji & Filipenko, 1984).

Death due to cocaine is very quick, occurring within minutes from the beginning of the symptoms. Excitement, psychotic behavior, seizures, and respiratory paralysis are reported. Because of the short time it takes to die from cocaine, treatment is extremely difficult unless the victim happens to be very near medical help. Few cocaine users, however, freebase or snort cocaine in or near a hospital.

Cocaine and the Heart. Cocaine constricts blood vessels, thus decreasing the blood supply to the heart and can disrupt heart rate. In addition, since cocaine also increases heart rate and blood pressure it should not be surprising that its use has been linked to angina pectoris (pain brought on by a decrease in the blood supply to the heart), stroke, and myocardial infarct (heart attack) (Mittleman & Wetli, 1987).

These effects of cocaine can be seen in apparently healthy young people who are not cocaine abusers. Many of the cardiovascular effects seem to be independent of the dose taken. The reasons why serious and frequently fatal cardiac problems can occur in healthy people is unknown but may be related to genetic factors or individual sensitivity (Goodwin, 1990). The heart attack may be a result of a sudden spasm of the coronary arteries or of blood clots blocking arteries that have been narrowed by the vasoconstricting effects of the drug (Roh & Hamele-Bena, 1990). Many times those experiencing these cardiovascular complications were unaware of any underlying problem, underscoring the fact that even occasional use of cocaine can have serious or fatal consequences.

Cocaine and the Brain. Cocaine can trigger seizure activity in the brain. Studies have indicated that cocaine taken over a prolonged period of time can have a **kindling** effect on the brain. What this means is that the brain appears to become more and more sensitive to cocaine and the seizure threshold is lowered (Post, Weiss, Pert, & Uhde, 1987). This *reverse tolerance* has been shown in humans and other animals and may account for the many reports of sudden death due to seizures in individuals who used cocaine occasionally with no unusual problems.

Cocaine can also apparently increase the risk of strokes. The term stroke is used to describe two different conditions. In the first, a blood vessel in the brain ruptures and blood flows into the surrounding tissue (hemorrhage). *Aneurysms* are balloon-like swellings in blood vessels and are a common cause of hemorrhaging. Another kind of stroke occurs when the blood supply to a portion of the brain is cut off when a blood vessel becomes blocked (*ischemia*).

Cocaine use is associated with an increase in either kind of stroke. Use of cocaine by snorting or injection seems to increase the risk of stroke caused by hemorrhage more than by ischemia, but freebase cocaine, especially crack, is associated with an increase in both types of stroke. Just how cocaine produces these effects is not clear but is probably related to increased blood pressure and constriction of blood vessels (Levine, Brust, Futrell, et al, 1990).

In addition to heart attack and strokes, use of cocaine has been linked to other problems such as panic attacks and palpitations (Louie, Lannon, & Ketter, 1989; Petronis & Anthony, 1989). Not everyone who uses cocaine will have a heart attack or a stroke, of course, and some people are probably at greater risk than others. The problem lies in not being able to determine ahead of time who will experience what problems. In addition, even if there is only a small chance of any of these problems occurring, the odds become worse each time the drug is used.

Chronic Use. Chronic use of cocaine can result in an infection of **septum,** the tissue between the nostrils, in those who snort cocaine, and hepatitis and abscesses in those who inject the drug (Chow, Robertson, & Stein, 1990). Of course, injection has been tied to the spread of AIDS as well (NIDA 1986), and there is some evidence that cocaine may directly harm the immune system (Jones, 1986).

Smoking cocaine in the form of crack can lead to its own problems. Since most crack users also smoke cigarettes or marijuana, precise effects are hard to determine, but crack users seem to be at greater risk for various acute respiratory tract problems including chronic cough, shortness of breath, and pneumonia (Karch, 1991). Other conditions include "black sputum," perhaps caused by the butane used to ignite the crack, coughing up blood, and chest pain (Tashkin, 1990).

Cocaine increases the amount of the neurotransmitter dopamine in the brain. Sufficiently high doses for a prolonged time can produce symptoms that are virtually identical to schizophrenia and manic disorders, both mental disorders linked to excess brain catecholamines (Lieberman, Kinon, & Loebel, 1990). One study found that daily use of cocaine increased the risk of psychotic experiences three-and-a-half times in otherwise normal individuals (Goodwin, 1990). The psychotic symptoms are similar to those reported for amphetamine on page 189.

Chronic use also can result in poor nutrition; remember that cocaine is an appetite suppressant. Other effects include fungal infections, tuberculosis, nutritional deficiencies, and additional health problems. Cocaine users often go for long periods of time without sleep and often permit their own personal appearance to deteriorate.

Cocaine Use in Pregnancy. An emerging problem that may have long-term impact on society is the use of cocaine, especially crack, by pregnant women. The extent of the problem is difficult to determine because most newborn babies are not tested for drug exposure, pregnant women are understandably reluctant to admit drug use, and because drug users are likely to use more than one drug. Taking all of these factors into consideration, one widely used estimate is that 375,000 babies are exposed to drugs each year.

Babies exposed to cocaine, especially crack, are of smaller birth weight, shorter in length, and have smaller heads than nonexposed infants. They are more likely to show physical abnormalities such as deformed kidneys and neural defects. In addition, since they show signs of withdrawal at birth, including irritability, bonding with the mother may be less likely to occur (Cole, 1990). Cocaine use also increases the risk of spontaneous abortion and fetal death. In cases of fetal death, the blood levels of cocaine and its metabolites may exceed those in the mother (Meeker & Reynolds, 1990).

To make matters worse, women sometimes take cocaine when they go into labor, in the belief that it will shorten labor and make the experience more positive (Skolnick, 1990). Cocaine use not only does not shorten labor, but may cause premature labor and other birth problems (Chasnoff, Griffith, MacGregor, Dirkes, & Burns, 1989).

The problems with cocaine-exposed babies does not end with birth. Since many of the babies are born premature and need hospital care, and since many end up being "boarder babies" (remaining in the hospital for foster care placement because their mothers are unwilling or unable to care for them), the cost to the hospital system is enormous. Babies born to mothers who smoke crack seem to require more care than babies born to mothers who used other forms of cocaine. The total cost nationwide is estimated to be $500 million a year (Phibbs, Bateman, & Schwartz, 1991). Remember, this is only for neonatal care!

While these and other studies indicate that cocaine use during pregnancy can cause serious problems, you should also be aware that most of these studies involve a small number of subjects and the long-term consequences of cocaine exposure are far from clear. Many other factors, like presence or absence of prenatal care, other drug use by the mother and socioeconomic variables, undoubtedly also affect the babies' health. While the dangers of cocaine exposure have received widespread publicity, some researchers urge caution about the interpretation of many of the findings. They fear that labels like "cocaine baby" can become self-fulfilling prophecies (Mayes, Granger, Bornstein, & Zuckerman, 1992). Many of the negative effects of exposure can be reduced if the mother stops using early in pregnancy. In addition, proper postnatal care and drug intervention programs for parents also help.

Tolerance and Dependence. From the discussion in chapter 2, you will remember that there are various types of tolerance. Regular use of cocaine can lead to physiological tolerance, reverse tolerance, and acute tolerance. Physiological tolerance develops with most of the physical symptoms of cocaine use, such as loss of appetite, increase in body temperature, and release of catecholamines. The physiological tolerance is not as dramatic as that of, say, the opiates, but it is a factor.

Reverse tolerance brings about the phenomenon of "kindling" discussed on page 180. Reverse tolerance can also increase the likelihood of hallucinations as well as cardiac arrhythmia described earlier. Acute tolerance, you will recall, occurs within a drug-taking episode when the effect of a drug is reduced after taking it a second or third time. During a drug-taking episode, cocaine users use more cocaine each time they snort, inject, or smoke the drug.

Physical dependence on cocaine also occurs. Withdrawal usually lasts for up to three days and is characterized by fatigue, depression, hunger, and increased appetite. Withdrawal symptoms are roughly the opposite of the cocaine experience itself.

The emotional roller coaster that cocaine produces also leads to continued use and could be considered a kind of dependence. The depression following the euphoria produced by cocaine can be relieved partially by more cocaine, but the ensuing "down" is even worse, and the user eventually uses more and more cocaine to chase after an ever more elusive high.

The process of withdrawal seems to follow three phases. First, the acute stage, which occurs when the cocaine is being removed from the system. During this period (three to four days) there is little craving. Following this is a longer period of intense craving lasting for days or weeks. Relapse is common during this time. Finally, there is the suggestion that neuropsychological changes occur which alter the ability of the central nervous system to regulate pleasure. This third stage of depression and anhedonia may last for months or years. Cocaine dependence is both physiological and psychological and is quite different than that of most other abused drugs (Gawin, 1991).

Economics of Cocaine

Imagine that you own a small farm on arid land in the southwestern United States. You make barely enough to stay alive by growing a small berry that local people make into a tea. Suddenly, you find that in a rich country in the Far East, these berries are worth hundreds of dollars an ounce. A buyer comes to you and offers you ten times your annual gross for the berries and assures you that they will be shipped immediately out of the country to this far-off land. Would you sell?

Assume that you did sell and now have enough money to buy a car, a VCR, good clothes, and even save a little. Representatives of this far-off country come to you and order you to stop growing the berries because their citizens are becoming dependent on them. They ask you to go back to your subsistence farming. You know of no one in your country who was harmed by the tea that they make. Would you stop growing your berry, plow your land under, and go back to near starvation? Or would you tell that stranger to get lost?

Much the same problem is faced by the growers of coca leaf. In fact, at every step of production of cocaine from the growing of the leaf to the sale of the powder, economic issues exert a tremendous influence. If the cocaine industry were listed in the Fortune 500 it would easily be in the top ten, along with Ford, General Motors, and others.

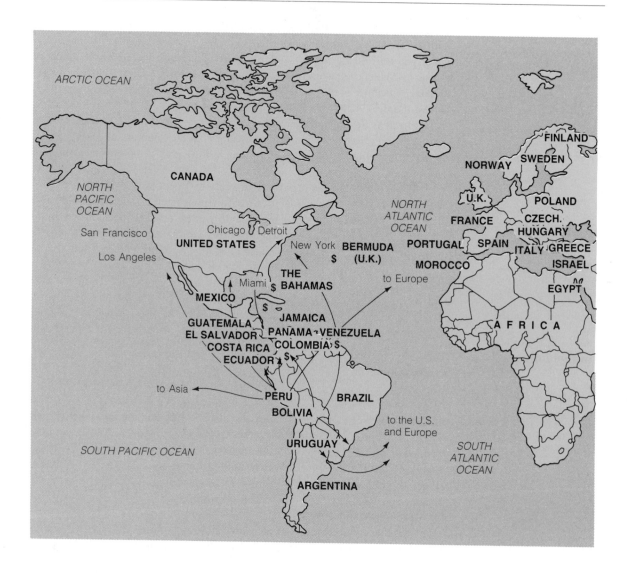

FIGURE 5.2

Major routes by which cocaine is smuggled into the United States. Coca leaves are usually shipped to Colombia where they are processed into cocaine before being shipped to the United States.

Figure 5.2 shows the geography of cocaine. Coca is grown in Colombia, Ecuador, Brazil, and Bolivia. Most of the cocaine reaches the United States from Colombia, although Ecuador, Peru, and Brazil also supply some. The profits to be gained from this trade are almost incomprehensible. The major dealers own banks, soccer teams, and entire islands. They assassinate those they can't buy off, and some even get elected to office in their countries (White, 1989).

In the early 1990s, the cocaine cartel of Colombia formed a group that called themselves the Extradibles and waged a terrorist campaign against the Colombian government. Colombia and the United States had, at that time, an agreement that allowed the United States to try the drug traffickers in this country where they were more likely to be punished. The cartel finally reached an agreement that they would stop the terrorist campaign in exchange for being tried in Colombia. By the way, another drug family quickly stepped in to take up the slack, and this cartel is thought to be even more ruthless than the Extraditables.

There still exists an understandable resentment of the drug eradication efforts by the United States, however. Many South American leaders think we are being hypocritical to do so little to help our addicts, while expecting so much from them (the South Americans). More than one official has pointed out, on or off the record, that "if you didn't buy it, we couldn't sell it."

The cocaine epidemic seems to have peaked, at least among the middle class, and use has reached its lowest level in many years, but the epidemic of "crack" continues unabated in lower socioeconomic groups. Of course these widely publicized trends do not mean that professionals and the middle class have completely given up cocaine since conservative figures indicate that up to one million people are still users, nor does it mean that crack use is universal in the ghettos, barrios, and inner cities. It does mean that while the flood of publicity about cocaine seems to be waning, the economic and health impact of this drug remains considerable.

Amphetamine

The story of cocaine and the story of amphetamine are similar. Although **amphetamine** is a synthetic compound with a relatively short history and does not resemble cocaine biochemically, its use parallels that of cocaine. The several stimulant epidemics of the late nineteenth and the twentieth centuries are interchangeable in their patterns, the only difference being that some involve cocaine and some amphetamine.

History of Amphetamine

Amphetamine was first synthesized in 1887 (Kramer, 1969), but its value for medical purposes was not recognized until the 1930s. **Benzedrine** was the first trade name for amphetamine and was marketed as a **bronchodilator** useful for treating asthma. Later it was found to be effective in treating narcolepsy and what is now called attention deficit disorder.

Narcolepsy is a condition in which the person afflicted has uncontrollable episodes of sleep. Many students and most faculty members think this condition is epidemic among college students, although it is, in fact, quite rare. If you fall asleep while your instructor is lecturing, you are probably normal. If your instructor falls asleep while lecturing, that is narcolepsy. Although narcolepsy is not in itself life-threatening, it obviously can be dangerous if one is driving a car and has an attack. Amphetamine is quite effective in treating this condition.

Attention deficit disorder (ADD) is the current term for what many know as hyperactivity. Most often diagnosed in childhood, attention deficit disorder is a complex illness. Symptoms include the inability to concentrate, accompanied by poor motor skills and a subsequent tendency to excessive activity. Amphetamine has been used with success in treating this condition although its use has also generated considerable controversy.

in depth

Why did crack become so popular? What are its effects? How can we help crack users? Will crack use continue to decline in the years to come? The answers to the problem of crack use involve understanding not only the pharmacology of cocaine but also political and socioeconomic factors as well.

As you have read, crack is a form of freebase cocaine formed by combining cocaine with sodium bicarbonate (baking soda), and a little water. The mixture is then heated to evaporate the fluid. Street cocaine is cocaine hydrochloride plus whatever has been added to dilute it. Crack on the other hand, is much purer since the hydrochloride salt has been combined with the sodium bicarbonate. In addition, crack melts at a lower temperature (about 80 degrees Centigrade instead of 180 for the cocaine). When heated, nearly 80 percent of the cocaine is made available for inhalation, a much more efficient route of administration even than injection (Nakahura & Ishigami, 1991).

Carefully controlled laboratory studies are difficult to do with crack and may not reflect the experience of the street user of the drug. First of all, experienced cocaine smokers must be recruited; second, crack is normally smoked in various different kinds of pipes, and inhalation techniques vary from user to user. Basically, however, laboratory studies confirm what you should already be able to predict from your knowledge of pharmacology: Compared to oral and nasal routes of administration the time to peak blood level of smoked cocaine is extremely rapid (although the intravenous route is the same as smoking), and the time to peak subjective effect is more rapid with crack than any other route (Jones, 1990).

The problem of helping crack users is complicated by political and socioeconomic factors. The major push against crack has involved the legal system. Crack users disproportionately come from lower socioeconomic classes and are not likely to have medical care plans that pay for drug abuse treatment. Government sponsored drug abuse treatment programs are overwhelmed and so the crack user often fails to get any help. This problem, combined with the general perception that crack use is difficult to treat, means the crack users are isolated from the mainstream of drug abuse treatment.

History has taught us that all drug epidemics eventually fade, and the same may be true for crack. The question is whether another drug will take the place of cocaine. Some studies have indicated that smoking of heroin is increasing, sometimes in combination with cocaine. One technique known as "chasing the dragon" involves smoking heroin a few minutes after smoking crack. The combination is supposed to increase the duration of the euphoria and reduce the depression that follows after cocaine.

In addition to the effects noted above, amphetamine is a powerful central nervous system stimulant. Students, truck drivers, and others who felt the need to stay awake for long periods of time or who felt they needed extra pep, quickly took to this drug. It is still prescribed to pilots of the United States Air Force to stay awake during long flights.

During World War II virtually every country issued amphetamine as if it were candy. Soldiers learned to appreciate its effects and when the war was over, amphetamine use spread to the civilian population. In Japan, an epidemic of amphetamine use broke out after the war. The drug was available without prescription, and huge stockpiles were available. A similar epidemic also occurred in Sweden.

In the United States, amphetamine use became quite common among respectable adults. It was prescribed for simple fatigue and to aid in weight loss while the abuse potential was largely ignored. Combinations of amphetamine and other drugs were also common. A particularly notorious combination was amphetamine and a barbiturate. Amphetamine provided the stimulation and appetite suppressant effect while the barbiturate acted like alcohol, producing a sedative, euphoric effect. In the late 1960s the use of amphetamines spread to the subculture of the hippies. Instead of taking a pill, however, a popular means of abusing this drug was injection.

The Speed Scene. No one really knows where intravenous injection of amphetamine started or how it spread. It was common in Sweden during its epidemic, and, of course, heroin users had been injecting their drug for many years. However it began, the practice of injecting amphetamine spread rapidly, in part because of the realization that it produced a virtually instantaneous rush. **Speed** was born.

The famous "Summer of Love" in San Francisco in 1967, when thousands of idealistic youth gathered to smoke marijuana, experience "free love," and end prejudice, war, and poverty lasted only a short time. Marijuana and LSD were crowded out by heroin and amphetamine, and the scene turned nasty (Lee & Schlain, 1985). The speed freak drove away the flower child.

Peer pressure is very powerful, and it was a substantial factor in the decline of speed. The speed freak on a run (an intravenous user who had been injecting for several days) is a hostile, paranoid, hyperactive, dangerous, and thoroughly unlikable person. Speed freaks were rejected by other members of the drug-using community. Speed doesn't necessarily kill, but speed freaks sometimes did, and no one wanted delusional, paranoid hyperaggressive drug users around who were actively hallucinating.

The very real dangers of injecting drugs, such as hepatitis, abscesses, and infection, also proved to be a substantial deterrent to the continued use of the amphetamine in injectable form. It seems likely, however, that the social disapproval of peers was the most potent influence in reducing amphetamine use (Brecher, 1972).

Current Use of Amphetamine. Amphetamine use today is by no means rare, although it is not as common as cocaine. Amphetamine is used as a substitute for cocaine or mixed with it. There is, however, a subculture of amphetamine users. **Crank** labs are common in rural areas that have ready access to major communities. Rural areas are preferred by operators of these labs because the odors involved in the synthesis of these drugs are quite distinctive and because it is easier to hide a laboratory in a bungalow down a private road than it is to hide in a suburban tract.

Designer Drugs

MDA(methylenedioxyamphetamine) use began in the late sixties and early seventies. Depending on how it is classified, it can either be considered a mescaline-like drug (see Chapter 8) or an amphetamine. Although MDA is usually classified as a hallucinogenic, its effects are not like those of LSD or mescaline, and many do not consider it hallucinogenic at all (Naranjo, Shulgin, & Sargent, 1967). MDA developed a reputation as a "love drug" (Thiessen & Cook, 1973) and is still fairly popular even today (Nichols, 1986). It is, however, illegal.

In 1914 Merck Company patented a drug that came to be called MDMA (methylenedioxymethamphetamine); in other words, MDA with a methyl group attached (Merck, 1914). Presumably, MDMA was to be used as an appetite suppressant. It failed to catch on, and little was heard of it for almost seventy years, until it emerged as Ecstasy.

As can be seen in figure 5.3, MDA and MDMA are similar to each other but different from other amphetamine-like drugs that cause hallucinations in that they are the only drugs that have the methylenedioxy structure that is indicated by the dotted lines on the figure. MDMA is reported to have less hallucinogenic potential than MDA, and this has been attributed to the methyl group as explained in the figure.

Careful laboratory studies indicate that the primary symptoms of MDMA are nausea, increased heart rate, tight jaw muscles, and headache (Hayner & McKinney, 1986). Subjective reports by users are much more positive, and some border on the fantastic. Both MDA and MDMA are reported to produce a strong need to be in the presence of, and talk to, other people. MDMA is supposed to induce a sense of "closeness" with others (Nichols & Overlender, 1990).

On 1 July 1985, the Drug Enforcement Administration made Ecstasy a Schedule I drug, along with heroin and other drugs for which there is high abuse potential and no medical use. The result of such classification was that conviction for trafficking could result in a jail term of fifteen years and a $125,000 fine. Until then the drug was as legal as tap water. The decision to ban its use was met with considerable controversy since some felt that it was useful as an adjunct in psychotherapy (Nichols, 1986; Grinspoon & Bakalar, 1986).

Recent evidence supports earlier findings that, like MDA, MDMA may cause brain damage (Ricaurte, Forno, Wilson, DeLanney, Irwin, Molliver & Langston, 1988). Doses of MDMA given to primates apparently caused damage to neurons that contain serotonin, as well as a decrease in the serotonin content of the brain. It should be noted, however, that the doses given were given twice a day for four days and were much higher than the dose usually taken by humans. On the other hand, MDMA seems more toxic to monkeys than to rats, leading to the possibility that it may prove even more toxic in humans. MDMA apparently exerts its effect by destroying the enzyme that produces serotonin (Schmidt & Kehne, 1990).

There is no clear-cut evidence that Ecstasy causes brain damage in humans; however, preliminary evidence suggests that recreational users of the drug may show some alteration of serotonin function (Price, Ricaurte, Krystal, & Heninger, 1989). These findings of brain damage in primates and possible altered serotonin function in humans are especially important in light of the fact that even after being placed on Schedule I status, Ecstasy use continues. In one study, 40 percent of college students at a major university reported at least experimental use of the drug (Peroutka, 1987). Although other studies have failed to confirm such a high percentage of use on other campuses, one estimate has 100,000 doses a month were being sold (Ricaurte, Finnegan, Irwin, & Langston, 1990).

In parts of the United States, "Raves" or all-night dance parties, have become popular. Ecstasy is supposed to be a popular drug at these events. Raves began in England, where it is now a fad to smear your body with vapor rub and take ecstasy.

As we shall see in chapter 9, in the discussion on "designer drugs" related to the opiates, it is a simple matter to alter a molecule of a restricted drug and produce a new one. Ecstasy was developed many years ago, but a more recent arrival on the scene is "Eve" (3, 4 methylenedioxyethamphetamine). Both of these drugs have been associated with several deaths thought to be the result of cardiac arrhythmias (Dowling, McDonough, & Bost, 1987).

Pharmacology and Physiology of Amphetamines

As far as the effect on the user is concerned, cocaine and amphetamine are virtually identical. The effects of amphetamine are dose dependent. At low, medically normal, doses, pupil dilation occurs, blood pressure increases, bronchial muscles relax, and blood-flow to the muscles increases. At moderate to high doses, the symptoms include increased respiration, slight muscle tremor, insomnia, and agitation. When the drug wears off, the user typically sleeps for a long period of time and awakens depressed and hungry.

If these effects do not seem startling, remember that amphetamine has historically been used to increase energy and decrease sleepiness, not to get high. The amphetamines were long considered a means to an end. It took the advent of injectable speed to change amphetamine from a pep pill to a killer (at least in the public's eye).

High doses produce a rush, paranoia, delusions, and behavior which is indistinguishable from paranoid schizophrenia (Levine, 1983). This pattern of behavior occurs in individuals with no past psychiatric history and seems to be the direct result of the biochemical changes induced by the drug in the brain. Some individuals who take large doses also get "crank bugs"—the feeling that insects are crawling under their skin. This delusion is so strong that users will dig into their skin to find the bugs.

In both humans and laboratory animals, high doses of amphetamines can result in what is called **stereotypy.** In laboratory animals this means that animals may gnaw continuously at the bars of their cage, or turn in rapid tight circles. In humans, stereotypy may result in repetition of a seemingly meaningless act for several hours.

Amphetamine exists in two forms; a "d," and an "l" form, so-called because of the way polarized light bends when it shines through a solution of the substance. The d stands for dextro and bends the light to the right, and the l stands for levo and bends it to the left. The d form has more central nervous system activity. A large number of amphetamine-like compounds also have been developed. These drugs vary in their potency as central nervous system stimulants and differ in other minor ways, but basically they are identical to amphetamine. The chemical structure of amphetamine and its cousins are shown in figure 5.3.

The terms "speed," "meth," "crystal," "crank," and others such as "bennies," "black beauties," and "cross tops" refer to amphetamine in its many forms. At present, most drug users of amphetamines take **methamphetamine,** which is also known as crank, meth, and crystal. Methamphetamine can be snorted, injected, or taken orally. In the form of **"ice,"** it can also be smoked.

Mode of Action. Amphetamine stimulates the release of norepinephrine and dopamine (Groves & Segal, 1984; Cheramy, Nieoullon, & Glowinski, 1978), and high doses can lead to an inhibition of neuronal firing. Like cocaine, amphetamine inhibits re-uptake of the catecholamines. Amphetamine alters the firing patterns of neurons in many parts of the brain including the reticu-

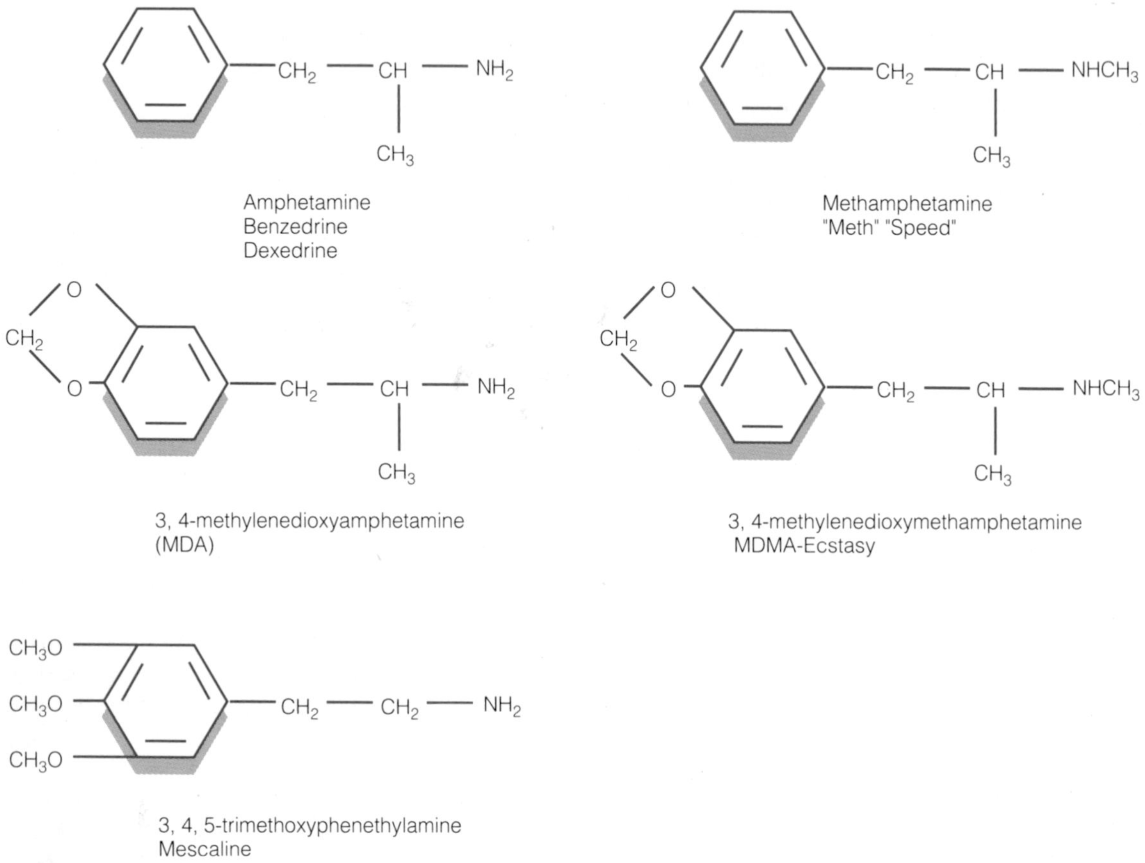

Amphetamine
Benzedrine
Dexedrine

Methamphetamine
"Meth" "Speed"

3, 4-methylenedioxyamphetamine
(MDA)

3, 4-methylenedioxymethamphetamine
MDMA-Ecstasy

3, 4, 5-trimethoxyphenethylamine
Mescaline

FIGURE 5.3
Molecular structure of amphetamine, methamphetamine, MDA, MDMA (Ecstasy), and mescaline. Compare them to norepinephine and dopamine (Figure 3.6)

lar formation, parts of the brain involved in motor movement, the hypothalamus, and the cortex (Groves & Tepper, 1983). As with cocaine, the behavioral effects of amphetamine cannot be explained completely by its effect on catecholamines.

The primary behavioral difference between amphetamine and cocaine is that the stimulant effects of amphetamine can last for several hours, while the duration of action of cocaine is measured in minutes. Drug dealers often take advantage of this fact and try to sell amphetamine as cocaine. They add a local anesthetic and tout their drug to the unsuspecting. Many buyers think they are getting superior cocaine because the stimulant effects last longer. What they are really getting is a drug that is much cheaper and more readily available.

In the last half of the 1980s, **ice** made its first appearance in the United States, mainly in Hawaii. Although popular press reports give the impression that ice is a new drug, it is not. The Drug Enforcement Agency reports that in Japan and Korea, ice has been known for a number of years.

• YOU READ IT HERE FIRST •

For a while, "ice," the popular name for smokeable crystal methamphetamine seemed to be a drug about ready to explode on the market. The relationship between ice and methamphetamine is virtually identical to that of crack and cocaine; ice and crack both are in a form readily absorbed through inhalation, while cocaine and amphetamine are usually snorted or injected (Cho, 1990).

Two important differences between cocaine and amphetamine need to be discussed, however. First of all, the psychoactive effect of amphetamine is much longer acting than that of cocaine. The exact duration of effect of ice is at present unknown, but is certainly many times longer than that of crack. What this means is that even if the cost of ice is initially greater, the user may end up spending less since the effects last longer.

The second difference is that cocaine comes from the coca leaf, which is grown only in South America. Amphetamine is a synthetic drug, manufactured in the United States. What this means is that a substantial part of the profit of the sale of cocaine goes into the pockets of members of South American drug cartels. Should ice ever become popular, the profits would go to those manufacturing the drug here in the United States. The possibility of billions of dollars going to clandestine laboratories and outlawed motorcycle groups—who are presently involved in the distribution of methamphetamine, or crank—frightens many law enforcement officials and should concern you as well. With virtually unlimited amounts of money, would the "icemen" be able to wreak the kind of havoc here that cocaine barons have in South America?

Although it is too soon to tell, the ice epidemic may never come to pass. The fact that it has not already become the scourge that crack has, is a good sign. There may be several reasons why. Crack is still plentiful and cheap, so the demand for ice is not great. Manufacture and distribution channels have not been established, and the using population has not had as much opportunity to sample the product. Also, while methamphetamine can be "cooked" in four days, some reports indicate that ice may take much longer than that to manufacture. The most important reason, however, may lie in the reinforcing properties of the drug itself. The euphoria does not seem to be as great, and the fact that its effects last for several hours may deter many users. Perhaps they prefer the short, intense effect of crack better.

It is, in reality, nothing more than the *d* isomer of methamphetamine hydrochloride, prepared so that it looks like little slivers of glass or ice. Some reports indicate that it melts and vaporizes at a lower temperature than crystal methamphetamine.

SUMMARY

Stimulants act upon the central nervous system to exert their effect, and the primary effect is on the arousal system. The three major groups of stimulants are the xanthines, cocaine, and amphetamine.

Coffee, tea, and chocolate all contain xanthines, and have had a long history in various societies. Like cocaine, and to an extent, amphetamine, they have been banned by law, revered as gifts of the gods, and used by a wide segment of society. Coffee contains caffeine, tea contains theophylline, and chocolate contains theobromine. All three of these drugs have various properties that make them useful as medicine as well as attractive as recreational drugs. They apparently act by increasing the activity of the second messenger system and by blocking the action of adenosine.

Coca leaves (the source of cocaine) have been used for thousands of years by the Indians of South America. Some fields of coca have been cultivated for centuries. The discovery of the cocaine molecule led to important discoveries in medicine, particularly in the area of anesthesia. At the same time, cocaine has been recognized as a potential drug of abuse for about as long as it has been recognized as an anesthetic. The use of cocaine as a recreational drug has fluctuated, and there have been several cocaine epidemics. The current one seems to be waning with some users at the same time that a form of cocaine, crack, has reached epidemic proportions with other members of society.

Amphetamines have a relatively short history. Originally introduced in the early part of the twentieth century, they were used by soldiers during World War II. After this war, use of amphetamines became widespread in some cultures leading to various crises. In the United States, the peak of amphetamine use came with the advent of the injectable form known as speed. Amphetamine and cocaine use are closely related.

The abuse potential of amphetamine and cocaine is considerable and is probably related to their effects on mood. Treatment for cocaine and amphetamine dependence has lagged behind that for other forms of drug abuse. Abuse of the xanthines is rare and, as presently used, they do not seem to represent a significant hazard, although it should be noted that in sufficiently high doses, caffeine and theophylline can be fatal.

REFERENCES

Altman, L. (1989). Lingering cocaine can cause heart attack weeks after use is discontinued. *New York Times Service,* December 1.

Burns, M., & Moskowitz, H. (1990). Two experiments on alcohol-caffeine interaction. *Alcohol, Drugs and Driving, 5,* 303–15.

Chaisson, R. E., Bachetti, R., Osmond, D., Brodie, D., Sande, M. A., & Moss, A. R. (1989). Cocaine use and HIV infection in intravenous drug users in San Francisco. *Journal of the American Medical Association, 261,* 561–65.

Chasnoff, I. (1988). Drug use in pregnancy: Parameters of risk. *Pediatric Clinical Medicine, 82,* 888–95.

Chasnoff, I., Griffith, D., MacGregor, S., Dirkes, K., & Burns, K. (1989). Temporal patterns of cocaine use during pregnancy. *Journal of the American Medical Association, 261,* 1741–44.

Chelsky, L., Cutler, J., Griffith, K. (1990). Caffeine and ventricular arrhythmias. *Journal of the American Medical Association, 264,* 2236–40.

Cheremy, A., Nieoullon, A., & Glowinski, J. (1978). In vivo changes in dopamine release in cat caudate nucleus and substantia nigra induced by nigral application of various drugs including GABAergic agonists and antagonists. In J. Garattini, J. F. Pujol, and R. Samanin (Eds.), (pp. 175–90). *Interactions between putative neurotransmitters in the brain.* New York: Raven Press.

Cho, T. (1990). Ice: A new dosage form of an old drug. *Science, 249,* 631–34.

Chow, J., Robertson, A., & Stein, R. (1990). Vascular changes in the nasal submucosa of chronic cocaine addicts. *American Journal of Forensic Medicine and Pathology, 11,* 136–43.

Christian, S. (1987). Bolivians fight efforts to eradicate cocaine. *The New York Times,* July 27.

Cole, H. (1990). Legal interventions during pregnancy. *Journal of the American Medical Association, 264,* 2663–70.

Cone, E., & Weddington, W. (1989). Prolonged occurrence of cocaine in human saliva and urine after chronic use. *Journal of Analytical Toxicology, 13,* 65–68.

Dorfman, L. J., & Jarvick, M. E. (1970). Comparative stimulant and diuretic action of caffeine and theobromine in man. *Clinical Pharmacology and Therpeutics, 11,* 869.

Dowling, G. P., McDonough, E. T., & Bost, R. O. (1987). "Eve" and "Ecstasy": A report of five deaths associated with use of MDEA and MDMA. *Journal of the American Medical Association, 257,* 1615–17.

Erickson, P. G., Adlaf, E. M., Murray, G. F., & Smart, R. G. (1987). *The steel drug: Cocaine in perspective.* Lexington, MA: Lexington Books, D. C. Heath and Company.

Forensic Drug Abuse Advisor (1991). *New cocaine metabolites, 3,* 1718.

Fried, R. E., Levine, D. M., Kwiterovich, P. O., Diamond, E. L., Wilder, L. B., Moy, T. F., & Pearson, T. A. (1992). The effect of filtered-coffee consumption on plasma lipid levels. *Journal of the American Medical Association, 267,* 811–815.

Garriott, J. C., Simmons, L. M., Poklis, A., & Mackell, M. A. (1985). Five cases of fatal overdose from caffeine containing "Look-alike" drugs. *Journal of Analytical Toxicology, 9,* 141–43.

Gawin, F. (1991). Cocaine addiction: Psychology and neurophysiology. *Science, 251,* 1580–86.

Gelles, P. (1985). Coca and Andean culture: The new dangers of an old debate. *Cultural Survival, 9,* 20–23.

Gomez, A. P. (1987). Cocaine and basuco: An overview of Colombia, 1985. In D. Allen (Ed.), (pp. 199–206). *The cocaine crisis.* New York and London: Plenum Press.

Goodwin, F. (1990). Cocaine euphoria and CMR rates. *Journal of the American Medical Association, 264,* 2495.

Greden, J. (1987). Caffeine. In S. Mule, (Ed.), (pp. 164–89). *Behavior in excess.* New York: The Free Press.

Griffiths, R., & Woodson, P. (1988). Reinforcing properties of caffeine: Studies in humans and laboratory animals. *Pharmacology, Biochemistry and Behavior, 29,* 419–27.

Griffiths, R., & Woodson, P. (1988). Caffeine physical dependence: A review of human and laboratory animal studies. *Psychopharmacology, 94,* 437–51.

Grinspoon, L., & Bakalar, J. B. (1986). Can drugs be used to enhance the psychotherapeutic process? *American Journal of Psychotherapy, 90,* 393–404.

Grobbee, D., Rimm, E., & Giovannucci, E. (1990). Coffee, caffeine and cardiovascular disease in men. *New England Journal of Medicine, 323,* 1026–32.

Groves, P. M., & Segal, D. S. (1984). Psychobiological foundations of behaviors induced by amphetamines. In C. M. Sharp (Ed.). *Mechanisms of tolerance and dependence.* NIDA Research Monograph 54. Department of Health and Human Services.

Groves, P. M., & Tepper, J. M. (1983). Neuronal mechanisms of action of amphetamine. In I. Cresse (Ed.), pp. 81–129. *Stimulants: neurochemical, behavioral and clinical perspectives.* New York: Raven Press.

Hammer, S., and Hazelton, L. (1984). Cocaine and the chemical brain. *Science News*, October.

Hanzlick, R. H., Gowitt, G. T., & Wall, W. (1986). Deaths due to caffeine in "look-alike drugs". *Journal of Analytical Toxicology, 10*, 126.

Hayner, G. N., & McKinney, H. (1986). MDMA: the dark side of ecstacy. *Journal of Psychoactive Drugs, 10*, 341–47.

Healy, K. (1985). The cocaine industry in Bolivia: Its impact on the peasantry. *Cultural Survivial, 9*, 23–29.

Heller, J. (1987). What do we know about the risks of caffeine consumption in pregnancy? *British Journal of Addiction, 82*, 885–89.

Hobhouse, H. (1986). *Seeds of Change*. New York: Harper & Row.

Inaba, T., Stewart, D. J., & Kalow, W. (1978). Metabolism of cocaine in man. *Clinical Pharmacology and Therapeutics, 23*, 547–52.

Jeri, F. R. (1987). Somatic disorders associated with the abuse of coca paste and cocaine hydrochloride. In D. Allen (Ed.), (pp. 177–90). *The Cocaine Crisis.* New York and London: Plenum Press.

Jones, R. (1986). Cocaine increases natural killer cell activity. *Journal of Chemical Investigations, 77*, 1387–90.

Karch, S. (1991). Introduction to the forensic pathology of cocaine. *American Journal of Forensic Medicine and Pathology, 12*, 126–31.

Kendal, S. (1985). South American cocaine production. *Cultural Survival, 9*, 10–11.

Kornetsky, C., & Bain, G. (1987). Neuronal bases for hedonic effects of cocaine and the opiates. In S. Fischer, A. Raskin, and E. H. Uhlenhuth (Eds.), (pp. 66–79). *Cocaine: clinical and biobehavioral aspects.* New York and Oxford: Oxford University Press.

Kramer, J. C. Introduction to amphetamine abuse. *Journal of Psychoactive Drugs, 2*, 27–32.

Lee, M., & Schlain, B. (1985). *Acid dreams: The CIA, LSD and the sixties rebellion.* New York: Grove Press.

Levine, S., Brust, J., & Futrell, N. (1990). Cerebrovascular complications of the use of the "crack" form of alkaloidal cocaine. *New England Journal of Medicine, 323*, 699–704.

Lieberman, H. R., Wurtman, R. J., Emde, G. G., Roberts, C., & Coviella, I. L. G. (1987). The effects of low doses of caffeine on human performance and mood. *Psychopharmacology, 92*, 308–12.

Lieberman, J., Kinon, B., & Loebel, A. (1990). Dopaminergic mechanisms in idiopathic and drug induced psychoses. *Schizophrenia Bulletin, 16*, 97–110.

Louie, A., Lannon, R., & Kester, T. (1989). Treatment of cocaine induced panic disorder. *American Journal of Psychology, 146*, 40–44.

Lubin, E., Ron, E., Wax, Y., Black, M., Funaro, M., & Shitrit, A. (1985). A case controlled study of caffeine and methylxanthines in benign heart disease. *Journal of the American Medical Association, 253*, 2388–92.

MacMahon, B., Yen, S., Trichooulos, D., Warren, K., & Nardi, J. (1981). Coffee; And cancer of the pancreas. *New England Journal of Medicine, 304*, 630–33.

Mayes, L. C., Granger, R. H., Bornstein, M. H., & Zuckerman, B. (1992). The problem of prenatal cocaine exposure. *Journal of the American Medical Association, 267*, 406–408.

Meeker, J., & Reynolds, P. (1990). Fetal and newborn death associated with maternal cocaine use. *Journal of Analytical Toxicology, 14*, 376–82.

Minton, J. P. (1985). Caffeine and benign breast disease. *Journal of the American Medical Association, 254*, 2408.

Mittleman, R. E., & Wetl, C. V. (1987). Cocaine and sudden "natural" death. *Journal of Forensic Science, 32*, 11–19.

Nakahara, Y., & Ishigami, A. (1991). Inhalation efficiency of free-based cocaine by pyrolysis of "crack" and cocaine hydrochloride. *Journal of Analytical Toxicology, 15*, 105–07.

Nanji, A. A., & Filipenko, J. D. (1984). Asystolic and ventricular fibrillation: Association with cocaine intoxication. *Chest, 85*, 132–33.

Naranjo, C., Shulgin, A. T., & Sargent, T. (1967). Evaluation of 3, 4, methylenedioxymethamphetamine (MDA) as an adjunct in psychotherapy. *Medicina et Pharmacologia Experimentalis, 17*, 359–64.

National Institute of Drug Abuse (1989). Drug abuse and pregnancy. U. S. Department of Health and Human Services.

National Institute of Drug Abuse Prevention Network (1986). *Cocaine Use in America*. U. S. Department of Health and Human Services.

Nichols, D. E. (1986). Differences between the mechanisms of action of MDMA, MBDB, and the classic hallucinogens: Identification of a new therapeutic class: Entactogens. *Journal of Psychoactive Drugs, 18*, 305–13.

Nichols, D., & Oberlender, P. (1990). Structure activity relationship of MDMA and related compounds: A new class of psychoactive drugs? In P. Whitaker-Azmita & S. Perouka (Eds.), (pp. 424–46). *The Neuropharmacology of Serotonin, Annals of the New York Academy of Sciences, 600*.

Noya, N. D. (1987). Coca paste effects in Bolivia. In D. Allen (Ed.), (pp. 191–98). *The Cocaine Crisis*, New York and London: Plenum Press.

Opler, M. K. (1970). Cross cultural uses of psychoactive drugs (ethnopsychopharmacology). In W. G. Clark & J. del Giudice (Eds.), (pp. 31–50). *Principles of Psychopharmacology*. New York: Academic Press.

Ott, J. (1984). *The Cacahuatl eaters: Ruminations of an unabashed chocolate addict.* Vashon, WA: Natural Products.

Petronis, K., & Anthony, J. (1989). An epidemiological investigation of marijuana and cocaine related palpitations. *DAD, 23*, 219–26.

Petrouka, S. J. (1987). Incidence of recreational use of 3, 4, methylenedioxymethamphetamine (MDMA-Ecstasy). on an undergraduate campus. *New England Journal of Medicine, 317*, 1542–43.

Phibbs, C., Bateman, D., & Schwartz, R. (1991). The neonatal costs of maternal cocaine use. *Journal of the American Medical Association, 266*, 1521–26.

Post, R., Weiss, S., Pert, A., Uhde, T. (1987). Chronic cocaine administration: Sensitization and kindling effects. In S. Fisher, A. Raskin, & E. Uhlenhuth (Eds.), (pp. 109–73). *Cocaine: Clinical and biobehavioral aspects.* New York and London: Oxford University Press.

Price, L. H., Ricaurte, G. A., Krystal, J. H., & Heninger, E. R. (1989). Neuroendocrine and mood response to intravenous L-tryptophan in 3, 4, methylenedioxymethamphetamine (MDMA) users. *Archive of General Psychiatry, 46*, 20–23.

Rall, T. W. (1980). Central nervous system stimulants: The xanthines. In A. G. Gilman, L. S. Goodman, & A. Gilman (Eds.), (pp. 592–607). *The pharmacological basis of therapeutics*. New York: Macmillan.

Randall, T. (1992). Cocaine, alcohol mix in body to form even longer lasting, more lethal drug. *Journal of the American Medical Association, 267*, 1043–44.

Ricaurte, G. A., Forno, L. S., Wilson, M. A., Delanney, L. E., Irwin, I., Molliver, M. E., & Langston, J. W. (1988). 3, 4, methylenedioxymethamphetamine selectively damages central serotonergic neurons in nonhuman primates. *Journal of the American Medical Association, 260,* 52–55.

Ricaurte, G., Finnegan, K., Irwin, I., & Langston, J. (1990). Aminergic metabolism in cerebrospinal fluid of humans previously exposed to MDMA, preliminary observations. In P. Whitaker-Azmita & S. Perouka (Eds.), (pp. 699–710). *The Neuropharmacology of Serotonin, 600 Annals of the New York Academy of Sciences, 600.*

Roberts, S., James, R., Simmons, H., & Harbison, R. (1987). Alcohol and cocaine-induced liver injury. *Alcohol Health and Research World,* 20–25.

Roh, L., & Hamele-Bena, D. (1990). Cocaine-induced ischemic myocardial disease. *American Journal of Forensic Medicine and Pathology, 11,* 130–35.

Schmidt, C., & Kehne, S. (1989). Neurotoxicity of MDMA: Neurochemical effects. In P. Whitaker-Azmita & S. Perouka (Eds.), (pp. 665–81). *The Neuropharmacology of Serotonin, 600 Annals of the New York Academy of Sciences, 600.*

Shultes, R. E. (1987). Coca and other psychoactive plants: Magico-religious roles in primitive societies in the New World. In S. Fisher, A. Raskin, & E. H. Uhlenhuth (Eds.). *Cocaine: Clinical and biobehavioral aspects.* New York: Oxford University Press.

Siegel, R. K. (1982). Cocaine and sexual dysfunction. *Journal of Psychoactive Drugs, 14,* 71–74.

Smart, R., & Anglin, L. (1987). Do we know the lethal dose of cocaine? *Journal of Forensic Science, 14,* 303–13.

Sun. M. (1980). FDA caffeine decision too early some say. *Science, 209,* 1500.

Tashkin, D. (1990). Pulmonary complications of smoked substance abuse. *Western Journal of Medicine, 152,* 525–30.

Thiessen, P. N., & Cook, D. A. (1973). The properties of e, 4, nethylene dioxyamphetamineII. Studies of acute toxicity in the mouse and protection by various agents. *Clinical Toxicology, 6,* 193–99.

Tien, Q., & Anthony, J. (1990). *Journal of Nervous and Mental Diseases, 178,* 473–80.

Turner, C. E. (1987). In D. Allen (Ed.), (foreword). *The Cocaine Crisis.* New York: Plenum Press.

Van Dyke, C. & Byck, R. (1982). Cocaine. *Scientific American, 240,* 128–34.

Weiss, R. D., Tilles, D. S., Goldenheim, P. D., & Mirin, S. M. (1987). Decreased single breath carbon monoxide diffusing capacity in cocaine freebase smokers. *Drug and Alcohol Dependence, 19,* 271–76.

Wethersbee, P. S., Olser, J. R., & Lodge, A. L. (1977). Caffeine and pregnancy: A retrospective study. *Postgraduate Medicine, 62,* 64–69.

Wetli, C. V., & Mittleman, R. E. (1981). The ''body packer'' syndrome—Toxicity following ingestion of illicit drugs packaged for transportation. *Journal of Forensic Sciences, 26,* 492–500.

Winek, C. L., Wahba, W., Rozin, L., & Janssen, J. K. (1987). An unusually high blood cocaine concentration in a fatal case. *Journal of Analytical Toxicology, 11,* 43–45.

Woods, J. H., Winger, G. D., & France, C. P. (1987). Reinforcing and discriminative stimulus effects of cocaine: Analysis of pharmacological mechanisms. In S. Fisher, A. Raskin, & E. H. Uhlenhuth (Eds.), (pp. 21–65). *Cocaine, clinical and biobehavioral aspects.* New York and London: Oxford University Press.

6

• • •

MARIJUANA

• • •

OBJECTIVES

When you have finished studying this chapter you should:

1. Know some of the uses of marijuana in the past.
2. Be able to discuss the economic significance of cannabis.
3. Be able to trace the history of marijuana.
4. Know why marijuana was such a symbol of rebellion in the 1960s.
5. Be able to list the three types of cannabis.
6. Know the most important psychoactive components of marijuana.
7. Understand the factors affecting the absorption and metabolism of cannabis.
8. Be able to discuss the effects of marijuana on thinking.
9. Separate fact from fiction concerning the health dangers of marijuana.
10. Know the relationship between smoking cigarettes and smoking marijuana.
11. Be able to decide if marijuana is ''addictive.''
12. Be able to discuss the role of marijuana and THC in the treatment of various medical conditions.
13. Understand how the potential medical uses of marijuana affect the concept of legalization.

KEY TERMS

amotivational syndrome
Harry Anslinger
antiemetic effects
assassin
autotitration
Baudelaire
behavioral tolerance
bronchodilator
cannabinoids
Cannabis indica
Cannabis ruderalis
Cannabis sativa
Club des Hachichins
contact high
delta-9-tetrahydrocannabinol
Dumas
Emperor Shen Nung
glaucoma
hash
hash oil
hasheesh
hashish
hashishiyya
immune system
Mahabharata
marihuana
marijuana
Marijuana Tax Act of 1937
Marinol
Napoleon
phencyclidine
Reefer Madness
reverse tolerance
salmonella
second messenger system
set and setting
sinsemilla
tachycardia
testosterone
the munchies

The plant that we call marijuana, *Cannabis sativa,* has been known by many names throughout history. It has been grown for its commercial, medicinal, and euphoric properties, has been considered a crop much like cotton, and has been condemned as a major scourge in our society. How did such a substance come to play these varied roles?

Known as hemp, it was made into rope and clothing, and was an important crop from the time of the Ancient Greeks until it was replaced by other sources after World War II. None other than the first president of the United States, George Washington, had extensive plantings of it. At the same time that the "Drug Czar" of the 1930s and 1940s, Harry J. Anslinger, was prosecuting marijuana use and claiming that smoking the drug incited violence and insanity, the Department of Agriculture was making a film showing farmers the best methods for growing hemp.

Used as a drug, tincture of cannabis was part of the official list of drugs, the U.S. Pharmacopoeia, until 1941, and it was recommended for a wide variety of ailments. Because of its unpredictable effects and because other, more effective, drugs were developed, its use as medicine ceased. Recently, however, there has been an increase in interest in **THC,** or tetrahydrocannabinol, the main active substance in marijuana, as a treatment for loss of appetite, muscle spasms, glaucoma, and especially nausea. Marinol, distributed by Roxanne Company, is a synthetic form of THC that can be legally prescribed and some individuals have won court cases to permit them to legally smoke marijuana itself.

On the other hand, marijuana is considered a dangerous drug. Multimillion dollar campaigns are being waged against its cultivation in the United States, and we spend more millions every year in aid to other countries, much of whose marijuana is imported into the United States. In the United States, federal agencies confiscated nearly 482,948 pounds of marijuana in 1991. Ironically, in the same year, a group of growers in Australia applied to their government for permission to grow 37,000 acres of marijuana to be made into paper. These growers, who call themselves Hemp for Paper, say that their marijuana produces paper that lasts several times longer than paper made from wood, is more environmentally sound, and would have little or no THC (*San Francisco Chronicle,* 24 March 1991).

A BRIEF HISTORY OF MARIJUANA

The first mention of what we call marijuana is found in medical texts in China, India, and Assyria, some of which go back almost five thousand years. It was recognized as a medicine, as a source of hemp, and as a substance that produced intoxication. Herodotus, writing in the fifth century B.C., speaks of smoking cannabis. A warship of Carthage, the great empire

FIGURE 6.1
Marijuana was widely grown in many parts of the world as a source of plant material for clothing and rope.

that existed before Rome, was recently excavated and large quantities of what turned out to be cannabis were found in the ship. It appears that the ship was sunk sometime near the end of the First Punic War (264–241 B.C.). The large quantity of marijuana found led the discoverer to conclude that it was probably there for the enjoyment of the crew (Frost, 1987). In India, where recreational and religious use of marijuana was, and is, quite common, clear references to it date back to 1300 B.C. The epic poem **Mahabharata** includes a warning against what we would now call the **amotivational syndrome** (Morningstar, 1985).

The next important reference to marijuana takes us to the Arab world of the early Middle Ages, where, according to legend, there was a group of political fanatics called **hashishiyya.** They were reputed to be followers of Sheik Hasan Ibn-Sabbah. One legend relates that they smoked hashish and while in this altered state, sallied forth to kill their political enemies (Abel, 1980).

Another legend has it that the political leaders recruited followers by inducing young men to smoke hashish. The would-be recruits were then introduced to certain beautiful young ladies in a magnificent courtyard. The events that transpired were supposed to be similar to what would be their eternal reward if they died in the service of their leaders.

Yet another, less fanciful, story is that the hashishiyya smoked hashish as a means of relaxing after they committed their nefarious deeds. Marco Polo, the noted adventurer, is the source for many of these legends, and there is considerable doubt as to their authenticity.

Examination of the available writings of the Muslim world during the Middle Ages reveals that hashish and marijuana were widely known and used. Virtually all of the supposed positive and negative effects of cannabis were widely recognized many hundreds of years ago. What we now call cannabis was supposed to make you crave sweets, make you high, make sex better, and stimulate creativity. On the other hand, it was also supposed to *decrease* the sex drive, make males effeminate (shades of the testosterone controversy!), produce insanity, and cause an amotivational syndrome remarkably similar to that described below (Rosenthal, 1971).

The same analysis of the written record suggests that rather than referring to a bloodthirsty group of political fanatics, the term assassin, or hashishiyya, probably was a term used to describe common criminals who also used hashish. Thus, the hashishiyya were not fanatical killers driven to their deeds by the evil drug, but, instead, petty thieves and murderers who also used hashish and were incidentally members of a religious sect. In modern day Mexico, similarly, the colloquial word *marijuaneros* is used to describe young men and women who smoke marijuana and support their habit through burglary and robbery.

Hashish or marijuana crops up again in Europe in the 1800s. The **Club des Hachichins** was formed by writers in France, including **Baudelaire** and **Dumas,** to smoke hashish and try out other drugs as an aid to their creative processes. While they and other writers and artists of the period tried hashish, and several wrote about the experience, both Baudelaire and Dumas eventually turned against the drug (Kusinitz, 1987).

The popularity of hashish in Europe probably was, in part, the result of the Napoleonic Wars. In the early 1800s, France, under the leadership of **Napoleon,** waged a campaign in Egypt. Napoleon apparently was concerned that his soldiers, who had picked up the habit of smoking hashish in Egypt, would bring the drug back to France, which seemingly they did. Others with exposure to the Middle East did the same and hashish became the rage of France and the rest of Europe.

Marijuana Comes to the United States

In the beginning of the twentieth century in the United States, recreational marijuana use was confined to Hispanics in the Southwest and blacks in the ghettos, and hence was of little concern to middle-class white America. During the twenties, however, immigration by Mexican laborers had increased rapidly in much of the Southwest. The immigrants, both legal and illegal, were badly needed as farm laborers, but they brought with them their habit of smoking marijuana for enjoyment and relaxation. Given the prejudice against these workers, it is not surprising that use of the drug became a matter of considerable concern (Inciardi, 1986).

Numerous violent crimes were blamed on the use of marijuana, which was supposed to release inhibitions and be a sexual stimulant (Inciardi, 1986). When the Depression of the thirties deepened, these immigrants, who by now had moved into the Midwest, became unwanted surplus laborers and prejudice against them and their choice of recreational drug increased (Musto, 1987).

By the 1930s the marijuana "menace" had been discovered. Movies like *Reefer Madness* were made to warn the populace of the danger of marijuana. In *Reefer Madness,* the hero not only engages in illicit sex but then kills his sweet virginal girlfriend (named Mary, no less), while under the influence of marijuana. This film has become something of an underground classic. With its stilted acting and unbelievable plot the audience is typically more amused than appalled.

The brief history of marijuana would not be complete without mentioning **Harry Anslinger,** who with the aid of the media, led a vendetta against the drug. Anslinger was chief of the Bureau of Narcotics for thirty years, from 1932 to 1962, and in 1936 described marijuana as the "foremost menace to life, health and morals in the list of drugs used in America" (Anslinger & Cooper, 1937).

Anslinger may have truly believed that marijuana was a threat to American civilization or he might have been a shrewd bureaucrat who saw the issue as a way of advancing his career and that of the Bureau or both, but whatever his motives, his methods were questionable (Inciardi, 1986). He publicized dubious "police reports" like the one below that inflamed public opinion. His crusade led to the signing of the **Marijuana Tax Act of 1937** that wrongly classified marijuana as a narcotic, placing it under the same regulations as the opiates. Marijuana retreated to the barrios and ghettos.

> An entire family was murdered by a youthful addict in Florida. When officers arrived at the home, they found the youth staggering about in a human slaughterhouse. With an ax he had killed his father, mother, two brothers and a sister. . . . The boy said he had been in the habit of smoking something called "muggles" a childish name for marijuana (Sloman, 1979).

Along came the sixties, with its hippies, psychedelic music, and revolution. Marijuana moved out of the ghetto and, along with LSD, became a popular drug of middle-class youth. Remember—as a result of the hysteria generated by Anslinger—marijuana possession was a serious felony. Suddenly, teenagers from respectable families were being arrested for possession. Something had to be done, and it was.

A presidential commission on marijuana headed by the then governor of Pennsylvania, William Shafer, whose son had been arrested for possession of marijuana, concluded that the marijuana menace was overstated, and penalties for its use were too severe. In 1970, the Comprehensive Drug Abuse Prevention and Control Act reduced the federal penalty for possession from a felony to a misdemeanor, and many, but not all, states followed suit.

Marijuana Today

Even though there has been a gradual decline in reported current marijuana use among young adults from a peak in 1979 of 35.4 percent to 13.4 in 1991, marijuana is still being used by a substantial number of adolescents. Furthermore, some of those who were introduced to marijuana during their high school years in the sixties and seventies continue to use it. Regular use of marijuana by adults has not changed nearly as much in the last ten years as has use by younger people. What this seems to mean is that many people try marijuana, and a few continue to use it for prolonged periods of time.

Where Does All the Marijuana Come From?

Most marijuana is still smuggled into the United States, but domestic production is on the rise. Colombia seems to be the major exporter of marijuana, although it is also grown in Mexico, the Caribbean, and Asia. In fact, cannabis is so easy to grow that virtually any country *could* be a supplier, and anyone with a spare closet and electricity for lighting *could* be a grower. Attempts to reduce marijuana use by attacking the source do not seem likely to succeed.

In Mexico and Colombia, marijuana is grown on large farms; in the United States, marijuana is usually grown in smaller quantities on isolated land, indoors, or even underground. As law enforcement develops better

methods of detection, marijuana growers try to develop better methods for avoiding detection. In a sense, then, attempts to stop marijuana cultivation in the United States have become a cat and mouse game.

In chapter 12, forfeiture laws are described in detail, but basically they mean that the government can take possession of any property associated with illegal drug trade. Land used to grow marijuana can be confiscated and sold. Growers have learned to grow marijuana on rented land or government property. Helicopters are now equipped with special devices to locate unusual sources of heat such as a collection of lights used to grow marijuana (or orchids) indoors, so growers have built elaborate underground shelters. Millions of dollars are spent every year to eradicate the marijuana crop, yet billions are still spent to purchase it.

Another tool being used by the federal government is exemplified by Operation Green Merchant. Agents have subpoenaed the shipping records of companies that ship equipment used to grow plants indoors. If the agents can then associate the purchase of the equipment with some other ''suspicious'' activity such as a sudden rise in the electric bill (presumably representing the use of grow lights) or a subscription to a magazine advocating legalized marijuana, they may have just cause for a search warrant. The rationale used in Operation Green Merchant troubles many people. After all, it is not against the law to subscribe to a magazine that advocates the legalization of marijuana, buy grow lights, or use more electricity than normal.

Most authorities admit that it is impossible to totally eliminate marijuana growing, and feel the most they can hope for is to make it difficult to

Woman Tells Judge
The Marijuana
Was for Her Iguana

Reuters

Ottawa

A Canadian woman escaped drug-trafficking charges by convincing a judge that the marijuana police found in her Ottawa house was food for her iguana, lawyer Jim Harbic said yesterday.

Cindy Havens said she discovered the marijuana growing near her house and started feeding it to her finicky iguana, Pogo Longtail.

Judge Bernard Ryan said that the marijuana was of poor quality and that it appeared Havens had no intention of selling it. Ryan fined Havens $435 for possession of about one pound of marijuana, then said he expects that "every drug trafficker in the city will now be buying iguanas."

grow it safely. An ironic result of success in this attempt has been to raise the price of marijuana, thereby making it more profitable to grow and encouraging people to take additional risks.

Why are people willing to spend billions of dollars a year on marijuana? What does it really do? Is it the scourge that some claim, or are its dangers overstated? On the following pages let's try to separate fact from fiction, opinion from evidence.

CANNABIS SATIVA, CANNABIS INDICA, MARIJUANA, MARIHUANA, WHAT?

The confusion concerning marijuana begins with its botanical nomenclature. The commonest form of the plant is **Cannabis sativa,** which was widely grown as a source of hemp. *Cannabis sativa* is a tall plant with a woody stem. Some botanists (and growers) claim that there is a second species, **Cannabis indica,** which came originally from India and is shorter and has a higher THC content. A third type of marijuana called **Cannabis ruderalis,** grows in northern Europe and parts of Asia. It is characterized by a short growth period from seed to flower, as befits the short growing season and low potency.

A22 The Sacramento Bee Final ● Saturday, June 22, 1991

Government halts giving pot to new patients

By Tom Webb
Knight-Ridder Newspapers

WASHINGTON – Government health agencies will no longer provide marijuana cigarettes to new patients with AIDS, cancer or glaucoma, despite claims that smoking the drug eases chronic symptoms of those diseases.

For a decade, the government has distributed marijuana to a small number of seriously ill patients nationwide. But fearing that the program sends mixed signals about drug use – and worried about a "rapid increase" in demand due to AIDS – officials said Friday they are virtually halting new approvals.

"It was felt that this might get out of hand, both in terms of the supply we might have and the government saying, rather successfully, that marijuana is not good for you," said Bill Grigg, a spokesman for the U.S. Public Health Service. "It might be (perceived as) saying that it's safe and effective, which is the standard for a new drug."

The new policy was angrily criticized by some activists, who believe that smoking marijuana eases pain and restores appetite in people ravaged by acquired immune deficiency syndrome.

"They're really saying to terminally ill people, 'Go die in agony,' " said Arnold Trebach, president of the Drug Policy Foundation, a drug think-tank. "With AIDS, many of the medications cause terrible problems, and this eases some of the discomfort, eases some of the nausea."

Under the new policy, the 34 Americans now approved to receive government-grown marijuana cigarettes will continue to get them. But new applications will be frowned on, and applicants must first prove that they had no response to the pill form of THC, the active ingredient in marijuana.

The use of marijuana as an AIDS therapy has been controversial, and public health officials – including those from the Food and Drug Administration and the National Institutes of Health – expressed concern that there's no scientific proof that it helps.

"There is great concern that the contaminants in natural marijuana might harm these immune-impaired patients," health officials said in a statement.

Most botanists believe, however, that all three types are subspecies and represent the product of selective breeding for height in the case of *Cannabis sativa* (it can reach twenty feet) or psychoactive strength in the case of *Cannabis indica*. These arguments may seem academic but have important legal implications. Someone arrested for possession of marijuana when legal statutes define it as *Cannabis sativa* cannot be prosecuted if the plant possessed is *Cannabis indica* or *Cannabis ruderalis* if the two are separate species.

Cannabis, of whatever species or subspecies, is the plant. The leaves, buds, and flowers mixed together are known by the Spanish term marijuana. **Marihuana** is simply the English language phonetic spelling of marijuana. **Sinsemilla** is Spanish, a combination of the word *sin* meaning "without" plus *semilla* meaning "seed." Sinsemilla is marijuana from the female plant that has not been allowed to be fertilized. If male plants are isolated from the female plants, the female plant produces more resin and flowers. The buds and flowers of the marijuana plant contain more THC than the leaves and stems, so sinsemilla is much stronger than ordinary marijuana.

Other Forms of Cannabis

Stronger even than sinsemilla is **hash, hashish, hasheesh,** or **hash oil.** The resin in the cannabis plant contains a high percentage of THC. It can be scraped from the plant by hand or extracted, usually by boiling the plant material in alcohol. THC is almost insoluble in water, but highly soluble in alcohol. After the mixture is boiled for a while it is strained and reduced further. The resin itself is usually called hash or hashish, while the reduced alcohol extraction is hash oil. THC content of hash and hash oil can exceed 60 percent.

While most marijuana or hash is smoked, it can be ingested orally. In the United States, marijuana is most often eaten after being baked in brownies, although it is sometimes mixed with butter. The effects of THC ingested orally are often different than when smoked, as we shall see.

Occasionally someone buys what is reported to be THC. You may be absolutely sure that there is no real THC on the street. **Delta-9-tetrahydrocannabinol** is unstable in light and needs to be refrigerated. Marinol is THC mixed in sesame oil in gelatin capsules. It is stable at room temperature and hence could be sold on the street. However, at present, strict regulations regarding the distribution of Marinol have prevented it from being diverted to the general population.

PHARMACOLOGY AND PHYSIOLOGY OF MARIJUANA

From a pharmacological standpoint, marijuana is a curious plant with some limited potential for medical use. While there are more than four hundred chemicals found in it, including sixty that occur in no other plant and hence are called **cannabinoids** (Turner, 1980), only four seem to have any biological, medical, or psychoactive significance (Compton, Dewey, & Martin, 1990). These four are delta-9 and delta-8-THC along with cannabidiol and cannabinol.

The primary difference between delta 9 and delta 8 is potency, with delta 9 being about twice as potent as delta 8. Cannabidiol and cannabinol do not seem to have any significant action themselves but may add to the overall effect of either of the other two active cannabinoids. Laboratory studies done with synthetic THC in animals or humans may not yield the same results as would be found if marijuana were smoked, because the other active cannabinoids are not found in synthetic THC.

To help solve these problems there is now a standard "research" marijuana cigarette offered with two different potencies (roughly 1.4 percent and 2.8 percent THC), available from the National Institute of Drug Abuse. There is also a placebo marijuana cigarette which contains no THC. The marijuana is grown in Mississippi on government owned land. Researchers there also are experimenting to find selective herbicides that will kill marijuana plants and leave other crops untouched.

Absorption and Elimination

In the United States, marijuana is usually smoked, and absorption is quite rapid. Exactly how long it takes for the drug to reach the brain, the time to peak effect, and the duration of action are dependent on so many factors that exact figures, while they are often presented, are virtually meaningless. One important problem is the definition of being "high." How do researchers quantify such a subjective phenomenon? In the laboratory a standard dose of delta-9-THC can be injected, taken orally, or smoked, and the results measured with precision. However, in real life, users smoke nonstandard joints containing various amounts of marijuana, inhale more or less deeply, and hold the smoke in their lungs for different lengths of time—yielding effects that are impossible to quantify.

One common belief, that holding marijuana smoke in the lungs for a long time produces a greater high, has not held up to laboratory research. In this study, subjects were asked to hold smoke in their lungs for one, ten, and twenty seconds. There were no differences in objective or subjective ratings between those who held marijuana in the lungs and those who exhaled it rapidly (Zacny & Chait, 1989).

For our purposes, it is sufficient to note that THC reaches the brain within seconds of being smoked and the psychological effects are often noted shortly thereafter. The duration of effect of marijuana depends on the definition of ''being high,'' but it is usually considered to be a few hours at most (Benedikt, Cristofaro, Mendelson, & Mello, 1986).

Similar rapid onset of action is seen with injection of THC, but different results are seen when marijuana is ingested. Since it is absorbed relatively poorly in the gastrointestinal tract, THC has a long latency before it takes effect. A person may eat a marijuana brownie at a party and not notice any effects until one or two hours later, after the party is over.

When taken orally the concentration of THC in the bloodstream is more difficult to titrate than when marijuana is smoked. Since users who smoke marijuana can usually tell in seconds or minutes how ''high'' they are, they are able to adjust their dosage accordingly, a phenomenon known as **autotitration.** The onset of action when marijuana is consumed is measured in hours, however, and the amount ingested is often impossible to determine. No wonder then that ingestion of marijuana is not nearly as popular as smoking, and the percentage of unpleasant experiences is quite high.

As is the case with alcohol, rate of elimination of marijuana is less variable than rate of absorption. Not only are the cannabinoids highly fat soluble, but also bind to protein (described in chapter 2). What this means is that the drug is rapidly eliminated from the bloodstream, but can remain in fatty tissue for two to three weeks after use (Mirin & Weiss, 1983). The cannabinoids are released slowly into the bloodstream and metabolized, and eventually excreted in the urine. The primary metabolites are called 11–nor-delta-9 (and delta-8) THC-9-carboxylic acid. The delta-9 metabolite is the one that is detected in the most widely used urine test.

The fact that trace amounts of metabolites of marijuana can be detected in urine by sophisticated tests days and weeks after being smoked does not necessarily mean that a person who smokes a joint is affected by the drug for that length of time. First, THC is bound to protein and fatty tissue; second, you should recall from chapter 2 that a threshold amount of the drug is required before an effect is seen. Well-meaning but misguided ''authorities'' to the contrary, an occasional smoker of marijuana is not continuously stoned.

Moreover, there is controversy over how long marijuana can be detected in the urine. Heavy smokers of marijuana may show metabolites of THC present for weeks, but someone who smokes one marijuana cigarette will not; nor can the usual urine tests distinguish between high levels of very recent use and lower levels of consistent use.

The metabolic breakdown of THC begins in the lungs when smoked (Turner, 1980). The THC that is not bound to protein or taken up by body tissue is rapidly metabolized, primarily in the liver and excreted in the feces and urine.

Physiological Effects   Given that most marijuana is smoked, we must consider both the effects of THC and the effects of smoking. The short-term physiological effects of smoking marijuana are dose dependent, relatively minor, and temporary. The effects of long-term use are more difficult to determine, in part because marijuana use in the United States did not become extensive until the 1960s.

Marijuana and the Central Nervous System

Despite years of research, surprisingly little is known about the effect of marijuana on the brain. Like alcohol, it probably disturbs the neuronal membrane, and there is evidence for involvement of neurotransmitters. Catecholamine neurotransmitters are involved; THC reduces norepinephrine activity while increasing dopamine activity (Markianos & Vakis, 1984). Marijuana has anticholinergic properties as well, and decreases the turnover of acetylcholine in the hippocampus, a brain structure involved in memory (Domino, 1981). Finally, some researchers believe that there exists a specific receptor on the neuron for cannabinol, especially delta-9-THC. As you saw in chapter 2 and will read in chapter 9, the discovery of a specific receptor for morphine led to the discovery of endorphins. Could there be an endogenous cannabinoid?

The changes in cortical brain wave activity after using marijuana are similar to those in a relaxed drowsy person. Marijuana does seem to interfere with REM (rapid eye movement) sleep. People awakened during REM sleep usually report that they had been dreaming. When marijuana use is stopped after several days use, there is REM rebound—in other words, increased dreaming (Jones, 1980). Unlike alcohol, marijuana does not seem to impair deep, or stage four, sleep.

Marijuana apparently has a different physiological effect on experienced as opposed to inexperienced users. Experienced marijuana smokers show an increased blood flow to the brain after smoking, while the blood flow of inexperienced smokers is decreased. Furthermore, these changes are matched by corresponding mood changes. In one study, inexperienced users felt sleepier, and were more depressed and anxious than experienced smokers, who reported being *less* anxious and depressed and who reported being *more* energetic (Mathew, Wilson, & Tant, 1989). In other studies, changes in cerebral blood flow have been found to be correlated with the same kind of psychological changes that follow marijuana use.

The most controversial topic related to marijuana and the brain concerns the consequences of long-term use. The popular press often reports that studies have shown clear neurological deficits with long-term use of marijuana. A few such studies do exist, but they are difficult to interpret. One of the best known studies (Campbell, Evans, Thomson, & Williams, 1971) involved ten young male cannabis users and found damage in the caudate nucleus, basal ganglia, and areas around the third ventricle (see chapter 3). They also reported finding enlarged brain ventricles.

Widespread criticism of these initial findings focused on the small number of subjects, the control group involved, and the fact that these subjects not only admitted to fairly extensive use of other drugs, but that several also had evidence of head injury and other factors that might produce similar results (Wert & Raulin, 1986a). Subsequent studies done with a technique known as a CAT scan, which is less dangerous and more sensitive, have largely failed to support these findings.

Well controlled studies on long-term effects of marijuana are difficult to do. Remember that most marijuana users also use other drugs. Also, it is difficult to estimate the degree of use, and it is difficult to control the possibility that preexisting factors may have contributed to the results. In a review of the research which took many factors into consideration, Wert and Raulin (1986) concluded that there was no clear evidence that marijuana produces either physical or functional changes in the brain of humans.

In the last several years, some studies have been done that may qualify that finding. The acute effects of marijuana on memory are well known. Like alcohol, marijuana produces a short-term memory deficit. The hippocampus, an important structure in the midbrain, is believed to be involved in the processing of memory, and injections of delta-9-THC cause disruption of the electrical activity in the hippocampus.

In animals, the same injections have been shown to disrupt memory, particularly for sensory information. The deficit caused by injection of THC is similar to that seen in animals with hippocampal damage. Finally, long-term administration of high doses of THC has, in rats, been shown to produce hippocampal damage (Deadwyler, Heyser, Michaelis, & Hampson, 1990).

The relevance of these animal studies to human behavior has not yet been determined. The dosages given to rats far exceed those that humans normally self-administer. For example, in the memory studies the human equivalent of the "high dose" condition is about 130 mg of pure THC. As a frame of reference, the standard NIDA-issued marijuana cigarette contains between 1.4 and 2.8 percent THC and weighs less than 1 gram, which means that a person would have to smoke more than 65 joints (allowing for loss of THC during burning and inhalation) to reach the equivalent dosage.

Of course, THC does accumulate in fatty tissue, and chronic, heavy use may produce different results than short-term administration. A preliminary study of ten marijuana-dependent adolescents concluded that at least some chronic heavy users of marijuana show short-term subtle memory deficits that may last at least six weeks after they stop smoking (Schwatz, Guenewald, Klitzner, & Fedio, 1989). It is unfortunate that little experimental research is presently being conducted with THC and marijuana. The drug research dollar has to be stretched a long way, and cocaine, crack, and other more glamorous drugs have taken a large share. If current trends in drug abuse continue, more money may be available for the kind of research described above, and better studies may clarify the confusion that currently exists.

The Cardiovascular System

Smoking marijuana causes an increase in the heart rate which is called **tachycardia.** In laboratory studies the increase in heart rate averages about fourteen beats per minute (Benedikt, Cristoforo, Mendelson, & Mello, 1986).

The previous study involved mature women who had never previously smoked marijuana, but the self-report by admitted users of marijuana confirms this finding (Petronis & Anthony, 1989).

Tachycardia could conceivably present a problem for people with cardiovascular problems, as it means that the heart is working harder. Furthermore, tachycardia is more common with inexperienced users and is sometimes interpreted as a symptom of fear. Therefore, tachycardia may be frightening to experimental users. Tolerance occurs rapidly, and tachycardia is rarely noticed by regular smokers.

Peripheral blood vessels may be dilated, producing bloodshot eyes and warm ears. Effects on blood pressure are variable and impossible to predict. In general, the effects of marijuana on the cardiovascular system may be thought of as similar to mild stress.

The Respiratory System

The effects of marijuana on the respiratory system are twofold. THC itself is a **bronchodilator,** and has been suggested as a treatment for asthma. Prior to 1941, extract of marijuana could be prescribed for such a purpose.

When smoked, however, marijuana can be harmful to lung tissue. Tobacco manufacturers go to great lengths to ensure that tobacco smoke is easy to inhale. Many of the additives in cigarettes are designed to make the smoke seem cooler or sweeter. Furthermore, the manufacturers have spent millions of dollars developing low tar and nicotine cigarettes.

Marijuana, is, by these standards, quite crude, and marijuana smoke quite harsh. Furthermore, a person smoking a marijuana cigarette typically inhales it very deeply, holds it in the lungs as long as possible (increasing the amount of contact with lung tissue), and often smokes it down to the very end.

Not surprisingly, then, studies have shown that chronic smoking of marijuana cigarettes causes lung irritation and decreased pulmonary function (Bernstein, 1980). Marijuana smoke, like cigarette smoke, contains cancer-causing substances known as carcinogens. Also, tars, carbon monoxide, and hydrogen cyanide levels are similar to those of cigarette smoke (Cohen, 1985). Actual examination of the lungs of regular marijuana smokers leaves no doubt that marijuana and cigarette smoking have similar effects on the lungs. *All* of the chronic marijuana smokers (defined as ten or more joints a week for at least five years) in one study showed pathological changes. Furthermore, those who smoked both tobacco and marijuana showed the most changes of all (Gong, Fligiel, Tashkin, & Barbers, 1987). No doubt exists whatsoever that inhaling the smoke of burning leaves is harmful, whether they are marijuana, tobacco, or lettuce leaves. The question is the extent of risk.

While marijuana smokers do not smoke as frequently as cigarette smokers it may be that one joint may be the equivalent of several tobacco cigarettes. Twenty years from now, will marijuana smokers report the same incidence of lung cancer and emphysema as do cigarette smokers? No one knows.

Sex and Reproduction　　　If I told a group of experienced marijuana users that marijuana can decrease their sex drive, they would probably burst out laughing. In our culture, marijuana is considered an aphrodisiac (see chapter 12). The euphoria, increased responsiveness to external stimuli, and other effects are often interpreted as increased sexual feelings. Nevertheless, studies do show that marijuana can decrease levels of **testosterone** in males (Kolodny, Masters, Kolodner, & Toro, 1974; Kolodny, Lessin, Toro, Masters, & Cohen, 1976).

On the other hand, the significance of decreased testosterone levels is a matter of debate since other researchers have found that the reduced testosterone levels were still within normal range (Cushman, 1975; Mendelson, Ellingboe, Kuehnle, & Mello, 1984; Cone, Johnson, Moore, & Roache, 1986). In healthy males, occasional use of marijuana has not been shown to cause any serious reproductive problems, although the effects of decreased testosterone production on very young males just beginning puberty should be a matter of some concern and future study.

Evidence suggests that there are also reproductive effects in women. Pregnant white women who are also regular marijuana smokers (defined as those who smoke two or three times a month or more), tended to have babies who were of low birth weight (less than five pounds) or who were small for their gestational age. Occasional use did not seem to affect birth weight or size. Nonwhite women who smoked marijuana regularly did not have smaller babies, probably because smaller babies are typical of nonwhite women in general (Hatch & Bracken, 1986).

What causes the decreased birth weight and shorter body length of babies whose mothers smoke marijuana—THC, some other active ingredient, or the act of smoking itself? THC does pass the placental barrier (see chapter 2) but animal studies of its teratogenic effects are inconclusive. In some species such as the rabbit, there is evidence that inhaling marijuana smoke during pregnancy results in an increased number of fetal deaths, although there was no evidence of teratogenic effects (Rosenkrantz, Grant, Fleischman, & Baker, 1986).

The Immune System　　　With the tragedy of AIDS, everyone knows about the immune system. Some test tube and animal studies have shown that THC can reduce immunity to infections, and there is some similar evidence in humans. However, a number of studies contradict the findings in humans, and the dosages in the test tube and animal studies that do show a link tend to be quite high (Hollister, 1988).

Most of the studies that have been done on the effects of marijuana on the immune system were done in the early 1970s and the relatively small number of recent studies would seem to indicate that the general consensus among researchers is that the possible dangers are quite small (Hollister, 1988).

If the effect is real, it is unlikely to have any consequences for the average, young, healthy, occasional marijuana smoker. Of course, anyone testing positive for the AIDS virus would not want to take any chances, and those who do test positive are routinely advised to avoid marijuana and alcohol. On the other hand, it is unfortunate that much of the antidrug literature includes uncritical statements about the presumed harmful effect of marijuana on the immune system. Inaccurate statements, even when made with best of intentions, often have results that are the exact opposite of those intended.

PSYCHOLOGICAL EFFECTS

The psychological effects of smoking marijuana are difficult to describe. Certain changes can be quantified and are consistent. Time perception is altered; time seems to pass more slowly. A smoker finds it more difficult to concentrate, and short-term memory is impaired (Ferraro, 1980). Anyone who has attempted to talk to someone who has been smoking marijuana will have no trouble recognizing the results of the above effects. These effects are temporary, meaning that a person who has just smoked marijuana would do poorly studying for or taking an exam. No clear evidence exists that marijuana smoking causes any permanent cognitive impairment (Wert & Raulin, 1986b).

Subjective Effects

The more subjective effects of marijuana include mood changes, heightened sensitivity to external stimuli, and an introspectiveness that may cause the smoker to be silent for prolonged periods. The mood changes usually involve euphoria and a sense of hilarity (marijuana smokers are notorious for getting fits of giggling), but can include sadness, anxiety, and paranoia (Tart, 1971).

Why would an inability to concentrate, forgetfulness, and a feeling that time is passing slowly, be seen as positive? Even if we throw in mood swings and a greater sensitivity to stimuli, it might be hard to imagine that marijuana has been and continues to be such a commonly used substance. Even more remarkable, inexperienced users of marijuana do not even experience most of these phenomena, neither the negative nor positive effects!

Apparently, inexperienced marijuana smokers have to learn to identify the changes that occur as a result of smoking and learn to label them as subjectively pleasant. Experienced smokers get just as much pleasure, and report themselves as being just as high when they smoke placebo cigarettes as when they smoke marijuana containing THC (Jones, 1971). This phenomenon is known as reverse tolerance and is another puzzling aspect of marijuana.

One clue to these confusing findings may be found in the details of the study reported above. One half of the experienced marijuana users reported getting high after smoking a placebo extract, but only 5 percent after taking a placebo orally. Perhaps even more telling is that while 72 percent of infrequent smokers reported getting high after oral administration of THC, only 32 percent of frequent users did so. In other words, more regular smokers got high smoking a placebo cigarette than regular smokers receiving THC orally.

These findings suggest that much of the high is conditioned to the frequent users' usual mode of ingestion, smoking. Set and setting play an important role in all drug effects, but particularly so with marijuana. The infrequent user who has no set for the effects relies on the actual changes that THC produces; the frequent smoker has past experience to fall back on and a shared history of what being high is supposed to be.

Controlled studies of the effects of Marinol also are instructive. About half of the subjects taking Marinol reported drowsiness, and 16 percent reported anxiety. Nearly half of the subjects receiving a placebo also reported drowsiness, and 24 percent reported anxiety. Those who received Marinol were, however, more likely to report muddled thinking and dizziness (Physician's Drug Reference, 1990).

In the study reported on page 210, cerebral blood flow was found to be greater in experienced users and less in inexperienced users. Furthermore, when experienced users were given a placebo marijuana cigarette, changes in blood flow were the same as when given a marijuana cigarette with THC (Mathew, Wilson, & Tant, 1989). Whatever the reason for the differences between experienced and inexperienced smokers, it has in part a physiological basis.

Described objectively, the psychological effects of marijuana do not seem either remarkable or positive. Apparently, the experienced user seems to have learned to appreciate the changes produced by marijuana and interprets them as positive. Similar changes in a different set and setting might be interpreted differently.

Amotivational Syndrome

In 1968, the first two modern reports describing the **amotivational syndrome** were published (McGlothlin & West, 1968; Smith, 1968). Heavy users of marijuana were supposed to be unable to concentrate, show little ambition or interest in achievement as traditionally defined, and would cease to be productive members of society. These studies were followed by numerous first person stories in magazines about "My son, the marijuana user."

A typical case history went something like this: John was a hard-working straight A student until his junior year in high school. He split wood on weekends to earn enough money to pay for the restoration of his 1959 Volkswagen. He went to church on Sunday and worked with the boys and girls in the Children's Hospital. All of a sudden he started to change; instead of working, he sat in his room and listened to rock-and-roll. He grew his hair long and started hanging out with a crowd that got in trouble in school. Finally his parents confronted him, and he admitted that he had been smoking marijuana. He stopped smoking and went into counseling for two years. Now he seems to be back on track, although he sometimes reports having difficulty concentrating. He looks back on his marijuana smoking with shame and regret.

Keeping in mind the long half-life of marijuana, it is likely that someone who smoked marijuana several times a day would always be under the influence of marijuana and perhaps content to listen to music rather than chop wood. The reader, however, must really ask which came first—the marijuana or the amotivational syndrome? Adolescents have gone through similar changes (including "getting well") for many generations before marijuana became popular. Why blame something that may be a symptom rather than the cause?

Studies of other cultures in which heavy marijuana use is common provide mixed support for the concept of the amotivational syndrome. Studies done in Jamaica (Rubin & Comitas, 1976) and Costa Rica (Carter & Doughty, 1976) examined long-term smokers of very high doses of marijuana and found no evidence of such a syndrome. In a recent follow-up of the Costa Rica group, some impairment was noted on cognitive tasks, and those who continued to use marijuana tended to have menial jobs, be less well adjusted and, in general to be rejected by polite society. The authors of the study cautioned, however, that it was impossible to determine if the marijuana use was the cause of the apparent lack of adjustment; it could as easily have been the result.

In both the Jamaica and Costa Rica studies, the marijuana users were employed at jobs that did not require much skill or cognitive ability. Perhaps individuals in a more modern, complex society might not be able to function as well (Cohen, 1985). One study conducted in the United States directly examines this hypothesis. Extensive testing was done on a group of heavy, prolonged marijuana users aged twenty-five through thirty-six. Put simply, the findings indicate no evidence of the amotivational syndrome. All the subjects worked steadily, and their IQ scores were very high (Schaeffer, Andrysiak, & Ungerleider, 1981).

On the other hand, another study of adult heavy marijuana users did show at least some impairment of functioning. One hundred and fifty subjects who smoked an average of 3 1/2 joints a day were studied. From these a sample of fifteen was tested and interviewed in depth. The authors concluded that while the subjects were functioning relatively well in society, most used marijuana to avoid dealing with personal or vocational issues. They smoked heavily, the authors felt, to compensate for perceived failures in other aspects of their lives or to enable them to ignore the requirements of adulthood (Hendin, Haas, Singer, Ellner, & Ulman, 1987).

Other studies also indicate that some people who smoke marijuana extensively have impaired function. Compared to pre-drug behavior, adolescents who smoked at least four times a week had low grades, stayed away from home, and were more likely to be involved in automobile accidents (Schwartz, Hoffman, & Jones, 1987). Of course, it should be noted that in both of these studies the user's marijuana consumption was high by anyone's standards. Nor does either study address cause and effect relationships.

The amotivational syndrome is difficult to define and difficult to demonstrate. Most researchers no longer believe that smoking marijuana (at least occasional smoking) invariably leads to lower productivity or decreased

in depth

One frequently overlooked problem with recreational drug use is that of quality control. Buyers can never be sure that the drug they think they are purchasing is the drug they are actually getting. Another problem is that the drug is frequently adulterated with other substances. Cocaine is cut with local anesthetics and heroin with quinine. The story below illustrates how adulteration of marijuana can be harmful.

In the winter of 1981, there was an outbreak of salmonella poisoning in Ohio. In all, there were thirty-six cases, most of them either involving young people between the ages of fifteen and forty or very young children. Normally, **salmonella** outbreaks are the result of eating contaminated food, particularly eggs, but these cases were puzzling. The victims had not eaten at the same restaurants, nor had they purchased the same food. Very few knew each other, and the outbreaks occurred in various parts of the area in a seemingly unconnected fashion.

The ages of the victims finally lead those in charge of the investigation to suspect marijuana.

Nearly all of the people who had fallen ill admitted to having used marijuana, and analysis of the marijuana they gave to the researchers revealed that it was contaminated with salmonella, as well as several other pathogenic bacteria.

What about the young children? The users apparently transmitted the bacteria to their young children. Anyone rolling a contaminated joint would have fingers contaminated with salmonella and anyone smoking that joint would contaminate his/her lips. Transmission, then, would be a simple process.

Where did the salmonella come from? The best evidence suggested that either the growers or the dealers added manure to the marijuana to increase its weight and bulk. One victim reported that the marijuana smelled and tasted funny. Indeed! The jury may be out on the amotivational syndrome or the effect of marijuana on the immune system, but there is no doubt that if you smoke manure you will get sick (Roueche, 1984).

---

motivation. It is just as likely that those who develop these problems also smoke large quantities of marijuana. Nevertheless, it is also valid to note that heavy marijuana use often accompanies behavior that might be described as amotivational.

Tolerance and Dependence

Tolerance to the effects of marijuana does occur, but the nature of the tolerance is complex. Behavioral tolerance reduces the effects of marijuana (Zinberg & Harding, 1982). That is, experience with low doses of marijuana will enable a user to compensate for the decreased concentration, coordination, and memory loss. Reverse tolerance also occurs, in that learning to appreciate the effects of marijuana results in a greater effect of a low dose in the experienced than in the inexperienced user (Jones & Benowitz, 1976), especially when the experienced user *wants* to be high. Finally, the traditional form of tolerance also occurs, in that high doses of marijuana over a long period of time produce less and less effect (Jones, 1980).

In animals, tolerance is easy to demonstrate and quite remarkable. It occurs in all animals that have been tested and in virtually all conditions, whether physiological or behavioral. Tolerance also occurs to the lethal or toxic effects of THC in both rats and pigeons. These doses, incidentally, are extremely high, the human equivalent of about 6,000 standard marijuana cigarettes per day. Tolerance occurs rapidly and is long-lasting (Compton, Dewey, & Martin, 1990).

In humans, evidence for tolerance to the lethal effects of THC is lacking because of the simple fact that there has never been a documented case of a single death due to an overdose of marijuana. There have been occasional reports of death due to marijuana overdose going back to the nineteenth century (Laurence, 1844; Heyndrickx, Scheiris, & Schepens, 1969; Nahas, 1971), but they have not been substantiated. Emergency room reports of drug overdoses reported through DAWN (Drug Abuse Warning Network) sometimes include marijuana but these deaths are always a result of marijuana in combination with other drugs.

Given the rapid development of tolerance, it is surprising that the question of physiological dependence is still being debated. Physical withdrawal signs have been reported but they are relatively mild. In humans, they include irritability, restlessness, sleeplessness, and changes in appetite (Jones & Benowitz, 1972).

It should be pointed out that in studies of withdrawal in humans, subjects were given relatively high doses of marijuana for up to twenty days. Upon cessation, their symptoms were observed. However, all of the subjects in the study were confined to a locked psychiatric ward and had been hospitalized there for a month with no contact with the outside world. One must question the extent to which irritability, restlessness, sleep difficulties, and other symptoms were the result of the setting as much as the withdrawal.

A more convincing argument for the possibility of dependence on marijuana comes from clinical reports of drug abuse professionals. By definition, craving, compulsive use, and frequent relapse to marijuana are indications of dependence, and these have been reported. Keep in mind that this dependence is almost undoubtedly psychological dependence, but regardless of the cause, some users are simply unable to stop when they want to.

The reasons for wanting to stop seem to be varied. The increasing use of drug testing (discussed in chapter 12), has encouraged some users to attempt to stop. Others, who initially sought treatment for abuse of other drugs and who were counselled to stop the use of all drugs, have found giving up marijuana difficult. Others have been alarmed by the effects of marijuana use on their respiratory systems, or have been disturbed by what they see as a difficulty in expressing emotions or experiencing intimacy. Still others have been influenced by the drug use and abuse of their own children and wish to set a better example (Zweben & O'Connell, 1988).

Clinical reports such as the one reported above are difficult to interpret. In particular, it is difficult to distinguish between psychological and physiological dependence in human subjects. Marijuana does not seem to result in dependence when a strict definition of *physical* dependence is adopted (Compton, Dewey, & Martin, 1990). Thus from the strict definition of addiction as presented in chapter 2, marijuana does not meet the criteria.

The Contact High

Part of the folklore of the sixties was the contact high. People who were susceptible were supposed to get stoned merely by being around actual smokers. Some believed that the effect was due to inhaling what is now called sidestream smoke. Others argued, quite reasonably, that being around people who were giggling and acting strangely led to similar effects in non-smokers.

With the current increase in urine testing, however, what was folklore has become an important issue. Is it possible to get high simply by inhaling marijuana smoke, and can a person in a room of smokers test positive on urine tests? The answer to both questions is a definite maybe.

Cone and Johnson (1986) exposed subjects to the smoke of either four or sixteen standard dose marijuana cigarettes for one hour a day for six days. The high dose group reported getting high and there were significant levels of THC in the blood. Using a very sensitive urine test, the subjects showed significant levels of THC metabolites, especially for the high dose (sixteen cigarettes). Using a less sensitive, but more commonly used criteria, the results were less clear. The subjective effects of being exposed to sixteen marijuana cigarettes for an hour was approximately equivalent to smoking one joint.

The most important critical factor in determining whether the subject would test positive was not the number of cigarettes inhaled, but the room air levels of THC (Cone & Johnson, 1986). Keep in mind that these subjects were exposed to four or sixteen marijuana cigarettes for an hour a day in a room that was eight-by-eight-by-six feet, hardly a situation likely to be encountered by the average person, nor one to be tolerated by anyone except a subject in an experiment.

Based on these findings as well as others, the possibility that someone will get high or test positive when exposed to the smoke of a single marijuana cigarette in a room for a short period of time is relatively small, but it can happen. If I knew that I were subject to regular, unannounced drug testing, I would be careful even of sidestream smoke. On the other hand, if someone tried to convince me that they had tested positive because they had been at a party where someone else had smoked marijuana, I don't think I would believe them.

Effect on Appetite

Another belief of recreational users is that marijuana makes the smoker hungry, especially for sweets—hence the term **"the munchies."** There has not been a great amount of research in this area but the clinical and experimental studies that do exist support the anecdotal evidence. Smoking marijuana seems to increase one's appetite for food—especially between-meal snacks

(Foltin, Brady, & Fishman, 1986). Increased appetite is sometimes mentioned as a possible useful side effect of marijuana for those undergoing chemotherapy (see below).

MEDICAL USES OF MARIJUANA

Cannabis was used for a wide variety of medicinal purposes for thousands of years. Its effectiveness, however, was limited by a lack of understanding of the active ingredient in the drug and by the fact that the THC content of marijuana varies widely from sample to sample. Consequently, as new drugs that had similar medicinal properties were discovered marijuana use tapered off. The new drugs could be administered in standard doses and their effects were more reliable.

An ironic consequence of the explosion of illegal marijuana use in the 1960s was a resurgence of interest in marijuana as a medicine. Research into its effects resulted in a better understanding of the chemistry of marijuana, and, consequently, refined methods of extracting THC were developed. Now that the relatively pure active ingredient had been discovered, it could be evaluated for possible medical uses.

Glaucoma

Glaucoma is a serious disease produced by the build-up of pressure inside the eye. This increased pressure damages the optic nerve, resulting in blindness. Marijuana lowers intraocular pressure and is an effective treatment for glaucoma. It does not cure the condition, but it can prevent blindness (Peterson, 1980). It is unlikely, however, that marijuana will become the drug of choice for glaucoma, since there are other drugs that are just as effective and have fewer unpleasant side effects. Nevertheless, marijuana may be useful in situations where other drugs fail.

Antiemetic Effects

Marijuana is quite effective in reducing vomiting and nausea. Cancer patients undergoing chemotherapy often experience prolonged nausea and vomiting which is extremely unpleasant, so much so that it is a major consideration for those beginning or continuing therapy. Marijuana has proved effective for some, though not all, patients undergoing chemotherapy, and for some it is effective where other treatments have failed (Peterson, 1980).

Since possession of marijuana is at least a misdemeanor in most states, and furnishing it to others a felony, medical doctors are understandably reluctant to provide it to their patients. However, *In Health* magazine reported a study by Kleiman and Doblin that found that 44 percent of the responding doctors said they recommended marijuana to their cancer patients (1991, vol. 5, p. 11). Moreover, in many hospitals, its use is discreetly ignored. For those who are more strictly law abiding, Marinol is available.

Marinol was discussed earlier. Since it is in capsule form, and is prescribed by a doctor, it may be more acceptable to some. The set and setting of a cancer patient taking a capsule to reduce vomiting is much different than that of a recreational user smoking a joint to get high. In one case, the person is a patient taking medication for a medical problem, in the other a user smoking for pleasure. However, there is some debate over the relative effectiveness of Marinol, which requires the oral route of administration as compared to a marijuana cigarette (Weiss, 1988). Those who are vomiting may find Marinol difficult to take, and titration is more difficult with the oral route as you learned in chapter 2.

Other Medical Uses

Marijuana also has been suggested as being useful in treating various other problems. THC seems to be a bronchodilator; that is, it increases lung capacity. However, since it is normally smoked and smoking decreases lung capacity, it is unlikely to be useful for treating asthma. In addition, there are other more effective bronchodilators with less variable action and fewer side effects. THC or marijuana has been recommended for its muscle relaxant (antispasmodic) properties, especially for those who are partially or completely paralyzed, its anticonvulsant, appetite stimulating, and analgesic properties, as well as in the treatment of multiple sclerosis (Peterson, 1980).

The use of marijuana for medical purposes seems to be gaining momentum. In September, 1988, the chief administrative law judge of the Drug Enforcement Agency recommended to the DEA that they reclassify marijuana to a less restrictive category so that it could be made available by prescription for those suffering from multiple sclerosis or chemotherapy-induced nausea. He called it ''one of the safest therapeutically active substances known to man'' (*Science News,* 1988).

Ironically, in 1992 the Drug Enforcement Agency suspended a program which supplied marijuana to doctors who could, under strict guidelines, give it to their patients as they might any new drug for testing and evaluation. Apparently there had been a sudden increase in requests for marijuana from AIDS patients who found that it helped them with the nausea and loss of appetite associated with this disease. The reason for the ban was that supplying marijuana was ''sending the wrong message.'' On the one hand, the reasoning went, efforts were being increased to stop marijuana use at the same time the government was providing it for medical use.

HOW SERIOUS IS THE MARIJUANA ''PROBLEM''?

Marijuana is a curious drug in many ways. Basically, it has had minor economic significance as a source of hemp for rope or clothing, some medical purposes, and psychoactive properties that are difficult to define. Its main claim to fame seems to be that it represented for an entire generation a symbol of rebellion against authority and the status quo. The ''other side'' accepted the thrown gauntlet, and the battle was on. As the ''smoke clears'' after more than twenty years, a rational perspective is beginning to emerge.

Marijuana is not a harmless drug. Since it is normally smoked, the act of smoking itself presents a clear danger. The dosages typically used by the recreational smoker have, until quite recently, been low, although this is a debatable point. No one knows what will happen if marijuana follows the trend of cocaine and so many other drugs and finds its way into the market in stronger and stronger forms. All drug effects are dose related and the mild effects described above may not apply to the marijuana of the 1990s.

• YOU READ IT HERE FIRST •

Hemp is, of course, marijuana, but the plant itself has had widespread use as raw material for rope, clothing, and paper. In the 1970s, legalization of marijuana was promoted on the grounds of individual rights and its relative harmlessness. Obviously that approach went nowhere. An interesting new approach is developing which piggybacks onto the environmental/ecological concerns. Some ''enthusiasts'' are promoting hemp as a substitute for nonrenewable energy sources such as petroleum and as environmentally sound alternatives to cotton and synthetic fiber.

In addition, the AIDS epidemic has had an interesting but little noticed consequence. Activists within the AIDS movement have emphasized that everyone needs to take more control over their own medical needs, and individuals are winning increasingly greater controls over obtaining prescription drugs. One offshoot of this may be an increased pressure to provide marijuana to individuals for their own personal use to treat medical conditions.

Keep in mind that *Cannabis sativa* is *Cannabis sativa,* whether you make rope or smoke dope. Advocates say that hemp grown for fiber has a low THC content, but it would be an impossible legal task to control the potency of the plant. Similarly, if patients gain the right to grow it for medicinal purposes, effective control over growing it for other purposes would essentially cease. Don't be surprised to see this back door approach to legalization heat up in the 1990s.

Dependence does occur in some people. Since it does offer a release and a chance to escape, it may be attractive to many who probably should not use it.

On the other hand, the generation of the sixties and early seventies, who were the heaviest users of marijuana in recent history, seem for the most part to have taken their place in corporate America. It seems that most smokers of that era ''gave up their dreams as they cut off their hair.'' Marijuana does not seem to cause most of the terrible effects that have been attributed to it. The amotivational syndrome may be more symptom than cause, the immunological and hormonal findings seem to be of little practical importance, and most of the other effects seem to be of short duration.

As the wave of cocaine use subsides, marijuana may very well become the next object of increased media scrutiny and government attention as it did in the 1960s. This time around, however, the proponents and opponents will be pushing different arguments to support their positions. The proponents are likely to emphasize the economic significance of marijuana, citing its potential usefulness as a source of energy, clothing, and paper, and its medical usefulness. Indeed there have been several congressional hearings on this topic alone (Randall, 1991). The opponents are likely to stress the supposed increased potency of marijuana (for which there is little objective evidence, incidentally) and recent studies on the toxicity of chronic THC in the brain.

SUMMARY

Like many other drugs, marijuana has had a long past. It has been used as a medicine, as a material to make clothing and rope, and as a recreational drug. In the United States marijuana briefly became a symbol for a large portion of an entire generation, who viewed smoking it as a symbol of rebellion and, at the same time, conformity.

The botany of the plant is a matter of some controversy and the active ingredient, tetrahydrocannabinol, is poorly understood. Marijuana has been used in various forms and its potency has also been variable. In recent years, the strength of marijuana has dramatically increased.

The physiological effects of marijuana are not remarkable and do not seem to be permanent. Much research has been conducted to determine how harmful the drug is; the results seem to indicate that at moderate doses the main harmful effects are similar to smoking tobacco. Many of the more lurid stories about marijuana use have not held up to scientific investigation.

The psychological effects are difficult to describe. For those who seek its effects, they are pleasant, but for others who may take THC by prescription, they may be unpleasant. The amotivational syndrome so often described is probably not a significant danger, and may be related more to the age of the typical user than to the drug.

Marijuana was once fairly widely used as medicine. Discovery of more reliable treatment for most conditions has blunted the role of marijuana in medicine. Recently, however, interest has been expressed in THC as a treatment for severe nausea and vomiting, and a prescription product known as Marinol is now available.

The dangers as well as the beneficial effects of marijuana have both been overstated. Although it is still an extremely popular recreational drug, adolescents seem to be using it less. Those young adults who appreciate its effects are moving into the mainstream of society. Whether they will continue to use the drug is a matter of debate.

REFERENCES

Abel, E. L. (1981). Marijuana and sex: A critical review. *Drug and Alcohol Dependence, 8,* 1–22.

Abel, E. L. (1980). *Marijuana: The first 12,000 years.* New York: Plenum Press.

Anslinger, H. J., & Cooper, C. R. (1937). Marijuana: Assassin of youth. *American Magazine, 24,* 19;153.

Benedikt, R. A., Cristoforo, P., Mendelson, J. H., & Mello, N. K. (1986). Effects of acute marijuana smoking in post-menopausal women. *Psychopharmacology, 90,* 14–17.

Bernstein, J. G. (1980). Medical consequences of marihuana use. In N. K. Mello (Ed.), (pp. 255–87). *Advances in substance abuse, behavioral and biological research, 1,* Greenwich, CT: JAI Press.

Campbell, A. G., Evans, M., Thomson, J. L., & Williams, M. J. (1971). Cerebral atrophy in young cannabis smokers. *Lancet, ii (7736),* 1219–25.

Carter, W. E., & Doughty, P. L. (1976). Social and cultural aspects of cannabis use in Costa Rica. *Annals of the New York Academy of Sciences, 282,* 2–16.

Cohen, S. (1985). *The substance abuse problem: volume II, New issues for the 80's.* New York and London: Haworth Press.

Compton, D. R., Dewey, W. L., & Martin, B. R., (1990). Cannabis dependence and tolerance production. *Advances in Alcohol and Substance Abuse, 9,* 129–46.

Cone, E. J., & Johnson, R. E. (1986). Contact high and urinary cannabinol excretion after passive exposure to marijuana smoke. *Clinical Pharmacology and Therapeutics, 40,* 247–56.

Cone, E. J., Johnson, R. E., Moore, J. A., & Roach, J. D. (1986). Acute effects of smoking marijuana on hormone, subjective effects and performance in male human subjects. *Pharmacology, Biochemistry and Behavior, 24,* 1749–54.

Cushman, P. (1975). Plasma testosterone levels in healthy male marijuana smokers. *American Journal of Drug and Alcohol Abuse, 2,* 269–75.

Deadwyler, S. A., Heyser, C. J., Michaelis, R. C., & Hampson, R. E. (1990). The effects of delta-9-THC on mechanisms of learning and memory. In L. Erinoff, (Ed.). Neurobiology of drug abuse: Learning and memory. *National Institute of Drug Abuse Research, Monograph 97.* U. S. Department of Health and Human Services.

Domino, E. F. (1981). Cannabinoids and the cholinergic system. *Journal of Clinical Pharmacology, 21,* 249s–255s.

Ferraro, D. P. (1980). Acute effects of marijuana on human memory and cognition. In *Marijuana Research Findings: 1980.* National Institute of Drug Abuse, Research Monograph 31.

Fink, M. (1976). Conference Summary (Re: Chronic cannabis use). *Annals of the New York Academy of Science, 282,* 427–30.

Foltin, R. W., Brady, J. V., & Fishman, M. W. (1986). Behavioral analysis of marijuana effect on food intake in humans. *Pharmacology, Biochemistry and Behavior, 25,* 577–86.

Frost, H. (1987). How Carthage lost the sea. *Natural History, 96,* 68–69.

Gong, H., Fligiel, S., Tashkin, D. P., & Barbers, R. G. (1987). Tracheobronchial changes in habitual, heavy smokers of marijuana with and without tobacco. *American Review of Respiratory Diseases, 136,* 142–49.

Hatch, E. E., & Bracken, M. B. (1986). Effect of marijuana use on pregnancy and fetal growth. *American Journal of Epidemiology, 124,* 986–97.

Hatch, E. E., & Bracken, M. B. (1986). Effect of marijuana use in pregnancy on fetal growth. *American Journal of Epidemiology, 124,* 986–93.

Hendin, H., Haas, A. P., Singer, P., Elliver, M., & Ulman, R. (1987). *Living high: Daily marijuana use among adults.* New York: Human Sciences Press.

Heyndrickx, A., Scheiris, C., & Schepens, P. (1969). Toxicological study of a fatal intoxication by man due to cannabis smoking. *Journal de Pharmacie de Belgigue, 24,* 371–76.

Hollister, L. E. (1988). Marijuana and immunity. *Journal of Psychoactive Drugs, 20,* 3–7.

Inciardi, J. A. (1986). *The war on drugs: Heroin, cocaine, crime and public policy.* Palo Alto, CA: Mayfield Publishing Company.

Jones, R. T. (1971). Marijuana-induced "high"; Influence of expectation, setting and previous drug experience. *Pharmacological Reviews, 23,* 359–69.

Jones, R. T., & Benowitz, N. (1976). The 30 day trip—Clinical studies of cannabis tolerance and dependence. In M. C. Braude and S. Szara (Eds.), (pp. 627–42). *Pharmacology of Marihuana, Volume 2.* New York: Raven Press.

Jones, R. T. (1980). Human effects: An overview. In Robert C. Peterson (Ed.). *Marijuana Research Findings: 1980. National Institute of Drug Abuse, Research Monograph 31.*

Kalant, O. J., Fehr, K. O., Arras, D., Amylin, L. (1983). *Cannabis: Health risks, A comprehensive annotated bibliography. 1844–1982.* Addiction Research Foundation.

Kolodny, R. C., Masters. W. H., Kolodner, R. M., & Toro, G. (1974). Depression of plasma testosterone levels after chronic intensive marijuana use. *New England Journal of Medicine, 290,* 872–74.

Kolodny, R. C., Lessin, R., Toro, C. L., Masters, W. H., & Cohen, S. (1976). Depression of plasma testosterone with acute marijuana administration. In M. C. Braude & S. Szara (Eds.), pp. 217–25. *Pharmacology of Marijuana.* New York: Raven Press.

Kusinitz, M. (1987). *Drugs and the arts.* New York and New Haven: Chelsea House Publishers.

Laurence, J. (1844). On the prevalence of, and ill effects resulting from the use of bhang and other narcotic drugs, in the native army. *Madras Quarterly Medical Journal, 6,* 274–78.

Lemberger, L., & Rubin, P. (1978). Cannabis: The role of metabolism in the development of tolerance. *Drug Metabolism Review, 8,* 59–68.

McGlothling, W. H., & West, J. L. (1968). The marijuana problem: An overview. *American Journal of Psychiatry, 125,* 1126–34.

Markianos, M., and Vakis, A. (1984). Effects of acute cannibis use on urinary neurotransmitter metabolites and cyclic nucleotides in man. *Drug and Alcohol Dependence, 14,* 175–78.

Mathew, R. J., Wilson, W. H., & Tant, S. R. (1989). Acute changes in cerebral blood flow associated with marijuana smoking. *Acta Psychiatrica Scandanavia, 79,* 118–28.

Mendelson, J. H., Ellingboe, J., Kuenhle, J. C., & Mello, N. K. (1978). Effects of chronic marijuana use on integrated plasma testosterone and lutenizing hormone. *Journal of Pharmacology and Experimental Therapeutics, 207,* 611–17.

Mirin, S. M., & Weiss, R. L. (1983). Substance abuse. In E. L. Bassok, S. C. Sclevonne, & A. J. Gelenberg (Eds.). *The Practitioner's Guide to Psychoactive Drugs,* (2d ed.). New York: Plenum Press.

Morningstar, P. J. (1985). Thandai and chilam: Traditional Hindu beliefs about the proper uses of cannabis. *Journal of Psychoactive Drugs, 17,* 141–65.

Moskowitz, H., Burns, M. M., & Williams, A. F. (1990). Skills performance at low blood alcohol levels. *Journal of Studies of Alcohol, 46,* 482.

Musto, D. F. (1987). *The American disease: Origins of narcotic control.* New York and Oxford: Oxford University Press.

Nahas, G. G. (1971). Lethal cannabis intoxication. *New England Journal of Medicine, 284,* 792.

Petersen, R. C. (1980). Marijuana and health. In Peterson (Ed.). NIDA, *31.*

Petronis, K. R., & Anthony, J. C. (1989). An epidemiologic investigation of marijuana and cocaine related palpitations. *Drug and Alcohol Dependence, 23,* 219–26.

Randall, R. C. (1991). *Muscle spasm, pain and marijuana therapy.* Washington, D.C.: Galen Press.

Rosenkrantz, H., Grant, R. J., Fleischman, R. W., & Baker, J. R. (1986). Marihuana-induced embryotoxicity in the rabbit. *Fundamental and Applied Toxicology, 7,* 236–43.

Rosenthal, F. (1971). *The herb: Hashish versus medieval muslim society.* Leiden, Netherlands: E. J. Brill.

Roueche, B. (1984). Annals of medicine: A contemporary touch. *The New Yorker.* August 13, 76–85.

Rubin, V., & Comitas, L. (1976). *Ganja in Jamaica.* New York: Anchor Books.

Schaeffer, J., Andrysiak, T., & Ungerleider, T. J. (1981). Cognition and long term use of ganja (cannabis). *Science, 213,* 465–66.

Schwartz, R. H., Hoffman, N. G., & Jones, R. (1987). Behavioral, psychosocial and academic correlates of marijuana usage in adolescents. *Clinical Pediatrics, 26,* 264–70.

Schwartz, R. H., Gruenewald, P. J., Klitzner, M., & Fedio, P. (1989). Short term memory impairment in cannabis-dependent adolescents. *American Journal of Diseases of Children, 143,* 1214–19.

Sloman, L. (1979). *Reefer madness: A history of marijuana in America.* Indianapolis: Bobbs-Merrill.

Smith, D. E. (1968). The acute and chronic toxicity of marijuana. *Journal of Psychedelic Drugs, 2,* 37–48.

Tart, C. T. (1971). *On being stoned: A psychological study of marijuana intoxication.* Palo Alto, CA: Science and Behavior Books.

Turner, C. E. (1980). Chemistry and metabolism. In Robert C. Petersen (Ed.). *Marijuana Research Findings: 1980.* National Institute of Drug Abuse, Research Monograph 31.

Weiss, R. (1988). Take two puffs and call me in the morning: Proponents of marijuana's medical benefits take their case to court. *Science News, 133,* 122–23.

Wert, R. C., & Raulin, M. L. (1986). The chronic cerebral effects of cannabis use: I. Methodological issues and neurological findings.

Wert, R. C., & Raulin, M. L. (1986). The chronic cerebral effects of cannabis use: II. Psychological findings and conclusions. *The International Journal of the Addictions, 21,* 605–28.

Zacny, J., & Chait, L. (1989). Breathhold duration and response to marijuana smoke. *Pharmacology, Biochemistry and Behavior, 33,* 481–84.

Zinberg, N. E., & Harding, E. M. (1982). Introduction: Control and intoxicant use: A theoretical and practical overview. In N. E. Zinberg & W. M. Harding (Eds.), pp. 13–35. *Control of intoxicant use: Pharmacological, psycholgoical, and social considerations.* New York: Human Services Press.

Zweben, J. E. & O'Connell, K. (1988). Strategies for breaking marijuana dependence. *Journal of Psychoactive Drugs, 20,* 121–27.

7

• • •

NICOTINE

• • •

OBJECTIVES

When you have finished studying this chapter you should:

1. Know how tobacco was introduced to Western Civilization.
2. Be able to discuss the role of tobacco in the American Revolution.
3. Know how the various forms of tobacco differ.
4. Be able to discuss why cigarette smoking became popular.
5. Understand the controversy surrounding passive smoking and ETS.
6. Know the effects of nicotine on the brain.
7. Be able to list the principle components of tobacco smoke.
8. Know how smoking relates to health problems.
9. Be able to discuss the effects of smoking on the fetus.
10. Know how quitting smoking affects health.
11. Understand the role of the tobacco industry in our economy.
12. Be able to list methods to stop smoking.
13. Understand why smoking is difficult to stop.

KEY TERMS

acetylcholine
apnea
carbon monoxide
COLD (Chronic Obstructive Lung Disease)
cotinine
emphysema
environmental tobacco smoke
Nicorette
nicotine
passive smokers
sidestream smoke
SIDS (Sudden Infant Death Syndrome)
social factor

Nicotine
"A custome loathsome to the eye, hateful to the nose,
harmful to the brain, dangerous to the lungs, and in the
black, stinking fume thereof, nearest resembling the horri-
ble Stygian smoke of the pit that is bottomless."
James I of England-
A Counterblast to Tobacco (1604)

"One Man's Death is Another Man's Living"
Ira Gershwin

HISTORY OF TOBACCO

Christopher Columbus reported that when he landed on the shores of San Salvador in the West Indies on 12 October 1492 the "Indians" presented him with gifts of fruit, other valuables, and some dried leaves. He and his crew apparently accepted the other gifts but threw away the leaves. The leaves were what we now call tobacco and it wasn't long before such leaves had become a prized commodity rather than something to be discarded. Tradition has credited two men of the Columbus crew as being the first Europeans to smoke tobacco.

Whoever the first European was, he certainly wasn't the last. No society that has ever adopted tobacco use has ever given it up. Customs change and the way tobacco is used changes, but by means of pipe, cigar, cigarette, or snuff, a chaw in the jaw, or a dip in the lip, tobacco use remains with us.

The Indians Introduce Tobacco to Europe

Not only did the Indians know the pleasures of tobacco, they also had found every effective means of delivering nicotine to the bloodstream that we now use. Long before Columbus "discovered" America (a discovery that must have been a shock to the natives already living in North and South America), Indians used pipes, cigars, cigarettes, snuff, and chewing tobacco (Heiman, 1960). Although there was ritual and medicinal use, most reports of the time indicate that the Indians also used the drug for recreational purposes.

When Europeans expanded their horizons even further and settled in Australia, they discovered that the original inhabitants of that part of the world, the Aborigines, also had discovered the usefulness of nicotine-containing plants. In addition to plants similar to the tobacco plant of North America, the Aborigines also used a plant called *pituri*. They used pituri and tobacco in a way that was similar to that of North American Indians, and for both groups of people, nicotine was seen as a powerful drug over which the culture exerted considerable control.

History records that the first use of tobacco in Western Europe was for medicinal purposes. Tobacco was recommended for a wide range of conditions

FIGURE 7.1

Sketch of a Mayan smoking what seems to be a cigar. The lack of ritual figures indicates that the cigar was in everyday use.

from migraine to intestinal problems. One theory held that tobacco smoke blown into the rectum would revive a drowning victim! The idea of tobacco as medicine was so well established that a prescription was needed to get tobacco in Connecticut in 1647 (Stewart, 1967).

The transition from tobacco as medicine to tobacco as recreational drug was rapid, however, and it was aided by what has finally been acknowledged by the Office of the Surgeon General in the face of considerable opposition from the tobacco industry: nicotine is addicting (Office of the Surgeon General, 1988). As medicine, tobacco and nicotine have no current use; as a recreational drug, however, tobacco is a multibillion dollar industry.

From the time of the American Revolution, tobacco has been a major crop in the South. One of the main sources of revenue for the Revolutionary army came from selling tobacco to France. As a result, major campaigns were waged against tobacco plantations by the British. George Washington was a leading tobacco grower and one of the richest men in the country. No wonder he was picked to lead the rebel forces.

The Advent of the Cigarette

Cigarette smoking, now the commonest method of ingesting nicotine, is a twentieth century phenomenon. In the United States, until just after World War I, most tobacco was chewed, snuffed, or smoked as a cigar. The cigar was the most popular form of smoking, with more than 6.5 billion cigars being produced in 1915. By contrast, only 29 million were manufactured in 1982 (Sharp, 1986).

Cigarette smoking more than took up the slack since worldwide sales increased from ''only'' two billion cigarettes at the beginning of this century

These young men are supposed to represent the height of elegance and sophistication in this drawing from the middle of the nineteenth century. Notice the long stem on the pipe: obviously only "gentlemen" would be able to smoke such an impractical pipe as this.

to nearly 5 *trillion* in 1986 (Morris, 1986). Part of the reason for the change to cigarettes was that a milder form of tobacco was developed ("bright"), and mechanical cigarette rolling machines were developed which made cigarettes cheaper than cigars. Modern rolling machines can make 8,000 cigarettes a minute (Morris, 1986). The cigarette also could be inhaled more easily than the cigar, leading to faster absorption of nicotine and more rapid addiction.

The middle part of this century was the heyday of cigarette smoking. Tobacco companies advertised that doctors endorsed Luckies as "less irritating to sensitive or tender throats than any other cigarettes." By 1946, a survey of 113,597 physicians reported that "More doctors smoke Camels than any other cigarettes" (Blum, 1985). How many didn't smoke at all was a statistic that was carefully ignored.

At the beginning of World War II, "Lucky Strike Green went to war," and cigarette manufacturers "patriotically" contributed a three-pack of cigarettes to the field rations for soldiers in combat. Is it just chance that smoking by men began to increase during World War II?

Such generosity continued until quite recently. The author of this text remembers getting cigarettes in rations that were issued during the Vietnam War. During the war with Iraq in 1991, you may recall that considerable controversy occurred over supplying cigarettes to soldiers. Although cigarettes

FIGURE 7.2

Do you think that the increase in cigarette smoking in the United States in the fifties had anything to do with the free cigarettes that soldiers received during World War II?

were not included in the MREs (Meals Ready to Eat), they were still available for purchase even though sale and consumption of alcoholic beverages were prohibited.

Since 1981 cigarette use has declined, both on a per capita basis and in overall consumption. In 1992 fewer people were smoking than at any time in recent history. Nevertheless, nearly 30 percent of the adult population still smokes despite health warnings on every pack of cigarettes and millions of dollars spent in antismoking advertising. Furthermore, the Centers for Disease Control reported in 1991 that 19.1 percent of young people smoked or used smokeless tobacco and that use was beginning at an earlier age than in the past.

Current Tobacco Use   The cigarette that is smoked today is a far cry from the cigarette of the twenties and thirties. Nearly everything that can be done has been done to make the modern cigarette "milder," meaning easier to inhale. The result, of course, is that inhalation produces more rapid absorption of nicotine and, some would claim, more rapid addiction, than other means of absorption.

There are several different kinds of tobacco, and several different means of curing them, yielding tobacco that is either mild or strong tasting and high or low in nicotine and tar. The blend of various kinds of tobacco in each brand of cigarette is considered a trade secret, but most contain a far milder combination than found in cigars or in earlier cigarettes. In addition, various additives are mixed with the tobacco to make it smoother burning and better tasting. Congress has specifically exempted tobacco cigarettes from regulations that require disclosure of what manufacturers put in their product (Bailey & Lamarine, 1986) but known additives include cocoa, licorice, spices, and even shellac.

Table 7.1 shows data from the National Household Drug Survey on current cigarette use. As you can see, cigarette use is declining in every age group. A more expanded view of cigarette use by the Centers for Disease Control breaks down the use by high school age students into sex and ethnic background as shown in table 7.2. It also specifically includes smokeless tobacco.

Starting in 1964, the year of the first U.S. Surgeon General's report on smoking, smokers have shifted to so-called low tar and nicotine (T/N) cigarettes. The vast majority of cigarettes now sold are advertised as low in tar and nicotine, with only 9 percent smoking unfiltered cigarettes (Stellman & Garfinkel, 1986). Curiously, the tobacco used in low T/N cigarrettes is actually *higher* in nicotine content than that used in nonfilter cigarettes; the reduction in nicotine comes from the filter (Benowitz, 1986).

In addition to the tobacco leaf, cigarettes also contain shreds made from the stems and other portions of the tobacco plant. Also, the tobacco used in cigarettes is freeze-dried and then exposed to various gases that fluff up the leaf, expanding the cells of the leaf and allowing it to absorb more additives.

While the tar and nicotine content of the smoke from a modern cigarette is considerably less than that of older cigarettes, the smoker does not necessarily receive less tar and nicotine. Evidence suggests that smokers who smoke low tar and nicotine cigarettes inhale more deeply, hold the smoke in their lungs for a longer time, or smoke the cigarette further down than do smokers of stronger cigarettes (Woodman, Newman, & Pavia, 1987; Russell, Sutton, & Iyer, 1982).

The ultra-low-yield cigarettes may be a different story. Ultra-low-yield cigarettes contain less than 1 mg of tar and less than 0.1 mg of nicotine. Smokers of these cigarettes seem to receive less tar and nicotine, and their carbon monoxide levels are lower than smokers of either high or low tar and

Table 7.1 Regular Cigarette Use by Percent of Various Age Groups

	1974	1976	1977	1979	1982	1985	1988	1990
Youth (12–17)	25.0	23.5	22.3	12.1	14.7	15.3	11.8	11.6
Young Adults (18–25)	48.8	49.4	47.3	42.6	39.5	36.8	35.2	31.5
Older Adults (25+)	39.1	38.4	38.7	36.9	34.6	32.8	29.8	27.7

Regular use is defined as use within the last month.
Data from the National Household Survey on Drug Use

nicotine cigarettes. While it seems that smokers can compensate for the lower yield of some cigarettes by inhaling more deeply and holding the smoke in the lungs longer, ultra-low-yield cigarettes are constructed in such a way that such compensation is not possible (Benowitz, Jacob, Yu, Talcott, Hall, & Jones, 1986). Interestingly, smokers reported that smoking these brands was less satisfying than smoking cigarettes with higher tar and nicotine content.

The widely advertised tar and nicotine content of various cigarettes is determined by machines that analyze the contents of a standard puff taken by the machine. However, people do not smoke like machines, and there is no such thing as a standard puff by a smoker. Smokers also block the air holes on some cigarettes, smoke the cigarette longer, and even remove the filter. Consequently, the advertised ratings may be misleading.

Clove Cigarettes

Clove cigarettes had a brief popularity in the 1980s among young people. Manufactured in Indonesia, they contain about 60 percent strong tobacco and 40 percent ground cloves which contain *eugenol*. Eugenol not only gives these cigarettes their distinctive aroma, but also anesthetizes the back of the throat, making it easier to inhale the smoke. Eugenol is the over-the-counter substance used to reduce toothache pain (Bailey & Lamarine, 1986).

Smokers have to learn how to inhale, and inexperienced smokers find cigarette smoke harsh. Clove cigarettes bypass the normal coughing reflex because of their anesthetic action (Bailey & Lamarine, 1986). Several deaths have been reported from the use of these cigarettes, and some states have banned their sale.

Smokeless Tobacco

Spittoons used to be a common sight when chewing tobacco was common. Concern about the spread of tuberculosis and other diseases and changing public opinion about the aesthetic nature of spitting, along with the rise of the machine manufactured cigarette, led to the decline of the use of chewing tobacco.

While people still chew tobacco, the use of what is now more graciously named ''smokeless tobacco'' has increased. In fact, it is the only type of tobacco product whose use has increased in recent years. Smokeless

Table 7.2   Cigarette Use by High School Students—1990

Category	Any Use	Cigarette Use	Frequent Use	Smokeless Use
Sex				
Male	40.4	33.2	13.0	19.1
Female	31.7	31.3	12.5	1.4
Grade				
9th	32.1	29.5	9.9	7.8
10th	33.9	30.0	10.8	10.9
11th	36.7	32.8	12.6	9.5
12th	41.2	36.7	17.7	11.9
Race/ethnic background				
White	41.2	36.4	15.9	12.6
Black	16.8	16.1	2.3	1.9
Hispanic	32.0	30.8	7.4	5.7
Total				
	36.0	32.3	12.8	10.1

Cigarette Use refers to use within the last 30 days.
Frequent Use refers to smoking at least 25 of the last 30 days.
Data Source: Centers for Disease Control—*The Morbidity and Mortality Weekly Report, 40*, 617–619. 1991.

tobacco comes in two forms: moist snuff and the same product encased in a small bag. The idea is to take a pinch of the snuff or one of the bags and place it between the cheek and gum. Absorption is through the mucous lining of the mouth into the bloodstream.

Advertisements for this product feature athletes and run in adventure and sports magazines, thereby appealing to young people, and adolescents have gotten the message. One study reported about virtually the same number of smokers as nonsmokeless tobacco users. Many in this sample do both, of course, but it is not too common. Smokeless tobacco is a common route to smoking cigarettes. Users typically report that they "progress" to cigarette use. A switch from cigarettes to smokeless tobacoo is far less common (Hatsukami, Nelson, & Jensen, 1991). Therefore, smokeless use could be seen as a gateway to cigarette smoking.

While a claim could be made that smokeless tobacco is a little safer than smoking (after all, one doesn't get lung cancer), it is far from safe. Smokeless tobacco has been shown to cause oral cancer, periodontal disease, and high blood pressure (Connolly, Winn, & Hecht, 1986). Another problem is gingival recession, in which the gums around the teeth retract, leaving them loose and in danger of infection (Wientraub & Burt, 1987).

The athletes most closely associated with tobacco use are baseball players. Part of the image of summertime is a batter entering the batter's box with a wad of tobacco in his cheek. Nor is this image far from the truth. One study showed that almost 40 percent of baseball players used smokeless tobacco in one form or another. Furthermore, nearly half showed signs of

Smoking in the Future

Is it reasonable to believe that cigarette smoking will ever be completely eliminated? As long as we live in a democratic society and as long as cigarettes are legal, it seems likely that some people will continue to smoke. Making tobacco illegal is certainly not the answer even if it were economically and politically feasible. Imagine the black market that would spring up two hours after tobacco was outlawed.

What does seem likely is that the demographics of smoking will change. That is, smokers increasingly will come from lower socioeconomic classes and from those with less education. A study that covered the years 1974 to 1985 concluded that education is a more important determinant of cigarette smoking than gender. Although smoking has declined in all education groups, the decline has occurred five times faster in the more highly educated (Pierce, Fiore, Novotny, Hatziandreu, & Davis, 1989a). Extending this trend to the year 2000) the estimate is that 30 percent of those with less than a high school diploma will be smokers, compared to 10 percent of those with a college degree (Pierce, Fiore, Novotny, Hatziandreu, & Davis, 1989).

Recently considerable criticism was mounted when cigarette firms attempted to market brands of cigarettes to two groups, blacks and women with high school educations, whose smoking remains at a high level. Furthermore, many believe that the advertisements for certain brands of cigarettes are focused toward young people. The use of "fun" images such as certain animals, or stereotypic masculine figures, is seen as an attempt to encourage cigarette use by teenagers (Cotton, 1990).

One event could change the whole face of cigarette smoking forever. On 13 June 1988 a federal court jury awarded the family of Rose Cipollone (who died of lung cancer in 1984) $400,000 damages. The jury ruled that while Cipollone was 80 percent responsible for her own death by smoking a pack a day for forty years, the cigarette company that manufactured her brand—Liggett Group Incorporated—was partly to blame because they failed to warn smokers of the dangers of cigarettes, dangers of which they were aware.

It was not a complete victory for the antismoking forces, since the award was based on the fact that until 1968 there was no warning on cigarettes. Had she not started smoking until after that time the jury would probably not have awarded damages. Moreover, she was held mostly responsible for her own death. Nevertheless, the award is considered a foot in the door and was the first time anyone had successfully sued a cigarette company. If it is upheld the precedent could be catastrophic for the cigarette industry. Imagine the families of the 350,000 people a year who die as a direct result of smoking winning lawsuits against the suppliers of these cigarettes. A. H. Robbins went bankrupt when users of the Dalkon Shield contraceptive devices sued and won their cases. Would the cigarette industry simply cease to exist? Then what would happen to all the smokers?

oral leukoplakia (white patches on the gum or cheek) and a third showed signs of other gum and tooth problems. Virtually no nonusers had evidence of these kinds of changes (Ernster, Grady, Greene, Walsh, Robertson et al, 1990). Since the average age of the ball players was twenty-three and they had only been using smokeless tobacco for about five years, one wonders what problems they will have in the future.

FIGURE 7.3
Structure of the nicotine
molecule.

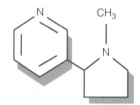

Since users of smokeless tobacco absorb the nicotine through the mouth, blood levels do not peak and decline as they do for cigarette smokers. Nevertheless, regular users can have nearly the same nicotine levels as smokers (Russell, Jarvis, Devitt, & Feyerabend, 1981). In fact, considering that smokeless tobacco users keep the product in their mouths for prolonged periods, the total amount of nicotine absorbed is actually greater than for cigarettes (Benowitz, Porchet, Sheiner, & Jacob, 1988). The general pattern of smokeless tobacco use indicates that it can result in both tolerance and dependence (Hatkusami, Nelson, & Jensen, 1991).

Given these facts it is no wonder that critics charge that advertising smokeless tobacco to young people is a strategy to guarantee another generation of addicted users. Tins of smokeless tobacco now carry the statement, ''This product is not a safe alternative to smoking cigarettes.''

PHYSIOLOGY AND PHARMACOLOGY OF NICOTINE

Nicotine, the primary active ingredient in tobacco, is a very toxic substance widely used as an insecticide. As little as 40 mg taken orally has proved fatal (Goldfrank, Melinek, & Blum, 1980). The structure of nicotine is very similar to that of **acetylcholine,** the neurotransmitter in the neuromuscular junction as well as the brain.

Nicotine also stimulates the release of norepinephrine, which partially accounts for the stimulating effect of the drug. At the dose absorbed by the typical cigarette smoker, the effect of nicotine seems to be the result of central nervous system activity; at higher doses there are direct effects on the central nervous system (Benowitz, 1986). In addition to the effects on the nervous system, cigarette smoking also increases levels of catecholamines and endorphins in the blood (Cryer, Haymond, Santiago, & Shah, 1976; Karras & Kane, 1980).

Absorption and Metabolism

Nicotine, like cocaine, is a base or alkaloid and is most rapidly absorbed in this form. When a cigarette is smoked, the nicotine is carried on the droplets of tar. The smoke of most American cigarettes is acidic, which means that nicotine is not readily absorbed in the mouth. Cigars, pipes, and some European cigarettes are made from a form of tobacco that remains alkaline when smoked, so that for these products absorption is rapid in the mouth. Smokeless tobacco is mixed with various ingredients to make it alkaline and hence speed up absorption (Benowitz, 1986).

Once the smoke from the inhaled cigarette, cigar, or pipe reaches the lungs, it doesn't matter what form it is in. It is absorbed very rapidly. Experienced smokers seem to be able to absorb nicotine much more efficiently than nonsmokers, probably because they have learned to inhale the smoke deeply into their lungs (Armitrage, Dollery, George, Houseman, Lewis, & Turner, 1975).

Nicotine absorbed into the bloodstream through the lungs is distributed very rapidly throughout the body. It passes the blood/brain barrier, the placental barrier, and is found in amniotic fluid and breast milk. It is even found in the fluid of the cervix in women (Benowitz, 1986).

Metabolism of nicotine primarily occurs in the liver, although some takes place in the lung and the kidney. The major metabolite of nicotine is **cotinine,** which reaches much higher levels in the blood than nicotine and is metabolized much more slowly. Cotinine is important because it forms the basis for various tests that can detect tobacco smoking for several days. These tests could be used to determine whether those who profess to have stopped smoking are sneaking cigarettes, or perhaps by insurance companies who offer lower rates for nonsmokers.

The half life of nicotine in the bloodstream is two hours. With regular smoking, however, nicotine accumulates and then persists overnight in the absence of smoking, enabling the smoker to sleep. This accumulation of nicotine also means that the regular cigarette smoker is exposed to nicotine twenty-four hours a day (Benowitz, 1986b).

Short-term Effects of Smoking

The best way to remember what the short-term effects of smoking are is to keep in mind that cigarette smoking produces a state of sympathetic nervous system arousal twenty-four hours a day. Available evidence suggests that nicotine is the drug maintaining this arousal.

Cardiovascular Effects

In healthy people, smoking a cigarette increases heart rate, and increases the output of the heart and the volume of blood that is pumped from the heart. Regular cigarette smokers show little tolerance to these effects. Except for early in the morning, the heart rate of smokers seems always to be higher than those who don't smoke. Those with heart disease may show opposite effects; reduced output and blood flow (Benowitz, 1986a).

Cigarette smoke contains from 1 to 5 percent carbon monoxide gas. Carbon monoxide combines far more readily than oxygen with hemoglobin, the portion of the blood responsible for carrying oxygen to the tissues. Because of their exposure to carbon monoxide, smokers lose up to 15 percent of the oxygen-carrying capacity of the blood, making the heart work even harder (Cole, Hawkins, & Roberts, 1972).

Smoking also increases the stiffness of the walls of the arteries, making them less flexible when blood pulses through (Caro, Lever, Parker, & Fish, 1987). As we shall see later, cigarette smoking is thought to increase the severity and risk of hardening of the arteries. If smoking temporarily increases the stiffness of the walls of the artery, hardening might be the result of a lifetime of smoking.

Cigarette smoking also results in constriction of the peripheral blood vessels, thus reducing skin temperature. The constriction of peripheral blood vessels is accompanied by an increased blood flow to muscles. The decreased blood supply to the peripheral blood vessels, and hence to the cells of the skin, may in part account for the fact that smokers show signs of aging far more quickly than nonsmokers.

Central Nervous System

Smokers typically report that smoking makes them feel more alert. This arousal function of smoking is supported by the finding that cigarette smoking decreases alpha wave activity and increases beta wave activity in the brain. Alpha wave activity is measured from the cortex and seen when a person is relaxing and not actively processing information. Beta activity is characteristic of an alert person. Nicotine seems to be responsible for the alerting activity of smoking, since drugs that block the action of nicotine block the alerting response (Benowitz, 1986a).

Smoking increases blood sugar levels and slows stomach contractions. In addition, cigarette smoke deadens the taste buds. These findings may account for the fact that smoking seems to decrease hunger. Smoking also causes an increase of norepinephrine and epinephrine, two stress-related hormones.

Passive Smoking from Environmental Tobacco Smoke

To most nonsmokers, cigarette smoke is offensive, but until recently they were forced to tolerate it. Of late, there has been a dramatic increase in the number of laws prohibiting public smoking. Cities, states, and the federal government have joined together to ban smoking in offices, restaurants, and public institutions. Smoking has even been banned in some jails and prisons (Fielding, 1986; Millar, 1986). These restrictions are part of an overall strategy to convince smokers and nonsmokers that smoking is socially unacceptable behavior (Sees, 1990).

Another factor in the recent legislation is the economic cost of cigarette smoking. One estimate is that smoking costs society $60 billion a year, and smoking employees cost the employer $1,000 a year more than nonsmokers. The reason for these staggering figures include health care costs, lost productivity, insurance premiums, effects of passive smoke, and even damage to property and furnishings. Part of the cost occurs as a result of smoking at home, but little can be done to alter smoking there. The workplace is another matter and that is where the current emphasis has been placed.

To listen to some of the more extreme opponents of cigarette smoking, you might think that a single exposure to cigarette smoke in a crowded restaurant was sufficient to cause lung cancer even in those sitting in the no smoking section. At the same time, the tobacco industry has worked very hard to convince you that the risk of environmental tobacco smoke is virtually zero and that the many reports to the contrary are all flawed or poorly done.

While the smoker is absorbing nicotine into her lungs, she is releasing cigarette smoke into the air.

The purpose of this textbook is to present the available evidence in a nonjudgmental manner to allow you to make up your own mind. Let's see what the evidence suggests.

First of all, it is important to understand what the justification for banning smoking is in the first place. Sidestream cigarette smoke contains more carcinogenic substances than does the smoke that the smoker actually inhales, and metabolites of nicotine found in the urine of noncigarette smokers who live with active smokers are similar to those found in light smokers. Furthermore, passive smoking is estimated to cause more deaths a year than any other environmental pollutant and the risk of dying because of exposure to passive smoking is 100 times greater than required for the Environmental Protection Agency to label a pollutant as carcinogenic and ten thousand times greater than the level required to label a *food* as carcinogenic (Goodin, 1989).

Environmental tobacco smoke (ETS) is composed of two elements: sidestream smoke and mainstream smoke. Sidestream smoke is the smoke that comes from the burning end of a cigarette. It is unfiltered and contains more toxins and carcinogens than exhaled smoke, known as mainstream smoke (Sepkovic, Haley, & Hoffman, 1986). Sidestream smoke composes two-thirds of all the pollution due to smoking (Schmeltz, Hoffman, & Wynder, 1975).

The majority of the research on ETS has focused on four areas: ETS and lung cancer, ETS and cardiovascular problems, ETS and pulmonary problems, and the effects of ETS on the health of children exposed to smoke from parents who are smokers. The U.S. Surgeon General's 1986 report on passive smoking was clear in its conclusions. First, involuntary smoking is a cause of disease, including lung cancer, in healthy nonsmokers. Second, children of parents who smoke have an increased frequency of respiratory infections and show reduced lung function as they mature. Finally, separation of smokers and nonsmokers in the same airspace reduces, but does not eliminate, the exposure to ETS (Sees, 1990).

Most researchers would agree that the Surgeon General's report is accurate in its broad scope, but, in the interest of fairness, you should be aware of some of the limitations of these statements. First of all, the best evidence that ETS causes cancer links it with lung cancer, for obvious reasons. Some of the studies that have been done indicate that exposure to smoking has no effect, some that it has a slight effect and some that it has a moderate effect. The studies showing the largest effect indicate that exposure to cigarette smoking doubles the risk of lung cancer in nonsmokers (Janerich, Thompson, Varela, Greenwald et al, 1990).

While this increase is statistically significant, you should keep in mind that lung cancer in nonsmokers is rare. The exact figures vary from source to source, but an estimate of about 12,000 deaths per year is probably close enough. The percentage of these deaths due to ETS is even more difficult to determine and this area is a source of a great deal of controversy. A figure of 3,000 is probably a fair consensus estimate, although some place it much lower. Even one death due to exposure to ETS is too many, of course, but it should also be noted that most studies indicate that the nonsmoker who develops lung cancer must be exposed for a period of many years.

Recent evidence suggests that the risk of death due to heart disease resulting from ETS is even greater than the risk of death due to lung cancer. Although the findings are somewhat controversial, a review of major studies indicates that the average nonsmoking male living with a smoker has a 9.6 percent chance of dying of heart disease by the age of 74 while a nonsmoking male has only a 7.4 percent chance. This difference may seem small, but it accounts for many thousands of unnecessary deaths per year, and the risk is

• YOU READ IT HERE FIRST •

The Backlash

While tobacco smoke is offensive to most nonsmokers, and spitting tobacco-stained saliva onto the sidewalk or into a jar is unlikely to be seen by anyone as an effective courtship ritual, some people, including some nonsmokers, feel that attempts to restrict smoking can, on occasion, go too far. A real concern exists among some professionals that a backlash by smokers is imminent.

You may have seen the overly zealous, called "nicotine Nazis" by some, wave their hands in front of their noses, make disgusted faces, and call loudly for a smoker to put his/her butt out, even when the smoker is at a considerable downwind distance. Just where and how can smokers indulge their habit? What happens when my right to smoke conflicts with your right not to be bothered by the smoke? Since no good studies show that occasional exposure to ETS, such as that likely to be encountered at a bar or restaurant, has significant health hazards, the issue is really an aesthetic one.

Several smokers' rights groups have formed (supported morally and sometimes financially by the tobacco industry) and insist that they are being unduly discriminated against. Just because someone's behavior offends someone else is no reason to pass a law against it, they argue. Just how far this issue can go is exemplified by the attempt of a group in Marin County, California, to declare public buildings "perfume-free" zones, since they claim that 10–15 percent of the population is allergic to perfume. Perfume-free zones have been established in restaurants and other public places across the country.

Smokers' rights groups feel that moral suasion, not legal regulation, is the route to take and they are supported by some in the restaurant and bar industry who feel that if regulations are passed to prohibit smoking in their town or city, the smokers will go to a restaurant or bar in another area. Evidence suggests, however, that most smokers are not as considerate as nonsmokers would like, and nonsmokers are very reluctant to ask smokers to stop—only 4 percent said they would do so in one study (Davis, Boyd, & Schoenborn, 1990).

The consititution of the United States guarantees the right to be outrageous, offensive, or rude. The next time you who are nonsmokers are near someone smoking and are irritated, examine your response to determine how much the irritation is due to the cigarette smoke and how much to your attitude toward smokers in general. Do smokers have rights? (By the way, the author is a nonsmoker.)

---

many times greater than that permitted by the federal government for other toxic environmental substances (Steenland, 1992).

The strongest evidence that ETS causes health difficulties comes from studies of children exposed to their parents' smoke. Children can be exposed two ways; either through prenatal nicotine because their mothers smoked during pregnancy or in the home after birth. The Centers for Disease Control (1991) estimates that 50 percent of all children have been exposed to environmental tobacco smoke before the age of five. The percentages are twice as high for blacks, those living in poverty, and those who have limited education.

The damage seems to occur in two areas; an increased incidence of respiratory symptoms and diseases such as cough, wheezing, asthma, chest colds, and bronchitis, and a decrease in pulmonary performance. Maternal smoking presents a greater risk than paternal smoking and the greatest effects are seen in children under the age of five. These findings should not be surprising since children under five spend most of their time at home and in the presence of their mothers. Older children do not spend as much time at home and seem to suffer less (Wu, 1990).

It is clear that exposure to cigarette smoke is harmful. Even though the effect is small, it is not insignificant. Most of the studies that have been done look at the spouses of smokers. The effect of ETS in the workplace has not been as extensively studied but is probably at least as great because of the length of time the nonsmoking worker spends there and the number of smoking employees.

Another rationale for banning smoking is that most people find it offensive. If rules prohibiting smoking in the workplace save money, help encourage smokers to quit, and improve the overall atmosphere of the work environment they are justified even if the overall improvement in the health status of nonsmokers is likely to be small.

Is Nicotine Addicting?

Nearly everyone knows someone who has tried to give up smoking. While some seem to be able to stop smoking without trouble, others seem to have an extremely difficult time. Simple observation should be enough to convince the average person that nicotine is addicting. Nevertheless, it was not until 3 May 1988 that the U.S. Surgeon General's report was released detailing how and why nicotine is addicting. The report is complex, but the major conclusions are as follows:

1. Cigarettes and other forms of tobacco are addicting.

2. Nicotine is the drug in tobacco that causes addiction.

3. The pharmacologic and behavioral processes that determine tobacco addiction are similar to those that determine addiction to drugs such as heroin and cocaine (Office of the Surgeon General, 1988).

As the report points out, many people are reluctant to see tobacco smoking as addicting because it is legal. However, as we have seen, the legality of a drug has little to do with its harmfulness or addictive characteristics. According to the report, nicotine meets the primary and most of the secondary criteria for dependence. Tobacco users engage in compulsive use, driven by strong urges. It can persist despite repeated attempts to stop. Nicotine is a reinforcer in both animal and human studies. Furthermore, tolerance occurs, withdrawal reactions trigger further nicotine intake, and the drug taking persists despite adverse physical, psychological, or social consequences.

FIGURE 7.4
This diagram shows the similarity of relapse rates for three commonly abused drugs. Keep in mind, however, that relapse is not permanent; most who want to will become drug-free.

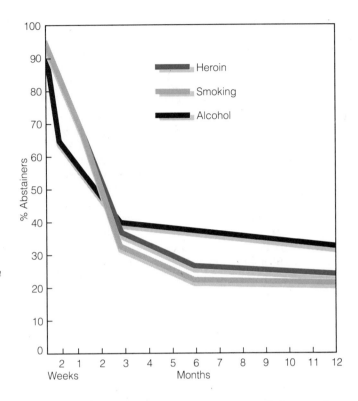

L. W. Barnett, et al., "Relapse Rates In Addiction Programs" in Journal of Clinical Psychology, *27: 455–56, 1971. Copyright 1971 by the American Psychological Association. Reprinted by permission of the publisher and author.*

The main reason for stating that nicotine is as addicting as heroin is the tendency for relapse, which is the same for most drugs of abuse. Figure 7.4 shows a graph showing the relapse for alcohol, heroin, and tobacco. You can see that the three curves are remarkably similar. In fairness, however, it should be noted that when all of the characeristics that define "addiction" are taken into consideration, most researchers conclude that, while nicotine is addicting, the addiction is not as strong as it is for cocaine or the opiates (Collins, 1990; Henningfield, Cohen, & Slade, 1991).

Regular Smoking and Health Consequences

The Office of the Surgeon General spends millions every year to inform the public of the health consequences of smoking and it appears that the information is beginning to sink in. Nearly all adults recognize that smoking can cause or aggravate lung cancer (94 percent), emphysema (90 percent) and cancer of the esophagus (79 percent), for example. However, less than half the population knows that smoking is a major cause of heart disease and only 35 percent associate smoking with an increased risk of bladder cancer (Thornberry, Wilson, & Golden, 1985).

Before we examine the specific health risks, consider this: Regular smokers increase their risk of death by lung cancer 700 percent, cancer of the larynx 500 percent, mouth 300 percent, esophagus 400 percent, bladder 100 percent, pancreas 100 percent. They increase their risk of death by

in depth

The Rights of Smokers

Most companies now have restrictions about smoking in the workplace. Over 85 percent of larger companies have such regulations and most of those that don't are considering them. What if the employers took the antismoking campaign one step further? Does a company have a right to discriminate in hiring against a cigarette smoker? Do companies have the right to demand that their employees stop smoking? How would the ban be enforced? Smokers lose far more days due to illness than nonsmokers and their medical costs can be staggering. Can a company forbid its workers from smoking off the job as well? How will the company know?

It is well within the capabilities of analytical chemistry to detect cigarette smoking up to fourteen days after the last cigarette in frequent smokers. It also is possible to detect recent, but infrequent, use of tobacco. Nicotine, cotinine (a metabolic product of nicotine), carbon monoxide, and sodium thiocyanate (a metabolic product of cyanide that is present in cigarette smoke) are all fairly sensitive and accurate measures of cigarette use.

Suppose the company you work for required that all employees stop smoking even at home and submit to periodic tests to see whether they have indeed stopped. After all, cigarette smoking increases health care costs to employers, and smokers have a higher absenteeism rate (Sees, 1990). Is this an unwarranted intrusion on your rights as a citizen or is it a reasonable demand by an employer trying to reduce expenses? Your answer probably depends on whether you are a smoker or not, but since court cases in several states have ruled that since cigarette smoking is not a constitutional right, more companies may do just that.

---

emphysema 1,300 percent, and heart disease 100 percent (Whelan, 1984). Note that these data refer to *death,* not just to the danger of acquiring these diseases. Note also that these risks are all combined.

Smoking and Pregnancy

The two major constituents of cigarette smoke that affect the fetus are carbon monoxide and nicotine. Carbon monoxide combines with hemoglobin to reduce the oxygen-carrying capacity of the blood (Visnjevac, 1986). The reduction can be as much as 15 percent. Only a 5 percent reduction can cause cognitive deficits in adults, and since the developing fetus gets its oxygen from the mother, the possibility exists that the decreased oxygen might pose a real hazard to the fetus (Longo, 1977).

The other ingredient in cigarettes that is clearly harmful to the fetus is nicotine. Nicotine passes the placental barrier, is secreted in breast milk, and has even been detected in amniotic fluid (Benowitz 1986a). Since it is a potent poison, nicotine is undoubtedly responsible for at least some of the effects of smoking.

Smoking seems to increase the risk of infertility in both men and women. In men, smoking is associated with decreased sperm motility (Abel,

1984). In women, smoking also is associated with a higher rate of spontane-ous abortion, with the risk approximately 1.5 times that for nonsmokers. Other effects include slower fetal growth, and increased risk of stillbirth, and preterm delivery (Friesen & Fox, 1986). It has been estimated that smoking by pregnant women is responsible for nearly 14,000 perinatal deaths each year. The cause of these and other fetal health problems such as placental abnor-malities, central nervous system defects, and cleft lip and palate are primar-ily the result of lack of oxygen, since the smoking mother's bloodstream has less oxygen available for the developing fetus (Friesen & Fox, 1986).

One of the most consistent findings of smoking on pregnancy is that babies born to smoking mothers tend to be smaller and shorter than those of nonsmoking mothers. Some women who have undergone a difficult birth with a large baby may not see this difference as a disadvantage, but most physicians disagree. Babies born to smoking mothers weighed, on an aver-age, about a half pound less than those of nonsmoking mothers and were a half inch shorter (Abel, 1980; McClaren & Nieburg, 1988).

There is also evidence that babies born to mothers who smoke have continuing physical and behavioral problems that show up months or years after birth. Smoking mothers have babies that are more likely to die from **Sudden Infant Death Syndrome** (SIDS), be more susceptible to respiratory disease, and be smaller even as young children (Golding, 1986). The in-crease in SIDS may be due to the fact that babies born to mothers who smoke show longer periods of **apnea** (cessation of breathing), a condition that has been linked to SIDS (Toubas, Duke, & McCaffree, 1986).

In addition to physical problems, children born to smoking mothers may show cognitive deficits as well. One study found that these children show attention deficits at age four (Streissguth, Martin, Barr, Sandman, Kirchner, & Darby, 1984). Longitudinal studies now are being conducted to see whether these differences persist into late childhood. The large number of health and behavioral problems associated with smoking has been called the Fetal Tobacco Syndrome (Tye, 1986).

It should be pointed out that these studies are mostly correlational. It is possible that some other factor that varies with cigarette smoking could be the real culprit in causing these problems. However, sophisticated statistical techniques reveal that smoking is the likeliest cause of these problems, even when most other factors are held constant.

Smoking and Cancer   In the early part of the twentieth century some medical students were called to witness an autopsy of a man who had died of lung cancer. They were assembled because the surgeon considered lung cancer so rare that he be-lieved the students might have a lifetime of practice before seeing another one. Lung cancer now is the commonest cause of death by cancers in both men and women (McGoldrick, 1986).

Smoking not only increases the likelihood of lung cancer but cancer of the esophagus, larynx, trachea, and just about every part of the body. Table

Table 7.3   Number of Deaths Attributed to Smoking in 1984

Disease	Males	Females	Total
Cancer of the:			
Mouth	3,958	1,110	5,068
Esophagus	3,717	1,257	4,974
Stomach	1,455	1,467	2,922
Pancreas	3,459	1,653	5,112
Larynx	2,385	274	2,660
Lung	65,659	27,170	92,829
Cervix	—	1,685	1,685
Circulatory Diseases:			
Hypertension	2,099	2,645	4,744
Heart desease	55,823	21,708	77,531
Strokes and aneurysms	14,336	19,249	33,585
Respiratory Diseases:			
Pneumonia	5,986	2,679	8,664
Bronchitis, emphysema, and airway obstruction	35,638	15,376	51,014
Pediatric Diseases:			
Low birth weight, Sudden Infant Death Syndrome, and others	1,475	1,069	2,544
Total (including other diseases)	209,057	106,063	315,120

Source: Adapted from the *Journal of the American Medical Association, 258 (19),* pp. 2648, 2652, Nov. 20, 1987. Used with permission.

7.3 shows the number of deaths from various diseases attributable to smoking. The trend toward smoking lower tar and nicotine cigarettes has not yet had a noticeable impact on deaths due to cancer, nor has the impact of the antismoking campaigns. Using lung cancer as a model, it has been estimated that for men, deaths should level off about 1990 and then decline gradually. For women, however, it appears that deaths will not peak until 2010 (Brown & Kessler, 1988).

The data are shown for both males and females. Note that most of the number of total deaths are lower for women than for men. This is probably due to the fact that women have not been smoking as heavily nor for as long as men. Trends indicate that for all cancer, the rate of death of women smokers is approaching that of men smokers. "Smoke like a man, die like a man!"

Women and Smoking

Women did not begin smoking like men until after World War II. Although by 1950, 70 percent of men in some urban areas were smokers, only about 25 percent of women smoked. The advent of the filter cigarette changed all that, and the percentage of women who smoked increased rapidly. At present, in fact, among seventeen- to nineteen-year-olds, more females than males smoke (Thornberry, Wilson, & Golden, 1986). The health consequences of smoking for women have not been as noticeable until recently because their smoking patterns have lagged behind those of men by twenty-five to thirty years.

Smoking and Heart Disease

The relationship between smoking and lung cancer is obvious; inhaling smoke many times every day ought to have harmful consequences. Surprisingly few people see the relationship between heart disease and smoking. In fact, the risk of a smoker dying of heart disease as a result of smoking is about the same as the risk of dying of cancer.

Nicotine and carbon monoxide both play a role in deaths due to cigarette smoking. Nicotine causes an increase in the heart rate and blood pressure, while carbon monoxide decreases the amount of oxygen delivered to the cells of the body, requiring that the heart work harder. Smoking increases the risk of arteriosclerosis or hardening of the arteries, stroke, and coronary heart disease (Office of the Surgeon General, 1983).

Smoking is a particular risk for women who use oral contraceptives. The rate of heart attack, stroke, and other cardiovascular diseases is increased in women who smoke and take the pill, compared to women who do not smoke. The risk of myocardial infarct (a kind of heart attack) is ten times as great in women who smoke and take the pill than in those who do neither (U.S. Department of Health and Human Services, 1982). The frequency of other kinds of cardiovascular problems such as stroke are also increasing in women. The woman who is a pack-a-day smoker has almost three times the risk of stroke as nonsmoking women (U.S. Department of Health and Human Services, 1989).

The good news about smoking and cardiovascular problems is that they seem to be reversible. Those former smokers who have not smoked in five to ten years have no higher risk of heart disease than nonsmokers, as shown in table 7.5.

Smoking and Chronic Obstructive Lung Disease (COLD)

COLD is a combination of chronic bronchitis and emphysema and is seen almost exclusively in smokers. Emphysema is a condition in which the ability of the air sacs in the lungs to hold oxygen decreases and the chest cavity expands in an attempt to get more oxygen to the bloodstream. The diaphragm that controls breathing then stretches, and each breath becomes shorter and shorter. The concentration of oxygen in the blood is decreased and the heart must beat faster to get less and less oxygen to the tissues.

Take the deepest breath possible, until your lungs are completely expanded, and then breathe rapidly with the shallowest breaths possible. What you are experiencing is part of what the person with emphysema experiences twenty-four hours a day, seven days a week. You can let the air out of your lungs and breathe normally; the person with emphysema cannot. Now imagine that your lungs are filled with mucous and take another deep breath. Try coughing without letting out much air, and you may have some idea of what the person with COLD experiences.

Chronic bronchitis occurs when the cilia, or hairlike cells, that normally protect the lung from dust and mucous are damaged by cigarette

FIGURE 7.5
Effects of smoking: (A) airways are narrowed and production of mucus that leads to smoker's cough is increased; (B) cilia are killed and the ability to clear the lungs of mucus and other secretions is impaired; (C) inflammatory cells increase and these release a substance the impairs the lung's ability to expand and contract leading to emphysema.

smoke. When the irritating effect of the smoke causes more mucous to be formed, the result is a racking cough that never brings up enough mucous to give relief and further exhausts the COLD sufferer. In an attempt to get enough oxygen to the blood, the person with COLD often has to breathe pure oxygen. You may have seen people walking around with what looks like a tank attached to a mask over their face. The vast majority of them are former (and possibly current!) smokers.

The person who has emphysema, chronic bronchitis, or the combination (COLD) dies when it is no longer possible to breathe, unless the heart gives out first. To make matters even cheerier, autopsies of smokers indicate that nearly every person who smokes regularly shows some signs of emphysema or bronchitis, regardless of age or cause of death. Furthermore, many,

FIGURE 7.6

Chances of dying of a smoking-related illness by the age of 85. Remember these are excess deaths that would not have happened if the person was a nonsmoker.

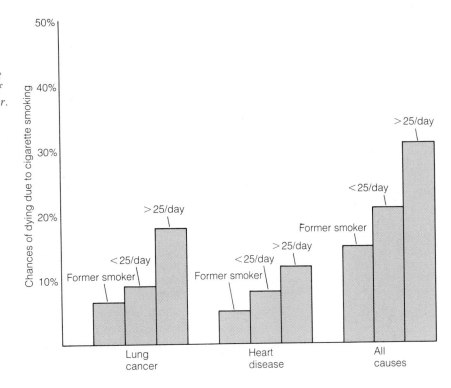

if not most, smokers also show evidence of what is called "carcinoma in situ," meaning that their lungs in particular show signs of cancers that are small and have not spread to other parts of the body or begun to grow rapidly. Yet.

It seems that cigarette smoke has been linked to nearly every conceivable human malady. Recent studies keep adding to that list. One which should be of practical concern is that smoking seems to cause premature wrinkling, especially when combined with exposure to the sun (Kadunce, 1991). Other problems associated with smoking include an increased risk of colon polyps, an increase in white blood cell count, and perhaps even an increased risk of AIDS (Zahm, 1991; Anderson, 1991; Halsey, Coberly, Holt, Coreil, et al., 1992).

Putting all this information together, figure 7.6 shows the chance of a thirty-five year old male smoker dying of a smoking related condition. Remember that all of the risks are substantially decreased if the person stops smoking.

Table 7.4 shows another way of looking at the same kinds of data. It presents the number of years your life will be shortened if you smoke cigarettes.

Table 7.4 Average Number of Years of Life Lost Due to Smoking		
	Males	**Females**
Whites	5.56	2.17
Blacks	12.07	4.85

Source: Adapted from the *Journal of the American Medical Assoc., 258 (19),* pp. 2648, 2652, November 20, 1987. Used with permission.

THE ECONOMICS OF THE TOBACCO INDUSTRY
Tobacco in Other Countries

Smoking has declined in the United States, Canada, and Western Europe in general. The same is not true for other parts of the world. In most Asian and third world countries the percentage of males who smoke is around 50 percent, with many having even higher rates (Council on Scientific Affairs, 1990; Yu, Mattson, Boyd, Mueller, Shopland, Pechacek, & Cullen, 1990). Moreover, in most countries smokers smoke unfiltered cigarettes. The health consequences of smoking are the same in Tunisia as they are in the United States and it is estimated that tobacco use is responsible for 2.5 million excessive or premature deaths worldwide every year, a figure that approaches 5 percent of all deaths. Lung cancer rates are increasing rapidly as well as deaths due to other smoking related causes. This effect is seen more in males than females in most countries, because rates of smoking are far higher in men than in women in most of the world.

Attempts to restrict smoking are increasing, as is legislation banning smoking in workplaces, and education to prevent smokers from ever starting. Even if these attempts meet with success, however, look for the toll of cigarette-related illness and death to increase for many years, since the lag time between smoking and the onset of health problems can be as long as twenty years.

In general, smoking increases in countries that are experiencing an increase in socioeconomic development and in disposable income, and then decreases when educational and literacy levels rise. In many countries, cigarette manufacturing is a state industry, so that the pressure to decrease smoking works at cross purposes with the profit motive. China, for example, controls the production of cigarettes and manufactures nearly twice as many as the next leading manufacturer, the United States. In 1987, for example, China produced a staggering 1,441 billion cigarettes.

The international trade in cigarettes is dominated by large companies in the United States, and to a lesser extent, Great Britain. American tobacco, especially the mild burley which makes up 90 percent of our production, is becoming increasingly popular in foreign markets. Our tobacco firms have made a concerted effort to expand their market in countries where demand is high or where they feel they can increase the demand. In Asia, for example, there was a 75 percent increase in U.S. cigarette imports in 1988 alone. The United States government has cooperated with the attempt to the extent of threatening sanctions against some countries which have attempted to restrict the importation of tobacco into their countries.

Not all of the exportation of tobacco is purely for profit. Because of an econonomic crisis in 1990, there was an shortage of cigarettes in the Soviet Union, and tobacco companies in the United States offered to ship billions of cigarettes there. Purely out of humanitarian concerns, of course.

WHY DO PEOPLE CONTINUE TO SMOKE?

If smoking is, as former Surgeon General Everett Koop has said, ''the chief preventable cause of death in the United States,'' and if nearly everyone knows that smoking is harmful, why do 30 percent of people still smoke? By law, there are warnings on all cigarette packages and on all advertisements for cigarettes. How could anyone who smoked ignore these warnings? Interestingly, studies indicate that the warnings on outdoor advertisements are not readable under ordinary driving conditions and most smokers cannot even recall the warnings on their own cigarette packs (Davis & Kendrick, 1989; Richards, Fischer, & Conner, 1989).

Understanding why people smoke will go a long way toward understanding how to help people stop smoking. First, you must consider that the average pack-a-day smoker delivers more than 200 doses of his drug to himself everyday. To the extent that these are reinforcing, the smoker reinforces his drug-taking behavior more than the user of any other drug, legal or illegal. Can you imagine a heroin addict shooting up 200 times a day, or an alcoholic drinking 200 drinks a day?

Two hundred ''hits'' a day of a rewarding drug builds up a considerable habit merely from the physical act of smoking. When combined with fact that smoking can be either stimulating or relaxing, and that our society has, at least until recently, tolerated, condoned, and even encouraged this behavior, it is not hard to see why it has continued.

Smoking, moreover, does not impair performance like drinking alcoholic beverages, smoking marijuana, or using other illegal drugs does. In fact, some studies show that it increases performance on some tasks (Office of the Surgeon General, 1988). Since there is no immediate decline in performance after a cigarette, smokers often see no real reason to quit.

The harmful effects of smoking tend not to occur until the drug has been used for years. To a twenty-year-old, the prospect of dying of cancer at sixty-five is so remote as to not be a deterrent at all. Surely a cure for cancer will be discovered by then. Furthermore, everyone knows someone who smoked two packs of cigarettes a day for fifty years without any obvious harmful consequences.

If I tell smokers that they have a 35 percent chance of dying of a smoking-related illness, they may tell me they have a 65 percent chance of *not* dying, and given the pleasure they get from smoking, they will take those odds. Young people, especially, tend to believe that they are invincible and immortal and engage in denial when confronted with the relationship between smoking and health problems (Hansen & Malotte, 1986).

Perhaps the most important reason why people continue to smoke is that nicotine is an addicting drug. Not everyone who smokes becomes addicted, just as not every drinker is an abuser, but for those who do, nicotine addiction is extremely powerful.

How to Stop Smoking

Look around—you are a witness to one of the most massive anti-drug campaigns in history and one which is finally beginning to work. The reduction in smoking among many groups is virtually unprecedented in history. Smoking is banned in the obvious places like hospitals, but also in places where smoking would seem to be the least concern—in jails and prisons (Skolnick, 1990a,b; Stillman, Becker, Swank, Hantula, Moses, Glantz, & Waranch, 1990).

The various changes in legislation that make it more and more difficult for the smoker to indulge in his habit are so numerous and are happening so rapidly that it is impossible to keep up with them. The result of all these changes both shapes and reinforces public opinion that it is no longer socially acceptable to smoke in public.

Given that you or someone you know is a smoker, and has decided to quit, how do you go about it? Not everyone who smokes has difficulty stopping, and people smoke for different reasons. Knowing some of the reasons *why* you smoke, may help you make some decisions about how to stop.

People smoke for many reasons, and many ways of classifying these reasons have been proposed. Basically, all can be divided into three categories; an inner need to smoke, a sensorimotor factor, and a social factor. The inner need to smoke may be because the smoker finds smoking either stimulating or relaxing or both. It may also result from pharmacological addiction and habit. The inner need to smoke is strongest in those that have the most difficulty stopping.

Smoking also provides enjoyment through the process of reaching for the cigarette, handling it, placing it in the mouth, lighting it, inhaling and exhaling, and watching the exhaled smoke. This sensorimotor factor can be quite rewarding. People whose smoking is partly maintained by this factor need to find something to do with their hands when they stop smoking. Smokers can get an idea of how important the sensorimotor factor is by smoking a cigarette in the complete dark. Many smokers report that their enjoyment is considerably lessened, unless there is at least a little light in the room when they smoke.

The social factor of smoking is involved when smokers are around others who smoke. Occasional cigarette smokers often feel no need or compulsion to smoke unless they are with someone who lights up. The social factor also comes into play when the smoker views smoking as a mark of maturity or sophistication. It is this aspect of smoking that cigarette advertisements often address. The social factors supporting smoking have lessened considerably although some concern has been raised that adolescents are beginning

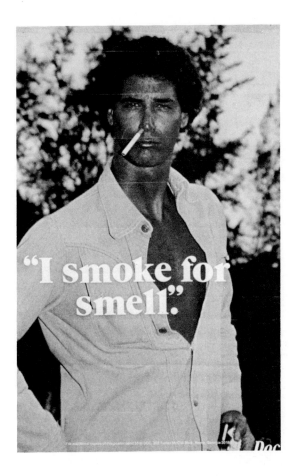

"I smoke for smell."

to associate cigarette smoking with risk taking, perhaps thereby increasing its attractiveness.

Keeping all of these factors in mind, you now should be able to formulate your own stop-smoking plan. Many smokers have become dependent on nicotine and can expect to experience withdrawal symptoms. These symptoms included craving for tobacco, irritability, anxiety, difficulty in concentrating, headache, drowsiness, inability to sleep at night, constipation, and dizziness (Cummings, Giovino, & Jaen, 1985). These symptoms tend to subside sharply during the first few days of withdrawal and then more slowly over the next few weeks (Gritz, Carr, & Marcus, 1991).

Ninety percent of smokers stop without help from anyone (Office of the Surgeon General, 1988). For others a variety of techniques are available. Nicotine fading (a form of tapering off) has been successful and is discussed in several readily available publications such as the *Pregnant Woman's Self-Help Guide to Quitting Smoking*. Hypnosis has been proven useful under some circumstances (Hudson, 1986), as have techniques ranging from acupuncture to aversion therapy (American College of Physicians, 1986). The crucial factor in any program is the smoker's motivation to quit, of course. In addition, successful stop-smoking programs are most effective when they emphasize the benefits of quitting rather than the dangers of smoking, when they offer a consistent plan for the maintenance of nonsmoking, and when they continue for a period of weeks or months (Bailey, 1986; Musk & Shean, 1986).

Formal smoking cessation programs are popular and widely advertised. Evidence suggests that they are more likely to be utilized by educated, middle-class people who are heavy smokers and have made previous attempts to quit. According to one study, 47.5 percent of those attempting to quit on their own succeed, while only 23.6 percent of those who use the programs succeed (Pierce, Fiore, Novotny, Hatziandreu et al, 1990). Of course, it should be noted that those who could stop on their own usually did, and thus the programs attracted a disproportionately large number of those who were more dependent on smoking.

If it is true that many people smoke because they are dependent on nicotine, then wouldn't it make sense to provide them with nicotine while they try to stop *smoking* and later try to withdraw them from the nicotine dependence? Various attempts have been made to do just that but have met with little success until recently. The introduction of a nicotine based chewing gum shows some promise.

Nicorette is the trade name for nicotine polacrilex. It is available by prescription only in the form of chewing gum. Each tablet contains 2 mg of nicotine. In Europe it also is available in a 4 mg form. When the gum is chewed nicotine is absorbed through the buccal cavity (mouth). The blood levels of nicotine that occur when a cigarette is smoked and when Nicorette is chewed are quite similar. However, as seen in figure 7.7, the pattern is quite different.

As you can see from the figure, smoking a cigarette results in a rapid rise in nicotine levels. Each subsequent cigarette produces another "spike." The absorption of nicotine through the mouth causes a more gradual absorption. To the extent that the smoker smokes in order to obtain that sudden increase in nicotine level, chewing gum is not particularly satisfactory. However, since the blood levels of nicotine are similar, Nicorette should reduce some of the withdrawal symptoms.

The results of clinical studies of attempts to stop smoking using Nicorette are in line with what you might expect given your new knowledge of the effects of drugs on the body. Simply giving the chewing gum to people trying to stop smoking has no more effect than chewing a placebo gum without nicotine. When the nicotine chewing gum was used as part of a stop-smoking clinic, it was significantly more effective than the placebo. When used alone the success rate was only about 11 percent, but when used in combination with a clinic, the success rate increased to 27 percent (Lam, Sze, Sacks, & Chalmers, 1987). Other studies have found similar rates of success (Daughton, Kass, & Fix, 1986).

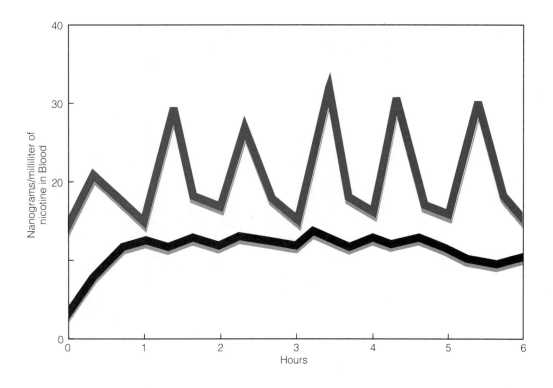

FIGURE 7.7

Changes in blood nicotine levels after smoking one cigarette per hour (top line) and using 4 mg of Nicorette per hour. As you can see the blood nicotine levels after Nicorette are lower and do not show the ''spike'' indicated after cigarette smoking.

Another technique for administering nicotine has recently been introduced. Transdermal nicotine administration by means of patch has been shown to be effective in a treatment program that also includes counseling. The major advantages of the transdermal patch over gum is that it provides higher levels of nicotine with less variability. The levels are similar to those found in cigarette smokers (Transdermal Nicotine Study Group, 1991). The transdermal patch is renewed every week, and remains in place in the upper torso or arm. The smoker (or would-be nonsmoker) has to remember to use the gum. Of course, as is the case with other methods of quitting, relapse rates are high once the patch is removed.

Nicotine dependence obviously is only part of the reason why people smoke. We need to address the other two factors mentioned on page 254: the sensorimotor and social factors. Let's assume you are an addicted smoker who wants to stop and have gone to a doctor. Even though, thanks to nicotine gum, you are not going through withdrawal, you are used to lighting up a cigarette and puffing on it. You have practiced the rituals of drug use hundreds of times a day for years. What will take its place?

The American Cancer Society has a number of suggestions that will help with the sensorimotor aspects of smoking. Chew gum or spices, eat fruit, or sip water whenever you have a craving to puff. Exercise vigorously; very few people smoke while they are jogging. Keep a pencil handy and manipulate it as you would cigarette. Some people go through the motions of smoking with a cigarette but eliminate the step of lighting it. They hold a cigarette, put it in their mouth and puff on it. A moment's reflection should reveal that this method is doomed to failure; it is too short a step to lighting up!

The social aspects of smoking also can be manipulated. Tell everyone you know, whether they care or not, that you have stopped smoking. Avoid people and situations previously associated with smoking. Throw away your ashtrays and lighters. If you rationalize keeping them around because guests might need them you are fooling yourself.

The new regulations against smoking help keep these restrictions in mind. Force yourself to pay attention to the no smoking signs being posted everywhere. Ask to sit in the no smoking section of restaurants and fly in the nonsmoking section of your plane.

What to Do If You Can't (Or Won't) Stop

The recidivism rate (the rate of return) for smoking is appallingly high. Given the best possible circumstances, smoking cessation clinics, and nicotine gum, only about 30 percent of smokers are still not smoking after one year (American College of Physicians, 1986). Of course, many of these might stop after the second or third or subsequent attempt, but what advice is available to those who can't or won't quit smoking? Can they reduce their risk of dying of all the diseases mentioned earlier? Perhaps.

1. Switch to a low tar/nicotine brand. This strategy will work only if you do not, as most smokers do, inhale low tar/nicotine cigarettes more deeply, smoke them to a shorter butt, and smoke more of them. This strategy is most effective with those who are not nicotine dependent.

2. Smoke fewer cigarettes. Make a list of the time and situations when you smoke a cigarette and how badly you need that cigarette. Simply keeping a list usually results in smoking fewer cigarettes. Try to avoid smoking in situations where your craving is not strong.

3. Smoke less of each cigarette. The tars and nicotine from a cigarette are filtered by the tobacco. The last half of the cigarette contains more than half of the tar and nicotine. Stomp out that butt. Also try taking fewer puffs.

4. Make cigarettes less available. Put them on the highest shelf of your kitchen. Don't carry them with you. Buy them by the pack, not the carton. Set aside a place to smoke, and smoke only there. Make that place as unattractive as possible: outside in cold weather, your basement, or standing on the toilet seat.

When the time comes that you decide to quit, quit. The benefits of quitting smoking are enormous, there are no good reasons to continue.

Table 7.5 Risks of Smoking and Benefits of Quitting

Shortened Life Expectancy
10–15 years after stopping, ex-smokers and nonsmokers have the same life expectancy.
Lung Cancer:
10–15 years after stopping, ex-smokers and nonsmokers have the same risk of lung cancer.
Larynx Cancer:
Risk declines with time, after 10 years no difference.
Mouth Cancer:
Risk declines with time, after 10 years no difference.
Cancer of the Bladder:
After 7 years, no difference between smokers and nonsmokers.
Coronary Heart Disease:
Rapid decline after one year, by ten years the same risk as for nonsmokers.
Bronchitis and Emphysema:
Excessive coughing disappears in a few weeks, lung function can improve.
Stillbirth and Low Birth Weight:
Can eliminate risk to fetus if you stop before fourth month.

The Health Benefits of Smoking Cessation

With all the health consequences that occur with smoking, it should not be surprising that if you quit smoking you will be a healthier person. What may be surprising, however, is how much healthier you are likely to be. One common excuse used by people who continue to smoke is "it hasn't hurt me yet," or when the health consequences do begin to appear, "the damage has been done." Common sense and behavioral psychology both agree that threatening someone with punishment in the future is not effective in stopping a behavior when the immediate consequences are positive. Telling yourself that one more beer is going to give you a hangover in the morning is not likely to stop you from having that beer because the immediate reinforcement is so strong. Similarly, telling cigarette smokers that they will die of cancer in twenty-five years is not likely to be much of an incentive to overcome their current addiction. Therefore it is important to emphasize the short-term as well as long-term benefits of smoking cessation.

Overall, smokers who quit before fifty years of age are only half as likely to die in the next fifteen years as those who continue. Stopping smoking cuts the risk of lung cancer nearly in half as well as reducing the risk of the various other cancers discussed. Even those whose cancer has already developed may be helped by smoking cessation. Certainly they are less likely to develop respiratory and cardiovascular problems that worsen their chance of surviving the cancer.

Cessation of smoking has even more dramatic effects on cardiovascular disease. Just one year after smoking cessation, the risk of developing heart disease is only one half that of those who continue to smoke, although it is still greater than nonsmokers. After fifteen years of not smoking, the risk of heart disease is the same as for those who never smoked. Once heart disease has been diagnosed, it still helps to stop smoking, since the risk of actual heart attack and death is also reduced by half. Similar benefits are seen with stroke, although the benefits may not show up for several years.

Stopping smoking can reduce the risk of developing COLD as well, and long-term abstinence can reduce the risk to that of nonsmokers. Once COLD has developed, little can be done except to treat the symptoms, but continuing to smoke makes symptoms worse and accelerates the damage. Other benefits from smoking cessation include a reduced risk of artery disease, abdominal aneurysm, and ulcer.

Earlier in this chapter you read of fetal nicotine syndrome and other health hazards to the fetus from mothers who smoke. Women who smoke, but stop smoking before pregnancy, eliminate these problems. Even if women wait until the fourth month of pregnancy to stop smoking, the benefits are the same. According to the U.S. Surgeon General cessation of smoking during pregnancy would prevent 10 percent of perinatal deaths, 35 percent of all low birthweight births, and 15 percent of preterm deliveries.

You also read of the effects of environmental tobacco smoke on children. Although data are scarce it would seem logical that if smoking increased the number of respiratory illnesses and slowing of lung growth, that cessation of smoking by parents would eliminate this problems. Perhaps the best reason for parents to stop smoking is modeling of harmful behavior. Children whose parents smoke are much more likely to smoke themselves.

A common belief among smokers is that smoking cessation will cause them to gain weight. Sometimes this belief is enough to deter smokers from attempting to stop, or encourage them to resume smoking once they have stopped. Roughly half of smokers believe that smoking helps control weight and nearly half of those who resumed smoking reported actual weight gain or fear of weight gain as a reason for relapse.

Ironically, research indicates that for most smokers not only is the weight gain small, but is largely outweighed by improved cholesterol levels and a healthier distribution of body fat. The average weight gain varies from study to study but is rarely more than six to eight pounds (Klesges & Meyers, 1989; Williamson, Madans, Anda, Kleinman, Giovino, & Byers, 1991). About ten percent of smokers report large weight gains (more than twenty pounds) and those who smoke heavily gain more than lighter smokers.

Although six pounds is not likely to cause any additional health risk, it does present a problem given our society's near obsession with thinness. The reasons for the weight gain are complex but may be related to an increased intake of sweets as well as to metabolic changes. Increasingly, weight control advice is being incorporated into smoking cessation programs.

SUMMARY

Nicotine is a widely used drug, although addicting and poisonous. Tobacco smoking, the most widely used form of nicotine use, is responsible for hundreds of thousands of deaths a year. The cigarette has evolved in the last one hundred years as an extremely effective means of delivering nicotine to the body, and the resultant cigarette industry is big business in the United States.

Considered a drug, nicotine can be considered both a sedative and a stimulant. Its effects are difficult to distinguish from the act of smoking itself, but nicotine addiction and cigarette smoking are believed to be responsible for cancer, heart disease, and difficulties with pregnancy. The Surgeon General of the United States has called smoking the most important preventable health hazard in the United States.

People smoke cigarettes for many reasons including the stimulation, the social reward, and sensory effects. For those who are addicted, the current campaign against smoking may not be effective unless the issue of addiction is directly addressed.

Smoking cigarettes in public is no longer considered socially acceptable by many, and the number of smokers has declined. The cigarette industry has responded to this challenge in a number of ways, some of which have drawn criticism. They have attempted to deny the link between smoking and health concerns, to diversify their holdings by buying companies that do not manufacture cigarettes, and to expand their markets to other countries.

Many people find it difficult to stop smoking. An understanding of why a person smokes in the first place may help them to stop. For those who are addicted, a nicotine substitute is available that is chewed in the form of gum. This product has helped many people stop. Even if smokers merely cut back and follow a few simple rules, they can reduce but by no means eliminate their risk of health consequences.

REFERENCES

Abel, E. L.,(1980). Smoking during pregnancy: A review of effects on growth and development of offspring. *Human Biology, 52,* 1980.

American College of Physicians (1988). Methods for stopping cigarette smoking. *Annals of Internal Medicine, 105,* 281–91.

Anderson, R., (1991). Passive smoking by humans sensitizes circulating neutrophils. *American Review of Respiratory Diseases, 144,* 570–74.

Armitrage, A. K., Dollery, C. T., George, C. F., Houseman, T. H., Lewis, P. J., & Turner, D. M., (1975). Absorption and metabolism of nicotine from cigarettes. *British Medical Journal, 4,* 313–16.

Bailey, W. C., (1986). Smoking cessation. *Southern Medical Journal, 79,* 223–26.

Bailey, W. J., Lamarine, R. J., (1986). Clove cigarettes: Problem or symptom? *Journal of School Health, 56,* 29–30.

Benowitz, N. L. (1986). The human pharmacology of nicotine. In H. D. Cappell, F. B. Glaser, Y. Israell, H. Kalant, W. Schmidt, E. M. Sellers, & K. C. Smart (Eds.), pp. 1–53. *Research advances in alcohol and drug problems, volume 9.* New York and London: Plenum Press.

Benowitz, N. L. (1988). Pharmacological aspects of cigarette smoking and nicotine addiction. *New England Journal of Medicine, 319,* 1318–30.

Benowitz, N. L., Hall, S. M., Herning, R. J. Jacob, P., Jones, R. T., & Osman, A. (1983). Smokers of low yield cigarettes do not consume less nicotine. *New England Journal of Medicine, 309,* 139–42.

Benowitz, N. L., Jacob, P., Yu, L., Talcott, R., Hall, S., & Jones., R. T. (1986). Reduced tar, nicotine, and carbon monoxide exposure while smoking ultralow but not low yield cigarettes. *Journal of the American Medical Association, 256,* 242–46.

Benowitz, N. L., Porchet, H., Sheiner, L., & Jacob, P. (1988). Nicotine absorption and cardiovascular effects with smokeless tobacco use: Comparison with cigarettes and nicotine gum. *Clinical Pharmacology and Therapeutics, 44,* 23–28.

Blum, A. (1985). When ''More doctors smoked Camels'': Cigarette advertising in the *Journal*. In A. Blum (Ed.). *The cigarette underworld: A front line report on the war against your lungs.* Secaucus, NJ: Lyle-Stuart.

Blum, A. (1985). Alton Ochsner, MD, 1896–1981: He cleared the air. In A. Blum (Ed.). *The cigarette underworld: A front line report on the war against your lungs.* Secaucus, NJ: Lyle-Stuart.

Caro, C. G., Lever, M. J., Parker, K. H., and Fish, P. T. (1987). Effect of cigarette smoking on patterns of blood flow: Possible insight into mechanisms underlying the development of arteriosclerosis. *Lancet, 15,* 11–13.

Centers for Disease Control (1991). *Children's exposure to environmental cigarette smoke before and after birth.* National Center for Health Statistics, U.S. Department of Health and Human Services, #202.

Charlton, A. (1984). Children's coughs related to parental smoking. *British Medical Journal, 288,* 1747–49.

Chassin, L., Presson, C., Sherman, S. J. (1985). Psychosocial correlates of adolescent smokeless tobacco use. *Addictive Behaviors, 10,* 431–35.

Cole, P. V., Hawkins, L. H., & Roberts, D. (1972). Smoking during pregnancy and its effects on the fetus. *Journal of Obstetrics and Gynecology of the British Commonwealth, 79,* 782–87.

Collins, A. C. (1990). An analysis of the addiction liability of nicotine. *Advances in Alcohol and Substance Abuse, 9,* 83–94.

Connolly, G. N., Winn, D. M., Hecht, S. S. (1986). The reemergence of smokeless tobacco. *New England Journal of Medicine, 314,* 1020–27.

Cotton, P. (1990). Tobacco foes attack ads that target women, minorities, teens, and the poor. *Journal of the American Medical Association, 264,* 1505–06.

Council on Scientific Affairs—The American Medical Association (1990). The worldwide smoking epidemic: Tobacco trade use and control. *Journal of the American Medical Association, 263,* 3312–19.

Cryer, P. E., Haymond, M. W., Santiago, J. V., & Shah, S. D. (1976). Norepinephrine and epinephrine release and adrenergic mediation of smoking-associated hemodynamic and metabolic events. *New England Journal of Medicine, 295,* 573–77.

Cummings, K. M., Giovino, G., & Jaen, C. R. (1985). Reports of smoking withdrawal symptoms over a 21-day period of abstinence. *Addiction Behaviors, 10,* 373–81.

Dalager, N. A., Pickle, L. W., Mason, T. J. (1986). The relation of passive smoking to lung cancer. *Cancer Research, 46,* 4808–11.

Daughton, D. M., Kass, I., & Fix, A. J. (1986). Smoking intervention: Combination therapy using nicotine chewing gum and the American Lung Association's ''Freedom from smoking'' manuals. *Preventive Medicine, 15,* 432–35.

Davis, R. M. (1987). Current trends in cigarette advertising and marketing. *New England Journal of Medicine, 316,* 725–32.

Davis, R. M., & Kendrick, J. S. (1989). The Surgeon General's warning in outdoor cigarette advertising: Are they readable? *Journal of the American Medical Association, 261,* 90–94.

Davis, R. M., Boyd, G. M., & Schoenborn, C. A. (1990). Common courtesy and the elimination of passive smoking. *Journal of the American Medical Association, 263,* 2208–10.

Ernster, V. L., Grady, D. G., Greene, J. C., Walsh, M., Robertson, T., Daniels, T. E., Benowitz, N., Siegel, D., Gerbert, G., & Hauck, W. (1990). Smokeless tobacco use and health effects among baseball players. *Journal of the American Medical Association, 264,* 218–24.

Fielding, J. E. (1986). Banning worksite smoking. *American Journal of Public Health, 76,* 957–59.

Friesen, C., & Fox, H. A. (1986). Effects of smoking during pregnancy. *Kansas Medicine, 87,* 7–9, 21–22.

Goldfrank, B., Melinek, M., & Blum, A. (1980). Nicotine. *Physician Assistant and Health Practitioner,* August, 34–35.

Golding, J. (1986). Child health and the environment. *British Medical Bulletin, 46,* 204–11.

Gritz, E. R., Carr, C. R., & Marcus, A. C., (1991). The tobacco withdrawal syndrome in unaided quitters. *British Journal of Addiction, 86,* 57–69.

Halsey, N. A., Coberly, J. S., Holt, E., Coreil, J., Kissinger, P., Moulton, L. H., Brutus, J. R., & Coulous, R. (1992). Sexual behavior, smoking and HIV-1 Infection in Haitian women. *Journal of the American Medical Association, 267,* 2062–66.

Hansen, W. B., & Malotte, C. K. (1986). Perceived personal immunity: The development of beliefs about susceptibility to the consequences of smoking. *Preventive Medicine, 15,* 362–72.

Hatsukami, D., Nelson, R., & Jensen, J. (1991). Smokeless tobacco: Current status and future directions. *British Journal of Addiction, 86,* 559–63.

Heiman, R. K. (1960). *Tobacco and Americans,* New York: McGraw-Hill.

Henningfield, J. E., Cohen, C., & Slade, J. D. (1991). Is nicotine more addicting than cocaine? *British Journal of Addiction, 86,* 565–69.

Hudson, B. (1986). Hypnotherapy and smoking cessation. *Journal of Family Practice, 23,* 18.

Iglehart, J. K. (1986). The campaign against smoking gains momentum. *New England Journal of Medicine, 314,* 1059–64.

Janerich, D. T., Thompson, W. D., Varela, L., Greenwald, T., Chorost, S., Tucci, C., Zaman, M. B., Melamed, M. R., Kiely, M., & McKnealy, M.F. (1990). Lung cancer and exposure to tobacco smoke in the household. *New England Journal of Medicine, 323,* 632–36.

Kadunce, D. P. (1991). Cigarette smoking: risk factor for premature facial wrinkling. *Annals of Internal Medicine, 114,* 840–44.

Karras, A., & Kane, J. M. (1980). Naloxone reduces cigarette smoking. *Life Sciences, 27,* 1541–45.

Klesges, R. C., Meyers, A. W., Klesges, L. M., & LaVasque, M. E. (1989). Smoking, body weight, and their effects on smoking behavior: A comprehensive review of the literature. *Psychological Bulletin, 106,* 204–30.

Koop, C. E. (1986). The campaign against smokeless tobacco. *New England Journal of Medicine, 314,* 1042–44.

Lam, W., Sze, P. C., Sacks, H. S. & Chalmers, T. C. (1987). Meta analysis of randomized controlled trials of nicotine chewing gum. *The Lancet,* 4 July, 27–29.

Longo, L. D., (1977). The biological effects of carbon monoxide on the pregnant woman, fetus and newborn infant. *American Journal of Obstetrics and Gynecology, 129,* 69–103.

McClaren, N. M., & Nieburg, P. (1988). Fetal tobacco syndrome and other problems caused by smoking during pregnancy. *Medical Aspects of Human Sexuality,* August, 69–72.

McGoldrick, K. E. (1986). Playing with fire: Women and tobacco. *Journal of the American Medical Women's Association, 41,* 2;28.

Millar, W. J. (1986). *Smoke in the workplace: A survey of health and welfare employee opinion.* Health and Welfare, Canada: Health Services and Promotion Branch.

Morris, J. E. (1986). This tobacco business, part XXIV: A century of cigarettes. *Tobacco International, 188,* 16;18;20;22;24.

Musk, A. W., & Shean, R. E. (1986). The treatment of cigarette dependence. *World Health Forum, 7,* 86–87.

Pierce, J. P., Fiore, M. C., Novotny, T. E., Hatziandreu, E. J., & Davis, R. M. (1989). Trends in cigarette smoking in the United States: Projection to the year 2000. *Journal of the American Medical Association, 261,* 61–65.

Richards, J. W., Fischer, P., & Conner, F. G. (1989). The warnings on cigarette packages are ineffective. *Journal of the American Medical Association, 261,* 45.

Russell, M. A., Jarvis, M. J., Devitt, G., & Feyerabend, C. (1981). Nicotine intake by snuff users. *British Journal of Medicine, 283,* 814–17.

Schmeisser, D. (1988). Pushing cigarettes overseas. *The New York Times Magazine,* July 10, 16–22;62.

Schmeltz, I., Hoffman, D., & Wynder, E. L. (1975). The influence of tobacco smoke on indoor atmospheres. *Preventive Medicine, 4,* 66–82.

Sees, K. L. (1990). The smokefree workplace. *Journal of Psychoactive Drugs, 22,* 79–83.

Sepkovic, D. W., Haley, N. J., & Hoffman, D. (1986). Elimination from the body of tobacco products by smokers and passive smokers. *Journal of the American Medical Association, 256,* 863.

Skolnick, A. (1990a). While some correctional facilities go smoke-free, others appear to help inmates light up. *Journal of the American Medical Association, 264,* 1509;1513.

Skolnick, A. (1990b). Jails lead prisons in smoking bans. *Journal of the American Medical Association, 264,* 1514.

Steenland, K. (1992). Passive smoking and the risk of heart disease. *Journal of the American Medical Association, 267,* 94–99.

Stellman, S. D., & Garfinkel, L. (1986). Smoking habits and tar levels in a new American Cancer Society prospective study of 1.2 million men and women. *Journal of the National Cancer Institute, 76,* 1057–63.

Stewart, G. G. (1967). A history of the medicinal use of tobacco. *Medical History, 11,* 228–68.

Stillman, F. A., Becker, D., Swank, R. T., Hantula, D., Moses, H., Glantz, S., & Waranch, R. (1990). Ending smoking at the Johns Hopkins Medical Institutions. *Journal of the American Medical Association, 264,* 1565–69.

Thornberry, O. T., Wilson, R. W., & Golden, P. M. (1986). *Health promotion data for the 1990 objectives. Estimates from the national health interview survey of health promotion and disease prevention.* U.S. Department of Health and Human Services, Public Health Service, National Center for Health Statistics, Vital and Health Statistics, NCHS Advance Data, #126.

Toubas, P. L., Duke, J. C., & McCaffree, M. A. (1986). Effects of maternal smoking and caffeine habits on infantile apnea; A retrospective study. *Pediatrics, 78,* 159–63.

Transdermal Nicotine Study Group. (1991). Transdermal nicotine for smoking cessation. *Journal of the American Medical Association, 266,* 3133–38.

Tsimoyianis, G. V., Jacobson, M. S., Feldman, J. G., Antonio-Santiago, M. T., Clutario, B. C., Nussbaum, M., & Shenker, I. R. (1987). Reduction in pulmonary function and increased frequency of cough associated with passive smoking in teenage adolescents. *Pediatrics, 80,* 32–35.

Tye, J. B. (1986). Fetal tobacco syndrome. *Journal of the American Medical Association, 256,* 862–63.

U.S. Department of Health and Human Services (1989). *Smoking tobacco and health: A fact book.* DHHS pub. no. (CDC) 87–8397.

Visnjevac, V., & Mikov, M. (1986). Smoking and carboxyhaemoglobin concentration in mothers and their newborn infants. *Human Toxicology, 5,* 175–77.

Warner, K. E. (1987). A ban on the promotion of tobacco products. *New England Journal of Medicine, 316,* 745–47.

Weiss, S. T., Tager, I. B., & Speizer, F. E. (1980). Persistent wheeze: Its relation to respiratory illness, cigarette smoking and level of pulmonary function in a population sample of children. *American Review of Respiratory Diseases, 122,* 697–707.

Whelan, E. M. (1984). Big business *vs* public health: The cigarette dilemma. *USA Today, 61,* 66.

Wientraub, J., & Burt, B. (1987). Periodontal effects and dental cases associated with smokeless tobacco use. *Public Health Reports, 102,* 30–35.

Williamson, D. F., Madans, J., Anda, R. F., Kleinman, J. C., Giovino, G. A., & Byers, T. (1991). Smoking cessation and severity of weight gain in a national cohort. *New England Journal of Medicine, 324,* 739–45.

Woodman, G., Newman, S. P., & Pavia, D. (1987). Response and acclimatization of symptomless smokers on changing to low tar, low nicotine cigarette. *Thorax, 42,* 336–41.

Wu, J. M. (1990). Summary and concluding remarks. In D. J. Ecobichon and J. M. Wu, (Eds.). *Environmental tobacco smoke; Proceedings of the International Symposium at McGill University, 1989.* Lexington, MA: Lexington Books.

Yu, J. J., Mattson, M. E., Boyd, G. M., Mueller, M. D., Shopland, D. R., Pechacek, T. F., & Cullen, J. W. (1990). A comparison of smoking patterns in the People's Republic of China with the United States; An impending health catastrophe in the middle kingdom. *Journal of the American Medical Association, 264,* 1575–79.

Zahm, S. H. (1991). Tobacco smoking as a risk factor for colon polyps. *American Journal of Public Health, 81,* 846–49.

8

• • •

HALLUCINOGENS
AND
INHALANTS

• • •

OBJECTIVES

When you have finished studying this chapter you should:

1. Be able to discuss the history of hallucinogens.
2. Know how peyote and mushrooms are viewed by Indian groups.
3. Be able to discuss the relationship of ergot and LSD.
4. Understand how LSD became so popular in the United States among some people.
5. Know how LSD is absorbed and metabolized.
6. Know how LSD affects the body and the brain.
7. Be able to discuss the psychological effects of LSD.
8. Know how the hallucinogens affect brain chemistry.
9. Understand the relationship between the amphetamines and mescaline.
10. Know why peyote is part of the ritual of the Native American Church.
11. Know how anticholinergic hallucinogens work.
12. Know what a dissociative anesthetic is.
13. Decide for yourself how dangerous PCP is.
14. List the various solvents and their effects.
15. Know how the solvents affect the body and behavior.
16. Be able to discuss how solvents differ from the hallucinogens.

KEY TERMS

aerosols
Amanita muscaria
anesthetics
atropine
belladonna
datura
dimethyltryptamine
Ecstasy
ergot
fly agaric
hallucinogens
Ipomoea violacea
Kaposi's sarcoma
Ken Kesey
ketamine
Timothy Leary
Lophophora williamsii
lysergic acid diethylamide (LSD)
mace
mandrake
MDA
mescaline
MDMA
myristicine
nitrous oxide
nutmeg
ololiuqui
peyote
phencyclidine (PCP)
psychedelic
psychotomimetic
Saint Anthony's Fire
scopolamine
serotonin
solvents
synesthesia
teonanacatl
toluene

WHAT ARE HALLUCINOGENS?

The ingenuity of the human race to use plants to survive is equalled only by its ingenuity to use them to alter consciousness. By a complicated process of trial and error, interspersed, no doubt, with moments of sheer brilliance, people learned that some plants and their products could relieve hunger and some were useless, some could cure illness and some cause sickness, some could be made into clothing and some into shelter.

Our ancestors learned also that some plants caused strange sensations when used properly and were considered sacred. These sacred plants enabled the user to see the spirits of the other world, to predict the future, and to experience indescribable visions. The chemical substances that modern man has isolated from these plants are those we call the hallucinogens.

There are probably more than half a million different species of plants, but only about 150 have been used for hallucinogenic purposes (Schultes & Hofmann, 1979). How did so-called primitive man discover the tiny needle in the giant haystack? Why would he even want to bother? How do these plants exert their effects on the brain? Why are they still being used? Are they still of any value? We will examine these and other questions in this chapter.

The first problem in understanding these drugs is one of terminology. Strictly speaking, the term **hallucinogenic** is somewhat misleading, since some produce true hallucinations only in high doses, and others do not produce hallucinations at all. However, every other term that is used to describe them is even worse. They are sometimes called **psychotomimetic** because they are supposed to produce the symptoms of psychoses (**psychoto** = psychoses and **mimetic** = acting like), but this term is inaccurate since psychotics report their experiences with the "hallucinogens" are not like true psychoses.

The term **psychedelic** is often used because it seems more neutral. However, this term has become associated with a particular lifestyle and has been used to describe so many things associated with that lifestyle that it has lost all precision. You can have psychedelic dreams, listen to psychedelic music (dressed in clothes dyed psychedelic colors), and collect psychedelic art. What, then, is a "psychedelic" drug?

Other terms have been suggested and the list is long: entheogens, deliriants, delusinogens, misperceptinogens, mysticomimetics, psychotogens, and schizogens, among many others (Schultes & Hofmann, 1979). Hallucinogen is the most widely used term, so it will be used here. It is easy to pronounce and is easily understood. Keep in mind, however, that it is not entirely accurate.

HISTORY OF THE HALLUCINOGENS

One of the oldest recorded references to a hallucinogenic drug is in the *Rig Veda*, a collection of hymns from India thought to be over 3,500 years old.

Areas in which halluncinogenic drugs are widely used.

This drug, called soma, is believed to be the **fly agaric,** a mushroom whose botanical name is **Amanita muscaria** (Wasson, 1971). Evidence exists that hallucinogenics were used even earlier, and it is safe to say that the use of plants as medicine and as mind-altering substances is equally ancient.

The diligence with which mankind searched for these substances is exceeded only by the ingenuity used in administering them. Some Bushman tribes in Africa cut their scalps and rub the bulb of a plant called *kashi* on the incisions. Some Indian tribes in Colombia, Venezuela, and Brazil blow a hallucinogenic snuff called *epena* into each others' nostrils through long tubes. The snuff causes them to cry and produces a large flow of mucous. After a period of time epena causes visions and disorientation. Others have even used plants such as water lilies and tobacco as enemas (Schultes & Hofmann, 1979; deSmet, 1985).

Perhaps the most unusual and determined method of ingesting drugs is found among the natives of Siberia who take fly agaric. Women of the tribes chew the mushroom to prepare it for the men who then eat it after it has been softened. Fly agaric causes hallucinations and delirium, and the user reports that objects suddenly become very large or small. The user experiences periods of excitation, interspersed with depression (Dobkin de Rios, 1984).

Unlike most other hallucinogenic drugs, the active chemicals in fly agaric are excreted unchanged in the urine. According to some accounts, the poorer members of the tribe wait around the huts of those who have taken the mushroom. When the richer men step outside to urinate, the poorer men collect the urine in the bowl and drink it. It is believed that this process can

Common hallucinogenic plants.

be repeated up to five times (Dobkin de Rios, 1984). Think of *that* the next time you drink warm beer.

The Indian of North and South America is credited with having discovered nearly 120 of the 150 known plant substances that are hallucinogenic. These plants were widely used and remain familiar to us. Peyote, magic mushrooms, even morning glory seeds, have, as we shall see, not only strong hallucinogenic properties, but cultural importance as well. What happened when hallucinogenics became popular among the youth of the 1960s demonstrates remarkably well the importance of set and setting.

The hallucinogenic drugs can be divided roughly into three categories based on their structure and their effect on the brain: those that resemble the neurotransmitter serotonin, those that resemble the catecholamines, and those that are anticholinergic. Keep in mind, however, as we shall see later, it appears that most of the hallucinogenic effects of most drugs can be attributed to their effects on postsynaptic receptors of serotonin-containing neurons. One drug often included among the hallucinogens defies such easy classification. Phencyclidine, or PCP, has unique properties and will be discussed separately.

HALLUCINOGENS THAT RESEMBLE SEROTONIN

Many drugs that are hallucinogenic resemble the serotonin molecule. The serotonin system influences vision and other important functions in the brain. The best known of these drugs is lysergic acid diethylamide-25 (LSD) (see figure 8.1).

Lysergic Acid Diethylamide (LSD)

The Middle Ages were characterized by war, epidemics, and intolerance. Among the epidemics were frequent outbreaks of a condition called **Saint Anthony's Fire.** Sufferers from this disease experienced burning of the hands and feet and one of two groups of symptoms. In the first type, there

FIGURE 8.1

Although they may not look similar to you, to an organic chemist LSD and serotonin are remarkably alike.

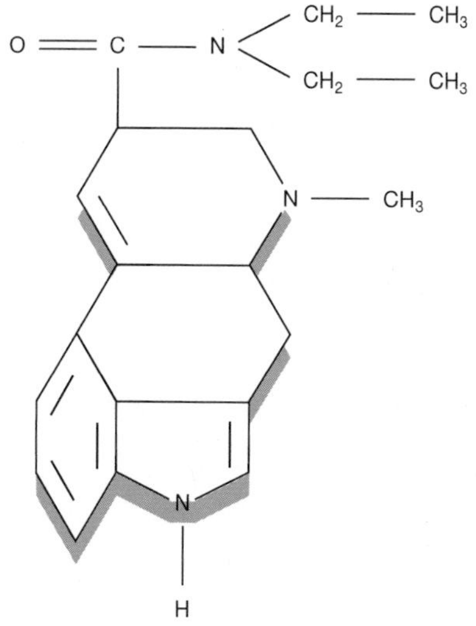

d-lysergic acid diethylamide (LSD)

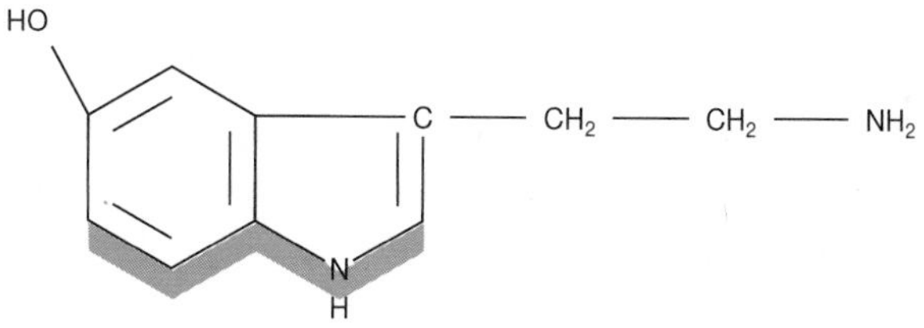

5-Hydroxytryptamine
(serotonin)

would be seizures and convulsions, while a second form was characterized by gangrene, spontaneous abortions, and skin blisters. Most sufferers also experienced hallucinations, and the disease was often fatal. Outbreaks of this disease have occurred as recently as 1953 (Schultes & Hofmann, 1979).

The disease was named Saint Anthony's Fire after a religious hermit who died in 356 in Egypt and whose remains were brought to France in 1070 where a shrine was built. In life, Saint Anthony was supposed to have performed miraculous cures; in death, he was the saint who protected people against fire, epilepsy, infection, and, of course, Saint Anthony's Fire. In 1090, a rich man pledged his fortune to the shrine if Saint Anthony would cure his son of the dread disease. The son recovered and the wealthy man built a hospital (Bove, 1970).

The cure was probably secular, not miraculous, since Saint Anthony's Fire is caused by a fungus called **ergot** that grows on rye, an important grain in the Middle Ages. The sufferer going to the holy shrine was probably cured because the shrine had become a hospital of sorts and undoubtedly had access to better food products than the average person (Schultes & Hofmann, 1979).

Ergot was long used as a medicine in Europe, and chemists of the early part of the twentieth century isolated a number of useful medicines from the fungus. In 1938, Albert Hoffman of Sandoz Pharmaceuticals extracted a chemical from ergot called **lysergic acid diethylamide.** He was looking for a drug that would stimulate the circulatory system. He developed a whole series of such compounds. None had any useful effect, so he gave up. On 16 April 1943, however, he decided to try one more time. He experimented with the twenty-fifth in the series, called, for obvious reasons, LSD-25.

Exactly what happened on that day, no one, not even Hoffman, knows. In any case, he managed to absorb some LSD. The effects were quite spectacular and included rapidly changing imagery and visions of brilliant colors. He lay down, and the effects subsided after about three hours. Three days later he intentionally ingested 250 micrograms (about five times the minimum dose necessary) and this apparently unimportant event started a chain of events that altered history (Cashman, 1966; Lee & Shlain, 1985).

Research with LSD

Scientific research developed along several lines and very rapidly. Use of LSD in psychotherapy was particularly common, with over 1,000 reports on its use by 1968 (Bliss, 1988). Because LSD in high doses produces hallucinations, and since many schizophrenics also experience hallucinations, LSD was seen as a model for this form of psychosis. Perhaps whatever LSD did to the brain, occurred naturally in schizophrenics. Furthermore, if science could develop a model for schizophrenia, various drug treatments could be tested. Finally, insight into the experience of schizophrenia might be obtained by taking LSD.

Unfortunately, this line of research did not produce useful results. The hallucinations of schizophrenia and of LSD are different. Most schizophrenics have auditory hallucinations; LSD hallucinations are usually visual. Loosening of associations and other thought disorders characteristic of schizophrenia are not seen with LSD. These and other findings led to the conclusion that LSD did not produce a ''model psychoses'' as had been hoped (Jaffe, 1980).

A second line of research used LSD as an adjunct to therapy. Therapists tried using LSD to help clients gain insight into their particular problem. The use of LSD became so popular that by 1965 it was estimated that nearly 40,000 mental patients around the world had been given LSD for psychotherapeutic purposes (Buckman, 1967). The overall evaluation of LSD as a therapeutic tool was fairly positive, patients seemed to show less defensiveness, responded better to their therapists, and experienced useful emotional responses called *abreactions* (Cohen, 1967).

There was also a flurry of interest in LSD as a treatment for alcoholics (Van Dusen & Wilson, 1967), and several researchers tried using LSD with terminal patients with generally positive results (Cohen, 1965; Kurland, 1967). In each of these cases, initial reports of success were followed by more negative reports, and the bad publicity of the late 1960s hastened the decline of LSD as a psychotherapeutic agent (Grinspoon & Bakalar, 1987). There is occasional interest in renewing this line of research (Metzger, 1978; Sellers & Kalant, 1978), and in fact research is being continued at the Maryland Psychiatric Research Institute in Baltimore.

A third line of research with LSD stemmed from the fantastic images and strange perceptual distortions the drug can produce. A number of experiments were done in which LSD was given to artists to see whether the drug could improve their creativity. Other studies tested ordinary people before, during, and after ingesting LSD. Once again, the results were mixed.

Artists generally enjoyed the experience but there was little objective evidence that it improved their creativity. One finding was virtually universal: attempting to translate the experience of LSD while the subject was under its influence was impossible. Visual artists, in particular, found that their ability to draw was greatly impaired (Krippner, 1985). LSD use spread throughout the artistic world, and even the theatrical community got into the act. One of the seemingly most unlikely users was Cary Grant, who admitted taking LSD as part of his psychotherapy (Berquist, 1959).

LSD and the Military   In the fifties and early sixties when much of the military "research" with LSD was being done, there was a widespread fear of mind control and brain washing. The then-director of the Central Intelligence Agency, Allen Dulles, would regularly give speeches denouncing the Red Menace and accusing Russia and China of having developed mind control techniques that could turn patriotic, brave American soldiers into zombie-like lackeys of communism (Lee & Schlain, 1985).

Not to be outdone by the Communists, the CIA and other agencies conducted and sponsored a large number of studies in which individuals were given various drugs to see whether they had any potential as a "truth serum" or for "mind control." Attention naturally turned to LSD. There were several names for this program, including Operation Bluebird, Operation Artichoke, and finally MK-Ultra. In these programs some of the most bizarre experiments imaginable were conducted, with results that were all too frequently tragic (Stevens, 1987).

In November 1953, a group of government scientists and technicians met for a retreat in Maryland. Unknown to them, a CIA agent spiked the after-dinner cocktails with LSD in order to observe the effects of LSD on unsuspecting people. Frank Olson, a specialist in biological warfare, was one of the scientists present. He experienced what would later come to be called a ''bummer'' or a ''bad trip'' and became depressed.

After he returned home, his behavior became more and more unusual. He was evaluated and found to be suffering from a psychotic state brought on by the LSD experience. The night before he was to have been hospitalized for treatment he jumped from the tenth floor window of a hotel in New York City (Lee & Schlain, 1985).

To the credit of no one, this incident was covered up. His wife was given a government pension, but not told of the likely reason for his suicide. LSD research was slowed down by this tragic event, but it still continued and no one was ever given so much as a reprimand. It wasn't until 1975 that the actual story came out and Olson's widow was given a settlement of $750,000 and an apology from President Gerald Ford.

In another project, *Operation Midnight Climax,* prostitutes were paid $100 a night to pick up men and take them to a San Francisco apartment where they were given drinks containing LSD. Their subsequent sexual activities and experiences were duly noted by agents observing through two-way mirrors (Lee & Schlain, 1985). These and other projects were conducted in a slipshod, unscientific manner by mostly untrained investigators.

The military was also involved in research with LSD and other hallucinogenic drugs. Edgewood Arsenal, Maryland, was a center for this research which involved giving various hallucinogenic drugs to military ''volunteers,'' who were seldom informed of the dangers involved and whose cases were rarely followed up. As a result of this research, a new hallucinogenic compound, BZ, was developed.

The obvious ethical problems, a changing political atmosphere, and economic factors resulted in the virtual abandonment of this line of research. In both series of experiments conducted by the CIA or the military, an analogy could be drawn to the ''research'' conducted in Nazi concentration camps. Very little useful information ever came of any of this research and it was clearly unethical.

LSD and the Sixties

Any attempt to understand the role of LSD in our culture would be incomplete without mentioning two men whose exploits virtually defined an entire decade.

Timothy Leary. In 1961, Timothy Leary was on the faculty of the psychology department at Harvard University. Earlier, in Mexico, he had taken psilocybin, the active ingredient in magic mushrooms, and the experience had been so interesting that he decided to conduct research on this drug. He and a colleague, Richard Alpert, began a series of studies to explore how psilocybin affected humans. One thing lead to another and by 1963, Leary and Alpert had the distinction of being the first two faculty members in the twentieth century to be fired from Harvard.

The early research of Alpert and Leary was carried out in the best scientific tradition. Leary apparently felt, however, that the laboratory was an inappropriate setting for his research. He began to administer psilocybin to

Timothy Leary

people in social gatherings, and conducted research without medical supervision. During this time he also discovered LSD. The notoriety that he and Alpert gained from their research and the questionable methods they used led to their dismissal.

Richard Alpert made a pilgrimage to India and became Baba Ram Dass. He is still pursuing this line of enlightenment today. Leary spent the next two years developing his beliefs, and in 1966 announced the formation of the League of Spiritual Discovery (LSD—get it?). He claimed that—like peyote for the Native American Church—LSD was a sacrament for his ''League.'' The next few years saw him in and out of jail on various drug charges.

He was released from jail in 1976 and now makes a living on the college lecture circuit. His message was always far less radical than most of his followers assumed. The famous phrase, ''Turn on, tune in, and drop out'' was meant to warn drug users that the enlightenment supposedly obtained from LSD was the result of hard work and much study. As early as 1964, he was saying that LSD was one path, but not an essential one, to understanding. For most people, however, Timothy Leary epitomizes the drug scene of the sixties.

Ken Kesey. Ken Kesey was a graduate student in creative writing at Stanford University in 1960 when Leary was on the faculty at Harvard. He participated in several experiments at a nearby Veterans Hospital where he was paid $75 to take various hallucinogenic drugs. He later worked as a ward attendant at the same hospital where he had further access to various hallucinogenic drugs.

While working at the hospital and sampling drugs, Kesey came up with the idea to write his famous book, *One Flew Over the Cuckoo's Nest.* Supposedly, the image of Chief Broom, the protagonist, came to him during an experience with peyote. A group began to form around him and his drug experiments at Stanford. Jerry Garcia, the famous guitarist of the *Grateful Dead,* Robert Stone, who wrote *Dog Soldiers, A Hall of Mirrors, A Flag for*

San Francisco Chronicle,
October 21, 1987 © 1987
Chronicle Publising Co.,
San Francisco, CA.

'Acid' Party May Close UC Co-op Hall

Barrington Hall, a Berkeley student housing cooperative that was almost shut down last year because of drug problems is in trouble again for a recent "acid punch" party that sent seven people to the hospital.

The party, at which the hallucinogen LSD was put into punch, has led to the resignation of Barrington manager Robert Dick and to new demands that the hall be closed or taken over by the university.

Sunrise, and *Children of Light,* and Larry McMurty, the author of *HUD, Terms of Endearment,* and the winner of the Pulitzer Prize for *Lonesome Dove,* all participated in the goings-on (Lee & Schlain, 1985).

Ken Kesey was the center of a group called the Merry Pranksters who toured the United States, dressed in outlandish clothing, sponsored huge parties in which LSD-spiked punch was freely offered and, in general, formed the nucleus and the role model for the "hippie" movement. Hippies spread throughout the United States carrying with them a vague, idealistic philosophy and a fondness for drugs like marijuana and LSD.

LSD quickly became a fad, and its use reached a peak in 1967 and 1968. By then the entire hippie movement had begun to fizzle out. Public outcry had made the drug illegal and publicity concerning the alleged dangers of the drug made it less popular. The fact that many of these bad experiences were not the fault of LSD was immaterial. There are reports that LSD seems to be making something of a comeback, so it is important to distinguish the truth from the myth.

Physiology and Pharmacology of LSD

The pharmacology of LSD can be described quite briefly. Absorbed readily through the gastrointestinal tract, it is the most powerful of the known hallucinogenic drugs. As little as 50 micrograms can produce significant changes in perception and mood (Cox, Jacobs, Leblanc, & Marshman, 1983). This amount, less than the weight of a period at the end of a sentence, is distributed throughout the body. Only about 1 percent is taken up in the brain.

To further complicate matters, the half-life of LSD is only about three hours, even though the behavioral effects often persist for six to eight hours.

What all this means is that there is an almost infinitesimally small amount of the drug absorbed into the body, distributed throughout the system, and rapidly metabolized. The unimaginably small amount that actually reaches the relevant receptors in the brain is sufficient to produce profound effects that last far longer than the drug itself does. Whatever LSD does to the brain, it is quite remarkable.

Metabolism occurs in the liver, and the drug is excreted in an inactive form. Tolerance to both the physiological and psychological effects of LSD develops so rapidly by the third or fourth day of consecutive daily use, the user could take virtually any amount of the drug without effect (Cox, Jacobs, Leblanc, & Marshman, 1983). When use of LSD ceases, sensitivity to LSD returns quickly.

Unless you are an elephant, LSD is, from a pharmacological point of view, a safe drug. The lethal dose for LSD in humans is unknown, since there has never been a documented case of death due to overdose. Not many elephants take LSD, but in one study, West, Pierce, and Thomas (1962) injected an elephant with 297 mg of LSD. The elephant promptly began to trumpet, went into seizures, and died. The dosage given to the elephant was about 70–100 times the dose required to produce psychological effects in humans, but similar to that required to see noticeable effects in other animals.

Because tolerance builds up so rapidly and because dependence is thought not to occur, there is no clear evidence of the effects of long-term use of LSD on the brain in humans. In animals, however, at least one study has shown that continuous exposure to 70 mg of LSD over seven days resulted in long-lasting behavioral and physiological changes that suggested brain damage (King & Ellison, 1989). In this study, the drug was administered slowly through a subcutaneous pump. The same effect was not seen when the same dose was injected daily. Furthermore, the dose given to the rats was about 500 times the dose usually taken by humans. Studies such as this and the more widely known elephant "study" emphasize the difficulty in comparing the effects of drugs on humans with those on other animals.

Physiologically, LSD is similar to other ergot compounds in that it stimulates the sympathetic nervous system, producing dilated pupils, increased blood pressure, and increased body temperature. Since it also stimulates uterine contractions and increases salivation, it has parasympathetic effects as well. Muscle weakness, muscle twitching, and numbness have also been reported (Cox, Jacobs, Leblanc, & Marshman, 1983).

LSD is included in the category of serotonergic hallucinogenics, but the effect of LSD cannot be explained simply on the basis of its effects on serotonergic neurons. They do, however, play an important role. The earliest, simplest hypothesis was that LSD blocked the action of serotonin, which in the peripheral nervous system it does (Gaddum & Hameed, 1954). However, brom-LSD, a similar drug that also blocks the action of serotonin, does not have hallucinogenic properties (Cerletti & Rothlin, 1955).

After several false starts, the effect of LSD and, indeed, most other hallucinogenic drugs on serotonin is finally becoming clearer. The understanding of how these drugs work is a result of increased knowledge about the basic structure of the neuron. Neurotransmitters such as norepinephrine, dopamine, and serotonin each have several different targets on the postsynaptic receptor. The protein molecules that make up the postsynaptic receptor can be of several different types and there may be as many as five for serotonin. Serotonin itself operates at all these receptor sites, but it appears that LSD and most other hallucinogens primarily affect one of these receptors, called 5–HT$_2$ (Jacobs, 1987). LSD may function either in an inhibitory or excitatory manner depending on which neurons are affected but the hallucinogenic properties are probably due to a stimulating effect on the receptor (Glennon, 1990). No one is certain just how this effect on the 5–HT$_2$ receptor translates into the profound effects seen when LSD or other hallucinogens are taken, and to futher complicate matters, LSD also affects other serotonin receptors.

It may be that since serotonin normally affects all five receptor sites simultaneously, affecting only some of them may sufficiently disrupt the normal functioning of the serotonin system so as to set off a cascade of unusual patterns of neuronal firing which the brain interprets as hallucinations and depersonalization. This is obvious speculation and the details of how the hallucinogens work will remain unknown until more is discovered about the relationship of brain to behavior.

We do know that several brain structures are affected by LSD and contain serotonergic neurons. In general, the cell bodies of serotonergic neurons are found in the brain stem, while the axons extend to all portions of the brain, including the cortex, specifically the visual cortex (Jacobs, 1987). The *raphe nuclei* are located near the reticular formation in the brain and are largely serotonin-containing neurons. Involved in sleep and wakefulness, the raphe nuclei also influence behavior by suppressing response to incoming sensory stimuli (Trulson, Jacobs, & Morrison, 1981). One effect of LSD is to shut down the functioning of the raphe nuclei (Cooper, Bloom, & Roth, 1985), presumably leading to a barrage of stimuli into the brain that had previously been suppressed.

The reticular formation also serves to inhibit sensory input, has both serotonin and adrenergic neurons, and is probably also involved in the effects of LSD. We are not normally aware of a number of incoming sensory stimuli, such as those arising from internal states and other sensory stimuli to which we have become accustomed. By disrupting the normal functioning of the raphe nuclei and the reticular formation, LSD may make the user aware of these stimuli and produce peculiar, distorted sensations.

Psychological Effects of LSD

So much has been written in the popular literature about LSD, both by its critics and its advocates, that it obscures what LSD really does. The effects of set and setting are of paramount importance with this drug. A "trip" in a quiet setting, with an experienced person familiar with what the drug can do, will have much different effects on the user than a similar trip in a threatening or unpleasant situation.

The psychological effects of LSD are dependent upon the dose taken, the set and setting, and the duration of the experience. The first effects are the result of physiological stimulation: dry mouth (the increase in salivation comes later), dizziness, and, occasionally, nausea. These effects are followed by changes in mood and sensory perception.

Such a wide variation in the effects of LSD occurs that it is impossible to be specific about what a given amount of the drug will do in a given situation, and no list could ever be complete. The following are a few of the effects that have been reported.

1. Synesthesia—the phenomenon of ''seeing'' sound or ''hearing'' colors.

2. Time distortion—seconds pass as minutes and minutes as hours.

3. Distortion of body image—portions of the body may take on deep significance, or the user may feel a floating sensation.

4. Loss of the boundary between the self and the environment—the user may melt into the chair or bed on which they are sitting.

5. Resurfacing of memories—these suddenly take on profound significance.

6. Mystical or religious experiences—a feeling of ''oneness'' with the universe (Cox, Jacobs, Leblanc, & Marshman, 1983).

These experiences gradually subside, and six to nine hours later the user has usually returned to normal. There may be a feeling of fatigue that lasts for a day or so. The rapid build-up of tolerance and the amount of time required for a single trip make it unlikely that the LSD user will immediately repeat the experience. It is rare for recreational users of LSD to use the drug more than once a week or so, at the most, by which time tolerance has worn off.

Negative Effects of LSD

Any drug that has such a disturbing influence on sensory awareness and perception of self is bound to produce unpleasant experiences at times. The negative effects of LSD can be divided into short-term and long-term effects.

Short-term Effects

The combination of depersonalization, sudden perceptual changes, and a general feeling of loss of control all contribute to what was called in the sixties a ''bad trip'' or a ''bummer.'' Under most circumstances, the person experiencing a bad trip needs nothing more than reassurance that what is happening is the result of taking a drug, that someone will remain with him or her until the drug wears off, and that the drug *will* wear off. Under some circumstances, especially if the panic state is severe, one of the antipsychotic drugs such as chlorpromazine (see chapter 11) is prescribed. These drugs are

• YOU READ IT HERE FIRST •

In the past few years, there has been a wave of nostalgia for the 1960s. Perhaps as a consequence, reports of LSD use are also on the increase. LSD availability seems at present to be limited to metropolitan areas and confined to a relatively small subgroup of basically middle-class users. The National Household Survey and the high school senior survey discussed in Chapter 1 do not reflect a spectacular rise; however, hospital emergencies have increased and there is circumstantial evidence to suggest that its use is more popular. In 1990 the Drug Enforcement Agency confiscated nearly 500,000 doses of LSD, making it the third largest category of drugs discovered (Law Enforcement News, 1991).

Curiously, only two major manufacturing operations have been discovered since the 1970s, suggesting that the production of LSD is concentrated among a very few people who must be cautious indeed. To give an idea of how 500,000 doses confiscated translates into doses on the street, consider that even with the millions spent on interdiction of cocaine, it is estimated that only 10 percent of the total is confiscated. If the analogy holds, 5 million doses of LSD were prepared last year. Retail price on the street is about $3–5, making LSD manufacturing a profitable business.

If the upward trend continues, expect to see a large increase in hospital admissions and serious reactions to this drug. The widespread street wisdom that prevailed when LSD was last popular is gone. Many modern users of these powerful drugs have no idea of how to control set and setting, which are so important in determining the nature of the experience. As experimental users with little preparation, they are at risk for very unpleasant "trips."

---

usually quite effective in reducing both the panic and the disturbed thinking, but are seldom necessary and have their own side effects.

Long-term Effects

The initial users of LSD tended to be basically stable, often artistic people, who took the drug in carefully designed surroundings. As LSD moved into the drug culture, more and more *less* stable people began experimenting with the drug, and neither the set nor the setting were conducive to a positive experience. There is no question that basically unstable people can be severely affected by LSD, and the brief panic attack discussed above can, in some people, trigger a long-term psychotic episode.

An often feared but poorly understood phenomenon is the *flashback*. Flashbacks occur days, weeks, or months after the last experience with LSD, long after the drug has been eliminated from the body. Sometimes considered evidence of long-lasting neurological damage produced by LSD, the flashback is usually a brief recurrence of the LSD experience, often involving sensory phenomena. Its cause is unknown, and the treatment is symptomatic—reassuring the individual that this experience will pass. The incidence of flashbacks decreases with time since the last LSD experience (Cohen, 1985).

The Mythology of LSD

In the heyday of the sixties various stories circulated about the effects of LSD. There were reports of murder and mayhem committed by people under the influence of the drug, stories of users being blinded by staring at the sun after taking it, and reports of birth defects in babies born to mothers who had taken LSD. None of these stories has more than the slightest foundation in fact.

Stories of atrocities committed by those under the influence of drugs have been told about marijuana, cocaine, amphetamine, alcohol, and virtually every mind-altering substance. Careful research into these reports inevitably reveals serious flaws. Since it is usually impossible to determine the actual contents of a drug sold on the street, and since drug dealers are not known for maintaining careful quality control, the possibility also exists that the untoward reactions attributed to LSD were caused by other drugs.

People under the influence of LSD are highly suggestible and may inadvertently commit acts that bring harm to themselves or others. Panic states brought on by LSD can lead users to attempt suicide if they think they will not recover from the bad trip. Common sense, however, could prevent most of these accidents. LSD is not a harmless drug, as it causes depersonalization and disorientation. The users are more likely to be victims rather than perpetrators of crimes, however.

Early studies showed that LSD did cause chromosomal breakage. However, this breakage was found in chromosomes of cells circulating in the blood. Numerous other drugs, including caffeine, cause such chromosomal breakage. There is no clear evidence of either chromosomal damage to the cells of the sperm or egg, or of birth defects caused by the ingestion of LSD in humans. In very high doses LSD does cause birth defects in fruit flies, mice, and monkeys, but these levels are not likely to be achieved by humans. In fruit flies, for example, the dose required to produce mutations is 100,000 times the equivalent dose in humans (Dishotsky, Loughman, Morgan, & Lipscomb, 1971).

Pregnant women should avoid all drugs, obviously, just to be safe, and the same goes for LSD. LSD is an **ergot** compound, and since ergot has been used to stimulate uterine contractions the possibility exists that LSD might do the same.

If in the years to come LSD use does increase substantially, will the same stories be resurrected? The unsigned warning reprinted in figure 8.2 and circulated in California in 1988 indicates just such a possibility. This warning has appeared in several states and the wording in every case is so similar that it is obviously a scare tactic rather than a genuine response to a real danger. If you read the text carefully you will readily see other evidence that it is what is called a "folk myth."

Ololiuqui

LSD-25 was first synthesized from the fungus, ergot. A similar substance is found in two species of morning glory seeds, *Turbina corymbosa* and *Ipomoea violacea*. These plants were well known to the Aztecs, who gave the plant the name **ololiuqui.** Seeds of the ololiuqui plants are ground up and mixed with water or an alcoholic beverage. When this concoction is drunk,

---

ALERT!   ALERT!   ALERT!   ALERT!   ALERT!   ALERT!   ALERT!   ALERT!

The Police Department has informed us that there is another danger in our community. It is a form of tattoo called "BLUE STAR" and it is sold all over the United States. It is a small sheet of white paper containing blue stars the size of a pencil eraser. Each star is soaked with LSD. Each star can be removed and placed in the mouth. The LSD can be absorbed also through the skin simply through handling the paper. There are also brightly colored paper tabs resembling postage stamps that have pictures of Superman, butterflies, clowns, Mickey Mouse and other Disney characters on them.

These stamps are packaged in a red cardboard box wrapped in foil. This is a new way of selling ACID to our young children. A child could happen upon these and have a fatal "trip". It is learned that little children could be given a free "tattoo" by older children who want to have some fun or by others cultivating new customers. A red stamp called "Red Pyramid" is also being distributed along with "Micro-Dots" in various colors and another kind called "Window Pane" which has a grid that can be cut out.

THESE ARE ALL LACED WITH DRUGS!! PLEASE ADVISE YOUR CHILDREN ABOUT THESE NEW DRUGS. IF YOU OR YOUR CHILDREN SEE ANY OF THE ABOVE . . . DO NOT HANDLE!!! THESE DRUGS ARE KNOWN TO REACT VERY QUICKLY AND SOME ARE LACED WITH STRYCHNINE.

SYMPTOMS ARE: Hallucinations, severe vomiting, mood change and change of body temperature. **GET TO THE HOSPITAL AS SOON AS POSSIBLE AND CALL THE POLICE!**

FIGURE 8.2

This message was circulated in California in 1988, not 1968. Virtually the same warning was reported in England in 1991, indicating that this is a widely circulated myth.

the user experiences visual distortions and hallucinations that, given the appropriate set and setting, were interpreted as messages from the gods (Dobkin de Rios, 1984).

The common morning glory, grown in much of the United States, is ***Ipomoea violacea.*** While it is possible to experience an LSD-like trip by taking morning glory seeds, several hundred are required, and commercial firms often coat their seeds with a substance that causes vomiting and diarrhea.

Like the mushroom, ololiuqui was a well kept secret among the Indian ancestors of the Aztecs. After the initial description of it in the seventeenth century, nothing was heard of it again until the middle of this century. At present it is primarily of interest to those who try to figure out how and why two plants, one a fungus and the other a vine, both produce a hallucinogenic substance.

Psilocybin

The Aztec Indians called the various species of psilocybin mushrooms **teonanacatl,** which can be translated as "divine flesh" or "God's flesh." Of all the hallucinogenic substances the Aztecs took, this one seemed to displease the Spanish conquistadors the most, perhaps because its name seemed sacrilegious to the priests who accompanied the conquerors. The Spaniards did such a good job of suppressing its use that it wasn't until the 1930s that the hallucinogenic mushroom was rediscovered by Western science. Its use had, of course, continued among the Indians (Schultes, 1987).

"Magic mushrooms" contain psilocybin which is chemically similar to LSD. The effect is also similar, although less intense and shorter acting. Technically, psilocybin is not hallucinogenic. It must be converted to psilocyn in order to exert its effect. A similar situation exists with heroin, which is really diacetyl morphine, and must be converted to morphine in the body.

This common garden flower has hallucinogenic properties. The seeds contain an LSD-like substance.

The Psilocybin *mushroom has been used for hundreds of years in Central and South America and similar mushrooms are found throughout much of the United States.*

When psilocybin mushrooms were rediscovered in the twentieth century, it was believed that only a few species had hallucinogenic properties. It is now known that psilocybin-containing mushrooms grow in a wide area of the United States, as well as in Mexico and Europe (Stamets, 1978). In some states it is legal to buy spores of psilocybin mushrooms, and they can be grown indoors although it is quite difficult. The collection of wild growing psilocybin-containing mushrooms is a dangerous proposition, as is the collection of wild mushrooms for other purposes. Many mushrooms are highly toxic and can cause death by liver failure.

Dimethyltryptamine (DMT)

Dimethyltryptamine is the active ingredient in a variety of hallucinogenic compounds used throughout the world. Typically these compounds are ingested as snuff, although DMT itself can be injected or smoked. One interesting characteristic of DMT is that it has a short duration of action, about one hour. Cohoba or epena, two snuffs that are used by Indians in South America also can cause muscle twitches.

DMT was popular for a brief period of time in the sixties. It was known as "businessman's LSD" because of its short duration of action. It rapidly fell from favor for reasons that are not clear. It is rarely seen today.

Other hallucinogenics that affect the serotonin system are ayahuasca and virola. These plants are found in South America and contain DMT. They are unique in that they are taken orally. Most DMT-containing drugs must be snorted (McKenna & Towers, 1985).

THE CATECHOLAMINE HALLUCINOGENS
Mescaline

Peyote is one of the oldest hallucinogenic plants known. A cactus whose scientific name is ***Lophophora williamsii,*** it grows in various parts of Texas and Mexico and was widely used by the Aztec Indians. Evidence of the use of peyote can be found in ancient cave paintings and the cactus itself is seen in sculpture and pottery of the Aztecs.

Considerable debate exists about the first appearance of humans in what we call the "New World." However, highly developed cultures certainly existed for thousands of years before their "discovery" by the Spanish conquistadors. Most of these groups had a form of religion in which a certain person (a shaman) served as a go-between from the seen to the unseen world. This shaman cured the sick, gave advice, and passed on the wisdom from the other side. The shaman accomplished this through mystic visionary experiences aided by psychoactive plants. For these cultures, then, the use of what we call hallucinogenic drugs is a sacred experience never to be taken lightly.

When Hernando Cortez first encountered the Aztecs, he found a flourishing culture that had acquired considerable knowledge about the medicinal and psychoactive properties of many plants. In order to eradicate what they felt was religious heresy, the conquistadors systematically destroyed virtually all traces of that knowledge. In the few records that survived, however, there was mention of a plant called peyotl. Despite the persecution, use of peyote, as it is now called, continued among many groups of Indians in Mexico and was rediscovered in the twentieth century by anthropologists and others.

The use of peyote by the Huichol Indians, originally from an area of Mexico near modern day Guadalajara, probably gives us the best insight into how this substance was employed for the thousands of years of civilization that preceded the conquest, since the Huichol traditions were largely untouched by the Spanish. Huichol society and religion is complex and closely interwoven and the peyote cactus plays an important part in both.

Grandfather Fire, Tatewari, and Our Grandmother, Tacutsi, are two central figures. Tacutsi is the mother of every living thing, and fire is the most important god. Father Sun was born in the peyote desert and turned the original ancient ones, the wolf people, into humans. Grandfather Fire communicates to humans through peyote visions to give wisdom and healing. Tacutsi also communicates knowledge through peyote.

The Huichol believe that corn and peyote are gifts of the Deer Spirits and make a pilgrimage to Wirikuta, the land where peyote grows. There they perform elaborate rituals to assure food and water for the coming year. Figure 8.3 shows a yarn painting by noted Huichol artist Mariano Valadez depicting a vision in which peyote is giving knowledge and abundance to humans. The various animals and figures, the fantastic forms that each takes, and the vivid colors are all related to religious peyote experience.

Peyote rituals by the Huichols and other Indians are performed to heal the sick, celebrate some great event, or to acquire specific information. They require much fasting, prayer, and other preparation and last all night and

FIGURE 8.3
Peyote poster.

into the next morning. Given the sacred beliefs that surround this cactus and the seriousness of its purpose, casual or recreational use is unthinkable among those who follow the peyote religions.

Several North American Indian tribes have adopted some of the peyote ritual and have incorporated aspects of the Christian faith to form the Native American Church. The Native American Church uses peyote as a sacrament in its religious ceremonies. It is recognized as a valid church by government authorities and its members may legally possess and use peyote buttons, which they buy (often from the Huichols) and ship through the mail. The Native American Church is a major religious group among Indians, with a membership estimated at more than 200,000.

On occasion, the ritual use of peyote by members of the Native American Church has caused legal difficulties. In 1990, the Supreme Court of the United States ruled against two members of the Native American Church who were also drug counselors. They had been fired when they failed a urine test. The Supreme Court ruled that while their right to religious freedom was guaranteed (meaning they were free to use peyote) their firing was correct since the rules of the agency hiring them forbid any drug use. In chapter 12, you will read of the further issues concerning the rights of individuals as opposed to the rights of society.

The peyote cactus is small (about three inches in diameter) and shaped like a top. The Indians who gather the plant cut off the crown and dry it. This dried cactus is sometimes referred to as a ''mescal'' or peyote button. Do not confuse the mescal button with mescal, the liquor, which is made from another cactus and has no hallucinogenic properties at all, unless you count what alcohol does. To further complicate matters there is also a mescal plant that produces toxic, but hallucinogenic, seeds. To avoid confusion, we shall use the term peyote.

Taking peyote requires more than a little dedication. The dried cactus has been described as smelling like a dead, wet dog on a warm afternoon. It has a bitter taste and initially causes nausea, vomiting, and diarrhea. These unpleasant sensations are followed by vivid hallucinations of intense colors and a sense of depersonalization. Despite its different biochemistry, the effects of peyote are remarkably similar to that of LSD.

Mescaline is the most important hallucinogen found in peyote and one of the first naturally occurring hallucinogens to be synthesized. Mescaline closely resembles norepinephrine and amphetamine, as can be seen in figure 8.4. It also has an effect on serotonin-containing neurons, which probably accounts for the similarity to LSD. When mescaline alone is taken the hallucinations last for about two hours and the drug remains in the system for about ten hours.

Tolerance develops rapidly, but dependence does not seem to occur. Individuals who have built up a tolerance to mescaline are also tolerant to LSD—a phenomenon known as cross-tolerance. This cross-tolerance further demonstrates that mescaline and LSD are quite similar.

DOM (STP), MDA, MDMA, and the Rest of the Alphabet

The effects of **Ecstasy** and **MDA** were discussed in Chapter 5 and need to be mentioned only briefly here. Even though these drugs are classified as affecting catecholamine systems and even though they resemble norepinephrine, they share many similarities with LSD and the serotonin hallucinogens. The primary difference is that they also have strong amphetamine-like effects. Amphetamine, you will recall, also resembles norepinephrine. The combination of amphetamine-like effects and hallucinogenic effects can be seen most clearly in dimethoxymethylamphetamine, or DOM.

DOM also is known as **STP** and has both hallucinogenic and euphoric properties, depending on dosage. It has both catecholamine and serotonin-like effects. Unlike most of the hallucinogens, DOM is not eliminated from the body for up to twenty-four hours. Apparently, the amphetamine-like effects of the drug are perceived as increasingly negative as the hours go by. DOM had a brief popularity but quickly faded from the market.

Nutmeg and Mace

A little nutmeg on your eggnog tastes good, a little mace in cookies improves the flavor, but who would ever think to eat the whole box? Nutmeg is the ground seed of an East Indian tree, while mace is made from the covering of the same seed. **Nutmeg** and **mace** were introduced into Europe as a

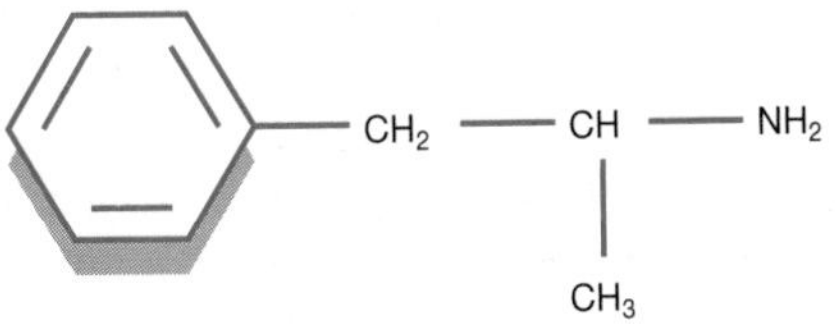

Amphetamine

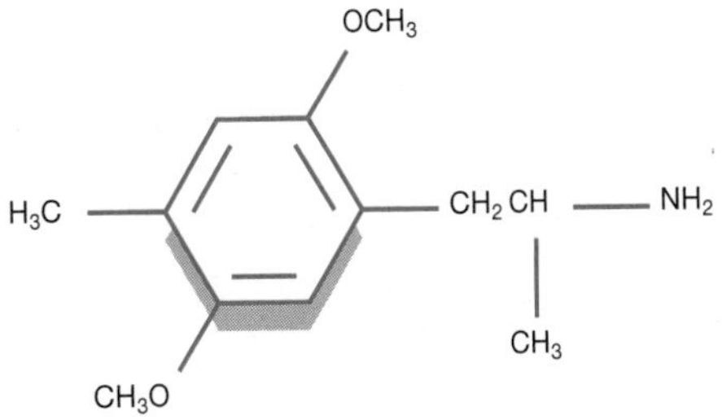

DOM (STP)
2,5-Dimethoxy-4-
Methylamphetamine

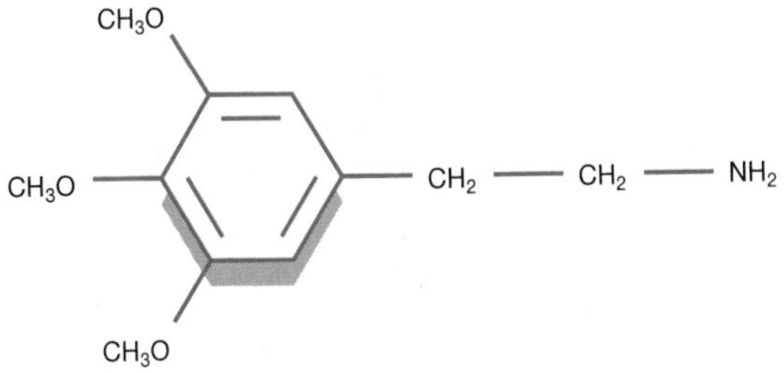

Mescaline
3, 4, 5-Trimethoxyphenethylamine

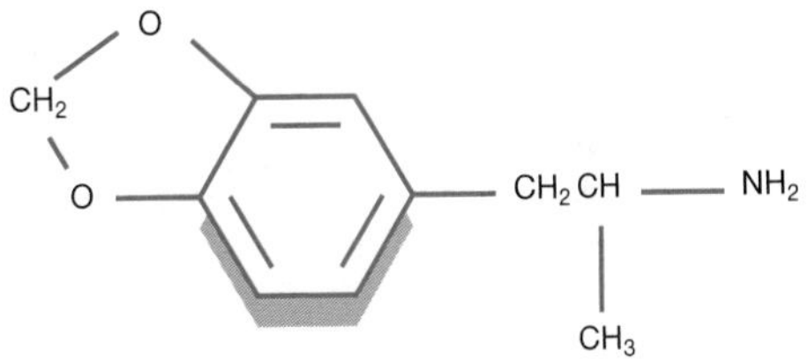

MDA
3, 4-Methylenedioxyamphetamine

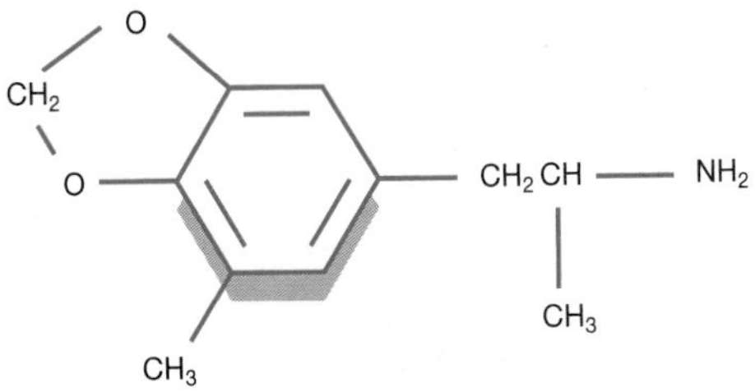

Methylenedioxymethylamphetamine
MDMA (Ecstasy)

FIGURE 8.4
Notice how similar all of these "hallucinogens" are to each other and how similar each is to amphetamine.

medicine, although there are reports that it was smoked in India as a substitute for hashish.

Nutmeg and mace contain myristicine, which has mescaline-like properties if taken in high enough doses. In order to experience any mind-altering effects, you need to take at least one or two teaspoons. Nutmeg intoxication is characterized by nausea, vomiting, severe headache, a floating sensation, and sensory distortions (Schultes, 1987). It is usually followed the next day by a very unpleasant hangover. About the only people who use this drug recreationally are those who can't get anything else and who are desperate. It is, for example, kept under careful scrutiny in prisons. Nutmeg and mace can be quite toxic in high doses.

ANTICHOLINERGIC HALLUCINOGENS

Plants that contain the anticholinergic hallucinogens have had a long history of use as medicine, as poisons, as beauty aids, and most interestingly, as aids in sorcery and witchcraft. The anticholinergic hallucinogens produce peculiar symptoms that most people would not consider particularly pleasant, and in high doses, most are quite toxic.

All of the important plants discussed here belong to the same family as the potato. They contain atropine, scopolamine, and other anticholinergic drugs in various concentrations. Although they are not commonly used at present they have an important past.

Datura

Many species of **datura** exist and have been widely used as a medicine and a sacred hallucinogen. The plants are often mixed with alcohol or smoked with cannabis. There is evidence of their use in China, India, Greece, and Africa, but datura use seems to have been most important to the Indians of North and Central America.

Probably the most familiar of the datura species is *Datura stramonium*, also called jimson weed or loco weed. American Indians used this and other species of datura in many rites and ceremonies. The Plains Indians would sometimes take datura if they thought some object had been lost or stolen. They believed that the person taking datura would either have a vision telling him who had stolen the lost object, or where it could be found. They also believed that the user might wander around in a trancelike state induced by datura until the object was located (Dobkin de Rios, 1984). This technique is not recommended the next time you lose your car keys.

Datura also was used by the Algonquin Indians in their puberty rites for adolescent boys. The boys would be given datura in sufficient doses to induce hallucinations that lasted for several days (Schultes & Hofmann, 1979). Once the datura had worn off, they frequently had no memory of anything they had said or done during that time. The purpose was to emphasize the break between childhood and adulthood. The Algonquins instituted a culturally-sanctioned period of craziness lasting several days. For many adolescents in the United States, the same culturally-sanctioned process takes many years.

Belladonna

The word **belladonna** is Italian and means beautiful lady. For centuries, the Italian women would use eyedrops to enlarge their pupils to make them seem more beautiful. Belladonna is an anticholinergic drug that enlarges pupils and prevents the eye from focusing, so women who used it had a kind of glassy, unfocused stare which was considered a mark of beauty.

Belladonna also is known as deadly nightshade and formerly was widely used as a poison. At low doses it provides a kind of delirium; in high

Throughout history, it was believed that the Mandrake plant had great medicinal value because of its resemblance to the human body. Can you see the resemblance?

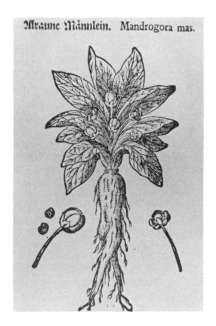

doses it is indeed toxic. The hallucinations induced by this drug, as noted in chapter 1, may have helped witches think they really could fly.

Mandrake

If you look at a mandrake root and have a *very* good imagination, you may see the shape of the human body. Mandrake has been considered an aphrodisiac and a hallucinogen by a number of cultures. In addition to its toxic properties, it was considered an important plant because of a theory called the doctrine of signatures.

The doctrine of signatures is a theory that holds that objects resembling a part of the body will affect that part. Plants, such as carrots or asparagus, for example, which resemble the sexual organs of humans were considered aphrodisiacs. The doctrine of signatures may seem ridiculous on one level—after all, no one really believes that an orchid is an aphrodisiac because it resembles a human testicle—but how many athletes believe that it takes meat (animal muscle) to build human muscle? Since the mandrake resembled the entire human body, it was considered good for whatever ailed you.

Mandrake root does contain anticholinergic hallucinogens, so it is easy to see how it would be considered a valuable medicine. Just how the belief, once common and mentioned in Shakespeare, that mandrake would shriek like a human when pulled from the ground and could be harvested only by being pulled out of the ground by a black dog is a little more difficult to understand (Schultes & Hofmann, 1979).

The anticholinergic hallucinogenics exert their effect in a number of ways and there is little difference between them. They increase heart rate, cause a dry mouth by inhibiting salivation, dilate the pupil, and in high doses produce a psychotic-like condition of mental confusion and hallucinations. One rather peculiar effect of the anticholinergics is that there is often amnesia for events that occurred while under the influence of the drug.

Scopolamine and **atropine,** the two major drugs found in most of the plants above, have medical uses. Scopolamine has been administered along with morphine to produce "twilight sleep" in women who are giving birth. The idea is that the morphine will reduce the pain and the scopolamine will not only dry up mucous passages, making breathing easier, but also will cause amnesia so the mother-to-be will forget the pain of childbirth. Unfortunately, women given scopolamine often have hallucinogenic or delirious episodes which both they and the medical staff find most unpleasant. Until recently, scopolamine was used in some over-the-counter sleeping aids and in cold remedies.

Atropine is used by ophthalmologists to dilate the pupil and by surgeons to reduce lung congestion during anesthesia. It also is used as an antidote for poisoning in some insecticides.

In recent years there have been numerous reports that prostitutes have begun using scopolamine to help them rob their clients. The prostitutes supposedly single out traveling businessmen wearing expensive jewelry or watches. They pose as teachers or businesswomen and go to the traveller's room where they slip some scopolamine into his drink. The businessman often falls asleep in a stupor and wakes up several hours later with neither his jewelry nor a clear recollection of what happened to him. For obvious reasons, many of these robberies go unreported to the police.

Phencyclidine (PCP)

Considerable controversy exists about phencyclidine (PCP), along with confusion and misinformation about nearly every aspect of the drug. To begin with, PCP should not be considered in the same category as the hallucinogens since it produces many effects but hallucinations are not among them. Second, despite (or perhaps because of) its reputation, PCP use is not as widespread as you might expect from media reports. The stories are spectacular and make good copy, but when objective reports are analyzed, it appears that PCP use is confined to a few cities and is used primarily by young adults, rather than high school age students (Thombs, 1989).

Phencyclidine was originally developed as a "dissociative anesthetic," which means that patients taking it may keep their eyes open and apparently be conscious and yet feel no pain. The patient seems to be "disassociated" from reality. In addition to being anesthetized, the patient usually also experiences amnesia for the time the drug is in his/her system. There are obvious advantages in surgery to such anesthetics, and phencyclidine was the subject of much enthusiasm (McCarthy, 1981).

It soon became obvious, however, that there were serious problems with PCP, one of which is called the "emergence phenomenon." Simply put, this means that the patient becomes disoriented, abusive, unmanageable, and sometimes violent as the drug is wearing off. Although not every subject showed these effects, enough did so that PCP, then known as Sernyl, was withdrawn from the market. That should have been the end of the story of PCP.

In 1967, however, PCP hit the streets. Known as angel dust, peace pill, horse tranquilizer, or various other names, it quickly became widely used, both on its own and as a substitute for LSD and other hallucinogens. Some believe that it was responsible for the majority of the "bad trips" that gave LSD such a bad reputation in the late sixties. Although its popularity has declined in the intervening years, it is still encountered in the drug culture.

The effects of PCP are, not surprisingly, dose dependent. In laboratory settings, low doses produce subjective effects of depersonalization and distortion of body image. Subjects report that the distinction between them and the world is blurred. Another common finding is that the subjects cannot concentrate, plan, or follow a train of thought. At slightly higher doses there is vertical movement of the eyes (nystagmus), difficulty in walking, and increasing confusion. At the dose that begins to produce anesthesia, the subjects become agitated and the confusion worsens. At very high doses, there is muscular rigidity. The subjects also exhibit a peculiar blank stare and often salivate excessively (Gallant, 1981; Young, Lawson, & Gacono, 1987).

As a street drug, PCP is mixed with parsley or marijuana and smoked, taken as a pill, or even injected. The effects reported above do not seem particularly pleasant, but street users sometimes say that the depersonalization and "floating" sensation is enjoyable. A large percentage reported that even though many of the effects of the drug were unpleasant, they continued to take it (Fauman & Fauman, 1981). It seems that the unpredictability of the effects of the drug is one of the important reasons that it is used. PCP seems to be attractive to a particular subculture of drug users who value a loss of contact with reality and disorientation.

One aspect of PCP use bears further scrutiny. Every police officer and most people familiar with drug users have heard the story about the PCP user who was shot any number of times (the author has heard up to fifteen) by police and still continued to fight arrest. A variation of this story is the one of the 97-pound young girl who, under the influence of PCP, became supernaturally strong and required ten policemen to subdue her. PCP use is widely associated in the drug subculture with violence.

The available evidence does not support the idea that PCP makes you supernaturally strong. What seems instead to happen is that the user is disoriented and confused and frequently hostile and paranoid. Because of the anesthetic properties of the drug, the user does not feel as much pain. Anyone foolish enough to resist arrest with all of their strength would be very difficult to subdue, especially if they could not feel the nightstick that hits them in the ribs or the punch to the jaw. PCP does not make you supernaturally strong, just supernaturally stupid.

The association of PCP use with aggression needs to be considered in the context of set, setting, and the personality characteristics of the user. People take drugs for various reasons, and a drug that has a reputation of causing violent behavior is likely to be attractive to a different type of person than one that has a reputation for causing giddiness and laughter. The available research is difficult to evaluate, for obvious reasons, and laboratory research can offer few clues about the effects of PCP on violence, but does seem clear that PCP users are more hostile and suspicious even when not using PCP (McCardle & Fishbein, 1989).

Many of the effects produced by PCP are similar to those of schizophrenia (Young, Lawson, & Gacono, 1987). Furthermore, when schizophrenics are given phencyclidine their psychotic symptoms become greatly intensified. The intensification of their symptoms may remain for weeks or months, far longer than the drug remains in the body.

On the street, chronic use of PCP has been associated with a long-lasting confusional state that continues for weeks after the subject stops taking the drug as well as with a long-lasting depression. A single dose can cause a psychotic reaction that is the direct result of the drug, or precipitate a reaction virtually indistinguishable from true schizophrenia that may last a month or more (Smith, 1981). High doses of PCP can be fatal, and there also is the real danger that those in a confused, hostile, disoriented state may harm themselves and others (Fauman & Fauman, 1981).

Treatment for overdose is often symptomatic. A dark, quiet room is often more effective than medication, although a sedative may sometimes be prescribed. About the only effective way to treat a PCP overdose is to increase the rate of elimination of the drug. This is accomplished by use of diuretics and acidification of the urine. Some authorities recommend large amounts of cranberry juice for this purpose (Done, Aronow, & Miceli, 1981). Once detoxification has occurred, or when a user comes to a clinic for help, outpatient treatment usually begins. PCP abuse is difficult to treat, however, since patients are typically not highly motivated to stop. It is not uncommon for PCP users to show up at treatment sessions under the influence of the drug (Gorelik, Wilkins, & Wong, 1989).

PCP use among pregnant women is not unknown and babies born to these women often show various symptoms similar to babies born to mothers who are narcotics users (Wachsman, Schuetz, Chan, & Wingert, 1989). In areas of the United States like Washington, D.C., where PCP is prevalent, up to 12 percent of babies born in some hospitals have been exposed to PCP. By the first year of age, the babies seem to be normal, but subtle differences cannot be ruled out. Animal studies, for example, show that exposure to PCP in the uterus can have long-term effects (Goodwin, 1989).

Ketamine

Ketamine is a drug that closely resembles PCP. It is widely used in medicine as an anesthetic, even though up to a third of patients report disturbing PCP-like symptoms postoperatively. There also is evidence that the drug is used recreationally by medical personnel with access to the drug. What is interesting about ketamine is that its effects are basically indistinguishable from PCP, yet in the hands of basically stable people with a legitimate source and knowledge of routes of administration the effects are much different than when virtually the same drug is taken on the street. The words set and setting should now be occurring to you.

INHALANTS

Anyone who has ever seen a cat smell catnip, or a dog with its head out the window knows that smells can alter consciousness. For humans, in a way, incense and other vapors were the first inhalants, although the concept of them as a means of substance abuse was not recognized until the 1950s, at least in the United States.

Almost everyone has had the experience of pumping gas, spilling some, smelling the fumes, and feeling a little disoriented as a result. Probably few readers have ever intentionally inhaled gasoline with the specific intent of becoming intoxicated. Gasoline sniffing and its first cousin, glue sniffing, however, is surprisingly common. To this list may be added an almost endless list of household chemicals, such as cleaning fluids, inks, and various other substances.

Inhalant use can be divided into four main classes: (1) volatile solvents such as glue, gasoline, and paint thinners; (2) aerosols such as hair spray, vegetable frying pan lubricants, and spray paint; (3) anesthetics such as ether and nitrous oxide; and (4) volatile nitrites including amyl and butyl nitrite. All four types are widely available in many different forms and quite legal. All three also have psychoactive effects, employed by different groups for different purposes.

Use of inhalants in order to get high first came to widespread public attention in the sixties when reports indicated that up to 50 percent of youths had tried sniffing glue (Cohen, 1973). Since then the list has lengthened considerably. For the most part, regular inhalant use is seen primarily in young adolescents and those who lack access to other drugs. Experimental use is undoubtedly far more common and is not likely to show up in drug surveys.

In the United States, the "typical" user, in addition to being young, often has been involved in criminal behavior and frequently comes from families in which there is other drug use. Gasoline sniffing is considered a serious problem among some Canadian and American Indians and in some Australian aboriginal communities (Smart, 1986). Inhalant use is common among other groups as well, with reports of abuse among poor, young Mexican Americans and young people in Singapore (The Journal, 1988).

While these groups attract the most attention, inhalant use is seen in young adults and among more highly educated individuals as well. Amyl or butyl nitrite use is common among some homosexual groups, and nitrous oxide use is far from rare among medical professionals (Pollard, 1990). Because possession is legal, nitrous oxide is sold openly at some rock concerts, and fads of other inhalant use occasionally are seen in high schools.

Volatile Nitrites

Amyl nitrite and butyl nitrite are similar compounds with similar effects. Amyl nitrite is a prescription drug used to treat angina, pain due to an insufficient blood supply to the heart and to treat cyanide poisoning. Butyl nitrite is not presently regulated by the Food and Drug Administration and is not considered a prescription drug. It is sold through magazine advertisements and in stores that specialize in drug paraphernalia or pornography. Some of its trade names give you an idea of the purposes for which it is sold: Rush, Climax, Heart-On, and, because of its odor—Locker Room.

The primary effects of these two drugs are peripheral vasodilation leading to flushing, and occasionally, fainting, relaxation of smooth muscle, feelings of warmth, and throbbing sensations. These last for a few minutes at most and are often followed by a severe headache and chills. Ringing in the ears, problems with vision, abdominal cramps, and diarrhea are also reported.

Nitrites are most popular among young adolescents and some homosexuals. Young adolescents apparently take them for the light-headedness and dizziness they produce, while others report that they increase the pleasure and prolong the experience of orgasm, although the headache, chills, and diarrhea would seem to take some of the initial pleasure away. In addition, nitrites are supposed to cause muscle relaxation, particularly the anal sphincter, thus making anal sex more pleasant.

The major concerns about nitrites have to do with their effect on hemoglobin, the oxygen-carrying substance in the blood, and the possibility that they might be carcinogenic. Use of nitrites is associated with the formation of methemoglobin, an abnormal form of hemoglobin. In normal individuals, hemoglobin is reformed from methemoglobin, but those with heart problems and other conditions can have serious complications. The carcinogenic properties of nitrites is a matter of debate. Amyl and butyl nitrite can form nitrosamines, among the most potent cancer-forming substances known. Some studies have linked nitrite use with the development of Kaposi's sarcoma, an otherwise rare form of cancer seen with uncommon frequency in homosexual men.

Volatile Solvents

The common ingredient in most solvents is **toluene,** an additive that is increasingly found in unleaded gasoline. The effects are not unlike that of alcohol, with effects on perception and coordination. Acute, heavy use can result in unconsciousness. While most users do not use solvents heavily, the dangers are still considerable. Acute intoxication can lead to death by cardiac arrest, and unconsciousness as a result of intoxication can result in asphyxia (Ikeda, Takahashi, Umetsu, & Suzuki, 1990). Chronic use can lead to brain damage resulting in hallucinations and self-mutilation, and peripheral nervous system damage leading to the destruction of nerves leading to various muscles. Kidney damage is also seen, along with liver problems.

An added danger is found in the other components of the substance that is sniffed. The lead in gasoline, for example, can be quite toxic when

NOTICE!

State law prohibits the sale of spray paint cans or any product containing Toluene to anyone under 18 years of age.

STATE OF CALIFORNIA BILL AB-797

sniffed. Hexane, benzoic acid, and other chemical substances found in various solvents or as metabolite by-products are also harmful. Laboratory studies on humans are impossible for obvious reasons, and it is hard to determine what chemicals are found in which abused solvents. Nevertheless, it is safe to say that volatile solvent abuse is extremely dangerous.

Solvent use has never developed the kind of mystique or mythology associated with marijuana or LSD. Attempts to reduce its use have focused on reducing the availability of toluene-based products to the population most at risk, young teenagers. In several states, for example, airplane glue cannot be sold to those under eighteen. These restrictions are not strongly enforced, however, and restrictions on the sale of other toluene products, such as gasoline, seem impossible.

Aerosols

The chemicals in aerosols that cause the most problems are called halogenated hydrocarbons, and are related to a commonly used anesthetic, halogen. Halogenated hydrocarbons are also found in typewriter correction fluid and fire extinguishers. Their primary toxic effect is seen on the cardiovascular system. They can cause a sensitization of the heart muscle with resultant runaway rapid heartbeat and death. Strokes and liver damage have also been seen. Added to the danger of these substances is the fact that they are often inhaled from a plastic bag, leading to a buildup of carbon dioxide and adding to the danger of heart attack (Pollard, 1990).

Anesthetics

Volatile anesthetics other than nitrous oxide are sometimes used and abused, but their use seems to be limited to medical personnel. **Nitrous oxide** use is fairly common, however, and can cause serious toxicity in addition to the desired effects of lightheadedness and euphoria. True pharmacological addiction to anesthetics is probably rare, but has been reported. The negative effects of prolonged use include numbness and tingling in the extremities, memory loss hallucinations, and paranoid delusions (Pollard, 1990). The abuse potential of nitrous oxide is indicated by the fact that it seems to affect the endorphin receptors.

The effects of all the inhalants are basically similar, but nitrous oxide has a reputation for producing giddiness, hence its common name of laughing gas. If you have inhaled nitrous oxide at the dentist, as the author has, you may be puzzled by this description. However, sitting in an awkward position undergoing uncomfortable or painful dental procedures is not the ideal setting for bursting into laughter.

On the other hand, at least one rock group is famous for being followed by bands of devotees. Nitrous oxide use is common at Grateful Dead concerts (along with marijuana, according to most reports). Perhaps the beatific smiles on the faces of the Deadheads is a result of something other than the music?

SUMMARY

There is evidence for the use of hallucinogenic drugs that dates back to the beginning of recorded history. The ingenuity of humans in finding hallucinogenic drugs is astounding. Indians of North and South America discovered a large quantity of these drugs and used them extensively in their religious rituals.

One problem with understanding the hallucinogenic drugs is that while their biochemistry and botany may differ, they have similar effects, which may or may not resemble what most people think of as "hallucinogenic." Classification of the hallucinogenics is therefore difficult. Basically, most seem to affect the serotonin transmitter system. However, they are generally classified because of their structure and other effects as serotonergic, catecholaminergic, and anticholinergic hallucinogens.

One hallucinogenic has become infamous. LSD was widely used in the 1950s and 1960s as a potential drug for understanding human nature, as a treatment for various psychological problems, and by the military as a possible weapon. None of these possible uses has stood up to scientific investigation and it is not currently being evaluated for any of these purposes.

In the 1960s writers and others began to explore the use of these drugs; these experiments, along with the exploits of people like Timothy Leary and Ken Kesey, helped launch the era of the "hippie." There is evidence for a resurgence in the use of this drug as 1960s nostalgia returns.

Peyote and psilocybin are other hallucinogenic drugs that have also been used and abused. Revered by the Aztecs and other Indians, peyote is still a sacrament for the Native American Church. Psilocybin mushrooms have been used by adolescents since they grow wild in various parts of the

United States. Gathering and eating them is dangerous, however, because they resemble some poisonous mushrooms.

Drugs which affect the cholinergic system can also be hallucinogenic and have had a long history of use. Datura was widely used throughout the world, as was belladonna and other anticholinergic drugs. Even the common spices, mace and nutmeg, can produce hallucinogenic-like effects.

One of the most peculiar of this class of drugs is PCP. Originally introduced as an anesthetic, it is now widely used and abused. Its effects can be quite extreme and those who take it are often a management problem to others. Ketamine, a related compound, is a widely prescribed anesthetic that occasionally crops up in reports of drug use by medical personnel.

Inhalant use has never been as popular as use of the true "hallucinogens." Experimental use has been common in the past and will probably wax and wane as a result of publicity or lack thereof. Among the economically disadvantaged, however, solvent use is more common. Its major "advantages" are its price and availability. The dangers are considerable, and among those who deal with solvent users there is considerable concern about its use.

REFERENCES

Bergquist, L. (1959). The curious story behind the new Cary Grant. *Look, September 1,* 50–58.

Bliss, K. (1988). LSD and psychotherapy. *Contemporary Drug Problems,* 519–63.

Buckman, J. (1967). Theoretical aspects of LSD therapy. In H. A. Abramson (Ed.). *The use of LSD in psychotherapy and alcoholism.* New York: Bobbs-Merrill.

Cashman, J. (1966). *The LSD story.* Greenwich, CT: Fawcett Publications.

Cerletti, A., & Rothlin, E. (1955). Role of 5 hydroxytryptamine in mental disease and its antagonism to lysergic acid derivatives. *Nature, 176,* 785–86.

Cohen, S. (1965). LSD and the anguish of dying. *Harpers, September,* 69–70.

Cohen, S. (1973). The volatile solvents. *Public Health Reviews, 2,* 185–214.

Cohen, S. (1978). Psychotomimetics and cannabis. In W. G. Clark & J. DelGuidice (Eds.), pp. 357–69. *Principles of psychopharmacology (2d ed).* New York: Academy Press.

Cooper, J. R., Bloom, F. E., & Roth, R. H. (1986). *The biochemical basis of neuropharmacology.* New York and Oxford: Oxford University Press.

Cox, T. C., Jacobs, M. R., Leblanc, A. E., & Marshman, J. A. (1983). *Drugs and drug abuse.* Toronto: Addiction Research Foundation.

deSmet, P. (1985). *Ritual enemas and snuffs in the Americas.* Amsterdam: CEDLA Publications.

Dishotsky, J. I., Loughman, W. D., Morgan, R. E., & Pipscomb, W. R. (1971). LSD and genetic damage. *Science, 172,* 431–40.

Dobkin de Rios, M. (1984). *Hallucinogens: Cross cultural perspectives.* Albuquerque: University of New Mexico Press.

Done, A. K., Aronow, R., & Miceli, J. N. (1981). Pharmacokinetic bases for the treatment of phencyclidine (PCP) intoxication. In E. F. Domino (Ed.). *PCP (phencylidine): Historical and current perspectives.* Ann Arbor, MI: NPP Books.

Fauman, M. A., & Fauman, B. J. (1981). Chronic phencyclidine (PCP) abuse: A psychiatric perspective. In E. F. Domino (Ed.). *PCP (phencyclidine): Historical and current perspectives.* Ann Arbor, MI: NPP Books.

Gaddum, H. H., & Hameed (1954). Drugs which antagonize 5-hydroxytryptamine. *British Journal of Pharmacology, 9,* 240–48.

Gallant, D. M. (1981). PCP—Clinical and laboratory diagnostic problems. In E. F. Domino (Ed.). *PCP (phencyclidine): Historical and current perspectives.* Ann Arbor, MI: NPP Books.

Glennon, R. A. (1990). Serotonin receptors: Clinical implications. *Neuroscience and Biobehavioral Reviews, 14,* 35–47.

Gorelick, D. A., Wilkins, J. N., & Wong, C. (1989). Outpatient treatment of PCP abusers. *American Journal of Drug and Alcohol Abuse, 15,* 367–74.

Grinspoon, L., & Bakalar, J. B. (1986). Medical uses of illicit drugs. In R. Hamowy (Ed.). *Dealing with drugs: Consequences of government control.* Lexington, MA: Lexington Books.

Ikeda, N., Takahashi, H., & Suzuki, T. (1990). The course of respiration and circulation in "toluene sniffing." *Forensic Science International, 44,* 151–58.

Jacobs, B. L. (1987). How hallucinogenic drugs work. *American Scientist, 75,* 386–92.

Jacobs, B. L., & Tralson, M. E. (1979). Mechanisms of action of LSD. *American Scientist, 67,* 396–494.

Jaffe, J. H. (1980). Drug addiction and drug abuse. In A. G. Gilman, L. S. Goodman, & A. Gilman (Eds.), pp. 535–84. *The pharmacological basis of therapeutics.* New York: Macmillan.

King, W., & Ellison, G. (1989). Long-lasting alterations in behavior and brain neurochemistry following continuous low level LSD administration. *Pharmacology, Biochemistry and Behavior, 33,* 69–73.

Krippner, S. (1985). Psychedelic drugs and creativity. *Journal of Psychoactive Drugs, 17,* 235–45.

Kurland, A. (1967). The therapeutic potential of LSD in medicine. In R. C. Debold & R. C. Leaf (Eds.). *LSD: Man and society.* Middletown, CT: Wesleyan University Press.

Law Enforcement News, 15 September 1991. LSD makes a comeback with middle class, *17,* 7.

Lee, M. A., & Schlain, B. (1985). *Acid dreams: The CIA, LSD and the Sixties Rebellion.* New York: Grove Press.

McCardle, L., & Fishbein, D. (1989). The self-reported effects of PCP on human aggression. *Addictive Behaviors, 14,* 465–72.

McCarthy, D. A. (1981). History of the development of cateleptoid anesthetics of the phencyclidine type. In E. F. Domino (Ed.). *PCP (phencyclidine): Historical and current perspectives.* Ann Arbor, MI: NPP Books.

McKenna, D. T., & Towers, G. H. (1985). On the comparative ethnopharmacology of malphigiaceous and mystericaceous hallucinogens. *Journal of Psychoactive Drugs, 17,* 35–39.

Metzger, R. (1978). Reflections on LSD: Ten years later. *Journal of Psychoactive Drugs, 10,* 137–40.

Pollard, T. G. (1990). Relative addiction potential of major centrally active drugs and drug classes—Inhalants and anesthetics. *Advances in Alcohol and Substance Abuse, 9,* 149–65.

Schultes, R. E., & Hofmann, A. (1979). *Plants of the gods: Origin of hallucinogenic use*. New York: McGraw-Hill.

Schultes, R. E. (1987). Coca and other psychoactive plants—magico-religious roles in primitive societies of the New World. In S. Fisher, A. Raskin, & E. H. Uhlenhuth (Eds.). *Cocaine: Clinical and biobehavioral aspects*. New York and Oxford: Oxford University Press.

Smart, R. G. (1966). A controlled study of lysergide in the treatment of alcoholism. *Quarterly Journal of the Studies of Alcohol, 27,* 469–82.

Smart, R. (1986). Solvent use in North America: Aspects of epidemiology, prevention and treatment. *Journal of Psychoactive Drugs, 18,* 87–95.

Smith, D. E. (1981). A clinical approach to the treatment of phencyclidine (PCP) intoxication. In E. F. Domino (Ed.). *PCP (phencyclidine): Historical and current perspectives*. Ann Arbor, MI: NPP Books.

Stamets, P. (1982). *Psilocybe mushrooms and their allies*. Seattle, WA: Homestead Book Company.

Stevens, J. (1987). *Storming heaven: LSD and the American dream*. New York: Atlantic Monthly Press.

Thombs, D. L. (1989). A review of PCP abuse: Trends and perceptions. *Public Health Reports, 104,* 325–28.

Trulson, M. E., Jacobs, B. L., & Morrison, A. D. (1981). Raphe unit activity during REM sleep in normal cats and in pontine lesioned cats displaying REM sleep without atonia. *Brain Research, 226,* 75–81.

Van Duran, W., Wilson, W. (1967). Treatment of alcoholism with lysergide. *Quarterly Journal of the Studies of Alcohol, 28,* 299–302.

Wachsman, L., Schuetz, S., Chan, L. S., & Wingert, W. A. (1989). What happens to babies exposed to phencyclidine (PCP) in utero. *American Journal of Drug and Alcohol Abuse, 15,* 31–39.

Wasson, R. G. (1971). *Soma: Divine mushroom of immortality*. New York: Harcourt, Brace & Jovanovich.

West, L. J., Pierce, C. M., & Thomas, W. D. (1962). Lysergic acid diethlyamide: Its effects on a male Asiatic elephant. *Science, 138,* 1100–02.

Young, T., Lawson, G. W., & Gacono, C. B. (1987). Clinical aspects of phencyclidine (PCP). *The International Journal of the Addictions, 22,* 1–15.

9

• • •

NARCOTICS

• • •

OBJECTIVES

When you have finished studying this chapter you should:

1. Know the role of opium in the ancient world.
2. Know how morphine is derived from opium.
3. Know the reason heroin was developed.
4. Be able to list the various opiate derivatives.
5. Understand the role of opium in the world scene of the nineteenth century.
6. Be able to discuss the history of narcotic addiction in the United States.
7. Know the physiological effects of the opiates.
8. Know the difference between agonists, antagonists, and agonist-antagonists.
9. Be able to discuss the role of morphine and the endorphins in pain perception.
10. Be able to discuss the various types of heroin "addicts."
11. Understand the relationship between opiates and the designer drugs.
12. Understand why AIDS has produced changes in patterns of opiate use.

KEY TERMS

Acquired Immune Deficiency Syndrome (AIDS)
agonist
antagonist
black tar heroin
celebrity addict
chasing the dragon
chipper
codeine
designer drugs
diacetylmorphine
endorphin
enkephalin
fentanyl
Harrison Narcotic Act
heroin
ice cream habit
LAAM
matured out
methadone
morphine
MPPP
MPTP
naloxone
naltrexone
opium
opioid peptides
Papaver somniferum
pentazocaine
propoxyphene
skin-popping
stand-up cat

O pium was, until the last century, virtually the only clearly effective remedy medical doctors could offer the sufferer of most diseases. Little wonder, then, that it was considered a miracle drug. Galen, the last great physician of ancient Rome and Greece, considered it a cure for everything from snakebites to asthma, and from depression to leprosy (Scott, 1969).

HISTORY OF OPIUM

The story of the first use of opium is lost in antiquity, but it is clear that it was known to the major civilizations from the beginning of recorded history. Evidence exists for its use among the Egyptians, Greeks, Romans, and Arabs, and that evidence indicates that opium was used recreationally as well as medicinally.

The Arabs, who shunned the use of alcohol, were responsible for spreading the message of the power of opium throughout the then known world. When Greek and Roman civilization declined, about A.D. 400, the Arab countries became the storehouse of accumulated knowledge. The Arabs made contact with the countries of the Far East and other parts of the world. Wherever they went, opium, like Mary's little lamb, was sure to follow (Owen, 1968).

In China, opium had been used for its medical properties since it was introduced, but it also had another use. Opium smoking was a popular pastime among the elite of China. Because it was fairly expensive and required pipes and other paraphernalia, the smoking of opium was initially restricted to the upper classes (Scott, 1976).

Most of the opium smoking of the Chinese in the eighteenth and nineteenth centuries came from India, since the quality was apparently better. You will recall from chapter 4 that the British were buying huge quantities of tea and silk from China. The Chinese insisted that the British pay for these products in silver, leading to a drain on the British economy.

The Chinese considered the British barbarians and had no use for any of their products. In order to retrieve some of their silver, the British, through the East India Company, provided smugglers with huge quantities of Indian opium. The Chinese by this time had become concerned about the harmful effects of opium smoking and had officially prohibited its importation.

All of these events led to a smuggling operation that was lucrative for everyone from the emperor of China to the lowest British seaman. Chinese merchants bought the opium from the British seamen and resold it at an enormous profit to middlemen, and so on up the line. This arrangement continued for many years until the Son of Heaven, Emperor Tao Kuang, who was genuinely opposed to the use of opium, declared a crackdown on its use in 1838. Henceforth, there was to be a two-year period of grace to give all opium smokers the chance to quit, and medical treatment was offered to those who wished it.

In 1839, the emperor took a fateful step in his anti-drug campaign when he appointed Lin Tse Hu to the post of imperial high commissioner for the port of Canton. Lin was a rare administrator in any government—he was scrupulously honest. The opium smugglers, used to trading with relatively low level officials of the emperor, did not at first appreciate the man they were dealing with. Lin carried with him the arrogance and power of the emperor himself. He demanded that the traders surrender all of their opium immediately.

After many threats the traders agreed, and 20,283 chests of opium worth about $500 each were surrendered. Lin was now the one with the problem. He had thousands of tons of opium on his hands. If he shipped it back to the emperor to show his success, it would likely be smuggled. At the same time, he couldn't burn tons of opium without polluting the atmosphere for miles around. He solved his problem by ordering that pits be dug so that the opium could be mixed with water, salt, and lime. When this mixture was decomposed it was released into the harbor.

The British government resented what it considered the high-handed treatment of its subjects and found an excuse to start the Opium War. The British defeated the Chinese, forced them to open several ports, give them the island of Hong Kong, and pay for the opium they had destroyed. As a result of the British victory, the supply of opium to China increased dramatically and opium smoking became even more popular, especially among the lower classes.

Narcotic Use in the United States

Opium was used in the United States during the 1700s primarily for medicinal purposes. The 1800s saw an explosion of narcotic use that is difficult to believe. Narcotic addicts were everywhere and of every social and economic class. The exact number remains a matter of controversy, but by 1900, there were probably more than 300,000 opiate addicts in the United States (Courtwright, 1982). The population of the United States at that time was only 76,000,000. In comparison, the estimate of narcotic addicts today is between 300,000 and 500,000 out of a population of 245,000,000.

The person most likely to be a narcotic addict in the nineteenth century was a woman, middle or upper class, middle-aged or older, probably residing in the South. These people were proper members of society, and their addiction was considered a matter of pity, but rarely one of disgust.

How did so many people become addicted? Most people had little access to physicians in the nineteenth century. Only the relatively wealthy and educated could afford to go to doctors. The physicians, for their part, could not cure most diseases. They did, however, have a drug which promised prompt symptomatic relief, the newly-discovered morphine.

Little wonder then that morphine was prescribed for "women's troubles," chronic headache, rheumatism, and a wide variety of other conditions

Notice that all of these patent medicines contain either opium or morphine.

The Anodyne Principle of Opium.

PAPINE.

PAPINE· is the *Anodyne or Pain-Relieving* Principle of Opium in a pleasant liquid form. Its advantages are: That it produces *the good effects* of Opium with less tendency to cause nausea, vomiting, constipation, etc. It is the *safest* and *most pleasant* of all the preparations of Opium, and is uniform in strength. It can be relied upon in all cases where Opium or Morphia *is indicated.*

ONE FLUID drachm represents one grain of Opium in Anodyne Powder.

AVERAGE DOSE, one half to one teaspoonful.

Prepared EXCLUSIVELY for Physicians' Prescriptions.

BATTLE & CO., Chemists,
St. Louis.

for which it is completely ineffective. Needless to say, only the middle and upper classes would be in a position to receive these "treatments" and hence become addicted.

The introduction of the hypodermic syringe made it even more tempting for the doctor. Relief of pain was now virtually instantaneous. Often the doctor left the syringe and a supply of morphine with his patients for them to self-administer. The addictive nature of morphine was not widely recognized and the physician undoubtedly thought he was doing his patient a favor. After the medicine was gone, withdrawal often began, which the patient interpreted as another disease, a disease that had a cure, patent medicines.

The names of patent medicines were legion and the cures they claimed as numerous as bottles themselves, but usually they had only two major ingredients, alcohol and either opium or morphine. The manufacturers were not required to list the contents of their "medicines" so that buyers never knew what they were taking. One medicine advertised as a treatment for morphine addiction actually contained a large amount of morphine!

The epidemic of morphine addiction in the later half of the nineteenth century is sometimes blamed on the fact that wounded Civil War soldiers were injected with morphine to relieve their pain. They supposedly became addicted, and returned home from the Civil War with this addiction. However, during the Civil War, morphine was typically sprinkled on wounds, an unlikely source of addiction. Furthermore, 60 percent of all narcotic addicts during this time were women, so the Civil War was probably a relatively minor influence on the rise of addiction (Courtwright, 1982).

Some became dependent on opiates through medicines, others through opium smoking. Opium smoking was introduced into our country by Chinese immigrants who came here in the middle of the nineteenth century. Many of them came to work in the gold mines, and others to help build the transcontinental railroad system. They brought with them their attitudes and their opium. By 1870, opium smoking had spread to the underworld and it was "discovered" to be a menace.

When labor was scarce, the Chinese worker was welcomed. He (they were almost invariably male) was hard-working, frugal, and rarely initiated trouble, but as unemployment rose, so did resentment of the Chinese laborer. Racial prejudice was common, and this prejudice focused on the one trait that differentiated the Chinese from the American or European worker, opium smoking. Lurid stories circulated about opium dens to which unsuspecting young (always Caucasian) women were lured and introduced to a life of degradation and prostitution. The other group that took to opium smoking, the gamblers and prostitutes, were already looked down upon.

About this time, the Bayer Company of Switzerland introduced a new drug that would relieve the symptoms of morphine addiction and yet not be addicting itself. This drug was so important that no ordinary name would be sufficient. It would be named after Hero, the Greek mythological character. Heroin, as we will see on page 309 is merely a different form of morphine.

After the passage of the **Harrison Narcotic Act** in 1914 (see chapter 12), opiate use began to decline among most sectors of the population. The reasons for this decline are complex and have little to do with the Harrison Act itself (Musto, 1987). The older population of morphine addicts, those addicted by their own doctors, or by patent medicines, aged and died.

As a result, opiate use retreated into the ghettos and the underworld, morphine became more difficult to come by, and heroin took its place. The typical opiate user changed in a few short years from a middle-class, southern, white woman to a young, city-dwelling, black man. The former was respectable, if pitiable; the latter, a criminal. The shift of the perception of opiates from medicine to addictive drug had less to do with increased understanding of the nature of these drugs than it did with economic conditions (Hoffman, 1990).

Modern Use of Opiates

The Vietnam War, like the Civil War more than a hundred years earlier, provided a short burst of notoriety for narcotics. During most American wars, the most popular drugs for soldiers, tobacco and alcohol, were legal. In

This very racist etching was published in Harper's Weekly *in 1880. Accompanying it was a story about the difference between alcohol and opiate abuse. The implication was that opium smoking resulted in apathy*

Vietnam, however, there was a different type of soldier and a different type of drug. Most soldiers were, of course, the same age as those back home who were protesting on campus, smoking marijuana, and marching on Washington.

Both marijuana and heroin were widely available in Vietnam, and the Armed Forces announced a number of highly visible crackdowns on illegal drug use (they were mostly silent about alcohol abuse). One result was a decline in the use of marijuana, which could be smelled easily, in favor of heroin, which was easier to hide and harder to detect. Although injecting heroin was not uncommon, most users in Vietnam mixed their heroin either with tobacco cigarettes or marijuana and smoked it (Rosenbaum, 1971). Inhalation of potent heroin will produce much the same experience as injecting it.

The military understandably became very concerned and set up heroin treatment centers in Vietnam. They adopted a slogan that heroin addiction "stopped at the South China Sea." Every soldier leaving Vietnam had to

in depth

Three Famous Opiate Users

With morphine addiction common among the educated and well-to-do, it is not surprising that some famous people of the nineteenth century were addicted. In most cases their addiction had harmful effects on their productivity, but in one case there seemed to be no effect at all.

William Halsted was one of the great physicians of the century, a founder of Johns Hopkins Medical School, a brilliant surgeon, devoted husband—and morphine addict for thirty-six years. He was one of the first medical researchers to experiment with cocaine and became dependent on it. After several unsuccessful attempts to stop using cocaine, he "cured" his problem by becoming a morphine addict. In fact, he did his most brilliant work while addicted to morphine and managed to keep his secret from his friends, his family, and all but one of his professional colleagues.

Thomas DeQuincey became addicted to laudanum (a mixture of alcohol and opium). If he had been born in 1950 instead of 1785, DeQuincey would have been a hippie. He ran away from his middle-class parents at seventeen and went to London. At first, he refused to accept money from his family, but finally gave in when he realized he would otherwise have had to go to work, an occupation unfit for a gentleman. During his career as a professional student, he cultivated the friendship of the major artists of the day.

His experience with opium is supposed to have begun one Sunday afternoon when he had a toothache.

He went to a druggist who suggested laudanum. He loved the experience he got from laudanum from the very first time he took it. Although he tried to regulate its use, he began taking more and more until he was essentially nonfunctional as a writer. It appears that he finally either reduced or gave up his opiate addiction and became able to write once again. His most famous work, *Confessions of an English Opium Eater,* is a description of his experience with the drug. His inability to work while taking opium is far more common than the successes that Halsted achieved.

Samuel Taylor Coleridge wrote *The Rime of the Ancient Mariner* and *Kubla Kahn*. Coleridge freely admitted that an opium-induced dream was the source of *Kubla Kahn* (remember that opium was not illegal), and internal evidence, plus what is known of his life, suggests that *The Ancient Mariner* was written while he was in a similar condition. At one point in his life, Coleridge was taking half a gallon of laudanum a week! He spent most of his life dependent on his friends who recognized his genius, especially William Wordsworth (Drabble, 1985).

Keeping in mind that opium was not illegal or even disapproved of, the nineteenth century saw widespread use of this drug among the famous and the common person. Others who were widely considered to be opium users, for medical or other reasons, include Edgar Allan Poe, Charles Dickens, and John Keats.

---

pass a urine test for heroin. Those failing were placed in treatment centers. The treatment programs were generally considered to be total failures and some reports indicate that servicemen used more heroin in the rehabilitation programs than they did when on active duty (Zinberg, 1972).

When the soldiers did return to the United States, moreover, many tried heroin again on the streets. Gradually, however, use of heroin declined

Heroin in Vietnam was inexpensive and potent. Many soldiers used heroin in Vietnam, but few continued this use when they returned to the United States.

for most users. Despite the fact that 85 percent of soldiers had been offered heroin, and at least 35 percent of the enlisted men were believed to have used it, of the perhaps 54 percent who became dependent on it only 12 percent were still using it three years after their return to the States (Robins, Helzer, Hesselbrock, & Wish, 1979). Furthermore, this study found that approximately 12 percent of the control group (the non-soldiers) were also addicts, implying that whatever caused narcotic addiction had little to do with exposure to the drug in Vietnam.

The fact that relatively few soldiers became dependent on heroin should not be too surprising, given what you now know about drugs. First of all, since it was quite potent, most users in Vietnam smoked heroin rather than injecting it. When the addicts returned to the States, they found the heroin weaker, so smoking was not an alternative—shooting up was necessary. While heroin was widely used in Vietnam, in the States it was deviant behavior. Heroin was seen by nearly all users as merely a temporary escape from an intolerable situation and was not considered part of a particular lifestyle as it was here (Zinberg, 1984).

In the nineties, heroin addiction has apparently stabilized. Accurate estimates of the number of addicts are difficult to obtain but a figure of 400,000 is probably close. Traditionally, heroin has come from the so-called Golden Triangle in Southeast Asia, although for a few years in the 1980s, Mexico was the primary source.

"Black tar" heroin at left contains many impurities. At the right of the picture is "pure" heroin.

Opium and Other Narcotics

Opium is derived from the tar-like substance that oozes from the seed pod of the Oriental poppy *Papaver somniferum* when it is cut. Why the poppy produces opium and why it produces it for only about a week after the petals fall and before the poppy seeds have developed, remains a considerable mystery.

The Important Narcotics

The term *narcotic* is used medically to indicate three different types of drugs: 1) the natural derivatives of opium such as morphine, 2) the semisynthetic drugs that are the result of chemical modification of the natural derivatives such as heroin, and 3) the synthetic drugs that have only a slight similarity to drugs such as morphine but have similar effects on pain, such as meperidine or Demerol.

Another way of describing these drugs is by their effect on the endorphin receptors. Although you read in chapter 3 that the proper term for endorphin is opioid peptide, endorphin is so much more familiar it will be used here. Drugs can be described as **agonists,** meaning that they increase the activity of the endorphin system, **antagonist,** meaning that they oppose the system, and **agonist-antagonist,** meaning that they have different actions on different endorphin receptors (Ternes & O'Brien, 1990).

Morphine is the standard against which all other narcotic drugs are measured. It is an agonist and a description of its effects define the entire groups of drugs except where mentioned. The two primary effects of morphine are on the central nervous system and the gastrointestinal tract. In the central nervous system morphine reduces pain, depresses respiration, suppresses cough, and causes nausea and behavioral changes. In the gastrointestinal tract, morphine decreases diarrhea.

The effect of morphine depends in part on the individual and in part on whether the person taking it is in pain. For many individuals, even those in severe pain, the effects are quite unpleasant and include nausea, vomiting, anxiety, and general depression lasting for several hours. For those in pain, morphine reduces the emotional component of pain as well as actually reducing the pain itself.

The onset of action for morphine is slow compared to codeine, heroin, and methadone, in part because it is not as lipid soluble. As you saw with cocaine, part of the rewarding effect of a drug can be explained by the speed of onset. Addicts, therefore, do not consider morphine as ''good'' as heroin or methadone, for example. Death due to morphine overdose occurs as a result of respiratory failure. Morphine suppresses the ability of the brain to respond to normal increases in carbon dioxide in the blood.

Codeine is another naturally occurring opiate found in morphine. Its chemical name is methylmorphine and is widely used both as an analgesic and as a cough suppressant. In the past, codeine was a common ingredient in cough medicines sold over the counter but has been largely replaced with synthetic cough suppressants such as dextrometorphan. Codeine is less effective as a cough suppressant and as an analgesic than morphine but is also less likely to cause dependence. Codeine can and has been abused however, especially by addicts unable to get morphine or heroin. One interesting characteristic that sets it apart from morphine is that it is actually more effective orally than by injection, because it is not as rapidly metabolized in the liver.

Heroin is **diacetylmorphine,** morphine with two acetyl groups attached. It is more lipid soluble than morphine, crosses the blood/brain barrier more rapidly, and has greater euphoric effects. It is also more potent as an analgesic than morphine. Illegal in the United States (it is a Schedule I drug) it is used in other countries where it is considered superior to morphine. The addictive potential of heroin is almost undoubtedly due to its rapid absorption because it is immediately metabolized to morphine in the brain.

There are two other drugs similar in structure to heroin that are legal in the United States. Hydromorphone (Dilaudid) and oxymorphone (Numorphan) are available by prescription. Hydromorphone, in particular, is so similar to heroin that addicts cannot tell the difference. Dilaudid is often the target of drug store robberies.

Methadone was first synthesized in Germany during World War II. Its trade name, Dolophine, supposedly is a tribute to Adolf Hitler. As a drug it is very similar to morphine, especially when injected, but has certain differences that have made it useful as a treatment for narcotic addiction. It is more readily absorbed orally than morphine and has a slow onset of action, giving it less abuse potential than some other drugs. Furthermore, its analgesic effects last about six hours, while blockage of withdrawal symptoms persists for more than twenty-four hours. When injected, however, it is virtually identical to morphine (Ternes & O'Brien, 1990). The use of methadone in treating narcotic addiction is discussed in chapter 13.

Levo-alpha-acetylmethadol (**LAAM**) is a drug with an interesting potential that has not been extensively explored. Unlike methadone, which must be taken every day, LAAM is a long-acting drug which needs to be taken only three times per week. It has even less dependence potential than methadone.

Propoxyphene (Darvon and others) is a well known drug that is less potent than codeine and has side effects which limit its potential for dependence. It is extremely irritating when injected, and high doses taken orally produce unpleasant, even psychotic, symptoms. Because of its low abuse potential it is widely prescribed.

Many over-the-counter cough medicines contain dextrometorphan, which is another synthetic opiate. It has little or no dependence potential and little analgesic properties. It does, however, reduce coughing. It is used because of concern about the dependence potential of codeine.

Agonists-Antagonists. Pentazocaine (Talwin) is an analgesic and can produce dependence if injected, but it is also an antagonist of some of the enkephalins and actually can produce withdrawal symptoms when given to people addicted to morphine. In some parts of the United States and especially Canada, it is mixed with antihistamine and injected.

Other mixed agonists-antagonists have varying characteristics, but in general have low dependence potential, rarely cause euphoria, and can cause withdrawal in those who are already morphine dependent. They are not widely used in the United States.

Antagonists. Naloxone and **naltrexone** are interesting drugs in that they produce very few effects themselves but reverse the action of other opiates. They do not produce analgesia, dependence, sedation, or any of the other effects associated with narcotics. They are useful in treating narcotic overdoses and also in helping those who are addicted. Naltrexone in particular has been used to help heroin and morphine addicts since its effects last several days. If the addict takes Trexan (its trade name), heroin and morphine have no effect, so it helps the highly motivated drug abuser stay clean by removing the temptation to inject, because if he or she did, there would be no euphoria.

PHYSIOLOGY AND PHARMACOLOGY OF NARCOTICS

Because of the extraordinary usefulness of the opiate drugs, a large number have been developed. The ideal opiate would be one that is a powerful analgesic, fast-acting, long-lasting, causes little or no respiratory depression, and has no abuse potential. Such a drug does not exist, but those that do, have the above properties to various degrees. Table 9.1 shows the common narcotic-based drugs and some of their effects on pain and other symptoms, as well as their abuse potential. Note that, as a general rule, the better they are at relieving pain, the higher the abuse potential.

The Endorphins, the Opiates, and Pain

In Chapter 3, you read about the neurotransmitters and how they function in the brain. You will recall that the term **endorphin** really refers to a number of different opiod peptides each with its own distribution in the body and the brain. Those in the brain are most properly called **enkephalins** and are involved in the central mediation of pain perception among other functions.

Table 9.1 Abuse, Dependence Potential and Effectiveness of Various Narcotics			
Drug	**Abuse Potential**	**Dependence Potential**	**Pain Relief**
heroine	High	High	High
hydromorphone (Dilaudid)	High	High	High
oxycodone (Percodan)	High	High	Moderate
fentanyl	High	Moderate	High
morphine	Moderate	High	Moderate
methadone (Dolophine)	Moderate	High	Moderate
meperidine (Demerol)	Moderate	High	Low
codeine	Low	Moderate	Low
propoxyphine (Darvon)	Low	Low	Low
pentazocine	Low	Low	Low
Talwin	Low	Low	Low

Abuse potential refers to the preference of the drug by addicts and probably is influenced by lipid solubility, euphoric effects and availability. Dependence refers to the actual physical dependence potential. Pain relief is estimated using a 10 mg subcutaneous dosage of morphine as the standard and designating that "moderate" pain relief. Drugs which are more potent and/or longer lasting are classed as "high" while those less potent or shorter acting are classed as low.

Source: Compiled from Ternes and O'Brian (1990) and Jaffe and Martin (1975).

Pain is a familiar phenomenon that we have all experienced and yet in many ways it is peculiar. Pain means various things to different people in different circumstances. Football players may play an entire game with a broken ankle and not notice the pain until the last quarter is over. On the other hand, the slight prick of the dentist's needle into your gum may make you flinch. One of the first researchers to explore the subjective nature of pain in an objective fashion was a physician during World War II who noticed that soldiers often required smaller amounts of painkillers than civilians undergoing surgery, even though the soldier's wounds were more severe (Beecher, 1946).

The severity of the soldier's wound often meant that they would be returned home. In fact, the term that was used was a "Million Dollar Wound," meaning that it would take the soldier out of combat. They recognized that they were in pain, but it didn't seem to "hurt." The civilian, on the other hand, did not have to face the possibility of battle and death and so interpreted the pain much differently. Pain can, therefore, be affected by feelings and hence by the central nervous system.

Physiologically, this translates into the fact that there are two separate anatomical systems for pain (Price & Dubner, 1977; Basbaum & Fields, 1979). One goes up the spinal cord to the thalamus, the central receiving center of the brain, and then to the sensorimotor cortex. It tells us where the pain is and how strong it is. Nerve fibers on this pathway carry their messages quite rapidly. Everyone has undoubtedly had the experience of hitting their thumb with a hammer, feeling the pain, pulling away their hand, and waiting for the throb. The second pain comes along more slowly and is a function of another system.

The second system goes to the reticular formation, especially the periaqueductal gray area (see chapter 3), to the thalamus, and to the limbic system, the emotional center of the brain. This system is the one that gives the emotional quality to the pain. Stimulating parts of this system produces analgesia, a lack of pain, in humans (Richardson & Akil, 1977), which means that this system not only "feels" pain but also inhibits it. This second system is affected by the opiates such as morphine and by the enkephalins. These fibers conduct rather slowly compared to fibers of the first system.

As we shall see, opiates produce the classic form of tolerance and physical dependence we call addiction. In addition, as you have already seen, they depress the respiratory centers and slow down gastrointestinal functioning. There is evidence that the tolerance to the analgesic effect occurs more rapidly than tolerance to the effects of the opiates on respiratory depression (Pasternak, 1988). Another characteristic of most opiates is that the pain relief increases with the dosage but a point is reached at which the dose response curve flattens out. From chapter 2 you should remember that this means that further increases in the dosage do not translate into further pain relief, although the side effects continue to increase.

In practical terms this means that addicts and those taking narcotics for pain relief who increase their intake because of tolerance increase the risk of side effects or even dying of respiratory depression. What is needed is to find a way of separating the pain-relieving effects of narcotics from the other effects, including dependence.

The Opiates and Alcohol

In the nineteenth century it was common knowledge among physicians and narcotics addicts that there was a close relationship between opiate addiction and alcohol dependence. In fact, a not uncommon cause of opiate dependence was the result of an attempt to reduce the symptoms of alcohol withdrawal (Siegel, 1986).

In recent years, there has been a flurry of revived interest in this connection, as you read in chapter 4. Alcohol and the opiates share many characteristics. They are both depressants and they potentiate the effects of each other. Many heroin addicts turn to alcohol when they stop using narcotics, and administration of narcotics will relieve some of the symptoms of alcohol dependence. Finally, narcotic antagonists have been shown to reverse the effects of severe alcohol intoxication.

As you read in chapter 4 some treatment programs for alcohol abuse explain the alcoholic's craving in terms of changes in the enkephalin in the brain. You also read that this explanation is at best only a partial one. The fact that heroin addicts often turn to alcohol can probably best be explained simply by the fact that alcohol is a cheap legal substitute for opiates. The interaction between the opiod peptides and alcohol is far too complicated to explain the connection.

Central Nervous System Effects

In general, the opiates are depressants. They depress the respiratory centers and have a specific attachment to the limbic system, the emotional center of the brain (see chapter 2). They also cause pupil contraction. Pupillary constriction is a classic sign of narcotic intoxication, and one that police officers often look for to determine if someone is under the influence of these drugs (Ryall, 1990). A stereotype of drug users either of stimulants or narcotics is that they wear sunglasses, presumably to hide either the dilation or constriction of pupils caused by the drug.

Death due to a true overdose of narcotics is the result of respiratory depression. The medulla, a part of the brain stem responds to changes in carbon dioxide. Opiates prevent this response. Drugs that antagonize the effects of the opiates can rapidly reverse this respiratory depression.

Gastrointestinal Effects

In modern Western society, the food we eat is rarely spoiled, sanitation is almost always excellent, and most gastrointestinal disorders are rare. It takes only one experience, however, with "Montezuma's revenge" or "New Delhi belly" or salmonella poisoning to remind us how devastating intestinal disorders can be. Morphine and its derivatives are excellent remedies for diarrhea, a major cause of death in the Third World.

Opiates also cause nausea and vomiting when first taken, although tolerance to these effects builds rapidly. The drugs also stimulate the smooth muscle of the intestine, which, on the one hand reduces diarrhea (Ryall, 1990), but in chronic users produces constipation. The smooth muscle of the urinary bladder is also stimulated and this can produce an unpleasant sensation of a constant need to urinate.

Narcotics and the "Cough Control Center"

The opiates are effective also in reducing cough. Although it is often useful to cough when you have a cold, especially if the cough will bring up mucus accumulating in the lungs, a nonproductive cough can be annoying and painful. Through their action on the medulla (see chapter 3), the opiates suppress the cough reflex. As you read earlier in this chapter, codeine was commonly used for this purpose until recently, although some research indicates that at the dosage typically taken (5 mg), it is ineffective in reducing cough.

ABUSE POTENTIAL OF THE OPIATES

Few drugs produce the classic symptoms of addiction as well as the opiates. Tolerance develops rapidly followed by physical dependence and withdrawal symptoms. However, the "classic symptoms" of addiction have strong psychological components as well, and opiate addiction rarely resembles the media image of it.

Since heroin is the most widely abused opiate drug, and since the heroin addict is often thought of as the prototype drug user, we will focus our discussion on addiction to heroin.

Tolerance

It is not particularly easy to become a heroin addict. Patterns of drug use that lead to heroin addiction vary from city to city and neighborhood to neighborhood, but many of those who eventually become addicts start by smoking or snorting the drug. For anyone not in severe pain, the commonest response on ingestion of heroin is nausea and vomiting. The snorter or smoker who persists in his habit and continues in spite of the nausea is sometimes rewarded with a feeling of euphoria.

The next step after snorting or smoking is **"skin-popping,"** or injecting the drug under the skin. Since the bags of heroin used in recent years contain as little as 5 percent heroin, the smoking or snorting stage is often bypassed and the user moves directly to skin-popping.

Eventually, the user is ready for mainlining, or injecting the drug directly into the vein. The need for mainlining seems to reflect the fact that the average bag of heroin is relatively impure and contains very little heroin. Soldiers in Vietnam could experience euphoria by smoking heroin. Users in the thirties and forties often could get by with injecting the drug into a large muscle group, since the potency of their heroin was fairly high. In order to get the same rush, today's addict has to inject the drug directly into a vein. Even after mainlining the drug, it may take several injections a day for a number of days to actually produce dependence.

Dependence and Withdrawal

The classic definition of dependence requires that the addict experience withdrawal when the drug is no longer present in the body. With addicts who have developed a strong dependence, withdrawal occurs in three stages. The first stage begins four to six hours after the last dose of opiates and lasts for two to three days. It includes craving for the drug, yawning, a runny nose, sweating, and crying.

Stage two begins about twelve hours after the last dose and is characterized by sleep disturbance, dilated pupils, loss of appetite, irritability, goose bumps, and muscle tremor. The third stage is the most severe. It begins after about twenty-four hours and reaches a peak about the third day of withdrawal. It is characterized by insomnia, yawning, muscle weakness, nausea, vomiting, diarrhea, chills and fever, flushing, and abdominal pain. The common term "kicking the habit" refers to muscle spasms of the lower extremities common in this stage. You should recognize that most of these symptoms are the result of a "rebound" from the effects of the drugs themselves.

If these symptoms, however unpleasant, do not seem terribly severe, consider that your concepts of addiction are affected by television which tends to exaggerate just about everything for dramatic effect. Furthermore, as you will see, many addicts do not even have a full-blown addiction and even for those that do, the withdrawal symptoms can be largely prevented with narcotic antagonists and a drug called clonidine. You should not underestimate the dangers of narcotic addiction, but it is also important to distinguish reality from dramatic license.

Contrary to popular belief, polydrug use is common among heroin users.

Dangers of Opiate Use

Any discussion of the dangers of opiate use must take into consideration the fact that possession of these drugs without a prescription is a felony. Even possession of narcotics paraphernalia, such as hypodermic syringes, is against the law. Many of the physical problems that heroin addicts have are more the result of the illegal nature of their drug taking than the effects of heroin itself. Addicts inject impure drugs, share needles, neglect their diet, and engage in other behaviors that are not conducive to good health.

The most serious short-term danger of heroin use is the overdose. The number of deaths due to narcotic overdose is not particularly large (about 4,000 a year) compared to those due to cigarette smoking or alcohol use, but the number of people using heroin is, of course, far less. As we have seen, the opiates are respiratory depressants. Remember that alcohol is also a respiratory depressant, and alcohol in combination with heroin is a particularly deadly mixture.

Death by heroin overdose is fairly slow, and effective treatment is available. Some users of heroin die suddenly, often within seconds after injection. These deaths are unlikely to be due to overdose. They probably are allergic reactions to the various substances used to adulterate heroin, such as quinine (Bourne, 1976; Brecher, 1972).

Other than death by overdose, the short-term effects of heroin are rather innocuous. The long-term health effects are not particularly remarkable either. Nearly all the physical problems associated with heroin abuse—abscesses, hepatitis, and even AIDS—are the result of injecting adulterated heroin with unsterile needles. Heroin is highly addictive, and a lifetime "on the nod" is rarely conducive to notable achievement. However, long-term use of heroin (or any other narcotic), given a pure drug and a safe means of administration is, apparently, not especially harmful to the body (Platte, 1987).

Behavioral Effects of Opiates

The heroin addict with a fully developed habit must mainline heroin several times a day to avoid withdrawal. He or she is often in poor health because of poor nutrition, usually suffers from abscesses stemming from the use of unsterile needles, and may have hepatitis or various other blood disorders as a result of sharing needles with other addicts. Constipation is a very common side effect of heroin addiction. Partly because of the depressant effects of heroin and partly because of poor health and nutrition, the heroin addict also has little or no sex drive. These unpleasant symptoms should cause you to wonder why anyone would use opiates in the first place. Do the behavioral effects compensate for the negative physiological effects?

When the heroin user first starts to inject the drug, he/she experiences a wave of pleasurable feeling when the drug reaches the brain. The euphoria is followed by sudden relief from anxiety and tension and the combination is referred to as a "rush." This rush is followed by a period of apathy, relaxation, and peacefulness, during which the addict may doze off in a twilight state between sleep and alertness. This is called being "on the nod" and is generally described as being quite pleasant. The user can be aroused from this condition but shows slurred speech, and has difficulty in paying attention.

As tolerance and dependence (and addiction) develop, however, even the euphoria diminishes, and the addict works very hard indeed, not to feel good, but to feel less bad. The goal of drug-taking is now to avoid withdrawal. The rush and the pleasurable state of relaxation become secondary and may even disappear entirely. The reward for drug-taking is no longer positive reinforcement, but negative reinforcement (see chapter 1). Even with the description of the effects of narcotics, it may be difficult to understand why people become addicts. Sociocultural factors play a role, as do personality characteristics, but, in the end, like so many other characteristics of drug use and abuse, the exact reasons remain an enigma.

Types of Heroin Addicts

While many heroin addicts fit the description above, there are many other users of heroin who do not. In fact, the "typical" heroin user of the nineties is unlikely to fit the above description. Most of the users of this decade are more likely to fit one of the following categories.

The Chipper

As unbelievable as it may seem to those whose image of the heroin addict has been picked up from the media, some individuals seem to be capable of recreational use of heroin (Zinberg & Jacobson, 1976). They use the drug occasionally and do not develop significant tolerance or dependence (Cox, Jacobs, Leblanc, & Marshman, 1983). No one knows how many "chippers" there are, since this kind of drug use is so socially disapproved that virtually no chipper would volunteer the information.

No one knows why some people remain chippers and others become compulsive users. It appears, though, that chippers use heroin more for recreational reasons than for escape and do not associate with compulsive users. They are careful also to regulate the situations in which they use heroin. Thus, both their set and setting are different than those of the addict (Zinberg, 1984).

The Ice Cream Habit

Not only are there large numbers of chippers (there are perhaps three to four times as many chippers as addicts), but many of today's "addicts" are not really addicted to heroin. The heroin available on the street today is often of such low potency that it is almost impossible to develop a serious addiction. Heroin addicts of the fifties had serious habits and experienced serious withdrawal.

Many of today's "addicts" are more addicted to the hustle and excitement of the lifestyle, the *idea* of being an addict, and to the experience of shooting up itself, rather than to heroin. A trend that concerns many law enforcement and drug abuse professionals is that the purity of a typical "bag" of heroin is beginning to increase and more potent forms of heroin are becoming more widely available. Not only is this likely to result in an increase in drug overdose deaths, but also in an increase in both the numbers of addicts and the seriousness of their addiction.

The Celebrity Addict

Except for a brief period in the sixties, most heroin addicts were from the lower socioeconomic classes. Recently, however, heroin use has once again been making inroads into the middle and upper classes. Many of these individuals have the money and the resources to obtain relatively pure heroin, use clean needles, and hide their addiction well. The only hint of most of these addicts comes from the occasional arrest of a dealer or a user who agrees to turn in his "friends" for a reduced sentence. Several rock and popular music stars of the past decade have reported a heroin addiction. For these addicts real addiction is possible and withdrawal is often most unpleasant.

The "Matured-Out" Addict

Another fact about heroin addiction that surprises many people is that the typical heroin addict is addicted for about six to eight years. It is rare to find heroin addicts who are in their thirties. There are several possible explanations for this phenomenon. It is possible that the addict finally succeeds in being cured after trying several heroin treatment programs. The rate of recidivism among heroin addicts within one year after completion of a detoxification program is more than 80 percent. Follow-up studies indicate, however, that by about six years after initial treatment the rate of addiction is reversed, with only 20 percent still being addicted.

Another possibility is that the individual problems that led the addict to become addicted have been reduced. Whatever life crisis the person was experiencing that made him/her turn to drugs was resolved, and the ex-addict becomes better able to cope, or more resigned.

It may also be that the hustle of being addicted just becomes too much of a grind, and addicts stop using drugs for the simple reason that they get tired. Consider the plight of an addict with a $150-a-day habit. Seven days a week, 365 days a year, he or she must come up with $150 in addition to normal living expenses, find a dealer, and take the time to shoot up three to four times a day.

Many addicts turn to theft or burglary, but still have to dispose of the goods. A fence, or dealer in stolen goods, rarely gives more than ten cents on the dollar, so the addict has to steal more than $1,000 worth of merchandise *every day*. No wonder most addicts are in their twenties and few in their forties.

Boy George has been arrested for heroin possession.

The "New" Addict

Most heroin addicts in the United States inject their drug intravenously, despite the numerous disadvantages of this method. The reasons range from the low potency of most street heroin to the fact that injection is the "style" in the same way that smoking marijuana or freebase has its own ritual. Recently, there has been a trend toward snorting heroin seen in several parts of the country where heroin use is common (AIDS Research, 1990; French & Safford, 1989).

Whether this shift from injecting heroin to snorting it is a result of a fear of AIDS, the increased purity of heroin, a general fear of needles, or some other factors is not clear, but some drug professionals feel that such a switch might be useful in reducing the prevalence of AIDS in the drug-using population. Ideally, of course, no one would use any of these drugs, let alone become addicted, but reality indicates that some people will continue to use narcotics and reason requires that something be done to minimize the harm they will do to themselves (Casriel, Des Jarlais, Rodriquez, Friedman, Stepherson, & Khuri, 1990).

AIDS, hepatitis, and other blood related diseases cannot be transmitted by snorting, but sniffing heroin has its own drawbacks, primarily destruction of nasal tissue. Furthermore, the combination of higher purity of heroin and a less dangerous method of administration may result in increased addiction by those who are deterred at the thought of giving themselves an injection. When heroin purity declines, as history indicates it will, these sniffers may be led to injection. Similarly, those who become addicted by sniffing may turn to injecting when their nasal passages become infected.

Despite these problems, expect to see increasing reports of sniffing heroin or perhaps even smoking it. In a few areas of the United States, **"chasing the dragon"** is already known. This phrase refers to smoking or sniffing heroin after smoking crack (Kramer, Fine, Bahari, & Ottomanelli, 1990). The ingenuity of drug users in pursuing easy euphoria seems to know

Opium Smoking Returns?

Opium smoking was widespread among the Chinese immigrants to the United States. Many parts of the country are experiencing a new wave of immigration from other parts of Asia. Laotian, Cambodian, and to a lesser extent, Vietnamese, refugees are entering this country in unprecedented numbers. In 1988, approximately 250,000 came to America, bringing with them their families, religions, and customs, including opium smoking.

In recent years, postal and U.S. Customs Service authorities have confiscated tons of opium being smuggled into the United States. While this opium has primarily been intended for Asian immigrants, other drug users who have become accustomed to smoking crack, marijuana, or even cigarettes, could become the next customers for smoking opium. Will the 1990s see a resurgence of opium smoking? Reports indicate the U.S. Department of Justice has stepped up its attempts to interdict the supply of opium reaching America perhaps with this possibility in mind.

no bounds and further argues against the possibility that we or any society will ever be without either drug use or drug abuse.

DESIGNER DRUGS

Fentanyl (Sublimaze) is one of the most useful anesthetic drugs ever developed. It is 100 times as potent as morphine and is very short-acting (about thirty to sixty minutes). Like morphine and heroin, it is highly addictive and produces euphoria. The trade name of fentanyl is Sublimaze, and it is widely used in surgery in the United States. The molecular structure of fentanyl is quite complicated, and there are a large number of compounds similar in structure that may also have similar effects.

Abuse of fentanyl by medical personnel is not unknown and some does reach the street, but a greater danger is the development of analogs—drugs similar in structure and effect but different enough so that they do not fall into the same legal category as fentanyl. In order to make possession of a drug illegal, that illegal drug must be so defined by law. Designer drugs are analogs of either fentanyl or Demerol (meperidine), a synthetic morphine derivative.

Known on the street by various names, including China White, these designer drugs are extremely dangerous. One of them, 3-methyl-fentanyl, is 3,000 times as potent as morphine so the possibility of an overdose is enormous. The addict used to injecting a bag of heroin containing 5 mg of heroin (which is approximately ten times as potent as morphine) would only have to inject about 15 micrograms of 3-methyl-fentanyl, an amount so small as to be virtually invisible.

The designer drugs based on meperidine are equally dangerous. One of them, which will be called **MPPP** because its chemical name is quite long, is easy to manufacture but is potentially very toxic. Following improper procedures in the manufacture of MPPP leads to the synthesis of **MPTP,** a drug which destroys the neurons in the substantia nigra, a portion of the brain which is involved in the control of muscle movement (see figure 9.1).

Users who accidentally inject MPTP develop muscular rigidity and a condition that is very similar to Parkinson's disease, a crippling condition that mainly affects the elderly. Since neurons in the brain, once destroyed, normally do not regenerate, the damage caused by injection of MPTP is permanent. The normal treatment for Parkinson's disease can reduce but does not eliminate the user's symptoms. Ironically, the discovery that this drug produced symptoms similar to Parkinson's disease revitalized research on this disease.

Given the fact that heroin is widely available, why develop designer drugs? The answer is simple: economics. According to one estimate, a $2,000 investment in glassware and chemicals could produce two *billion* dollars worth of 3-methyl-fentanyl (that was no misprint: two billion dollars) (Baum, 1985).

To make matters more intriguing, there is considerable reason to believe that the discovery of 3-methyl-fentanyl, and perhaps MPPP, was made by one scientist who may have made enough so that he or she could retire fabulously wealthy (Baum, 1985). The rationale for this belief lies in the fact the synthesis of such a drug is so complicated that it could have been accomplished only by someone who set out to do just that.

As preposterous as it may seem, there are drug abuse experts who believe that somewhere in the world there is a person with a suitcase containing a few hundred grams of various powders. Whenever he or she is in need of a hundred thousand dollars or so, out comes the suitcase, the proper contacts are made, and more China White appears on the scene. If you like to deal in intriguing speculation, consider this—perhaps there are drugs more powerful even than 3-methyl-fentanyl.

NARCOTICS AND AIDS

Acquired Immune Deficiency Syndrome (AIDS) is the bubonic plague of the last twenty years of the twentieth century. In most parts of the United States, AIDS has hit hardest among homosexuals, with intravenous drug users being the second highest at-risk population. In Europe and in New York, the intravenous drug-using population is at greatest risk. In Africa, the heterosexual population is at greatest risk and there is considerable evidence that AIDS is spreading to the heterosexual population in the United States as well, since most intravenous drug users are heterosexual. Education has made inroads on the gay population in America but has been less successful with addicts.

AIDS is not easy to acquire. The surest way is through the exchange of infected blood. One characteristic of heroin addicts and intravenous cocaine users is that they share needles, making them a population at extraordinary

FIGURE 9.1
The diagram shows some common opoids. There are many more, both natural and synthetic. The shaded boxes indicate the drugs that have for various reasons, the highest abuse potential.

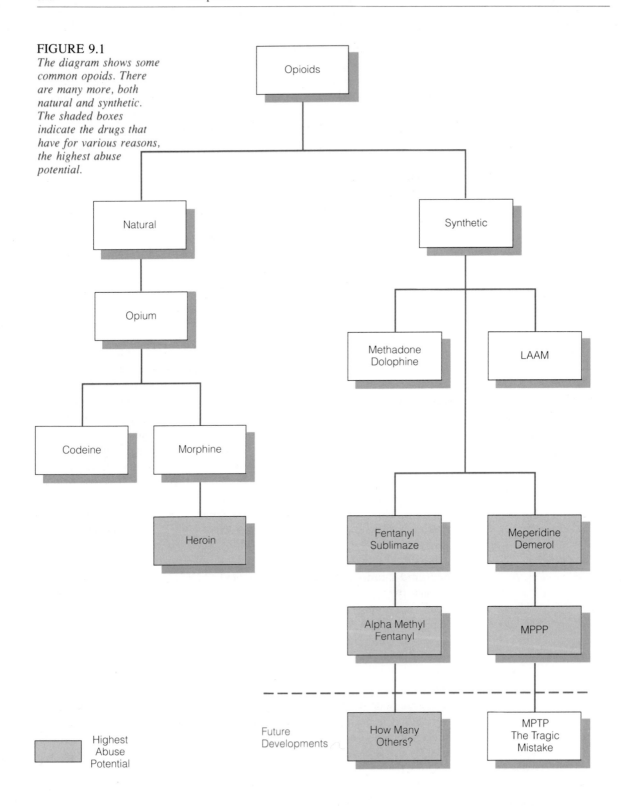

risk. It would seem to be a simple measure to reduce the risk of infection—make sure that addicts use clean needles. Reality is, as always, far from simple, however.

The attitudes of narcotics addicts make any such simple solution extremely difficult to employ. Many addicts do not believe that AIDS is a risk for them, and others have a fatalistic attitude that results from the nature of their addiction. Since they must work very hard simply to assure themselves of tomorrow's supply of heroin, they are unlikely to be impressed by authorities who tell them they have a good chance of dying several years hence.

A growing number of health professionals in the United States have proposed supplying addicts with free hypodermic syringes. An even more popular idea is needle exchange, where clean needles can be obtained by bringing in used ones. The federal government has been strongly opposed to this measure contending that it is ineffective; they believe that habits are so ingrained that addicts would still share needles, and free access to them would give many a false sense of security. The ready availability of hypodermics might also encourage non-addicted people to experiment.

In Europe, most countries that have adopted needle exchanges have found them effective, especially when the needle exchange is accompanied by a methadone program and an extensive public information campaign (The Journal, 1988). Authorities in Switzerland, Denmark, Holland, and other countries that have instituted such programs feel that they have helped slow the spread of this disease. San Francisco, New York, and some other metropolitan areas are beginning to explore such exchanges and many individuals have risked arrest to distribute these needles as a way of establishing a test case.

The cost of hospitalization and treatment of each AIDS patient in his or her final months can reach several hundred thousands of dollars and the number of potential victims vastly exceeds the available beds. What is going to happen in the next few years is anyone's guess, but AIDS is going to have a major economic impact on society, and any program which proves effective in reducing AIDS transmission must, at least, be considered.

The AIDS epidemic has also increased the pressure to provide more methadone programs. As you will read in chapter 13, some people oppose methadone treatment because it supposedly subsititutes one form of addiction for another. The AIDS epidemic has, to some degree, made this argument moot since if addicts continue to shoot up heroin, they will almost surely eventually contract AIDS. Methadone is not injected and thus reduces the transmission of this disease. Whether methadone is the ideal treatment, it is an essential part of the overall strategy to fight AIDS (Cooper, 1989; Dole, 1989).

SUMMARY

The opiates are among the most useful of all drugs. Without morphine, Demerol, codeine, and other drugs, many surgical procedures would be unbearable and the suffering of humankind immense. Interestingly, evidence suggests that opiates relieve the emotional aspect of suffering as much as they do the actual pain.

These posters, in Spanish and English, are based on a secondary prevention model. If users do not protect themselves, then their loved ones must take precautions. Elements of peer pressure are also obvious.

El no dejó de inyectarse drogas... por eso lo dejé.

No sé si compartió con otros las agujas. Solo sé que se inyectaba, y eso es peligroso. Creo que yo no le importaba tanto como para dejar las drogas. El sabía que los dos podíamos adquirir el SIDA, y le rogué que no lo hiciera. Hasta le pedí que buscara consejo y tratamiento contra las drogas. Yo hice todo lo posible, pero él no me hizo caso. Por eso . . . lo dejé.

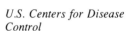

AMERICA
RESPONDE
AL SIDA

1-800-344-SIDA
1-800-344-7432

Este ha sido un mensaje del Centro para el Control
de las Enfermedades de los Estados Unidos

U.S. Centers for Disease Control

He wouldn't give up shooting up... so I gave him up.

I don't know if he shared needles. All I know is that he shot up. That's bad enough. And he didn't care enough about me to stop. He knew we could both get AIDS, and I begged him to stop. I even asked him to get some counseling and drug treatment. I did all I could, but he just wouldn't listen. So I left.

AMERICA RESPONDS TO AIDS

1-800-344-SIDA
1-800-344-7432

This has been a message from the
U.S. Centers for Disease Control

Opiate addiction has been a serious problem for centuries. It was partly responsible for several wars, played a role in the opening of feudal China to trade, affected a substantial portion of middle-class America in the eighteenth century, and now threatens serious economic hardship upon our health care system.

Addiction to heroin is the most prevalent opiate addiction in the United States and takes many forms. Many of the "facts" that the average person believes about heroin addiction are not true, and this misinformation has hindered attempts to help addicts. It may very well be that the majority of present heroin users are not even addicted to the drug.

The spread of AIDS is linked to intravenous drug use, and the concern about this disease has lead some authorities to suggest and even implement programs such as free needle exchange that would have been unheard of only a few years ago.

REFERENCES

AIDS Research (1990 Spring). New Jersey IV drug users' shift to snorting heroin may be linked to fear of AIDS. p. 19.

Basbaum, A., & Fields, H. (1979). The origin of descending pathways in the dorsolateral funiculus of the spinal cord of the cat and rat: Further studies on the anatomy of pain modulation. *Journal of Comparative Neurology, 187,* 513–22.

Baum, R. M. (1985). New variety of street drugs poses growing problem. *Chemical and Engineering News, 9 September,* 7–16.

Beecher, H. D. (1946). Pain in men wounded in battle. *Annals of Surgery, 123,* 96-105.

Brecher, E. M. (1972). *Licit and illicit drugs.* Boston: Little, Brown.

Casriel, C., Des Jarlais, D., Rodriguez, R., Friedman, S., Stepherson, B., & Khuri, E. (1990). Working with heroin sniffers: Clinical issues in preventing drug injection. *Journal of Substance Abuse Treatment, 7,* 1–10.

Cooper, J. R. (1989). Methadone maintenance and acquired immunodeficiency syndrome. *Journal of the American Medical Association, 262,* 1664–68.

Courtwright, D. T., (1982). *Dark paradise: Opiate addiction in America before 1900.* Cambridge, MA: Harvard University Press.

Cox, T. C., Jacobs, M. R., Leblanc, A. E., & Marshman, J. A. (1983). *Drugs and drug abuse.* Toronto: Addiction Research Foundation.

Drabble, M., (1985). *The Oxford companion to English literature.* Oxford and New York: Oxford University Press.

Hoffman, J. P. (1990). The historical shift in the perception of opiates: From medicine to social menace. *Journal of Psychoactive Drugs, 22,* 53–61.

Jaffe, J. H. and Martin, W. R. (1975). Narcotic analgesics and antagonists in L. S. Goodman, and A. Gilman. *The Pharmacological Basis of Therapeutics, fifth edition,* pp. 245–83.

Kramer, T. H., Fine, J., Bahari, B., & Ottomanelli, G. (1990). Chasing the dragon: The smoking of heroin and cocaine. *Journal of Substance Abuse Treatment, 7,* 65.

Musto, D. F. (1987). *The American disease: Origins of narcotic control.* Oxford and New York: Oxford University Press.

Owen, D. E. (1968). *British opium policy in China and India.* Hamden, CT: Archon Books.

Pasternak, G. W. (1988). Multiple morphine and enkephalin receptors and the relief of pain. *Journal of the American Medical Association, 259,* 1362–67.

Platt, J. J. (1986). *Heroin addiction: Theory, research and treatment.* Malabar, FL: Krieger.

Price, D. D. & Dubner, R. (1977). Neurons that subserve the sensory discriminative aspects of pain. *Pain, 3,* 307–28.

Richardson, D. E., & Akil, H. (1977). Pain reduction by electrical brain stimulation in man. *Journal of Neurosurgery, 47,* 178–83.

Robins, L. N., Helzer, J. E., Hesselbrock, M., & Wish, E. (1979). Vietnam veterans three years after Vietnam. In L. Brill & C. Winick (Eds.). *Yearbook of substance abuse,* New York: Human Services Press.

Rosenbaum, B. J. (1971). Heroin: Influence of the method of use. *New England Journal of Medicine, 285,* 299–300.

Scott, J. M. (1969). *The white poppy: A history of opium.* New York: Funk & Wagnalls.

Siegel, S. (1986). Alcohol and opiate dependence: Reevaluation of the Victorian perspective. In H. D. Cappell, F. B. Blaser, Y. Israel, H. Kalant, W. Schmidt, E. M. Sellers, & R. C. Smart (Eds.), pp. 279–306. *Research advances in alcohol and drug problems: Volume 9.* New York: Plenum Press.

Ternes, J. W., & O'Brien, C. P. (1990). The opioids: Abuse liability and treatments for dependence. *Advances in Alcohol and Substance Abuse, 9,* 27–45.

Zinberg, N. E. (1972). Heroin use in Vietnam and the United States: A contrast and critique. *Archives of General Psychiatry, 26,* 486–88.

Zinberg, N. E. (1984). *Drug, set and setting.* New Haven and London: Yale University Press.

Zinberg, N. E., & Jacobson, R. C. (1976). The natural history of chipping. *American Journal of Psychiatry, 133,* 37–40.

10

•••

THE LEGAL DRUGS I: OVER-THE-COUNTER MEDICATION

•••

OBJECTIVES

When you have finished studying this chapter you should:

1. Know how over-the-counter (OTC) and prescription drugs came to be.
2. Recognize the categories of OTC drugs.
3. Be able to differentiate the three types of aspirin-like drugs.
4. Know why acetominophen and ibuprofen are not necessarily safer or more effective than aspirin.
5. Know how aspirin relieves pain.
6. Know the difference between cold remedies and antihistamines.
7. Know how antacids work.
8. Be able to decide for yourself if you should take vitamins.
9. Know how "sedatives" work and if you should take them.
10. Know what OTOC stimulants are.
11. Understand the relationship between amphetamines and the OTC appetite suppressants.

KEY TERMS

acetominophen
acetylsalicylic acid
analgesics
antacids
antihistamines
antioxidant
antitussives
beta carotene
broncodilators
decongestants
diet aids
enteric coating
expectorant
Food, Drug, and Cosmetic Act of 1938
Food and Drug Act of 1902
generics
Harrison Narcotic Act of 1914
ibuprofen
OTCs
patent medicines
phenylpropanolamine
prostaglandin
Retin-A
Reye's syndrome
sedatives
stimulants
Tretinoin
vitamins

W hile the main focus of this book is on drugs taken for their psychoactive properties, over-the-counter and prescription drugs also must be considered, since many of these drugs have psychoactive effects. Furthermore, our attitude toward these drugs and the role they play in society help us to understand our fascination with other drugs. Taking drugs is a deeply ingrained part of our culture. When we grow up believing that every ailment, major or minor, can be "cured" with some drug, it is not difficult to see why we turn to them for other purposes as well.

THE HISTORY OF THE LEGAL DRUGS

As we have seen in several contexts in previous chapters, the use of medicine for most of recorded history was based more on magic and wishful thinking than on scientific knowledge. Along with the few useful substances, such as opium, there were a vast number that were either useless or downright harmful. This situation prevailed almost until the beginning of the twentieth century.

Only a little more than 100 years ago, Oliver Wendell Holmes, whom we met in Chapter 1, could facetiously, but correctly, claim that if "the whole materia medica, as now used, could be sunk to the bottom of the sea, it would be all the better for mankind—and all the worse for the fishes" (Morgan, 1981). The phrase "materia medica" refers to the drugs and other substances used in treating illness.

Until the twentieth century in the United States, the vast majority of people lived on farms or in small towns where medical doctors were rare. Doctors in these areas were often poorly trained and less well equipped. Medical treatment, such as it was, was often prescribed by a trusted friend, a family member, or a druggist. Hospitals were even rarer, and no one who could help it ever went to them, except to die.

At that time, there were no distinctions between over-the-counter and prescription medicines, and once a patient saw a doctor and obtained a prescription, he/she owned it and could refill it at will. Druggists were as free to prescribe medicine as doctors and the former was often in competition with the latter. The doctor was also free to sell medicine, and in rural areas he often was a traveling pharmacy.

To further confuse the issue, remedies could be purchased through the mail and were widely advertised in magazines. Most of the **patent medicines,** as they were called, were useless, and those that did provide some relief did so because, as we saw in Chapter 9, they contained opium and alcohol.

By the end of the nineteenth and beginning of the twentieth century, several factors combined to alter the public view of medicine and drugs. The temperance movement drew attention to the problems of alcohol abuse, and

JULY 30, 1898.   HARPER'S

NEVER HAS ANYTHING BEEN SO HIGHLY AND SO JUSTLY PRAISED AS

VIN MARIANI

MARIANI WINE, the FAMOUS TONIC for BODY, NERVES and BRAIN.

GEN. SIR EVELYN WOOD Says:

"Regarding the infantry marching in the recent manœuvres, it was the best seen during my command at Aldershot. Many officers availed themselves of the tonic and reconstituent properties of the well-known Mariani Wine, the most certain as well as the most palatable method of inducing resistance to fatigue."
From "The London Sketch."

MAX O'RELL,
The Renowned Writer and Lecturer, Writes:

Your Vin Mariani is positively marvellous; one glass put me on my feet; one bottle made a new man of me.
Yours gratefully,   **MAX O'RELL.**

ALL DRUGGISTS.

MARIANI WINE is invaluable at this season of the year, when, owing to trying climatic conditions, the system is especially susceptible to attacks of debility and prostration.

VIN MARIANI (MARIANI WINE) has stood the test of thirty = five years' trial. It has written endorse= ments from more than 8000 Amer= ican physicians, in addition to having received cordial recommendations from royalty, princes of the Church and of the State, and many notable personages.

MARIANI WINE is a tonic pre= pared upon careful scientific princi= ples. It contains absolutely no in= jurious properties. It gives power to the brain, strength to the entire nervous system, firmness and elas= ticity to the muscles, and richness to the blood. It has been aptly de= scribed as a promoter of good health and longevity.

MARIANI WINE is specially indi= cated for General Debility, Weakness from whatever causes, Overwork, Profound Depression and Exhaus= tion, Throat and Lung Diseases, Consumption, Malaria and La Grippe.

MARIANI WINE is an adjuvant in convalescence and a powerful reju= venator. For Overworked Men, Del= icate Women, Sickly Children it Works Wonders. Taken with cracked ice, it relieves Summer Prostration quickly and effectually. It soothes, strengthens and sustains the system.

To those who will kindly write to MARIANI & CO., 52 West 15th Street, New York City, will be sent, free, book containing portraits with endorsements of Emperors, Empress, Princes, Cardinals, Archbishops, and other interesting matter.

AVOID SUBSTITUTIONS.

PARIS: 41 Boulevard Haussman.   LONDON: 83 Mortimer Street.   MONTREAL: 28-30 Hospital Street.

the addictive nature of the opiates was realized. Doctors and druggists became better organized and better educated, while science could now offer cures for some disorders instead of symptomatic relief.

As a consequence, public opinion began to turn against patent medicines. For a long time, few physicians and fewer laymen realized that morphine and opium were addictive. Patients taking large doses of opiates interpreted the withdrawal symptoms they developed as another disease, which was effectively treated with more opium or morphine. Infants and babies given these medicines often became addicted to opiates, and one wonders how many adult addictions had their start in the nursery.

With the discovery of the nature of addiction, the praise once heaped on combinations of alcohol and opium turned to scorn. One prominent doctor is quoted in 1882 as saying, "There is a triad of infant murderers, and their names are Godfrey's Cordial, Paregoric, and Mrs. Winslow's Soothing Syrup" (Morgan, 1981). Godfrey's Cordial, Paregoric (which is still available), and Mrs. Winslow's Soothing Syrup were popular remedies for sedating children and contained varying amounts of alcohol and opium.

As doctors and druggists became more professional and as their education increased, prescriptions became more common and drugs became more uniform in quality and preparation. The **Harrison Narcotic Act of 1914** required that druggists and doctors keep records of their prescription writing. Gradually, during this time, our present system evolved. We now have two categories of drugs, those for which a prescription is not needed (over-the-counter) and those for which a prescription is required.

Occasionally, prescription drugs can move into the nonprescription market. Cases in point include diphenhydramine (Dramamine) and ibuprofen (Advil, others), both of which were originally available only by prescription but are now OTC drugs. Rarely do drugs move in the opposite direction, although codeine-based cough medicines formerly were far more widely available. Now many states require either recordkeeping or a prescription.

OVER-THE-COUNTER DRUGS (OTCs)

The over-the-counter drug market is enormous. Americans spend $7 billion annually on nonprescription drugs, many of which have no effect on the conditions for which they are taken. Vitamins are a good example. It has been said that Americans have the most expensive urine in the world. Many people take unnecessarily large amounts of vitamins, most of which are water soluble and promptly excreted; some estimates indicate that we spend more than $3 billion a year on these substances alone (Ratto, 1987). On the other hand, as you will read later, some advocates claim that at least some vitamins *can* have health benefits.

Until the **Food and Drug Act of 1902,** there were no restrictions on medications sold in the United States. The Food and Drug Act required that food and drugs be labeled properly and not misbranded. It was this law that resulted in the cocaine being removed from Coca-Cola. The company never acknowledged that cocaine was actually present in its drink, but did agree to change the formula.

The **Food, Drug, and Cosmetic Act of 1938,** required that *new* drugs also be safe as well as properly labeled. This law led to the widespread testing of animals for possible harmful effects of drugs and cosmetics. The cosmetic industry recently has come under considerable criticism for its alleged cruelty to animals in these screening tests. The companies reply that they are meeting the requirements of federal law.

Somewhat surprisingly, it was not until 1962 that the Kefauver–Harris amendment to the FDC Act required that OTC drugs be proved to be effective. And this requirement applied only to *new* drugs. The thousands of drugs already on the market could be sold and advertised as usual until they were tested. This testing did not begin until 1972, and only recently was completed.

The U.S. Food and Drug Administration (FDA) has three categories of over-the-counter drugs. Category I consists of drugs that are generally recognized as safe, effective, and properly labeled. Category II drugs are those that are not generally recognized as safe or effective, or that are mislabeled. Note that a drug does not have to be harmful to be placed in this category. A safe, but ineffective drug, could also wind up in Category II. Category III is the catchall category for all drugs for which there is insufficient evidence to decide if they are safe and effective. Presumably, drugs in this category will be reclassified when sufficient data are available.

Suppose I am a manufacturer of a profitable drug that has been tested and placed in Category II or III. Do I have to take it off the market? Not necessarily. If I am willing to spend the money, I can challenge the decision of the FDA in a formal hearing or in court. As long as the case is being decided, I can still market my product. As anyone who has ever been in a court case knows, this process can take years.

There are hundreds of different brand names of OTC medications. The vast majority of these are various combinations of a relatively few drugs. The FDA has established twenty-six different categories for OTC drugs, including anti-nailbiting compounds, toothpastes, dandruff products, and hemorrhoid compounds. Only a few of the categories need to be discussed in detail, although a brief description of each may be found in Table 10.1.

Analgesics

Aspirin is one of the true wonder drugs. Because it is so common and can be purchased over the counter, many people fail to realize how valuable it is. Aspirin has three extremely valuable properties: It is effective against some kinds of low-to-moderate levels of pain, it reduces inflammation, and it decreases fever. It also has a wide safety margin, rarely causes an allergic reaction, and is generally well tolerated. Aspirin is not, however, totally safe, and improperly used can be quite dangerous.

The active substance in aspirin is **acetylsalicylic acid.** A similar substance is found in willow bark, which has been used for centuries to reduce

Table 10.1 The Over-the-Counter Drugs (OTCs)

Classification	Purpose	Example
Antacids	Treat "acid indigestion," stomach acidity	Maalox, Alka-Seltzer
Antidiarrheals	Treat diarrhea	Kaopectate, Pepto-Bismol
Laxatives	Treat constipation	Ex-Lax, Correctol
Emetics	Induce vomiting	Ipecac
Antiemetics	Prevent vomiting and treat motion or sea sickness	Dramamine
Antiperspirants	Reduce perspiration	Arrid
Sunburn prevention and treatment products	Reduce sunburn and treat pain of sunburn	Coppertone, Ban-de-Soleil
Vitamin/Mineral products	Supplement diet with necessary vitamins and minerals	One-a-Day
Antimicrobial products	Treat superficial wounds. Must be applied to the surface of the skin.	Tinactin, Mycitracin, Anbesol
Dandruff products	Treat dandruff	Head and Shoulders, Tegrin
Oral hygiene aids	Treat sore throat, bad breath; reduce bacteria in the mouth	Listerine, Micrin
Hemorrhoidal products	Treat hemorroids, other rectal problems	Preparation H, Anusol
Hematinics	Increase hemoglobin count, treat anemia	Geritol, Femiron
Bronchodilator and antiasthmatic products	Dilate bronchial tubes	Sudafed, Primatene
Analgesics	Relieve minor pain	Bayer, Advil, Tylenol
Sedatives and sleep aids	Reduce sleep onset	Sominex
Stimulants	Increase mental alertness	NoDoz, Vivarin
Antitussives	Reduce coughing	Benadryl, Triaminicol
Allergy treatment products	Reduce symptoms of allergies, sneezing, watery nose and eyes	Contact, Dristan
Cold remedies	Relieve cold symptoms	Nyquil, Dristan
Antirheumatic products	Treat rheumatoid arthritis symptoms	Bufferin, Advil
Opthalmic products	Reduce eye irritations	Murine
Contraceptive products	Prevent pregnancy	Trojans
Miscellaneous dermatological products	Treat skin disorders	Clearasil, Stridex, Rhuli-gel
Dentrifrices and dental products	Clean, brighten teeth, relieve toothaches, reduce teething pain	Colgate, Orajel
Miscellaneous OTC products	Everything else not mentioned above. Appetite suppressants, diuretics, and other minor medications	Ayds, Dexatrim, Acutrim Doan's, Aquaban, Diurex

fever and pain (Stanitski, 1987). Aspirin was first introduced into medicine in 1899 and was probably developed as a substitute for quinine (Flower, Moncada, & Vane, 1980). Quinine, known in the nineteenthth century as

Peruvian or Jesuit's bark, was used to reduce fevers. It was so effective that it became rare, and hence, expensive.

The Effects of Aspirin   We saw in chapter 9 on narcotics that there are two separate pathways for pain. There are also two different subjective experiences of pain, a sharp insistent pain that you feel when you hit your thumb with a hammer, for example, and the dull throb that follows it. Aspirin is far more effective against the latter and is therefore widely used in post-operative recovery, for muscle aches, and for arthritis. It is not effective against pain not associated with inflammation. For example, two aspirin will not reduce the pain felt while a tooth is being extracted, but will help with the ache afterwards.

The effectiveness of aspirin in alleviating the symptoms of arthritis is partly the result of the reduction of pain and partly the result of aspirin's anti-inflammatory properties. Aspirin is particularly useful in rheumatoid arthritis, provided high doses are taken in order to maintain a high level of aspirin in the bloodstream.

Aspirin also reduces fever, and the effect is quite rapid. Aspirin, in fact, is one of the best antipyretic (fever-reducing) drugs known. Reducing fever, incidentally, may not always be desirable, since many bacteria and quite a few viruses are killed by temperatures only slightly above normal body temperature.

Another condition that aspirin apparently helps is migraine. Anyone who has ever suffered from a migraine knows that the pain can be excruciating. While aspirin may not relieve the pain, there is evidence that it may reduce the number of migraine attacks that occur by 20 percent (Buring, Peto, & Hennekens, 1990). The way in which aspirin prevents migraine is not clear, but may be related to its tendency to slow blood clotting.

How does such a miracle drug work? The way in which aspirin reduces inflammation and fever has been known for some time, but despite the fact that aspirin has been around since the beginning of the twentieth century, its mode of action in relieving pain was not really understood until about ten years ago when the importance of substances called prostaglandins was first appreciated.

Even today, **prostaglandins** are still somewhat of a mystery, despite many years of research on them. For our purposes, we need to know that they are chemicals that are synthesized by virtually every cell and are released when the cell is damaged. Among many other functions, they increase inflammation, and affect the temperature-regulating function of the hypothalamus (see chapter 3). Aspirin blocks the synthesis of the prostaglandins, thus reducing fever and inflammation (Flower, Moncada, & Vane, 1980).

The prostaglandins also have an effect on pain. When injected in very high doses, they cause pain and headache. They probably do not exert their effect directly, since such high levels of prostaglandins are rarely seen except as a result of injection. At lower levels they seem to sensitize the pain receptors, so that these receptors will fire when stimulated at levels that would not normally trigger a response (Yaksh, 1982).

One way to understand this effect of prostaglandins is to recall the last time you had a bruise or swelling. Merely touching the area caused pain, while touching a nearby area with the same force had no such effect. This condition is called hyperalgesia. Apparently the release of prostaglandins sensitizes the normal pain receptors in the injured area. Aspirin, because it inhibits the production of prostaglandin, reduces the pain associated with inflammation, then, but does so indirectly. The sharp pain caused by direct stimulation of the pain receptors is better relieved by the opiates and by cocaine applied locally.

Side Effects of Aspirin

Although it is usually considered to be safe, aspirin is not without side effects. The most common problem is stomach upset and blood loss. Nausea, vomiting, and other gastrointestinal problems occur in many people, and the irritating effect of **acetylsalicylic acid** on the stomach lining can cause a sufficient amount of blood loss to produce iron deficiency anemia. Aspirin can aggravate peptic ulcers and even cause hemorrhage.

In one study, four to five grams of aspirin a day (about fifteen tablets) for a month caused up to 8 ml of blood loss a day, a significant amount (Leonards & Levy, 1973). While fifteen aspirin tablets may seem like a lot, the dosage is not uncommon for arthritis sufferers. For the occasional user, of course, the blood loss is much smaller, and hence not particularly important. It could, however, make a difference under certain circumstances.

Many aspirin products supposedly protect against such stomach upset. There is little evidence that the addition of a buffering solution will do much to help reduce gastrointestinal distress (Stanitski, 1987). Furthermore, to the extent that the buffering solution causes the urine to become more alkaline, it may increase the rate at which aspirin is excreted and thus shorten its half-life (Flower, Moncada, & Vane, 1980).

Some brands of aspirin have an **enteric coating** that supposedly protects against gastrointestinal problems by preventing the aspirin from being absorbed until it reaches the small intestine. While there is some evidence that this coating does reduce the damage caused to the stomach lining, there also is evidence that the enteric tablets are less well absorbed (Thiessen, 1982; McDonald, 1982). Timed-release capsules, another well publicized "advance," are not any more effective than plain aspirin, since aspirin has a long period of action in the body.

There Is Aspirin and Then There Is Aspirin

Despite what advertisers spend millions of dollars telling us, for the relief of minor pain such as that of headache or muscular aches, all of the various brands of aspirin are identical. So your best bet is to buy the cheapest. The difference in price can be quite substantial. In 1991, in one store in California, for example, you could purchase 500 of the store brand of aspirin for $3.59 (.7 cents per aspirin) or pay $3.21 for 30 (10.7 cents per aspirin) of a famous name brand!

You can be sure you are getting a safe, effective product, regardless of the price, because the FDA goes to great lengths to ensure that all drugs are labeled accurately and are identical in quality. Those pills sold under the label "aspirin" are called **generics.** As we shall see in chapter 11, generics are a controversial issue in the pharmaceutical industry.

If you have problems taking aspirin, you should always take them with a full glass of water, or even better, milk. Food also helps reduce gastrointestinal symptoms, but may interfere with absorption. You have probably seen many people take two aspirin and wash them down with just a sip of water. They are basically wasting their time and money and are possibly giving themselves a stomachache. Aspirin dissolves poorly in water, so the pills end up unchanged in the stomach and intestine where they can cause severe distress.

Aspirin also prolongs bleeding time. Two aspirin approximately doubles bleeding time for four to seven days. While this is not a serious problem for most people, those undergoing surgery probably should stop taking aspirin at least one week before surgery. Hemophiliacs and those with other bleeding problems probably also should avoid aspirin.

Since aspirin is so widely used, and for every possible reason, many people fail to realize that it can be fatal. Aspirin toxicity results in ringing in the ears, headache, sweating, thirst, hyperventilation, and other unpleasant symptoms. Death has been reported after ingestion of as little as forty aspirin, although one person is reported to have taken 450 and survived (Flower, Moncado, & Vane, 1980).

According to the Drug Abuse Warning Network (DAWN), which monitors 744 hospital emergency rooms and seventy-five medical examiners' offices nationwide, aspirin was the eighth most common drug mentioned in emergency room cases of overdose, and was responsible for at least 115 deaths in 1989.

As of 1988, all products containing aspirin must contain the following statement: "WARNING: Children and teenagers should not take this medicine for chicken pox or flu symptoms before a doctor is consulted about Reye's syndrome, a rare but serious illness." This warning must precede all other warnings and cautions. The FDA made this requirement as a result of a large scale study showing that there was a correlation between the use of aspirin and the development of Reye's syndrome.

Reye's syndrome can result in coma, brain damage, and death. Milder cases are characterized by vomiting and strange personality changes. Reye's syndrome is rare—fewer than 0.1 percent of children with flu or chicken pox who take aspirin will develop symptoms, and 90 percent of all cases occur in children under fifteen years of age. Furthermore, no one knows *how* aspirin is related to the condition. However, since virtually every person who was diagnosed with Reye's had taken aspirin, a strong statistical argument can be made.

Since the publicity about the relationship between Reye's and aspirin, both the use of acetylsalicylic acid in children with flu-like symptoms and the incidence of Reye's has declined substantially, furthering arguing for some causal link (Zamula, 1990). The number of cases of this syndrome is so small that you may wonder why the FTC went to all the trouble in the first place. The use of aspirin to treat fever with chicken pox or flu is not absolutely necessary. Not only is the fever relatively mild, but there are other ways of treating it (with acetaminophen or ibuprofen) that do not increase the risk of Reye's. Therefore there is no *need* to take the risk.

One other problem with aspirin mentioned in chapter 5 should be repeated here. Aspirin decreases the activity of gastric alcohol dehydrogenase when taken on a full stomach (Roine, Gentry, Hernandez-Munoz, Baraona, & Lieber, 1990). What this means is that taking two extra-strength aspirin before a meal and then ingesting alcohol can raise your BAl as much as 26 percent. Considering how many products contain aspirin this is an important finding to consider if you drink.

Substitutes for Aspirin

Given all these dire warnings, plus others not even mentioned, should we all switch to such non-aspirin pain relievers as Tylenol, Datril, or Advil? You would have to have lived in a hermetically-sealed container for the past ten years not to have heard of these drugs. Are they really any better than plain old acetylsalicylic acid? Advertisers spend millions of dollars to convince us we should, but the real evidence is mixed.

Of all the pain relievers sold over the counter, the one most likely to give aspirin a run for its money is **ibuprofen.** Originally marketed as a prescription drug, it is now available without a prescription under the names Advil, Nuprin, and others. It is also known as a *non-steroidal anti-inflammatory drug,* or NSAID for short. NSAIDs include aspirin (but *not* acetaminophen, discussed below), as well as indomethacin, phenylbutazone, naproen, and others. For reasons that are not entirely clear, NSAIDs have been linked to liver problems (Gay, 1990).

Ibuprofen has virtually the same antipyretic, analgesic, and anti-inflammatory properties as aspirin although it seems to be less upsetting to the stomach. If you are sensitive to the gastrointestinal effects of aspirin, ibuprofen may be better for you. On the other hand, it can produce gastrointestinal problems, including ulcers, and the danger is that the person taking it might take a greater number of tablets, and thus trigger the same effect as aspirin does.

Acetaminophen, a drug which is closely related to two others that have been around since the beginning of the twentieth century, phenacetin and acetanilide, rounds out the OTC analgesics. Acetanilide was sold as U-RE-KA Headache Powders, Telephone Headache Powders, and other names. It produced serious toxic side effects primarily involving the oxygen-carrying capacity of the red blood cells and was overtaken by aspirin.

In the 1940s and 1950s there was a pill whose name was nearly as famous as aspirin itself. APCs were a combination of aspirin, phenacetin, and caffeine and were prescribed for nearly every ailment. The Armed Forces of the United States bought enormous quantities of the drug and dispensed them (and a glass of water) with abandon. The use of APC declined when it was discovered that phenacetin could cause liver damage and sedation (which was why caffeine was also included in the combination).

Acetaminophen is the metabolic by-product of phenacetin and is the active ingredient in Tylenol and numerous other OTC drugs. According to the DAWN survey of 1986, it is the *seventh* most common drug mentioned in hospital emergency rooms, surpassing aspirin, and was responsible for twice as many deaths as aspirin. In high doses it can, like phenacetin, cause liver damage, especially in heavy drinkers. Most of the deaths caused by overdose of acetaminophen are the result of hepatic (liver) failure (Flower, Moncada, & Vane, 1982).

Because it is less likely to cause stomach upset, it has been advertised widely as a substitute for aspirin. However, acetaminophen is different than aspirin in that it is not an effective anti-inflammatory drug, so it does not relieve most of the symptoms of arthritis. Like aspirin, it does reduce fever, but it does not prolong bleeding time, suggesting that it is not an effective anticoagulant.

The available evidence is not absolutely clear, but some studies have linked acetaminophen to an increase in blood pressure, cardiovascular disease, and kidney problems. Keep in mind that acetaminophen is very similar to phenacetin, a product that is no longer available in the United States. In England, where it is still used, phenacetin use has been associated with an increased risk of high blood pressure, cardiovascular disease, and cancer and kidney disease (Dubach, Rosner, & Sturmer, 1991). At doses normally taken, acetaminophen is undoubtedly safe for almost everyone taking it, but under certain circumstances, it, like every drug, can cause problems.

If you aren't confused by now, take a look at some of the popular advertised brand name products and you will see that some contain both acetaminophen and aspirin. Many of them also contain caffeine. What is caffeine doing in a headache pill? The answer is no one knows. The FDA has not found that caffeine adds anything to aspirin, acetaminophen, or ibuprofen. Could it be there just as a little "pick me up"? Or could it be more sinister? Could some headaches be the result of caffeine withdrawal? If so, caffeine would relieve the headache—and continue the dependence.

If everyone has basically the same product that does the same job in the same way, why do different manufacturers spend so much money trying to convince you that their product is best? Does the fact that Americans spend more than $2 billion a year on nonprescription pain relievers alone give you a clue?

COLD REMEDIES

The term *cold remedies* is a misnomer, since there is no remedy for the common cold. The scientist who discovers the cure for the common cold will undoubtedly go down in history along with Pasteur, Lister, Salk, and other heroes of medicine, even though colds are self-limiting. Self-limiting means that colds will go away with or without treatment. The fact that most

Aspirin and Heart Attack

In January 1988, the *New England Journal of Medicine* published a special report on the effects of aspirin in preventing acute myocardial infarct (known to the layman as a heart attack). Although it was a preliminary report, it generated an enormous amount of interest and controversy. Within days, advertisements were broadcast advising people to take one aspirin every other day to help prevent heart attack. Shortly after that the Food and Drug Administration warned aspirin manufacturers that advertisements making such claims would be considered misleading and the manufacturers agreed to "voluntary restraint" on any further promotion. Since nearly everyone has heard of this study, it might be worthwhile to see what it *really* found.

The study was conducted on male physicians in the United States between forty and eighty-four years of age. After excluding those with existing heart conditions and other medical problems, as well as any who were currently taking aspirin or Vitamin A supplement, the researchers were left with 22,000 volunteers. Half took one aspirin every other day, the other half took a placebo. The physicians did not know which group they were in. After 4.8 years, those taking the aspirin had 47 percent fewer heart attacks than those taking the placebo. Another part of the study, to determine if beta carotene (discussed later in this chapter) can prevent cancer is ongoing, but the results of the aspirin study were so spectacular that an advisory group recommended stopping the research and putting the placebo half on aspirin.

Can you really decrease your risk of heart attack by half simply by taking one aspirin every other day? Consider these facts: The 22,000 were selected from an original volunteer group of 59,000 primarily because they *were* healthy to begin with. Statistically, there *should* have been 733 deaths in this group of 22,000, yet there were only 88 in *both* groups. Male doctors who volunteer for such a study are hardly representative of the population at large. A more interesting question might have been, why was the observed rate of heart attack so low in *both* groups? Second, the rate of death by stroke actually increased significantly, although the actual numbers were quite small. Third, a British study using even higher doses of aspirin taken daily showed no significant protection from heart attack.

Will aspirin reduce *your* risk of heart attack? If you are a male physician in good health, preferably health-conscious enough to volunteer for such a study, yes. What if you are an overweight, unhealthy college professor with a high cholesterol count? Or a black woman of childbearing years, or anyone else? The answer is less clear. Another matter of concern is the *increase* in strokes. Are you merely decreasing your risk of a common cardiovascular condition while increasing your risk of a less common one? No wonder the FDA was concerned about those advertisements.

diseases are self-limiting is what gave rise to most over-the-counter medicines in the first place. If you have an illness and take a pill, when the condition goes away you will likely give the pill the credit.

Cold remedies can relieve some of the symptoms of a cold, making the patient feel better, but some of the symptomatic relief may actually make matters worse in the long run. Nevertheless, Americans spend nearly $2 billion annually on a large number of different cold remedies usually without reading the names of the drugs listed on the side of the package and the bottle. If we did, we would realize that all of the cold remedies contain various combinations of the same drugs.

There are five types of drugs that make up all cold remedies: **antihistamines, antitussives, bronchodilators** (now rarely used in cold remedies), **decongestants,** and **expectorants.** In addition, some add aspirin, caffeine, or alcohol to enhance or counteract the effects of the basic five. Antihistamines and bronchodilators are effective for allergies or asthma, but don't relieve the symptoms of a cold. Expectorants don't really work, you don't always want antitussives to work, and bronchodilators can cause a rebound. What's a person to do?

Antihistamines

Antihistamines block the release of histamine, a substance released in the body when allergens are present. If you have an allergy and take antihistamines, they may relieve your symptoms, but colds are not caused by allergies and the antihistamines do not relieve congestion caused by a cold. In addition, they cause drowsiness, particularly when combined with alcohol and can actually make a cough less productive.

Nyquil is a good example of one type of cold remedy. A popular OTC drug combination, a tablespoon contains the equivalent of three standard acetominophen tablets, pseudoephedrine (a decongestant), dextromethorphan (a cough suppressant), and doxylamine succinate (an antihistamine) in a solution of 25 percent alcohol. The directions call for up to four one-ounce doses per day, taken six hours apart.

Doxylamine succinate is approximately as effective as secobarbital (a prescription barbiturate) in causing sleep onset. This potent sedative is combined with 50 proof alcohol, which we know from chapter 4 is also a potent sedative. A one-ounce dose (or shot) is the recommended dosage. Since alcohol and antihistamines are additive in their effects the combination should be quite effective in producing sleep.

No wonder Nyquil is advertised as the "Nighttime Cold Medicine"! The advertising on the labels reads: "Take at bedtime . . . relieves the major cold and flu-like symptoms to let you get the restful sleep your body needs," but neither the antihistamine nor the alcohol helps relieve cold symptoms. Combined, they will sure help you get to sleep, though.

Antitussives

Antitussives are substances that suppress coughing. Codeine (where legal) and dextromethorphan are the two most common antitussives. They work by affecting the central nervous system to raise the threshold of stimulation necessary to trigger the cough reflex. There are basically two types of coughs; productive and nonproductive. You do not want to suppress a productive cough, since it is caused by excess mucous secretions and foreign matter in the lower respiratory tract. Productive coughing thus actually improves respiration (Franklin, 1982).

From time to time, a fad crops up, typically in junior or senior high school, of consuming large quantities of a cough syrup which contains dextrometorphan, which can have narcotic-like effects in high doses. This "discovery" brings about the usual congressional hearing at the state or national level and then nothing is done, mainly because the fad passes and because drinking a whole bottle of cough medicine is not particularly pleasant. In addition, policing sales of such products would place a considerable burden on grocery stores, supermarkets, and drugstores. Imagine having to prove you were a certain age to buy a cough medicine.

Coughs can be unpleasant. In the case of a nonproductive cough, you might want to consider a cough suppressant, since this kind of cough can cause irritation to the throat. Of course, a sour hard candy will sooth your throat and stimulate saliva secretion much more inexpensively. Expectorants are substances that supposedly increase mucous secretion in the lower respiratory tract and thus make a cough productive. However, at the doses normally employed, expectorants such as terpin hydrate probably do not work. Incidentally, expectorants and antihistamines would be expected to counteract each other, so combining the two would be useless.

Decongestants

Decongestants such as pseudoephedrine or phenylpropanolamine really do work. They constrict the blood vessels in the nasal passages and increase air flow. They also can reduce the annoying release of secretions into the back of the throat (postnasal drip). However, decongestants also can cause a significant "rebound" when you stop taking them. The blood vessels expand again when the drug wears off and this expansion is often greater than it was originally. The "cure" is more decongestant, which then can cause more rebound. In a sense the nasal passages become addicted to the decongestant (Reif, 1986). **Phenylpropanolamine** is also the active ingredient in OTC appetite suppressants and sufficiently high doses can produce an amphetamine-like effect on the taker.

If these drugs are not really all that effective, why do we (and the author includes himself) continue to buy them? By now the word placebo should spring immediately to mind. Any time you take a drug you think will help you, the psychological boost you get from it will likely make you feel better. Since you can't cure a cold, feeling better is what it is all about anyway. But there is more to a cold remedy than a simple placebo effect.

Cold remedies do help a little. Judiciously used, decongestants can make us more comfortable and certainly more pleasant companions. Antitussives can reduce an annoying, hacking, cough. Many colds are accompanied by or confused for allergies, so antihistamines might be of some help; certainly, their sedative properties can be quite valuable. The aspirin or aspirin-like substances can reduce fever and relieve inflammation as well as help with the headache that often accompanies a cold. Even the alcohol, in moderation, might make you feel better.

The primary argument against most cold remedies is that they are a combination of products. A cold pill might contain up to eight different ingredients, many of which are not necessary, and some of which might be counterproductive. Also, the more drugs you take, the greater the possibility of developing an allergic reaction to one of them.

Is there any way to become an intelligent consumer of cold remedies or any other OTC drug? Perhaps the best thing to do is to buy a book like the *Physicians' Desk Reference for Nonprescription Drugs* and consult it regularly. When you have a cold, check to see which products have the ingredients that will help your particular combination of symptoms. Expensive is not always best, and a combination of a large number of drugs is rarely necessary. The cheapest, simplest product is probably as good or better for you than the most heavily advertised combination of products.

ANTACIDS

Many people are convinced that their stressful lifestyle and dietary habits give them "heartburn," "acid indigestion," and assorted other stomach problems. As a society we spend nearly a billion dollars a year on products like Alka-Seltzer, Tums, Maalox, and Mylanta. Do they work? Many must think so, since we spend so much money for them. Advertising for these products is quite effective and the potential market is tremendous, since almost half of us report having occasional attacks of stomach indigestion.

So-called acid indigestion is apparently caused by hydrochloric acid irritating the lining of the stomach. Normally, the stomach is highly acidic and must be to prepare food for digestion. The antacids reduce stomach acidity somewhat and, thus, presumably allow the lining of the stomach to heal itself. While most do work, none is without its problems. Furthermore, they offer only temporary, symptomatic, relief. If the irritation is due to a more serious condition, such as an ulcer, the symptomatic relief of the antacids could lead to a delay in treatment.

If you read the list of ingredients of the most popular antacids, you will find that nearly all are composed of either sodium bicarbonate, calcium carbonate, or magnesium and aluminum salts. All of these, as well as the less common ones, reduce stomach acidity, and each has its drawbacks.

Sodium bicarbonate is baking soda, and the kind you have in your refrigerator or kitchen cabinet is just as good as the kind with the fancy label that you spend far more to purchase. If you have high blood pressure or some other reason for restricting your sodium intake, you want to avoid this product, since it does contain high levels of sodium. You will find sodium bicarbonate is the ingredient in Alka-Seltzer and other products.

Calcium carbonate contains no sodium and is now being advertised widely because it is an additional source of calcium. However, it can cause a "rebound" similar to that seen with decongestants, and may actually increase stomach acidity when its effect wears off (Reif, 1986). Furthermore, those with kidney stones may find them aggravated by this product. Tums is the best known calcium–carbonate–containing antacid.

The salts of magnesium and aluminum reduce stomach acidity, but aluminum salts are constipating. The magnesium salts are added because they counteract the effects of the constipating aluminum salts by causing diarrhea.

While for most people, these products do not create problems, those with intestinal conditions such as "irritable bowel syndrome" may want to avoid them. Rolaids contains aluminum, while Digel, Maalox, Mylanta, and others contain the combination of aluminum and magnesium.

Worth remembering are the FDA guidelines for using antacids. First, these products are for temporary relief. Do not use them for more than two weeks. Second, be aware of the sodium content of some, the rebound effect of others, and constipating or diarrheal properties of others. Third, the FDA has found that the liquid antacids are more effective than those in tablet form. Tablets should be chewed thoroughly and followed by a full glass of water. Finally, the FDA believed it necessary to warn people that the effervescent tablets must be dissolved in water before they are taken!

VITAMINS

Nearly everyone has an opinion about vitamins. Many in the medical establishment maintain the nearly $3 billion a year we spend on them is not only a waste of money, but potentially dangerous. On the other hand, there are nutritional experts who swear by the necessity of a handful of different tablets every day. Vitamins are believed by some to prevent cancer, treat the common cold, relieve premenstrual syndrome, restore sexual potency, make skin look younger, provide energy, and relieve the symptoms of stress.

Seventy million Americans report that they take vitamins, and the majority of these are health-conscious people aware of the importance of good nutrition and the dangers of smoking and alcohol—just the people who are least likely to *need* vitamins (Ratto, 1987). Even most nutritionists take them, more than 60 percent in one study (Worthington-Roberts & Breskin, 1984). According to another study, nearly half of those over sixty take vitamins, and 94 percent felt they obtained some health benefits from them (Schneider & Nordlund, 1983). Most people seem to see vitamins as a kind of insurance; they can't hurt and perhaps they will make up for poor eating and sleeping habits, and maybe even contribute to good health.

Moreover, we seem to pride ourselves on the high level of stress we like to think we endure. After all, successful people have many demands placed upon them and along with success comes stress. Since we like to think of ourselves as successful, we, too, must be under stress. Medical research recognizes that physical stress, such as illness, increases our need for vitamins, and we are told that mental stress must do the same. We see advertisements for High Potency Vitamins for High Stress People and buy them.

Another argument for taking vitamins is based on the "if a little is good for you, a lot is better" school of thought. The minimum daily requirement (MDR) of a given vitamin was established to prevent vitamin deficiency. The reasoning of some people is that, for example, since vitamin E deficiency in rats leads to sexual difficulties, extra vitamin E will turn me into a sexual superstar. Although the former is true, there is no evidence whatsoever for the latter.

Not everyone always pays attention to every meal to be sure that it contains a balanced combination of nutrients, so a multipurpose vitamin might do many people some good. Pregnant women might want to consider use of a multipurpose vitamin, since some evidence exists that multivitamin use might prevent some cases of neural tube defect, a rare condition in which the spinal cord and backbone fail to develop normally. Pregnant women who took vitamins were significantly less likely to have babies with this defect (Mulinare, Cordero, Erickson, & Berry, 1989). Keep in mind, however, that the vitamins had to have been taken around the time of conception, that the effect was not seen for blacks, and a host of other, related factors may account for the results (Holmes, 1989).

With so many people taking so many vitamins, you might assume that the average person knows just what vitamins are and what they do. In fact, most people have only a vague notion of what vitamins do and an even vaguer idea of where they come from. For the most part vitamins function by helping regulate chemical process in the individual cells. They function as "cofactors" for catalysts. A catalyst is a compound that facilitates a chemical reaction without being affected itself. The presence of vitamins is necessary for the catalysts to function. Vitamins are found in food although vitamin D is also produced in the skin and vitamin K by some intestinal bacteria (Hendler, 1990).

Vitamins cannot relieve stress, nor does the physical stress of a broken leg produce the same vitamin needs as the stress of a job. In 1986, one pharmaceutical company was fined $25,000 and ordered to halt advertising a stress vitamin formula because it proclaimed that "stress can deplete your body of water soluble vitamins." While this is true of physical stress, the ad showed a worried businessman (Ratto, 1987).

Natural vitamins, with one exception, are no more "natural" than synthetic vitamins. Vitamins are vitamins, and both the chemical formula and the product are the same whether the vitamin was synthesized in a laboratory or extracted from a fruit. The "natural" part that is advertised is everything else that goes into the pill: the coating, the other ingredients, and any preservatives.

The one exception to this general rule is vitamin E. "Natural" vitamin E is derived from vegetable oil, and is more biologically active than the vitamin E made synthetically. Even so, the FDA requires that this be taken into consideration when a product is labeled. The unit of strength that the FDA uses is the International Unit (IU). Two vitamin E tablets with the same IU number will be the same strength, even though the synthetic one will contain more vitamin E.

Vitamins can be dangerous. While an overdose of water soluble vitamins (vitamins in the B complex and C) will generally result in nothing more than a vitamin-rich urine, the fat soluble vitamins (A, D, E, and K) are another story. More than 4,000 cases of vitamin poisoning are reported each year, with most of the toxic effects due to vitamin D (Dubick & Rucker, 1983).

In children, toxic effects of vitamin D can be seen after no more than four or five times the recommended daily allowance for adults. Adults have to take at least 50,000 IU for a long time (the MDR is only 400), but overly zealous health conscious people have been known to take such megadoses (Hathcock, 1984). Vitamin A is toxic at only five to ten times the MDR, an amount quite easy to reach, and an overdose can lead to liver damage, not to mention skin problems and hair loss. Some overdoses occur because of sensational media reports that have described it as a cancer preventive, leading some people to take huge quantities. Liver is a rich source of both A and D, and some experts feel that, given the number of people taking supplemental doses of A and D, liver should be eaten sparingly.

Although this book is primarily about psychoactive drugs, and vitamins are not generally considered drugs, many do have psychoactive properties, and there is so much information (and misinformation) about them that a brief discussion is warranted. Table 10.2 shows the major vitamins and minerals.

Vitamin A

Vitamin A and its derivatives have recently gained a great deal of attention. If you are over the age of thirty you have probably heard of **Retin-A,** but may not be aware that it is a derivative of vitamin A. As **Tretinoin,** it is regularly used to treat acne, but in the late 1980s it had a brief fad as a "miracle" wrinkle cure. If you were given Retin-A your wrinkles were supposed to disappear. You may recall the enormous publicity this finding produced. As might be expected there was an equally fierce backlash. As it stands now, it appears that if you have wrinkles and are given Retin-A your wrinkles are still there but less noticeable, especially if the light is right and the person doing the noticing really likes you.

If you are under thirty, you have probably heard of Tretinoin, but may also be familiar with Accutane. Accutane is a very powerful vitamin A derivative, like etretinate, that is useful in treating a form of acne. These drugs are quite effective but also have a major drawback; they can cause serious birth defects if taken by a woman during pregnancy. Etretinate remains in the body for weeks or months, while Accutane is probably completely gone in a few days.

While anyone with severe acne considers their medical problem serious, vitamin A has had application in even more serious conditions. Vitamin A apparently is effective in helping the immune system fight off infection and it has been very effective in reducing diarrhea and other conditions, especially in Third World countries where nutrition is poor (Keusch, 1990). Where nutrition is adequate, vitamin A may still be effective but the doses required can be quite toxic.

Beta carotene, the precursor of vitamin A, is far less toxic, and research with it is ongoing. Interest has particularly focused on the use of vitamin A and beta carotene to prevent cancer. It appears that people whose intake of beta carotene is low are at greater risk for lung and several other forms of cancer. It apparently works by being an **antioxidant** (Hendler,

Table 10.2 Minimum Daily Requirements for Vitamins and Minerals		
Vitamin*	**Men**	**Women**
Biotin (mg)	0.3	0.3
Folic acid (mcg)	400	400
Niacin (mg)	18	15
Pantothenic acid (mg)	10	10
Pyridoxine (mg)	2.2	2.0
Riboflavin (mg)	1.6	1.2
Thiamin (mg)	1.4	1.0
Vitamin A (mcg)	1000	800
Vitamin B$_{12}$ (mcg)	3	3
Vitamin C (mcg)	60	60
Vitamin D (mcg)	5	5
Vitamin E (mg)	10	8

*mcg = microgram mg = milligram. A microgram is a thousandth of a milligram.
The data are for individuals between 23 and 50. Pregnant and nursing women may need more of some of these. Obtaining two-thirds of these requirements will prevent symptoms of deficienices.
Source: National Academy of Sciences and Food and Drug Administration.

1990). Oxidation by chemicals is thought to lead to cancer development. Antioxidants prevent this deterioration.

One side effect of beta carotene is that in Caucasians it can cause an orange tint to the skin. Believe it or not, the product has been marketed as a means of obtaining a tan without exposure to the harmful rays of the sun. Beta carotene is highly fat soluble and taken in large doses it accumulates in the fatty deposits under the skin. Its orange color then makes the skin look the same. Some people are willing to pay money to turn the color of a carrot! At least one death has been associated with intake of a synthetic beta carotene called canthaxanthin taken for tanning purposes (Bluhm, Branch, Johnston, & Stein, 1990).

Vitamin A and its close relative, beta carotene, seem to be useful in stimulating immunity, helping to prevent the development of cancer and in fighting skin disorders. At the same time it is toxic at high doses and can cause birth defects.

Vitamin B

Thiamin. Thiamin deficiencies can cause any number of problems, including mental confusion and muscle weakness. The disease produced by thiamin deficiency is called beriberi. Thiamin deficiency is common in severe alcoholics and may be a problem for less heavy drinkers as well. There are unproven claims that it can also increase intelligence and even act as an insect repellent when taken orally! Thiamin deficiency is a serious problem; except for heavy drinkers, however, most of us get enough of this vitamin.

Niacin. Some evidence exists to suggest that niacin taken as a supplement will lower cholesterol. The decrease is modest but real. Along with other cholesterol-lowering drugs, however, it is effective (Chashin-Hemphill et al., 1990). It was also suggested as a treatment for schizophrenia, but the results were not impressive. An excess of niacin can produce an unpleasant facial flush and cardiac arrhythmia.

Vitamin B12. The picture you saw of John Wayne in Chapter 2 showed him getting an injection of some drug. Since he was on a set and the picture dated from the fifties, it might have been an injection of vitamin B12. This vitamin has a reputation of increasing energy and being a general "feel good" drug. Rumors circulate occasionally that President Kennedy used to get regular injections of this vitamin. The evidence supporting the claim is not very good, but it has become part of the mythology of drug use.

Vitamin C

An entire book the size of this text could and has been written both for and against the vitamin C. Clinical studies are suggestive but not conclusive by any means that it may have some beneficial effect if taken in higher than recommended dosages. Beware, however, of those claims which suggest that it can do everything from curing cancer to preventing the common cold.

Vitamin C is an antioxidant and can prevent the formation of cancer-causing chemicals called nitrosamines which are found in cigarette smoke, malt beverages, and cured meat products. There is some evidence therefore that it might *prevent* cancer. As you are undoubtedly aware, evidence suggests that it may also help lessen the severity of a cold. It is also important to note that smokers have lower levels of vitamin C in their blood and white blood cells. They are also more prone to colds and, of course, cancer.

Vitamin D

The exception to the general rule of how vitamins work, D acts as a hormone. Produced by the skin in response to energy from the sun, it can also be obtained from fatty fish, liver, and egg yolks. In children, a deficiency of D results in rickets, a growth disorder which is now rare in the Western world. It aids in the metabolism of calcium, a mineral necessary for strong bones. In addition there is some evidence that, like vitamin A, it may have properties that protect against some forms of cancer and aid the body's immune system. In addition there may be a connection between vitamin D and the aging process.

Vitamin E

This is another of the vitamins about which much has been written but little is really known. Some would claim that it can do everything from cure cancer to increase the size of the male sex organ. It is quite toxic in high doses and can cause high blood pressure and hormonal disturbances among other things. There is not enough evidence to recommend taking it as a supplement.

SEDATIVES

In addition to, or perhaps because of, our national preoccupation with stress and upset stomach, Americans also seem to be a nation of insomniacs. Most of us have had trouble sleeping on occasion, and almost one-fifth of us suffer from chronic insomnia. A wide variety of prescription medications are available to treat insomnia (see chapter 11), but we also spend millions on over-the-counter sleep aids, with rather dubious results. The vast majority of OTC sleeping aids are nothing more than antihistamines.

Every drug has some side effects, but the definition of a side effect is dependent on the definition of the *main* effect. If you took an antihistamine to combat an allergy, drowsiness would be a side effect. However, if you took it to become drowsy, stuffiness and dry mouth would be side effects. The two most common antihistamines to be found in OTC medications are pyrilamine maleate and doxylamine succinate, which is discussed on page 341. Both of these are antihistamines whose potency in causing drowsiness is about the same as their antiallergic properties.

Although antihistamines may make you drowsy, their effect is rather limited. If you are having difficulty sleeping because of severe anxiety or pain, antihistamines are unlikely to help. For common, everyday, garden variety sleeplessness, other, nondrug techniques discussed in chapter 11 are probably just as effective. Even if they work for you, reliance on OTC sleeping aids has an additional drawback; it further reinforces the belief that any problem, whether it is sleeplessness, anxiety, boredom, pain, or unhappiness, can be treated with a pill.

STIMULANTS

Over-the-counter stimulants, such as No-Doz or Vivarin, have been as common as a beer party among young college students for many years. Older college students also are familiar with them as a way of combatting drowsiness while driving or performing some other boring task. For some reason, it always surprises a large number of users when they look at the label and find they have merely been taking caffeine.

The amount of caffeine in an OTC stimulant can be considerable—up to 200 mg, or the equivalent of two to three cups of coffee. While caffeine is generally considered to be safe and effective by the FDA, you should recognize that it is banned by the International Olympics Committee and is also present in coffee, tea, many soft drinks, and some cold remedies. As of March 1989, caffeine is the only drug permitted in OTC preparations sold as stimulants (Food, Drugs & Cosmetic Law Report, 1988).

With all of the possible sources of caffeine, a student or anyone else could easily consume enough of the drug to produce the toxic symptoms discussed in chapter 5. Two OTC tablets washed down by a couple of cups of strong coffee, followed by a soft drink and a cold tablet could easily induce caffeinism.

Careful use of OTC stimulants is not harmful, but caution should be urged. Drugs are drugs, and overdoses are overdoses, regardless of the source of the drug. As we saw in chapter 5, caffeinism is probably far more common than most people realize. Unfortunately, they rarely make the connection between their own use of a legal drug and the conditions it can produce.

DIET AIDS

In our society it has been said many times, you can't be too rich or too thin. Diet books and cookbooks consistently top the best-seller lists. People spend enormous sums of money for liposuction, exercise classes, and a wide variety of medications that supposedly reduce weight. The FDA regularly cracks down on products that ''melt away'' the pounds or are promoted as permitting you to eat all you want without gaining weight. Over-the-counter drugs are sold as appetite suppressants to aid in weight loss.

Amphetamines were widely prescribed as appetite suppressants in the 1950s and into the 1960s. One particular drug, no longer available, combined a barbiturate with amphetamine. The effect of these two drugs was interesting. The amphetamine not only was an appetite suppressant, but, of course, increased alertness and general well-being. The barbiturate reduced some of the nervousness that often accompanies amphetamines and also produced a general feeling of well-being. The abuse potential of this combination was obviously quite high.

While studies indicate that subjects who take amphetamines and go on a diet lose more weight than those on a placebo and diet, it is difficult to determine whether this effect is due to appetite suppression or some other factor. At any rate, tolerance develops rapidly, and the anorectic effect wears off after a few days of use. Consequently, drugs containing amphetamine or amphetamine-like substances are rarely, if ever, used today as appetite suppressants.

Use of amphetamines as an appetite suppressant declined drastically when amphetamine abuse became widespread in the 1960s and early 1970s. **Phenylpropanolamine** (PPA) has largely taken its place. PPA is structurally very similar to amphetamine, as you can see in figure 10.1. Because it has less central nervous system activity, however, it may be sold over the counter. Virtually all OTC diet aids contain PPA, and all but one are manufactured by the same company even though they are marketed under several different names.

The appetite suppressant effects of PPA are mild, although controlled studies do show that people on a diet who take PPA lose more weight than those who take a placebo (Griboff, Berman, & Silverman, 1975; Altschuler, Conte, Sebok, Marlin, & Winick, 1982). The difference is not typically very large (four to five pounds), but it does occur. Moreover, PPA, even though it resembles amphetamine structurally, functions as an appetite suppressant in a different way (Wellman, 1990).

At the recommended dose of 75 mg a day, PPA does not increase blood pressure, produce amphetamine-like mood changes, or have any other notable side effects (Liebson, Bigelow, Griffiths, & Funderburk, 1987; Morgan, Funderburk, Blackburn, & Noble, 1989). Nevertheless, it should not be taken by anyone with high blood pressure or by anyone who suffers from depression. Remember, too, that these studies were all done with the recommended dosages of PPA. Phenylpropanolamine is often found in cold remedies as well as in diet aids, and higher doses of PPA may be toxic. You

FIGURE 10.1

Note how similar phenylpropanolamine (used in appetite suppressants) is to amphetamine.

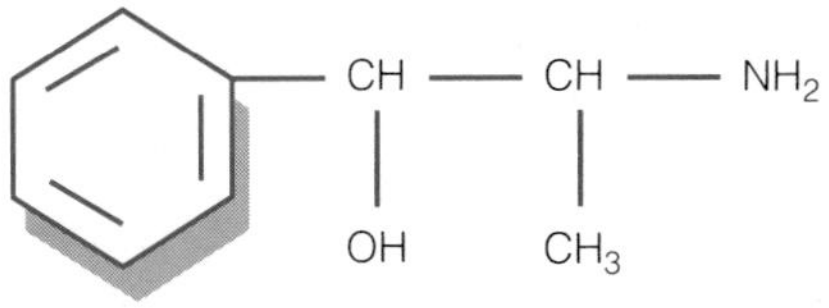

Phenylpropanolamine

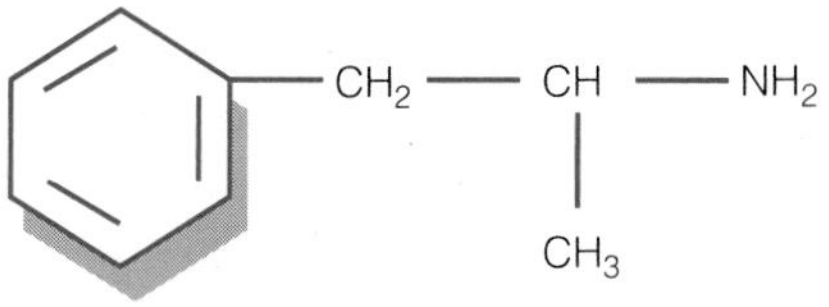

Amphetamine

should be quite careful about taking diet pills if you are also taking cold medication.

If you look carefully at the various brand names for diet aids you will find they all contain exactly the same active ingredient, 75 mg of phenylpropanolamine. One contains 37.5 mg but recommends two tablets a day. Others advertise "maximum strength" or the "strongest appetite suppressant you can buy without a prescription." Some are also available in time-release capsules. No matter how they are packaged or advertised, they are all exactly the same drug.

The only way to lose weight is to burn off more calories than you take in. No diet aid is going to provide willpower or cause you to exercise more. The most they can do is dull your appetite temporarily. Recent evidence from research in psychology and physiology indicates that obesity is a far more complicated issue than previously believed. There are evolutionary advantages to being able to gain weight easily. Obesity is in part a psychological and sociological phenomenon, in part a physiological process, and in part the result of long-established past habits, none of which is likely to be changed by a simple pill.

Over-the-counter drugs are self-medication taken to treat self-limiting conditions. While most can help relieve some symptoms, they cannot treat the underlying cause of the condition being treated. To a great extent our use of OTC drugs reflects the belief prevalent in American society that there exists a pill to cure all ills. That pill must act quickly and with no further action on our part. Unfortunately, such simplistic thinking has little relation to reality.

SUMMARY

Over-the-counter drugs are a multibillion dollar industry in the Unites States, and its products have been sold for more than a hundred years. Their effectiveness only recently has been studied, however, and as a result many drugs were removed from the market. Now, in order for a drug to be sold, it must be generally recognized as both safe and effective. OTC drugs are taken for the same reasons that other drugs are taken and have the same advantages and drawbacks. Several of these drugs are important to our overall understanding of the role of drugs in society.

Analgesics are drugs designed to relieve pain. The most common are aspirin, acetaminophen, and ibuprofen. All three seem to relieve dull, aching, throbbing pain very well. In addition to relieving pain, aspirin and ibuprofen also are anti-inflammatory. All three drugs reduce fever. While they are probably the most common drugs used in our society, they are by no means totally safe and are responsible for hundreds of deaths a year. They, like all drugs, should be used with caution.

Cold remedies are misnamed since they don't remedy colds. They do, however, relieve some of the symptoms of a cold, which may or may not be good in the long run. Many of the symptoms of a cold are actually beneficial, and overuse of cold remedies may make a cold last longer. Colds are self-limiting, and the cold medications cannot alter the duration of a cold. Nevertheless, they are valuable to enable sufferers to function.

Antacids relieve stomach acidity, which supposedly is the cause of "upset stomach." However, the stomach is supposed to be acidic and antacids should be used only for short-term relief. Anyone on a sodium restricted diet or who has intestinal problems should be cautious about taking the drugs. Finally, some of the antacids can actually cause acidic rebound, making the upset stomach even worse.

Vitamins have a useful function in our hectic society. Again, however, they are not a panacea. A person on a proper diet has no real need of vitamins, although so few of us have the time to plan our diets that vitamins can be helpful. Overdose on vitamins can be quite harmful, and particular caution must be taken with the fat soluble vitamins. Vitamin overdose is a particular concern for children, since the toxic level of some of the vitamins is surprisingly easy to reach.

As a result of FDA regulations, nearly all sedatives sold as OTC medications are antihistamines. While antihistamines do cause drowsiness in some people, they, like virtually all OTC drugs, are symptomatic. They relieve the symptoms, but not the cause of insomnia. Taken in moderation, they are not harmful, but they should not be combined with alcohol and should not be relied upon as a cure. Nondrug techniques for inducing drowsiness are probably just as effective.

Stimulants sold as OTC drugs are, quite simply, caffeine. Given the widespread use of caffeine as an additive to soft drinks and the levels of caffeine that we consume in coffee and tea, caffeinism ought to be of greater concern than it is. While they are generally recognized as safe and effective as stimulants, the OTC drugs should be viewed as expensive and less enjoyable ways of having a cup of coffee.

Diet aids also are potent drugs that should be used sparingly. The ingredient in them is structurally quite similar to amphetamine, and while it is less centrally active than amphetamine, it shares many of the same properties.

Diet aids cannot provide willpower or motivation. Obesity is in part a cultural and in part a physiological phenomenon that cannot be "cured" by a pill.

REFERENCES

Altschuler, S., Conte, A., Sebok, M., Marlin, R., & Winick, C. (1982). Three controlled trials of weight loss with phenylpropanolamine. *International Journal of Obesity 6*, 549–56.

Bluhm, R., Branch, R., Johnston, P., & Stein, R. (1990). Aplastic anemia associated with canthaxanathin ingested for "tanning" purposes. *Journal of the American Medical Association, 264*, 1141–42.

Buring, J. E., Peto, R., & Hennekens, C. H. (1990). Low dose aspirin for migraine prophylaxis. *Journal of the American Medical Association, 264*, 1711–13.

Cashin-Hemphill, L., Mack, W., Pogoda, J., Sanmarco, M., Azen, S., & Blakenhorn, D. (1990). Beneficial effects of colestipol-niacin on coronary atherosclerosis. *Journal of the American Medical Association, 264*, 3013–17.

Council on Scientific Affairs (1988). Treatment of obesity in adults. *Journal of the American Medical Association, 260*, 2547–51.

Dubach, U., Rosner, B., & Sturmer, T. (1991). An epidemiological study of abuse of analgesic drugs: Effects of phenacetin and salycylate on mortality and cardiovascular morbidity (1968–1987). *New England Journal of Medicine, 324*, 155–160.

Dubick, M. A., & Rucker, P. B. (1985). *Journal of Nutritional Education, 47*.

Flower, R., Moncada, S., & Vane, J. (1980). Analgesic antipyretics and acute inflammatory agents: Drugs employed in the treatment of gout. In A. G. Gilman, L. S. Goodman, & A. Gilman (Eds.). *The Pharmacological Basis of Therapeutics, 6th Ed.* New York: Macmillan.

Food, Drugs & Cosmetic Law Reports (1988). Final monograph on OTC stimulants issued. *No. 1320*, March, p. 1.

Franklin, N. (1982). Dubious drugs for coughs and colds. *Medical Self Care, 17*, 38–41.

Gay, G. (1990). Another side effect of NSAIDS. *Journal of the American Medical Association, 264*, 2677–88.

Griboff, S., Berman, R., & Silverman, H. (1975). A double-blind clinical evaluation of a phenylpropanolamine–caffeine–vitamin combination and a placebo in the treatment of exogenous obesity. *Current Therapeutic Research, 17*, 535–43.

Hartney, T. J. (1988). The physician's health study: aspirin for the primary prevention of myocardiac infarction. *New England Journal of Medicine, 318*, 924.

Hathcock, J. L. (1985). *Pharmacy Times*, May, 104.

Hendler, S. S. (1990). *The doctor's vitamin and mineral encyclopedia.* New York: Simon & Schuster.

Holmes, L. B. (1988). Does taking vitamins at the time of conception prevent neural tube defects? *Journal of the American Medical Association, 260*, 3181.

Keutsch, G. (1990). Vitamin A supplements—Too good not to be true. *New England Journal of Medicine, 323*, 985–86.

Leonards, J. R., & Levy, G. (1973). Gastrointestinal blood loss during prolonged aspirin administration. *New England Journal of Medicine, 289*, 1020–22.

Liebson, I., Bigelow, G., Griffiths, R. R., & Funderburk, F. R. (1987). Phenylpropanolamine: Effects on subjective and cardiovascular variables at recommended
over-the-counter dose levels. *Journal of Clinical Pharmacology, 27,* 685–93.

McDonald, J. W. (1982). Effects of acetylsalicylic acid on gastric mucosa. In H. Barnett, J. Hirsh, & J. F. Mustard (Eds.). *Acetylsalicylic acid: New uses for an old
drug.* New York: Raven Press.

Mann, C. C., & Plummer, M. L. (1988). The big headache. *The Atlantic Monthly,* October, 39–57.

Morgan, H. (1981). *Drugs in America: A social history, 1800–1908.* Syracuse University Press.

Morgan, J. P., Funderburk, F. R., Blackburn, G. L., & Noble, R. (1989). Subjective
effects of phenylpropanolamine: Absence of stimulant or euphorgenic effects at
recommended dose levels. *Journal of Clinical Psychopharmacology, 9,* 33–38.

Mulinare, J., Cordero, J. F., Erickson, J. D., & Berry, R. J. (1988). Periconceptual use
of multivitamins and the occurrence of neural tube defects. *Journal of the
American Medical Association, 260,* 3141–45.

Nutrition Reviews, *42,* February, 1984, p. 49.

Ratto, T. (1987). Vitamin ABCs. *Medical Self Care,* January-February, 28–34; 56.

Reif, R. (1986). Sneak addictions to over-the-counter drugs. *Self,* August, 116–19.

Roine, R., Gentry, T., Hernandez-Munoz, R., Baraona, E., Lieber, C. S. (1990). Aspirin increases blood alcohol concentration in humans after ingestion of ethanol.
JAMA, 264, 18, 2406–408.

Schneider, C. L., & Nerdlund, D. J. (1983). Prevalence of vitamin and mineral supplement use in the elderly. *Journal of Family Practice, 17,* 243–47.

Science News (1988). FDA warns aspirin makers. 12 March, p. 165.

Stanitski, C. (1987). Pharmacological adjuncts to the management of musculoskeletal
injuries in sports. In R. H. Straus (Ed.). *Drugs and performance in sports.* Philadelphia: W. B. Saunders.

The Steering Committee of the Physicans Health Study Research Group Preliminary
Report (1988). Finding for the aspirin component of the ongoing physicians'
health study. *New England Journal of Medicine, 381,* 262–64.

Thiessen, J. J. (1982). Pharmacokinetics of Salicylates. In H. Barnett, J. Hirsh, & J. F.
Mustard (Eds.). *Acetylsalicylic acid: New uses for an old drug.* New York:
Raven Press.

Wellman, P. (1990). A review of the physiological bases of the anorexic action of
phenylpropanolamine (d,l-norephedrine). *Neuroscience and Biobehavioral Reviews, 14,* 339–55.

Worthington-Roberts, B., & Breslin, J. (1983). *Journal of the American Dietetic Association, 84,* 795.

Yaksh, T. (1982). Central and peripheral mechanisms for the antianalgesic action of
acetylsalicylic acid. In H. Barnett, J. Hirsh, & J. F. Mustard (Eds.). *Acetylsalicylic acid: New uses for an old drug.* New York: Raven Press.

Young, F. E., Nightingale, S. L., & Temple, R. A. (1988). The preliminary report of
the finding of the aspirin component of the ongoing physicians' health study.
Journal of the American Medical Association, 259, 3158–60.

Zamula, E. (1990). Reye's syndrome, decline of a disease. *FDA Consumer,* November, 21–23.

11

• • •

THE LEGAL DRUGS II: PRESCRIPTION MEDICATION

• • •

OBJECTIVES

When you have finished studying this chapter you should:

1. Know how prescription drugs came into existence.
2. Be able to describe the most important antianxiety drugs.
3. Understand how antianxiety drugs affect the brain.
4. Know the relationship between the amino acid neurotransmitters and the benzodiazepines.
5. Be able to discuss the role of catecholamines and serotonin in mood disorders.
6. Know how affective disorders are treated with antidepressants.
7. Know how antidepressants work in the brain.
8. Know how prescription sedatives work.
9. Know the limitations of sedatives.
10. Be able to discuss the drug treatment of schizophrenia.
11. Know the role of drug treatment in schizophrenia.
12. Be able to discuss the characteristics of the various schedules of drugs.
13. Know how to read a prescription.

KEY TERMS

anhedonia
antianxiety agents
antipsychotics
barbiturates
benzodiazepines
beta blocker
bipolar affective disorder
catecholamine theory
dexamethasone suppression test
fluoxetin
Halcion
Librium
MAO inhibitors
meprobamate
neuroleptics
Prozac
re-uptake inhibitors
Saint Barbara
Schedules I, II, III, IV
sedative hypnotics
tricyclic antidepressants
Valium
Xanax

357

I n chapter 10, we saw how over-the-counter medications worked and why they were considered so safe that no prescription was necessary to obtain them. In this chapter we will consider several types of medications that are available only by prescription, the effects they have, why they are classified as prescription drugs, and their psychoactive properties. The primary focus of this chapter is on drugs with psychoactive properties although that term includes drugs often prescribed for other purposes.

WHY WE HAVE PRESCRIPTION DRUGS

Generally, prescription drugs are both more potent and have more dangerous side effects than do OTC drugs, thus requiring closer supervision by a physician. They can be purchased only through a pharmacy and require a written form with carefully specified instructions. Many cannot be refilled without permission and, in the case of some drugs, careful records must be kept of which medications doctors are prescribing to which patients.

While cynics might argue that OTC drugs are legal because they don't work very well, and that prescription drugs are so labeled to ensure that pharmacists and doctors maintain a suitable standard of living, the fact is that many prescription drugs would be dangerous if improperly or indiscriminately used. In countries where powerful drugs such as antibiotics and tranquilizers are available without prescription, numerous problems have been seen.

In this chapter we will consider four categories of prescription drugs that have important psychoactive properties: antianxiety drugs, antidepressant (and antimanic) drugs, sedative/hypnotic, and the antipsychotics. The effectiveness of many of these drugs in treating mental disorders has provided important insights into possible biochemical mechanisms that may be involved in these disorders.

In addition, we will look briefly at other drugs that relate to the purpose of this book, as well as some general considerations that are important to informed consumers of *any* drugs. Most of the issues we have explored in previous chapters apply also to our understanding of how prescription drugs fit into an overall view of drugs and our society.

ANXIETY AND DRUGS

Anxiety in its many forms is familiar to all of us: the feeling you get when your instructor springs an exam you didn't expect, the vague uncomfortable feeling you get when you are relaxing when you think you should be working, or the rapid heartbeat and dry mouth you experience when you have to give a talk to a group of people.

Many psychologists make a distinction between fear and anxiety—fear being an appropriate response to a threatening situation, and anxiety being a

Prescription medications are purchased only from a pharmacy, which must follow strict controls for dispensing and refilling prescription drugs.

fear-like response to an inappropriate situation (Goodwin, 1986). While such a distinction may be useful under some circumstances, for our purposes, the term anxiety will be used to define both conditions, since the physiological response involved is the same.

When anxiety becomes debilitating, it is often treated with drugs. Considerable controversy exists about the terminology of the drugs used to treat the condition. Confusion exists in many people (including quite a few physicians and other health professionals) concerning the difference between tranquilizers and sedatives—and between so-called "major" and "minor" tranquilizers.

If I am worried and cannot go to sleep, a doctor may prescribe a sedative. If I am anxious because of stressful life events and am unable to function normally during the day, my doctor may prescribe a "minor" tranquilizer. If I become psychotic and need to be hospitalized, I may be given a "major" tranquilizer. How do these types of drugs differ?

The fact is that none of the terms (sedative or major or minor tranquilizer) is entirely accurate. Many drugs have sedative properties (alcohol is one) and are not medically prescribed as sedatives. Sedatives may be used, either with or without a prescription to relieve anxiety. The "minor" tranquilizers, prescribed to relieve anxiety, also have sedative properties, and the "major" tranquilizers often are given to agitated psychotic patients for their sedative properties even though the symptoms that the patients exhibit have nothing to do with anxiety.

Moreover, the so-called major and minor tranquilizers and the sedatives have different modes of action and different physiological effects. While it might sound logical to take a minor tranquilizer for minor problems and a major one for major problems, the fact is that these drugs are prescribed for entirely different reasons. In order to avoid these difficulties in terminology, the term **antianxiety drugs** will be used to describe the minor tranquilizers. The major tranquilizers will be called **antipsychotic drugs** and the sedatives will be labeled **sedative hypnotic.** The sections that follow discuss each of these classes, as well as drugs whose primary effect is to relieve depression and otherwise alter mood.

Antianxiety Drugs

The most famous tranquilizer of the 1950s was Miltown, the trade name for **meprobamate,** a drug derived from a muscle relaxant. Equanil is another trade name for the same drug. These drugs are not prescribed very much today because of the low safety margin. The dosage required to relieve anxiety is only about half of that required to produce dependence. In addition, meprobamate has virtually no advantage over the barbiturates, which it was supposed to supplant (Baldessarini, 1980). The popularity of meprobamate, however, paved the way for the concept that anxiety is a "disease" treatable by drugs.

The drugs that replaced meprobamate are a group of drugs known as the **benzodiazepines.** The early benzodiazepines were Valium and Librium, and they quickly took the market away from Miltown and Equanil. Other antianxiety drugs followed, all of them benzodiazepines, including Atarax, Serax, Tranxene and Xanax. These drugs vary from Librium and Valium in their length of action, strength, and relative sedating properties. For a while **Valium** and **Librium** (both made, incidentally by the same company) were the most frequently dispensed of *all* prescription drugs.

Their supposed advantage over Miltown, Equanil, and the barbiturates (see below) concerned their supposed selective antianxiety effect at less than sedative doses. Theoretically, what this meant was that these drugs would relieve anxiety at dosages lower than those that caused sedation, were less dependence-producing, and were safer than other drugs, especially the barbiturates.

These supposed advantages are true only to a certain extent. All of the benzodiazepines can cause dependence, all have sedative properties at high doses, and all can cause a fatal overdose. For various reasons, **Xanax** has overtaken both Valium and Librium and is now not only the most often prescribed antianxiety drug but also the fifth most often prescribed of *all* drugs. Table 11.2 shows a list of the most commonly prescribed prescription drugs.

From chapter 2 you will recall that drugs differ in their duration of action. Another factor that has been discussed repeatedly in this text is the time to onset of a drug. In general, the more rapidly the drug reaches the brain the higher the abuse potential. The various benzodiazepines, while sharing the same basic structure, vary greatly in their duration of action and

Table 11.1 Common Antianxiety Drugs

Generic Name	Brand	Time to Onset	Half-Life
buspirone	BuSpar	very slow	2–8
diazepam	Valium	very fast	20–50
chlordiazepoxide	Librium	moderate	5–30
oxazepam	Serax	slow	5–20
clorazepate	Tranxene	fast	30–100
lorazepam	Ativan	moderate	10–15
prazepam	Centrax	very slow	30–100
alprazolam	Xanax	moderate	6–20
flurazepam	Dalmane	very fast	40–250
temazepam	Restoril	very fast	10–20
triazolam	Halcion	very fast	2–3

These benzodiazepines are prescribed for various purposes depending on their half life and speed of onset.
Source: Preston and Johnson, 1991.

time to onset. Some benzodiazepines are prescribed as antianxiety drugs and some as sedative hypnotics.

In general, benzodiazepines with a long duration of action are classified as antianxiety drugs, while those with a short duration of action are classified as hypnotic. The function of hypnotics in treating insomnia is discussed later in this chapter. It is important to remember that whether the drugs are prescribed for anxiety or insomnia, they are all basically the same drug and their effects are additive. Table 11.1 shows various antianxiety drugs and their characteristics.

Tolerance to the antianxiety effects of benzodiazepines develops, although there is little or no tolerance to the lethal dose (Westermeyer, 1986). This means that a person who increases his/her dosage to obtain the same antianxiety effect can rapidly approach the lethal dose. The development of dependence requires high doses for a long time, but the withdrawal symptoms can be severe (Allquander, 1978).

The question of dependence on benzodiazepines and the method of treatment is yet another example of how our attitudes toward drugs has changed over the last twenty or so years. When they were first introduced, benzodiazepines were seen as virtually harmless with little or no abuse potential. A reaction set in and in the 1970s and early 1980s benzodiazepine use declined with the realization that dependency did occur. In recent years, a general consensus has begun to emerge about the abuse potential of these drugs.

First of all, it should be noted that most people who take benzodiazepines do not find them reinforcing and usually take less than is prescribed. Those with a preexisting drug problem such as alcohol dependency are different however, and frequently seek out these drugs. The dosage prescribed

Table 11.2 Most Frequently Dispensed Prescription Drugs (1990)		
Rank	**Name**	**Use**
1.	Amoxil (amoxicillin)	antibiotic
2.	Lanoxin (digoxin)	increases heart contractions
3.	Zantac (ranitidine)	anti-ulcer
4.	Premarin (estrogen)	estrogen replacement
5.	Xanax (alprazolam)	anxiety reliever
6.	Dyazide	anti-hypertensive
7.	Cardizem (diltiazem)	anti-anginal anti-hypertensive
8.	Synthroid (levothyroxine)	thyroid replacement
9.	Ceclor (cefaclor)	antibiotic
10.	Seldane (terfenadine)	antihistamine

Source: U.S. Food and Drug Administration.
Note that four of the top ten most often prescribed drugs are for stress-related conditions, including ulcers, hypertension, and anxiety.

also differentiates the abuse potential of these drugs as does the length of time over which they are taken. The person who uses these drugs on an occasional basis is in little danger of developing a dependency; for those who are abusers of other drugs and are taking high doses of benzodiazepines, the danger of dependence is much greater and withdrawal can be difficult (Woods, Katz, & Winger, 1988; Morgan, 1990; Ashton, 1991; Busto & Sellers, 1991).

Gradual withdrawal, known as tapering off, is recommended for those taking daily, low doses of the benzodiazepines for more than one month, while those taking high doses for more than eight months may need more careful treatment including possible hospitalization. In general, withdrawal symptoms represent an exaggeration of the conditions for which they were prescribed, and include tension, restlessness, sleep disturbance, and panic attacks. In severe cases, convulsions and hallucinations have been reported (Marks, 1988; Alexander & Perry, 1991).

Benzodiazepines are sometimes prescribed during alcohol withdrawal (Jaffe, 1980; Linnoila, 1983), although this practice has been criticized on the grounds that it merely amounts to substituting a potential addiction for a demonstrated one. Alcoholics may have long recognized what research has just recently demonstrated: alcohol and benzodiazepines operate on the same receptor systems, and as many as 20 percent of alcohol abusers have also abused benzodiazepines (Schuckit, Greenblatt, Gold, & Irwin, 1991). On the other hand, the benzodiazepines are safer than alcohol and easier to control, so they may be useful during withdrawal.

An enormous amount of research has been done on the biochemistry of the benzodiazepines and, as a result, their mode of action in the brain is fairly well understood. A specific receptor exists in the brain which responds to the benzodiazepines, just as one exists for morphine. This receptor is widespread throughout the brain and is found in about 30 percent of all neurons, and in virtually every animal.

The benzodiazepines seem to work by potentiating or increasing the activity of GABA and similar amino acids which are the primary inhibitory neurotransmitters. The GABA neurotransmitters decrease the likelihood that a given neuron will fire in response to stimulation; thus by increasing their action, the benzodiazepines have a wide range of effect in many parts of the brain. Alcohol has a functionally similar effect, but appears to act more directly, as you read in chapter 5.

Antianxiety drugs have proved to be useful in the symptomatic relief of severe anxiety that is limited in time. They were not meant, nor should they be used, for the treatment of the long-term, mild anxiety that is experienced by so many people in our society. Anxiety is a symptom, not a disease, and drugs that relieve it should not be confused with a cure. Other methods such as relaxation, meditation, and behavior modification are more effective in the long run, although more time consuming, at least initially.

The benzodiazepines, particularly Valium, also are effective muscle relaxants and often are prescribed for that purpose. However, care should always be taken to remember that taking a drug for its muscle relaxant properties does not negate the fact that it is a potentially addictive, sedative drug. Nor should anyone ever forget that their effects are additive with alcohol.

Benzodiazepines have another effect that has only recently been recognized. These drugs can result in a kind of memory deficit known as anterograde amnesia which occurs when there is a failure of recall of information learned while the drug is in the system. Previously learned information (prior to taking the drug) is not affected, nor is short-term memory. What seems to happen is that the benzodiazepines prevent the formation of long-term memory. Subjects taking the benzodiazepines may remember information for a short period of time, but be unable to recall what they had learned after the passage of a few minutes. Most of the benzodiazepines share this property and it can be of considerable significance especially when patients take these drugs for prolonged periods of time (Curran, Schiwy, & Lader, 1987; Anthenelli, Monteiro, Blunt, & Shuckit, 1991).

Recently, the strong amnesic effects of some benzodiazepines have been recognized as being useful. Administered during painful or unpleasant surgical procedures, the patient remains conscious but has no subsequent memory of the procedure. Most patients report that since they don't remember the pain, the operation was not unpleasant.

Next to dying, the fear of standing up in front of a group of people is the commonest fear we have. Actors have had careers ruined because of stage fright, and teachers have had to change their profession after being unable to conquer it. The benzodiazepines have been used to treat this form of anxiety, but they also can cause confusion, muddled thinking, and amnesia.

The actors are experiencing tremendous anxiety. Would they remember their lines better if they had taken a beta blocker or would they suffer amnesia if they had taken benzodiazepine drug?

Recently a fad has swept over the performing arts. Musicians, actors, and even dancers are taking a ''new'' drug that does not cause sedation and maintains mental clarity, yet relieves the symptoms of anxiety. Furthermore, since it is not active in the central nervous system, it does not cause dependence. Most fascinating of all, it is not really a *new* drug, but has been used for many years in the treatment of high blood pressure.

Propanalol (Inderal) is a **beta blocker,** meaning that it reduces heart rate, blood pressure, and other symptoms of hypertension. Basically, there are two different kinds of receptors (alpha and beta) in the peripheral and central nervous system which respond to epinephrine and norepinephrine. Each of these *adrenergic* receptors is composed of two subtypes and may be located on either the presynaptic or postsynaptic membrane (Cooper, Bloom, & Roth, 1986).

Alpha receptors are in both the peripheral and central nervous system as well as the heart and smooth muscle. Beta receptors are primarily localized in the body, although there are beta receptors in the brain. Stimulation of beta receptors increases cardiac output, dilates the bronchial tubes, and produces vasodilation. Beta blockers, then, reduce heart rate and lower blood pressure. They constitute a major type of drug taken to counteract high blood pressure.

When taken in a situation of great stress, propanalol seems to prevent the normal arousal response that, taken to extreme, is the cause of stage fright (Skoler, 1988). It does not cause confusion and is perfectly legal.

Among musicians, propanalol is especially useful since it reduces muscle tremor which interferes with the ability to play nearly every instrument, from the violin to the tuba (Lockwood, 1989). Consequently, as many as 27 percent of performers report at least occasional use of the drug (Lockwood, 1989).

DRUGS AND MOOD DISORDERS

We all know people who are depressed, and many of us assume that depression is synonymous with sadness, crying, and misery. While depressed people feel these emotions, a more basic underlying symptom is **anhedonia,** the inability to feel pleasure. It may seem like an unimportant distinction to make, but the inability to feel pleasure is a much more essential characteristic of the depressed person than is sadness.

Sadness is a normal response to a severe loss or to death. There is usually a specific focus or cause of the sadness, and even the most inconsolable person can report moments of pleasure. The wake for the dead, so common in early decades of this century, is a good case in point. After a person died, the mourners would gather and carry on throughout the night. By the next day, the sadness would have lifted somewhat and by the time everyone went home, there was a general air of frivolity and merriment.

You would be a callous person indeed not to be sad when your father or mother died, but if uncontrollable crying and inability to carry on the usual affairs of life occur without any obvious reason, a more likely diagnosis is depression. Depression can be triggered by sudden loss, but it outlasts what would be considered a normal period of mourning.

Depressed people are unable to feel pleasure in the everyday events of life, cannot see themselves as ever getting better, and often know no reason for these feelings. Depressives obviously are at great risk for suicide and often suffer from a wide variety of physical complaints. Psychotherapy often has been used to help people with depression, and it has proved effective. Drugs are also used and are also effective. In fact, evidence supports that both psychotherapy and drug treatment can be equally effective, and a combination is not necessarily better than either one separately (Robinson, Berman, & Neimeyer, 1990).

Antidepressants, drugs used to treat disorders of affect (mood) or feeling, are basically of three types: **MAO inhibitors,** which are less commonly prescribed than when they were first introduced, **tricyclic antidepressants,** and **drugs that inhibit serotonin turnover.** The tricyclics have been widely prescribed for many years while the serotonin turnover inhibitors are the new rage in treating depression.

Monoamine Oxidase (MAO) Inhibitors

MAO inhibitors work at the presynaptic level (see chapter 3). You should recall that the catecholamines and indoleamines are taken back up into the presynaptic neuron (re-uptake). Monoamine oxidase in the presynaptic space metabolizes these neurotransmitters and thus regulates their concentration. The MAO inhibitors prevent this process and hence increase available amounts

FIGURE 11.1

Norepinephrine, dopamine, and serotonin are taken back into the presynaptic membrane. MAO metabolizes these neurotransmitters. MAO inhibitors prevent this and so increase available neurotransmitters.

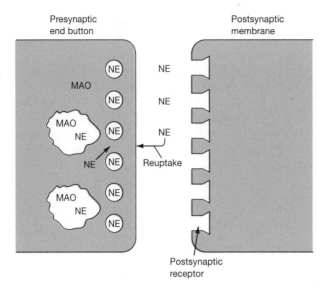

of norepinephrine and serotonin (see figure 11.1). An increase in these two neurotransmitters is thought to help reduce depression.

Unfortunately, the MAO inhibitors can be quite dangerous, since they also increase levels of tyramine, a common amino acid present in many foods. An increase in tyramine can result in fatal increases in blood pressure, as well as headaches, palpitations, flushing, and nausea. In addition, MAO inhibitors cause a wide range of side effects, ranging from dry mouth to agitation (Persad & Rakoff, 1987). Those taking MAO inhibitors must avoid such diverse food and drugs as cheese, liver, herring, beer, figs, red wine, most preserved meats, diet pills, amphetamines, and cold preparations, among a longer list.

Some hope, however, remains for the MAO inhibitors. Recently it was discovered that there are two types of MAO which affect different neurotransmitters. MAO-A oxidizes the norepinephrine and serotonin transmitters, while MAO-B oxidizes tyramine, tryptophan, and dopamine. Thus, a drug that inhibited MAO-A, without affecting MAO-B would be safer to use. Such drugs have been developed but none are now available in the United States, although they can be obtained in some other countries (Marsden, 1991).

Tricyclic Antidepressants

The **tricyclic antidepressants** prevent the re-uptake of catecholamines into the presynaptic area. This also is the primary mode of action of cocaine, you will remember, even though the tricyclics do not produce euphoria in the normal individual. In addition, tricyclic antidepressants have anticholinergic effects as well, which somewhat limit their effectiveness. The primary anticholinergic effects are dry mouth, blurred vision, and urinary retention. Other side effects include sedation, nausea, heartburn, and diminished sex drive (Persad & Rakoff, 1987).

FIGURE 11.2

A primary method of terminating the action of NE and DA is re-uptake. Cocaine and some antidepressants prevent re-uptake and increase available NE and DA.

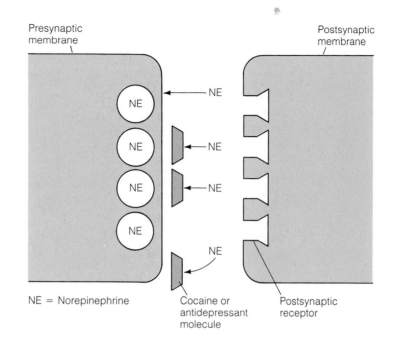

Presynaptic membrane

Postsynaptic membrane

NE

NE

NE

NE

NE

NE

NE

NE = Norepinephrine

Cocaine or antidepressant molecule

Postsynaptic receptor

Tricyclics also affect serotonin metabolism as well. There are specific antidepressants that alter serotonin metabolism without affecting the catecholamines, as you will read shortly. The triciclics however have a broader effect. One might conclude, therefore, that they are more effective antidepressants, but the fact is that some patients do not respond to them but do to the serotonin antidepressants, and vice versa. Drug treatment for depression is very complicated and requires careful monitoring. Table 11.3 shows the effect of the most common antidepressants on the serotonin and norepinephrine systems.

Two curious facts stand out about the tricyclic antidepressants. First, three to four weeks typically pass before they exert their effect, and second, only unpleasant side effects are experienced by the nondepressed individual. This first characteristic can present problems. As we have seen in many previous chapters, Americans are accustomed to their drugs, like their food, being fast, fast, *fast*. Depressed people often get discouraged when they take a drug daily for weeks without any noticeable change. Careful counseling is sometimes necessary to prevent them from becoming even more depressed.

While the unpleasant side effects of the antidepressants can further discourage depressed patients, they also virtually guarantee that these drugs will not become drugs of abuse. A drug that makes a depressed person feel normal gives him or her a strong incentive to continue its use, but a drug that inhibits urination, makes it difficult to see, and decreases sex drive is

Table 11.3 Effect of Common Antidepressants on Norepinephrine and Serotonin

Generic	Brand	Norepinephrine	Serotonin
imipramine	Tofranil	++	+++
desipramine	Norpramin	+++++	0
amitriptyline	Elavil	+	++++
Nortriptyline	Aventyl	+++	++
protryptyline	Vivactil	++++	+
trimipramine	Surmontil	+	++++
doxepine	Sinequan	+	++++
maprotiline	Ludiomil	+++++	0
amoxapine	Asendin	++++	+
trazodone	Desyrel	0	+++++
fluoxetine	Prozac	0	+++++

Key: 0 = No effect
     + = Degree of effect
Source: Preston and Johnson, 1991.

unlikely to be a big hit on the underground market. As a consequence, there is no black market for antidepressants.

Serotonin Antidepressants

In 1988, a new antidepressant was introduced—**fluoxetine,** known as **Prozac.** Unlike the tricyclic antidepressants, fluoxetine is believed to exert its effect by altering serotonin metabolism. Fluoxetine inhibits the re-uptake of serotonin into the presynaptic membrane. The tricyclics do the same, but fluoxetine is much more specific and effective. Another advantage of fluoxetine is that it has fewer anticholinergic side effects, and this is more likely to be tolerated by depressed patients. Finally, it has a long half-life and accumulates in the blood so that even if the depressed person "forgets" to take the drug, it will continue to exert its effects for days or weeks.

On the other hand, it is similar to the tricyclics in that a period of weeks may elapse before its effects are noticed and it has its own side effects, including loss of appetite. Furthermore, its long half-life, under most circumstances an advantage, could create problems when the drug is discontinued or if other medication is given which might interfere with it.

Estimated users of Prozac approach 5 million, generating sales of nearly $1 billion. It was probably inevitable, therefore, that some problems with its use have emerged. First, since it has so few side effects, there is a temptation to give the drug to people who may not need it. Feeling a little down or even mildly depressed may not automatically require medication. Like the benzodiazepines before it, fluoxetine may be prescribed when the doctor feels the need to do *something*.

One side effect of fluoxetine is weight loss, and the drug has been prescribed for this purpose. Given the complicated relationship between obesity, life style, personality, and other factors, it would seem of little value to take an antidepressant to lose weight. It is a little like killing a mosquito with a shotgun.

A more serious issue has emerged recently. Some psychiatrists feel that this drug is associated with a worsening of suicidal impulses and are concerned that some people have committed suicide as a result. Suicide is an ever-present danger in depressed people, of course, and suicidal thoughts are considered a symptom used to diagnose the disorder. Whether Prozac makes them more depressed is extremely difficult to determine. Even if it does, how would *you* weigh the positive effects of the drug for millions, against an increase in suicidal thoughts for a few? In 1991, the Food and Drug Administration held hearings which became quite heated, but concluded that, as prescribed, fluoxetine was a safe drug.

Which Antidepressant Is Best?

A curious fact about the antidepressants is that the drugs are highly variable in their effect. Some people respond to one tricyclic antidepressant and not to others, some respond better to fluoxetine, and some even respond best to MAO inhibitors. For the person being treated, as well as for the physician, these individual differences can be a source of frustration (Cole, 1989).

There is no accurate method of determining who will respond to which antidepressant, just as there is no clear method of diagnosing depression itself. Some tests and methods have been developed but they are not particularly useful in individual cases. For example, many depressed people begin their first REM sleep (dream sleep) cycle earlier than nondepressed people.

A common test is known as the DST or **dexamethasone suppression test.** In this test, dexamethasone, a synthetic cortisone, is given and the patient's reaction is monitored. In normal persons, the production of cortisol, a hormone secreted by the adrenal glands, is reduced. In about 50 percent of depressed people this suppression does not take place. Although a lack of suppression is probably a fairly good indication of depression, the reverse is not true and it has not been possible to use this test to predict the effectiveness of antidepressants.

In most cases, the tricyclic or serotonin antidepressants are the drug of choice because of their lower incidence of side effects. However, the MAO inhibitors seem to be useful when the depression is accompanied by anxiety or phobias (irrational fears). In addition, some people seem to respond to the MAO inhibitors better than the tricyclic antidepressants (Joyce & Pakel, 1989).

A seemingly unrelated use for the "antidepressants" is in the treatment of obsessive-compulsive disorders. Obsessive-compulsive disorders involve recurrent thoughts of a disturbing nature and repeated behaviors the person feels an overwhelming need to perform. Just why the antidepressants work, and all three types seem to be effective for some people, is not known. It may be that obsessive-compulsive disorder and depression share a similar biochemical basis, but this is pure speculation.

Drugs and Mania   At the other end of the continuum of depression is elation. We all experience short periods of depression, while at other times everything goes well and nothing can go wrong. But those suffering from a **bipolar disorder** experience these mood swings to an extraordinary degree. The term bipolar disorder has replaced a term that many are more familiar with—manic depression.

People with a bipolar disorder are on an emotional roller coaster that ranges from suicidal depression to grandiose behavior during which they are convinced they can do just about anything—make a killing in the stock market, write the great American novel, or reform the world—today. While some creative artists seem to show evidence of a bipolar disorder and in fact may harness the energy in their creative work, for most people with a bipolar disorder the condition is destructive to themselves and their families.

In addition to those with depression and those with a bipolar disorder, some people experience only the manic aspect of the mood disorders. They do not experience the mood swings from depression to elation, but only a swing from relatively normal to elation. Both the bipolar and manic disorders are treated with lithium salts, and like the antidepressants, just how these salts work is something of a mystery.

Like the tricyclic antidepressants, lithium salts have no psychoactive properties in normal individuals, but are effective in reducing manic behavior. Manic patients have a higher level of the primary metabolic product of norepinephrine in their cerebrospinal fluid, indicating that they have higher levels of norepinephrine in the brain. Treatment with lithium decreases these levels and the decrease is associated with a reduction in symptoms (Swann et al, 1987). Thus, lithium apparently decreases the amount of norepinephrine in the brain.

By now you should be seeing a pattern emerge. A drug which increases catecholamines at the synapse relieves symptoms of depression, and a drug which decreases available catecholamines reduces the symptoms of manic affective disorder. The **catecholamine theory of affective disorders** is a more complicated version of this observation and states that depression results from a deficiency of catecholamine at important receptors, while mania is the result of an excess of catecholamine.

The evidence for the theory, as logical as it might appear, is less than completely convincing. There are numerous problems with such a simple theory. First of all, the increase in brain catecholamines after antidepressants are given occurs far more rapidly than does the decrease in depressive symptoms. Second, there are tricyclics which do not affect catecholamine reuptake and yet are effective antidepressants (Cooper, Bloom, & Roth, 1986).

Moreover, cocaine, which has virtually the same biochemical effects as the tricyclics, is *not* an effective antidepressant, and lithium *is* effective against bipolar affective disorder which involves depression. Perhaps most damaging to the theory is the finding that most antidepressants cause the postsynaptic receptors to become *less* sensitive to catecholamines (Sulser, 1982). This effect should result in decreased activity of the catecholamine system.

Finally, there is the problem of the serotonin antidepressants that have little effect on catecholamine metabolism. Lithium also has an effect on the serotonin system, in part by enhancing serotonin function (Price, Charney, Delgado, & Heninger, 1989). In chapter 2, you read a warning against reductionism; trying to equate behavior with events that happen at the level of the synapse. Nowhere is this warning more appropriate than in the treatment of the affective disorders.

THE SEDATIVE DRUGS

Most of us occasionally have trouble going to sleep. As we saw in the previous chapter, antihistamines are effective in producing drowsiness. Sometimes, however, physicians will prescribe a **sedative hypnotic** drug when the OTC compounds prove ineffective. These are potent drugs and should be used with extreme caution.

Barbiturates

The use of barbiturates as sedative hypnotics peaked in the 1950s and 1960s. They are derived from barbituric acid, a compound discovered in 1864 by a German chemist, Dr. Bayer, whose name has become synonymous with headache relief in the United States. Legend has it that he celebrated his achievement at a tavern frequented by artillery officers. That day was also the feast day of **Saint Barbara,** who was the patron saint of artillery officers in Germany. After a few steins of lager, the story goes, Bayer is supposed to have named his new substance after her.

Just why Saint Barbara is the patron saint of artillery officers (and firemen, by the way) is not clear, since she was beheaded. Perhaps the connection is that she is supposed to intercede for those who experience sudden death. She also is connected with protecting people from death by lightning. Another, more mundane story about the naming of this compound is that Bayer named the drugs after a former girlfriend. Whatever the source of the name, the barbiturates have come to play an important part in the history of psychoactive drugs.

The barbiturates were the first sedative hypnotic, so called because they have a calming effect at low doses and produce unconsciousness at higher doses. They affect the reticular formation (see chapter 3) and reduce input that would normally produce an arousal response. There are basically four types, differentiated by their duration of effect, as can be seen in Table 11.4.

The barbiturates have been widely used as sleeping pills, even though they interfere with a major phase of sleep. REM (rapid eye movement) sleep occurs several times during an evening of sleep. During REM sleep all major muscle movement is suppressed, while the eyeballs dart back and

Table 11.4 Various Types of Barbiturates

Type	Drug	Duration of action
1. Ultra-short Acting	Thiopental	less than 3 hours
2. Short Acting	Pentobarbital Nembutal Secobarbital Seconal	up to 3 hours
3. Intermediate Acting	Amobarbital Amytal Butabarbital Butisal	up to 6 hours
4. Long Acting	Phenobarbital	up to 12 hours

forth in a rapid fashion. If awakened during this time, the subject is likely to report dreaming. REM sleep is very important to normal functioning. Subjects deprived of REM sleep have difficulty concentrating, and may eventually hallucinate.

Barbiturates depress REM sleep and hence reduce dreaming (Cox, Jacobs, Leblanc, & Marshman, 1983). A person who has taken these "sleeping pills" often feels groggy the next day and may take stimulants to keep going. Since these stimulants might interfere with sleep the next night, the barbiturates are repeated. Moreover, when the user stops taking barbiturates, there is often a REM rebound, with disturbing nightmares and extended periods of dreaming. These disturbing dreams may induce the user to return to the pills to get a good night's sleep.

Barbiturates also have an additive effect with alcohol. The 1986 DAWN reports indicate more than 2,000 emergency room cases of barbiturates in combination with other drugs (most often alcohol). Just about half of these were suicide attempts. The same liver enzymes that metabolize alcohol also metabolize the barbiturates. This means that those with a tolerance to one also will have a tolerance to the other. It too means that, to the liver, there is no difference between the barbiturates and alcohol.

The barbiturates have largely been replaced by nonbarbiturate sedatives and the benzodiazepines as both antianxiety and sedative medications. Despite years of research and the introduction of many new barbiturate sleeping pills, sales of these drugs have declined. Nevertheless, they are still useful for their anesthetic and anticonvulsive properties.

Dependence on barbiturates develops slowly, but withdrawal is severe. Seizures are not uncommon, and even death can result. Barbiturate withdrawal is generally considered to be more unpleasant than heroin withdrawal and lasts longer. In this regard it is similar to alcohol withdrawal. The lethal dose of barbiturates is only about ten times the effective hypnotic dose.

Benzodiazepines

You read previously that benzodiazepines with a short duration of action and fairly rapid onset are prescribed more as sedatives than as antianxiety drugs. Three of these drugs are widely used: temazepam (Restoril), Flurazepam (Dalmane), and triazolam (**Halcion**). They differ primarily in their rate of metabolism and, hence, their half-life, with triazolam being the shortest (Gillin & Byerley, 1990). Halcion, like Prozac, has been the object of controversy. In 1991, the British equivalent of the Food and Drug Adminstration suspended its use because of concerns about its safety. It continues to be very popular in the United States.

There is little to recommend any of the sedative hypnotics for regular use when the abuse and dependence potential is taken into consideration. As sleeping pills, they may be useful for short-term emergency situations. However, for normal insomnia, the transient insomnia experienced by all of us, the advice in Table 11.5 is far more effective. If none of this advice works, stronger means may be called for, but sleeping pills should be considered a last resort.

One other effect of using sedatives is the phenomenon of rebound upon withdrawal. Rebound means that after the person stops taking the drug, there is a paradoxical increase in symptoms. In other words, if you take the benzodiazepines because of insomnia, you may experience *more* insomnia once you stop taking them. Rebound anxiety has also been reported (Oswald, 1983; Gillin & Byerley, 1990).

DRUGS AND PSYCHOSES

Schizophrenia is a serious mental disorder that afflicts about 1 percent of the population at some point in their lives. It is characterized by delusions (unshakable beliefs that are obviously untrue), hallucinations (hearing, seeing, or otherwise perceiving things that are not there), thought disorders, and other physical and mental problems. A common misconception of schizophrenia is to confuse it with the multiple personality disorder, an entirely different problem. Schizophrenics do not switch from one personality to another, nor do they act perfectly normal at one time and in a bizarre manner shortly after. Schizophrenic behavior is usually sufficiently disturbed that it is quite easy to identify, although difficult to treat.

The various forms of schizophrenia are typically treated with drugs that are called major tranquilizers, **antipsychotics,** or **neuroleptics.** It is important to remember, however, that these drugs only modify the symptoms, they do not cure the condition. They may help the schizophrenic to deal with reality and to benefit from psychotherapy, but the underlying cause of the disease remains.

The development of the antipsychotics, beginning with chlorpromazine in 1954, has revolutionized the treatment of those afflicted with mental disorders (Snyder, 1984). The initial success of chlorpromazine (Thorazine) has led to the development of a number of other antipsychotics, including Haldol, Stelazine, Prolixin, and Mellaril, to name a few.

Table 11.5 What to Do When You Can't Sleep

1. Don't Take Sleeping Pills.
    Unless prescribed by a doctor for a temporary situation, prescription sleeping pills make matters worse by causing drowsiness, depressing REM sleep, and creating tolerance.

2. Listen To Your Body.
    Some people have an internal clock that tells them to go to sleep early and others to go to sleep late. This internal clock can be changed, but the process might take weeks or months. If you can't get to sleep, try changing your sleeping times.

3. Tire Yourself Out.
    Don't drink coffee or tea, smoke cigarettes, eat a heavy meal or exercise 3 to 4 hours before you go to bed. Avoid daytime naps.
    Plan a procedure to help you relax. Take a bath, learn to relax, read a boring book, do breathing exercises, have sex, or pray. Make the procedure a routine that you follow every night.

4. Don't Drink Alcohol.
    The effects of alcohol are similar to most prescription sleeping pills; it disrupts REM sleep, causes lethargy the next day, and can be habit forming.

5. Remember: Beds Are For Sleeping.
    Don't worry, watch television, or write the great American novel. If you can't get to sleep after 20 minutes, get up and do something else until you are sleepy.

Source: Adapted from Heckman, 1988.

A discussion of the effectiveness, side effects, and indications for use of the antipsychotics would require a volume longer than this entire book and is not relevant to our purposes. Suffice it to say that these drugs, the antipsychotics, are rarely abused by the normal population. They are not addictive and have a large safety margin, but their side effects can be relatively unpleasant, and, since they possess no stimulating or euphoric properties, are not considered potential drugs of abuse. They do, however, provide clues as to how other drugs work and some insight into the cause of schizophrenia itself.

The drugs used to treat schizophrenia work by blocking the action of dopamine in the brain. As you will remember, dopamine is a catecholamine neurotransmitter that has widespread effects. Many drugs of abuse, especially cocaine and amphetamine, alter dopamine metabolism, and in high doses for prolonged periods of time can produce symptoms that are indistinguishable from true schizophrenia. These drugs increase dopamine in the brain, while the schizophrenic drugs decrease it and reduce symptoms. This observation along with other research has lead to the *dopamine hypothesis of schizophrenia.*

A textbook on drugs and life is not the place for a prolonged discussion of the dopamine hypothesis, but a brief description is called for. There are at least five different receptors in the brain that respond to dopamine. Numerous lines of evidence indicate that the D_2 receptor is involved in schizophrenia. Not surprisingly, one of these lines of evidence is that the

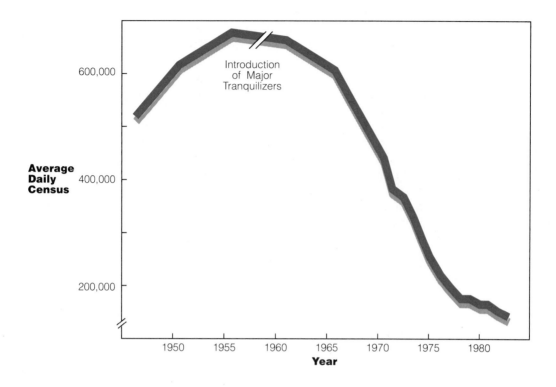

600,000

Average Daily Census 400,000

200,000

Introduction of Major Tranquilizers

1950   1955   1960   1965   1970   1975   1980

Year

The number of patients in psychiatric hospitals declined drastically after the introduction of the phenothiazines.

potency of most antischizophrenic drugs depends on their effectiveness at this receptor. These drugs also cause side effects related to dopamine metabolism.

For the long-term user of antipsychotics, the side effects are usually relatively mild, and include skin rashes and unusual sensitivity to sunlight. Some are quite serious, however, such as tardive dyskinesia, an irreversible condition involving involuntary movement of the mouth, tongue, and lips, and parkinsonism, a serious muscle tremor. Both tardive dyskinesia and parkinsonism are believed to result from damage to dopamine receptors.

Another use of antipsychotics seems to be on the upswing. With a growing population of elderly and the increasing number of chronically mentally ill persons who are not hospitalized, there is an increasing need for long-term care facilities. The vast majority of the elderly are obviously competent and capable of taking care of themselves. However, many also eventually require assistance in living. The number of nursing care homes under whatever name has drastically increased across the United States.

In some of these, antipsychotic medication is prescribed for the patients. Considerable concern has been raised about use of these drugs. Are they being prescribed to treat legitimate problems or to ensure that the residents are more manageable? Is there proper supervision over the prescription and dispensing of these drugs? Are the side effects, such as tardive dyskinesia, recognized as side effects or as the normal consequences of aging?

Keep in mind that 40-to-70 percent of nursing home patients suffer from some kind of mental illness that is related to a brain disorder such as Alzheimer's disease. Many of these patients are destructive to themselves and to others. Physical restraints such as special chairs and wrist and ankle cuffs are used under some circumstances, while drugs are used in other cases. Up to 50 percent of all nursing home patients and nearly 75 percent of those with mental disorders receive some medication (Slone et al, 1991).

The problem arises because nursing homes are frequently understaffed and always underpaid. There is a fine line between prescribing a drug for a person in the mild stages of Alzheimer's and prescribing for a cantankerous patient who is rebelling against what is, even in the best of nursing homes, a difficult situation. As the population of elderly increases, the issue of medication is bound to become more prominent.

THE PRESCRIPTION

Many people feel cheated when they go to a doctor and leave without a prescription. Yet few do more than glance at the slip of paper they are given. Were they to look carefully at it, even fewer would be able to understand what they saw. The prescription is a kind of shorthand, easily understood by the doctor and the pharmacist. It is a shorthand that you would do well to learn, too.

Figure 11.3 shows a prescription form with various numbers. A properly written prescription includes the following. The top line is for the *date* (1), followed by the *name and address of the patient* (2) to ensure that appropriate records are kept. Next comes the *symbol* R_x (3). The exact meaning of this familiar symbol is obscure, but most sources state that it stands for the Latin "take thou," or for the Latin word meaning "recipe." Following that is the *inscription,* or the name of the drug, to be taken (4).

The inscription can be written two ways, by generic or by proprietary (brand) name. Drugs with the same generic name may have different trade names, and the drug may be available by its generic name alone. At present, if the doctor writes a trade name in the inscription, the pharmacist *must* dispense that product. If he/she writes a generic name the pharmacist is free to dispense any drug with the same generic name. The debate between writing a prescription by generic or trade name has been going on for some time.

The *subscription* (5) contains the instructions to the pharmacist, telling him or her how to dispense the drug; the number of tablets, for example, or the quantity of a liquid drug. The *signature* (6) is not the physician's signature, but the instructions to the patient to be written on the label, such as how many pills to be taken, when they should be taken, and any special instructions. More and more, these instructions are written in English (or what passes for English in a doctor's handwriting). Some doctors still prefer Latin inscriptions such as *b.i.d.* (twice a day), or *q.i.d.* (four times a day),

FIGURE 11.3
The numbered lines of the prescription form are explained in the text.

Prescription Form

1.

2. Rosa Fulano Age 23
   235 Redwood Way
   Citrus Heights, California
3.
4. Tenormin 50 mg
5. Dispense 30 tablets
6. Label: Take one tablet before breakfast
7. Do not refill
8.
                                    Sven Larson, M.D.
                                    DEA No. AB4758699
                                    1423 Flood Road
                                    Cool, California 95603

but there is no reason for such usage, since the instructions are written in English by the pharmacist.

The *refill information* (7) is in the lower left-hand corner. Current law dictates how often various drugs can be filled and the physician must adhere to these requirements. The final portion of the prescription is the prescriber's signature, address, and a number that certifies that the doctor is authorized to prescribe such a drug (8). This is the Drug Enforcement Agency registry number. Physicians convicted of various offenses may be permitted to practice medicine, but may have their prescribing authority restricted.

Many pharmaceutical companies maintain that all generic drugs are not equal and that their trade drug is superior by virtue of more careful manufacturing processes and better ingredients used to make the inert part of the pill (the filler and the capsule, for example). The FDA insists that all drugs that have the same generic name are identical, and that the cheapest is as good as the most expensive. The FDA claims that its quality control requirements ensure that the drugs are the same.

Of course, the pharmaceutical companies would like to sell their more expensive trade drugs, since included in their cost is the cost of developing and advertising their products. They sometimes view the maker of the generic drug as a Johnny-come-lately who is reaping the profits of their research. To further complicate matters, however, some companies sell the same drugs under generic *and* trade labels. This issue will undoubtedly be debated through the 1990s.

Prescription Drugs and Advertising

Another issue that is beginning to have an impact is what is referred to as "direct to consumer" advertising. In 1985 after considerable discussion the

Generic Drugs

The chemical name for aspirin is, as we saw, acetyl-salicylic acid, and the price difference between a nationally advertised brand and one that is produced by a supermarket chain can be enormous. The same principle applies to prescription drugs. Inderal, for example is the name that is used by one manufacturer (Ayerst) of propanalol. Other companies offer what they claim is the same drug and call it, not surprisingly, *propanalol*. The name given to the drug by the company that first produced it is called the *innovator* or *product* name and is considered a trademark. The *generic* name is also called the *nonproprietary*, or *trivial* name. The *chemical* name is based on careful rules formulated by the international chemical societies.

In recent years there has been considerable controversy over generic as opposed to innovator drugs. Are the two kinds of drugs really the same? Could a pharmacist substitute a generic drug for a trademarked drug? Did the pharmacist have to follow the physician's instructions exactly? In the 1950s numerous state laws were passed which required that pharmacies dispense exactly the brand of drug prescribed by the physician. Pressure slowly grew to permit substitution of generic drugs and by 1982 all such laws had been repealed. In 1984 a federal law, the Drug Price Competition and Patent Term Restoration Act was passed to clarify the situation.

The basic idea behind generic drugs is simple in theory; if two drugs are equivalent they can be used interchangeably. As always, in reality, the issue is more complicated. There are three different types of equivalence, and drugs listed as equivalent at one level may not be equivalent at others. *Chemical equivalence* means that two drugs contain the same amount of the therapeutic ingredient in the same dosage form. However, chemical equivalence applies only to the active ingredient. There are binders, fillers, and coatings that may differ between manufacturers, and two drugs that are chemically equivalent may have quite different effects when taken.

Biological equivalence means that two drugs will deliver an amount of drug to the same site of action sufficient to produce the same response. This is the current standard that is used by the Food and Drug Administration. However, biological equivalence may not always mean *therapeutic equivalence*. Therapeutic equivalence means that the two drugs will not only get to the same site but will exert the same effect.

As an example of how biological and therapeutic equivalence may differ, consider the fact that in the 1930s a manufacturer marketed an extract of sulfanilamide (an antibacterial drug no longer used) dissolved in diethylene glycol. Diethylene glycol is essentially antifreeze and has a sweet taste. The sulfanilamide reached the site of action but the diethylene glycol killed more than 100 children (Strom, 1987).

Drug companies may spend millions of dollars developing, testing, and advertising new drugs and are understandably less than enthusiastic when another company comes along and markets the generic equivalent of the same drug. To this end the 1984 law provides for a five year period during which the company that develops the drug has exclusive rights to it.

On the other hand, if a drug can be manufactured by one company for a fraction of the cost that another charges for it, and the two drugs are the same, why should anyone pay the higher price? Consumer groups and others have supported the companies that manufacture generics. Look for this issue to heat up in the 1990s, with the debate focused on whether or not generics and innovative drugs are therapeutic as well as biological equivalents.

Food and Drug Administration permitted consumer advertising within certain limits. You have undoubtedly seen these advertisements on television. Some are disease specific in that they discuss some condition such as high blood pressure and recommend seeing a doctor for medication to treat it.

Others are more specific and indicate in their advertisements that a specific product exists, but do not name it. Consumers are encouraged to ask their physician about the medication. Some advertisements go further and mention specific drugs and describe their advantages and disadvantages. Cable television programs aimed at health professionals are the likely targets of these ads. Of course, anyone can watch them and get the information and the name of the drug (Kessler & Pines, 1990).

On the one hand, the commercials might provide a service by informing the viewer who may be unaware of a given health problem or who has previously given up on other drugs. On the other hand, some feel that advertising to the consumer might disrupt the doctor–patient relationship or encourage unnecessary prescribing. Whatever the rationale, prescription drug advertising is big business; more than $70 million is spent every year trying to get you to buy products that will treat hair loss, reduce allergy symptoms, get you to stop smoking, or reduce your blood pressure. Expect to see both the commercials and the controversy expand in the next few years.

Legal Aspects of Prescription Drugs

There are numerous legal requirements concerning prescription drugs. Some cannot be prescribed at all, while others have strict regulations about how often they may be prescribed. These regulations are the result of the Comprehensive Drug Abuse and Control Act of 1970 which has been amended several times. Table 11.6 shows a summary of this act.

While Table 11.6 may seem confusing, it is, in fact, quite simple to understand. **Schedule I** drugs have no medical use, have a high potential for abuse, and cannot be manufactured except under strict controls. Included are the narcotic drugs that are most often abused, such as heroin, and the derivatives of fentanyl (the "designer drugs" discussed in chapter 9). In addition, MDMA (Ecstasy) and similar drugs are on the list, as well as the less dangerous drugs such as marijuana, LSD, and mescaline.

Schedule II drugs are similar in their potential for abuse, but do have medical uses. Schedule II contains one notorious error. Cocaine is listed as a narcotic, which, of course, it is not. Nevertheless, the penalties for possessing cocaine are the same as those for possessing narcotics and are greater than those for possessing other Schedule II drugs, such as amphetamine and methamphetamine, which it more closely resembles.

Schedule III drugs are those having less capacity to produce dependence than Schedule I or II and have a medical use. Paregoric is in Schedule III, as is glutethimide (Doriden), a popular "sleeping pill." Not many familiar drugs are found in Schedule III because Schedule IV drugs are generally just as effective and are less likely to be abused.

Table 11.6 Controlled Substances

Schedule	Description	Examples
I	Virtually all the drugs in this group are illegal. All of them have a high potential for abuse and currently do not have an accepted medical use. These drugs are not prescribable.	Benzylmorphine, dihydromorphine, heroin, LSD, marijuana, mescaline, nicocodeine, peyote.
II	Like Schedule I drugs, these have a high potential for abuse and can lead to serious physical and psychological dependence. Unike Schedule I drugs, however, they have an accepted medical use. Most of them are stimulants, narcotics, or depressants. Prescriptions for them cannot be renewed.	Amphetamine, cocaine, codeine, meperidine, morphine, secobarbital.
III	Drugs in this group have a lower potential for abuse than those in the Schedules I and II, but they can nevertheless lead to dependence. Prescriptions for Schedule III drugs can be refilled up to five times in six months if the prescriber authorizes it.	· Acetaminophen with codeine, aspirin with codeine, methyprylon (sleeping drug), benzphetamine (appetite suppressant), phendimetrazine (appetite suppressant).
IV	The drugs in this group have a potential for abuse lower than Schedule I-III drugs. The regulations for refilling prescriptions are the same in most states as for Schedule III drugs.	Chloral hydrate (sleeping drug), diazepam (antianxiety drug, muscle relaxant), ethchlorvynol (sleeping drug), phenobarbital (anticonvulsant), prazepam (antianxiety drug).
V	These drugs have a low potential for abuse. For the most part, they are preparations that contain small amounts of narcotics.	(Note: These are all brand-name combination preparations.) Lomotil (antidiarrheal), Parepectolin (antidiarrheal), Cheracol (cough suppressant), Robitussin AC (cough suppressant), Tussi-Organidin liquid (cough suppressant).

Source: AMA Guide to Prescription and Non Prescription Drugs, Random House, 1988, p. 13.

Schedule IV drugs are the most familiar. They include most of the antianxiety drugs such as Librium and Valium, many barbiturate sedative hypnotics, and other drugs with relatively low potential for abuse and definite medical uses. Even these drugs have more abuse potential than the Schedule V drugs, and you still need a prescription to obtain them.

Schedule V drugs can be purchased in many states without a prescription. The Comprehensive Drug Abuse and Control Act of 1970 does not require a prescription, although it does require the pharmacist to keep records of such sales, limit the amount sold, and obtain positive identification of the purchaser. Some states have stricter regulations and require prescriptions for Schedule V drugs that are mainly codeine-based antitussives (see chapter 10) and opium compounds to treat diarrhea.

Very few sufferers of acute diarrhea will take enough of these drugs to produce dependence, but narcotics addicts frequently use them and the codeine antitussives when stronger narcotics are not available. The positive identification, quantity limits, and reporting requirements are, therefore, designed to prevent someone from buying large amounts of these drugs.

The various schedules of drugs have different regulations concerning refilling of prescriptions, recordkeeping, and security. A prescription for a Schedule II drug, for example, cannot be refilled. In addition, separate records must be kept, and a report must be made by the pharmacist to the Drug Enforcement Agency of all prescriptions dispensed. Further, these drugs must be kept in a secure vault or safe.

For Schedule III and IV drugs, refills are permitted, but with a limit of five refills in six months. These drugs must be kept in a secure area, but a separate vault is not required. Prescription records do not have to be reported directly to the DEA but they must be readily available.

All of these safeguards are designed to regulate the availability of drugs with potential for abuse. Keep in mind, however, that they limit only *legal* availability of drugs. Any drug can be obtained by anyone with the right contacts and enough money. Their other purpose is to identify patterns of abuse by doctors writing the prescriptions, either for themselves or for others. Those who write any prescription for a price are called "script doctors" or "script writers."

Drug regulations are effective in the same way as a lock on the door of your house. It tells honest people that you are not at home and they should not enter. Burglars are not deterred by most locks, as our rising burglary rates readily demonstrate. Drug regulations may prevent the casual user from overdosing or becoming dependent unintentionally, but the determined drug user simply bypasses legal channels. Therefore, regulations, no matter how strict, are no deterrent to him or her at all.

SUMMARY

While over-the-counter drugs are used in self-medication, prescription drugs, because of their abuse potential, potentially harmful side effects, or other considerations are available only with a prescription written by a physician. Of the many thousands, the prescription drugs most important to this text are those used to treat psychological disorders.

Antianxiety drugs are the drugs formerly referred to as minor tranquilizers. They are useful in the treatment of acute anxiety brought on by temporarily stressful life events. Because of their abuse potential they should not be taken for prolonged periods of time. They are also useful in inducing sleep.

Drugs used to treat affective disorders alter levels of serotonin and the catecholamines. They are often quite effective when proper dosages are determined and when taken long enough to exert their effect. Because those suffering from affective disorders may be potentially suicidal, or engage in some other self-destructive behavior, they may quite literally be life-saving.

Unlike the drugs used to treat affective disorders, those used to treat schizophrenia really only reduce the symptoms, enabling the person with this disorder to function better and perhaps be amenable to psychotherapy. They have serious side effects with prolonged use, and their prescription must be carefully monitored.

Many people suffer from sleep disorders, and drugs are sometimes used to help them. It should be remembered that these drugs are only a temporary measure. They are sedative hypnotics and really don't produce *sleep* as much as they induce consciousness. Like every drug, they can have potentially serious side effects and should be used cautiously.

The legal classification of drugs is based on a given drug's medical use and potential for abuse. Various restrictions on prescription refilling and recordkeeping accompany each of the schedules. The combination of a requirement for medical use and the degree of abuse potential leads to some curious classifications. Marijuana, for example, is a Schedule I drug (the most restrictive category), while cocaine is a Schedule II.

Ideally, prescription drugs are classified as such because more controls are necessary to prevent danger or abuse. Like any drug, they should be taken with care.

REFERENCES

Alexander, B., & Perry, P. J. (1991). Detoxification from benzodiazepines. *Journal of Substance Abuse Treatment, 8,* 9–17.

Allquander, C. (1978). Dependence on sedative and hypnotic drugs. *Acta Psychiatrica Scandinavia, 270,* 1–120.

Anthenelli, R. M., Monteiro, M. G., Blunt, B., & Schuckit, M. A. (1991). Amnestic effects of intravenous diazepam in healthy young men. *American Journal of Drug and Alcohol Abuse, 17,* 129–36.

Ashton, H. (1991). Protracted withdrawal syndromes from benzodiazepines. *Journal of Substance Abuse Treatment, 8,* 19–28.

Baldessarini, R. J. (1980). Drugs in the treatment of psychiatric disorders. In A. G. Gilman, L. S. Goodman, & A. Goodman (Eds.). *The Pharmacological basis of therapeutics.* New York: Macmillan.

Busto, U., & Sellers, E. M. (1991). Pharmacological aspects of benzodiazepine tolerance and dependence. *Journal of Substance Abuse Treatment, 8,* 29–33.

Cole, J. (1988). Where are those new antidepressants we were promised? *Archives of General Psychiatry, 45,* 193–94.

Cooper, J. R., Bloom, F. E., & Roth, R. H. (1986). *The biochemical basis of neuropharmacology.* New York and Oxford: Oxford University Press.

Cox, T. C., Jacobs, M. R., Leblanc, A. E., & Marshman, J. A. (1983). *Drugs and drug abuse: A reference text.* Toronto: Addiction Research Foundation.

Curran, H. V., Schiwy, W., & Lader, M. (1987). Differential amnesic properties of benzodiazepines: A dose response comparison of two drugs with similar elimination half times. *Psychopharmacology, 52,* 358–64.

FDA Consumer (1991). Top 10 drugs in 1990, July/August, p. 5.

Gillin, J. C., & Byerley, W. F. (1990). The diagnosis and management of insomnia. *New England Journal of Medicine, 322,* 239–46.

Goodwin, D. W. (1986). *Anxiety.* New York: Ballantine.

Heckman, J. (1988). Beating insomnia: How to get the sleep of your dreams. *Hippocrates, 2,* 42–43.

Jaffe, J. H. (1980). Drug addiction and drug abuse. In A. G. Gilman, L. S. Goodman, & A. Gilman (Eds.). *The pharmacological basis of therapeutics, 6th ed.* New York: Macmillan.

Joyce, P. R., & Paykel, E. S. (1989). Predictors of drug response in depression. *Archives of General Psychiatry, 46,* 89–99.

Kessler, D. A., & Pines, W. L. (1990). The federal regulation of prescription drug advertising and promotion. *Journal of the American Medical Association, 264,* 2409–15.

Lockwood, A. H. (1989). Medical problems of musicians. *The New England Journal of Medicine, 320,* 221–27.

Marks, J. (1988). Techniques of benzodiazepine withdrawal in clinical practice: A consensus workshop report. *Medical Toxicology, 3,* 324–33.

Marsden, C. A. (1991). The neuropharmacology of serotonin in the central nervous system. In J. P. Feighner, & W. F. Boyer (Eds.). *Selective serotonin re-uptake inhibitors.* New York: Wiley.

Morgan, W. W. (1990). Abuse liability of barbiturates and other sedative hypnotics. *Advances in Alcohol and Substance Abuse. 9,* 67–75.

Persad, E., & Rakoff, V. (1987). *Use of drugs in psychiatry.* Toronto: Hans Buber Publishers.

Preston, J., & Johnson, J. (1991). *Clinical psychopharmacology.* Miami, FL: MedMaster.

Price, L. H., Charney, D. S., Delgado, P. L., & Heninger, G. R. (1989). Lithium treatment and serotonergic function: Neuroendocrine and behavior response to intravenous tryptophan in affective disorder. *Archives of General Psychiatry, 46,* 13–19.

Robinson, L. A., Berman, J. S., & Neimeyer, R. A. (1990). Psychotherapy for the treatment of depression: A comprehensive review of controlled outcome research. *Psychological Bulletin, 108,* 30–49.

Schuckit, M. A., Greenblatt, D., Gold, E., & Irwin, M. (1991). Reactions to ethanol and diazepam in healthy young men. *Journal of Studies on Alcohol, 52,* 180–87.

Skoler, M. (1988). Upstaging fright with a pill. *Hippocrates, 2,* 26–27.

Slone, P. D., Mathew, L. J., Scarborough, M., Desai, J. R., Koch, G. G., & Tangen, C. (1991). Physical and pharmacologic restraint of nursing home patients with dementia. *Journal of the American Medical Association, 265, 1278–82.*

Snyder, S. (1984). Medicated minds. *Science 84,* November, 141–42.

Squires, L. F., & Brasestrup, C. (1977). Benzodiazepine receptors in rat brain. *Nature, 266,* 732–34.

Strom, B. L. (1987). Generic drug substitution revisited. *New England Journal of Medicine, 316,* 1456–61.

Sulser, F. (1982). Antidepressant drug research: Impact on neurobiology and psychobiology. In E. Costa & G. Racagini (Eds.). *Typical and atypical antidepressants.* New York: Raven Press.

Swann, A. C., Koslow, S. H., Katz, M. M., Maas, J. W., Javaid, J., Secunda, S.K., & Robins, E. (1987). Lithium carbonate treatment of mania. *Archives of General Psychiatry, 44,* 345–59.

Westermeyer, J. (1986). *A .clinical guide to alcohol and drug problems.* New York: Praeger.

Woods, J. H., Katz, J. L., and Winger, G. (1988). Use and abuse of benzodiazepines: Issues relevant to prescribing. *Journal of the American Medical Association, 260,* 3476–80.

12

• • •

DRUGS AND THE LAW

• • •

OBJECTIVES

When you have finished studying this chapter you should:

1. Be able to discuss the history of drug laws.
2. Understand the legal attempts to limit alcohol use.
3. Know how the government attempts to control drug use.
4. Be able to explain how seizure and forfeiture laws are used to control drug use.
5. Be able to discuss three ways of attacking drug sales.
6. Understand the special problems of corruption.
7. Know how our attitudes toward drunk driving have changed.
8. Be able to discuss the problems of controlling drunk driving through legal means.
9. Know why drug testing has become so popular.
10. Know why so many authorities are concerned about the constitutional questions of drug testing.
11. Understand how drug testing works.
12. Be able to distinguish between false positives and false negatives and tell why they are important.

KEY TERMS

Harry Anslinger
Boggs Act
Comprehensive Drug Abuse Prevention and Control Act of 1970
conspiracy
Drug Abuse Act of 1988
Drug Czar
Drug Enforcement Agency
Drug-Free Workplace Act of 1988
Eighteenth Amendment
EMIT
false positive
false negative
Federal Bureau of Narcotics
Harrison Narcotic Act of 1914
Marijuana Tax Act of 1937
Mr. Big
Narcotics Control Act of 1956
National Commission on Drug-Free Schools
paraphernalia
preemployment screening
Pure Food and Drug Act of 1906
Quick, Caught, and the Dead
RICO
Benjamin Rush
seizure and forfeiture
SYVA
Uniform Drug Act of 1937
Volstead National Prohibition Act
war on drugs
Women's Christian Temperance Union

THE HISTORY
OF DRUG LAWS

The attempt to regulate or prevent drug use by legal means has a long history. In this section we will concentrate on how legislation in America has shaped our view of drugs, both legal and illegal. Keep in mind that whether a drug is legal or illegal has little to do either with its capacity to produce dependence or its lethality. The rationale behind scheduling drugs as legal or illegal has as much to do with our political and cultural history as with medical science.

At one time or another virtually every drug, even those considered comparatively harmless today, such as caffeine, have been banned. Coffee drinking was considered a sacrilege in Arab countries shortly after its introduction. Attempts to enforce laws against tobacco smoking go back to its introduction into the Western Hemisphere. Sultan Murad IV decreed the death penalty for smokers, and tobacco was banned in China shortly after its introduction. Attempts to regulate drugs more widely recognized as addictive, such as opium, were just as common but no more successful. No society has ever eradicated any drug by passing laws against its use, and there is no reason to believe we will be any more successful.

In the United States, various states had individual laws against tobacco, cocaine, opiates, and alcohol during the eighteenth and nineteenth centuries but no federal laws existed. By and large, America was a drug fiend's paradise until the passage of the **Pure Food and Drug Act of 1906, and the Harrison Narcotic Act of 1914.** These two acts capped a growing anti-drug movement that had led to passage of laws restricting the use of cocaine in forty-six states and opiates in twenty-nine (Abadinsky, 1989). There were a few attempts prior to this, including a presidential commission into the use of cocaine either in soft drinks or mixed with wine (see chapter 4), while federal laws were passed against opium in the Philippines, at the time an American territory.

The Pure Food and Drug Act of 1906 was designed to correct incredible abuses in the food industry and to regulate the use of certain drugs in over-the-counter medications (see chapter 10). One effect of the regulations was that medicine had to list certain drugs, thus effectively reducing the use of cocaine, opiates, and alcohol in patent medicines. The Harrison Narcotic Act of 1914 was directed specifically at drugs and was spearheaded by Congressman Francis Harrison, who, ironically, was reported to have been a very heavy drinker if not an alcoholic. It required that anyone dealing in opiates or cocaine had to register and pay a tax of one dollar (Abadinsky, 1989).

While such a restriction may seem minimal, the act also made it illegal to sell or give away these drugs except with a special order form and made

This postcard dates back to the beginning of the twentieth century and is a protest against illegal sale of drugs by pharmacists. It may date to early Prohibition days.

DRUGGIST
Such dope and booze you serve, they say,
Your counter's like a bar all day—
You'll feel at home, and we'll thank our stars
When you are safe behind the bars.

their possession without the form illegal. The U.S. Treasury Department would not allow anyone other than a medical doctor to register and thus gave the medical profession a monopoly over the prescription of these drugs (Abadinsky, 1989). Doctors could still prescribe narcotics to addicts or cocaine to anyone, and those who were already addicts could, at least theoretically, maintain their addiction. The federal government began to chip away at this privilege, and physicians gradually stopped prescribing to addicts.

The various states passed their own laws regulating drug use in the aftermath of the Harrison Narcotic Act. These laws differed greatly, and enough pressure eventually was felt so the federal government developed a model set of laws called the **Uniform Drug Act of 1937.** This law regulated opiates and cocaine, legally considered a "narcotic" since 1922, but made no provisions for marijuana. Most of the states adopted these guidelines and all banned marijuana separately. The problem was that virtually no one paid any attention to any of these laws.

Meanwhile the **Federal Bureau of Narcotics,** under **Harry Anslinger,** whom we met in chapter 6 was trying to do something about marijuana. Because the Bureau was not sure it could get Congress to pass legislation banning the drug outright, it proposed the **Marijuana Tax Act of 1937** which placed a tax of $100 an ounce on the marijuana. Harry Anslinger then orchestrated a campaign to ensure passage of the law.

As a result of such legislation, law-abiding citizens stayed away from these drugs; after all, they had alcohol. Illegal drug use was largely confined to ghettos, to criminals, some musicians, and others about whom society was not particularly concerned. No one protested; indeed, very few people even were aware of these laws. In 1951, the difference between marijuana, the opiates, and cocaine was eliminated by the **Boggs Act,** and penalties for all of these substances were substantially increased.

The penalties were increased even more by the **Narcotics Control Act of 1956** which made sale of heroin to anyone under eighteen punishable by the death penalty. There were periodic adjustments to these acts in the years that followed, but the next big change occurred in 1965 when Congress passed the Drug Abuse Control Amendments which gave jurisdiction over some of the drug issues to the Food and Drug Administration, and the Narcotic Addicts Rehabilitation Act of 1966 which permitted involuntary commitment of addicts to treatment rather than putting them in jail.

The next major drug prevention bill was the **Comprehensive Drug Abuse Prevention and Control Act of 1970.** It eliminated the Federal Bureau of Narcotics and created the Bureau of Narcotics and Dangerous Drugs with authority over violations of the laws relating to drugs and added the jurisdiction over importation and smuggling. At the same time, it liberalized many of the existing penalties and provided for separate programs for drug prevention and education under the National Institute of Mental Health. This is the act that established the five schedules of drugs you read about in chapter 11.

In 1973, the **Drug Enforcement Agency** was formed within the Department of Justice and in 1982 the Federal Bureau of Investigation (FBI) and the Department of Defense were brought into the act, widening the scope of law enforcement activities and bringing the United States military forces into play on the **war on drugs.**

The legal authority in the current war on drugs is the Anti-Drug Bill of 1988 signed into law by President Reagan on 18 November 1988. It has several hundred provisions with the goal of making America drug-free by 1995. Drug-free means, of course, illegal drugs. The many provisions include the following:

Civil Penalties

Civil penalties of up to $10,000 can be imposed for possession of small amounts of illegal drugs, with the provision that the records of those given these fines would be erased if the person remained drug-free for three years. The concept of civil penalty is important because many of the provisions of criminal law, including the concept of guilty beyond a reasonable doubt, do not prevail. No jury trial is necessary and rules of evidence are relaxed.

Penalties for ''Casual Users''

In addition to the civil penalties, individuals convicted of drug offenses can be denied federal benefits such as loans for five years for a first, and ten years for a second, offense. Welfare, Social Security and a few other benefits are exempted. The offender can reinstate benefits by completing a drug rehabilitation program.

Legal Penalties

The Act establishes the death penalty for drug "kingpins" and anyone convicted of a drug-related killing. It regulates those supplying precursor chemicals (which can be made into illegal drugs) and increases penalties for drug traffickers.

Further provisions involve funding to states to establish alternative sentencing programs, such as house arrest and "boot camps," for nonviolent drug offenders and to expand programs to eradicate the domestic marijuana crop. As we will see later in this chapter the Act also establishes procedures for widespread drug testing programs.

The Drug Czar

The Act establishes a cabinet level position for the Director of the Office of National Drug Control Policy who is responsible for the entire federal drug budget.

As part of this Act, the Drug Czar is required to submit a yearly summary and a national drug control strategy to update and focus efforts on the war on drugs. Some major priorities from the 1991 report, for example, call for: (1) user accountability; (2) providing effective treatment; (3) expanding precursor chemical programs; (4) continuing efforts to eradicate the domestic marijuana crop; (4) halting diversion of legal drugs to the illegal market; and (5) focusing on money laundering schemes (The White House, 1991).

One spinoff of the war on drugs has had a direct effect on college campuses. **The Drug-Free Workplace Act of 1988** applies to college campuses. What this means is that illegal drug use is forbidden on college campuses, and alcohol use is severely restricted. All employees are required to report any convictions related to drug use and their employment could be terminated. Employees must sign a statement that they are aware of these regulations. Students convicted of drug-related offenses can be denied federal funds including grants and scholarships. Interestingly, no such regulations exist for other crimes. It is possible, therefore, for a murderer to get a federal scholarship that would be denied to someone convicted of drug possession.

The **National Commission on Drug-Free Schools** which was mandated by the **Drug Abuse Act of 1988** issued a final report in 1990 setting goal of drug-free schools by the year 2000. It makes the following recommendations (National Commission on Drug Free Schools, 1990). How many are being followed in your school? How many do you think *will* be in place by 2000?

1. Colleges should develop and enforce policies that prohibit the use of all illegal drugs.

2. Colleges and universities should conduct mandatory drug education and prevention orientation sessions for all students.

3. Colleges should include drug prevention education in curricula for educators and other professionals who work with youth.

4. At colleges, require all organized group residences to develop risk management plans.

5. College presidents should establish a drug education and prevention task force to assess drug problems, student and staff attitudes, and the relevant policies, practices, and programs of the school.

6. Every college should provide leadership training for its top administrators.

7. Every college should provide staff members in-service training on alcohol and other drugs.

8. Prohibit alcohol and tobacco use at all college sporting events(!).

9. State clearly the school rules regarding alcohol and cigarette use and possession in school and at school events, and ensure the rules are strictly enforced.

10. Prohibit all alcohol and tobacco advertising in school newspapers, at stadiums, and at all school events.

11. Include alcohol and tobacco in the school's drug prevention curriculum.

12. To help counter the influence of advertising, teach students the basic concepts of marketing alcohol and tobacco products and the ways in which marketers seek to initiate and increase product consumption through audience targeting, celebrity endorsement of products, and other means.

13. Provide adequate support programs for students and staff who need help combatting drinking or smoking problems.

14. Colleges should recognize individuals and groups that demonstrate a leadership role in drug prevention activities.

15. Colleges should consider alternative sanctions for students who violate drug laws.

To give teeth to these regulations, the government has the right to withhold most federal funds, including research grants, if these conditions are not being met. In 1991 a faculty member at Stanford University in Palo Alto, California, was suspended because he said he had used MDA (see chapter 5), recommended it to others, and carried it in his knapsack on campus. He is also said to have provided an underage drinker with alcohol. Do you feel that this kind of threat (to withold funds) might produce an atmosphere in which an instructor's right of free inquiry is lessened, or do you feel that the Stanford instructor went too far? By the way, he was never convicted of any offense related to his statements.

THE LEGAL CONTROL OF ALCOHOL

You have just read how our legal system has attempted to control narcotics, stimulants, and marijuana use. Alcohol is, at present, a legal drug, but has not always been so and many of the patterns seen in the present attempts to control illegal drug use first appeared when our society attempted to control alcohol. So many similarities exist between the consequences of attempts to regulate alcohol and attempts to regulate other drugs that you would think we would have learned valuable lessons from the past. Unfortunately, we have not, and we seem to continue to make the same mistakes our forefathers (and foremothers) did.

For the first two hundred years of our country's existence, alcoholic beverages were considered not only harmless, but absolutely essential. Alcohol was a beverage when water was unsafe to drink and a medicine when virtually nothing other than opium was available. As you have already read, the Puritans drank beer, wine, and hard cider, while most of the rest of the colonists seem to have lived their lives from childhood to old age in a mild alcohol-induced haze. Children were given alcohol from an early age and until the early nineteenth century, many, if not most, people who could afford it started their day off with a drink (or two or three). In the Army and Navy, soldiers and sailors got two to four ounces of hard liquor as their daily ration *first thing in the morning(!)* (Furnas, 1973).

Until the revolution, the only legal controls over alcohol were taxes on its manufacture or sale, in the same way that nearly every business now pays taxes. These attempts were not primarily aimed at controlling drinking, but at gaining revenue from a sure source and encouraging the sale of wine, beer, and cider at the expense of imported hard liquor. In order to understand the basis of our laws about alcohol, it is important to remember that distilled liquor was considered a different beverage than beer and wine, which were fermented or brewed. Lacking a clear understanding of what alcohol, the chemical, was, our ancestors for much of our history did not even consider beer or wine to be intoxicating. Also, they had little or no concept of addiction.

The first hints of what our liquor laws would eventually become can be found in a pamphlet written in 1774 by Anthony Benezet, a Quaker, called *The Mighty Destroyer Displayed, in Some Account of the Dreadful Havock Made by the Mistaken Use as Well as Abuse of Distilled Spiritous Liquors,* and a more famous article published in 1784 by one of the greatest minds of the eighteenth century, **Benjamin Rush,** *Inquiry into the Effect of Ardent Spirits.* These titles refer to what we call hard li- quor. Both Benezet and Rush were proponents of *temperance,* not prohibition. Rush's article not only set the tone for nearly every anti-alcohol article written for the next 150 years or so, but came out in favor of at least considering making liquor illegal (Furnas, 1973).

This woodcut from the nineteenth century satirizes both dueling and heaving drinkers. Many duels resulted in a harmless exchange of gunfire because both participants were drunk.

From the end of the Revolutionary War until the 1840s the United States went on a hard liquor binge unparalleled before or since. The abuse was so notorious that it eventually spawned numerous temperance societies, such as the American Temperance Union and even the Congressional Temperance Society, an organization of Congressmen and Senators. Keep in mind that virtually no one was as yet advocating abstinence or calling for legislation. The idea behind these groups was to promote moderation and they were largely made up of middle-class, Protestant men. Eventually, other groups, notably the Washingtonians, began to attract members of the lower working classes (Tyrrell, 1979).

The first real attempt to prohibit alcohol was an act in 1834 that prohibited the sale of liquor to Indians under federal jurisdiction. In 1838, the state of Massachusetts passed a law forbidding the sale of less than fifteen gallons of liquor at one time. Of course, the wealthy could afford that much, so the law was primarily a way of keeping the poor from drinking too much. Enterprising drinkers and sellers soon figured out a way to get around the law. The purchasers simply bought fifteen gallons and one *gill* (1/4 pint). He (they were always male) drank the gill on the spot and sold the fifteen gallons back to the seller.

The first serious attempt at controlling alcohol was made in Maine in 1846. Officially titled ''Act for the Suppression of Drinking Houses and

Tippling Shops'' it went through several revisions and eventually provided penalties for the manufacture, sale, and possession for sale of *distilled* liquor. Many states followed suit and the Maine law became famous among temperance advocates. However, the people of Maine were just as ingenious as the people of Massachusetts, and numerous strategies were developed to get around the law.

While the law prevented the sale of spirits, shopkeepers could and did sell crackers for a few cents and give the liquor away. A drinker could pay admission to get into a room where the drinks were provided free. One trick resulted in coining a new word that is still sometimes seen today. A ''blind pig'' now means a place where liquor is illegally sold. In Maine in the 1850s, it referred to a trick of selling admission to see an animal, a pig with a blindfold, or a striped pig (a pig painted with stripes). After paying admission, the viewer got a free drink.

The laws were unenforceable and were soon repealed in most states. The Civil War further weakened the Temperance movement, but it picked up steam in the latter part of the 1800s and another round of legislation passed in many states. The difference, however, was that these were *Prohibition* laws, preventing the sale or manufacture of any alcoholic beverage. The switch from temperance to prohibition came about for several reasons; a scientific understanding of the similarity between various types of alcoholic beverages, a religious revival, the beginning of the understanding of the nature of addiction, and prejudice against certain ethnic groups, notably Germans and Irish (Tyrell, 1973).

Both Germans and Irish were seen as brewers, distributors, and consumers of large quantities of alcoholic beverages. Furthermore, they and other immigrant groups brought with them to the United States their own drinking habits which were at odds with those already developed in this country. The saloon, the beer garden, drinking on Sunday, women drinking along with men in public, were widely disliked by many native-born Americans, but accepted practice among many immigrants.

Three organizations spearheaded Prohibition: the Women's Christian Temperance Union, the Prohibition Party and the Anti-Saloon League. They joined forces just before the entry of the United States into World War I, and their combined influence plus anti-German sentiment finally tipped the scale. In January 1919 the Eighteenth Amendment was ratified and Prohibition became law, to be effective one year later. The **Volstead National Prohibition Act** implemented the Eighteenth Amendment and provided penalties of five years in jail and $10,000 fine for *selling* alcoholic beverages. Possession and drinking were still legal, and physicians could still prescribe alcohol.

Virtually everyone believes Prohibition was a failure, but it did have its positive aspects, as least initially. Incidence of cirrhosis of the liver declined, as did alcohol-related automobile accidents and arrests for public drunkenness. Although actual figures are impossible to come by, by most measures per capita alcohol intake decreased by about 50 percent (Goode,

1989). Looking back at that time we remember the images of the speakeasies and alcohol smugglers and assume that everyone behaved the same way. During Prohibition, however, the average person drank less and didn't begin to increase intake until well after its repeal.

Repeal occurred in 1933, although in 1932, President Franklin Roosevelt declared that beer with less than 3.2 percent alcohol was "nonalcoholic." The impetus for its repeal was not only the realization that it had not succeeded in its goal, but because the taxes that could be raised from its manufacture and sale would help reduce income and corporate tax. Another reason was the fear that the disrespect for the law that prohibition had produced would combine with the dissatisfaction and growing unrest in the country as a result of the Great Depression to destabilize the entire country. Finally, the rise of the middle class, especially those of non–Anglo–Saxon backgrounds created a market for alcohol and a reaction against the restrictive attitudes of the past.

After repeal of Prohibition, the government wisely decided to get out of the business of attempting to legislate consumption and restricted itself to regulating production and marketing of alcoholic beverages. The Bureau of Alcohol, Tobacco, and Firearms within the U.S. Treasury Department now has jurisdiction. Its regulations are confined to discouraging sales to underage and intoxicated persons, maintaining purity standards, and other minor issues. The other regulatory agencies are the various Alcohol Beverage Control commissions of each state. They are responsible for most of the day-to-day regulation of the marketing of alcoholic beverages that exist in your state.

Recently, various acts of Congress have provisions which have served to alter some regulations that are technically under the jurisdiction of the states. For example, states that do not maintain a minimum drinking age of twenty-one lose highway funds. Given the changing attitude in our society toward drug use in general and the declining consumption of alcoholic beverages in particular, further regulations are likely. No one, however, realistically expects to see a return to Prohibition, not even the remnants of the Women's Christian Temperance Union, once perhaps the most powerful lobbying force for Prohibition.

DRUGS AND CRIME

That drugs and crime go hand-in-hand is so obvious, it hardly needs to be stated. The statistics to demonstrate this relationship leap out at us from the newspaper, magazines, television, and other media. For example, in 1991 the combined populations in state and federal prisons approached 800,000 with another 450,000 in local jails (Department of Justice, 1991). This figure is in addition to the nearly three million offenders on probation or parole (the term parole is used when a prisoner is released under supervision *before* his/her sentence is completed, while probation usually refers to supervision in lieu of a prison sentence). Another way of looking at this statistic is to consider that almost 4 percent of the entire adult male population of the United States is either in prison, jail, or on probation or parole.

Of that enormous total (the highest percentage of any country that keeps such statistics), two-thirds of those in state prisons were convicted of trafficking or manufacturing illegal drugs, and one-third of state prisoners, one-quarter of jail inmates, and two-fifths of youths convicted of a violent crime said they were under the influence of an illegal drug at the time of their offense. Approximately 80 percent of prisoners in all facilities admit to having used drugs at some point in their lives, and about a third of prisoners admitted they needed help with alcohol or drug abuse.

All but the first of these figures were based on self-report, which is notoriously unreliable. Direct measurements of the relationship between drugs and crime are even more frightening. In a recent study, individuals who had been just arrested were asked to provide a urine specimen. Amazingly, 80 percent complied, and of 10,554 male and 3,215 female arrestees, 68 percent of the men and 63 percent of the women tested positive for some illegal drug (Department of Justice, 1991).

Considering crimes related directly to drugs, more than one million drug arrests are made every year, about 80 percent are prosecuted, and 50 percent actually go to jail. Increased penalties and requirements about the minimum amount of time served that have been passed as a result of the Anti-Drug Act of 1988 and more recent rulings, insure that these prisoners will spend most of their sentence behind bars instead of on parole.

The economic expense related to the criminal justice system is enormous, as is the amount of money spent on drugs themselves. According to the Office of National Drug Control Policy (ONDCP), illicit retail sales of drugs amounted to $40 billion in 1990 which, according to ONDCP, reflects a decline from $49.9 billion in 1989 and $51.6 billion the year before. Both the decline and the actual figures are doubted by many and are probably low estimates. In terms of expense the government spent $47 billion on the drug war in 1990, and the total criminal justice system expenditure for 1988 (the last year figures were available) was nearly $61 billion. Considering that roughly half of all crime expenditures are related to illegal drugs, combining these figures reveals the enormous cost of drugs and crime in this country.

While these statistics are impressive, they do not tell us *how* drugs and crime are related. A traditional point of view says that there are three ways: psychopharmacological, economic compulsive, and systemic. A psychopharmacological relationship is one in which the drug user commits a crime because of some drug-induced change in mood, or physiological function, or an increased impulsivity due to drug use. Examples might include a fight or assault when someone was high on cocaine, or a murder as a result of drug-induced paranoia.

Economic compulsive reasons for crime involve committing a crime to obtain money to buy drugs. Heroin addicts are notorious for stealing everything in sight, and in many parts of the country burglary and robbery are used to obtain money to feed a crack habit. Even the so-called victimless

Table 12.1 Drug Use by Male Arrestees*

CITY	% POSITIVE ANY DRUG*	2+ Drugs	Cocaine	Marijuana	Amphetamines	Opiates	PCP
MALES							
Philadelphia	80	30	70	19	0	8	1
San Diego	80	50	45	37	30	17	6
New York	79	36	67	24	0	20	4
Chicago	75	46	59	38	0	27	10
Houston	70	18	57	21	**	6	0
Los Angeles	70	28	54	19	0	16	5
Birmingham	69	21	50	18	0	6	0
Dallas	66	20	44	32	0	7	0
Cleveland	65	22	49	26	0	4	1
Portland	64	21	24	40	13	10	0
San Antonio	63	26	30	39	2	17	1
St. Louis	62	18	48	26	0	4	2
Ft. Lauderdale	61	18	47	27	0	**	0
New Orleans	60	22	51	20	**	6	3
Phoenix	60	20	27	38	9	5	**
Indianapolis	60	19	22	48	0	3	0
Wash., D.C.	59	24	49	12	**	15	6
Denver	59	16	30	37	1	3	**
San Jose	58	23	32	26	8	8	8
Kansas City	57	12	38	26	**	2	**
FEMALES							
Cleveland	88	29	80	14	0	4	0
Wash., D.C.	85	33	78	12	**	20	6
Philadelphia	81	28	64	14	0	16	0
Ft. Lauderdale	79	22	60	28	0	1	0
Kansas City	76	23	66	22	5	1	0
Portland	76	36	43	34	20	19	0
Los Angeles	73	30	59	12	0	16	**
New York	71	31	67	6	0	24	4
Dallas	71	29	57	25	0	15	0
San Diego	70	34	34	16	38	18	4
St. Louis	69	16	54	15	0	7	0
Phoenix	69	31	38	25	8	16	**
Houston	66	30	56	13	5	11	0
Birmingham	66	33	40	11	0	6	0
New Orleans	65	26	57	16	0	14	0
San Jose	64	24	31	10	5	20	22
Denver	62	15	46	15	4	3	0
Indianapolis	56	18	18	35	0	10	0
San Antonio	44	20	18	11	4	17	0

Source: National Institute of Justice/Drug Use Forecasting Program

* Positive urinalysis, January through March 1990. Drugs tested for include cocaine, opiates, PCP, marijuana, amphetamines, methadone, methaqualone, benzodiazepines, barbiturates, and propoxyphene

** Less than 1%. The positive drug test results in various cities underscore the relationship between drug use and crime.

Drug users often commit crimes for drug money.

crimes such as prostitution are often fueled by the need for money to obtain drugs.

The systemic reasons are a little more complicated. Drive-by shootings that you watch on television, rip-offs of buyers and sellers of drugs, murders committed to eliminate rivals in the drug trade, and perjury or bribery to avoid conviction are all examples. Being part of the drug culture in some communities requires evidence of criminal activity as a means of acceptance.

You should be aware, however, that the relationship is not quite so simple. While there is a strong relationship between drugs and aggression, for example, don't be too hasty in concluding that correlation is causality. People who get violent when they use alcohol or cocaine are often violent to begin with, and the drug use may be a way of releasing, or excusing, the violent behavior. The need for drugs does bring about an increase in crime, but it is not at all clear that a desire for drugs is what leads to crime in the first place. There is considerable evidence to suggest that for many, involvement in criminal activity actually precedes drug use; the crime provides the money to experiment with expensive drugs. After the use is established, of course, drugs fuel crime (Abadinsky, 1989).

Even the systemic view of drugs and crime is more complicated than it might seem. Increased law enforcement can lead to an escalation on the part of the criminal. The more profitable drugs are, the more willing drug dealers are to engage in violent activity to keep their investments and profits. The enormous profits of cocaine trafficking has led to widespread bribery in other countries and in the United States. One reason for the enormous profit, paradoxically, is the success of law enforcement efforts to interdict supply.

The relationship between drugs and crime is incredibly complex and the methods used to attack them are equally so. In addition to the obvious approach of jailing offenders for trafficking in drugs, other means of combatting the problems are also used. These involve regulations relating to conspiracy, tax violations, and seizure and asset forfeiture. While these are potent weapons, they trouble many people in and out of the legal profession.

The Internal Revenue Service requires that we pay taxes on all income we receive. They do not make a distinction between legal and illegal income. Most readers will remember Al Capone, the notorious Prohibition era gangster. Capone was eventually imprisoned, not for murder, smuggling, prostitution, or the numerous other crimes he committed, but for income tax evasion. If the IRS can determine a criminal's net worth at a given time and subtract it from the estimate of his/her worth at a later time, the IRS can prosecute the taxpayer for not reporting the income. The IRS does not even have to prove where the income came from.

Another weapon in the anti-drug arsenal is to impose a tax on the drug in question. Some states now impose a tax on the sale of marijuana, for example. Even if such a sale is illegal, the dealer still owes the tax. If the dealer is convicted, the state can then collect the tax and impose whatever other penalties are called for.

Conspiracy Laws

The laws of **conspiracy** are extremely complicated but in their simplest form mean that two or more persons agree to commit a criminal act. The *agreement* then becomes the crime, not the act committed. In fact, the crime of conspiracy is punishable even if the act the conspiracy was formed to commit is never carried out. The only requirement is that one of the conspirators commits a single act to further the conspiracy. If you plot with another person to smuggle opium in the United States and one of you rents a storage space to hide the shipment, you both have committed the act of conspiracy. Furthermore, each person in a conspiracy is responsible for the acts of others in the conspiracy, so if your partner in crime commits murder, you can both be prosecuted, even if you did not participate in or even know about the murder.

The conspiracy statutes are very broad and some feel they offer the opportunity for harassment and unfair prosecution. For example, conspiracy is a felony, even if the act that you conspire to commit is a misdemeanor. How far can conspiracy be defined? If you are selling a product used to commit a drug offense and know the buyer's intent are you also guilty of conspiracy? In other words, could you be prosecuted for selling manure to a marijuana grower if you knew he was going to put it on his plants? Look for law enforcement agencies to increase their use of conspiracy statutes and look for a reaction to this to step up in the next few years.

Seizure and Forfeiture of Assets

State and federal laws provide that property used in the commission of a crime or secured with the fruits of criminal activity can be confiscated. Most people are aware that any drugs seized in a criminal case may be disposed of without a court order. You also may be aware that the state and federal government may confiscate what is called *derivative contraband,* meaning anything used in the furtherance of a criminal act. Therefore, airplanes, cars, and boats can be forfeited even though they are not illegal to possess.

In addition to the obvious seizures, the law also provides for forfeiture of direct proceeds (any money that proceeds from the illegal activity) or derivative proceeds (anything bought with that money, such as real estate, stocks, or jewelry). The argument behind these laws is that the criminal should not be allowed to profit from criminal activity. With the enormous profits from drug dealing, these forfeitures have been a valuable tool to combat drug trafficking.

What is troubling to many is that the forfeiture proceedings do not necessarily follow the same rules as criminal proceedings. Criminal forfeiture requires that the defendant be convicted of a criminal offense first, and is therefore entitled to all the protection that the criminal laws in the Constitution provide. Civil forfeiture is different, however. There is no jury, and the prosecutors have to prove only a "preponderance" of evidence that a crime has been committed rather than proving guilt beyond a reasonable doubt. Civil proceedings can occur even when the defendant is found not guilty in criminal court or even when no criminal case is brought at all.

What does all this mean? Suppose you are arrested for attempting to smuggle marijuana into the United States from Mexico. Your new car is confiscated along with you. You are released from custody, but the government can still proceed against your car. The forfeiture laws are directed against property, not persons. Whether you find this troubling probably depends on your confidence in the legal system.

Another issue might have occurred to you. Suppose you lend your car to someone who smuggles drugs into the United States without your knowledge and is arrested. Can you get your car back? If you can convince the authorities that you knew nothing about the criminal activity and if you act fast enough, yes, but your legal fees are likely to be substantial. The law also protects banks and lending institutions. If you borrow money to buy a car, the bank owns the car. If you are arrested, the bank gets the car back. They could, theoretically, give it right back to you.

The conspiracy and forfeiture laws relating to drug use are largely the result of the Racketeer Influenced and Corrupt Organizations statute of the Organized Crime Control Act of 1970 (called **RICO**) and the Comprehensive Forfeiture Act of 1984. Seizure and forfeiture is not only a powerful weapon against crime but a substantial source of revenue for federal and state governments.

LEGALIZATION OF DRUGS

Toward the end of the Vietnam War, a political writer facetiously suggested that the way to end the war was to declare ourselves the victor and get out. Some critics of our drug policy feel that we are doing exactly that in the war on drugs. As you read in chapter 1, surveys indicate that experimental and occasional use of illegal drugs is declining (provided that you accept the validity of the surveys). Politicians talk of "turning the corner" on drug use even though we "still have a long way to go." Meanwhile, however, the number of those with serious drug problems does not seem to have changed much, if at all.

Given the enormous costs to maintain drug offenders in the penal system and the tremendous cost in crime committed to obtain drugs, some have suggested making drugs legal. Granting that drug use is unhealthy, the argument runs that it should be treated the same way as other unhealthy activities such as cigarette smoking and alcohol drinking or even overeating, motorcycle racing, and professional football.

Those proposing the legalization of drugs come from a wide spectrum of American politics, ranging from the arch-conservatives to the extreme liberals. Economists, psychologists, criminologists, and physicians have added their voices (Boaz, 1990). Even national news magazines had drug legalization as lead articles in the late 1980s. On the surface, the idea seems ludicrous and the results almost unimaginable. Would it mean that you could stop off at the nearest convenience store and pick up a pack of marijuana cigarettes? Would crack be advertised on television?

Keep in mind, however, that virtually every study that has been done has shown that, while casual use is down, abuse is up, and the attempt to interdict drugs into this country is a failure. Furthermore, unless most Americans are willing to give up the constitutional rights we already have, legal efforts are not likely to make the situation any better.

Surprisingly strong arguments can be advanced in favor of the concept of legalization (Nadelman, 1989):

1. Costs of drug law enforcement, currently estimated in excess of $8 billion dollars a year would be substantially reduced.

2. The drugs could be produced at low cost, thus reducing the need for criminal activity to buy them.

3. Taxes could be levied and the subsequent money would defer the cost of treatment for those who became addicted.

4. Those with a drug problem could lead more normal lives. Opium and morphine addicts at the end of the nineteenth and beginning of the twentieth centuries were not seen as criminals and essentially could lead relatively normal, crime-free lives, if they so chose.

5. The criminal organizations that now support the illegal drug industry would have a product no one would buy and thus go out of business.

6. Many of the medical costs of drug abuse could be reduced. The risk of AIDS might lessen, since addicts could obtain free needles and drugs. Other medical complications from drug use such as hepatitis or hospitalization for accidental overdose, might also be reduced.

Drug Paraphernalia Laws

All drug use is accompanied by certain rituals and special **paraphernalia.** Some people have a special way of pouring their beer into a special glass. Coffee mugs are a popular sales item, personalized with names or cartoons. Tobacco humidors, cigarette lighters, and crystal decanters are all paraphernalia used in the consumption of legal drugs. Illegal drug users have their own paraphernalia and rituals as well. One way of attacking drug use is to prevent the sale of items primarily used to ingest or inject illegal drugs. Prosecution of sale of such paraphernalia also sends a message that drug use is not acceptable. Does it make sense to pass laws stating that cocaine possession is a felony, if the sale of coke spoons is a minor industry?

In 1979 the federal government proposed a Model Drug Paraphernalia Act which is intended to be used as a guideline by the states to control the sale of paraphernalia. The act is too long to reproduce here but the following excerpt gives a good idea of what is prohibited:

The term *drug paraphernalia* means all equipment, products, and materials of any kind which are used, intended for use, or designed for use, in implanting, propagation, cultivating, growing, harvesting, manufacturing, compounding, converting, producing, processing, packaging, repackaging, storing, containing, concealing, injecting, ingesting, inhaling or otherwise introducing into the human body a controlled substance in violation of this Act [meaning the Controlled Substances Act].

The Act then goes on to describe everything from kits used to plant any species of plant, testing equipment, scales, and balances, to capsules, balloons, pipes, roach clips, and cocaine spoons. A broad interpretation of this act would include just about anything in your kitchen or garage.

The Act qualifies drug paraphernalia to mean anything that is used primarily for drugs, thereby excluding your garden hose, your brother's toy balloon, and your mom's kitchen scale, but even these could be considered paraphernalia depending on statements made by the owner, proximity to controlled substances, the manner in which the items are displayed, and a host of other factors. According to Article II it is a crime to possess, manufacture, or sell (or even give away) such paraphernalia.

The idea of this Act is to eliminate "head shops," places where paraphernalia is openly sold, to crack down on advertisements in some magazines that offer growing equipment and, in general, to make it more difficult to grow, plant, manufacture, or measure any drug. Few would argue that the head shop of the sixties and early seventies was in existence to sell souvenirs, nor does it take a great deal of imagination to read between the lines of some advertisements.

It is interesting, however, to note that nearly every store the author has been in that sells tobacco products also sells rolling papers, and every electrical supply house has a whole range of alligator clips that look suspiciously like roach clips. While these stores are in no danger of being closed down, the federal government has subpoenaed the records of a number of stores that specialize in indoor growing supplies and issued warrants based on these records to search the houses of those who ordered large amounts of this equipment.

As convincing as these arguments may seem, there are counter-arguments that are equally compelling:

1. The illegality of drugs deters at least some people from trying them. Making drugs widely available would undoubtedly increase at least experimental use, and some of those would go on to develop abuse-related problems.

2. While it seems that some people do use 'drugs like cocaine and even heroin on a recreational basis, the exact abuse potential of any drug that is currently illegal is a matter of speculation. We think we know, based on the percentage of users who become abusers, but this percentage could increase if the drugs were widely available.

3. Even if it is relatively ineffective, we have developed social control over the use of legal drugs such as alcohol and tobacco. Among most drinkers, solitary drinking, drinking and driving, and being intoxicated are not socially sanctioned, while drinking moderately, with family and friends, and taking precautions about driving are encouraged. No such controls prevail over heroin, cocaine, or marijuana use.

4. Legal access to drugs, while taking away the stigma of being an addict, might reduce the incentive to the addict to get treatment.

5. The cost to society of those drugs that are legal, alcohol and tobacco, is enormous. We certainly don't need to add any more problems by increasing the availability of other drugs.

The arguments for and against drug legalization could and do fill whole books, and the issue will not be resolved any time in the near future. Nor is it likely, given the current political climate, that legalization will be seriously considered. In the interests of free inquiry, however, two aspects of the problem need to be considered since they are frequently overlooked. If the debate is to be over legalization of drugs, both the word *drug* and the word *legalization* need to be carefully defined.

What exactly is meant by drug in the phrase drug legalization? Based on what you know of short- and long-term effects, the dependence potential, and the toxicity of various drugs, would you place marijuana, cocaine, and nitrous oxide in the same category? Does it make sense to have virtually the same criminal sanctions against all drugs?

Similarly, what does the term legalization mean? What about decriminalization? How is it different? There are a number of different definitions of the word legalization, ranging from very restricted to totally libertarian. The most restrictive use of the term would mean availability of a drug only through government controlled facilities and only for a short period of time. Any other dispensing would remain illegal. One step further toward liberalizing drugs would be to permit physicians to dispense drugs like heroin or cocaine either for treatment or maintenance just as they presently do other prescription drugs. These two systems have been attempted in England with heroin addiction with limited success.

Less restrictive legislation would permit presently illegal drugs, or at least some, to be sold by the government, which could then regulate time and amount of sale, provide buyers with anti-drug counseling and information, and use the profits to provide treatment for those with drug problems. In some states a similar system is presently employed in the sale of alcohol. State run drugstores with government supplied drugs would help eliminate the profit motive, a concern that troubles even the most ardent proponents of legalization.

The ultimate legalization would be to have any and all drugs available, with sale and distribution controlled by the private economy. Presumably even this system would restrict sales of drugs to minors. While your imagination could run wild thinking of commercials of crack or marijuana, it is important to remember that this is precisely the control (or lack thereof) that is in place with tobacco products and alcohol.

Decriminalization usually refers to a halfway step between the present system and complete legalization. It could mean making possession of small amounts of a drug legal, but selling or manufacturing the drug illegal (the system in effect during Prohibition). It could mean making possession of the drug a civil rather than a criminal offense. The obvious problem with decriminalization is that it simply moves criminal sanctions one step backward in the supply chain. If cocaine were legal to possess under this system, but sale were illegal, how would you legally obtain it?

The issue of changing our drug laws is so laden with political, social, and ethical concerns that it is not possible to summarize it. Unless some miracle occurs and drug use suddenly plummets to near zero, these issues will continue to be debated into the next century.

DRUG LAW ENFORCEMENT STRATEGY

There may be debate about what proportion of the money to fight the war on drugs should be spent on law enforcement, but no one would argue that drug law enforcement should not be pursued. The issue in question is what strategy will produce the best results. Not all approaches can be pursued with equal vigor, and economic considerations must also play a role. In short, the question is, how can law enforcement best attack the problem of illegal drugs? The various strategies below all have their advocates, as well as advantages and disadvantages, and need to be examined individually (Kleiman & Smith, 1990).

Going after Mr. Big

Advocates of this approach maintain that the way to enforce drug laws is go after the main operators. Certainly there is logic in this method. Low level dealers can be easily replaced and there are so many of them that they are presently clogging the legal system. Why should the street dealer go to jail, when the big bosses live in palatial estates, free of harassment? Stopping the head of a drug cartel will shut down the entire system.

Stopping cartel leaders like Noriega is one strategy of drug law enforcement.

The difficulty with this approach is that it is extremely time consuming and incredibly expensive. It involves infiltrating the drug network with informants, setting up elaborate undercover operations, searching through financial records such as bank transactions, and maintaining surveillance. Mr. Big got to the top because he was smart, careful, ruthless, or a combination of all three. He is not going to be easy to catch.

Further complications arise when the Mr. Bigs live in another country. Extradition is always difficult and sometimes impossible, regardless of the evidence. As you read in chapter 4, the heads of cocaine smuggling rings in some South American countries have so much power that they can thwart the legal system of their own country. Even if the boss lives in the United States, he is usually insulated from day-to-day operations that would link him to specific crimes.

Another problem arises when Mr. Big is caught. If he is successfully prosecuted, justice has prevailed in his case, but there is no reason to assume that his organization will crumble or, even if it does, that another organization will not take its place. Continued prosecution of big time drug dealers may eventually have an impact, but it runs the risk of eliminating only the weaker ones while leaving the smartest, and thus strengthening the enterprise as a whole. Darwin, of course, referred to this as the survival of the fittest, and what applies to antelopes and lions may also apply to police and criminals.

The definition of a Mr. Big depends on the law enforcement agency. For the federal government, it might mean the head of an entire cocaine smuggling ring centered in Colombia, but for local law enforcement it might mean the main distributor in your town or city. The problems, however, are the same.

Cracking Down on Retail Sales

If you know the right section of virtually any city or town, you can find dealers selling drugs out in the open. Other drug sales take place in bars, office buildings, and living rooms. Cracking down on dealers involves making the intervention at the point of purchase. If it is successful it serves a number of goals: it reduces availability and presumably consumption, hurts the organization by cutting into profits, and protects the community from dealers.

The problems, however, are many. This method is time consuming, and clogs the judicial system. It produces a revolving door policy of arresting and then releasing dealers who go right back to dealing. Penalties are not a deterrent for most low level dealers, who often have an extensive police record. Cracking down on low level dealers can and has led to the recruitment of young children as couriers or dealers. The advantage to this method (to the dealer, of course) is that children are protected from most prosecutions.

Other problems involve the possibility of harassment of citizens going about their own business, and illegal searches. Moreover, such street sweeps often simply move the operation from one part of town to another, rather than eliminate the problem. Another problem that might seem trivial but in fact is quite important is that drug dealing usually occurs during the evening hours, when police are busiest with other emergencies. In smaller cities and towns there might only be a few police officers available to respond to drunk driving arrests, assault and battery cases, and accidents, all of which peak at the same hours as drug dealing.

A variation of this approach is to focus efforts on a selected area where drug sales are rampant. Saturating this area with law enforcement personnel will usually clear it, at least for a while. Of course, the dealers may and probably will move to another site, but some sites are more convenient to users than others and it might be possible to reduce demand in this way. The ideal would be to clear an area and have that area stay clear with the support of local residents, then move on to another area until all pockets of drug dealing are eliminated. The current phrase for this practice is "weed and seed."

Going after the Gangs

Like any manufacturer of any product, drug dealers need to distribute their goods to the consumer. Increasingly the task of distribution has been taken over by gangs of adolescents and post-adolescent youth. Although they have not reached all parts of the United States yet, these gangs have had a major impact in several western states. Two of the major organizations are known as the Bloods and the Crips, both of whom got their start in Los Angeles. On the east coast other groups, some of whom have roots in Jamaica, serve a similar purpose.

These gangs have taken over the sale of drugs, and the profits have gone to buying arsenals of weapons that would seem to rival those of some Third World countries. These weapons have then escalated the level of crime and intergang warfare in many neighborhoods. The gang members have considerable group loyalty and are difficult to infiltrate since the members are often recruited from the neighborhood. All of these factors make police action and drug law enforcement difficult.

One strategy is to make the very insignia they wear to identify themselves a signal for intense police scrutiny. Close surveillance of these gangs and monitoring their movements to prevent them from becoming established in other communities are some tactics that are currently used. These gangs are new and do not have the complicated organization of their adult counterparts, so they may be easier to disrupt.

There are other strategies that are beyond the scope of this textbook. They include providing political pressure, and financial and law enforcement assistance to countries where many drugs originate and to others that are through-points for drug smuggling. Crop eradication programs, incentives to plant legal crops, and even military assistance are all on the agenda as part of a concerted effort to stop drug use at every level. One unfortunate outcome of these methods is that the smugglers may simply change their markets. There is evidence, for example, that cocaine and heroin sales in Japan and Europe have begun to climb as the market in the United States has become less profitable.

It should be kept in mind that these enforcement strategies are best employed before drugs have taken hold in a community. The drug/crime problem is more severe and close to intractable in areas where drug use is rampant and has been established for some time. The drug law enforcement system can do only so much. In the next two chapters you will read about treatment and education which many think are far superior ways to win the war on drugs.

The Special Problem of Corruption

The enormous profits in drug trafficking and the hidden nature of dealing in general make corruption a real problem at every level of law enforcement and at the political level. The cop in the ghetto and the sheriff in a rural county in West Virginia are both vulnerable, and law enforcement officers throughout the country have, unfortunately but understandably, given in to the temptation of huge amounts of untraceable income.

Police have demanded protection money from smugglers, participated in the distribution themselves, and acted as lookouts and guards during drug deals. Rural police have taken bribes to permit planes to offload drugs on rural landing strips. Undercover police who have succumbed to the lure of drugs have become dependent themselves. Others have stolen drugs from

This crash is one example of how drinking and driving don't mix.

evidence rooms and diverted confiscated drugs before they even reached the police station.

On the other hand, a good argument could be made that what is remarkable is not the extent of corruption, but the fact that it is rare. Given the almost constant temptation, drug law enforcement officers have done an excellent job of maintaining their own integrity. While newspapers carry such stories almost every day, the stories of honesty and lack of corruption do not make headlines and are far more common.

DRINKING, DRIVING, AND DRUGS

A good case could be made that the area of drug law enforcement that is likely to have the greatest impact on the reader of this text concerns drinking and driving. Most people drink and virtually everyone drives. The combination of these two factors guarantees that at least some people will drive after they drink, and altogether too many may even drive *while* they drink. The issue is further complicated when we consider the role of drugs in driving and the role of both alcohol and other drugs in the operation of trucks, planes, and boats.

Not too long ago, within the memory of the author of this text, in fact, a drunken driving conviction was considered a minor inconvenience. Among some groups, it was virtually a badge of honor or a rite of passage. Eventually, some people felt, you were bound to get your first DUI and while it might result in a small fine, there was no stigma attached.

Much has changed in our attitudes toward drugs in the last twenty years and the attitude toward driving while intoxicated has been one of the most dramatic. More than 500 laws have been passed by various states to control drinking and driving in the last ten years. Virtually all of these laws have been in the direction of increasing penalties or making it more difficult for people to drink and drive. In addition, an extensive education program has been undertaken to inform the public of the dangers of drinking and driving.

**The Dangers of
Drinking and Driving**

The combination of drinking and driving is as dangerous a behavior as most people are ever likely to engage in, as the following statistics indicate. About 24,000 people die every year from alcohol-related automobile crashes. This comes out to one fatality every twenty-two minutes. More than 500,000 others are injured, nearly 50,000 of them seriously. You have a 40 percent chance of being involved in an alcohol-related crash sometime during your lifetime. Nearly two-thirds of all people killed in crashes had been drinking, and about 40 percent had a blood alcohol level over .10 (National Highway Traffic Safety Administration, 1989).

The reason that drinking and driving don't mix is very simple: alcohol impairs driving performance (Moskowitz & Burns, 1990). Furthermore, the impairment occurs at low levels of blood alcohol. In fact, the most important skills involved in driving are impaired at *any* blood alcohol level. For example, although heavy drinkers may not be as greatly affected as occasional drinkers, alcohol affects the coordination and balance of both. Vision is also impaired although in a complicated way. Alcohol seems to impair the ability of the brain to process visual information so that the alcohol-impaired driver pays more attention to the center of his/her field of vision and scans to the periphery less.

The ability of the brain to interpret and respond to complicated input is also impaired. Visually, driving requires rapidly processing information from many sources simultaneously. Pay attention to all of the incoming stimuli the next time you drive down a busy street. Alcohol impairs this ability, as well as the ability to make rapid adjustments in steering. The effect of alcohol on tracking, as it is called, is impaired at very low blood alcohol levels. Next time you are driving at night notice if the driver ahead of you is having a hard time making smooth steering changes. If so, chances are you are observing someone who is driving impaired.

Alcohol also has significant effects on other driving-related abilities. Drivers have to read and respond to street signs, and divide their attention between tasks such as steering and observing road conditions. Blood alcohol levels (BAL) as low as .02 percent can adversely affect these tasks. A BAL of .02 is about *one drink*! Since drinking is legal, and driving is a privilege, there is a clear legal precedent to permit laws to regulate a behavior like drinking and driving which causes so many problems. The goal, of course, is deterrence—to stop people from drinking and driving.

In order for drinking and driving (or any other) laws to be effective three conditions have to be met. The driver has to believe that the consequences of drinking and driving are severe, certain, and swift (Ross, 1990;

Any drug use is dangerous and illegal when combined with driving.

Hingson & Howland, 1990). The recent spate of legislation has largely been directed at attempting to ensure these principles that underlie any attempt at controlling behavior by legal means. The question is, how effective have these laws been to assure severity, swiftness and certainty?

Certainty   If you drink and drive, will you be caught? For most drivers, the answer, unfortunately, is no, at least not for a long time. Exact data on how many people drive intoxicated are impossible to come by, since self-report can hardly be credited and since no way exists of testing every driver. However, the best available estimates are not encouraging. If you drive with a blood alcohol level over 0.15 (about a six-pack of beer in a short period of time for a 150-pound male) you have only a 1 percent chance of being arrested. At 0.10, the legal limit in most states, the risk is between 1:500 and 1:1000. Put another way, if you drive monthly with a BAL over 0.10 you have at most a 6 percent chance of being arrested in any year (Phelps, 1990).

Every time a new law increases penalties for drunken driving, arrest rates and accident rates seem to go down, but only for a short period of time. A moment's reflection will indicate why. If you drink and drive and read about the new law, you will moderate your behavior, but then when you do drive after drinking and don't get caught, the law loses its effectiveness. Even alcoholics are seldom arrested. In one study only 17 percent of hospitalized alcoholics had had a DUI in the last six years.

Although it may seem flippant, some researchers divide drivers who drink into three groups: the Quick, the Caught, and the Dead (Perrine, 1990).

The Quick are those who drink and don't get caught, the other two are obvious. A considerable body of evidence exists to indicate that most (but certainly not all) of the Caught have several characteristics that increase the likelihood of being apprehended. They drink more heavily (about 50 percent admit to *normally* drinking five or more drinks in a given drinking session), tend either to be assaultive or depressed, and have more accidents and violations.

There seems to be a spectrum from the Quick to the Caught to the Dead, and these three constitute a separate group from those who normally don't drink and drive. Those with DUI convictions frequently acknowledge that they have a problem with drinking, drink more heavily, and are likely to become very intoxicated. There are exceptions, of course, but the person who shows up in a DUI class is not likely to be a light drinker who overindulged ''just this once'' to celebrate a birthday or a wedding. Not only are these celebrants unlikely to be caught, they probably have enough sense not to attempt to drive.

Swiftness

If we have not been successful in assuring certainty of being caught, we have done a better job of speeding up the process of conviction once an arrest takes place. Two kinds of laws have contributed to this improvement in law enforcement practice. The first is called *criminal per se,* which means that demonstrating that an arrestee had a given BAL is sufficient to ensure conviction. Prior laws required that the prosecution prove *impairment,* not just a given BAL. Impairment is more difficult to prove and far more subjective.

The second change is relatively new. *Administrative per se* laws mean that the arresting officer can immediately confiscate the driver's license of anyone arrested for drunken driving. Under certain circumstances in some states, drivers are permitted to drive in the interim and in all states their driving rights are restored if they are found not guilty. In a few states, there is essentially no appeal; if the driver has a BAL above the legal limit as determined by a test at the time of arrest, the suspension is automatic.

The benefit of these per se laws is still being studied, but it appears that they do reduce certain measures of intoxicated driving. Suspension itself, although it is widely flaunted, does seem to be an effective deterrent. Even though many drivers still drive on suspended licenses, they tend to drive more carefully.

Severity

States that impose mandatory jail sentences on convicted drunk drivers have generally found that they produce mixed results, but even the positive results are slight. First of all, in most communities jails are already overcrowded and there is little room for prisoners convicted of DUI, so many are given alternative sentences. Second, driving while intoxicated is often an impulsive act and since the likelihood of getting caught is small, the thought of a short jail sentence probably is not much of a deterrent (Hingson & Howland, 1990; Nichols, 1990). Jail sentences for convicted drunk drivers may not act as much of a deterrent, but they do satisfy the public demand that ''something be done.'' The fact that a jail sentence is at least a possibility may have a deterrent effect that is difficult to measure statistically. The criterion used in most studies to determine the effectiveness of jail sentences is recidivism, the tendency to repeat the previous offense. However, it is possible that the threat of a jail sentence may deter the occasional drinker from driving. Since the probabilities of arrest are low, this person may not show up in the data, but nevertheless modify his/her behavior.

In addition to jail sentences, there are other costs to a DUI that may act as more of a deterrent. There are legal expenses, healthy fines in every state, and increased insurance costs. The total cost of a single DUI infraction may be many thousands of dollars. Many, if not most, of us probably would rather sit in jail for forty-eight hours than lose $5,000, so perhaps financial penalties may prove to be more effective in the long run.

What has caused the decline in alcohol related crashes? Using as a measure of effectiveness the number of fatal crashes involving alcohol, it seems that Americans are becoming more sensible about drinking and driving (Fell, 1990). How might we account for this decline if legal sanctions have had only a modest effect?

1. Widespread media coverage and public information programs have heightened our awareness of the problem.

2. Sobriety checkpoints and increased sentencing have had some deterrent effect.

3. The raising of the drinking age to twenty-one has reduced the number of alcohol-related fatal crashes among young drivers.

4. Programs such as designated driver programs and free rides for intoxicated drivers have given drinkers an opportunity to exercise options about drinking and driving.

5. The population of young drivers, those most prone to alcohol-related crashes, is declining.

6. Overall, for many reasons, Americans are drinking less.

No one factor is going to substantially reduce drinking and driving. Law enforcement is only one element of an overall plan, but the total effort seems to be working. As long as there are drinkers and as long as there are cars, there will be those who drink and drive. It is reasonable, however, to expect that the damage they do can and will be reduced.

Marijuana, Motor Coordination, and Driving

On 4 January 1987 a train collision between a Conrail freight train and an Amtrak passenger train resulted in the death of sixteen people and caused injuries to 175. Both the Conrail engineer and brakeman tested positive for, and later admitted having used, marijuana shortly before the crash (Fram, 1988). This tragedy led to numerous calls for mandatory testing for marijuana and other drugs, and a focus on the relationship of marijuana to driving.

The available evidence does not permit a clear statement about the extent of the danger in driving under the influence of marijuana (Gieringer, 1988). Laboratory studies using perceptual and motor skills associated with driving, driving simulation studies, and other measures have shown that marijuana reduces attentiveness, impairs short-term memory, and affects certain tasks such as lane changing ability, that would normally be associated with an increased likelihood of accidents (Smiley, 1986).

On the other hand, marijuana produces a *decrease* in risk-taking behavior and speeding, the exact opposite effects from those seen with alcohol (Smiley, 1986). Some of the negative effects may be the result of using subjects who are relatively inexperienced with marijuana, since tolerance does seem to reduce some of the harmful effects on driving-related skills (Peck, Biasotti, Boland, Mallory, & Reeve, 1986). Criticism also has been directed to the relevance of these laboratory conditions to real life driving situations.

One finding seems clear: that alcohol and marijuana have additive effects, so that a combination of the two produces worse deficits than either alone (Chesher, 1986). Studies of those killed in traffic accidents further supports these laboratory findings. In one study, the investigators assigned proportional responsibility to the drivers in each accident. Those who had ingested both marijuana and some other drug, typically alcohol, were assigned a 95 percent responsibility rate; for those who drank only alcohol, the rate was 92 percent; for drug-free drivers it was 71 percent. Curiously, for those who had used marijuana only, the rate of responsibility was only 53 percent (Williams, Peat, Crouch, Wells, & Finkle, 1985). It should also be noted that the engineer of the Conrail train had had eleven traffic convictions, two license suspensions, and a recent arrest for drunk driving.

Nearly all studies of traffic fatalities have shown that the overwhelming majority of marijuana users also had significant levels of alcohol in their bloodstreams at the time of the accident, and anywhere from 68–83 percent were legally intoxicated (Mason & McBay, 1984; Cimbura, Lucas, Bennet, & Simpson, 1982; Fortenberry, Brown, & Shelvin, 1986). These findings should be considered in light of the fact that marijuana users tend to belong to a group that is more accident prone to begin with, since most are young adults (Terhune, 1986). Young adults also tend to show a high rate of alcohol use.

While the extent of the risk factor of marijuana alone on driving must await further and more precise studies, it seems clear that those who combine both alcohol and marijuana increase their risk of being in a fatal accident by a factor of ten or more (Gieringer, 1988). Since 90 percent of marijuana users also drink alcohol (Gieringer, 1988) the safest rule seems to be, if you smoke don't drive, if you drink don't drive, and if you smoke *and* drink don't even *think* about driving. Of course, someone who both smokes and drinks probably won't be thinking very much anyway, so in addition, look out for the other driver.

Drinking and Flying

Not nearly as many people fly as drive; excluding commercial pilots, there are approximately 700,000 people licensed to fly an airplane. Pilots, like drivers, drink, and some fly while intoxicated. Those of us who trust our lives to commercial flights probably have little to fear. There has never been a fatal accident in the commercial sector for which alcohol was considered a causative agent, and the recent widely publicized case of three airline pilots who flew (successfully) while intoxicated points out how swift and severe the punishment is for those who violate the rules.

General aviation, the term used to describe all civilian flights not for hire, is another story, however. Depending upon the study, from 10–30 percent of all airplane crashes due to pilot error involved pilots with a measurable BAL, and nearly half of those had BALs in excess of 0.10. Civilian and commercial pilots drink at about the same rate as the general population and many are not aware of the profound effects that alcohol has on flying skills. Impairment on many tasks can be measured with a BAL as low as 0.03.

The regulations for commercial pilots and general aviation are strict. No one may fly or act as a crewmember with a BAL of 0.04 or greater, while using any drug that may affect performance, or who has consumed any alcohol in the last eight hours. Drug testing for illegal drugs is also mandatory for commercial pilots, but not for civilians (Modell & Mountz, 1990). Although the problem may be small, due to the number of pilots, the amount of alcohol that is necessary to produce impairment is also small, and anyone who flies or is a passenger should be more than a little cautious.

Drinking and Boating

The thought of flying with someone who has been drinking is frightening, and massive programs seem to be successful in convincing Americans that drinking and driving is dangerous, but we seem to be much more casual about drinking and operating a boat. Boats seem safer and slower although anyone who has ever fallen off water skis knows that the water can be hard indeed. Two men with fishing poles and an ice chest of soft drinks and beer on a lake in the middle of July is an image that many of us associate with summertime. However, alcohol is alcohol and it impairs the ability to operate a boat the same way it impairs flying or driving a car.

Since we associate boating with recreation, and recreation with drinking, boating and drinking is common. In one study conducted in Nevada, 90 percent of the boats inspected had alcoholic beverages on board. While it is illegal to drink while driving a car or to have an open container of alcohol in a car, no such laws apply to boats. Nevertheless, the Coast Guard estimates that alcohol is involved in 85 percent of boating accidents, and 51 percent of those involved in fatal boating accidents were impaired. The Coast Guard maintains that a BAL of .035 percent can affect a boater's ability to respond appropriately.

Recognizing the danger, most states have laws prohibiting operating a boat under the influence of alcohol, and the federal government provides a $1,000 civil penalty plus criminal penalties of up to $5,000 and a year in jail

FIGURE 12.1

for anyone who operates a boat on water under federal jurisdiction with a BAL in excess of 0.10. Like commercial flying, commercial boating is under more severe restrictions. Enforcement of these regulations is spotty, however, and there are no lakeside sobriety tests.

Although legal sanctions are in place, most of the efforts to control drinking while boating have been educational and have emphasized the importance of safety, as can be seen in figure 12.1. Very few data exist to compare the relative effectiveness of various campaigns, or even if drinking and boating accidents are increasing or decreasing. Don't be surprised, however, to see this issue gain prominence as our attitude toward excessive drinking in general continues to become more negative.

DRUG TESTING AND THE LAW

One of the most controversial issues relating to drug use concerns the testing of urine, blood, or other body products for the presence of drugs. Of course, breath, urine, and blood tests for alcohol have been common and available for many years. Recently, however, testing for other drugs also has become popular, and new types of tests involving both hair and saliva have been developed. For legal and scientific reasons, urine testing has been the most common technique for determining the presence of illicit drugs.

Nearly half of the Fortune 500 companies now employ drug testing procedures, and testing itself has become a big business with hundreds of millions of dollars spent every year. A counter-industry has also emerged, which sells clean urine and conducts tests for individuals. Testing can either be conducted as part of the hiring procedure (**preemployment screening**), periodically or randomly during employment, or when job impairment has been documented (testing for cause). Testing for cause is the least controversial, while preemployment screening has serious economic and legal drawbacks.

Drug testing is mandatory for government employees in sensitive positions, police officers, and those in both public and private sectors whose positions entail great public responsibility, such as pilots, truck drivers, and air traffic controllers. Supreme court decisions have upheld the legality of preemployment screening, random testing, and testing for cause, under appropriate circumstances, but the issue continues to be controversial.

The Issues of Drug Testing

No one wants an airline pilot to try to land a plane, a surgeon to attempt to operate, or a diplomat to attempt delicate negotiations while stoned on marijuana, high on cocaine, or sleepy from narcotics. Many employers feel that their employees engage in jobs which demand utmost caution, considerable mental acuity, and/or physical ability. Why should they take a risk on someone who is using illegal drugs that clearly impair his/her performance? As a result many people agree that drug testing is a simple issue. Anyone testing positive for drug use should be removed from his/her job and offered treatment. If treatment is refused or if the problem persists, the person should be fired.

A number of assumptions are hidden in the sentence above, however, that are frequently not examined. It assumes the validity of drug testing. It assumes that a relationship between drug use and employee performance exists. It assumes that drug use off the job is in the same realm as drug use on the job. It assumes that all jobs are equally affected by drugs, and it assumes that treatment is effective. Are these assumptions true? Furthermore, drug testing raises some serious constitutional issues that need to be considered.

The Cost of Drug Abuse

You may have read a number of widely published statements about the cost of drug abuse in the workplace. Drug abusers have three to four times as many accidents, five times as many injuries, and use sixteen times as much sick leave. Keep in mind that these are estimates, and most often compare those with serious abuse problems to non-users. Studies which actually examine the relationship between drug use and job performance come up with more modest, but still significant, differences between users and non-users.

The best method to determine whether drug use is related to job performance is to test job seekers before employment and then follow up both users and nonusers to see if they differ. Only a few studies have actually done this. One of them, of postal workers, looked at those testing positive for marijuana and cocaine and found that those with marijuana-positive urines had 55 percent more industrial accidents, 85 percent more injuries, and were absent 78 percent more. Those testing positive for cocaine showed similar rates. These differences are significant but not nearly as great as previous

• YOU READ IT HERE FIRST •

Urine testing has a number of disadvantages. It can be cumbersome, not to mention embarrassing, to carry out, and is limited in that it cannot detect very recent use, cannot really quantify drug use, and cannot detect drug use after a few days. Two recent developments in testing have attempted to get around some of these problems and you are sure to hear about them in the future.

Hair Analysis

The hair follicle and particularly the root of an individual strand of hair lies close to blood vessels. Capillaries, which go from arteries to veins extend inside the hair shaft. Trace amounts of drugs can be isolated from the cortex, or keratin layer, of the hair shaft. Basically, any amount of drug found in the blood will end up in a hair follicle. Analysis of hair by GC\MS, the method discussed in this chapter, is widely recognized by forensic toxicologists as a valid measure of exposure to a wide variety of chemicals, including drugs. Recently, a method of analysis using a method similar to RIA (used by the military to test urine) was developed.

Testing hair has definite advantages over urine testing. Hair grows at a steady rate of about half an inch per month, so a strand of hair six inches long could be cut into lengths and give an estimate of drug use for the previous year. The well known methods of fooling urine tests would have no value against hair analysis and virtually the only method of fooling the test would be to shave your entire head and body.

There are disadvantages as well, of course. The exact rate of hair growth differs between individuals and races, and during different times of the year. The accuracy of the method in avoiding false positives has not been thoroughly tested, and other issues have yet to be resolved. In 1991, the Food and Drug Administration ruled that hair analysis could *not* be used to test for illegal drug consumption. The possibility remains, however, that this method may be used in the future. If this method becomes widespread, would you hire an employee who had a crewcut?

Saliva Testing

Another more recently developed method is analysis of saliva. The composition of saliva is basically that of blood, so any drug appearing in the bloodstream will appear in equal concentration in the saliva. It will detect drug use over only a one or two day period, but is difficult to tamper with. The method currently being developed and tested involves a small pouch which contains a saliva stimulating agent. The pouch is placed in the mouth for eight minutes and it collects a small amount of saliva which can then be analyzed.

The major disadvantage is that drugs which are bound to protein (see chapter 2) will not show up in the bound form in the saliva. Most illegal drugs are not bound to protein but some other drugs, such as Valium and testosterone, are. The amount of alcohol in the blood correlates very highly with the amount in the saliva, but the exact relationship between saliva and blood are presently being studied. Look for this method to become popular if the preliminary testing proves to be accurate.

estimates. Incidentally, cigarette smokers also had higher rates of absence and injuries (Zwerlin, Ryan, & Oray, 1990).

The other studies also showed significant but relatively modest evidence of performance impairment. The cost of preemployment screening can be considerable and must be weighed against the amount of money saved by not hiring drug users. Keep in mind that because of the characteristics of testing, no distinction can be made between occasional users and those who are dependent. It seems intuitive, but unproven, that those who are heavy users would have even worse performance. It might also be the case, however, that those who are occasional users would not differ at all from nonusers. Assuming that drug use does affect productivity and that testing is cost effective, what about the legal aspects of testing?

Legal Considerations

The Fourth Amendment to the Constitution of the United States guarantees an individual the freedom from "unreasonable searches and seizure" *by the government*. The taking of blood and urine samples has been amply demonstrated to be a seizure as defined in the Constitution. The important word, here, then, is *unreasonable*. The government is within its rights to make *reasonable* searches and seizures as long as it can demonstrate the reasonableness of the act. The courts have tended to consider the threat to public safety and the intrusiveness of the drug testing policy against the employees' constitutional rights (Bittle, Pahler, & Sernett, 1986).

Most of the concern about testing has taken place in the government sector where federal regulations tend to be strict. In the private sector (businesses and nongovernment agencies) the rules are somewhat relaxed, but businesses do owe their employees some rights against search and seizure. At this point another distinction needs to be made. Preemployment screening is subject to fewer restrictions than postemployment testing. We will return to this issue shortly.

The Fifth Amendment says that the government may not deprive an individual of life, liberty or property without due process. *Due process* means that the method used must be fair. The courts have held that due process would be violated if the drug tests were unreliable, if they were handled in an unreliable manner, or if one cannot show some relationship to job impairment. In addition, public employees are guaranteed a fair "trial" should they prove positive. Similar regulations for the private sector have been a matter of considerable debate, but in general are less stringent.

It should also be noted that alcoholism and drug addiction are considered *handicaps* under federal and most state laws. This means that the government agencies have the obligation to assist the abusers in the same way they must assist a wheelchair-bound employee. Moreover, *no* company or government agency may discriminate against an employee on the basis of having previously undergone drug or alcohol rehabilitation.

What Is Drug Testing Anyway?

How does drug testing work? Since urine testing is the commonest form of drug testing, our discussion will focus on it. Two basic types of urine testing for drugs are in present use. The first, which is intended for basic screening, is an immunoassay test. There are two types of immunoassay: the EMIT test and the RIA. The **EMIT** test is produced by **SYVA** Company in Palo Alto, California and is the basis for all the tests conducted by laboratories certified by the National Institute of Drug Abuse. The RIA involves a radioactive immunoassay (hence the name) and is used by the military. Since the EMIT is the most common, let's see how it works. Using the testing for marijuana as an example, the process goes roughly like this. Goats are injected with a metabolite of the active ingredient in marijuana, delta-tetrahydrocannabinol. This metabolite is known as THC carboxy acid. The goat develops an antibody to this foreign substance. The antibody is extracted and used in the assay. Similar antibodies are developed for each of the five drug groups tested: marijuana, cocaine, opiates, phencyclidine, and amphetamines. SYVA produces a separate kit for each of the groups.

Each kit contains the antibody, an enzyme, and a substrate. An enzyme is a protein that produces changes in other substances without being changed itself. The enzyme is related to the drug being tested. The substrate is the substance that does the changing. Assume you have provided a sample, and the kit is mixed with the urine. If there is no drug present, the antibody binds to the enzyme and prevents it from changing the substrate. If there is a drug present, the antibody binds to it, leaving the enzyme free to work. The product produced by the action of the enzyme on the substrate is then measured. If no product is detected, the sample is negative. The presence of a certain amount of the product indicates a positive test.

The EMIT test is not quantitative, it cannot tell how much of the drug is present, only if the drug is present at a certain concentration *or greater*. This concentration is the cut-off point. The fact that the test is not quantitative is important, as you will see.

Note that immunoassay testing is done for the presence of the metabolic product of most drugs, including marijuana and cocaine, rather than for the drug itself. If other drugs produce similar metabolites, the goat's antibodies can be fooled. The immunoassay cannot determine how long the metabolite has been in the blood, let alone how much of an illegal drug the subject has taken. Thus a person who has smoked one joint of marijuana in the past few hours might test the same as his friend who has smoked several joints a week before.

The second test is far more accurate. It is a gas chromatograph, mass spectrometry test, called, for short, GC/MS. The GC/MS test is too complicated to describe here but involves extracting the drug to be tested, heating it, sending it through a special column which measures its presence, and analyzing the molecular structure of every substance contained in the urine sample. The GC/MS measures the actual substances in the urine directly and is extremely accurate at very low concentrations. It is also expensive.

According to guidelines established by NIDA, all positive immunoassay tests are followed up with a GC/MS assay. A positive on both is virtually certain evidence of drug use. Experts on the legal defensibility of testing agree that a combination of the immunoassay and a GC/MS is fully defensible against legal challenge (Hoyt, Finnigan, Nee, Shults, & Butler, 1987). Other experts go so far as to claim that the EMIT–GC/MS is so accurate that false positives *never* occur in well run laboratories (Fretthold, 1990). Unfortunately, however, because of the expense, the GC/MS test is not always done, and action against an employee, or more commonly a failure to hire, is based on the immunoassay test alone.

Table 12.2 Legal Defensibility of Urine Testing Results of a Survey

Substance	EMIT	RIA	EMIT, GC/MS
Amphetamines	3.9	3.9	1.0
Barbiturates	4.0	4.0	1.0
Benzodiazepines	4.0	4.0	1.0
Cannabinoids	3.9	3.9	1.0
Cocaine	3.9	3.9	1.0
Opiates	4.0	4.0	1.0
Phencyclidine	3.9	3.9	1.0

Based on a survey of experts. Rating Scale: (1) fully defensible against legal challenge; (2) somewhat defensible; (3) difficult to defend; (4) unacceptable for legal defense.

Source: From Hoyt/Finnigan/Newe/Shults/Butler. *Journal of the American Medical Association* 258: 504–509. Copyright 1987, American Medical Association. Reprinted by permission of the publisher and the author.

The Problem of False Positives and False Negatives

A false positive occurs when a person who has not been using a drug is tested as positive for use, and a false negative occurs when a person who *should* test positive does not. Which of the two, false positives or false negatives, is more serious depends on one's point of view. If I were a non-drug-using prospective employee, I would be more concerned with the former; if I were an employer, I would be more concerned with the latter.

False positives occur when the method of testing cannot differentiate the metabolites of illegal or prohibited drugs from other, legal substances. A number of common substances can cause the immunoassay test to be positive. So much publicity resulted from the finding that some OTC painkillers such as ibuprofen can produce false positives, that the producers of the EMIT changed their procedures and claim to have taken care of the problem.

Nevertheless, other drugs can still cause a false positive. OTC cold remedies and diet aids contain drugs similar to amphetamine which will cause a false positive on the EMIT but not on the GC/MS. Others, such as the ingredient in Vicks Inhaler, can fool both tests. By the time you read this, the immunoassay and GC/MS tests are likely to have been changed to prevent such false positives. As soon as a problem appears, the rush is on to solve it. One false positive, however, has so far proven resistant.

Poppy seeds found in bagels and poppy seed cookies can cause a positive response on both the EMIT and the GC/MS (Struempler, 1987; Zebelman, Troyer, Randall, & Batjer, 1987). The reason for this is that the poppy seeds are from Papaver somniferum, the opium poppy, and actually contain small amounts of morphine and codeine. The amount required to produce a positive test is within the range of normal consumption of poppyseed bagels, moreover, and should be taken into consideration whenever a positive for opiates is found.

Even the number of poppy seed bagels shown in the photo could produce a positive urine test for opiates.

False positives also occur when the testing laboratories make a mistake. The accuracy of such laboratories is a matter of debate. The best laboratories are excellent and rarely, if ever, produce false positives. They have high standards that are strictly adhered to. The problem is that, in most states, there is little or no regulation or control over testing laboratories. Virtually anyone could start one, and quality control in many of these is not good. While it is possible to develop techniques that go a long way to ensure the accuracy of drug testing, all too often these techniques are not used. In an attempt to regulate the industry the National Institute of Drug Abuse has a certification procedure and has published a list of approved laboratories, but unapproved laboratories can still function.

False negatives are more of a problem than false positives. They occur when a drug user fools the urine test. Experienced drug users have diligently pursued means of fooling these tests, and many methods have an almost legendary quality. It is extremely difficult to fool the GC\MS test, but keep in mind that if the EMIT test is negative, the second test is not run. Therefore the techniques that have been developed are aimed at the EMIT test.

Many users believe you can fool a drug test by adding anything from detergent or salt to diesel fuel to the urine sample and cause the immunoassay to misread the outcome (Wimbish, 1987). The salt or detergent can be hidden underneath a fingernail and added to the sample. The adulterant stops the enzyme activity and produces a false negative. Most of these techniques can be detected by additional tests or prevented by proper guidelines for collection of urine.

Perhaps the easiest method to fool the urine test is to obtain a sample of ''clean'' urine and hide it until the urine test, and then pour it into the specimen bottle. Clean urine can be obtained from someone else, or guaranteed clean and dried urine can be purchased from at least one source. The clean sample can be taped to the inside of the thigh or hidden in the clothing and then poured into the specimen bottle.

Use of someone else's urine usually can be detected by the temperature of the sample, since a bottle held against the body will be of a lower temperature than an actual urine sample (Person & Ehrenkranz, 1988). To indicate how far some people will go, there are even reports, hopefully mythical, of drug users voiding their bladder and refilling it with clean urine through a catheter. One story concerns an athlete who used his girlfriend's urine. While he was clean for steroids, the tests indicated he was pregnant (Murray, 1987).

Another widely reported technique for cheating the urine test involves the reluctance of most people to observe a sample being taken. If the subject who wishes to cheat can figure a way to be left alone for a moment or two, he/she can dilute the urine sample with water from the toilet bowl. Some companies provide a toilet with colored water to prevent such a possibility but the coloring agent must be added to the tank as well as the bowl and the fresh water supply must be turned off for the duration of the test.

Consuming huge quantities of water prior to a suspected drug testing is an effective way of avoiding detection, provided that the person being tested is not a heavy user. The resultant dilution of the urine will usually fool most tests. Of course, as you read in chapter 2, consuming large quantities of water is not without its dangers.

All of the information just discussed is widely known in the drug using community, meaning that these and even more sophisticated techniques for avoiding detection are available to drug abusers, thereby decreasing their likelihood of being detected. The experimental or occasional user may not have such information, and this lack of knowledge, combined with the potential for false positives, raises the possibility that the relatively innocent may be punished far more often than genuinely guilty parties are detected.

The issue of laboratory accuracy is also important. Results of accuracy have varied widely. One problem has to do with the issue of ''blind testing''; submitting a sample without the knowledge of the laboratory. If a drug testing company knows that it is being evaluated, and which samples are the probes (open testing), their accuracy will undoubtedly improve. Blind testing has its own problems, so determining the accuracy of urine testing is quite difficult. In one recent well controlled study, only 1.6 percent of samples submitted blind were labeled as containing a drug when none was present (false positive). However, 31 percent were incorrectly labeled as negative when they contained drugs (Davis, Hawks, & Blanc, 1988).

Table 12.3   Reliability of Urine Testing

Drug	Percent Correctly Identified	
	Open	Blind
Cannabinol (high amount)	100	95
Cannabinol (low amount)	66	69
Amphetamine	88	72
Cocaine	77	62
Morphine	58	53
Phencyclidine	80	49

"Open" means that the laboratory knew it was being tested. "Blind" means that it was unaware. Subtract each percentage from 100 to get the percentage of *false negatives*—samples that are reported "clean" but in fact contain the drug.

From Kenneth H. Davis, et al., "Assessment of Laboratory Quality in Urine Drug Testing: A Proficiency Testing Pilot Study," *Journal of the American Medical Association* 260: 1749–54. Copyright 1988, American Medical Association. Reprinted by permission of the publisher and the author.

Other Issues Related to Drug Testing

Stringent guidelines are required to ensure that a urine sample is what it is supposed to be. Ideally, either someone should actually observe while the urine sample is being given, or if any privacy is to be permitted, colored dye must be placed in the toilet to prevent dilution. The temperature and specific gravity of the sample must be determined immediately after the sample is presented. Finally, the sample must be sealed and a continuous record kept to ensure that the sample is not altered on the way to be tested.

Actual observation of urination is distasteful to most Americans and raises a real issue about the invasion of privacy. Maintaining a "clean room," where a urine sample can be taken, and ensuring an unbroken chain of security are both difficult and expensive. All too often neither procedure is followed, allowing ample opportunity for the dishonest to escape detection.

Another issue of concern is the length of time after use a drug or its metabolite can be detected. Marijuana can be detected in the regular user an average of thirty days after use, according to one study, and in the occasional user (weekly or less often), an average of thirteen days. Cocaine is essentially gone after two to four days, as is heroin. Alcohol is not usually detectable after a few hours and is not even tested in the EMIT, RIA, or GC/MS methods.

Since marijuana can be detected longer than alcohol, could drug testing actually encourage those who wish to alter their consciousness to drink alcohol, as opposed to using marijuana? Does this present a problem, when most experts would agree that at present levels of usage, alcohol is a greater health problem than marijuana?

The final issue concerns when testing should be permitted. Remember the three types of testing: preemployment, regular testing (at random or scheduled), and testing for cause. Testing for cause seems to produce the least opposition. If an employee has frequent absences, if performance has declined, or if there is some accident, few would argue that testing is helpful in determining the cause of the problem. Other types of testing are more controversial.

On the one hand, most professional organizations such as the American Medical Association, the Association for Occupational Medicine, and many others are opposed to mandatory, random testing. Unions as well are concerned that testing could be used to harass unpopular employees. The primary objection is that such testing implies a lack of trust when the vast majority of workers do not use drugs. On the other hand, the argument could be raised that in some occupations, the employer cannot wait for evidence of impairment, since failure to act could result in the death of many people. Must we wait, they would argue, for an airline pilot to crash a plane before we test him/her?

Canal Cleaner/Laborer

Applications being accepted thru Dec. 30th at ———. Temporary position only (approx. 3 mo. project), $5.50 per hr. Applications must be accompanied by proof of identity & U.S. work authorization. Applicants req. to submit to preemployment physical exam, including drug test. (This advertisement appeared in a newspaper in December of 1988. Do you think they have gone too far? Does a canal cleaner need to prove that he has not smoked marijuana or used some other illegal drug? What would happen if he/she showed up for the interview with a hangover?)

Preemployement screening is the most controversial of all. While guidelines exist in both private and government sectors concerning what can be done when an employee tests positive, the rules are much looser with regard to preemployment screens. There is no requirement of confirmation with a GC\MS test for positive EMIT tests. Furthermore, the prospective employee has little or no legal recourse. While there are strict rules concerning discrimination against racial and ethnic groups and discrimination on the basis of sex and age, few other rules exist.

As an employer, I do not have to hire blondes, people who wear brown shoes with blue suits, or people who smoke cigarettes. I most definitely do not have to hire someone who fails a drug test, even if the drug test is not reliable. Since I have no obligation to the prospective employee and since I have a number of people who have passed the test, why should I take a chance?

With the knowledge that an employer is going to test for drugs, a drug user would not have to be too intelligent to avoid an illegal drug for a few days. What this means is that the preemployment screen is going to catch very few drug users. What *this* means requires a little mathematics.

Suppose that the EMIT test was 100 percent effective in spotting drug users (it is not) and that it has a false positive rate of 1 percent (which is very generous). Assume further that in a group of 100 prospective employees who take the test, one has recently taken an illegal drug. Since the test is 100 percent effective, that person will be caught, but another person (the 1 percent false positive) will also. Therefore, under these circumstances there is a 50/50 chance that a positive test is a false one. Anytime there is a very low rate of drug use, the chance of a person testing positive actually being innocent is high.

Another argument against preemployment screening is cost. The EMIT test is relatively inexpensive ($15–20), but assume that a large company decides to test all 1,000 prospective employees and 3 percent fail. Is it worth $20,000 to find thirty drug users? If you include the GC\MS on these thirty, the price goes up even more.

With all the furor over drug testing, do you find it curious that little or no mention is made of testing for legal drugs? The typical drug screening tests do not test for alcohol, although ordinary Breathalyzer tests are available to measure acute use. Moreover, there are several tests that can identify chronic heavy alcohol users (Salaspuro, 1986). What about cigarette smokers, heavy users of prescription drugs like Valium, or those taking sedatives for insomnia?

SUMMARY

Throughout history society has attempted to control drug use through legislation with little result. Severe penalties have not stopped the spread of tobacco, alcohol, or any other drug and there is little hope that our society can reasonably expect to be drug free in the forseeable future.

A good example of the problem of drug legislation has been the attempts to control alcohol in American society. The Prohibition movement started out as a Temperance movement with the goal of reducing, not eliminating, alcohol use. Legislation against alcohol never succeeded, although the results were not as catastrophic as many think.

A primary issue relating to drug use is the relationship between it and crime. In part because drugs are illegal, criminal activity is an integral part of drug use. At present, nearly one half of all prisoners are in jail for drug-related offenses.

Many different approaches have been used to stop drug use and related criminal activity. Each has its own advocates and problems. None has proved successful alone, unless demand is also affected.

Two concerns that are most likely to impact the average person are the relationship between drug use and driving, and drug testing. Drug use affects driving, and drunken driving, in particular has been a major target of the criminal justice system. Drunk driving fatalities seem to be on the decline, but whether legal sanctions are responsible is an open question.

Drug testing is a complex issue and troubles many concerned with civil liberties. Where do the rights of individuals end and the needs of society begin? How far can we constitutionally go to prevent the terrible toll that drugs take?

REFERENCES

Abadinsky, H. (1989). *Drug abuse: An introduction. Chicago: Nelson-Hall.*

Boaz, D. (Ed.) (1990). *The crisis in drug prohibition.* Washington, D.C.: The Cato Institute.

Bureau of Justice Statistics Bulletin (1990). Jail population in 1990, August.

Bureau of Justice Statistics Bulletin (1990). Prisoners in 1990 National Highway Traffic Safety Administration (1989), Fact sheet on alcohol impaired driving, May. U.S. Department of Health and Human Services.

Cimbura, G. B., Lucas, D. M., Bennett, R. C., & Simpson, H. M. (1982). Incidence and toxicological aspects of drugs detected in 484 fatally injured drivers in Ontario. *Journal of Forensic Science, 27,* 855–67.

Fell, J. C. (1990). Drinking and driving in America: Disturbing facts—encouraging reductions. *Alcohol Health and Research World, 14,* 18–25.

Fortenberry, J. C., Brown, D. B., & Shelvin, L. T. (1986). Analysis of drug involvement in traffic fatalities in Alabama. *American Journal of Drug and Alcohol Abuse, 12,* 257–67.

Fram, A. (1988). Associated Press report 0730, 26 February.

Furnas, J. C. (1973). *The late demon rum.* New York: Capricorn Books.

Gieringer, D. H. (1988). Marijuana, driving and traffic safety. *Journal of Psychoactive Drugs, 20,* 93–101.

Goode, E. (1989). *Drugs in American Society, 3d ed.* New York: Alfred Knopf.

Kleiman, M., & Smith, K. D. (1990). State and local drug enforcement: In search of a strategy. In M. Tonry & J. Q. Wilson (Eds.). *Drugs and crime: volume 13.* Chicago: The University of Chicago Press.

Mason, A. P., & McBay, A. H. (1984). Ethanol, marijuana and other drug use in 600 drivers killed in single-vehicle crashes in North Carolina (1978–1981). *Journal of Forensic Sciences, 29,* 987–1026.

Modell, J. G., & Mountz, J. M. (1990). Drinking and flying—The problem of alcohol use by pilots. *New England Journal of Medicine, 323,* 455–60.

Moskowitz, H., & Burns, M. (1990). Effects of alcohol on driving performance. *Alcohol Health and Research World 14,* 12–14.

Nadelman, E. A. (1989). Drug prohibition in the United States; Costs, consequences and alternatives. *Science, 245,* 939–46.

National Commission on Drug Free Schools (1990). Toward a drug free generation: A nation's responsibility.

National Drug Control Strategy (1990). The White House.

Nichols, J. L. (1990). Treatment versus deterrence. *Alcohol Health and Research World, 14,* 44–51.

OSAP Prevention Monograph—1 (1989). Stopping alcohol and other drug use before it starts: The future of prevention. U.S. Department of Health and Human Services.

Peck, R. C., Biasotti, A., Boland, P. N., Malory, C., & Reeve, V. (1986). The effects of marijuana and alcohol on actual driving performance. *Alcohol, Drugs and Driving, 2,* 135–54.

Perrine, M. W. (1990). Who are the drinking drivers? *Alcohol Health and Research World, 14,* 26–35.

Phelps, C. E. (1990). Control of alcohol-involved driving through impersonal prevention. *Alcohol Health and Research World, 14,* 52–56.

Ross, H. L. (1990). Drinking and driving: Beyond the criminal approach. *Alcohol Health and Research World, 14,* 58–62.

Salaspuro, M. (1987). Conventional and coming laboratory markers of alcoholism and heavy drinking. *Alcoholism: Clinical and Experimental Research 10, Supplement 52,* 53–125.

Smiley, A. (1986). Marijuana: On-road and driving simulator studies. *Alcohol, Drugs and Driving: Abstracts and Reviews, 2,* 121–34.

Terhune, K. W. (1986). Problems and methods in studying drug crash effects. *Alcohol, Drugs, and Driving, Abstracts and Reviews, 2,* 1–14.

Tyrell, I. R. (1979). *Sobering up: From temperance to prohibition in antebellum America, 1800–1860.* Westport, CT: Greenwood Press.

Williamns, A. F., Peat, M. A., Courch, D. J., Wells, J. K., & Finkle, B. S. (1985). Drugs in fatally injured young male drivers. *Public Health Reports, 100,* 19–25.

Zwerling, C., Ryan, J., & Endel, J. O. (1990). The efficacy of preemployment drug screening for marijuana and cocaine in predicting employment outcome. *Journal of the American Medical Association, 264,* 2639–43.

13

• • •

SUBSTANCE ABUSE AND SUBSTANCE ABUSE TREATMENT

• • •

OBJECTIVES

When you have finished studying this chapter you should:

1. Be able to describe the three models for addiction.
2. Be able to describe three personality disorders associated with substance abuse.
3. Know why the question of controlled drinking is so important.
4. Be able to describe both medical and psychological treatment for alcohol abuse.
5. Be able to discuss strategies used to prevent relapse.
6. Know why Alcoholics Anonymous (AA) is so prominent.
7. Be able to discuss some criticisms of AA.
8. Know how medical treatment is used to aid those undergoing heroin withdrawal.
9. Understand how methadone works.
10. Know how therapeutic communities work.
11. Be able to discuss the concept of spontaneous remission.

KEY TERMS

abstinence
acetaldehyde
Alcoholics Anonymous
Antabuse
antisocial personality
aversion therapy
borderline personality
clonidine
controlled drinking
covert sensitization
detoxification
emetine
methadone
MFS
naloxone
Narcotics Anonymous
Oxford Group
PAWS
Rational Recovery
SOS
spontaneous recovery
Synanon
Twelve Steps
WFS

S ubstance abuse is like pornography. Everyone knows what it is until
     faced with the prospect of defining it. Brendan Behan, the Irish poet
(and alcohol abuser of grand proportions) said that an alcoholic "is someone
you don't like who drinks more than you do." As we saw in chapter 2, the
problem of substance abuse is entwined with our concept of addiction. In the
case of alcohol, the Diagnostic and Statistical Manual of the American Psychiatric Association distinguishes between abuse and dependence (addiction),
but what about an "addiction" to gambling, television, or sex?

Assuming we have solved the problem of defining who is a substance
abuser, and what is substance abuse, what do we do next? How do we get
help for the person? Are some methods of treatment better than others? Is it
possible that some people get better without help? Is there any way of determining who will benefit from which program? What is our responsibility to
society at large? Can we require that people accept treatment for their
abuse?

SUBSTANCE ABUSE

In chapter 1, we examined the varied types of drug users and saw that drug
use was a complicated phenomenon. Experimental users cannot be considered in the same category as regular users, and regular use is different than
intensified use. The goal of helping substance users or abusers then also
must be different. Moreover, the task of defining (and treating) substance
abusers reveals a great deal about attitudes toward drug use in general.

Some of the definitions of substance abuse focus upon the drug, and
thus we have the terms *cocaine addiction* and *alcoholism*. Others emphasize
pharmacological criteria such as the presence of dependence and withdrawal
signs. Still other definitions rely on medical tests or complications such as
abnormal liver function or cirrhosis. Included in some but not all of the definitions are psychological concepts such as craving or the inability to stop
drug use.

Among the best known and most carefully worked out definitions are
those of the World Health Organization, the American Psychiatric Association (found in the Diagnostic and Statistical Manual III), that of the National
Council on Alcoholism, and the Feighner Research Criteria (Westermeyer,
1986). These definitions focus on different criteria, involve different drugs,
and were devised for different purposes. The American Medical Association
definition builds on that of the World Health Organization and is the most
widely used for diagnostic purposes in the United States. This definition
may be seen in chapter 5.

We have seen in previous chapters that while most people use drugs in
some form, most use them sensibly. Therefore, we must also ask why so

The typical alcoholic American

young

old

male

female

black

white

rich

poor

employed

unemployed

executive

laborer

student

doctor

immigrant

native born

**There's no such thing as typical.
We have all kinds. Nine million alcoholic Americans.
It's our number one drug problem.**

NATIONAL INSTITUTE
ON ALCOHOL ABUSE
AND ALCOHOLISM
NATIONAL INSTITUTE OF MENTAL HEALTH

many people *abuse* drugs. Theories proposing to explain drug abuse involve many levels of explanation, from events occurring at the level of the synapse to events occurring at the level of society, with all gradations in between. While we will look at several of these independently, it is important to remember that they are not mutually exclusive.

Genetic/
Neurobiological Level

Numerous neurobiological and genetic theories exist to explain substance abuse. In chapter 5, we reviewed the evidence for a genetic predisposition for alcohol abuse. A neurobiological model of opiate addiction has so much logical consistency that it almost seems self-evident. The neurobiological explanation for addiction to the opiates, for example, invariably involves a hypothesized lack of endorphins (Levinthal, 1988). The cause for the lack of endorphins may be a matter of debate, but to the neurochemist, addiction can be explained at the level of the synapse.

Nearly all of the neurobiological theories of opiate addiction are some variation of the following theme: Some individuals are born with or develop, perhaps as a result of childhood deprivation, a deficiency of endorphins in the brain. They feel the emotional component of pain more readily than others and are prime candidates for the development of dependence on the synthetic endorphin-like substances such as morphine and heroin. This priming leads them to increased use and subsequent tolerance, dependence, and withdrawal.

An alternative to this theory is that psychological and sociological factors predispose certain individuals to use narcotic drugs. As a result of this continued action, which may or may not be objectively pleasant, neurobiological changes occur, requiring the continuation of opiates. In this case, the initial reason for drug abuse is psychosocial, but the mechanism remains neurobiological (Trachtenberg & Blum, 1987).

Some neurobiological theories assume that the deficiency is irreversible, so the treatment lies in replacing the hypothesized deficiency permanently. A corollary of this theory would be that a heroin addict is similar to a diabetic who needs a daily dose of insulin (Fincher, 1979). No one blames a diabetic for *needing* insulin. Why should anyone blame a heroin addict for *needing* heroin?

Such theories downplay the psychological component of addiction. They do not explain, for example, why some addicts find the act of shooting up itself reinforcing. Nor can they explain why at least some narcotic addicts give up their dependence as they get older. Unless one presupposes the innate lack of endorphins, neurobiological theories cannot explain why drug users continue to use a drug that initially made them sick.

Although we have, so far, concentrated on opiate addiction, other drugs of abuse need to be considered. Elaborate neurobiological models also have been proposed to explain addiction to stimulants (Sunderwirth, 1985), barbiturates (Okamoto, 1984), and other drugs. The clearly demonstrated depletion of catecholamines after repeated use of amphetamines or cocaine provides the basis for most neurobiological theories of stimulant abuse. The initial withdrawal is followed by a prolonged period of depression due to a disordered dopamine metabolism in the brain, meaning that the user cannot feel pleasure as readily as others and craves cocaine or amphetamines to restore this ability.

For alcohol addiction, numerous neurobiological models have been suggested, depending on the presumed underlying deficiency that leads to abusive drinking. One problem with any of the models is that alcohol abuse is not a single disorder. Heavy drinking is a behavior brought about by a number of causes. Neurobiological models cannot hope to explain every case of alcoholism, nor do they attempt to do so.

Without being too specific, neurobiological theories of alcohol abuse suggest that for various reasons, some people respond differently to alcohol; either they respond more positively to its effects or they require more of the drug initially than do others. These individuals are more likely to drink heavily, which leads to neuronal adaptation at the cellular level, further increasing their tolerance. Once they have been drinking heavily for a long time, the neuronal changes are sufficient to produce dependence, meaning that without the alcohol, withdrawal takes place, leading to a further continuance of alcohol use (Wise, 1988).

You have read in chapter 5 about the genetic theories of alcohol abuse. Genetic factors alone cannot account for all alcohol abuse, and an environmental interaction is essential in those cases where genetics does play a role. The real danger of accepting a genetic theory uncritically is twofold. Those who do not believe they have the gene might feel that they were immune to the ill effects of alcohol, and those who do feel they have the gene might come to believe that they are "destined" to become alcoholics. Neither belief has any basis in research or common experience (Searles, 1989).

Another theory attempts to link the neurobiological with the psychological approach, by suggesting that an underlying neurological disturbance centering in the frontal lobes of the brain accounts for some alcoholism. Individuals who have this problem, so the theory suggests, have psychological characteristics such as attention deficits, impulsiveness, high activity levels, and rapid changes of emotion brought about by a neurological disorder, and these are seen before alcohol use becomes abusive. The same neurological disorder influences the way the person will respond to alcohol and thus alcohol abuse is a combination of neurobiological and psychological factors (Miller, 1990).

Treatment for substance abuse that follows the neurobiological/genetic model obviously has a focus on medical treatment. Drugs have been developed to help in the treatment of various types of substance abuse, including alcohol dependency, opiate addiction, and stimulant abuse. All of these medical treatments are based on the underlying principle that drug addiction can best be described at the neurobiological or genetic level.

Psychological Models   Psychologists interested in drug dependency ask a variety of questions. Some of these were addressed in chapter 1. Why, for example, can we expect that approximately 10 percent of the users of virtually any drug will develop problems with dependence? Is there a dependent or addictive personality? Are some people more likely to become abusers than others? As we have already seen, the major difficulty in answering these and similar questions lies in determining whether the personality characteristics that differentiate substance abusers are the cause or the result of drug abuse.

Research has indicated that abusers of alcohol and other drugs do seem to share certain personality characteristics. Depression, for example, is seen far more frequently in alcohol and drug dependents than in normal populations (Meyer, 1986; Kennedy, Konstantareas, & Homatidis, 1987). Sex differences also have been found. Men who abuse drugs are more likely to have symptoms of antisocial personality disorders, while women are more likely to show characteristics of borderline personality disorders. Although numerous other personality traits have been suggested as being related to substance abuse, the evidence for them is less clear. If there is to be a common psychological factor in drug abuse, it will likely be found in the characteristics of the depressive, antisocial, and borderline personalities.

You read about the characteristics of depression in chapter 12. It is easy to understand how depression might be both a predisposing factor as well as a result of substance abuse. Depressive people might find the mood-altering effects of drugs more rewarding than those who are not depressed. Those who begin using drugs to excess and are unsuccessful in controlling that behavior also might become depressed. Finally the physiological effects of excessive drug intake might produce depression.

Antisocial and borderline personality disorders are technical terms that come from the Diagnostic and Statistical Manual III of the American Psychiatric Association. Personality disorders are pervasive patterns of behavior that are the result of both experience and other, probably inherited, characteristics. Those who have personality disorders are not psychotic; that is, they have not lost touch with reality. They have, however, developed deep-seated and maladaptive (at least to others) ways of dealing with the problems of everyday life.

Perhaps the best way to define these personality disorders is to describe the characteristics of the two that are most often associated with substance abuse. Persons with an **antisocial personality** tend to be cold, callous, and dogmatic in their opinions. They are intolerant of frustration, have a very low tolerance for boredom and routine, and tend to jump from one exciting episode to another. They have very short tempers and are easily provoked to anger.

They are, ironically, usually quite aware of the feelings of others, but use these and manipulate them for their own ends. They are frequently intelligent and often quite charming in a superficial way. They are difficult, if not impossible, to help, extremely manipulative, and, from the standpoint of

---

Table 13.1 The Antisocial Personality

The antisocial personality typically displays at least four of the following characteristics:

1. Inability to sustain consistent work behavior
2. Lack of ability to function as a responsible parent
3. Failure to accept social norms with respect to lawful behavior
4. Inability to maintain enduring attachment to a sexual partner
5. Irritability and aggressiveness as indicated by repeated fights and assaults
6. Failure to honor financial obligations
7. Failure to plan ahead, or impulsivity
8. Disregard for the truth as indicated by repeated lying, etc.
9. Recklessness, as indicated by DUI ["driving under the influence"] or recurrent speeding

Source: Adapted from the DSM-III.

---

those trying to help them, thoroughly unlikable (Beck, Freeman, & Associates, 1990).

The **borderline personality** is more difficult to describe. Those with this condition have wide mood swings with very intense emotions. They are impetuous, erratic, impulsive, and occasionally self-destructive. They seem to keep repeating maladaptive behavior and never seem to "get it together." They seem to have no direction in life and follow every passing whim. They appear aimless and are often highly dependent on others (Beck, Freeman, & Associates, 1990).

It is easy to see how these two personality types might become substance abusers. They seem to share an impetuousness and an inability to learn from their actions. Antisocial personalities are constant thrill-seekers who are easily bored. Borderline personalities have wide mood swings and may use drugs to self-medicate. Both seek instant self-gratification.

Before accepting these personality disorders as an *explanation* of drug abuse, you should keep in mind that many substance abusers do not fit these categories. The personality disorders may be a function of the substance abuse rather than the other way around. Substance abusers are notorious for stealing, lying, and otherwise doing whatever is necessary to obtain their drug. However, these traits may have developed as a way of adapting to drug dependence. Similarly, a substance abuser often is subjected to chemically-induced mood swings and other traits that are characteristic of the borderline personality.

The Societal Approach

In general, and to simplify, psychological theories, like genetic theories, place the source of the abuse or addiction within the individual. Other theories focus on the role of society. The difference is the level of explanation. Neurobiological/genetic theories refer addiction to the synapse while psychological

---

Table 13.2   The Borderline Personality

To be classified as a borderline personality the person must exhibit at least five of the
following:

   a. A pattern of unstable relationships characterized by extremes of over-idealization and
      devaluation

   b. Impulsivity in behaviors such as spending, sex, or substance abuse

   c. Marked shifts in moods lasting a few hours to a few days

   d. Inappropriate anger or lack of control of anger

   e. Recurrent suicidal threats or self-mutilating behavior

   f. Marked identity disturbance about self-image, long-term goals, and preferred values

   g. Chronic feelings of boredom

   h. Frantic attempts to avoid real or imagined abandonment

---

theories refer it to the psyche. Societal theories attribute drug use to sociological factors.

In addition to neurobiological deficiencies and psychological factors,
substance abuse may also be a function of societal roles. Some groups
within a culture engage in drug use that other groups in that culture would
label substance abuse. Members of the using group are nevertheless under
considerable pressure to abide by the norms of their subculture. Those growing up where heroin addiction and alcohol abuse are common, such as a
ghetto, barrio, or slum, might be considered deviant if they did *not* engage
in such behavior. By the same token, a member of a group in which any
drug use causes ostracism would have a powerful incentive to be opposed to
any drug use.

Some substance abuse prevention and treatment programs emphasize
role models, both within and outside the family, and attempt to change the
social milieu that fosters drug abuse, substituting positive role models in its
place. Many drug education programs are aimed at convincing those at risk
for drug use that they can and should resist the pressure of their social group
and identify with other, non-using, groups.

SUBSTANCE ABUSE TREATMENT

For those who abuse drugs (as well as those associated with drug abusers),
the choice of treatments must seem bewildering. Choices range from those
based on the neurobiological/genetic model that involves pharmacological intervention (such as Antabuse for alcohol, or Traxene for heroin addition) to those
emphasizing the requirement for a total restructuring of the abuser's world
(such as Alcoholics Anonymous or Synanon). In between are innumerable
groups that attempt to integrate different aspects of substance abuse treatment within the patient's own physiological and psychological framework.

One basic distinction is between outpatient and inpatient programs. As the
names imply, inpatient programs involve a period of residence in a hospital

or clinic along with intensive medical and psychological treatment and extensive follow-up programs. Outpatient programs are designed to be integrated into the abuser's ongoing lifestyle and are less intense. They may involve medical treatment, psychotherapy and all of the trappings of inpatient treatment, but the patient's life is less disrupted. It is very difficult to evaluate the two types of programs, because of the great variability in the types of people who go to each, the types of programs, and the standards for evaluation. As a rule, however, the two types of programs seem about equally effective (Nance, 1989; Peele, 1990; Wallace, 1990).

Although abusers of various drugs probably share some characteristics, treatment for abusers varies with educational level, socioeconomic status, availability of facilities, and type of drug abused. Probably the best way to look at substance abuse treatment is to classify it by type of drug abused.

Alcohol Abuse Treatment

About 10 percent of all drinkers can be classified as abusers, alcoholics, or alcohol dependent, depending on whose terminology is used. Since there are upwards of 100 million drinkers in the United States, we can conclude that there are at least 10 million who drink alcohol in a way that significantly impairs their functioning. The methods used to help alcohol abusers are as varied as the theories of alcoholism. Behavioral techniques, medical management, and self-help groups abound. Because of the acute and long-term physiological changes accompanying alcohol withdrawal, an inpatient program is often recommended.

The best known model for inpatient treatment of alcoholism is called the Minnesota Model, named, not surprisingly, after a program developed over a period of years in Minnesota. It accepts the disease concept of alcoholism and has total abstinence as its goal. It incorporates psychotherapy, medical treatment, and lectures on the effects of alcohol.

Medical Approach

Treatment for alcoholism that focuses on the medical aspect of the disorder usually has two concerns: treating the alcoholic during the withdrawal process and use of drugs to foster sobriety.

Treating Withdrawal. Acute withdrawal from alcohol abuse is often characterized by nervousness, anxiety, muscle tremor (the shakes), and even hallucinations (the delirium tremens, or d.t.'s) and seizures. As we saw in chapter 11, the benzodiazepines are often prescribed to relieve some of these symptoms. As we saw also, there is some concern about the advisability of substituting one dependence-producing drug for another. Nevertheless, the benzodiazepines have their place in the treatment of acute alcohol withdrawal.

For alcoholics who have serious physical problems or who have been abusing alcohol for a prolonged period of time, inpatient hospitalization is usually recommended. For others (probably the majority), outpatient treatment or a social approach to withdrawal is probably sufficient even during the acute stage of withdrawal (National Institute on Alcohol Abuse and Alcoholism, 1989).

After the acute period of withdrawal, there is usually a period referred to as **PAWS** (Prolonged Alcohol Withdrawal Syndrome). The withdrawing alcoholic experiences anxiety, insomnia, depression, and physiological changes that indicate a period of central nervous system hyperexcitability. The existence of PAWS might be easy to understand if you recall that alcohol is a depressant and that these symptoms are a rebound brought on by prolonged exposure to alcohol.

During PAWS, there is a considerable risk of relapse. The alcoholic naturally finds this withdrawal unpleasant and seeks to find relief. Craving for alcohol is high during this period. The length of time for this withdrawal phase is not clear, but probably lasts for several weeks after initial withdrawal (National Institute for Alcohol Abuse and Alcoholism, 1989; U.S. Department of Health and Human Services, 1990).

Fostering Sobriety. Antabuse is used in the long-term medical management of alcohol abuse. You should recall from chapter 6 that alcohol is metabolized first to **acetaldehyde,** then to acetic acid, and eventually to carbon dioxide and water. Antabuse prevents acetaldehyde from being metabolized to acetic acid. The subsequent build-up of this chemical produces flushing, nausea, vomiting, and a drop in blood pressure. Acetaldehyde is an extremely toxic substance. People taking Antabuse can suffer severe reactions as a result of exposure to minute amounts of alcohol such as that found in mouthwash, hair tonic, or even vanilla extract.

Antabuse is a useful drug to help those who are highly motivated to stop drinking and maintain abstinence, but it is not a cure for alcohol dependence. It is administered in pill form, and the alcohol abuser must "remember" to take it every day. Determined abusers can find ways of avoiding the effects of Antabuse by "forgetting" or by only pretending to take the drug. Antabuse may prove useful for those motivated to stop drinking, but it is not a substitute for, nor does it provide, motivation in the first place. Antabuse also can produce fairly serious side effects, and its use needs to be monitored carefully.

Other drugs have been tested for helping alcoholics through the period of recovery. Some of these are designed to help overcome the craving, others to treat psychological problems associated with alcohol abuse, still others to treat other drug problems in polydrug abusers (Litten & Allen, 1991). Many of these drugs are in the early stages of testing, but the most promising are the serotonin re-uptake inhibitors discussed in chapter 11, which are prescribed for reducing craving.

Psychotherapy for Alcohol Abuse

Individual and group psychotherapy make up an important part of both outpatient and inpatient models of alcohol abuse treatment. Even if you accept a biological cause of alcoholism, psychological factors still play an enormous role. Moreover, the alcohol abuser has undoubtedly learned maladaptive ways

in depth

Codependency

Words and phrases often come into everyday usage and become entrenched in our thinking before they are even carefully examined. One such term is "codependent." Most alcohol and other drug abusers are married, and all have mothers, fathers, other relatives, and friends. To some in the field of substance abuse treatment, all of these are "codependents." Codependency is defined in numerous ways. According to some it is a disease that, untreated, can lead to death (Schaef, 1986; Young, 1987). According to one researcher codependency has fourteen categories of behaviors that total 241 characteristics (Beattie, 1987). In nearly every case when the term is used, the implication is that the codependent has a problem at least as severe as the abuser. Furthermore, according to some theories, the spouse or close family member may even be the cause of the abuse.

While it is entirely reasonable to wonder why someone stays with an alcoholic or other drug abuser who is violent, antisocial, or self-destructive, it is another matter to imply that the spouse has a disease that is in need of treatment. The term codependent is applied far too loosely and has come to acquire a meaning that is so moralistic and negative that it hurts rather than helps both the spouse and the abuser (Harper & Capedevila, 1990). No matter what you may read in the popular literature, there is very little agreement among professionals whether codependency even exists as a psychological disorder. The disease concept has a long history and has been quite useful in helping abusers overcome their alcohol and other drug problems. Applying the same concept to family and friends of abusers probably does little except increase the feelings of guilt of all involved.

of dealing with problems during the period of abuse. Group and individual psychotherapy are designed to help alcoholics deal with their problems and to avoid relapse by helping them develop new ways of coping without alcohol.

Most alcoholics are married and many have families. Alcohol abuse in one person can have an effect on everyone in the family, so family and marital therapy has been used to help the drinker, the spouse, and the other members of the family cope with their feelings, their bad past experiences, and adapt to the new lifestyle of the nondrinking spouse.

Social Skills Training

A variation on group and individual psychotherapy geared toward problem drinkers is called social skills training. Some alcoholics may never have learned basic methods of dealing with other people, or their original skills may have eroded as a result of years of drinking. Social skills training helps drinkers develop methods of communicating with others, dealing with anger and frustration, learning assertiveness, and avoiding peer pressure. These skills are designed to help the individual avoid a relapse when treatment has been completed.

Much confusion and controversy exists over how effective psychotherapy is, which type is best for which alcoholic, and so on. Almost everyone involved agrees, however, that it is useful and plays an important part in recovery. One problem in determining how effective therapy is, lies in the difficulty of defining "effective." Is the goal abstinence? If so, for how long? Is the goal to help abusers improve their lifestyle? If so, how is that variable measured?

Behavioral Treatment

While the disease concept of alcoholism is widely accepted, as we have seen in chapter 4, some researchers view alcohol abuse as a learned behavior rather than a disease. For them and for others who see behavioral techniques as useful in helping problem drinkers, the road to sobriety or moderation takes a different path. Behavioral treatment emphasizes punishing unwanted behavior and reinforcing desirable behavior.

From the standpoint of a behavioral model, Antabuse is a form of aversion therapy. Through the process of classical conditioning, drinking is associated with the unpleasant aftereffects of acetaldehyde build-up. *Not* drinking is reinforced by the absence of these effects. In chapter 1, you read about *negative reinforcement* in which behavior is reinforced by removal of an unpleasant or aversive stimulus. Therefore, with Antabuse, drinking is associated with punishment, and not drinking with negative reinforcement.

Another, even more direct form of aversion therapy involves giving alcohol abusers **emetine,** a drug that causes nausea and vomiting. The sight, smell, taste, and thought of alcohol become unpleasant instead of pleasant by pairing the drinking of alcohol with the immediate effects of this drug. In aversion therapy treatment, as it is commonly used, the sessions take place as part of hospital treatment. Subjects are instructed to take a small amount of an alcoholic beverage into their mouths just prior to the onset of the effects of emetine (Miller & Barlow, 1973). Several such pairings as well as one or more follow-up sessions after the patient has left the hospital is typically recommended (Weins & Menustick, 1983). Another technique involves pairing drinking with electric shock (Blake, 1965, 1967).

Another technique is called **covert sensitization** and involves *imagining* nausea and vomiting and pairing these thoughts with the behaviors associated with drinking. Imagined scenes of not drinking are paired with positive thoughts (Cautela, 1970). As with the case of other forms of aversion therapy, booster sessions are given at intervals after initial training. One advantage of covert sensitization is that it overcomes the natural reluctance of patients to experience chemically-induced vomiting with its ethical and medical considerations.

Some researchers have found that aversion therapy is effective (Weins & Menustick, 1983). However, you should realize by now that it is not sufficient to *prevent* someone from drinking. The person giving up one habit (drinking, for example) must receive something in return in order for true change to occur (Vaillant, 1983). Aversion therapy seems most useful for the short term, when the goal is to stop drinking. It is less useful in the long run, when the goal is to refrain from drinking (Vaillant, 1983). Aversion therapy is not widely used now, although there are occasional attempts to revive its use (Howard & Jenson, 1990). The main objections are ethical and perhaps aesthetic rather than practical, since it does appear to work.

Other behavioral approaches to the treatment of alcohol abuse are more complex. They involve attempts to understand and alter the reinforcement schedules that maintain drinking. Instead of seeing drinking as a sign of an underlying disease, they view it as learned behavior maintained by reinforcement. Those using this technique manipulate the reinforcements that underlie both drinking and abstinence so as to cause extinction of the drinking behavior and an increase in abstinence.

Controlled Drinking

Individuals who present themselves for alcohol treatment programs have, by definition, been unable to control their drinking. For them, abstinence is probably the ideal. Perhaps with effort some of them may be able to drink in a controlled fashion, but we must remember that "controlled" drinking—setting up times and places where alcohol may be consumed with precise monitoring of the amount consumed—is not the same as the typical drinking pattern of the non-alcohol-abuser, who seldom thinks about when or how much he or she is going to drink and still drinks moderately.

Why would anyone with a demonstrated drinking problem want to take the chance and risk a return to abuse? Are the rewards of drinking really that great? I know that if I play Russian roulette with a six-shot revolver, I *probably* will not be killed the first time I pull the trigger, but the thrill is not worth the risk. Many feel that the controlled drinking imposes the same kind of risk and that those abusive drinkers who want to return to "normal" drinking are denying the reality of their problem.

On the other hand, there are those who maintain vehemently that emphasis on abstinence serves as a deterrent to effective alcohol abuse treatment, especially when the abuser is in the early stages of the disorder. Those who hold this point of view do not deny that the alcohol dependent person should stop drinking. They believe that total abstinence may not be called for if the disorder is caught in its early stages, before the drinker becomes a serious abuser and/or dependent on alcohol. In support of this view, it appears that those who are successful at controlled drinking have fewer signs of alcohol abuse and begin their attempt relatively early in their drinking career (Ogborne, 1987).

Early intervention is an important goal for those who hold this point of view. They reason that an excessive drinker who is not yet dependent may be unwilling to go for treatment if he or she thinks that the only alternative to drinking is abstinence. Many, they feel, will wait until they are, in fact, dependent, in which case they must stop. Such reluctance would, in turn, reinforce the idea that total abstinence is necessary, producing a vicious circle.

The Sobell and Sobell Experiment

Perhaps the most famous, or infamous, depending on your point of view, experiment dealing with the behavioral method of treatment for alcohol abusers was done by Sobell and Sobell (1973;1976). It was based on a behavioral model, and through instruction and reinforcement the authors attempted to train a small group of problem drinkers to become controlled or social drinkers. This experiment, which involved a very few subjects and which was not intended to be a model for *all* alcohol treatment, generated an enormous amount of controversy.

The author's report of a successful return to controlled drinking were questioned by others who criticized the research and accused the two researchers of professional misconduct, at the least, and at the worst, outright fraud (Pendery, Maltzman, & West, 1982). They were cleared of any wrongdoing by a panel of eminent researchers (Marlatt, 1983) although, as is often the case, their exoneration did not gain the headlines that their accusation did.

Debate still rages about the validity and even morality of this experiment. Exploratory though it was, it challenged a basic tenet of faith of some important professionals in the field—that total abstinence is the only appropriate goal for alcohol abusers. More importantly, the furor over the research obscured the fact that the Sobells' finding was not new. A number of studies have reported, both before and after their research was published, that at least some problem drinkers do return to social drinking patterns. The real question is not *if* problem drinkers can moderate their drinking but whether such drinking should be considered a *goal*.

The disease and abstinence model advocated by Alcoholics Anonymous and the National Council on Alcoholism has had such a strong influence on alcohol treatment that the early intervention model has rarely been tested in a controlled, scientific way. Of course, well designed and well controlled studies of the effectiveness of Alcoholics Anonymous are also rare, mainly because they are extremely difficult to do (Glaser & Ogborne, 1982). Later in this chapter we will look at a phenomenon that has been widely observed but rarely studied, **spontaneous remission,** or self-cure. Some of the evidence that comes from these recent studies will shed some light on the concept of early intervention.

Relapse and After-Treatment Strategies

It is relatively easy to stay sober in an inpatient setting and most alcohol abusers can go for weeks or even months without drinking under certain circumstances. The difficulty occurs as time passes and the external cues to drinking remain while the vows to remain sober weaken. Most studies show that the great majority of alcohol abusers go back to drinking, and treatment is successful only for about 25–30 percent of alcoholics. In spite of, or perhaps because of, these odds it is essential to look at ways of preventing relapse.

This diagram shows the similarity of relapse rates for three commonly abused drugs. Keep in mind, however, that relapse is not permanent; most who want to will become drug-free.

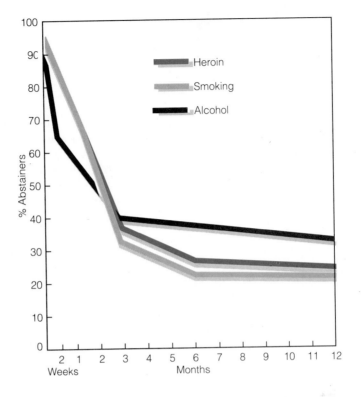

Undoubtedly the best known method, not only of getting off the bottle, but staying off, is Alcoholics Anonymous.

Alcoholics Anonymous (AA)

Alcoholics Anonymous was started in 1935 by two men, Bill W. and Dr. Bob S. (AA encourages members to use only their first names). Bill W. was a New England stockbroker who had been hospitalized several times for alcohol abuse. During the last of these episodes he had a spiritual conversion, joined a religious organization called the **Oxford Group,** and moved to Akron, Ohio, where he made his first convert, Dr. Robert S., a surgeon. The two formed Alcoholics Anonymous, incorporating the theories of Carl Jung and William James, and the Oxford Group. Eventually they developed their own justly famous Twelve Steps (Shore & Luce, 1976).

Alcoholics Anonymous emphasizes a group approach to the solution of problem drinking. AA maintains that alcoholism is a disease, but that the *treatment* (there is no cure) is not medical but social. AA emphasizes that total abstinence is essential to recovery and that this is best achieved through the assistance of those who have been there (other alcoholics). AA has developed twelve steps which members work on to aid them in their quest for sobriety.

Table 13.3 The AA Twelve Steps

1. We admitted that we were powerless over alcohol, that our lives had become unmanageable.

2. We came to believe that a Power greater than ourselves could restore us to sanity.

3. We made a decision to turn our will and our lives over to the care of God as we understood Him.

4. We made a searching and fearless moral inventory of ourselves.

5. We admitted to God, to ourselves, and to another human being the exact nature of our wrongs.

6. We were entirely ready to have God remove all these defects of character.

7. We humbly asked Him to remove our shortcomings.

8. We made a list of all persons we had harmed, and became willing to make amends to them all.

9. We made direct amends to such people wherever possible, except when to do so would injure them or others.

10. We continued to take personal inventory and when we were wrong promptly admitted it.

11. We sought through prayer and meditation to improve our conscious contact with God as we understood Him, praying only for knowledge of His will for us and the power to carry that out.

12. Having had a spiritual awakening as a result of these steps, we tried to carry this message to alcoholics and to practice these principles in all our affairs.

From Alcoholics Anonymous

Alcoholics Anonymous is without doubt the best known of all alcohol treatment programs and is, for many, life saving. The structure of AA follows many themes dominant in American society: individualism, equality, and spirituality, which undoubtedly accounts in part for its popularity (Trice, 1983). There are AA groups in other countries, but the movement has found its greatest success in the United States.

A brief description reveals just how "American" AA is. While AA members admit that they have lost control over their alcohol intake—which might seem to contradict the American emphasis on individualism—they also stress that the choice to commit themselves to the Twelve Steps is an individual decision and that each person must find the way to sobriety on his/her own. One of our proudest American traditions is that of rugged individualism.

AA conspicuously avoids even the appearance of a hierarchy. There is no central authority, and there are no officers other than a secretary in AA groups. Even the role of secretary changes hands frequently (Kurtz, 1987). The avoidance of last names further emphasizes the egalitarian aspects of American society. Even the intentionally broad definition of spirituality is in keeping with an American consciousness that places great emphasis on church attendance and at least a passing interest in religion itself.

Does AA work? For those who stay with the group, who work the Twelve Steps, who accept the underlying message of AA, the answer is yes.

Even AA's harshest critics (and there are many) admit that for many people Alcoholics Anonymous is a useful pathway to sobriety. The members of AA have all been abusive drinkers, are dedicated to helping others stop drinking, and provide a wide support basis for those who truly want to stop. You undoubtedly know people who have managed to gain and maintain sobriety through this group. Without denying its usefulness, it is important to see what the critics have to say.

The critics of AA question, for the most part, whether AA is good for *everyone* (Tournier, 1983). AA seems to be most effective for those who respond well to its social and religious aspects. A basically gregarious person with a background in traditional religion would seem the best candidate for AA. Others may be turned off by these very aspects that are so effective for the majority. AA keeps no records, and the drop-out rate is high. Those who remain with the group are, by definition, successful in controlling their drinking; those who disappear are lost to recordkeeping (Fingarette, 1988).

It is very common for inpatient programs for alcohol abusers to include AA meetings in their curriculum. When abstinence and relapse rates are studied in these groups, AA does seem to help individuals maintain sobriety (Cross, Morgan, Mooney, Martin, & Rafter, 1990). However, degree of involvement with AA after treatment is a significant factor because there is a strong tendency for the positive influence of AA to wane after one or two years of sobriety (Alford, Koehler, & Leonard, 1991).

Not everyone can benefit from the AA program. Perhaps the greatest stumbling block for some people is the emphasis that AA places on a "higher power." AA feels very strongly that it is impossible to stop drinking without believing in something greater than yourself, even if the higher power is the AA group itself. One of the core problems that alcoholics have, according to AA, is the belief that they have control, that they are God. Since AA maintains that the alcoholics cannot stop by themselves, it follows that a greater power has to help. Seven of the Twelve Steps make a reference to a higher power.

For the small minority of people in the United States who have no faith in a higher power, AA would seem to have little to offer. To be fair, there is no such requirement for being a member of AA and the emphasis is on "God as you know him to be." Furthermore, there are a number of agnostics and atheists within AA. Although the group downplays any specific religious point of view, for some people *any* reference to a higher power is a significant deterrent to joining such an organization.

Other critics find fault with the emphasis on powerlessness. AA members feel that to admit their powerlessness is the first step to recovery. Critics feel that such an admission leads from a dependency on alcohol to a dependency on the group. If the alcoholic is individually powerless to stop drinking then something must provide that power. Sometimes, say critics, AA members become so wrapped up in the group that they are nearly as dysfunctional as when they were drinking.

• YOU READ IT HERE FIRST •

Alternatives to AA

Alcoholics Anonymous has been the leading model for self-help alcohol groups since its inception in the 1930s. In fact, for most of that time it was the *only* model. Despite its undeniable success and the widespread public image of it as the cure for alcoholism, it is not for everyone. Other groups have emerged for those who find elements of AA unacceptable. The degree of similarity between their principles and those of AA vary widely.

The most recent arrival is called Rational Recovery. Its principles are most unlike AA of any of the alternatives. One of the mottos gives a good idea of the difference between the two groups. Instead of finding strength in admitting powerlessness over alcohol, it proclaims "If it is to be, it's up to me." The basic concepts of RR stem from Rational Emotive Therapy, a psychotherapeutic approach developed by Albert Ellis. The alcoholic drinks because he/she interprets events that happen in an irrational way and has learned to cope with the subsequent emotion by drinking. According to RR, if you learn to like yourself for who you are, you will not need to drink.

According to RR, all drug dependencies are the same, so, unlike AA, any drug user is welcome. While abstinence is seen as the goal, individuals who are trying to moderate their drug use are also welcome. In direct opposition to AA, RR rejects the concept that a higher power is essential for sobriety and, in fact, claims that belief in such a power slows recovery. While not rejecting the belief in a supreme being, RR seems to feel that such a belief is irrelevant to recovery from drug dependence.

Another difference is that, according to RR, once a person masters the need to drink or use drugs, meetings become increasingly irrelevant. The ex-alcoholic or ex-addict is encouraged to strike out alone because RR feels that the reliance on a group is substituting one form of dependence for another. Related to that is

the rejection of AA's well known slogan, "One day at a time." Instead, the user is encouraged to develop a "Big Plan," and that is never to drink again under any circumstances. Rather than see sobriety as a day-to-day event, it is seen as a long-range goal. Founded in 1990, it has grown to over 250 groups as of 1992.

A somewhat similar group is called SOS, which stands for both Save Our Selves and Secular Organizations for Sobriety. SOS shares a few more characteristics with AA than does RR. It focuses on *sobriety* as the primary goal of the group and advocates the "one day at a time" approach. Like RR, it believes that sobriety comes from the individual, not from a higher power and makes no distinction between the various forms of chemical addiction. Members of SOS are encouraged to acknowledge that they are alcoholics or addicts, and that they cannot and do not drink or use drugs, no matter what. They also share their thoughts and feelings with others to help maintain their and others' sobriety. The phrase that SOS uses is "Sobriety Priority."

Two other groups share a similar name and also position themselves some distance from the principles of AA. **Women for Sobriety** and **Men for Sobriety,** like all support groups, have abstinence as a goal. WFS was the original group, founded because of a perception that many of the ways AA uses to gain and maintain sobriety are more effective for men than for women. **WFS** and **MFS** have a spiritual basis, but emphasize the role of the individual and of positive emotions, particularly love. Instead of the Twelve Steps, these groups have Thirteen Statements of Acceptance. Some of the statements give a clear indication of their approach: I am what I think; Love can change the course of the world; The past is gone forever; The fundamental object of life is emotional and spiritual growth.

continued on page 447

• YOU READ IT HERE FIRST •

Alternatives to AA

continued from page 446

WFS and MFS accept that alcoholism is a disease, and see themselves as more of a recovery group for individuals who have already stopped drinking. AA, the WFS founder has stated, is good for getting people to stop drinking initially, but the emphasis on weekly meetings, humility, and powerlessness is not conducive to remaining sober. Instead, there is an emphasis on overcoming humility, finding strength, getting rid of the past, and feeling competent. Like RR, WFS and MFS feel that once the alcoholic learns to cope with the problems of life, the group becomes irrelevant.

Two other groups 1) the Calix Society and 2) Jewish Alcoholics, Chemically Dependent People, and Significant Others (JACS) are not alternatives to AA, but are support groups for those with a particular religious orientation. Calix is nondenominational but offers the opportunity for members to grow spiritually through traditional Catholic activities such as mass and communion, retreats, and Days of Reflection. JACS is primarily for those who wish to maintain their sobriety within a framework of Jewish culture and values.

The percentage of people who attend AA meetings and then stick with the program is small, although the overall number is large. Alternatives are needed, therefore, for people who find AA unhelpful. Watch for these groups to become more popular as they become better known. Our society is changing its attitude toward drug use and also getting away from a single point of view about those with alcohol and drug problems. As is stated at the end of this chapter, whatever approach works for a given individual, works for that person, and all approaches should be considered by anyone seeking help. The addresses of all the organizations are found at the end of this chapter.

If you keep in mind that alcoholism is a disorder with many causes, it stands to reason that its treatment will take many forms. Some people will be helped by inpatient treatment with or without AA. Some will recover independent of any treatment. Some will join a group for a short period of time and then leave and remain abstinent. Some might even make a return to social drinking. Some will join AA and stay in the fellowship for life, helping many others to gain sobriety. Unfortunately, many will go back to abusive drinking and suffer the consequences.

New Approaches to Relapse

Preventing relapse is at least as important as stopping in the first place. Recently, approaches have been developed that emphasize what is called the cognitive approach. The essence of this approach is that the ex-drinker recognize the environmental cues to drinking, develop ways of coping in situations that present a high risk of drinking, and develop personal confidence in the ability not to drink. Another element of relapse prevention is to look at the almost inevitable tendency to take a drink as a "lapse," not a relapse.

Three situations typically cause a relapse (or a lapse), according to the theory: (1) negative emotional states such as frustration, boredom, or depression; (2) interpersonal conflicts; (3) social pressure, such as being offered a drink in a situation in which it is hard to refuse. Most often, the relapse occurs when the person is in a high-risk situation which is encountered unexpectedly. If the individual copes successfully, probability of a relapse decreases. If not, then the individual sees their behavior in one of two ways, as a sign of weakness that triggers a full-blown relapse or as a simple lapse.

A lapse is an occasion where the person who has decided to be abstinent takes a drink. Rather than view this as a full-blown relapse and see it as indicating an inevitable return to heavy drinking, this approach maintains that the violation should be analyzed to determine why it occurred and to find ways of preventing it from happening again. Another important element of this approach is that it views craving as a temporary occurrence brought on by a variety of factors. Craving, therefore, is temporary and can be resisted. The approach is relatively new, but preliminary studies indicate that it may be effective (Annis, 1990; Amodeo & Kurtz, 1990; Mackey & Marlatt, 1990–91).

Because alcohol is so pervasive in our society, alcohol abuse is likely to remain a serious problem for the foreseeable future. For those who go on to develop a drinking problem, there are a variety of approaches that may help them recover. Unfortunately, just as we know very little about what causes alcoholism, we do not know exactly why some programs work with some people and others don't. More research is needed to determine which individuals are likely to be helped by which approaches (Levy, 1991).

Treatment for Narcotics Addiction

As we saw in chapter 9, the actual number of heroin, morphine or other opiate addicts is difficult to estimate, but it is probably close to 500,000. The importance of these addicts is much greater than their numbers would indicate because the vast majority must engage in criminal behavior to maintain their dependence.

Although there is considerable controversy about how much crime is actually committed by addicts, some estimates place it as high as 50 million crimes a year, including the crime of drug sale. (Ball, Rosen, Flueck, & Nurco, 1982). The total cost to society exceeds $85 million a year, or an estimated $20,000 per addict per year (Deschenes, Angline, & Speckart, 1991).

Since heroin seems to be the drug of choice among addicts in the United States, the term heroin addict will be used in the discussion that follows. Bear in mind, however, that other forms of opiate addiction occur. Methods of treatment range from psychotherapeutic to medical, with all the stops in between. As with treatment for alcohol abuse, heroin addiction treatment must be viewed from an acute as well as a chronic viewpoint.

Withdrawal and Detoxification

The first problem is one of withdrawal or detoxification. As we saw in chapter 9, heroin withdrawal is vastly overrated. The symptoms are similar to those of the flu and seldom last more than a few days. Even addicts are ambivalent about the severity of their symptoms. It is almost as if they feel that their symptoms **should** be worse than they really are. This statement by a heroin addict is a good example of the confusion:

Is it as bad as they make out?

> No, I don't think so. It's bad, really, but you can't explain it like. . . . a lot of people say this happens and that happens but when I done my turkey [experienced withdrawal], it wasn't as bad as I was expecting. But it was bad, if you know what I mean. . . . It was unbearable, like, but it wasn't as bad as I was expecting. (in Pearson, 1972, p. 152).

Moreover, even these relatively mild symptoms of withdrawal can largely be prevented with a combination of **clonidine** and **naloxone.** Clonidine was developed originally to treat high blood pressure, but it also eliminates most of the subjective symptoms of withdrawal (Riordan & Kleber, 1980). Use of clonidine for this purpose is not approved by the FDA, but it has proven helpful, even though users often experience side effects such as sedation (Kleber & Kosten, 1984). Naloxone is a very specific antagonist for opiates, that works at the level of the synapse. It occupies the postsynaptic receptor and prevents the opiates from binding there (O'Brien & Woody, 1986), and shortens the period of withdrawal (Resnick et al, 1977).

As with alcohol abuse, getting a heroin addict through withdrawal is the easy part. Keeping him or her clean is the hard part. Earlier studies of relapse indicated that virtually all heroin addicts who had been treated for their addiction either died or went back to using (Pescor, 1938; Hunt & Odoroff, 1962). However, subsequent studies indicate that these data were not entirely accurate. Relapse immediately after treatment does seem to be the rule rather than the exception, but the passage of years and often subsequent attempts to stop bring about a higher abstinence rate. Vaillant (1966), for example, found that in a twelve year follow-up of a group of heroin addicts, "only" 46 percent were still addicted.

A long-term study (Simpson & Marsh, 1986) is both pessimistic and optimistic. Most addicts (75 percent in this study) return to daily heroin use, at least for a time, but 75 percent were not daily users at the end of twelve years. This means that relapse from heroin treatment should be seen as a temporary problem. Most heroin addicts do manage to stop using heroin.

There is far more to being a narcotic addict than being addicted to an opiate, and treatment must take this fact into consideration. As we saw, many "addicts" are not really addicted at all. Heroin "addicts" take the drug for a variety of reasons: to enjoy the high, to relieve withdrawal, to be part of a group, or to demonstrate alienation from mainstream society.

Not to be minimized is the importance to some of being a "stand-up cat." Although the term has undoubtedly gone out of favor as slang among heroin users, the phenomenon remains. Stand-up cats are those who have the courage to take on a challenge, in this case the challenge of using heroin without becoming addicted. The worse the description of addiction and withdrawal, the greater the challenge to the ''stand-up cat'' to prove that he or she can handle such a dangerous drug (Feldman, 1968).

Medical Treatment

Three types of medical treatment are commonly used in various parts of the United States and elsewhere in the world to help the heroin addict: administration of naltrexone (Trexan), maintenance with dolophine (Methadone), or maintenance with heroin itself. The first two are preferred in the United States, while heroin maintenance is used, along with other methods, in England.

Naltrexone. A standard dose (50 mg) of Trexan will block the pharmacologic effect of heroin or other opiates for at least twenty-four hours. By increasing the dose, it is possible to increase duration of the blockade for up to three days. A person who has taken Trexan and who also injects heroin will experience none of the normal effects of the injection, since the opiate receptors at the synapse are occupied by naltrexone. Naltrexone, by itself, has little or no biological activity.

The primary advantage of Trexan treatment is that it helps prevent relapse. Many heroin addicts will shoot up shortly after they have completed treatment or detoxification. If they take heroin while on Trexan, nothing will happen, and thus they will not be motivated to continue drug use. Trexan will help them remain drug free while they make enough changes in their lifestyle to remain off narcotics without its use.

Naltrexone treatment is a useful adjunct for opiate-dependent people who are highly motivated to stop. In this regard it is similar to Antabuse with alcoholics although its effects are different. Naltrexone must be combined with psychotherapy or group therapy and the addicts must be willing and able to change their previous lifestyle. Various studies have shown that it is more effective with middle-class addicts than with street addicts (Washton, Pottash, & Gold, 1984; Greenstein, Arndt, McLellan, O'Brien, & Evans, 1984).

Buprenorphine. An interesting new treatment that is presently being evaluated helps the addict during the transition between heroin or methadone dependence and the drug-free state. Buprenorphine is a narcotic agonist (see chapter 9) with virtually no abuse potential. It produces a feeling of well being rather than a euphoric rush and blocks the effects of withdrawal (Goodwin, 1989). Addicts treated with buprenorphine seem to be more likely to stay in treatment, and it has been proposed as a transition between addiction and maintenance on naltrexone (see below). Other evidence suggests it may also be helpful in treating cocaine addiction (NIDA Note, 1990).

Methadone. Methadone is probably the best known medical treatment for narcotic addiction. Unlike Trexan, which blocks the action of the opiates, methadone is a form of narcotic substitution. Basically, methadone treatment involves substituting a legally prescribed narcotic for an illegal one. Since the addict does not have to steal in order to obtain the drug, the addict will presumably have the time and the motivation to change lifestyle. Additionally, intravenous users of drugs and homosexual males are the two largest at-risk populations for AIDS. Since methadone is taken orally, methadone can help save lives.

Methadone is dolophine hydrochloride. It was developed in Germany during World War II as a substitute for morphine. The FDA permits its use as an analgesic, for acute withdrawal from opiates, or for maintenance of opiate-dependent individuals. It does not produce the euphoria seen with heroin, but does block the craving. Methadone is not a cure for heroin addiction, and the former addict taking the drug is still dependent on opiates.

The addictive aspect of methadone has been responsible for fairly widespread criticism of its use. Methadone maintenance does nothing to change the underlying societal or psychological problems that may have led to addiction in the first place. Some have even charged that methadone maintenance provides an acceptable way for the addict to avoid dealing with psychological issues and that genuine treatment is impossible with an addict using methadone (Casriel & Bratter, 1974).

Methadone was introduced as a treatment for heroin addiction by Dole & Nyswander (1965). It has become the drug of choice for most programs that have a biological approach to narcotic addiction. At the time, many believed methadone would enable heroin addicts to get off opiates permanently, a belief, incidentally, that was not shared by Dole and Nyswander (Platt, 1987). Methadone would block the action of heroin, remove the necessity for crime, and enable the addict to change his/her lifestyle. Once this miracle had been accomplished, the addict would detox from methadone.

In reality, **detoxification** from methadone is about as difficult as from heroin. Few succeed in withdrawing, and those who do have to be selected and monitored carefully during withdrawal (Woody & O'Brien, 1986). Without becoming too dramatic, it appears that, for many, methadone maintenance is a life sentence. While this may be an acceptable alternative to a life of crime and an early death due to illicit intravenous heroin addiction or AIDS, methadone maintenance may not be appropriate for the majority of present day addicts whose addiction is not deeply rooted. For those addicted more to a lifestyle than a drug, alternatives which emphasize changing the addict's lifestyle may be preferable.

Keep in mind that the reasons most addicts report for giving up drug use have little to do with any treatment. Treatment may *help* but a look at Table 13.4 reveals that most reasons are personal.

Your family physician cannot legally prescribe methadone (or any other drug) for the purpose of *maintaining* a drug habit. Addicts have to enroll in a methadone maintenance program. These programs are supervised carefully by the Food and Drug Administration. Strict recordkeeping is

Table 13.4 Reasons for Quitting Daily Opioid Use (N = 372)	
Availability	
Not available	21.0%
Bad quality	35.8%
High cost	39.9%
No money	34.1%
Psychological/emotional	
Tired of hustle (measure of dysfunction)	83.2%
Needed change after "hitting bottom" (despair)	81.7%
Other personal/special events	65.8%
Influence of religion	22.2%
Health/physical	
Had health/medical problem	20.9%
Fear of overdose	31.0%
Legal Involvement	
Sent to jail	29.6%
Fear of being jailed	56.6%
Fear of parole/probation violation	29.1%
Family/friends	
Had family responsibilities	56.3%
Became divorced/separated	15.7%
Pressure from family	27.0%
Death of significant other	22.4%
Pressure from close friends	6.2%
Relocation	
Relocation (moved)	17.8%
Employment	
Obtained new or better job	22.6%
Fear of losing job	19.4%

Notice how little lack of availability mattered and how personal factors were of importance.
Source: *NIDA Treatment Research Report*, DHHS Pub. No. ADM 88–1420.

required and the drug may be given only in its oral form. Any qualified physician, however, may prescribe methadone for pain relief.

In practical terms, this means that addicts must go to methadone maintenance programs set up so that they serve a large number of addicts in one, presumably central, location. There are advantages to this method. Many addicts have serious behavior problems and are accustomed to a lifestyle of crime (Woody & O'Brien, 1987). Methadone maintenance programs bring these addicts to a center where individual and group psychotherapy, as well as other forms of counseling, medical treatment, and support are available.

On the other hand, would you want a methadone maintenance program next to your house? Loitering is a significant problem at many community programs and most residents are justifiably reluctant to have a group of people who have committed robbery, burglary, prostitution, and other crimes hanging around their neighborhood. Social contact is the primary purpose of most loitering, but drug dealing and alcohol use are fairly common (Hunt, Lipton, Goldsmith, & Strug, 1984).

Other drugs have been developed recently which offer even greater promise in the treatment of heroin addiction. LAAM is the abbreviation for l-alpha-acetylmethadol hydrochloride. A synthetic analgesic with most of the properties of methadone, it prevents withdrawal symptoms for up to three days, giving it an advantage over methadone which has to be administered daily (Platt, 1987).

The use of LAAM has been stymied in part because it is the kind of drug often referred to as an "orphan." Given the low political visibility of most heroin addicts, and the fact that few have health care plans which pay for their treatment, there is little economic incentive to develop new drugs to assist them in overcoming their addiction. However, since many health experts believe that the heterosexual intravenous drug user is likely to be the source of the feared spread of AIDS to the heterosexual population at large, the development of drugs such as LAAM may prove to be economically justifiable (Drugs and Drug Abuse Education Newsletter, 1988).

Heroin Maintenance. At this point you ought to be asking yourself, wouldn't it be simpler just to give heroin to the addicts? Such a program has been tried in England, with mixed results. There are relatively few addicts in England and the attitude of society toward heroin is much different than it is in the United States, making comparisons difficult to interpret. However, so much has been written about the English system that you should know some of the facts.

When heroin maintenance was first introduced to England, individual physicians were permitted to prescribe it. For various reasons, this system was replaced by one in which the addict had to register as a heroin addict and get the supply from one of several central supply locations. Various problems developed with this method as well, and at present in England methadone has replaced heroin as the treatment of choice for addicts.

Heroin maintenance in England was not the abject failure that some have claimed (Inciardi, 1986). The factors that led to its downfall could probably have been prevented (Trebach, 1987). However, it is not likely to be adopted in the United States. In a more ideal world than ours, the concept of heroin maintenance would be sound. Dispensed by a private physician as part of a comprehensive treatment program, the stigma of its use would be removed and the addict could learn to adjust to society. Heroin is certainly no more or less dangerous than methadone or other narcotics, so what is the purpose of switching dependencies?

There have been a number of impassioned and eloquent pleas for such a plan (Trebach, 1982; 1987) and even for the complete legalization of heroin (Michaels, 1987), but political and practical realities seem to preclude this. For those who cannot stop using narcotics, methadone or a similar drug seems a preferable alternative (Platt, 1987). No one believes, however, that medical treatment alone is sufficient to get the addict out of the environment that supports heroin use. To accomplish this, more complicated programs are necessary.

Therapeutic Communities. Therapeutic communities are a highly structured environment in which addicts learn the skills necessary to make it in a straight world, while learning to get off drugs. These programs include psychotherapy, behavior modification, vocational training, and social skills training, and generally last from 9–12 months. Typically, there is a period during which the addict takes on increasing responsibility in the program, learns to reenter the community and continues contact with the community even after he/she leaves.

When these programs were first developed, they tended to be rigid and relied heavily on those who had been in the program previously. Recently, however, some of the stricter regulations have been relaxed and outside people have been brought in. All programs insist on total abstinence from all illegal drugs and alcohol and have an absolute prohibition against violence. By and large they have been both useful and cost effective. As you might expect they are not cheap, but in general, those who stay at least three months seem to have lower rates of recidivism and crime than less intensively treated addicts. The longer the addict stays in the program the better the results.

If only a few thousand addicts (of the 500,000 who commit up to 50 million crimes a year) can be helped by these programs, millions of dollars will be saved and society will be the gainer. When the cost of medical treatment for AIDS patients and the likelihood of intravenous drug users contracting AIDS, as well as the possibility that the intravenous user may spread AIDS to the general, heterosexual, population is added to the crime figure, it seems obvious that, like the use of methadone or LAAM, therapeutic communities, whatever their rate of effectiveness, should be encouraged.

Community Outreach Programs

Community outreach programs attempt to combine many of the features of both medical treatment and therapeutic communities. These programs work with addicts on an outpatient basis, often when they are on methadone or LAAM maintenance. They provide individual and group psychotherapy, job training, and other programs. They combine the skills of professionally trained counselors with those of ex-users and serve a wider population than the therapeutic communities. Many of the clients of these centers are abusers of drugs other than narcotics. All stress abstinence from drugs of any kind.

These programs are roughly as effective as therapeutic communities and like them, the rule of thumb is the longer the stay the better the prognosis. Some of these outreach programs include methadone treatment and those that do seem to be more effective than those that do not. Evaluation of any of these programs is difficult, for the reasons mentioned in several other contexts, but as you just read, they are useful for society in reducing crime and the economic impact of AIDS.

Table 13.5   The Twelve Steps of NA

1. We admitted that we were powerless over our addiction, that our lives had become unmanageable.

2. We came to believe that a Power greater than ourselves could restore us to sanity.

3. We made a decision to turn our will and our lives over to the care of God as we understood Him.

4. We made a searching and fearless moral inventory of ourselves.

5. We admitted to God, to ourselves, and to another human being the exact nature of our wrongs.

6. We were entirely ready to have God remove all these defects of character.

7. We humbly asked Him to remove our shortcomings.

8. We made a list of all persons we had harmed, and became willing to make amends to them all.

9. We made direct amends to such people wherever possible, except when to do so would injure them or others.

10. We continued to take personal inventory and when we were wrong promptly admitted it.

11. We sought through prayer and meditation to improve our conscious contact with God as we understood Him, praying only for knowledge of His will for us and the power to carry that out.

12. Having had a spiritual awakening as a result of these steps, we tried to carry this message to addicts, and to practice these principles in all our affairs.

From Narcotics Anonymous

Narcotics Anonymous is another self-help group that has achieved considerable success. It is based on the principles of Alcoholics Anonymous, and the Twelve Steps of NA seen in Table 13.5 are virtually identical to the steps of AA seen on page 444. NA members also can be AA members, but the groups are separate since many in both groups believe that the needs of their members are best served by focusing on either narcotics or alcohol, rather than both simultaneously (Kurtz, 1987).

COCAINE TREATMENT

The recent cocaine epidemic has brought an unusual category of drug-dependent individuals to treatment. Alcoholics tend to be older, narcotics addicts poorer, and other abusers in general less well established than the cocaine addict. The cocaine abuser is young, often affluent, and likely to have health insurance as well, a rare commodity among narcotics users, at least. Numerous programs have been developed to aid the cocaine abuser, some of them quite innovative and most quite expensive. Nearly all, however, could be placed in our previous categories.

Medical Treatment

Treatment for the acute effects of cocaine is symptomatic. Even the toxic psychosis accompanied by delusion and paranoia, the result of heavy abuse of cocaine, is over in a few days. Many addicts, however, are severely depressed for weeks or months after they stop using cocaine. As we saw in chapter 5, the depression that follows minutes after the euphoria of cocaine wears off is a powerful incentive to continue its use. A more general depression often is seen when the cocaine user has stopped using the drug completely.

After the initial phase of cocaine withdrawal has subsided, medical treatment often is used to help alleviate the prolonged depression. Various antidepressants and other mood altering drugs have shown some promise (Kleber & Gawin, 1986) in treating this phase of recovery. You should remember from chapter 11 that antidepressants inhibit the re-uptake of norepinephrine and dopamine just as cocaine does, so their effectiveness should not be surprising.

Is depression so often seen after cocaine abuse the result of the drug use or is it the initial reason for cocaine abuse? In either case, of course, we must remember that extensive studies of depression have shown that both psychotherapy and drug treatment work for many depressives, and there is no clear reason why one should choose one treatment over the other.

Psychological Treatment

Like other drugs, treatment for cocaine addiction involves psychological treatment. One difference is the treatment tends to be more intense and involves learning skills to gain internal control. Relapse is a real problem for cocaine abusers. The almost immediate rush from taking the drug, lifestyle of the typical cocaine addict, as well as other factors make cocaine addiction a little different than alcohol or heroin addiction.

THE CRACK ADDICT

While the so-called private tier (treatment programs paid for by insurance or health benefits) provides ample opportunity for the middle-class cocaine addict to get help, treatment programs for those dependent on crack are another story. Crack use is most common in the inner cities, and the characteristics of crack dependency have not been widely studied. Most treatments have centered on acute detoxification, usually in an emergency ward, with relatively little emphasis being placed on long-term treatment. Control of the crack epidemic has focused upon reducing the supply by arresting high and middle level dealers, but relatively little has been done to reduce the demand for the drug.

The result of such a method of treatment, if it can be called that, is a revolving cycle of addiction, detoxification, and readdiction, as well as a revolving cycle of jail. Money for treatment has simply not funnelled down to the streets where most crack addicts live. Although there is some evidence that treatment will begin to get a bigger share of the drug war dollar, it remains to be seen how much will be used to treat crack addicts.

SPONTANEOUS REMISSION

Many people who abuse drugs go, willingly or otherwise, to drug treatment programs, and many are helped by the biological or psychosocial treatment available to them. You undoubtedly know others, however, whom you would have sworn had a ''problem'' but who managed to straighten themselves out *without* going to a drug abuse agency. How did they do it?

Spontaneous remission from drug use has been a widely noted but little studied phenomenon. Spontaneous remission might describe the process of "maturing-out" from narcotic abuse, the return of the former alcohol abuser to social drinking or to abstinence without intervention, or the cigarette smoker who simply decides to stop smoking and does so. If spontaneous recovery does occur, isn't it just as important to try to discover how these users managed to stop or at least regulate their use, as it is to discover techniques to help those who have not been able to achieve this formidable task without help?

Some professionals in the field of drug abuse would claim that anyone who managed to regulate his or her drug use or to stop spontaneously was not really a drug abuser or an addict in the first place. A moment's reflection would reveal, however, that this argument is circular. Presupposing the definition that drug addicts or abusers cannot stop without help, these experts then claim that anyone who can is not really an abuser. On the other hand, sobriety, or at least temperance, is the goal of most members of society, and it would behoove the reader to consider the *possibility* of spontaneous remission. It is in this light that the evidence below is presented.

Spontaneous remissions from drug abuse of whatever kind seem to share certain characteristics. Stall and Biernacki (1986) have identified three stages that seem to be common to those who recover from drug abuse without formal treatment. The first step seems to involve a "psychic change," the occurrence of "significant accidents," and a decision to quit, as well as several attempts at quitting. This is followed by a stage in which the abuser acknowledges the problem to others and, in Stage III, changes his/her identity, loses the craving, and successfully reintegrates into society.

The idea of a "psychic change" seems to be related to an alteration in the user's perception of substance use. This change is often accompanied by "significant accidents," events that seem to have little importance to the outside observer but are seen as crucial to the drug user. For example, an alcohol-dependent person may be arrested for drunken driving, or even arrive home safely after an evening of drinking without getting caught. While either of these behaviors may have occurred several times in the past, the abuser now sees them as important. Together with his or her changing view of drug use and the significant accidents, the user makes a decision to quit and makes attempts. In the parlance of Alcoholics Anonymous, the user has "hit bottom."

Stage II is characterized by a public pronouncement to quit. The user tells friends and family that he or she is quitting and begins to develop an identity as a non-user. Those who are successful are often able at this point to gain support from significant others. Stage II is a period of crisis and the user may resort to retelling the story of the "significant accident" to reinforce the commitment to stop.

If the abuser is successful in the attempt to stop he/she successfully stabilizes a new social identity, and usually finds that after about two years

Table 13.6 Stigmatized or Potentially Stigmatized Identity	
Stage 1	Problems Associated with Substance Use (Economic Costs)
	Possibility of Significant Accidents
	"Psychic Change"—Gradual or Sudden Change in
	Perspective Toward Substance Use
	Decision to Quit and/or Initial Attempts to Quit Using
	Continuing Possibility of Significant Accidents
Stage 2	Public Pronouncement of Decision to Quit Using Substance
	Claim to a New, Nonstigmatized Identity
Recidivist	*"Chipper"*
	Spontaneous Remitter
Stage 3	Ability to Successfully Renegotiate Identity
	Successful Eliciting of Significant-Other Support
	Ability to Manage Cravings
	Initial Integration into Nonusing Social Networks
	Lessening of Cravings—Disappear after 2 Years
	Resolution/Stabilization of New Social Identity

Source: Stall & Biernacki, 1988.

the cravings lessen and finally disappear. Not everyone is successful, however, and some go back to drug use at an abusive level. Others revert to occasional use, carefully hidden from friends and family.

It is not clear how many follow these steps without formal help, since they are unlikely to come to the attention of drug abuse professionals or those who study abusing populations. To get an idea, however, note that the Surgeon General's report on nicotine as an addiction estimates that 90 percent of those who stop smoking do so on their own, and the same report equates the strength of nicotine addiction with heroin addiction.

Should research indicate that spontaneous remission does occur frequently, care must be taken to avoid making those who do need help feel inadequate or weak. Just as there are many paths to substance abuse, and no simplistic theory can explain them all, there are many paths to recovery.

The goal for those whose substance use has become dysfunctional is to return to a productive life, however the individual defines the term. No method is better than any other, but by the same token no method works for everyone—a lesson that should be kept in mind by everyone who interacts on a daily basis with drug users. Since that group includes all of us, you should remember that no one has the answer to substance abuse. If you know someone who swears that she has cured her problem by praying to her shoelaces, do not question her method. Every treatment program, from Alcoholics Anonymous to methadone maintenance, has its critics. Objective measurement may, in the future, reveal that some methods are more effective than others, but keep in mind this analogy: if you were drowning, would you question the politics, the religion, or the philosophical belief of those who throw you a life ring?

SUMMARY

Substance abuse is easy to observe but difficult to define. There are various models for describing substance abuse and each model leads to a treatment method. No description of substance abuse is complete without considering all of these models. Effective treatment often involves several different methods as well.

There does not seem to be a particular psychological portrait of the substance abuser although those who have certain characteristics are more likely than others to become abusers. Many of the personality characteristics of the abuser are the *result* rather than the cause of the abuse, a fact that is often overlooked.

Many different treatment methods exist and they tend to focus on different aspects of the problem of substance abuse as well as being specific to the various drugs that are abused. In the case of alcohol abuse, Alcoholics Anonymous is the best known and most successful. Some, however, do not respond well to AA and for them, other methods of treatment are available. Treatment with Antabuse has helped some who are motivated to stop drinking but, like AA, it is not a universal cure.

Heroin addiction and the abuse of other opiates is complicated by socioeconomic factors. To be successful, treatment for the heroin addict has to consider the psychological and socioeconomic needs of the abuser, and various groups exist to provide this help. Medical treatment is also varied and ranges from giving long-acting narcotic antagonists to supplying the addict with heroin itself.

Stimulant abusers, especially those of cocaine, are often difficult to treat because depression is common with prolonged stimulant use. The depression often complicates the course of treatment, although promising results have been reported which involve the use of antidepressants. The treatment of crack users has not kept up with the pace of the epidemic and may be an important problem in the future.

ADDRESSES OF SELF-HELP ORGANIZATIONS

American Atheist Addiction Recovery Group (AARG), Box 6120, Denver, Colorado 80206.

Alcoholics Anonymous (AA), Box 459, Grand Central Station, New York, New York 10163.

CALIX–The Society, 7601 Wayzeta Boulevard, Minneapolis, Minnesota 55426.

JACS, 197 East Broadway, Room M7, New York, New York 10002.

Men for Sobriety (MFS), Box 618, Quakertown, Pennsylvania 18951.

Rational Recovery Systems (RRS), Box 800, Lotus, California 95651.

Secular Organizations for Sobriety (SOS), P.O. Box 5, Buffalo, New York 14215.

Women for Sobriety (WFS), Box 618, Quakertown, Pennsylvania 18951.

REFERENCE

Alcohol Alert (1989). Alcohol withdrawal syndrome. *National Institute on Alcohol Abuse and Alcoholism, No. 5,* 1–4.

Alford, G. S., Koehler, R. A., & Leonard, J. (1991). Alcoholics Anonymous—Narcotics Anonymous: Model inpatient treatment of chemically dependent adolescents: A 2-year outcome study. *Journal of Studies on Alcohol, 52,* 118–26.

Amodeo, M., & Kurtz, N. (1990). Cognitive processes and abstinence in a treated alcoholic population. *The International Journal of the Addictions. 25*, 983–1009.

Annis, H. M. (1990). Relapse to substance abuse: Empirical findings within a cognitive learning approach. *Journal of Psychoactive Drugs, 22*, 117–23.

Ball, J. C., Rosen, L., Flueck, J. A., & Nurco, D. N. (1982). Lifetime criminality of heroin addicts in the United States. *Journal of Drug Issues, 72*, 225–38.

Beattie, M. (1987). *Codependent no more*. Center City, MN: Hazelden.

Beck, A. T., Freeman, A., & Associates (1990). *Cognitive therapy of personality disorders*. New York: The Guilford Press.

Blake, B. G. (1965). The application of behavior therapy to the treatment of alcoholism. *Behavior, Research and Therapy, 3*, 75–85.

Blake, B. G. (1967). A follow-up of alcoholics treated by behavior therapy. *Behavior, Research and Therapy, 5*, 89–94.

Cahalan, D. (1988). *Understanding America's drinking problem: How to combat the hazards of alcohol*. San Francisco: Jossey-Bass Publishers.

Casriel, D. H. & Bratten, T. E. (1974). Metabolism, maintenance, treatment: A question of procedure. *Journal of Drug Issues, 4*, 359–75.

Cautela, J. R. (1970). The treatment of alcoholism by covert sensitization. *Psychotherapy: Theory, Research and Practice, 7*, 86–90.

Cross, G. M., Morgan, C. W., Mooney, A. J., Martin, C., & Rafter, J. A. (1990). Alcoholism treatment: A ten-year followup study. *Alcoholism: Clinical and Experimental Research. 14*, 169–73.

Deschenes, E. P., Anglin, M. D., & Speckart, G. (1991). Narcotics addiction: Related criminal careers, social and economic costs. *Journal of Drug Issues. 21*, 383–411.

Dole, V. P., & Nyswander, M. E. (1965). A medical treatment for diacetylmorphine (heroin) addiction. *Journal of the American Medical Association, 193*, 546–650.

Feldman, H. W. (1968). Heroin as a challenge. "Standup Cat." Controlling heroin use is seen as a challenge. They are certain they can control heroin use. *Journal of Health and Social Behavior, 9*, 131–39.

Fincher, J. (1979). Natural opiates and the brain. *Human Behavior, 2*, 28–32.

Fingarette, H. (1988). *Heavy drinking: The myth of alcoholism as a disease*. University of California Press.

Gawin, F. H., & Kleber, H. (1987). Issues in cocaine abuse treatment. In S. Fisher, A. Raskin, & E. H. Uhlenhuth, (Eds.), pp. 174–92. *Cocaine: Clinical and biobehavioral aspects*. New York and Oxford: Oxford University Press.

Glaser, F. B. & Ogborne, A. C. (1982). What we would most like to know: Does AA really work? *British Journal of Addiction, 77*, 77–78.

Goodwin, F. K. (1989). Buprenorphine and heroin addicts. *Journal of the American Medical Association, 261*, 970.

Greenstein, R. A., Arndt, I. O., Melellar, T. A., O'Brien, C. P., & Evans, B. D. (1981). Naltrexone: A clinical perspective. *Journal of Clinical Psychiatry, 2*, 25–29.

Harper, J., & Capedevila, C. (1990). Codependency: A critique. *Journal of Psychoactive Drugs, 22*, 285–92.

Howard, M., & Jenson, J. M. (1990). Chemical aversion treatment of alcohol dependence. Validity of current criticisms. *The International Journal of the Addictions, 25*, 1227–62.

Hunt, D., Lipton, D. S., Goldsmith, D. S., & Stong D. L. (1984). Problems in methadone treatment. In J. Grabowski, M. C. Stitzer, & J. E Henningfield (Eds.). *Behavioral intervention techniques in drug abuse treatment.* National Institue of Drug Abuse, *Monograph 46.*

Hunt, G. H., & Odoroff, M. E. (1967). Follow-up study of narcotics addicts after hospitalization. *Public Health Reports, 77,* 41–54.

Inciardi, J. A. (1986). *The war on drugs: Heroin, cocaine and public policy.* Palo Alto, CA: Mayfield Publishing Company.

Jaffe, J. (1980). Drug addiction and drug abuse. In A. G. Goodman, L. S. Goodman, & A. Gilman (Eds.), pp. 525–84. *The pharmacological basis of therapeutics.* New York: Macmillan.

Kennedy, B., Konstantareas, M., & Homatidis, S. (1987). A behavior profile of poly-drug abusers. *Journal of Youth and Adolesence, 16,* 115–27.

Kissin, B. (1977). Theory and practice in the treatment of alcoholism. In B. Kissin & H. Bergleiter (Eds.). *The biology of alcoholism, volume 5,: Treatment and rehabilitation of the chronic alcoholic.* New York: Plenum Press.

Kleber, H. D., & Kosten, T. R. (1984). Naltrexone induction: Psychological and pharmacological strategies. *Journal of Clinical Psychiatry, 2,* 29–34.

Kurtz, Ernest (1988). *AA: The story.* San Francisco: Harper & Row.

Levinthal, C. F. (1988). *Messenger of paradise; Opiates and the brain.* New York: Anchor Press, Doubleday.

Levy, M. S. (1990). Individualized care for the treatment of alcoholism. *Journal of Substance Abuse Treatment, 7,* 245–54.

Litten, R. Z., & Allen, J. P. (1991). Pharmacotherapies for alcoholism: Promising agents and clinical issues. *Alcoholism: Clinical and Experimental Research, 15,* 620–33.

Mackay, P. W., & Marlatt, G. A. (1990–91). Maintaining sobriety: Stopping is starting. *The International Journal of the Addictions, 25,* 1257–76.

Michaels, R. J. (1987). The Market for heroin before and after legalization. In Robert Hamowy (Ed.). *Dealing with drugs: Consequences of government control.* Lexington Books.

Miller, L. (1990). Neurodynamics of alcoholism and addiction; Personality, psychopathology and cognitive style. *Journal of Substance Abuse Treatment, 7,* 31–49.

Miller, P. M., & Barlow, D. H. (1900). Behavioral approaches to the treatment of alcoholism. *Journal of Nervous and Mental Disease, 157.*

Nace, E. P. (1989). The natural history of alcoholism versus treatment effectiveness: Methodological problems. *American Journal of Drug and Alcohol Abuse, 15,* 55–60.

NIDA Notes (1990). Buprenorphine may reduce craving for cocaine: New studies will examine treatment potential. *5,* 1–2.

O'Brien, C. P., & Woody, E. (1986). The role of naltrexone in the treatment of opioid dependence. In H. D. Cappel, F. B. Glaser, Y. Israel, H. Kalant, W. Schmidt, E. M. Sellers, & R. C. Smart (Eds.) *Research advances in alcohol and drug problems, Volume 9.* New York: Plenum Press.

Ogborne, A. C. (1987). A note on the characteristics of alcohol abusers with controlled drinking aspirations. *Drugs and Alcohol Dependence, 19,* 159–64.

Okamoto, M. (1984). *Barbiturate tolerance and physical dependence: Contribution of pharmacological factors.* National Institute of Drug Abuse Research, *monograph 54.*

Pearson, G. (1987). *The new heroin users.* Oxford: Basil Blackwell Incorporated.

Peele, S. (1990). Why and by whom the American alcoholism treatment industry is under siege. *Journal of Psychoactive Drugs, 22,* 1–13.

Pendery, M., Maltzman, I., & West, L. (1982). Controlled drinking by alcoholics: New findings and a reevaluation of a major affirmative study. *Science, 217,* 169–75.

Pescor, M. J. (1938). A statistical analysis of the clinical records of hospitalized drug addicts. *Public Health Reports, Supplement no. 143.*

Resnick, R. B. (1977). Naloxone-precipitated withdrawal: A method for rapid induction. *Clinical Pharmacology and Therapeutics, 214,* 208–13.

Riordan, C. E., & Kleber, H. D. (1980). Rapid opiate detoxification with clonidine and naloxone. *Lancet, 14,* 1079–80.

Searles, J. S. (1989). The role of genetics in the pathogenesis of alcoholism. *Journal of Abnormal Psychology, 97,* 153–67.

Shore, R. S., & Luce, J. M. (1976). *To Your health: The pleasures, problems and politics of alcohol.* New York: The Seabury Press.

Simpson, D. D., Joe, W., & Lehman, W. E. K. (1986). *Addiction careers: Summary of studies on the DARP followup.* National Institute of Drug Abuse Treatment Research Report.

Simpson, D. D., & Marsh, K. L. (1986). *Relapse and recovery among opioid addicts: 12 years after treatment.* National Institute of Drug Abuse Research, *monograph 72.*

Sixth Special Report to the United States Congress on Alcohol and Health. January 1987. U.S. Department of Health and Human Services, National Institute on Alcoholism and Alcohol Abuse.

Sobell, M. B., & Sobell, L. C. (1973a). Individualized behavior therapy for alcoholics. *Behavior Therapy, 4,* 49–72.

Sobell, M. B., & Sobell, L. C. (1973b). Alcoholics treated by individualized behavior therapy: One year treatment outcome. *Behavior Research and Therapy, 11,* 599–618.

Stall, R., & Biernacki, P. (1986). Spontaneous remission from the problematic use of substances: An inductive model derived from a comparative analysis of the alcohol, opiate, tobacco and food/obesity literatures. *The International Journal of the Addictions, 21,* 1–23.

Sunderwirth, S. (1985). Biological mechanisms: Neurotransmission and addiction. In H. B. Milkman, and H. J. Shapper (Eds.). *The addiction: Multidisciplinary perspectives and treatments.* New York: Lexington Books, D. C. Heath.

Tournier, R. E. (1979). Alcoholics Anonymous as treatment and as ideology. *Journal of Studies on Alcohol, 40,* 230.

Trachtenberg, M. C., & Blum, K. (1987). Alcohol and opioid peptides: Neuropharmacological rationale for physical craving of alcohol. *American Journal of Drug and Alcohol Abuse, 13,* 365–72.

Trebach, A. S. (1982). *The Heroin Solution.* New Haven: Yale University Press.

Trebach, A. S. (1987). *The Great Drug War.* New York: Macmillan.

Trice, H. (1983) Alcoholics Anonymous. In David A. Ward (Ed.). *Alcoholism: Introduction to theory and treatment, (2d ed.).* Dubuque, IA: Kendall/Hunt.

Vaillant, G. E. (1966). A twelve year followup of New York narcotic addicts: The relation of treatment to outcome. *American Journal of Psychiatry, 122,* 727–37.

Wallace, J. (1990). Controlled drinking, treatment effectiveness, and the disease model of addiction: A commentary on the ideological wishes of Stanton Peele. *Journal of Psychoactive Drugs, 22,* 261–84.

Weins, A. N., & Menustik, C. E. (1983). Treatment outcome and patient characteristics in an aversion therapy program for alcoholism. *American Psychologist, 38,* 1089–96.

Westermeyer, J. (1986). *A clinical guide to alcohol and drug problems.* Praeger.

Wise, R. A. (1988). The neurobiology of craving: Implications for the understanding and treatment of addiction. *Journal of Abnormal Psychology, 97,* 113–32.

Woody, E., & O'Brien, C. P. (1986). Update on methadone maintenance. In H. D. Cappell, F. B. Glaser, Y. Israel, H. Kalant, W. Schmidt, E. M. Sellers, & R. C. Smart (Eds.), pp. 261–78. *Research advances in alcohol and drug problems, volume 9.* New York: Plenum Press.

Zinberg, N. E. (1972). Heroin use in Vietnam and the United States. *Archives of General Psychiatry, 26,* 486–88.

Zinberg, N. E. (1976). The natural history of chipping. *American Journal of Psychiatry, 133,* 37–40.

14

• • •

DRUG EDUCATION AND DRUG ABUSE PREVENTION

• • •

OBJECTIVES

When you have finished studying this chapter you should:

1. Be able to list the three types of drug education programs.
2. Know the goal of primary prevention.
3. Be able to discuss the history of primary prevention programs.
4. Know how current primary prevention programs work.
5. Be able to discuss the role of the parents in drug education programs.
6. Understand how the community can aid drug education programs.
7. Know the philosophy behind secondary prevention programs.
8. Be able to discuss how the alcohol industry promotes secondary prevention programs.
9. Be able to discuss the role of tertiary drug abuse programs.
10. Know how employee assistance programs are organized.
11. Be able to discuss the future of drug education programs.

KEY TERMS

adult user
affective approach
BACCHUS
Contract for Life
cognitive inoculation
Drug-Free School Zones
employee assistance program
Entertainment Industry Council, Inc.
FCC
interdiction
Just Say No
Mothers Against Drunk Driving (MADD)
Office of Substance Abuse Prevention
Parents' Resource for Information on Drug Education (PRIDE)
primary prevention
Students Against Drunk Driving (SADD)
SAODAP
secondary prevention
self-esteem
tertiary prevention
values clarification

V irtually everyone knows that cigarette smoking is harmful, and yet 30 percent of the population smokes; we are inundated with information about alcoholism, and yet the majority of Americans drink, and millions have a problem with alcohol. Most Americans believe that illegal drug use is the most important problem we face, and yet in the latest data, 28.7% have used an illegal drug within the last year. Does all this mean that drug education and drug abuse prevention is a failure, or does the fact that use of all drugs, even tobacco and alcohol, is declining mean that our programs are finally beginning to succeed? Are we focusing on the right aspect of the problem? What is drug education all about anyway?

Drug education and drug abuse prevention programs can be divided into three groups: those which try to prevent drug use from occurring in the first place (**primary prevention**), those geared for early intervention (**secondary prevention**), and those aimed at helping the drug abuser after abuse is established (**tertiary prevention**). Each of these programs is geared to specific tactics, and each has had its day in the sun, with millions of dollars being poured into the prevention pipeline. Only now are we beginning to attempt to come up with an integrated approach, incorporating all three kinds of programs, but we still have a long way to go.

PRIMARY PREVENTION

Primary prevention would seem to be the ideal—the goal being to get to the potential user/abuser *before* he or she has an opportunity to begin using drugs. Programs with this approach have to start very early, since recreational use of licit and illicit drugs is beginning at an earlier and earlier age. Many programs begin in grade school, and it is generally acknowledged that *primary prevention* programs aimed at high school students are equivalent to teaching fish to swim.

The First Attempts

There are trends in primary prevention programs, just as there are trends in clothing, automobiles, and psychotherapy methods. The earliest programs were based on the entirely reasonable assumption that rational people do not do harmful things to themselves, and that revealing the danger of drugs would be an effective deterrent. Many of us remember seeing programs like these in high school. The presenter would show slides of cancerous lungs, then smoke a cigarette through a handkerchief and display the tars and residue that the filter did not remove. Slides of abscesses on the arms of addicts would be followed by lurid details of the horrors of drug withdrawal. The conclusion might be a gory film of traffic accidents caused by drunken drivers.

To counteract advertising, the National Cancer Institute provides these posters that emphasize the short-term effects of using snuff and the long-term dangers.

Unfortunately, these programs did not work. Many of them went so far overboard on the dangers of drugs that they produced overkill. In fact, many experts believe that emphasizing the dangers of a drug only serves to make it more attractive to precisely those who are at greatest risk for developing a pattern of abuse. Young adolescents and preteens often are attracted to the element of danger in any endeavor, and drug use could be seen by them as daring behavior.

Furthermore, much of the information presented was inaccurate. The stories of people taking LSD and staring at the sun until they were blinded, hideous murders being perpetrated by "marijuana addicts," and instantaneous death due to heroin overdose, were either patently untrue or greatly exaggerated. When the experimental user discovered, through personal experience, that marijuana did not cause permanent insanity, disbelief led to skepticism and the user ignored "advice" on other drugs by these same "experts." After all, it is not irrational to think that if the authorities were wrong about marijuana they were also wrong about heroin.

Only slightly better than the focus on the dangers of drugs were the *drug education* programs. These were supposedly nonjudgmental discussions of the pros and cons of drug use and of specific drugs. The assumption was that people used drugs because of misconceptions and a lack of knowledge about their effects. Take away the mythology (LSD dissolves the ego and enables you to see God), be honest and correct about the dangers, and the drug problem will disappear.

Consider, however, that very few teachers also are experts in pharmacology, psychology, and medicine. The programs tended to be conducted either in a perfunctory manner (remember your classes on sex education in high school?) or were directed by traveling ''road show'' experts who went from school to school with occasional one-shot, one-hour lectures. Somehow these methods were expected to counteract a lifetime of learning about drugs from adults and peers (Weisheit, 1983). Another drawback to these programs was that a percentage of students actually *were* deterred by the supposed dangers of drugs, no matter how exaggerated, and dispelling some of the more outrageous myths had a paradoxical effect.

Imagine the despair of the drug abuse establishment when evaluations of these programs revealed that they may actually have led to an *increase* in drug use (Bernard, Fafoglia & Perone, 1987)! In April 1973 the **White House Special Action Office for Drug Abuse Prevention** (SAODAP) called a moratorium on the production of all federally-funded drug information material, and eight months later published guidelines for subsequent material. The guidelines called for an end to all scare tactics, stereotyping of drug users, and dogmatic statements such as ''use of drug *X* always causes problem *Y*.'' At the same time they called for excluding information that demonstrated the proper use of illegal drugs (Resnik, 1978).

In all probability the increase in drug use resulting from these programs was in experimental use and did not reflect any basic flaw in the programs. Any discussion of any topic is bound to produce an increase in awareness and often arouse curiosity. If I did not know, for example, that I could get light-headed by sniffing gasoline and heard about it in class, I might decide to try it the next time I had to mow the lawn. In the late 1960s, there was a brief fad of banana peel smoking. Rational, intelligent people by the thousands scraped the inside of banana skins, baked the result in an oven and smoked it. They were inspired by newspaper reports that smoking banana peels would get you high.

The Self-Esteem Approach

These first drug abuse prevention programs were replaced by programs that often were so tangentially related to drug use as such that drugs frequently were never mentioned at all! In the late 1970s, the momentum in programs shifted from the drug to the person taking the drug. The philosophy behind these programs came from the humanistic psychology movement and can be explained partly by the graph below. There is a limit to how good you can feel and how much a drug can simulate that feeling. If you already feel good about yourself, then a drug will have little effect (see figure 14.1). Drugs have their greatest effect on those who aren't happy to begin with.

Drug abuse prevention programs following this model focused on developing self-esteem and teaching such skills as coping and communication.

FIGURE 14.1

The shaded area represents the improvement in feeling that a drug will give. If you feel good about yourself, so the theory goes, drugs will not be as rewarding.

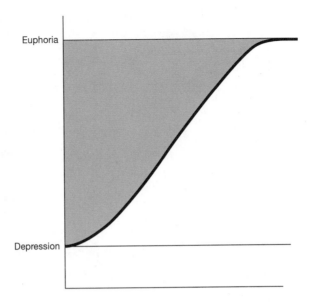

Values clarification was a catchword for these programs which were quite popular until recently. Of course, the poor hardworking high school teacher was no more experienced in values clarification than in pharmacology. High school teachers, especially, typically use a fact-oriented approach to teaching and are less experienced than, say, elementary school teachers in dealing with small groups and utilizing what came to be called the **affective approach.**

Many politically conservative and religious groups objected to values clarification believing that these programs were teaching "moral relativity." Others, although not upset by the humanistic underpinnings of this approach were critical because they thought self-esteem was too complex to be altered in programs that at most lasted only an hour or so a week. Perhaps the most difficult problem facing these programs was convincing taxpayers that teaching high school students how to climb mountains or feel good about themselves was going to keep them off drugs, when drugs were never mentioned. After all, isn't it reasonable to assume that a drug prevention strategy should focus on drugs?

Evaluations of these programs generally showed that they failed to alter drug-taking behavior. Although a few showed some positive effects, the majority of studies failed to support these claims. Furthermore, no program that relied on a values clarification approach could demonstrate that changes in values were related to changes in drug taking behavior. In short, the critics were right; the *affective* or "feel good" programs did not substantially alter drug use (Polich, Ellickson, Reuter, & Kahan, 1984).

When he finishes climbing this 5.9 route, this individual will undoubtedly be proud of himself. Will someone who learns to climb a cliff be less likely to abuse drugs?

The New Approaches

Recently a third type of drug abuse prevention program has been developed. These are based on a *social pressure* model and have a wider focus than previous programs. Rather than looking at drug use as a problem of education or as a result of some psychological deficiency on the part of the user, the programs look at the environmental and social factors involved in drug use. They emphasize the importance of the media and role models, both adult and peers. These programs relate much drug use to the desire of the younger person to appear grown up. Their goal is to provide positive role models for abstinence from drugs.

A number of programs have been developed, including QUEST and HERE'S LOOKING AT YOU. Because it was so closely associated with Nancy Reagan, nearly everyone remembers the JUST SAY NO program so widespread in the late 1980s, but few understand its theoretical basis. Just Say No and programs like it are based on the theory of **cognitive inoculation,** a very influential concept developed by McGuire (1981). This theory and those that have sprung from it offer an analogy between biological and cognitive inoculation. Because you received smallpox, diphtheria, whooping cough, polio, and other inoculations as a child, your body produces antibodies that make you immune to these diseases. Cognitive inoculation is supposed to work in a similar fashion.

In a variation of the cognitive inoculation theory, students first are taught about the pressures to which they will be exposed to use drugs and then are taught various strategies to resist them. Present anti-drug programs are much more complicated than a simple exhortation to say no to drugs. Students are encouraged to model behavior that precludes drug use, to avoid social situations

Programs like these are targeted at elementary school children to discourage them from even starting *drug use.*

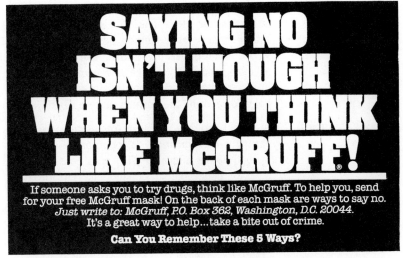

McGruff is a registered trademark of the National Crime Prevention Council, Washington, D.C., and the symbol for the Citizen's Crime Prevention Campaign. Used by permission.

in which drug and alcohol use is present, and to change the subject or walk away.

Students often are encouraged to make a public commitment not to use drugs. The purpose of this strategy is to fight the "everybody is doing it" mentality and to provide reinforcement for positive nondrug-related behavior. Such public commitments also help change the consensus of those participating to the idea that "everyone is not doing it."

Anti-drug programs are geared to a much younger group than was traditionally targeted. The focus of many of these programs is junior high school, since most studies now indicate that seventh and eighth grade is where much experimental drug use begins, especially of illicit drug use such as marijuana and cocaine. Even more recently, programs have been developed for elementary schools, since attitudes toward licit drugs such as alcohol and nicotine are formed quite early.

One Model Program   A model program for drug prevention has been developed by the U.S. Department of Education. It incorporates elements of all three approaches described above and also takes into consideration the cognitive and emotional level of development of students. The program is divided into four objectives: (1) to value and maintain sound personal health: to understand how drugs affect health; (2) to respect laws and rules prohibiting drugs; (3) to recognize and resist pressures to use drugs; and (4) to promote activities that reinforce the positive, drug-free elements of student life (U.S. Department of Education, 1986).

This model program suggests various learning activities for elementary and secondary school levels. For the elementary schools they tend to be broadly based and do not have a specific focus on illicit drugs or alcohol. One sample topic suggested for elementary schools under objective 1 is: the effects of poisons on the body; the effects of medicine on body chemistry; the wrong drug may make a person ill (U.S. Department of Education, 1986). For objective 3, the model recommends a topic on ways to make responsible decisions and deal constructively with disagreeable moments and pressures.

For secondary schools, the suggested topics focus more on drugs of abuse. For example, one suggested exercise involves examining advertisements for drugs to decide what images are being projected and whether the ads are accurate (objective 3). For objective 4, a suggestion is to form action teams for school improvement, with membership limited to students who are drug-free (how to make sure the participants are drug-free is not mentioned). Another suggestion: serving as peer leaders in drug prevention programs. You should be able to recognize elements of the social inoculation, information, and affective approaches in these suggestions.

Very few school systems have the resources to design a drug abuse education program from scratch, so a market opened up for already designed programs. A large number of these exist under various names. Each of them has a slightly different approach and all are competing with each other. The ultimate test of any program is that drug use declines after the program is instituted, but such a simple method of evaluation has many hidden problems.

Trends and fads in drug use have come and gone in the United States, and now seem to be on the downward slope of a wave of such use. Any program will show a decrease in drug use if it is measured against norms established a few years ago. Carefully controlled studies in which drug use in one school with the program is compared to drug use in another school without the program are virtually impossible to carry out because of the expense and the difficulty in finding equivalent schools.

Another problem is that these programs produce great social pressure to deny drug use, even if it does exist. In addition to any real effect, one thing the programs teach is to answer "no" when anyone asks if you use drugs. For example, in a survey conducted by the author on drug use, one physical education program had a zero prevalence of steroid use. Not coincidentally, the coach had an almost fanatical attitude against steroids. While it is possible that he managed to convince every single member of the football and wrestling team that steroids were dangerous, it is also possible that the students were less than honest in their answers, especially since he insisted on being present while the questionnaire was being administered.

A third difficulty in evaluating drug education programs is that their long-term impact is difficult to evaluate. Immediately after the program is over, its impact is still strong, but what happens as time goes on? By definition, everyone successfully completing a stop-smoking clinic or an inpatient alcohol treatment program is drug-free at the time of graduation. As we have seen, however, relapse rates within a year approach 80 percent.

Keeping all of these problems in mind, there is some evidence that these programs have an impact. One long-term study showed that drug education in junior high reduced cigarette and marijuana use in both high- and low-risk students and that these effects were still measurable after fifteen months. The program was less successful in reducing alcohol use (the effect was short-lived) and not at all successful in helping those who were already cigarette smokers (Ellickson & Bell, 1990).

There are certain other drawbacks in any school-based drug education program that limit its usefulness. In addition to teaching academic skills, such as reading, writing, and arithmetic, Americans expect schools to instill patriotic and moral values, foster social justice and the brotherhood of man, and at the same time instill good manners, teach sex education, and beat the Japanese on standardized math tests. Whenever there is a problem in our society, we seek a program in the schools to cure it.

Problems with School-Based Programs

School-based drug prevention programs often set unrealistic goals and do not challenge the unrealistic expectations of society (Bernard, Fafoglia, & Farone, 1987). Prevention programs that seek to eradicate drug use are doomed to failure if they are evaluated on that basis, and yet this is often the expected goal. Consider the example of alcohol. More than 90 percent of high school seniors reported using alcohol, with significant alcohol use beginning *before* junior high school. By seventh grade 22 percent of the girls and 30 percent of the boys in one study admitted to having had a "drink" rather than a "sip" within the previous month (Zucker & Harford, 1983). Given the pressure to drink in our society, is it reasonable to expect that any school-based program could eradicate drinking? As one group of researchers suggests,

"The present societal environment, at least in North America, is permeated with messages about alcohol and drugs (even if only the licit 'mood altering' kind) that range from tolerance to glamorization. In such an environment, any effort to teach youngsters abstinence from such substances is a little like trying to promote chastity in a brothel!" (Mauss, Hopkins, Weisheit, & Kearney, 1988, p. 59.)

A second problem is that most school-based programs are limited in time and scope. As we saw previously the demands on teacher and student time may preclude spending the hours each week that would be necessary to promote self-esteem, work on communication skills, practice strategies for refusing drugs, and learn factual information about drugs. Furthermore, teachers and even administrators often lack an understanding of the complex theoretical model on which contemporary drug abuse prevention programs are based.

Another problem is that school based-programs are limited by the nature of the participants. Not everyone likes school or participates enthusiastically in programs such as these. By the time students are in high school, a significant number have dropped out, so school-based programs do not reach this group at all. The student most likely to get involved in such programs may be the student *least* likely to get into trouble in the first place. Conversely, many of the students most likely to need the program may ignore it or view it with scorn.

Children and adolescents approach school with a wide variety of backgrounds and psychosocial traits. The characteristics that we associate with decreased drug use—high self-esteem, good decision-making skills, and an achievement orientation—may be the result of factors that are beyond the capacity of drug abuse programs to affect. While drug education programs address things that *ought* to be related to drug use, they may actually contribute very little to the overall determinants of drug use since they cannot create social change or improve mental health (Mauss, Hopkins, Weisheit, & Kearney, 1988).

Factors Affecting School-Based Programs

In evaluating school-based programs care must be taken to consider the social and cognitive aspects of elementary and secondary school students as well. Elementary students think on a simplistic, concrete, and egocentric level. They might readily interpret the message "If you drink and drive you could get into an accident" into "If you drink and drive, you will die," and be terrified when Dad has a beer and then goes out to the store. On the other hand, secondary school students are capable of more complex levels of thinking and could appreciate the humor and the message seen in figure 14.2.

High school students also are capable of subtle behavior that is not only beyond the capacity of elementary school students but also might raise

FIGURE 14.2

questions about the sophistication of those who advocate drug prevention programs. In California, for example, May brings graduation and a wide-spread dissemination of "Sober Graduation" bumper stickers for cars. Some students put these on their cars in the belief that the police will be less likely to stop them while driving. Just for good measure some add a "Don't Drink and Drive" or even a "One Day at a Time" (an AA slogan) sticker.

High school students are quite capable of cynicism as well as subtlety. Given the difficulty of getting into a good college and with an acute aware-ness of the need to appear to be a "well-rounded student" some students see participation in drug abuse programs as a good extracurricular activity to put on their high school transcript. They join groups more out of ambition than commitment.

On the other hand, just getting students to use these stickers or attend the meetings, for whatever reason, might have some impact. Attendance at meetings might expose the student to role models and authority figures who are opposed to indiscriminate drug use. Moreover, numerous studies of attitude

What we do speaks more loudly than what we say.

change have found that arguing a position opposite to one's beliefs produces an attitude change. Perhaps some students who make presentations against driving and drinking do so for motives that are less than pure, but the act of doing so may alter their attitude and subsequent behavior.

Realistically, school-based programs must be linked to the world beyond school if they are to be effective, which means that drug prevention programs have to reflect an understanding of the impact of society, especially the influence of parents and peers. The phrase "what you do speaks so loudly I cannot hear what you say" should be remembered before school boards approve yet another drug abuse program.

At-Risk Youth

Recognizing that most high school students are not abusers of drugs, and that the drug prevention dollar can go only so far, an increasing number of prevention programs are being geared to at-risk youths. At-risk youths are those who studies show are most likely to become abusers. Research has shown that five main categories influence the adolescent's decision to use drugs. These are: (1) genetic and family factors (2) peer factors (3) psychological factors (4) biological factors (5) community factors (Office of Substance Abuse Prevention, 1989).

A family history of either alcoholism or antisocial behavior increases the risk of alcohol or other drug use. As you saw in various chapters, the effect may be genetic or the result of modeling. In addition, inadequate parent direction and discipline, as well as the attitude of parents toward drug use play a role. Parents with poor parenting skills and those who model inappropriate drug and alcohol use increase drug use in their children.

FARLEY by Phil Frank.

Occasionally, newspapers report children turning in their parents and parents turning in their children for drug use. These reports have led some to satirize what they feel is an ominous change in family relationships.

Peers play an important role, as we have seen. One chooses one's friends on the basis of similar interests, and youths who have drug-using friends or older siblings, and who orient toward these peers over adults are also at risk.

Psychological factors include rebelliousness, alienation, school failure, low interest in school, and antisocial behavior. Youth at high risk for drug abuse tend to lack in empathy, desire immediate gratification, and don't seem to respond to punishment. Moreover, they don't seem to respond well to adults, making most antidrug programs difficult to implement.

The feel-good nature of most drugs is also a potent factor. Once dependence has developed, of course, the biological factors play an important role. Finally, the community also plays a role. Living in a community with high levels of mobility, where there is little to do and delinquent behavior is common, the at-risk youth is hard pressed to avoid drug use. Poverty, social disorganization, and deprivation add to the danger.

Programs intended to help at-risk youth stay off drugs, therefore, need not only address drugs. Community outreach, athletic teams, opportunities to deal with issues of parenting, and other seemingly unrelated programs are also important in helping at-risk youth.

SECONDARY PREVENTION

Of the three types of prevention, secondary prevention has been studied the least. Secondary prevention is basically the attempt to minimize the harm caused by drug use with a high-risk population or with a group that is involved in experimental or occasional use. Occasionally, secondary prevention is seen as early intervention involving drug users in initial stages of abuse. In high schools, secondary prevention frequently involves alcohol or tobacco use. Recognizing that most high school students use alcohol occasionally, secondary prevention attempts often focus on the issue of drinking and driving.

Other secondary prevention programs involve crisis counseling and drug abuse counseling for those whose drug use has gone beyond experimental or occasional use. On the principle that early intervention is better than intervention after serious harm has occurred, these programs often involve drug counseling centers and some of the other nonresidential programs discussed in the previous chapter. With the advent of the AIDS epidemic, secondary prevention has been extended to providing intravenous drug users with bleach to sterilize their needles and even, in some cases, needles themselves.

The concept of secondary prevention is one that needs to be explored further. The problem with focusing on this issue is that it seems to condone drug use. Most programs, implicitly or explicitly, have abstinence as their goal. Despite the fact that this goal is highly unrealistic, an attempt to change to a program that would minimize harm rather than promote abstinence would be highly controversial, to say the least.

It is difficult, if not impossible, to imagine Senator X, Governor Y, or the head of the National Institute of Drug Abuse publicly making a statement to the effect that "we will never completely eradicate drugs, so rather than spend millions or billions in an impossible attempt, let's change our focus—discourage drug use but also find ways to help those who continue to use drugs to do so safely." In the present social and political climate, such a comment would be political suicide, although it mirrors the private opinion of many experts.

TERTIARY PREVENTION

Tertiary prevention overlaps with secondary prevention and was the focus of chapter 13. Once a drug abuse problem is well established, society has provided numerous resources for the abuser to get help. Tertiary prevention attempts involve medical treatment, residential facilities, and rehabilitation. Once a drug abuse problem has become established, abstinence is usually considered the only appropriate goal. Like primary prevention, tertiary prevention has been well funded. Since the goal for both primary and tertiary prevention is abstinence, it is not difficult to see why these programs are funded at the expense of secondary prevention.

THE ADULT USERS

All of the programs mentioned so far have involved elementary and high school students. Nearly all experts would agree that the earlier the start the better, but the fact remains that college students of whatever age and other adults also use drugs. As the preferred drugs of these groups are alcohol and tobacco most programs are geared to them. However, during the recent epidemic of cocaine snorting, some programs were addressed to that drug.

Since alcohol and tobacco are legal drugs, and since the target is an adult population, the emphasis of these programs is different. For alcohol, abstinence is rarely the aim. Most of these programs are informational and attempt to increase awareness of the effects of alcohol and to decrease the harm that its use can do. Various distilling companies, as well as beer and wine producers have begun to emphasize moderate use and caution against drinking and driving. **Mothers Against Drunk Driving** (MADD) and similar groups also advocate a moderate approach with the emphasis on minimizing harm.

A good example of secondary prevention. Assuming the drug user is going to continue, this poster warns him or her to at least be careful.

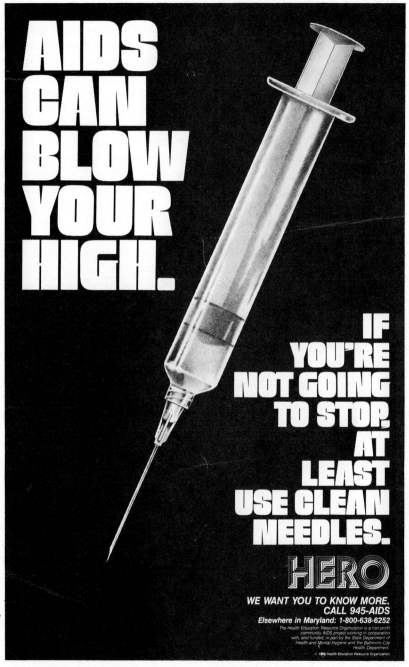

H.E.R.O (The Health Education Resource Organization) 101 West Read Street, Suite 825, Baltimore, Maryland 21201.

Slogans like "Friends Don't Let Friends Drive Drunk" and the "designated driver" campaign in which one person in a group agrees not to drink, also are based on the same principle. Another example of minimizing risk concerns fetal alcohol syndrome. Numerous programs have been developed for counseling pregnant women about alcohol and drug use, and educational efforts have had a considerable impact. Most people now are aware that drinking can cause damage to the fetus.

At the college level, recognizing that most students drink alcohol at least occasionally, local and national organizations exist to encourage responsible alcohol use. **Students Against Drunk Driving** (SADD), for example, has chapters in over 1,500 colleges, and has an offshoot called Student Athletes Detest Drugs geared toward the problem of drug use by athletes. SADD is probably best known for its **Contract for Life,** an agreement between parents and teenagers to prevent drunk driving.

Another group is called **BACCHUS** (Boost Alcohol Consciousness Concerning the Health of University Students). Aimed more directly at college students,it works with resident hall assistants, fraternal organizations, and other groups to foster sensible attitudes toward drinking. It opposes underage drinking and abusive drinking by anyone. A student organization, it has almost 500 chapters on campuses throughout the United States.

Other secondary prevention programs for alcohol include the ubiquitous self-quizzes about problem drinking, and television ads that emphasize getting help *before* abuse ruins family and career. Perhaps the best example of secondary prevention are the **Employee Assistance Programs** (EAPs).

EMPLOYEE ASSISTANCE PROGRAMS

Most people in the United States are employed outside the home, so worksite programs to discourage drug use are becoming increasingly popular. Moreover, the majority of illicit drug users are employed. Of course, the majority of these employed people also drink alcohol, and many smoke cigarettes. Programs to help stop tobacco use, develop healthy attitudes, including moderating alcohol use and in general improve lifestyles, are being instituted in many companies in the belief that they are cost effective. Healthy employees not only work more productively but cost their employers less in health costs. For those whose alcohol or other drug use causes problems, most companies have an employee assistance program.

There have been employee assistance programs for more than forty years (Trice & Beyer, 1983). Earlier programs focused on alcohol abuse and alcoholism, while later programs broadened the concept to include other drug use, as well as help with personal problems that might impair job performance. Employee assistance programs have proliferated in recent years and there are many types. Some are voluntary—that is, the employee can choose to use the services of the EAP—while participation in others is required as a condition of continued employment. Some companies hire employees whose duties are to provide drug prevention, intervention, and counseling services, while others use external providers.

Anheuser-Busch sponsored "Know When to Say When" contest for college students.

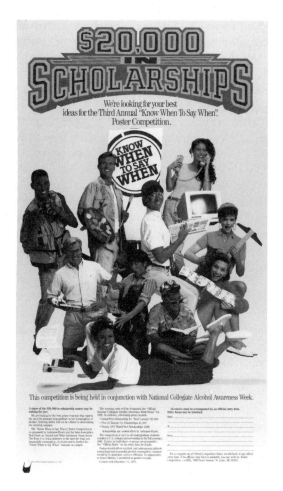

Employee assistance programs have been quite successful in part because they provide economic and social motivation. Many employ a technique known as "constructive confrontation" wherein a supervisor or counselor confronts an employee whose job performance is deteriorating with two options that might be expressed as "face up or face out" (Trice & Beyer, 1983). Faced with the potential loss of a job, often devastating in our society, the employee has an economic motive to get treatment. Other employees also help provide a social motive as well. The workplace is a source of considerable socialization, and social pressure also is brought to bear to persuade the employee to get treatment.

EAPs have evolved to the point where drug and alcohol treatment has become a part of the employee benefit package. Because of economic factors, this treatment is increasingly being provided by prepaid health plans and medical insurance. Inhouse EAPs have certain advantages, but the cost effectiveness prevents smaller businesses from establishing their own.

Not only are EAPs beneficial to the employee, but they are economically advantageous to the employer. They reduce absenteeism and increase productivity of the impaired worker. Virtually every study indicates that the employer saves thousands of dollars per employee treated for drug or alcohol abuse (Luckey, 1987). No wonder then that most companies provide these services, with more and more coming to rely on health care providers.

Even those who provide health care find that it is advantageous to provide drug and alcohol treatment. As can be seen on the next page, health care costs typically rise sharply immediately prior to treatment for alcohol or drug abuse. The abuser is using health services more, the family is under stress, and stress-related illnesses usually increase for them as well. Studies conducted over the past fifteen years indicate that the cost of treatment for alcohol and drug abuse is recouped within two to three years by reduced need for health care services (Luckey, 1987).

PREVENTION STRATEGIES WITH A FAMILY FOCUS

Alcohol and drug use in children and adolescents is correlated with families in which communication is poor, harsh physical punishment is used, and where the parents behave inconsistently. Parents' attitudes toward drugs also affect use by their children. It should come as no surprise that there is a correlation between parents' attitudes and behavior toward drugs and those of their children. The nature of the relationship is quite complex, however.

The data relating drug use and attitudes of parents and subsequent use by children are difficult to interpret. The general consensus, however, is that while both peers and parents play a role in determining drug use, the relative impact of peers is greater for boys, and the role of parents is greater for girls. Interestingly, negative parental attitudes toward drinking may be associated with drinking problems in adolescents who do, nonetheless, drink. Perhaps such parents are reacting to their child's alcohol use or perhaps their attitudes resulted in rebelliousness without providing their children a positive role model for social drinking.

Until recently, research on parents' effects on children's drug use has focused on the parents' use of alcohol and cigarettes. However, the children of the 1960s generation are now reaching the decision-making age for drug use. What effect will a parent's former or current marijuana or cocaine use have upon the children's choices? At present, the evidence is not sufficiently clear to draw a conclusion, but this is a question that will need to be addressed in the future.

PREVENTION IN THE COMMUNITY

Expanding the viewpoint on prevention effects one step beyond the family, communities are organizing to prevent drug and alcohol abuse. Community action can be effective by demonstrating a lack of tolerance for drug use and by fostering programs that support nondrug use. You may be aware of

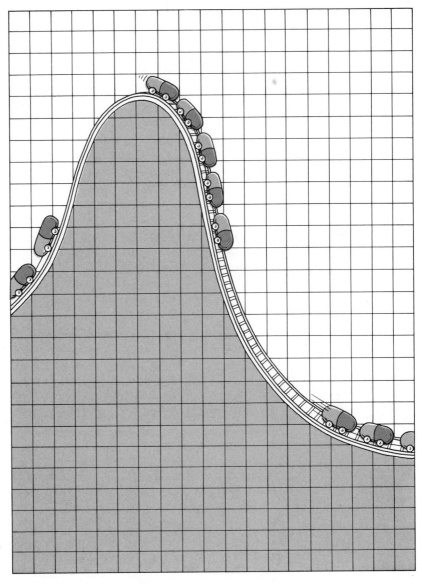

Research documents a trend toward a sharp rise in health care costs prior to alcoholism treatment and declining costs following treatment.

Source: Alcohol Health and Research World. National Institute of Alcohol Abuse and Alcoholism.

communities that support parades or races with an anti-drug message. Communities can participate in assuring that needed funds are spent for prevention and treatment.

Specific programs for communities are geared to reducing availability by restricting licenses for sale of alcoholic beverages, by enforcing existing alcohol beverage control regulations, and by supporting what is called *community-oriented policing.* Community-oriented policing is bureaucratic terminology for increasing police presence by foot patrols and other techniques.

A specific program that is gaining rapid support is the establishment of *drug-free zones* around schools. This program also serves an important law enforcement function as well. Communities cooperate by passing laws which make drug possession or sale a severe penalty within a specified distance from a school. Not only does this reduce availability, but it presumably scares dealers away from one of their primary outlets for drugs. Furthermore, a law increasing the penalty for drug offenses near a school is easier to pass than a law increasing penalties in general. By making the drug-free zone quite large, law enforcement has gained another weapon.

A potential drawback to these programs is that they simply force the undesirable behavior out of a specific community and into another. While this may satisfy the local community, it also can mean that drug use may be concentrated in communities that do not have as much political clout or local interest. Also, it may encourage drug consumption of a particularly destructive nature, such as binging.

Using alcohol as an example, the author can remember when alcohol sales were prohibited after 12:00 midnight on Saturday night in the state where he attended college. Unfortunately, two other states with more liberal laws were within a few minutes' driving distance. After "last call" it was traditional for many students (not the author, of course) to pile into a car and drive to the adjoining state, thereby virtually assuring drinking and driving long distances by immature drivers.

Many college towns still have laws prohibiting alcohol sales within a specified distance from a college. A drive through such towns is instructive, since inevitably there is a ring of liquor stores and bars exactly that distance in virtually every direction. Most colleges are now discouraging or prohibiting alcohol use on campus; unfortunately, this may lead to students driving off campus to drink and then attempting to drive back.

The concept of discouraging drug use by community action is remarkably similar to the approach used by the Temperance movement in the nineteenth century. Rather than pass nationwide laws against alcohol, the idea developed that the same effect could be obtained by passing laws community by community. Each community that passed the law became a model for neighboring communities to do the same, and eventually the entire country would be covered community by community. You will recall from chapter 12 that the Temperance movement culminated its effort with the constitutional amendment referred to as Prohibition.

For those interested in participating in drug prevention at the community level, the U.S. Government has a publication called *Citizen's Alcohol and Other Drug Prevention Directory: Resources for Getting Involved.* It is available from the Office of Substance Abuse Prevention and lists hundreds of local, state, and federal agencies that have programs concerned with drug prevention.

DRUGS AND THE MEDIA: ROLE OF THE ENTERTAINMENT INDUSTRY

What influence do movies, television, magazines, advertisements, and music have on drug use? Is it possible that a media focus on the dangers of drugs might actually make them more popular? Does rock and roll music and the example of rock musicians encourage or discourage drug use? How much drug use occurs in typical television programs and how does it affect us? How effective are advertisements in promoting and/or discouraging drug use? The importance of these influences on our lives in general and drug use in particular needs to be examined.

Drugs and Popular Music

References to drugs can be found in music of many types and many cultures. Most of these references are to alcohol, but whatever drug is mentioned, music reflects the attitude of the society and musician to that drug. Isn't it reasonable to assume, then, that these lyrics affect the behavior of the listeners?

The 1960s saw the rise in popularity of both rock and roll and drugs, and references to illicit drug use became common. As a result, considerable controversy arose concerning the influence of these songs, so much so that in 1971 the Federal Communications Commission issued a series of warnings that essentially required broadcasters to screen music for "language tending to promote or glorify" drugs. The warnings were ambiguous and did not demand censorship, but did imply that the broadcasters had "responsibility" and assumed a causal link between the lyrics and drug use (Schwartz, Feinglass, & Drucker, 1973).

Is the relationship really causal? There have been innumerable songs extolling alcohol use. Have these caused anyone to become an alcoholic? Can the lyrics of a song really influence someone to try marijuana, for example, if marijuana is not readily available? Do rock and roll entertainers really have that much influence?

Before trying to answer these questions, one should see how explicit the lyrics really were. Many of the lyrics were cryptic and made only veiled references to drug use. *Lucy in the Sky with Diamonds,* by the Beatles, is supposed to be about LSD and its effects, but anyone listening casually would never understand the references in the lyrics. To an extent, lyrics like these provided a secret language understood only by those who had experienced the effects of the drugs or wanted others to think they had.

Other lyrics were much more explicit, specifically mentioning various drugs and leaving no doubt as to what they were about. The majority of these songs were about marijuana and the psychedelics, although later, cocaine lyrics became more common. Most rock groups of the eighties have avoided or skirted the issue of drugs, although some lyrics have a strong antidrug bias. Instead, explicit sexual lyrics became more common, and public concern has recently centered on these songs and their supposed effect.

Do songs affect behavior? Surprisingly little research has been done in this area. What research has been reported tends to indicate that music has relatively little impact on drug use. First of all, most people listening to songs either do not pay attention to or cannot understand the lyrics. In one study, only about 20 percent of the subjects either heard the lyrics or understood what they meant (Schwartz, Feinglass, & Drucker, 1973). Furthermore, the contents of the songs, at least in the late sixties and seventies were about equally divided, with half giving a positive, but an equally large number, a negative message.

Since the FCC suggested that stations examine the lyrics of songs to avoid those with a drug content, very few such songs have become popular, at least very few have gained extensive play over the air. Anyone who is interested in music knows that songs are released as singles and as albums. Popular music stations play only a small percentage of all songs and albums released every year. Those songs that are not played are recorded by groups outside the mainstream of popular music, but nevertheless are widely known. Album sales and concert appearances provide the main source of income for these groups (along with the ever-present t-shirts and other paraphernalia).

While it may be true that Top-40 music has been purged of drug lyrics, the same is not necessarily true for albums by alternative groups. Some groups record songs which take free speech and free expression to the limit. Every year or two a controversy erupts over the content (sexual, violent, or drug-related) of these songs and just as quickly fades. While some individuals might carefully listen to and perhaps even understand the lyrics, the vast majority of listeners neither understand nor are concerned about the meaning of the words.

Finally the evidence suggests that references to specific drug use seem to *follow* rather than precede drug use (Schwartz, Feinglass, & Drucker, 1973). With the messages being ambiguous, with so few listeners actually understanding them, and with an equal number of pro- and anti-drug messages, it seems unlikely that popular music played then, or plays now, a direct role in drug use.

Even if the lyrics of rock songs did glorify drug use and promoted drug taking, the life (and death) of many rock stars in the sixties and seventies should have provided a potent antidote to excessive drug use. Like the deaths of athletes due to use of cocaine in the middle to late eighties, deaths due to drug abuse among rock stars were given wide publicity. A recent trend has been for the artists to publicly acknowledge their past drug use, check in for treatment at a famous treatment center and then begin a ''new'' career, drug and alcohol free. While most of them are undoubtedly sincere, the ensuing publicity probably doesn't hurt either.

Drugs harmed so many musicians the same way and for the same reasons that cocaine has proved to be such a trap for so many athletes. Fame, in sports or in music, often occurs suddenly and departs just as suddenly. It is accompanied by constant media attention and huge amounts of money. Those who are the recipients are typically young and often immature. With any drug being available at the right price, and with the crowds of hangers-on that typically surround the suddenly famous, it is almost a wonder that

in depth

Elvis Presley

Elvis Aaron Presley was born 8 January 1935 and died 16 August 1977. For many people he remains a figure of almost mythical proportions, a true cult hero, so much so that periodic reports appear in sensational tabloids that he is still alive. Although he had a mediocre voice and could barely play the guitar, he had an undeniable attractiveness and stage presence that made him the most popular entertainer of the late 1950s and early '60s. He made (and gave away) a fortune, was the object of countless editorials, sermons, letters to the editor, and symbolized for adolescents growing up in the fifties the very essence of the term ''generation gap.''

In his later years, as his popularity among adolescents waned, he became a less controversial figure and began playing to more mature audiences in such places as Las Vegas where he remained enormously popular. When he died of supposed heart failure, he again made headlines. The home that he built in Memphis, Tennessee, is now a shrine to his memory and is visited by millions of people a year.

Very few of these visitors know (or maybe care) that Elvis Presley was also a polydrug abuser of massive proportions. At a time when possession of marijuana was a felony punishable by long jail terms and President Nixon was waging one of a seemingly endless series of wars on drugs, Elvis Presley was consuming legally prescribed medications at an astounding rate. The day before he died, he had been preparing for a two week tour. On that day, 15 August 1976, Presley's physician prescribed for him the following drugs:

- 112 capsules, or ampules, of *amytal,* a powerful barbiturate
- 150 tablets of *Quaalude,* a non-barbiturate sedative with such a severe abuse potential that it was subsequently removed from the market
- 100 tablets of *dexedrine,* a form of amphetamine

- 100 tablets of *biphetamine,* known as Black Beauties (Biphetamine is a powerful combination of the two forms of amphetamine discussed in chapter 6.)
- 100 tablets of *Percodan,* an opiate prescribed for relief of severe pain
- 50 four milligram tablets and 20 ccs of *dilaudid* (Dilaudid is a powerful narcotic analgesic. The recommended dosages for moderate to severe pain are 1–2 milligrams subcutaneously or intramuscularly every 4–6 hours *or* one *two-milligram* tablet every 4–6 hours.)

The official cause of death was cardiac arrhythmia, or irregular heartbeat, accompanied by cardiovascular disease. This autopsy finding has never been changed and Presley's physician was cleared of any wrongdoing in his death. Nevertheless, one laboratory reported finding thirteen different drugs in Elvis' bloodstream at the time of his death.

It is difficult to imagine who but a confirmed drug abuser would need two hundred doses of stimulants, two hundred doses of sedatives, and two hundred doses of narcotic analgesics for a two-week concert tour. Were it not so tragic, it would be quite ironic to note that at the time of his death Presley was an agent of the Drug Enforcement Agency and a sworn law officer in a number of different cities.

What is even more amazing, perhaps, is that those who flock to Graceland continue to buy Elvis Presley albums and revere his memory, and ignore the fact that his drug use was widely publicized after his death. Could the reason be that all of the drugs were legal, prescription, drugs authorized by a physician? Is someone less of an addict if they obtain their drugs legally? In 1992, the U.S. Postal Service issued a stamp in honor of Elvis Presley. More than one million people voted to express their preference for a stamp in honor of an admitted drug addict!

any young athlete or musician ever escapes without serious drug involvement.

Drug abuse among musicians (and athletes) is not, by the way, a new phenomenon. Alcohol was the primary drug of abuse for many jazz musicians who also used marijuana, cocaine, and the opiates. Bessie Smith had a serious alcohol problem, and Charlie Parker abused both narcotics and alcohol. Others whose deaths were caused or accelerated by drugs include Lester Young and Billie Holiday (Berendt, 1962).

Drugs and Television

Television is a potent socialization force in our society. How many of us secretly believe that somewhere there are families that have breakfast as they do in the television ads: with sunlight streaming through the window of a nice suburban house, Mom and Dad dressed in their finest, and milk being poured from a glass pitcher into glasses placed on a breakfast table that has a bowl of flowers in the middle? Television affects our speech, dress, and food preferences. Does it also affect our drug taking?

The beer and wine industries must think so, or why else would they spend millions of dollars promoting one brand of beer or wine over another? The Federal Communications Commission must think so, since they banned cigarette and hard liquor advertising. The cigarette companies must think so, because they sponsor athletic events like the Virginia Slims tournament, and pay for advertising on billboards and walls that can be seen on TV during athletic events.

Brands of liquor, beer, and cigarettes are advertised in another way on television and in movies. Many manufacturers pay handsomely to have their product used by the actors in their scenes. You may rest assured that when a television or movie character takes a beer out of a refrigerator and the label of the can is visible, that a sum of money has been paid. The price varies depending on the circumstances, but can be in excess of $20,000.

Drug use is quite common on television and in the movies. The drug use is, of course, legal drug use, mostly cigarettes and alcohol. In recent years, fewer and fewer actors are seen smoking cigarettes. Watch an old movie on late night television, and you would think that everyone in the United States smoked constantly. Now it is rare to see a main character smoking.

The amount of alcohol use, however, is astounding. One study (Wallack, Breed, & Cruz, 1987) found that 80 percent of prime time television programs in the fall of 1984 included the appearance of drinking. Dramatic series were even more alcohol laden, with nine of ten episodes making some reference to alcohol. In all, a person watching an evening of television would see more than twenty drinking acts per evening.

Does all this boozing have an effect? Surprisingly, the evidence suggests that the effect is not as great as might be expected. Picking studies carefully from the published literature could lead to conclusions that such exposure has no effect, affects the choice of beverage, increases some type

Beer Advertising

Beer is typically consumed by men, and most advertising is geared to that fact. In order to sell their product, beer manufacturers appeal to what they apparently see as the traditional values of men. Postman, Nystrom, Strate, and Weingartner (1987) analyzed the content of beer commercials on television and came up with the following conclusions. Keep them in mind the next time you watch a beer commercial on television and see if you agree.

In beer commercials men work and play hard. Their labor is primarily physical and performed for its own value, to benefit society as a whole, or for acceptance by other men. Commercials rarely show an intellectual or a white collar worker with a beer in his hand.

Even at rest, men in beer commercials continue to compete with each other and with themselves to do the best they can. They rarely display any deep affection, but joke or compete with each other in sports like pool. Public displays of affection, unless placed in a joking context, are considered inappropriate.

Many commercials tap into these beliefs by portraying beer as a reward for a job well done, as the product of skilled craftsmanship—much like the work the men do—or an indication of male dominance. Having a beer together is sign of camaraderie and acceptance and an invitation to the society of males.

Beer commercials stress that beer consumption is done in a group, perhaps to counteract the belief that solitary drinking is a sign of a problem drinker. Men are expected to show self-restraint and to be egalitarian. Beer is the bond that holds men together and a shared beer is a reminder of good times past. Boys become men by working hard, showing courage, and taking pride in their work. They are initiated into male society when an older man offers them a beer.

This group consumption is often done in a bar. Have you ever noticed, though, that men are rarely seen either entering or leaving the bar? No issue of drinking and driving is ever raised. How did these men get to the bar and how are they going to get home? No one is ever drunk and all the men are portrayed as friendly and gregarious.

Women are conspicuously absent in most beer commercials except as an ornament. When the men act silly, the women present indicate their approval. Men signal that they are interested in a woman by offering her a beer and she indicates her availability by accepting it. "Candy is dandy, but liquor is quicker." Men in beer commercials apparently would rather spend time with their male friends than with women, and the women seem to accept this role.

Please keep in mind that these are not the author's editorial comments but are the conclusions of the Postman et al, study cited above.

Do these themes and issues affect alcohol use? Do beer drinkers choose their particular brand because they empathize with the people in the commercials? Perhaps not, but advertisers must think so, given the millions of dollars they pay for these commercials.

of alcohol use, or even decreases use (Kohn & Smart, 1987). One thing is for sure: advertising increases our awareness of alcoholic beverages, especially among children. In a study done in the Washington, D.C. area, eight-to-twelve-year-old children could name an average of 5.2 alcoholic beverages but only 4.8 presidents (Center for Science in the Public Interest,

1988). One ten-year-old girl could name only four presidents but knew the names of fourteen products.

Positive Aspects of Media Influence

Recognizing that the media can influence people both in a positive and negative way, an organization called the **Entertainment Industry Council, Inc.** was formed in 1983 to address social concerns such as drug and alcohol abuse, drunk driving, AIDS, and traffic safety. Through cooperation with the National Institute of Drug Abuse and the Office of Substance Abuse Prevention they have launched a number of campaigns to promote awareness of drug and alcohol problems.

A major emphasis is to encourage those in charge of television programing to include appropriate material in their shows. You have undoubtedly seen the effects of some of their efforts without being aware you were being sent a message. A character on your favorite program may be a designated driver or suggest that a guest not have another drink. You may see every character in a scene be offered "a drink" and have one of them ask for a soft drink. The Entertainment Council regularly publishes suggested guidelines about how to treat various issues. One such guideline concerns how a woman's response to alcohol or to drug addiction may be different from a man's.

Another program is the Musicares billboard campaign cropping up all over the country. This program is targeted to high-risk youths who may not be reached by school-based prevention programs and features popular musicians along with a hotline number to call. Some of the musicians include those who have had well publicized drug problems such as David Crosby and Bonnie Raitt, while others, such as Paula Abdul, Young MC, and Gloria Estefan were chosen because some high-risk adolescents may identify with them.

Television, music, movies, and other forms of the media probably have a subtle influence on behavior, but the amount of that influence is difficult to quantify. Social conventions, religious beliefs, drug education programs, personality variables, and a host of other factors interact as well. How much of each contributes to drug use is a moot point.

If drug abuse is going to be stopped and if drug abuse prevention is going to be anything other than an empty political slogan, efforts must be made at every level. Neither primary, secondary, nor tertiary prevention will work exclusively. Clearly a concerted effort similar to that which has been conducted with cigarette smoking is needed. Something has to be done at every level and at every opportunity. To repeat a phrase from the end of chapter 1—We have no other choice.

SUMMARY

Drug abuse prevention and education is an admirable goal and the ideal way to prevent substance abuse. Actually affecting substance abuse by education has proven to be an elusive goal. Prevention methods have focused on three goals: primary, secondary, and tertiary prevention, with the greatest emphasis being placed on primary and tertiary prevention.

Primary prevention involves educating prospective users *before* they have begun to use drugs. Various techniques have been developed to accomplish this goal but most have had limited success and some have actually *increased* drug use. The current emphasis is on social inoculation. Social innoculation programs have had some success with some individuals; notably, these programs seem to be partly responsible for a decline in cigarette use among middle-class youth.

Secondary prevention is an area that seems ripe for growth. Secondary prevention techniques are now mostly geared to alcohol use by adults. Tertiary prevention is better known as substance abuse treatment, and its problems and successes have been noted elsewhere.

An important issue that needs to be addressed is the role of parents and other adults as models and as leaders in prevention programs. More and more programs are being geared to elementary school children, and parents need to play a role in these developments.

Employee assistance programs have been developed for working adults who have been impaired by drug use. They have proven quite successful in many cases and their role is expanding. Business has come to realize that these programs not only help employees but are cost effective as well.

REFERENCES

Berendt, J. (1962). *The new jazz book.* New York: Hill and Wang.

Bernard, B., Fafoglia, B., & Perone, J. (1987). Knowing what to do and not to do reinvigorates drug education. In *Schools and drugs: A guide to drug and alcohol abuse prevention,* (pp. 1–18). Office of The Attorney General of California.

Center for Science in the Public Interest (1988). Kids are as aware of booze as presidents, survey finds. News release. 4 September.

Ellickson, P. L., & Bell, R. M. (1990). Drug prevention in junior high: A multi-site longitudinal test. *Science, 247,* 1299–1305.

Gfroerer, J. (1987). Correlation between drug use by teenagers and drug use by older family members. *American Journal of Drug and Alcohol Abuse, 13,* 95–198.

Kohn, P. M., & Smart, R. G. (1987). Wine, women, suspiciousness and advertising. *Journal of Studies on Alcohol, 48,* 161–66.

Luckey, W. (1987). Justifying alcohol treatment on the basis of cost saving: The "offset" literature. *Alcohol Health and Research World,* Fall, 8–15.

Mauss, A. L., Hopkins, R. H., Weisheit, R., & Kearney, K. A. (1988). The problematic prospects for prevention: Should alcohol education programs be expected to reduce drinking by youth? *Journal of Studies on Alcohol, 49,* 51–61.

McGuire, W. (1981). Theoretical foundations of campaign. In R. Rice and W. Paisley (Eds.). *Public Communication Campaign.* Beverly Hills, CA: Sage Publications.

Postman, N., Nystrom, C., Strate, L., & Weingartner, C. (1987). *Myths, men and beer.* Falls Church, VA: AAA Foundation for Traffic Saftey.

Resnick, H. S. (1978). *It starts with people: Experiences in drug abuse prevention.* NIDA pub. no. 79–590. U.S. Department of Health Education & Welfare.

Ryan, B. E., & Segars L. (1987). Minimarts and maxiproblems: The relationship between purchase and consumption location. *Alcohol Health and Research World,* Fall, 26–29.

Schwartz, E. S., Feinglass, S. J., & Drucker, C. (1973). Popular music and drug lyrics: Analysis of a scapegoat. In *Drug use in America: Problem in perspective,* (pp. 719–46). The technical paper of the second report of the National Commission on Marijuana and Drug Abuse.

Trice, H. M., & Beyer, J. M. (1983). Social control in the workplace: Using the constructive confrontation strategy with problem drinking employees. In D. A. Ward (Ed.), pp. 314–42. *Alcoholism: Introduction to theory and treatment.* Dubuque, IA: Kendall/Hunt.

U.S. Department of Education (1986). *What works: Schools without drugs.*

U.S. General Accounting Office (1987). *Report to the Select Committee on Narcotics Abuse and Control, House of Representatives: Drug abuse prevention: Further efforts needed to identify programs that work.* Human Resources Branch B-228715.

Wallack, L., Breed, W., & Cruz, J. (1987). Alcohol and prime time television. *Journal of Studies on Alcohol, 48,* 27–34.

Westermeyer, J. (1987). A *clinical guide to alcohol and drug problems.* New York: Praeger.

GLOSSARY

abreaction: A sudden discharge of emotion.

abstinence: Refraining from the use of drugs.

acetaldehyde: A metabolic by-product of the metabolism of alcohol.

acetaminophen: An analgesic drug often used as a substitute for aspirin.

acetylcholine: A neurotransmitter in the brain and the neuromuscular junction.

acetylsalicylic acid: The technical name for aspirin.

Acquired Immune Deficiency Syndrome (AIDS): A fatal disease caused by a virus often transmitted through intravenous drug use.

action potential: The process of the transmission of the nerve impulse down the axon.

acute alcohol amnesia: Amnesia produced by alcohol during a single drinking episode.

acute tolerance: The development of tolerance with repeated doses of a drug during the same drug taking session.

administrative per se: Carrying out some penalty provisions of a law prior to conviction of a crime.

adrenaline: A hormone secreted by the adrenal gland which produces a sympathetic nervous system arousal response. A synonym is epinephrine.

adult children of alcoholics: Those who grew up in a family in which one or both parents were alcohol abusers.

affective approach: An approach to drug prevention which emphasizes helping people to feel good about themselves.

alcoholic hepatitis: A serious liver condition brought on by alcohol abuse.

alcoholic fatty liver: The condition that occurs when fat is stored in the liver. A common occurrence after a few days of heavy drinking.

al kohl: "The essence": A phrase in Arabic used to describe distilled alcohol.

amanita muscaria: The mushroom known as fly agaric. Contains hallucinogenic substances.

amethystic agent: A drug that counteracts the effects of alcohol.

amino acid transmitter: Any one of several, primarily inhibitory, transmitters found in the brain.

amotivational syndrome: Lethargy or lack of ambition thought by some to be the result of heavy marijuana use.

amphetamine: A stimulant formerly used as an appetite suppressant, now primarily prescribed for the treatment of attention deficit syndrome and narcolepsy.

amyl nitrate: A drug which causes a sudden dilation of blood vessels. Prescribed for angina pectoris, sometimes used to enhance sexual enjoyment.

anabolic steroids: Drugs used to increase muscle mass. Related to testosterone, they are abused by some athletes.

analgesic: Pain killer.

anaphrodisiac: A drug that reduces sexual desire or performance.

angel dust: A street term for phencyclidine (PCP).

anhedoneia: An inability to feel pleasure.

anions: A negatively charged ion.

antabuse: The product name for disulfiram, a drug that produces a severe reaction when combined with alcohol.

antipyretic: A drug that reduces fever.

aphrodisiac: A drug that increases sexual desire or performance.

ascending reticular activating system: The system of the brain that alerts the cortex to important incoming sensory stimuli.

attention deficit disorder: Formerly called hyperactivity, a condition in which individuals are unable to inhibit incoming stimuli.

autonomic nervous system: The part of the nervous system that controls breathing, heart rate, etc. without conscious awareness.

autoreceptor: A receptor located on a neuron which responds to the same neurotransmitter that the neuron secretes.

barbiturates: A class of drugs used as sedative/hypnotics and in surgery.

basal ganglia: Brain structures involved in motor movement located near the thalamus.

basuca: A colloquial term for cocaine paste, often smoked in South America and the Bahamas.

behavioral tolerance: A learned ability to overcome some of the physical effects of a drug.

belladonna: "Beautiful lady" in Italian, the name of a drug used to dilate the pupils.

beta blocker: A drug which blocks the action of adrenaline or epinephrine especially in the heart muscle, used to reduce blood pressure, and by some performers and athletes to reduce anxiety.

biological equivalence: Drugs that have the same physiological effect on the body.

blackout: A loss of memory for an extended period of time after the consumption of alcohol. Considered a sign of alcohol abuse.

blind pig: An illegal bar or saloon. So named after the practice in these establishments of charging admission to view a ''blind pig'' (a blindfolded pig) and giving away a ''free'' drink.

blood/brain barrier: A barrier made up of cells in the capillaries of the brain that permit the passage of some chemicals.

body packers: People who attempt to smuggle drugs by ingesting drug-filled condoms or balloons.

bronchodilator: A drug that relieves symptoms of congestion by dilating the bronchial tubes in the lungs.

buccal route of administration: Absorption of a drug across the mucous membrane in the mouth.

bummer: A colloquial term describing an unpleasant drug experience.

cacahuatl: The Aztec term for a form of chocolate.

caffeine: A stimulant drug found primarily in coffee and soft drinks.

CAGE: A mnemonic device for four questions that may reveal a person with alcohol problems.

cannabinoids: The class of unique compounds found in marijuana.

Cannabis indica: A subspecies of cannabis that has a higher THC content than other forms.

Cannabis ruderalis: A subspecies of cannabis found in Northern Europe and Russia. It has a low THC content but a fast growing season.

Cannabis sativa: The common form of cannabis, also grown as hemp.

cantharidin: Also known as Spanish Fly. A blister agent mistakenly thought to be an aphrodisiac.

China White: A colloquial term for several synthetic and powerful forms of fentanyl.

chipper: An occasional user of heroin.

cholinesterase: The enzyme that blocks acetylcholine.

cholinesterase inhibitor: A substance that blocks the enzyme, cholinesterase, that metabolizes actylcholine.

Chronic Obstructive Lung Disease (COLD): Emphysema and chronic bronchitis.

chuspa: A word used in South America to describe a bag used to hold coca leaves.

cirrhosis:
Scarring of the liver, sometimes produced by alcohol abuse.

cognitive inoculation: A term used in drug prevention, it involves teaching potential users to avoid drug use.

COLD: Chronic Obstructive Lung Disease.

congeners: Forms of alcohol other than ethanol; found in some alcoholic beverages.

conspiracy: The act of two or more people planning or performing an overt act that leads to a crime.

constructive confrontation: A technique used to help drug abusers see that they have a problem.

contact high: A feeling of euphoria brought on without drug use, experienced by some people who are around users of drugs, particularly marijuana.

cotinine: A metabolite of nicotine used to measure the amount of nicotine ingested.

crack: A smokeable, highly potent form of cocaine made by mixing cocaine with baking soda and heating it.

crank: A term for any of several kinds of amphetamine, particularly methamphetamine (meth).

criminal per se: Laws which define certain behaviors, such as having a BAL of more than .08 as inherently illegal.

cross-tolerance: A change in responsiveness to one class of drugs after exposure to a different class. Cross-tolerance occurs between various hallucinogens and between alcohol and barbiturates.

curanderos: In Mexico and other Latin countries, those who have obtained knowledge of the medicinal properties of various plants and who are believed by others to be able to cure illnesses.

curare: An extract of bark that blocks the action of acetylcholine at the neuromuscular junction.

cyclic AMP: A chemical that operates in the postsynaptic area to modify neural transmission.

DAWN: Drug Abuse Warning Network.

dendrite: Part of the neuron that carries neural impulses to the cell body.

dependence: A change that takes place so that there is a physiological or psychological need for a drug in order to function normally.

designer drugs: Drugs similar to various synthetic opiates that are typically much more potent. The term is sometimes used incorrectly to describe various types of amphetaminelike drugs.

dexamethasone suppression test: A method of evaluating depression.

dimetylsulfoxide: A solvent that rapidly crosses the skin barrier, carrying with it any substance dissolved in it.

disease concept of alcoholism: The widely accepted idea that alcoholism is a disease like hypertension and diabetes.

dissociative anesthetic: A drug that causes a lack of pain perception without causing loss of consciousness.

distillation: The process of producing ethanol by heating alcoholic beverages.

doctrine of signatures: The belief that plants that resemble body parts will affect that portion of the body. Plants that resemble the sex organs, for example, are supposed to be aphrodisiacs.

dopamine: A catecholamine neurotransmitter found in various parts of the brain. Thought to mediate some of the effects of cocaine and other stimulants.

dose-response relationship: The relationship between the effect of a drug and the amount taken.

double-blind study: Research in which neither the experimenters nor the subjects know what, if any, drug the subjects are receiving.

Ecstasy: A term used to describe methylenedioxymethamphetamine. Ecstasy has been used in psychotherapy, but is now a Schedule I drug.

EMIT test: A urine test to detect the presence of various drugs.

Employee Assistance Programs: Programs designed to help those who abuse alcohol or other drugs overcome their problems and remain employed.

end button: The terminal portion of the neuron that contains the vesicles.

endorphin: A term used to describe a class of endogenous morphine-like substances found in the brain and the body.

ergogenic aids: Substances taken to build muscle mass and to increase physical performance. Ergogenic aids range from caffeine to steroids.

ergot: A fungus found on grain that contains many chemical substances that have profound effects on humans.

ethnobotany: A branch of science which studies the use of plants for medicinal purposes.

experimental use: Usually defined as use of a drug ten or fewer times.

false negative: In the context of drug use, the finding that no drug is present in a sample of blood, urine, or tissue when, in fact, the drug was taken.

false positive: In the context of drug use, the finding that a drug is present in a sample of blood, urine, or tissue when no drug was taken.

fentanyl: A synthetic analgesic and sedative, many times more potent than morphine.

fermentation: The conversion of sugar to alcohol by yeast.

fetal alcohol syndrome: A group of symptoms including retardation, facial deformities, and other problems presumably brought about by excess consumption of alcohol by pregnant women.

fetal tobacco syndrome: A group of symptoms including low birth weight presumably caused by use of tobacco by pregnant women.

fluoxetin: Prozac, an antidepressant that inhibits re-uptake of serotonin.

fly agaric: *Amanita muscaria*, a hallucinogenic mushroom.

fusel oils: By-products of fermentation and distillation thought by some to contribute to the experience of a hangover. Fusel oils are a higher order form of alcohol.

GABA: Gaba amino butyric acid, an inhibitory neurotransmitter.

GC/MS: Gas Chromatograph Mass Spectometry, a method for analyzing the content of some substances such as blood or urine.

generic drugs: Drugs not protected by a trademark.

glutamic acid: An amino acid neurotransmitter with excitatory properties.

gynecomastia: Enlargement of breast tissue in males.

Halcion: The brand name of a drug frequently used to induce sleep.

half life: The time required for one half the concentration of a drug to be metabolized.

hallucinogens: Drugs that cause perceptual distortions.

hashish: A potent form of marijuana, made from the resinous secretions of the plant.

hashishiyya: Supposedly, a group of assasins in Arab countries in the Middle Ages who used marijuana.

heavy use: Frequent use of a drug that impairs performance.

holiday heart syndrome: Rapid or irregular heart beat caused by excess consumption of alcohol over a period of several days.

hypertension: High blood pressure.

hypothalamus: A group of cell bodies just below the thalamus in the brain. The hypothalmic nuclei control many body functions, including eating and sexual behavior.

ibuprofen: An analgesic, antipyretic, anti-inflammatory drug often used as an aspirin substitute.

ice cream habit: A heroin "addict" who uses so little actual heroin that true addiction does not develop.

inhalation: A method of absorbing drugs through the lungs.

intramuscular route: Absorption of drugs by injecting them into muscle tissue.

intravenous route: The most direct route of drug administration, it involves injecting the drug directly into the bloodstream.

ion channels: Pathways in the cell body and axon though which anions and cations can pass.

jimson weed: The plant known as Datura stramonium, with poisonous and hallucinogenic properties.

Kaposi's sarcoma: A rare form of cancer found frequently in AIDS patients.

ketamine: An anesthetic related chemically to phencyclidine. Ketamine is widely used in surgery.

Korsakoff's syndrome: Deterioration of the brain brought on by alcohol abuse and poor nutrition; a major symptom is memory loss.

L-alpha-acethylmethadol hydrochloride: A long-acting substitute for methadone.

League of Spiritual Discovery (LSD): The name given by Timothy Leary to a group that wanted to make LSD a religious sacrament.

lecithin: A substance found in many vegetables, including soybean and corn, that is a precursor of acetylcholine.

limbic system: Structures in the brain that mediate various emotions such as aggression.

lipid layer: The layer of fat in cell walls that provides a barrier to some drugs.

lock-and-key principle: The idea that neurotransmitters function in a manner analogous to a key going into a lock.

look-alike drugs: Drugs such as caffeine and ephedrine packaged to look like prescription or illegal drugs.

LSD: Lysergic acid diethylamide, a hallucinogenic derivative of ergot.

magic mushrooms: A name given to various types of mushrooms presumably containing psilocybin.

mainlining: Injecting directly into a blood vessel.

malathion: An insecticide commonly used by gardeners; it has anticholinesterase properties.

MAO inhibitors: Drugs that inhibit the action of monoaxamine oxidase and thus increase catecholamines. Used as antidepressants.

Mariani, Angelo: An Italian who made a fortune selling a combination of wine and cocaine called Vin Mariani.

marijuana: The name given to the seeds, leaves, stems, and flowers of various cannabis plants.

marinol: The product name for delta-9-tetrahydracannabinol used medically to treat the symptoms of nausea and vomiting as a result of chemotherapy.

MAST (Michigan Alcoholism Screening Test): A relatively brief test to determine the possiblity of alcohol abuse.

MDMA (methylenedioxymethamphetamine): A drug related to amphetamine. See Ecstasy.

medial forebrain bundle: In some animals, the reward system in the brain.

medulla: The structure of the brain that controls breathing, heart rate, and other vegetative functions.

meperidine: Also known as Demerol, it is a widely used opiate analgesic.

methadone: A synthetic form of morphine used in pain relief and as a substitute for heroin with heroin addicts.

methamphetamine: Amphetamine with the addition of a methyl group, commonly known as crank or speed.

methylenedioxyethamphetamine: MDA, an amphetamine-like drug similar to MDMA or Ecstasy.

MK-ULTRA: The code name for a series of "experiments" in the 1950s on the effects of LSD and other drugs on unsuspecting subjects.

MPPP: A powerful designer drug based on meperidine.

MPTP: A drug produced by a mistake in the synthesis of MPPP that destroys dopamine receptors and produces a condition similar to Parkinsonism.

mules: those who smuggle drugs across the borders.

myristicine: the hallucinogenic chemical found in nutmeg and mace.

naloxone: An opiate antagonist, it blocks the action of heroin and morphine.

naltrexone: Similar to naloxone but longer-acting.

narcolepsy: Intrusion of REM sleep patterns into the waking state. Those with narcolepsy appear to fall asleep uncontrollably.

narcotraficante: Drug traffickers in Central and South America.

negative reinforcement: The removal of a punishing stimulus, negative reinforcement increases the likelihood of a behavior.

neurohormone: A chemical substance released by neurons that works at a distance, typically in the body.

neuromodulator: A substance that subtly alters the function of a neuron in a manner not completely understood.

neurotransmitter: The chemical substance that crosses the synapse to institute a neural impulse.

nicotine: The addictive substance found in tobacco, nicotine is a potent poison that has both stimulating and sedative properties.

norepinephrine: A catecholamine involved in sympathetic nervous system arousal and in mood alterations.

ololiuqui: The Aztec word for morning glory seeds; used as a hallucinogen.

opium: The gummy substance secreted from the opium poppy. It has analgesic and sedative properties.

parenteral use: Drug taken by injection into the body.

passive smoking: Absorption of the smoke as a result of being in the presence of smokers.

patent medicine: In the 19th century, manufacturers were allowed to keep the ingredients of their over-the-counter drugs a secret. They had a ''patent,'' hence patent medicine.

PAWS: Post Alcohol Withdrawal Syndrome: the behaviors that last for several weeks after an abusive drinker stops drinking.

PCP (Phencyclidine): A dissociative anesthetic that has been widely abused.

Peace pill: Another name for PCP.

peliosis: Formation of pools of blood in the liver.

peptide: A sequence of amino acids that can function as neurotransmitters.

phencyclidine: See PCP.

phenylpropanolamine: A drug available over-the-counter for appetite control. Structurally, it resembles amphetamine.

physical dependence: Alteration of tissue function so that a drug is now necessary for normal physiological processes to occur.

physiological tolerance: A physiological change in the body so that more of a drug is necessary to produce the same effect.

pituitary: The master neurohormone-producing structure in the brain.

placebo: A supposedly inert substance that can exert some psychological or physiological effect.

positive reinforcement: Some stimulus that increases the likelihood of a behavior.

postsynaptic membrane: The membrane that contains the postsynaptic receptor.

postsynaptic receptor: The structure that initiates the neural impulse after alteration by the neurotransmitter.

premorbid personality: Personality characteristics found before an illness or episode of drug abuse.

presynaptic area: The structures found in the neuron such as the end button and the vesicles.

PRIDE: Parents' Resource for Information on Drug Education.

Primary prevention: The attempt to stop people from using drugs by helping them not to start.

propanalol: A drug used as a beta blocker for the treatment of hypertension or, sometimes, anxiety.

prostaglandins: Hormones produced in response to damage to tissue damage and which sensitize pain receptors.

Prozac: The brand name for fluoxetin.

pruno: An alcohol beverage made from vegetable scraps, often made in prisons.

psilocybin: The active hallucinogenic substance found in some mushrooms.

psilocyn: The actual psychoactive metabolite of psilocybin.

psychedelic: A term used to describe drugs that cause perceptual alterations. Also a term used to describe some types of music, art, and clothing.

pulque: An alcohol beverage made from corn.

raphe nuclei: A group of cells located in the brain stem.

receptor binding: The tendency for chemical substances to bind to postsynaptic, presynaptic, or auto-receptors.

resting potential: The difference in charge between the outside of the axon compared to the inside, approximately -70mV.

reticular formation: A structure in the brain stem that activates the cortex when important or novel stimuli occur.

reverse tolerance: A decrease in the amount of a drug required to produce a given effect.

Reye's Syndrome: A rare paralytic condition that sometimes accompanies a viral infection. Aspirin is believed to be a risk factor for the development of Reye's Syndrome.

Saint Anthony's Fire: A disease brought on by ingestion of contaminated grain. It is characterized by gangrene, spontaneous abortion, and psychological disturbances.

schizophrenia: A severe psychological disorder characterized by hallucinations, delusions, and thought disorders.

scopolamine: An anticholinergic drug formerly used in OTC medications as a sedative. It can produce hallucinations and amnesia in high doses.

secondary prevention: Education directed at minimizing the harmful effects of drug use by emphasizing temperance rather than abstinence.

second messenger system: The events occurring in the postsynaptic region which increase or decrease the likelihood of the occurrence of a neural impulse.

sedative hypnotics: Drugs which decrease the latency to sleep and reduce motor activity.

serotonin: A primarily inhibitory neurotransmitter which is involved in the ARAS and in vision. Recent evidence indicates that serotonin may also be involved in mood disorders.

set and setting: The expectation of what a drug will do and the effect of the situation that the user is in during the drug experience.

sidestream smoke: Smoke from the burning cigarette as well as the exhaled smoke from the lungs of a smoker.

significant accidents: The events that occur to those under the influence of a drug that leads them to realize they have a drug problem.

skin popping: Injection of opiates into the subcutaneous space.

smokeless tobacco: Chewing tobacco, snuff, or tobacco pouches.

social inoculation: The attempt to reduce drug use through principles of social pscyhology.

sodium potassium pump: The process that restores the resting potential in the axon.

Spanish Fly: A blistering agent believed by some to be an aphrodisiac.

speed: A term used to describe methamphetamine or any other amphetamine-like drug.

speed freak: An abuser of amphetamine or methamphetamine, typically by injection.

spontaneous remission: A decrease or cessation in drug use without the intervention of outside groups.

stacking: The use of several types of ergogenic aids.

standard safety margin: A formula to determine the safety of a particular drug based on the relationship between the effective and the lethal dose.

stereotypy: A repetitive behavior brought on by drug use, particularly of some stimulants.

subcutaneous route: Injection of a drug just underneath the skin.

substance abuse: A term, criticized by some, that is used to specify abuse of various drugs, both legal and illegal.

Substance p: A peptic neurotransmitter.

Sudden Infant Death Syndrome (SIDS): A poorly understood fatal ''disease'' occurring among seemingly healthy babies under the age of two; also known as crib death.

Summer of Love: A media-invented term describing events that occurred in San Francisco in the summer of 1967.

teonanacatl: The Aztec word for peyote.

teratogen: A substance causing birth defects.

Tertiary prevention: Treatment for those who have been affected by drug abuse.

theobromine: A xanthine, or stimulant, found in chocolate. The name means ''food of the gods.''

theophylline: A stimulant drug, one of the xanthines, found in tea; sometimes used to treat asthma.

3-methyl-fentanyl: A particularly potent form of fentanyl; also known as China White.

time-response relationship: The changing effect of a drug during its absorption and metabolism.

titration: The process of adjusting drug use to maintain a given concentration.

tolerance: Generally, the lessening of effectiveness of a drug as a result of exposure.

toluene: An ingredient in airplane glue, gasoline, and other inhalants that causes disorientation and dizziness.

transdermal: Absorption of a drug across the intact skin barrier.

Triangle Trade: The purchase and sale, by New Englanders of the 18th century, of slaves, sugar, and rum. The Triangle Trade ran from New England to Africa to the Caribbean and back.

tricyclic antidepressants: Drugs which relieve symptoms of depression by inhibiting the re-uptake of the catecholamines and serotonin.

tryptophan: The precusor of serotonin.

Twelve Steps: A series of statements of belief and of challenges used by Alcoholics Anonymous to help members maintain sobriety and alter their lives.

Type II (male-limited): A kind of alcoholism characterized by early onset of abuse and associated with a high level of criminal behavior. Seen in males.

Type I (milieu-limited): A kind of alcoholism seen in both males and females. Relatively mild in its symptoms, it seems to occur only where the environment fosters or condones heavy drinking.

Vin Mariani: A combination of wine and cocaine very popular in the 19th century.

withdrawal: Physical or psychological symptoms that occur when drug use ceases.

xanthine: The class of stimulant drugs that includes caffeine, theophylline, and theobromine, the active ingredients in coffee, tea, and chocolate.

• • •

CREDITS

TEXT/LINE ART

Precision Graphics:

Figures 1.1; 2.1; 2.4; 2.5; 2.6; 2.7; 3.1; 3.2; 3.3; 3.4; 3.5; 3.6; 3.7; 3.8; 3.9; 3.11; 3.12; 4.1; 4.2; 4.3; 4.4; 5.1; 5.2; 5.3; 7.3; 7.4; 7.5; 7.6; 7.7; 8.2; 9.1; 10.1; 11.2; 11.3.
TA 1.6 (p. 14); TA 8.1 (p. 269); TA 8.4 (p. 276); TA 11.3 (p. 375); TA 13.2 (p. 443); TA 14.8 (p. 483).

Rolin Graphics

Figures 2.3; 3.10; 8.1; 8.4; 11.1; 14.1. TA 3.4 (p. 71).

PHOTO

Chapter One

Page 9: © Alan Carey/ The Image Works, Inc.; page 10: © James L. Shaffer; page 11: © Hiroji Kubota/ Magnum Photo Library; page 12: © James L. Shaffer; page 24: Photo courtesy of Kevin McEnnis; figure 1.2: © Bill Bachman/ Photo Researchers, Inc.

Chapter Two

Page 35: Photo courtesy of the Museum of the American Indian, Heye Foundation, NY; page 39: © Ian Berry/ Magnum Photo Library; figure 2.2: © Photo courtesy of the Drug Enforcement Agency; page 41: © Wayne Miller/Magnum Photo Library; page 47: © Eugene Richards/ Magnum Photo Library.

Chapter Three

Page 75: The Bettmann Archive; page 97: Photo courtesy of Kathleen Walker; page 98: AP/Wide World Photos, Inc.

Chapter Four

Page 126: © Steve Kagan/Photo Researchers, Inc.

Chapter Five

Pages 159, 161, 173: Photos courtesy of Kevin McEnnis; page 171: Photo courtesy of the Museum of the American Indian, Heye Foundation, NY; page 172: © Eugene Richards/Magnum Photo Library.

Chapter Six

Figure 6.1: Photo courtesy of the Drug Enforcement Agency; page 205: © Hiroji Kubota/Magnum Photo Library.

Chapter Seven

Figure 7.1: © Arents Collection, The New York Public Library, Astor, Lenox, and Tilden Foundations; figure 7.2: Bettmann Archive; page 241: © Gregory Saenz; page 242: © Bob Coyle.

Chapter Eight

Page 270 right: © Howard A. Miller, Sr./Photo Researchers, Inc.; page 270 left: Photo courtesy of the Drug Enforcement Agency; page 275: AP/Wide World Photos, Inc.; page 283: © Robert H. Wright/Photo Researchers, Inc., The National Audubon Society Collection; page 283: Photo courtesy of the Drug Enforcement Agency; page 289: From *Medical Botany: Plants Affecting Man's Health* by Walter H. Lewis. Copyright © 1977 John Wiley & Sons, Inc. Reprinted by permission of John Wiley & Sons, Inc.

Chapter Nine

Page 308: The Bettmann Archive; page 309: Photo courtesy of the Drug Enforcement Agency; page 316: © Ian Berry/Magnum Photo Library; page 319: AP/Wide World Photos, Inc.

Chapter Eleven

Page 359: Photo courtesy of Shirley Butticci; page 364: © 1975 The Saul Zaentz Company. All rights reserved.

Chapter Twelve

Page 397: AP/Wide World Photos, Inc.; page 404: AP/Wide World Photos, Inc.; page 407: AP/Wide World Photos, Inc.

Chapter Thirteen

Page 431: Photo courtesy of the NIAAA.

Chapter Fourteen

Page 470: Photo courtesy of Gregory Saenz; page 476: Photo courtesy of Shirley Butticci.

VISUALS

Figure 1.1

From L. Johnston and P. O'Malley, "Why Do the Nation's Students Use Drugs and Alcohol? Self-Reported Reasons from Nine National Surveys" in *Journal of Drug Issues,* 16(1): 29–66. Copyright © 1986 Journal of Drug Issues. Reprinted by permission.

Figure 2.1

From John W. Hole, Jr., *Human Anatomy and Physiology,* 3d. ed. Copyright © 1984 Wm C. Brown Publishers, Dubuque, Iowa. All Rights Reserved. Reprinted by permission.

Figure 2.6

Copyright © Harry Avis.

Figure 2.7

The Department of Motor Vehicles in cooperation with the California Highway Patrol, the Office of Traffic Safety, the Department of Alcohol and Drug Programs and the Department of Justice.

Figure 7.6

Adapted from Mattson, Pollack and Cullen, *American Journal of Public Health,* 77(4):425–531 (1987).

Figure 7.7

From McNaab, Ebert, and McCusker, *Journal of the American Medical Association, 248:* 365–368. Copyright © 1982, American Medical Association.

Illustration page 375

Reproduced from: Ray and Ksir, *Drugs, Society and Human Behavior,* 4th ed., St. Louis, 1987, Times Mirror/Mosby College Publishing.

Page 389

L. W. Barnett, et al., "Relapse rates in addiction programs" in *Journal of Clinical Psychology,* 27: 455–56, 1971. Clinical Psychology Publishing Company, 4 Conant Square, Brandon, VT 05733.

Woodcut page 392

Food and Drink: A pictorial archive from nineteenth century sources, 3 ed, Dover Publications, New York.

Illustration page 443

L. W. Barnett, et al., "Relapse rates in addiction programs" in *Journal of Clinical Psychology,* 27: 455–56, 1971. Clinical Psychology Publishing Company, 4 Conant Square, Brandon, VT 05733.

Page 467

Source: National Cancer Institute/National Institutes of Health.

INDEX